MEGARRY'S ASSURED TENANCIES

AUSTRALIA
LBC Information Services
Sydney

CANADA
Carswell
Toronto

NEW ZEALAND
Brooker's
Auckland

SINGAPORE AND MALAYSIA
Thomson Information (S.E. Asia)
Singapore

MEGARRY'S
ASSURED TENANCIES

SECOND EDITION

by

T. M. Fancourt
M.A. (Cantab.)
of Lincoln's Inn, Barrister

Being the Second Edition of Volume 3 of
THE RENT ACTS
(ELEVENTH EDITION)

by

Rt. Hon. Sir Robert Megarry
M.A., LL.D. (Cantab.), Hon. LL.D. (Hull, Nottingham,
The Law Society of Upper Canada, and London), F.B.A.
Sometime the Vice-Chancellor; a Bencher of Lincoln's Inn; an Honorary Fellow of Trinity Hall, Cambridge

and

Andrew Arden
Q.C., LL.B. (Lond.)
of Gray's Inn, Barrister

LONDON
SWEET & MAXWELL
1999

First Edition	(1939)	*By the author*
Second Edition	(1946)	*By the author*
Third Edition	(1947)	*By the author*
Fourth Edition	(1949)	*By the author*
Fifth Edition	(1950)	*By the author*
Sixith Edition	(1951)	*By the author*
Seventh Edition	(1953)	*By the author*
Eighth Edition	(1955)	*By Ashley Bramall and P. V. Baker*
Ninth Edition	(1961)	*By Ashley Bramall*
Tenth Edition	(1967)	*By the author*
Eleventh Edition		
Vols. 1 *and* 2	(1988)	*By J. S. Colyer Q.C. and the author (General Editors) and contributors*
Vol. 3	(1989)	*By the author and Andrew Arden*
Second Edition	(1999)	*By T. M. Fancourt*

Published in 1999 by
Sweet & Maxwell Limited
100 Avenue Road
London NW3 3PF

Printed and bound in Great Britain by
Butler & Tanner Ltd, Frome and London

A CIP catalogue record for this book is available from the British Library

ISBN 0421–62720–4

PREFACE

Over ten years have passed since the Housing Act 1988 and its new creature, the assured tenancy, came into force; ten years, too, since Sir Robert Megarry's and Andrew Arden's first edition of Volume 3 was published to celebrate the birth of the assured tenancy. Much in that book that at the time was necessarily tentative and untested has been proved to be correct and full of insight by ten years of experience and exegesis. Other matters have been subjected to learned judicial disagreement. Yet more matters have arisen that could not have been foreseen at the time the first edition was written, not least of these the refinements and extensions that Parliament has made to the law of residential landlord and tenant. All in all, it was time for a new edition.

Like its predecessor, this book attempts to set out a comprehensive statement of the law governing assured tenancies and related matters. Although the Rent Acts properly so called have continued to exercise judicial minds at the highest levels, the assured tenancy is by now a widely familiar creature, and is properly deserving of a text in its own right. Where the first edition sought to make comparisons to the Rent Acts, and to incorporate by reference some of the existing text in Volumes 1 and 2, this edition seeks wherever possible to address more of the applicable law within its own covers. At the same time, needless repetition and reproduction of text, where not centrally important to assured tenancies, has been sought to be avoided, and on occasions the reader will find himself referred to Volume 1. There is, after all, still much of relevance to assured tenancies that can be elicited from almost a whole century of learning on the Rent Acts; and this book, though now a separate publication, is intended to remain closely related to Sir Robert's classic text. Whether this approach is the best of both worlds or falls between two stools, I must leave to the pens and purses of others to judge.

Of the developments over the last decade, the most significant has been the emergence of the assured shorthold tenancy as the standard assured tenancy, and this is reflected in the amendments to the Act of 1988 made by the Housing Act 1996 which give it primacy. That Act has also introduced a new regime for "social landlords" in place of existing housing associations legislation, and a new homelessness code, each of which has some impact on assured tenancies. A new scheme for long residential tenancies has emerged from the Local Government and Housing Act 1989, under which assured tenancies will come into existence at the end of the long terms, and, owing to transitional provisions, it is only now beginning to be considered in practice. Important changes have been made by the Family Act 1996 to the rights of spouses, ex-spouses and co-habitant in relation to property, replacing the Matrimonial Homes Act 1983. Many judgments have been given, of course, and a lot of these are concerned with the validity or otherwise of notices for or relevant to recovering possession under assured tenancies, and with the statutory tort of unlawful eviction.

The enormous procedural changes contained in the new Civil Procedure Rules and the associated Practice Directions were at an insufficiently advanced stage when the manuscript and first proofs were completed for them to have been included in the book. The early indications, however, are that no substantial changes will be made to the special procedures relevant to the Act of 1988. Any that there are will be considered fully in the next edition of the Cumulative Supplement.

In expressing gratitude to those who have helped me with this book, I must start with the learned authors of the first edition, who created a remarkably clear and helpful structure, part by part and chapter by chapter, which I have not changed. Indeed, the only addition to the structure is Chapter 10, dealing with long residential tenancies, and these are one of the new developments cited above. As ever, I am indebted to the publishers for their support and understanding and, more tangibly, for the production of the tables of cases, statutes and statutory instruments, and for the production of the appendices and index. Emily Windsor brought unrivalled experience of county court possession actions to bear on the proofs and in doing so made many useful suggestions and comments that I have been able to incorporate.

The law is stated as at April 1, 1999, but I have been able to include a few citations of cases reported after that date.

FALCON CHAMBERS T. M. FANCOURT

CONTENTS OF VOLUME THREE

PART FIVE: RENT

TABLE OF CASES

TABLE OF STATUTES

Bold type indicates where the text of the statute has been reproduced.

TABLE OF STATUTORY INSTRUMENTS

AN INTRODUCTORY SURVEY

This book replaces Volume 3 of the eleventh edition of *Megarry's The Rent Acts*. It is also an independent book in its own right. Its main subject consists of the provisions made by the Housing Act 1988 for residential tenancies in the private sector. These provisions are gradually replacing the provisions of the Rent Acts that are dealt with in Volumes 1 and 2 of *The Rent Acts*, though the process is necessarily a slow and gradual one, and is likely to take many years to complete. Before considering the details of the Act (which will be called the "Act of 1988"), it may be helpful to set out a brief survey of this volume and of some of the main concepts of the Act of 1988.

1. Arrangement

This volume is arranged in five parts. Part One is general: the two Chapters deal with the relevant statutes, and also with the jurisdiction of the courts and rent assessment committees. The eight chapters of Part Two are concerned with the application of the Act of 1988. The first two chapters (3 and 4) set out the requirements for being an assured tenancy and the categories of tenancy which cannot be assured tenancies. Then Chapters 5 and 6 consider other tenancies (and especially their conversion into assured tenancies), and the nature of assured tenancies. The four last chapters (7–10) deal with statutory periodic tenancies, assured shorthold tenancies, assured agricultural occupancies and long tenancies at a low rent.

Part Three is concerned with dispositions of tenancies, Chapter 11 with dispositions *inter vivos*, and Chapter 12 with transmission on death. Part Four covers security of occupation. Chapter 13 considers restrictions on the landlord's right to possession, and the next two chapters respectively set out the mandatory and the discretionary grounds for possession under the Act. Chapter 16 examines protection from eviction as extended by the Act of 1988. Finally, in Chapters 17 and 18, Part Five discusses rent and the limited provisions made for the determination of rents by rent assessment committees for assured periodic tenancies and assured shorthold tenancies respectively.

2. The Housing Act 1988

Part I of the Act of 1988 came into force on January 15, 1989, two months after the Act received the Royal Assent. One of the main effects of the Act was to divide residential tenancies of dwellings in the private sector into two categories, depending on whether or not the tenancy was entered into before January 15, 1989 or pursuant to a contract made before that date.

(a) Old tenancies

If a tenancy was entered into before January 15, 1989 (or pursuant to a contract made before that date) and was a protected or statutory tenancy under the Rent Act 1977 (as amended), it continued after that date to be a protected or statutory tenancy under that Act. The same applies if the existing tenant is granted a new tenancy by the same landlord, or, if the court so directs, where the tenant is provided with alternative accommodation. The Act of 1988 has made some amendments to the Act of 1977, but it has not repealed it, and in its amended form the Act of 1977 continues to govern what for brevity may be called "old tenancies". Yet there are some circumstances in which a protected or statutory tenancy may be taken out of the Act of 1977 on being converted into another type of tenancy. Thus where there is a transmission on the death of an original protected or statutory tenant on or after January 15, 1989 and the successor is the tenant's spouse, the transmitted tenancy will continue as a statutory tenancy under the Act of 1977; but if instead the successor is merely a member of the tenant's family, the tenancy will become an assured tenancy, and the Act of 1977 will apply no longer. And a second transmission under the Rent Acts will give rise to an assured tenancy. Again, where the landlord's interest is transferred from the private sector to the public sector, a protected or statutory tenancy will normally become a secure tenancy, but the reverse does not generally apply, with the result that a tenancy may become an assured tenancy even though, by birth, it was an "old" tenancy.

(b) New tenancies

A tenancy entered into on or after January 15, 1989 (unless in pursuance of a contract made before that date) will not be a protected tenancy under the Act of 1977 but will be an assured tenancy under the Act of 1988, provided it satisfies various requirements as to residential occupation, level of rent, and not being an excepted tenancy. The tenancy may be periodic or for a fixed term, however long or short. There is also a special kind of assured tenancy called an "assured shorthold tenancy", which has proved by far the most important during the first ten years of life of the Act of 1988, and its importance has been reflected in amendments made by the Housing Act 1996 to give primacy to assured shorthold tenancies.

It is sometimes said that the Act of 1977 is being "phased out";[1] but this is misleading, for there is no phasing. The Act of 1988 will prevent the creation of many new protected tenancies, but mainly it will produce a slow and prolonged period during which more and more protected and statutory tenancies

[1] See Act of 1988, Pt. I, heading to Chap. V.

under the Act of 1977 will come to an end, and any new letting of the dwelling will be an assured tenancy under the Act of 1988. This process may be contrasted with that under the Act of 1923, whereby dwellings became completely decontrolled as soon as the landlord obtained actual possession of them. Under the Act of 1988, the process is not the removal of all protection, but the replacement of a greater protection by a lesser.

(c) The dual systems

There are thus now two systems in operation, one under the Act of 1977 (as amended) and the other under the Act of 1988. They will operate side by side, probably for many years. Both are covered by the two volumes of *The Rent Acts* and this book, together with the Cumulative Supplement, which will be updated during 1999. Further Cumulative Supplements will be published from time to time to keep the text up to date. When the first edition of Volume 3 was published (1989), the Introductory Survey pronounced that "for some time to come, the law governing old tenancies will be the law most commonly applicable". This proved rapidly not to be the case, and assured tenacies, in particular assured shorthold tenancies, are now the lifeblood of the practitioner in the private residential field. There remain, of course, many protected and statutory tenancies under the Act of 1977, and Volume 1 of *The Rent Acts* and the Supplement will continue to deal with these. Volume 2 contains the statutes up to the time of the Act of 1988, and new statutes applying to the subject matter of Volume 1 (such as the new regime for long tenancies under Schedule 10 to the Local Government and Housing Act 1989) will be published in the Supplement. The law governing new tenancies is set out in this book, and the Supplement will keep this up to date too. Many provisions of the Act of 1988, however, are identical with earlier statutory provisions that have been fully discussed in Volume 1, or are closely similar to them; and although this volume is intended to be independent, needless repetition has been avoided by sufficiently indicating the point and giving the appropriate page references to Volume 1. But in other respects the whole of the law governing new tenancies in the private sector is considered in detail in this volume.

(d) A proliferation of categories

For many years to come, one of the problems for practitioners and others will be that of making the correct classification of the type of tenancy with which they are concerned. There seem to be ever more classes; probably too many. Quite apart from business tenancies,[2] agricultural holdings,[3] farm business tenancies,[4] secure tenancies,[5] and "introductory tenancies",[6] and the impact that they

[2] Under Landlord and Tenant Act 1954, Pt. II.
[3] Under Agricultural Holdings Act 1986.
[4] Under Agricultural Tenancies Act 1995.
[5] Under Housing Act 1985, Pt. IV.
[6] Under Housing Act 1996, Pt. V.

sometimes have on tenancies under the Act of 1988,[7] residential tenancies in the private sector fall into the following categories of statutory control:

(1) Protected tenancies and statutory tenancies under the Act of 1977.
(2) Assured tenancies.
(3) Protected occupancies and statutory tenancies under the Rent (Agriculture) Act 1976 ("the Act of 1976").
(4) Assured agricultural occupancies.
(5) Restricted contracts under the Act of 1977.
(6) Housing association tenancies under Part VI of the Act of 1977.
(7) Long tenancies at a low rent under Part I of the Landlord and Tenant Act 1954.
(8) Long tenancies at a low rent under Schedule 10 to the Local Government and Housing Act 1989.
(9) Statutory periodic tenancies.
(10) Protected shorthold tenancies.
(11) Old assured shorthold tenancies.
(12) New assured shorthold tenancies.
(13) Assured tenancies held of registered social landlords under Part I of the Housing Act 1996.

Thankfully, at least old assured tenacies under the Housing Act 1980 have ceased to exist.[8] But the remaining array is formidable, and even it conceals some sub-categories, such as original and derivative assured shorthold tenancies. "Complexity can be an evil in itself".[9]

3. Assured tenancies and assured shorthold tenancies

(a) The tenancies

Assured tenancies and assured shorthold tenancies are the two most important types of tenancy under the Act of 1988. Assured tenancies were originally introduced by the Housing Act 1980. Under this, they were confined to certain types of landlord and certain categories of dwellings. Assured tenancies under the Act of 1988 are no longer restricted in this way, but are generally available to all. Further, apart from assured tenancies then subject to a pending application for a new tenancy, on January 15, 1989, all existing assured tenancies under the Act of 1980 became assured tenancies under the Act of 1988.

An assured shorthold tenancy is an assured tenancy. There are two categories of shorthold tenancy under the Act of 1988, dependant on whether the tenancy was entered into before or pursuant to a contract made before February 28,

[7] Case law on secure tenancies has been particularly fruitful in the last ten years, and often of direct applicability to the Act of 1988.
[8] See *infra*.
[9] Vol. 1, p. 211.

1997: "old" and "new" assured shorthold tenancies. Old assured shorthold tenancies were granted for a fixed term of not less than six months, under which the landlord had no power to determine it during the first six months, and after the landlord had given the tenant a warning notice that the tenancy was to be a shorthold. Such a tenancy is best called an "original" old assured shorthold tenancy, because if when it ends a new assured tenancy of the same premises between the same parties comes into being, it too will be an assured shorthold tenancy. This is so even if it satisfies none of the requirements for an original assured shorthold tenancy and is, for example, a tenancy for one month, or a weekly tenancy. Such tenancies will be called "derivative" assured shorthold tenancies. The above restrictions on the grant of an original assured shorthold tenancy were abolished with effect from February 28, 1997 by the Housing Act 1996. On or after that date, any tenancy granted which is an assured tenancy is an assured shorthold tenancy, regardless of the length or type of term granted, the terms of the tenancy, and despite the absence of any warning notice, unless it falls within a few exceptional cases where the tenancy cannot be a shorthold tenancy. So even a week's tenancy will be a new assured shorthold tenancy. Some measure of security of tenure is afforded a tenant under such a tenancy by restricting the landlord's right to possession of the dwelling-house before six months have expired from the commencement of the original tenancy. Both in terms of possession and rent control, the distinction between an original and a derivative new assured shorthold tenancy is unimportant, save that it is necessary to be able to identify when the original tenancy started.

(b) Rent

The rent under an assured tenancy is free from any restriction to a statutory "fair rent" under the Act of 1977, or to any rent registered under that or any other Act. In general, the tenant must pay whatever rent he has agreed to pay, and cannot get it reduced by applying to a rent officer or a rent assessment committee. To this general rule there are three important qualifications.

(i) ASSURED PERIODIC TENANCY. First, if the landlord seeks to increase the rent payable under an assured periodic tenancy by serving a statutory notice of increase, the tenant may apply to the rent assessment committee for the determination of the rent at which the dwelling might reasonably be expected to be let in the open market by a willing landlord under the assured tenancy. The rent so determined will become the rent payable by the tenant. But, except in the case of a statutory periodic tenancy, no such increase can be made before the end of the first year of the tenancy; and if the landlord refrains from attempting to increase the rent, the tenant remains liable to pay the agreed rent, however unreasonable he considers it to be. The rent under an assured fixed term tenancy cannot be referred to the rent assessment committee. But periodic assured shorthold tenancies do fall within this category.

(ii) ORIGINAL OLD ASSURED SHORTHOLD TENANCY. Secondly, a tenant under an original old assured shorthold tenancy may at any time refer the rent to the rent assessment committee for a determination of the rent that the landlord "might reasonably be expected to obtain" under the tenancy, and the rent so determined will replace the agreed rent. But no such determination can be made unless the committee considers that the rent is "significantly higher" than the level of rents under assured tenancies in the locality and there is also a sufficiency of "comparables". There is no such right to refer the rent of a derivative old assured shorthold tenancy to the committee, though if it is a periodic tenancy and the landlord serves a statutory notice of increase, the tenant may apply to the committee under the previous paragraph.

(iii) NEW ASSURED SHORTHOLD TENANCY. Thirdly, a tenant under a new assured shorthold tenancy may refer the rent to the rent assessment committee for a determination on the same basis and subject to the same restrictions as apply in the case of an original old assured shorthold tenancy, above. The right of a new assured shorthold tenant to refer his rent does not depend on whether his tenancy is original or derivative; but his right so to refer the rent ends after the lapse of six months from the beginning of the original tenancy. So, if a three month tenancy is first granted, and it is either renewed or a statutory periodic tenancy is deemed to be granted, the tenant has three months after the start of the new, replacement tenancy to refer his rent. But once the six months have expired, the grant of a new tenancy will not give the tenant the right to refer his rent unless either the dwelling-house which is the subject of the new tenancy is not substantially the same as that let under the previous tenancy, or the identity of the landlord or the tenant has changed.

(c) Security of tenure

Statute provides a substantial degree of security of tenure for assured tenancies, but very little for assured shorthold tenancies. For assured tenancies, security of tenure rests not on a statutory tenancy arising on the determination of the contractual tenancy, but on the statutory preservation of the assured tenancy, or its replacement by a contractual periodic tenancy. The Act of 1988 provides that an assured tenancy cannot be brought to an end except by an order of the court, or, if the tenancy is for a fixed term, by the landlord exercising a power of determination in the tenancy, *e.g.*, under a break clause in it. If an assured tenancy for a fixed term does come to an end, then unless it does so by virtue of an order of the court or a surrender or other action by the tenant, the tenant is entitled to remain in possession of the dwelling under a periodic tenancy arising under the Act; and the terms of this tenancy may be varied by the rent assessment committee. The grounds on which the court may make an order for possession resemble those under the Act of 1977, though there are many important differences. The grounds, some discretionary and some mandatory, include mandatory grounds where the landlord intends to demolish or reconstruct the dwelling, or where at least eight weeks' rent is unpaid.

Assured shorthold tenancies are completely different. If the tenancy is an old assured shorthold tenancy for a fixed term, the landlord can obtain an order for possession as of right at the end of the term, provided that he has given the tenant two months' prior notice that he requires possession. If the tenancy is an old periodic assured shorthold tenancy, the landlord is similarly entitled to an order for possession as of right, though here the two months' notice must specify a date for possession that coincides with the last day of a period of the tenancy. In both these cases, the tenant is entitled to retain possession under a periodic tenancy until the landlord secures an order of the court, and to this extent some limited security of tenure is provided.

In the case of new assured shorthold tenancies, the notice requiring possession provisions are the same as for old assured shorthold tenancies. Here, some limited further security is given by the restriction that the court may not make an order for possession of a dwelling-house let on a new assured shorthold tenancy to take effect earlier than six months from the beginning of the original tenancy.

4. Other tenancies and contracts

There are other types of tenancy and contract which continue to be subject to the law as it stood before the Act of 1988 came into force.

(a) Housing association tenancies and secure tenancies

Tenants of housing associations, housing trusts and the Housing Corporation were, prior to the Act of 1988, usually secure tenants under Part IV of the Housing Act 1985, as well as being housing association tenants. The Act of 1988 treats such tenancies in much the same way as it treats protected or statutory tenancies under the Act of 1977. If the tenancy was entered into before January 15, 1989 (or pursuant to a contract made before that date), it remains a housing association tenancy within Part VI of the Act of 1977, and a secure tenancy; and the same applies if the existing tenant is granted a new tenancy by the same landlord. But, subject to those provisions, no new housing association tenancies can be granted after January 15, 1989, and the ''housing association group'' of landlords[10] cannot satisfy the ''landlord condition'' for the grant of a secure tenancy after that date.

(b) Protected shorthold tenancies

Those who were protected shorthold tenants, or protected or statutory tenants subject to the mandatory protected shorthold ground for possession, on January 15, 1989, continue to be subject to the Acts of 1977 and 1980. But if such a tenant is thereafter granted a new tenancy by the person (or one of the persons) who was his landlord under that tenancy, the new tenancy will be an assured shorthold tenancy if it otherwise satisfied the requirements of the Act of 1988 for an assured tenancy.

[10] *i.e.* those identified above.

(c) Protected agricultural occupancies

Those who were protected occupiers under the Rent (Agriculture) Act 1976 on January 15, 1989, continue to be subject to that Act. But no new occupancy can be granted after that date except pursuant to a contract made before it or by way of re-grant to an existing protected occupier or statutory tenant under the Act of 1976.

(d) Restricted contracts

Restricted contracts existing on January 15, 1989, continue to be subject to the Act of 1977. No contract made on or after that date can be a restricted contract unless it was made pursuant to a contract made before that date. If a restricted contract is varied on or after that date, the question whether this has given rise to a new contract will usually be decided according to the general law. But if a variation affects the amount of rent, the contract must be treated as a new contract unless the variation is merely an increase or decrease in the rent that is made by a rent tribunal, or is made by the parties in order to make the rent the same as the registered rent.

Part One

GENERAL

Chapter 1

The Acts

Sect. 1. The Acts

1. Housing Act 1988

The provisions of the Act of 1988 relating to assured tenancies are found in Part I of the Act and its Schedules. Part I of the Act is divided into six Chapters. **1–01**

Chapter I (sections 1–19) and Schedules 1 and 2 contain the main provisions governing assured tenancies. Chapter II (sections 19A–23) and Schedule 2A set out further provisions that apply to assured shorthold tenancies, while Chapter III (sections 24–26) and Schedule 3 are concerned with assured agricultural occupancies. Chapter IV (sections 27–33) makes substantial amendments to statutory provisions for protection from eviction and against harassment, for protected and statutory tenants under the Rent Act 1977 as well as for assured tenants and agricultural occupiers under the Act of 1988. Chapter V (sections 34–39) and Schedule 4 enact transitional provisions, including certain amendments to the Rent (Agriculture) Act 1976 and the Rent Act 1977, which will be discussed in this book only so far as they are relevant to assured tenancies.[1] Chapter VI (sections 40–45) contains a number of general provisions.

Part I came into force on January 15, 1989.[2] Substantial amendments were made (in addition to other earlier, minor amendments) by the Housing Act 1996 with effect from various dates in 1996 and 1997. These relate principally to assured shorthold tenancies and grounds for possession. **1–02**

2. Other Acts

In addition to the Housing Act 1988 (which will usually be cited as the "Act of 1988"), certain other Acts are of importance in this book. They are mainly the following: **1–03**

[1] For other amendments, see the Cumulative Supplement to *The Rent Acts*.

[2] Act of 1988, s.141(3), also applying to Pt V with various exceptions; and see *post*, para. 5–08.

Rent (Agriculture) Act 1976 (sometimes referred to for convenience as the "Act of 1976");
Rent Act 1977 (usually referred to as the "Act of 1977");
Protection from Eviction Act 1977;
Housing Act 1980;
Housing Act 1985;
Local Government and Housing Act 1989; and
Housing Act 1996.

Occasional references to earlier Rent Acts will normally be made in the shortened form used in Volume 1,[3] for example "Act of 1968".

3. Application

1–04 Part I of the Act of 1988 applies to England and Wales.[4] It also applies to the Isles of Scilly, but subject to such exceptions, adaptations and modifications as the Secretary of State may by order direct.[5] Any such order must be made by a statutory instrument which will be subject to annulment in pursuance of a resolution of either House of Parliament.[6] Part I does not apply to Northern Ireland,[7] or to Scotland.[8]

4. Information

1–05 Local authorities are authorised to publish information for the benefit of landlords and tenants with respect to their rights and duties under the Act of 1977 and certain other Acts.[9] This authority now extends to the corresponding provisions of the Act of 1988.[10]

Sect. 2. Construing the Acts

1–06 In general, what has been said in Volume 1 about construing the Rent Acts[11] appears to apply equally to Part I of the Act of 1988. Where they cover the same ground, the two sets of statutory provisions have broadly similar objectives which they seek to achieve by comparable means. Further, the Act of 1988 adopts much of the terminology of the Rent Acts and, unless the context other-

[3] See Vol. 1, p. 10.
[4] Act of 1988, s.141(5).
[5] *ibid.*, s.139(1). No such order has been made.
[6] *ibid.*, s.139(2).
[7] *ibid.*, s.141(6).
[8] The comparable statute for Scotland is Housing (Scotland) Act 1988, Pt. II.
[9] Act of 1977, s.149; Vol. 1, pp. 348, 349.
[10] Act of 1988, s.43, applying to Pt. I, Chaps I to III (*i.e.* ss.1–26).
[11] Vol. 1, pp. 12–18.

wise requires, those terms were presumably used with the meanings that they had acquired. But two qualifications must be made to this general approach. First, the Act of 1988 differs from the Act of 1977 in that the Act of 1977 was primarily a consolidation Act[12], and the Act of 1988 is not. The Act of 1988 is accordingly not affected by the presumption that the provisions of a consolidation Act have the same effect as had the earlier provisions that they replace.[13] Secondly, the housing and social background which obtains when an Act relating to tenancies is passed may affect the construction of the Act.[14] Thus, for example, the court has refused to treat the Housing Act 1980[15] as having provided for the creation of a statutory tenancy or similar right, even though the Act of 1920 had been held to give rise to a statutory tenancy in comparable circumstances.[16] And in relation to the Act of 1988, the courts have shown on occasions a willingness to adopt a more purposive and even liberal approach to the construction of statutory requirements, where previously a stricter approach to a statute conferring security of tenure on tenants would have prevailed.[17]

Sect. 3. No Contracting Out

1. The rule

The general principle under the Rent Acts that it is impossible to contract out of the Acts, as examined in Volume 1[18] and recently reaffirmed by the House of Lords,[19] plainly applies with equal force to Part I of the Act of 1988. This principle is fortified under the Act of 1988 by an express provision that renders ineffective any obligation or document entered into or made by the tenant on or before the tenancy is granted or deemed to be granted if it will terminate the tenancy while it is an assured tenancy.[20] **1–07**

2. Transactions outside the Act of 1988

(a) Genuine transactions

Under the Rent Acts there is nothing to prevent the parties from so arranging matters that there is nothing to which the Acts can apply, for example because **1–08**

[12] See Vol. 2, p. 488 for the list of statutes consolidated.
[13] Vol. 1, p. 13.
[14] See *Harrison v. Hammersmith and Fulham L.B.C.* [1981] 1 W.L.R. 650 at 661, 666, CA.
[15] Now Housing Act 1985, Pt. IV (secure tenancies).
[16] *Harrison v. Hammersmith and Fulham L.B.C., supra*; and see *post*, para. 7–06 for differences in machinery.
[17] Compare *Marath v. MacGillivray* (1996) 28 H.L.R. 484 at 495, CA, *per* Sir Iain Glidewell (on possession notices under the Act of 1988) with *Torridge D.C. v. Jones* (1985) 18 H.L.R. 107 at 114, CA, *per* Oliver L.J. (on possession notices under the Housing Act 1980).
[18] Vol. 1, pp. 26–30.
[19] *Antoniades v. Villiers* [1990] A.C. 417.
[20] Act of 1988, s.5(5); see *post*, para. 6–13.

there is multiple sharing of the dwelling, or because a tenant is required to share living accommodation with his landlord. Thus the Acts do not apply to the common type of flat-sharing arrangements under which no occupant has any right to the exclusive possession of any part of the flat, even if in practice each is the sole occupier of a bedroom. This was established in a case where four people each made separate arrangements with the owner of a flat, at different dates and on different terms, whereby each was permitted to use the flat in common with not more than three others;[21] and it makes no difference if the arrangements are made simultaneously and in identical terms.[22] Such transactions create mere licences; they will not be treated as being joint tenancies dressed up as licences, and unless they create individual tenancies of individual rooms the Rent Acts have no application.[23] It seems clear that similar principles must apply under the Act of 1988: if the arrangement is genuinely one that falls outside the Act, its provisions do not apply to the arrangement in question.

(b) Shams and pretences

1–09 Under the Rent Acts the distinction between evasion and avoidance is firmly established. If in truth and substance a transaction falls outside the Acts, the courts will not treat it as being within the Acts on the ground that the landlord is trying to escape them.[24] But if a transaction is merely dressed up so as to look as if it is outside the Acts, whereas in reality it falls within them, the courts will disregard the dressing up and apply the Acts.[25] The courts will consider the reality of the transaction and disregard mere shams. Yet although astute to detect and frustrate sham devices, the court will approach the question even-handedly, and only if, viewed in that light, some feature seems to be a pretence will the court consider whether there is an attempt to evade the Acts.[26] This doctrine too appears to be fully applicable to the Act of 1988.

1–10 Recently, the doctrine of disregarding shams has been further developed. At one time a transaction would not have been held to be a sham unless all the parties had the common intention that it was not to create the legal rights and obligations that it appeared to create.[27] Today, such a common intention seems to be no longer required,[28] and in any case the courts will disregard any provision which is a mere "pretence", "disguise", "smoke screen" or "window dressing", as they have been variously described,[29] even if a common intention is lacking. The courts give effect to the real, and not to the unreal, however skil-

[21] *A.G. Securities v. Vaughan* [1990] A.C. 417 (reported with *Antoniades v. Villiers, supra*).
[22] *Stribling v. Wickham* (1989) 21 H.L.R. 381, CA.
[23] *A.G. Securities v. Vaughan, supra.*
[24] *ibid.*
[25] *Antoniades v. Villiers, supra.*
[26] *Stribling v. Wickham* (1989) 21 H.L.R. 381, CA; and see *Brennan v. Lambeth L.B.C.* (1997) 30 H.L.R. 481, CA.
[27] See *Snook v. London and West Riding Investments Ltd.* [1967] 2 Q.B. 786 at 802, CA, applied in *Antoniades v. Villiers* [1988] 3 W.L.R. 139, CA, reversed *infra.*
[28] See *Antoniades v. Villiers* [1990] A.C. 417 at 468G–470A, 475G–477C.
[29] *ibid.* at pp. 454F, 463, 469B, E–F.

fully and powerfully drafted. This was established by *Antoniades v. Villiers,*[30] where a man and a woman living together were each granted simultaneous and identical "licences" to "use" a furnished two-roomed flat containing a double bed, each paying separate but equal monthly sums to the owner. Apart from the drafting, all the circumstances pointed to the grant of a joint tenancy; and joint tenants the House of Lords held the "licensees" to be. This was so despite the attempt to split a single transaction into two, and despite the presence of clauses negativing any right to the exclusive use or possession of any part of the flat, and reserving a right for the owner to use and permit others to use the flat together with the licensees, as well as other anti-tenancy provisions. In particular, the owner's right to use the flat himself and authorise others to use it was held to be merely an attempt to exclude the Rent Acts that was never intended to be used, except possibly for bringing pressure to bear in order to obtain possession. The court must consider all the surrounding circumstances of the transaction, including the relationship between the occupiers, the course of negotiations, the nature and extent of the accommodation, and the intended and actual mode of occupation.[31] What matters is the true substance of the transaction, not mere unrealities or labels; those seeking a home may well agree to anything in order to obtain it, but their agreement to terms that seek to show that what is really a tenancy is merely a licence will be ineffective as being an attempt to contract out of the Acts.[32]

The grant of a licence to occupy a single small room which contained provisions negativing any right to exclusive possession, allowing the licensor to permit others to use the room, and depriving the licensee of any right of occupation for ninety minutes a day (the licensor retaining a set of keys), will create a tenancy where these provisions are wholly unrealistic pretences, and the retention of a set of keys is not *per se* inconsistent with the existence of a tenancy.[33] Where a licence to occupy a whole house[34] was granted on similar terms, a tenancy was created, the true bargain being that the licensees were entitled to exclusive occupation unless and until the owner actively sought another occupant.[35]

The astuteness of the courts to ensure that arrangements which are in truth tenancies are not covered up by carefully drafted language to the contrary must not be taken too far, however. Thus where a licence agreement was of a familiar type which provided for hostel accommodation and which, for the better running of the hostel, allowed the hostel managers to move occupants from room to room, the court was not required to be astute to ignore the clear wording of the agreement and to say that it was arguable that the agreement was a sham.[36]

30 [1990] A.C. 417.

31 *ibid.* at pp. 458G–H, 462E, 476F–477A. Subsequent conduct, though irrelevant to construction, is relevant to genuineness: see p. 469C.

32 See *City of Westminster v. Clarke* [1992] 2 A.C. 288 at 302, *per* Lord Templeman.

33 *Aslan v. Murphy (No. 1)* [1990] 1 W.L.R. 766, CA.

34 Such that there was at least the practical ability to introduce a sharer or sharers.

35 *Duke v. Wynne* [1990] 1 W.L.R. 766, CA, and see also *Family Housing Association v. Jones* [1990] 1 W.L.R. 779, CA. *Sed quaere*: the "licensees" either had exclusive possession or they had not. If the "licensor" genuinely had the right to introduce others, they did not have a tenancy whether or not in fact the right was exercised.

36 *Brennan v. Lambeth L.B.C.* (1997) 30 H.L.R. 481 at 485, *per* Brooke L.J. See also *City of Westminster v. Clarke, supra*, and the observations of Lord Bridge of Harwich in *A.G. Securities v. Vaughan* [1990] A.C. 417 at 454C.

(c) Division into pre-ordained steps

1–11 There is another aspect of the matter. Statutory protection for a tenancy cannot be excluded by splitting up the grant of the tenancy into two or more pre-ordained steps and then relying upon the absence of protection for the result of the last step: the courts will give effect to the transaction as a whole and disregard the separate steps.[37] But there are limits to the extent to which actual dispositions of interests in land can be disregarded. And if a landlord, seeking to prevent any security of tenure arising, refuses to let a dwelling to anyone except a limited company on terms which preclude sharing or parting with possession or occupation of the dwelling but permit it to be occupied by a nominee of the company, the letting will not create an assured tenancy vested in the nominee; for both in form and in substance the letting to the company was what was intended, and in no sense was the company merely the nominee's agent.[38] The same has been held to apply even if the occupier is a person who, with the landlord's knowledge, purchased a company and had the tenancy granted to it in order to be able to occupy the dwelling as the company's nominee.[39] The matter now appears to be beyond argument,[40] the approach in these cases seeming to be consonant with the decisions of the House of Lords in *A.G. Securities v. Vaughan*, *Antoniades v. Villiers* and *City of Westminster v. Clarke*.[41] The same approach will doubtless also apply under the Act of 1988.

(d) Diminished protection

1–12 Similar principles apply where the question is not the exclusion of security of tenure but its diminution. Thus, where protected tenants of a house had no protection against eviction by the mortgagee because their tenancies had been granted subsequently to the mortgage without the requisite consent of the mortgagee, the landlord's wife was held to be unable to evict them after taking a transfer of the mortgage; for the reality was that she was claiming possession not as a mortgagee seeking to enforce her security but as agent for the landlord.[42] Similarly, where Rent Act protected tenants, whose tenancies pre-dated a mort-

[37] *Gisbourne v. Burton* [1989] Q.B. 390, CA (grant of tenancy of farm by husband to his wife and then grant of sub-tenancy by wife to proposed farmer: farmer held to be direct tenant of husband and wife a mere agent or nominee for the landlord).

[38] *Estavest Investments Ltd. v. Commercial Investments Ltd.* (1987) 21 H.L.R. 106, CA (decision under the Rent Acts: company, not nominee, a protected tenant).

[39] *Hilton v. Plustitle Ltd.* [1989] 1 W.L.R. 149, CA (leave to appeal refused [1989] 1 W.L.R. 310, HL), unwittingly disposing of the suggestion to the contrary at first instance in the *Estavest* case, *supra*, at p. 110.

[40] The Court of Appeal again declined to interfere with the trial judge's finding that a company letting was genuine and reflected the true intentions of the parties in *Kaye v. Massbetter* (1990) 62 P. & C.R. 558.

[41] *Supra*.

[42] *Quennell v. Maltby* [1979] 1 W.L.R. 318, CA, where the mortgage was for far less than the value of the house, and the mortgagee had refused to evict the tenants. See also *Barrett v. Morgan* [1998] 3 E.G.L.R. 3, CA.

gage, agreed to the mortgagee's having priority to their interests, their security of tenure under the Act of 1977 was unaffected.[43]

3. No contracting in

Like the Rent Acts, the Act of 1988 cannot be made to apply to a transaction that is not within it; yet there similarly seems to be no reason why the parties should not by contract give the tenant what in effect are similar rights.[44] Indeed, compared with the Rent Acts, the Act of 1988 is more firmly based on contract in that it maintains the existence of the contract by fettering the landlord's power to determine it, rather than by substituting a statutory tenancy when the contract has ended. A party to a tenancy cannot estop himself from denying that the Act of 1988 applies any more than in relation to the Act of 1977.[45] The reason is that such an Act applies as a matter of statute and not because the parties agree that it does.[46] But if parties can agree expressly that a collection of rights binds them, which rights are equivalent to those that would bind them if the tenancy were within the Act, there seems to be no reason *in principle* why an estoppel to the same effect cannot arise.[47] **1–13**

In limited respects, the application of the Acts of 1977 and 1988 is a matter of agreement between the parties, and to this extent an estoppel may arise which has the effect that protection under the Acts exists where otherwise it would not. So, for example, where under the Act of 1977 an incoming tenant may become the statutory tenant of the dwelling in substitution for the previous tenant by agreement between the tenants and the landlord,[48] a landlord may by his conduct estop himself from denying that the incoming person is the statutory tenant.[49] **1–14**

[43] *Woolwich Building Society v. Dickman* (1996) 72 P. & C.R. 470, CA. The decision is not altogether satisfactory, having been decided on the basis that the protected tenancies were overriding interests under Land Registration Act 1925, s.70(1)(k) which could not be postponed to the subsequent registered chargee's interest. But the earlier decision of the Court of Appeal in *Paddington Building Society v. Mendelssohn* (1985) 50 P. & C.R. 244, which held that overriding interests could by even an *implied* agreement be postponed, was not apparently cited to the court. A better basis for the decision would have been that the agreement with the mortgagee was with someone claiming under the landlord and not with title paramount, and as such amounted to contracting out of the Rent Acts.

[44] Consider *Clays Lane Housing Co-operative Ltd. v. Patrick* (1984) 49 P. & C.R. 72, CA (unprotected tenant given by contract some but not all of the security of a secure tenant).

[45] See *Daejan Properties Ltd. v. Mahoney* [1995] 2 E.G.L.R. 75, CA.

[46] Consider *Guestheath Ltd. v. Mirza* (1990) 22 H.L.R. 399, QB.

[47] Though it is suggested that a mere representation by words or conduct that the Act applies will not suffice, for a party cannot be estopped from denying that legal consequence. *Semble* the representation would have to be to the effect that the landlord was willing to treat the tenant as if he had equivalent rights.

[48] *i.e.* under Act of 1977, Sched. 1, Pt. II, para. 13.

[49] *Daejan Properties Ltd. v. Mahoney* [1995] 2 E.G.L.R. 75, CA (landlord estopped from denying that second statutory successor was mother and daughter jointly, rather than just mother, so that daughter remained statutory tenant after death of mother).

Chapter 2

Jurisdiction

Jurisdiction under the Act of 1988 will be considered under four heads. These are:

(1) County Courts;
(2) Appeals from County Courts;
(3) The High Court; and
(4) Rent Assessment Committees.

Sect. 1. County Courts

1. Jurisdiction

2–01 On July 1, 1991, a new scheme of general application for distribution of work between the county courts and the High Court, specifying the jurisdiction of each, came into effect.[1] Essentially, the limits to county court jurisdiction have been removed;[2] county courts and the High Court are given co-extensive jurisdiction;[3] and proceedings may be commenced in either.[4] There are, however, a number of specified cases (none relevant to the Rent Acts or to the Act of 1988[5]) in which proceedings must be brought in the High Court, or in a county court.[6] Otherwise both the High Court and county courts are given wide discretionary

[1] Courts and Legal Services Act 1990, s.1; High Court and County Courts Jurisdiction Order 1991 (S.I. 1991 No. 724).
[2] County Courts Act 1984, s.15, as amended.
[3] County Courts Act 1984, s.38, substituted with effect from July 1, 1991 by Courts and Legal Services Act 1990, s.3; S.I. 1991 No. 1364.
[4] 1991 Jurisdiction Order, *supra*, art. 4.
[5] But see *post*, n. 11.
[6] 1991 Jurisdiction Order, *supra*, arts. 2(2)–(7), 5, 6.

powers to transfer proceedings at any stage, or to allocate them to the most appropriate forum for trial.[7]

The experience of the courts since 1991 has been that it is the county courts that generally exercise jurisdiction under the Rent Acts and the Act of 1988. The Act of 1988 provides that, with three exceptions, a county court has jurisdiction to hear and determine any question arising under any provision of Part I.[8] The exceptions are: **2–02**

(1) Sections 29–33, which are the sections of Chapter IV dealing with protection from eviction, other than sections 27 and 28 dealing with damages for wrongful eviction. But these excepted provisions are either amendments to the Protection from Eviction Act 1977, where the substantive jurisdiction is exercised under that statute, as amended, or definitional provisions, where there is no substantive jurisdiction to exercise. This ''exception'' therefore seems more illusory than real.
(2) Chapter VI (comprising sections 40–45), which contains certain general and administrative provisions.
(3) Any question falling within the jurisdiction of a rent assessment committee by virtue of any of the provisions in Part I,[9] apart from those in (1) or (2) above.[10]

2. Extensions of jurisdiction

Where any proceedings under the Act of 1988 within the county court's jurisdiction are brought there, that court also has jurisdiction to hear and determine other proceedings joined with those proceedings, notwithstanding that the county court would not otherwise have such jurisdiction.[11] **2–03**

3. Costs in the High Court

The costs sanction for bringing proceedings under the Act of 1988 in the High Court where the county court has jurisdiction has been repealed.[12] Instead, the taxing master in the High Court has a general power to reduce the amount of costs to be awarded by up to 25 per cent where the proceedings should have **2–04**

[7] County Courts Act 1984, ss. 40, 41, 42, amended and substituted with effect from July 1, 1991 by Courts and Legal Services Act 1990, s.2(1), (3); S.I. 1991 No. 1364; 1991 Jurisdiction Order, art. 7. See also *Practice Direction (County Court: transfer of actions)* [1991] 1 W.L.R. 643, QB.

[8] Act of 1988, s.40(1).

[9] See *post*, paras. 7–21, 17–16, 18–04, 18–27.

[10] Act of 1988, s.40(1).

[11] Act of 1988, s.40(3). After the amendment to County Courts Act 1984, ss. 15, 38, this would appear to embrace only title to tolls, fairs, markets and franchises, libel and slander, judicial review, and certain relief specified in the County Courts Remedies Regulations 1991 (S.I. 1991 No. 1222), as amended by S.I. 1995 No. 206.

[12] Act of 1988, s.40(4), repealed on July 1, 1991 by Courts and Legal Services Act 1990, s.125(7), Sched. 20; S.I. 1991 No. 1364.

been commenced in the county court.[13] It will therefore remain both appropriate and advisable to bring straightforward cases under the Act of 1988 in the county courts.

4. Procedure

2–05 The County Court Rules have been amended to provide an accelerated procedure, commenced by originating application supported by an affidavit rather than by summons, for landlords claiming possession from assured tenants on certain mandatory grounds, and from assured shorthold tenants.[14] These are discussed in detail in Chapter 14.[15] The County Court (Forms) Rules provide, by amendment, prescribed forms for the landlord's application and affidavit in such cases.[16] In other cases, a fixed date summons must be issued.

Sect. 2. Appeals from County Courts

2–06 The Act of 1988 makes no special provision concerning appeals from county courts to the Court of Appeal, and in general the discussion in Volume 1,[17] updated by the Supplement to include the County Court Appeals Order 1991,[18] applies equally to proceedings under the Act. Any order that included the giving or refusal of possession of land required leave to appeal.[19] As From January 1, 1999, all appeals (other than exceptional matters unrelated to assured tenancies) are subject to a requirement of leave unless either the appeal was set down by that date or an application for an extension of time was lodged before that date.[19a] As under the Rent Acts,[20] the decision of a county court on the apportionment or aggregation of rateable values is final;[21] and there is no appeal on any questions of fact in possession actions brought on the discretionary grounds,[22] where an order for possession can be made only if it is reasonable to do so.[23]

[13] Supreme Court Act 1981, s.51(8), (9), substituted with effect from October 1, 1991 by Courts and Legal Services Act 1990, ss.4(1), 124(3); S.I. 1991 No. 1883.
[14] County Court Rules 1981, Ord. 49, rr. 6, 6A.
[15] *Post*, paras. 14–03 *et seq.*, 14–86 *et seq.*
[16] County Court (Forms) Rules 1982 (S.I. 1982 No. 586), r. 2, Sched., Forms N5A, N5B.
[17] pp. 50–58.
[18] S.I. 1991 No. 1877.
[19] Supreme Court Act 1981, s.18(1A), inserted by Courts and Legal Service Act 1990, s.7; Rules of the Supreme Court 1965, Ord. 59, rr. 1B(1)(d), applying to all appeals set down or applications for leave to appeal lodged on or after October 1, 1993.
[19a] RSC, Order 59, rr. 1B, substituted by the Rules of the Supreme Court (Amendment No. 2) Rules 1998 (S.I. 1998 No. 3049), rr. 3, 4.
[20] Vol. 1, pp. 50, 51, 346.
[21] See *post*, para. 4–06.
[22] *i.e.* Act of 1988, Sched. 2, Pt. II, Grounds 9 to 17.
[23] County Courts Act 1984, s.77(6)(ee), inserted by Act of 1988, s.140(1), Sched. 17, para. 35(2); and see *post*, para. 15–05.

Sect. 3. High Court

Apart from the provision as to costs considered above,[24] there are no special provisions concerning the jurisdiction of the High Court in relation to the Act of 1988; and in general the discussion in Volume 1[25] applies equally to that Act. The out-of-date requirement that, where a claim is for possession of land, the writ be indorsed with a statement showing whether the claim relates to a dwelling-house and, if so, whether the rateable value exceeds the limits for the application of the Rent Acts,[26] does not now suffice for assured tenancies in the post-domestic rates world. The same applies to the certificate or affidavit required on an application for leave to enter judgment for possession in default of appearance or of defence.[27] **2–07**

Sect. 4. Rent Assessment Committees

The Act of 1988 confers jurisdiction on rent assessment committees to determine the rent of periodic assured tenancies where the landlord has served a statutory notice of increase, to determine the rent of assured shorthold tenancies,[28] and to vary the terms of statutory periodic tenancies.[29] These jurisdictions are considered under the substantive topics.[30] **2–08**

[24] *Ante*, para. 2–04.
[25] pp. 58–60.
[26] RSC, Order 6, r.2(1)(c). *Practice Direction (Queen's Bench: 10)*, at para. 720, hopelessly fails to provide a sensible suggestion for dealing with the effect of the arrival of assured tenancies and the disappearance of domestic rates!
[27] See Vol. 1, p. 59.
[28] Act of 1988, ss. 13, 14, 22; *post*, paras. 17–16 *et seq*; paras. 18–04 *et seq*.
[29] *ibid*., s.6; *post*, para. 7–21.
[30] See nn. 28, 29, *supra*.

Part Two

APPLICATION OF THE ACT

1. The statutory provision

Under the Act of 1988, ''a tenancy under which a dwelling-house is let as a separate dwelling is for the purposes of this Act an assured tenancy if and so long as'' it complies with three conditions.[1] These are:

(a) the tenant or, as the case may be, each of the joint tenants is an individual; and
(b) the tenant or, as the case may be, at least one of the joint tenants occupies the dwelling-house as his only or principal home; and
(c) the tenancy is not one which, by virtue of certain statutory provisions,[2] ''cannot be an assured tenancy''.[3]

2. The six requirements

There are thus six main requirements, five positive and one negative:

(1) There must be a ''tenancy''.
(2) There must be a ''dwelling-house''.
(3) The dwelling-house must be ''let as a separate dwelling''.
(4) The tenant (or each joint tenant) must be an ''individual''.
(5) The tenant (or at least one joint tenant) must occupy the dwelling-house as ''his only or principal home''.
(6) The tenancy must not fall within any of the statutory exceptions.

[1] Act of 1988, s.1(1).
[2] *ibid.*, s.1(2), (6); Housing Act 1996, s.209.
[3] Act of 1988, s.1(1).

These requirements will be considered in turn in this Part of the book, before turning to the relationship between assured tenancies and certain other tenancies. This Part will also examine the characteristics of assured tenancies, statutory periodic tenancies, assured shorthold tenancies, assured agricultural occupancies, and long residential tenancies.

3. "If and so long as"

The words "if and so long as" govern all six requirements.[4] They require the matters to be considered as they stand when the question arises. A tenancy which is an assured tenancy when granted will cease to be an assured tenancy as soon as any requirement ceases to be satisfied, and a tenancy which initially is not an assured tenancy may become one if later all the requirements are satisfied. The question whether a tenancy is an assured tenancy thus usually has to be resolved when the question arises, though there are some matters that depend upon what the terms of the tenancy are, for instance whether the premises are let "as" a separate dwelling.[5]

4. The Crown

(a) The Crown bound

In general, the provisions of Part I[6] of the Act of the 1988 apply to the Crown. They apply in relation to premises in which there subsists, or at any material time subsisted, a Crown interest as they apply in relation to premises in relation to which no such interest subsists or ever subsisted.[7] A "Crown interest" means an interest which belongs to Her Majesty in right of the Crown or of the Duchy of Lancaster, or to the Duchy of Cornwall, or which belongs to a government department, or is held in trust for Her Majesty for the purposes of a government department,[8] thus excluding the private property of Her Majesty. Where the interest belongs to Her Majesty in right of the Duchy of Lancaster, then for these purposes the Chancellor of the Duchy of Lancaster is deemed to be the owner of the interest.[9]

(b) Qualifications

These provisions for the application of the Act to the Crown are subject to three qualifications:

[4] The phrase is also used elsewhere: see, *e.g.*, ss.1(2), 2(1), 20(4).
[5] See Vol. 1, pp. 87–94.
[6] *i.e.*, ss.1–45.
[7] Act of 1988, s.44(1).
[8] *ibid.*, s.44(3).
[9] *ibid.*, s.44(4).

(1) Crown tenancies cannot be assured tenancies.[10]
(2) No action for damages lies against the Crown for unlawful eviction.[11]
(3) The other provisions of the Act providing protection against eviction[12] bind the Crown to the extent that they require proceedings to be taken in court for the recovery of possession, or that they confer powers on the court.[13]

[10] *ibid.*, s.44(1), Sched. 1, para. 11: see *post*, paras. 4–36 *et seq.*
[11] *ibid.*, s.44(2)(a), excluding ss. 27, 28: see *post*, para. 16–26.
[12] *ibid.*, ss. 29–33: see *post*, paras. 16–02 *et seq.*
[13] *ibid.*, s.44(2)(b), applying Protection from Eviction Act 1977, s.10.

Chapter 3

Requirements for an Assured Tenancy

This chapter will consider the five positive requirements for the existence of an assured tenancy. The sixth, the negative requirement that the tenancy is not one that is excepted from the Act, will be dealt with in Chapter 4.[1]

Sect. 1. Tenancy

3–01 Only a tenancy can be an assured tenancy;[2] but any form of tenancy will suffice, whether for a fixed term, periodic, at sufferance, at will or by estoppel.[3] Such tenancies are necessarily contractual: there are no "statutory tenancies" under the Act of 1988. Even the "statutory periodic tenancy"[4] is contractual. Chapter 3 of Volume 1[5] considers the distinction between tenancies and other relationships, and its analysis applies in general to the Act of 1988 too.[6] Whether a tenancy or some other relationship exists is a question of law to be decided on the facts proved.[7]

Since Volume 1 was published, there have been further developments in the law of licences and many new reported cases, and these are considered below.

1. Licences

3–02 As a licence is not a tenancy, no licence can be an assured tenancy.[8] The discussion of licences in Volume 1 applies equally to the Act of 1988; but it has been

[1] *Post*, p. 32.
[2] Act of 1988, s.1(1).
[3] There can be no tenancy by estoppel where a licensor, whom the licensee knows to have no title to the dwelling-house, expressly grants a licence to the occupier, even though the occupier enjoys exclusive possession: *Bruton v. London & Quadrant Housing Trust* [1998] Q.B. 834, CA. An appeal to the House of Lords is pending.
[4] See *post*, paras. 7–01 *et seq.*
[5] pp. 66–83.
[6] The text is updated by the Cumulative Supplement, to which reference should also be made.
[7] *Cole v. Lejeune* [1951] 2 T.L.R. 308 at 311, CA.
[8] But for assured agricultural occupancies, see *post*, para. 9–05.

supplemented by the decisions of the House of Lords in *Antoniades v. Villiers*[9] and *A.G. Securities v. Vaughan,*[10] in each of which the decision of the Court of Appeal[11] was reversed, and in *City of Westminster v. Clarke*. *Antoniades v. Villiers* has already been considered in relation to shams and pretences,[12] whereas *A.G. Securities v. Vaughan* was a decision on arrangements that were perfectly genuine, truly reflecting the bargain between the parties. In that case, the owner of a flat made four separate agreements, on different dates, on different terms, and for different periods, which gave each of four persons the right to "share in the use" of the flat with not more than three others, subject to the right of the owner to grant a further sharing licence to another person when the number of the licensees fell below four. Such an arrangement could not create any tenancy, for it gave no occupant any right to the exclusive possession of any part of the flat, and they could not be held collectively to be joint tenants of the whole flat.[13] A proper zeal for frustrating attempted evasions of the Acts must not force upon an honest transaction a nature that it lacks, and four separate licences could not be construed as creating a joint tenancy[14] when all the requisite unities of a joint tenancy (possession, interest, title and time[15]) were absent. Similarly, where there is a genuine obligation on the licensor to provide services to the dwelling, there is no grant of exclusive possession, even if the licensee later forbears to enforce the obligations.[16]

In contrast, where the circumstances showed that the substance of a transaction was the grant of a right of exclusive possession of a furnished two-roomed flat containing a double bed to a man and a woman who were cohabiting with each other, the creation of a joint tenancy will not be precluded by the existence of artificialities such as carrying out the transaction by making separate (though simultaneous) agreements with each, under which each was to pay the owner separate but equal monthly sums. This is so even though each agreement negatived any right to the exclusive use or possession of any part of the flat, and reserved to the owner the right to use the flat and permit others to use it.[17] The two agreements will be read together and the unrealities ignored.[18] Thus read, the agreements created an ordinary joint tenancy; the provision for each to pay what in effect was half the rent was not inconsistent with a joint tenancy, and in fact each would be jointly and severally liable for the whole rent.[19] **3–03**

[9] [1990] A.C. 417.
[10] *ibid.*
[11] Considered in Vol. 1 at pp. 28, 69, 70, 750.
[12] See *ante*, para. 1–10.
[13] It was not argued that they might have individual tenancies of their individual rooms: see at pp. 459H–460A, 466C, 471B, 473B.
[14] As the majority of the Court of Appeal had held (see Vol. 1, p. 69); this was a process that required "the highest degree of artificiality": *per* Lord Bridge of Harwich at p. 454C–D.
[15] See Megarry and Wade's *Law of Real Property* (5th ed. 1984), pp. 419–422.
[16] *Huwyler v. Ruddy* (1995) 28 H.L.R. 550, CA.
[17] *Antoniades v. Villiers, supra.*
[18] *ibid.*, and see *Nicolaou v. Pitt* (1989) 21 H.L.R. 487, CA.
[19] *Antoniades v. Villiers, supra*, at pp. 460H–461D, 469H. Contrast *Mikeover Ltd. v. Brady* [1989] 3 All E.R. 618, CA (genuine agreement under two identical licences to be responsible for one half of the rent: no joint tenancy as no unity of interest) (leave to appeal refused: [1990] 2 All E.R. xix, HL). Consider also *Street v. Mountford* [1985] A.C. 809 at 825, apparently taking the

3–04 Yet although the grant of a right of exclusive occupation at a rent will normally establish a tenancy, it will not do so if the circumstances are such as, objectively, to negative any intention to grant exclusive possession. A subjective but uncommunicated intention of the landlord that the right of occupation will only be for a short time does not prevent a tenancy arising.[20] The touchstone appears to be whether, on the proper construction of the agreement permitting occupation and in the light of all the surrounding circumstances, there must have been an intention that the occupier should have the right of exclusive possession of the dwelling.[21] So, where a licence agreement granted a non-exclusive right to occupy and expressly negatived the intention to grant exclusive occupation; where the premises were unspecified accommodation in a local authority-run hostel for vulnerable, homeless, single men; and where the objectives of the council were to provide supervision and assistance to the occupiers, many of whom were mentally or physically unwell, there was a strong inference that no such intention could rationally have existed.[22] Where such an inference arises, effect should be given to an unambiguous term of the agreement negativing an intention to grant exclusive possession unless it is established that the statement did not reflect the true intentions of the parties.[23] This inference will generally arise if a licence is expressly granted in circusmtances ''where there are arrangements which are *prima facie* familiar as arrangements for a hostel where lodgers are allowed to reside, where for the better management of the hostel the hostel managers are allowed to move the lodgers around from room to room''.[24] Similarly, no tenancy was created under a licence for 13 weeks granted by a local authority under its statutory duty to provide a temporary home for the homeless, for this negatives any tenancy.[25] Until January 20, 1997, that decision was given a statutory basis in relation to assured tenancies under the Act of 1988 itself.[26] In this particular category of case, the decision may equally turn on the conclusion that such temporary accommodation is not a dwelling-house let as a dwelling,[27] or at least not as a separate dwelling,[28] so that even if there is a tenancy, no statutory protections arises.

3–05 A further category of cases exists in which the existence of a tenancy is negatived by some particular relationship or agreement between the parties, to which

view that in *Somma v. Hazelhurst* [1978] 1 W.L.R. 1014, CA, there was a joint tenancy despite the absence of any joint obligation to pay the total rent.

20 *Brent L.B.C. v. Cronin* (1997) 30 H.L.R. 43, CA.

21 This is no different from the test applied with other types of tenancy: see *Evans v. Tompkins* [1993] 2 E.G.L.R. 6, CA (agricultural holding) and *Esso Petroleum Company Ltd. v. Fumegrange Ltd.* [1994] 2 E.G.L.R. 90, CA (business tenancy). For a borderline case in the residential context, see *Mehta v. Royal Bank of Scotland plc* [1999] *The Times*, January 25, QB (long-term occupation of hotel room agreed: licence not tenancy).

22 *City of Westminster v. Clarke* [1992] 2 A.C. 288.

23 *Camden L.B.C. v. Shortlife Community Housing Ltd.* (1992) 25 H.L.R. 330, Ch.; and see also *Shepherd's Bush Housing Association Ltd. v. HATS Co-operative* (1991) 24 H.L.R. 176, CA.

24 *Brennan v. Lambeth L.B.C.* (1997) 30 H.L.R. 481 at 485, CA, *per* Brooke L.J.

25 *Ogwr B.C. v. Dykes* [1989] 1 W.L.R. 295, CA. But see *Family Housing Association v. Jones* [1990] 1 W.L.R. 779, CA.

26 Act of 1988, s.1(6),(7); and *see post*, paras. 4–67 *et seq.*

27 *Mohamed v. Manek* (1995) 27 H.L.R. 439, CA.

28 See *Parkins v. Westminster C.C.* (1997) 30 H.L.R. 894, CA; see *post*, paras. 3–15 *et seq.*

the enjoyment of exclusive possession is properly attributable. In such cases, there is no compulsion to draw an inference of tenancy from the enjoyment of exclusive possession for a term, and the law does not draw it. The most common of these is where a tenant enjoys possession in contemplation of the formal grant of a tenancy, or where he holds over after the termination of an earlier tenancy or a superior tenancy. Even where payment is made for the occupation, a tenancy will not be created if it is clear from the circumstances that the parties can have had no intention to create a tenancy in that manner.[29] Other cases are where a close relationship between the parties suggests that the intention was the grant of a licence to share, rather than a sub-tenancy.[30] But the question is one of fact in each case: the existence of such a relationship will not *per se* prevent the creation of a tenancy.[31]

In general, these principles appear to be as fully applicable to the Act of 1988 as to the Housing Act 1985 or the Act of 1977, in relation to or under which statutes many of the cases were decided. But there may be a difference where there is a reservation by the landlord of a right to share occupation with the tenants in the future.[32] That right (if valid) would, when exercised, at common law convert the tenancy into a licence and thus terminate the tenancy, though the Rent Acts would "protect the occupiers from eviction".[33] Under the Act of 1988, if a tenant "executes, signs or gives any surrender, notice to quit or other document which . . . has the effect of bringing the tenancy to an end at a time when it is an assured tenancy", the surrender, notice to quit or other document as the case might be "shall be of no effect".[34] This arguably renders ineffective any such right to share occupation at a future time; yet it can also be said that what "has the effect of bringing the tenancy to an end" within the meaning of the provision is not the document, but the subsequent exercise by the landlord of a right under it.[35] **3–06**

2. Service occupiers and others

There are well established categories of relationship where, despite the enjoyment by one party *de facto* of exclusive occupation or even *de jure* of exclusive **3–07**

[29] See, generally, *Javad v. Mohamed Aqil* [1991] 1 W.L.R. 1007, CA, *Vaughan-Armatrading v. Sarsah* (1995) 27 H.L.R. 631, CA, and *Dreamgate Properties Ltd. v. Arnot* (1998) 76 P. & C.R. 25, CA. See also the cases under "Service occupiers and others", *infra*.

[30] *Monmouth B.C. v. Marlog* (1994) 27 H.L.R. 30, CA.

[31] *Nunn v. Dalrymple* (1989) 59 P. & C.R. 231, CA (family relationship outweighed by occupiers' giving up council tenancy and renovating the dwelling); *Ward v. Warnke* (1990) 22 H.L.R. 496, CA (retention of key by parents and occasional use of cottage by them not negativing tenancy in favour of daughter and son-in-law).

[32] As opposed to a right exercisable at any time so to do. In that case, a tenancy would never have been created.

[33] *Antoniades v. Villiers*, *supra*, at p. 461, *per* Lord Templeman: *semble* as statutory tenants and not, because of sharing with the landlord, under a restricted contract; see Vol. 1, p. 102.

[34] Act of 1988, s.5(5). See *post*, para. 6–13.

[35] The other limb of this provision, relating to the tenant entering into an obligation to do "any act" which will cause the tenancy to come to an end (see *post*, para. 6–13), also seems to be inapplicable; an obligation not to impede the landlord in the exercise of his rights of sharing is

possession of a dwelling-house, he is not the tenant of the other party to the relationship. These are service occupiers, spouses, trespassers, purchasers under contracts of sale, and mortgagors in possession. In general, their positions under Part I of the Act of 1988 are as under the Rent Acts.[36] In addition to these, a beneficiary under a trust, who is entitled to possession as such, will not be a tenant even though he pays a periodic sum for his exclusive occupation.[37]

A service occupier (as distinct from a service tenant[38]) is merely a licensee, and so cannot have an assured tenancy; but one type of service occupancy, an ''assured agricultural occupancy'', which is not an assured tenancy, is nevertheless to be treated ''as if it were such a tenancy''.[39] A service occupancy is created where either the agreement requires the employee to reside in specified premises and doing so assists him in the discharge of his duties, or (though the agreement is silent) it is necessary for him to live there in order to discharge his duties.[40] A term may be implied in a contract of employment that the employee is required to live in certain premises for the better performance of his duties.[41] An agreement may create a service occupancy even if the servant is, in the event, never able to perform his duties, provided that it was contemplated that he would do so within a reasonable time of taking up occupation.[42] It is of the nature of a service occupancy that the right to occupy the dwelling-house terminates with the employment. Accordingly, where an employer, subject to an unfair dismissal claim, gave evidence that he would pay compensation rather than reinstate the employee in the event that unfair dismissal was proved, the employer was entitled to possession of the dwelling without waiting for the termination of the industrial tribunal case.[43]

3–08 For spouses, the Matrimonial Homes Act 1983 was made applicable to assured tenancies;[44] and now the Family Law Act 1996 applies to assured tenancies as it applies to tenancies under the Rent Acts.[45] Like the Rent Acts, the Act of 1988 does not protect trespassers, and so will not protect even a former tenant who, when Part I came into force, was holding over after the determination of his tenancy.[46] Further, nothing in Part I relates to proceedings for possession of a dwelling-house brought by a mortgagee[47] who has lent money on the security of an assured tenancy of the dwelling.[48]

hardly an obligation to do an ''act'', though possibly a positive obligation to ''share occupation'' would be.

36 See the treatment of these categories in Volume 1 at pp. 76, 80, 81, 72, and 83 respectively.

37 *Gray v. Taylor* [1998] 1 W.L.R. 1093, CA.

38 See Vol. 1, p. 76.

39 Act of 1988, s.24(3); *post*, para. 9–05.

40 *Hughes v. Greenwich L.B.C.* (1993) 69 P. & C.R. 487, HL.

41 *South Glamorgan C.C. v. Griffiths* (1992) 24 H.L.R. 334, CA. See also *Greenfield v. Berkshire C.C.* (1996) 73 P. & C.R. 280, CA.

42 *Norris v. Checksfield* [1991] 1 W.L.R. 1241, CA (coach driver unable to obtain licence to drive).

43 *Whitbread West Pennines Ltd. v. Reedy* (1988) 20 H.L.R. 642, CA.

44 Act of 1988, Sched. 17, paras. 33, 34, repealed with effect from October 1, 1997 by Family Law Act 1996, ss.66(3), 67(3), Sched.10; S.I. 1997 No. 1892.

45 Family Law Act 1996, Pt. IV, s.30(4)(b); see *post*, para. 11–17.

46 See *Harrison v. Hammersmith and Fulham L.B.C.* [1981] 1 W.L.R. 650, CA (on Housing Act 1980, Pt. I, replaced by Housing Act 1985, Pt. IV: secure tenancies).

47 Within the meaning of Law of Property Act 1925; see s.205(1) (xvi).

48 Act of 1988, s.7(1); *post*, para. 13–44.

Sect. 2. A Dwelling-house

1. "Dwelling-house"

The second requirement is that there must be "a dwelling-house",[49] though a dwelling-house "may be a house or part of a house".[50] The language is the same as that of the Rent Acts, and the authorities under those Acts[51] seem to be equally applicable to the Act of 1988. A wooden bungalow, resting on concrete pillars on land, but not otherwise attached to it, was held to be a fixture and therefore part of the land, and a dwelling-house within the meaning of the identical language of the Rent Acts.[52] **3–09**

2. Other land

(a) Inclusion

If a tenancy of a dwelling-house includes other land, *i.e.* land other than the site of the dwelling-house, the general rule is that the other land will be treated as part of the dwelling-house. Thus, where a dwelling-house "is let together with" other land, the land is treated as part of the dwelling-house "if and so long as" the main purpose of the letting is the provision of a home for the tenant (or, where there are joint tenants, for at least one of them).[53] But this inclusive provision is not to affect any question whether a tenancy is precluded from being an assured tenancy by falling within the provisions excepting certain tenancies from the Act.[54] The most pertinent exception here is that in relation to agricultural land exceeding two acres.[55] **3–10**

(b) Exclusion

On the other hand, where a dwelling-house is let together with other land, but at any time the main purpose of the letting is not the provision of a home within (a) above, then at any such time "the tenancy shall be treated as not being one under which a dwelling-house is let as a separate dwelling",[56] with the result that it cannot be an assured tenancy. Further, "if and so long as" the tenancy **3–11**

49 Act of 1988, s.1(1).
50 *ibid.*, s.45(1). *Quaere* whether a landlord who has made alterations to the premises so that this requirement is not satisfied can take the point: *Prince v. Robinson* (1998) 31 H.L.R. 89, CA.
51 See Vol. 1, pp. 84–86.
52 *Elitestone Ltd. v. Morris* [1997] 1 W.L.R. 687, HL.
53 Act of 1988, s.2(1)(a).
54 *ibid.*, s.2(2), referring to Sched. 1; *post*, Chap. 4.
55 See *infra*.
56 Act of 1988, s.2(1)(b).

is one ''under which agricultural land, exceeding two acres, is let together with the dwelling-house'', the tenancy cannot be an assured tenancy.[57]

(c) Let under a tenancy

3–12 The use of the present tense (''is let'') seems to show that what must be considered is the state of affairs existing at the time when the question arises, and not merely the position when the tenancy was granted. So, if the terms of a tenancy have been varied so as to include other land, this head will apply to it even though initially that land was not included.[58] Similarly, if a tenancy is varied so as to remove part of the demised premises from the tenancy, the position with regard to any remaining land must be considered after the variation. In considering the ''main purpose'' of the letting, the words ''if and so long as'' emphasise that the inclusive test is to be applied at the time when the issue arises, with the consequence that such a tenancy could move from being an assured tenancy to a tenancy not falling within Part I of the Act of 1988, and back again, depending on the land comprised in the tenancy and the main purpose of the letting from time to time.

(d) ''Let together with''

3–13 It will be apparent that, for inclusion, the dwelling must be ''let together with'' the land, whereas for the agricultural exclusion, the land must be ''let together with'' the dwelling. A similar contrast and style of drafting in the Rent Acts led to the conclusion that the relative importance of house and land must be considered to determine which is the adjunct of which.[59] Although the drafting of the Act of 1988 is different in that it makes explicit the question of the main purpose of the letting,[60] in dealing with the exception relating to agricultural land it seems to have perpetuated some of the complexities of the Rent Acts authorities. For although the inclusionary provision speaks of ''a dwelling-house . . . let together with other land'', the agricultural exception is in terms of ''land . . . let together with the dwelling-house'', and nothing in *inter alia* the terms of the inclusionary provision is to affect the quesion of whether the exception relating to agricultural land applies.[61] There are therefore two different reasons why a tenancy which includes land other than the site of the dwelling-house may not be assured. First, if the main purpose of the letting is not the provision of a home for the tenant. In such a case, the tenancy is *treated as* not being one under which a dwelling-house is let as a separate dwelling.[62] Secondly, if more than two acres of agricultural land is let together with the dwelling-house. In

[57] *ibid.*, s.1(2), Sched. 1, para. 6(1). See *post*, para. 4–15.

[58] The result as a matter of law would be a surrender and re-grant in any event, and hence the grant of a new tenancy of dwelling-house with land from its inception: *Friends Provident Life Office v. British Railways Board* [1996] 1 All E.R. 336, CA; *J.W. Childers Trustees v. Anker* [1996] 1 E.G.L.R. 1, CA.

[59] See Vol. 1, pp. 131–134.

[60] See Act of 1988, s.2(1).

[61] *ibid.*, s.2(2).

[62] *ibid.*, s.2(1)(b).

such a case, the tenancy cannot be an assured tenancy.[63] What is unclear is whether the second reason applies despite the fact that the main purpose of the tenancy is the provision of a home, or whether the words of the exclusion relating to agricultural land itself denote the fact that the home is not the main purpose. It is suggested that the former is the case, for otherwise the exception relating to agricultural land would be otiose.[64]

(e) "A home"

This condition, which is relevant only where the dwelling-house is let together with other land and which will not usually apply where a flat is let, must be distinguished from the fifth main requirement, which is perfectly general, namely that the tenant (or at least one tenant) "occupies" the dwelling as "his only or principal home".[65] Under this specific condition, the provision of a secondary home suffices for the land to be treated as part of the dwelling-house, and the tenancy therefore has the potential to become assured if and when it is occupied by the tenant as his only or principal home. Further, the fifth, general requirement depends upon the state of actual occupation for the time being, whereas the present head is concerned with the purpose of the letting; and this may change or remain unchanged whatever the state of actual occupation. The Act of 1988 does not define "home", but there seems to be no material difference between the concept of a residence, as under the Rent Acts,[66] and a home.[67] Both imply a degree of permanence and settled habitation.[68] **3–14**

Sect. 3. "Let as a Separate Dwelling"

The requirement that the premises should be "let as a separate dwelling"[69] is identical with the requirement that has long appeared in the Rent Acts,[70] and it **3–15**

[63] Act of 1988, s.1(2).

[64] It follows from this reasoning that there can be no difference in substance under the Act of 1988 between the phrases "land let together with the dwelling-house" and "dwelling-house let together with other land". This happy conclusion would avoid some of the intricacies of the decisions under the Rent Acts.

[65] Act of 1988, s.1(1)(b): see *post*, p. 30.

[66] Act of 1977, s.2(1)(a); and see Vol. 1, pp. 235 *et seq.*

[67] *Crawley B.C. v. Sawyer* (1987) 20 H.L.R. 98, CA. There is, however, a difference between occupation as an only or principal home and the test of residence under the Rent Acts: see *post*, para. 3–24.

[68] In *Curl v. Angelo* [1948] 2 All E.R. 289 at 290, CA, Lord Greene M.R. considered that the word "dwelling" in Increase of Rent and Mortgage Interest (Restrictions) Act 1920 meant "home". More recently, in *Mohamed v. Manek* (1995) 27 H.L.R. 439, CA, temporary accommodation provided to a homeless man in a hostel was held not to be "occupied as a dwelling under a licence" within Protection from Eviction Act 1977, s.3(2B) because the nature of the occupation was transient and limited. Clearly, the three concepts of "dwelling", "residence" and "home" are very closely related.

[69] Act of 1988, s.1(1).

[70] Now in Act of 1977, s.1.

clearly bears the same meaning.[71] Where living accommodation[72] is shared, the Act of 1988 enacts provisions that in most respects are closely similar to those in the Rent Acts. They are set out below.

1. SHARING WITH LANDLORD: NO ASSURED TENANCY

1. Tenants

3–16 If the tenant of a dwelling-house shares living accommodation in it with his landlord, his tenancy cannot be an assured tenancy. This is, simply, because the dwelling-house is not ''let as separate dwelling'':[73] part of what is comprised in a dwelling is shared, and therefore the dwelling is not let separately.[74] The position is similar to that under the Rent Acts, save that those Acts gave such a tenancy the protection of being a restricted contract,[75] whereas the Act of 1988 does not. The right of the landlord to share must be clearly reserved in the tenancy.[76] A term of an oral tenancy agreement which required the tenant to share the kitchen, bathroom and lavatory with whomsoever the landlord might specify was insufficiently precise to amount to a sharing of occupation with the landlord.[77] But a genuine contemplation of sharing coupled with a real prospect of doing so suffices.[78] Where such a right was clearly reserved in the tenancy agreement, the fact that the landlord's interest subsequently became vested in a limited company did not change the legal consequences.[79]

2. Sub-tenants

3–17 For sub-tenancies, the position is also closely similar to that under the Rent Acts. A sub-tenant who shares living accommodation with the tenant has no assured tenancy as against him; but as against the landlord or any superior

[71] The different aspects of the meaning of this phrase are considered in detail in Vol. 1, pp. 87–117. Sections 1, 2, 3 and 5 of that Chapter, on the meaning and significance of the words ''Is let'', ''as'', ''a'' and ''dwelling'', are equally applicable to the Act of 1988; the meaning of ''separate'' under the Act of 1988 is governed by specific provisions of the Act, and is considered *infra*.

[72] The concept of ''living accommodation'' was fashioned out of the wording of earlier Rent Acts (the words are nowhere expressly used): see *Neale v. Del Soto* [1945] K.B. 144, CA; *Cole v. Harris* [1945] K.B. 474, CA. Decisions under those Acts have resulted in a slightly odd distinction, whereby a kitchen and a sitting room are ''living accommodation'', but a bathroom is not. See Vol. 1, pp. 95–97. Act of 1988, s.3(5) seems to preserve this established meaning, without making it clear that that is what the Act of 1988 is doing.

[73] Within Act of 1988, s.1(1).

[74] Even if it were ''let as a separate dwelling'', the tenancy would usually be subject to the ''resident landlord'' provisions, and would thereby be prevented from being an assured tenancy: Act of 1988, Sched. 1, para. 10, Pt. III; see *post*, paras. 4–21 *et seq.*

[75] See Vol. 1, pp. 102, 103.

[76] *Miller v. Eyo* [1998] 10 C.L. 421, CA.

[77] *Gray v. Brown* (1992) 25 H.L.R. 144, CA (a case on the equivalent provisions of Act of 1977).

[78] *ibid.*

[79] *Mortgage Corporation Ltd. v. Ubah* (1996) 73 P. & C.R. 580, CA (decided under Act of 1977, s.21).

landlord, no part of the dwelling is to be treated as being "excluded from being a dwelling-house let on an assured tenancy by reason only that the terms on which any person claiming under the tenant holds any part of the dwelling-house include the use of accommodation in common with other persons".[80] So the tenant is not excluded from the protection of the Act of 1988 because he sub-lets part or parts (but not the whole) on terms that, as between him and the sub-tenant, involve sharing of living accommodation. But this does not affect the rights and liabilities between the tenant and those claiming under him.[81]

2. SHARING WITH OTHERS: DEEMED ASSURED TENANCY

1. Deemed assured tenancy

The Act of 1988 continues the familiar distinction between sharing with the landlord and sharing with others.[82] Where living accommodation is shared by the tenant with a person other than the landlord, the tenant has the equivalent protection under the Act of 1988 as if a dwelling-house were let to him as a separate dwelling. So, if under a tenancy a tenant has "the exclusive occupation of any accommodation" (called "the separate accommodation"), and two further conditions are satisfied, the separate accommodation is deemed to be a dwelling-house let on an assured tenancy.[83] The conditions are that: 3–18

"(a) the terms as between the tenant and his landlord on which he holds the separate accommodation include the use of other accommodation" ("the shared accommodation") "in common with another person or other persons, not being or including the landlord"; and

(b) by reason only of condition (a), the separate accommodation would not, apart from the deeming provision, be a dwelling-house let on an assured tenancy.[84]

So, where a tenant has the exclusive occupation of a bedroom on terms that entitle him to share a kitchen, bathroom and sitting room with other tenants of other bedrooms in the house, the bedroom is deemed to be a dwelling-house let on an assured tenancy. The word "only", in condition (b), emphasises that the deeming provision has no effect if there is any other ground on which, or reason why, the tenancy cannot be an assured tenancy.[85]

[80] Act of 1988, s.4(1), modelled on Act of 1977, s.23(1); see Vol. 1, p. 107.

[81] *ibid.*, s.4(2).

[82] See Vol. 1, pp. 102, 103 for this distinction, and its effect, under the Rent Acts.

[83] The result is quite different in the absence of such a deeming provision, for example under Housing Act 1985, Pt. IV (secure tenancies): *Parkins v. Westminster C.C.* (1997) 30 H.L.R. 894, CA (licence to occupy a flat with three bedrooms and communal living and cooking facilities together with other persons so authorised: no exclusive possession of a dwelling-house).

[84] Act of 1988, s.3(1).

[85] The wording of Act of 1988, s.3(1) is arguably defective in seeking to bring about this clearly-intended result: it is not just the separate accommodation that would not, apart from condition (a), be a dwelling-house let on an assured tenancy, but the separate accommodation and the shared accommodation together. The separate accommodation alone, *i.e.* the bedroom in the example

Regard must be had to the entitlement to share the shared accommodation if it is necessary, for the purposes of establishing whether the tenancy cannot be an assured tenancy under any of the provisions of Part I of Schedule 1 to the Act of 1988, to make an apportionment under Part II of that Schedule to determine the rateable value of the separate accommodation.[86] Thus, in the example given above, the rateable value of the bedroom will reflect the value of the right to share the shared accommodation.

2. Protection under deemed assured tenancy

3–19 Where under these provisions there is deemed to be an assured tenancy of the separate accommodation, various provisions are made to protect the tenant against a diminution of his rights in relation to the shared accommodation. These are similar to provisions under the Rent Acts.[87]

(a) Possession of shared accommodation

3–20 While the tenant is in possession of the separate accommodation, no order can be made for possession of any of the shared accommodation, on the application of the landlord or any superior landlord, unless a like order is or has been made in respect of the separate accommodation.[88] This in effect gives the shared accommodation the same protection as the separate accommodation. This principle, *i.e.* that the entitlement to share the shared accommodation is coterminous with the tenancy of the separate accommodation, applies to rent assessment committees in fixing the terms of a statutory periodic tenancy.[89]

(b) Modification of rights to use shared accommodation

3–21 (i) MODIFICATION BY THE LANDLORD. While the tenant is in possession of the separate accommodation, any term of the tenancy terminating or modifying the tenant's right to use any of the shared accommodation which is "living accommodation" (or providing for such termination or modification) is of no effect.[90] "Living accommodation" here means "accommodation of such a nature that the fact that it constitutes or is included in the shared accommodation" would, but for the deeming, be "sufficient . . . to prevent the tenancy from constituting an assured tenancy of a dwelling-house".[91] It is suggested that this perpetuates the meaning of living accommodation established, by a process of judicial inter-

given, could not itself be a dwelling-house. But the intended result is so clear that a purposive construction must be applied.

86 Act of 1988, s.3(2).

87 See Vol. 1, pp. 105–107.

88 Act of 1988, s.10(1), (2), corresponding to Act of 1977, s.22(5).

89 *ibid.*, ss.6, 10(2); see *post*, para. 7–24.

90 Act of 1988, s.3(3).

91 *ibid.*, s.3(5); and see s.10(1); Vol. 1, pp. 95–97.

pretation, under the Rent Acts.[92] But this invalidation of terms does not prevent any terms of the tenancy from having effect so far as they provide that, at any time during the tenancy, the persons in common with whom the tenant is entitled to use the shared accommodation can be varied or their number can be increased.[93] Nor does it prevent a term relating to non-living accommodation from having effect.[94]

(ii) MODIFICATION BY THE COURT. There are two respects in which the court, on the application of the landlord, can make such order as it thinks just.[95] First, such an order may terminate the right of the tenant to use the whole or any part of the shared accommodation except living accommodation.[96] Secondly, the order may modify the tenant's right to use the whole or any part of the shared accommodation, whether by varying the persons entitled to the use of that accommodation or by increasing their number or otherwise;[97] and this power does not exclude living accommodation.[98] But the court can order no such termination or modification if (apart from the statutory invalidation of such terms[99]) it could not be effected by or under the terms of the tenancy.[1] In view of this restriction, it is unclear what jurisdiction the court has that the landlord has not under the terms of the tenancy. 3–22

Sect. 4. "An Individual"

The fourth requirement is that "the tenant or, as the case may be, each of the joint tenants is an individual".[2] Thus no limited company or other corporation (except possibly a corporation sole) can be an assured tenant.[3] This sharply contrasts with the Rent Acts, under which a corporation could be entitled to the protection of the Acts as to rent (as a protected tenant), but could never be a statutory tenant because it was incapable of the requisite personal occupation of the dwelling.[4] Instead of this partial exclusion from the statute, the Act of 1988 wholly disables corporations from being assured tenants. Presumably what has to be considered is the direct relationship between landlord and tenant, disreg- 3–23

[92] See Vol. 1, pp. 95–97, and *ante*, p. 26, n. 72.
[93] Act of 1988, s.3(4).
[94] See also *infra* for the court's powers.
[95] Act of 1988, s.10(3), corresponding to Act of 1977, s.22(6), which gives the power only to the county court.
[96] Act of 1988, s.10(3)(a).
[97] Enabling the landlord to apply to the court for variation if the tenancy itself does not provide for it.
[98] Act of 1988, s.10(3)(b).
[99] *ibid.*, s.3(3), *supra*.
[1] *ibid.*, s.10(4).
[2] *ibid.*, s.1(1).
[3] This produces the curious result that, under Landlord and Tenant Act 1987, Pt. I (Tenants' Rights of First Refusal), a corporate tenant would be a "qualifying tenant" within the meaning of that Part, with consequential rights in connection with acquisition of the reversionary interest of its landlord, whereas an individual, being an assured tenant, would not: *ibid.*, s.3(1)(d).
[4] See Vol. 1, p. 156, and *ante*, para. 1–11.

arding any trusts[5], so that while a corporation could not hold an assured tenancy on trust for an individual, and a tenancy could no longer be assured after being vested in a trust corporation, an individual may be able to hold an assured tenancy on trust for a corporation if under the trust he[6] occupies the dwelling as his only or principal home. The letting of a dwelling to a company so that its nominee can live in it will not, if genuine, be treated as a letting to the individual, even if that individual bought the company for the purpose of the transaction because the landlord refused to let the dwelling except to a company.[7]

Sect. 5. "Only or Principal Home"

3–24 The fifth requirement is that "the tenant or, as the case may be, at least one of the joint tenants occupies the dwelling-house as his only or principal home".[8] There is no material difference between the word "home" and the word "residence" as used in the Rent Acts,[9] but there is a difference between the test of occupation as an only or principal home within the Act of 1988 and the test of occupation as a residence under the Rent Acts. The Act of 1988 introduces a stricter test.[10] Where a person is no longer in physical occupation of a dwelling, the onus lies on him to satisfy the court that he is still occupying it as his principal home. That question is to be determined by an objective assessment of the actions and motives of the tenant, and not by his subjective intention or motives.[11] So, where the tenant had left the dwelling, taking with him all his personal effects, but leaving his furniture and a sub-tenant in occupation, he was no longer occupying it as his main residence.[12]

Both under the Rent Acts[13] and under the Act of 1988[14] there is nothing to prevent a person having two homes at once. But whereas under the Rent Acts the tenant may be a statutory tenant of them both, under the Act of 1988 no person can be an assured tenant of more than one; only his "principal home" can be held on an assured tenancy. Which of two homes is the tenant's "principal home" is essentially a matter of fact and degree,[15] so that it depends on all the circumstances, including the average time spent at each home by him and his immediate family, whether he owns one of them, where he keeps his papers, any constraints of his place of work (*e.g.*, in requiring him to live mainly

[5] Consider the principle of *Schalit v. Joseph Nadler Ltd.* [1933] 2 K.B. 79, DC.

[6] Or, in the case of joint tenants, one of them: see *infra*.

[7] *Hilton v. Plustitle Ltd.* [1989] 1 W.L.R. 149, CA (leave to appeal refused [1989] 1 W.L.R. 310, HL) and *Kaye v. Massbetter* (1990) 62 P. & C.R. 558, CA, cases on the Rent Acts: see *ante*, para. 1–11.

[8] Act of 1988, s.1(1).

[9] See *ante*, para. 3–14.

[10] *Ujima Housing Association v. Ansah* (1997) 30 H.L.R. 831, CA.

[11] *ibid.*

[12] *ibid.*

[13] See Vol. 1, pp. 239–241.

[14] See *Crawley B.C. v. Sawyer* (1987) 20 H.L.R. 98, CA.

[15] See *Frost v. Feltham* [1981] 1 W.L.R. 452 at 455, Ch. (the taxpayer's "only or main residence" within Finance Act 1974, Sched. 1, para. 4(1)(a)).

in the home which is nearer to his work,[16]) and many other matters. The words "only or principal home"[17] or similar words (*e.g.*, "only or main residence"[18]) may be found in other statutes, but in considering any authorities on them differences in the purposes of the Acts must be borne in mind.[19]

A dwelling does not cease to be a person's only or main residence merely because he sub-lets part of it,[20] or because of his absence from it if, objectively, he can be adjudged to be occupying it still as his main residence;[21] but a conditional intention to return, which under the Rent Acts has been held to be too contingent to be effective,[22] will almost always be insufficient under the Act of 1988. **3–25**

A cohabiting couple, or a husband and wife, though happily married, may each have a different dwelling as his or her main residence.[23] And a tenant will be treated as occupying a dwelling-house as his or her only or principal home if his or her spouse occupies it pursuant to matrimonial home rights as an only or principal home.[24] But this vicarious occupation only applies where the occupying spouse is there pursuant to the statutory rights, and not if he or she has a legal estate in the dwelling-house[25] or a contractual right to live there.[26] **3–26**

Sect. 6. Not Within the Statutory Exceptions

The sixth and last requirement for an assured tenancy is the negative requirement that the tenancy should not fall within any of the statutory exceptions. There are 14 of these, and they are addressed individually in the next Chapter. **3–27**

[16] See *Frost v. Feltham, supra* (publican in Essex, "main residence" in Powys).

[17] Housing Act 1985, s.81.

[18] Leasehold Reform Act 1967, s.1(2); Finance Act 1974, Sched. 1, para. 4(1)(a), now Income and Corporation Taxes Act 1988, s.355(1)(a).

[19] See *Poland v. Earl Cadogan* [1980] 3 All E.R. 544, CA, esp. at 549.

[20] See *Harris v. Swick Securities Ltd.* [1969] 1 W.L.R. 1604, CA (Leasehold Reform Act 1967, s.1(2)).

[21] See *Ujima Housing Association v. Ansah, supra.*

[22] *Robert Thackray's Estates Ltd. v. Kaye* (1988) 21 H.L.R. 160, CA.

[23] *Fowell v. Radford* (1969) 21 P. & C.R. 99, CA (Leasehold Reform Act 1967, s.1(2): his at Stoke Poges, hers at Ealing).

[24] Family Law Act 1996, s.30(4)(b), replacing Matrimonial Homes Act 1983, s.1(6) with effect from October 1, 1997: S.I. 1997 No. 1892. See *post*, para. 11–18.

[25] *i.e.* if the spouse is a joint tenant.

[26] Family Law Act 1996, s.30(1), (2), (4), (9). A spouse with an equitable interest only is deemed not to have the right to occupy, even though as against the other spouse he or she has the right. If the title to the dwelling is unregistered, the spouse cannot protect his or her interest by registration; a contractual purchaser can.

Chapter 4

Tenancies Excepted from the Act

1. The exceptions

4–01 Under section 1(1) of the Act of 1988, the sixth and last requirement for an assured tenancy (and the only negative requirement) is that "the tenancy is not one which, by virtue of subsection (2) or subsection (6) below, cannot be an assured tenancy". Subsection (2) is the main provision. By it, "if and so long as" a tenancy falls within any paragraph in Part I of Schedule 1 to the Act, "it cannot be an assured tenancy". These paragraphs are considered in detail below. Subsection (6) is confined to certain tenancies granted by arrangement with local housing authorities to provide accommodation for the homeless, where the application for housing or assistance with housing was made before January 20, 1997. It has now been repealed,[1] but has been replaced with new provisions to substantially the same effect.[1a]

2. Classification

4–02 In its original form, Part I of Schedule 1 contained 13 paragraphs, each setting out a particular type of tenancy that could not be an assured tenancy. Two of these types depended upon the rateable value of the dwelling,[2] and so they had to be revised when domestic rating was abolished.[3] This has been done by replacing the two paragraphs concerned by five new substantial paragraphs.[4] These

[1] Housing Act 1996, ss.227, 232(3); S.I. 1996 No. 2959, art. 2, Sched., para. 1. The repeal does not apply in relation to an applicant whose application for accommodation or assistance was made before January 20, 1997.

[1a] Housing Act 1996, s.209. See *post*, p. 62, n. 24.

[2] Act of 1988, Sched. 1, paras. 2 (dwelling-houses with high rateable values), and 3 (tenancies at a low rent).

[3] Under Local Government Finance Act 1988, with effect from April 1, 1990. The community charge, which replaced domestic rates then, proved short-lived, and was itself abolished by Local Government Finance Act 1992 in favour of the council tax with effect from April 1, 1993.

[4] Para. 2 has become paras. 2 and 2A, and para. 3 has become paras. 3, 3A and 3B, with a para. 3C that is merely ancillary to them: see References to Rating (Housing) Regulations 1990 (S.I. 1990 No. 434), Sched., paras. 29, 30.

changes, though important (and complex) in detail, have not affected the substance of the exclusion of these two particular types of tenancy that cannot be assured tenancies. There continue to be 13 of these types in all, and there have been some minor amendments to some of them since the Act of 1988 came into force.

Like the exceptions under the Rent Acts,[5] the exceptions under the Act of 1988 defy classification. Nevertheless, it is possible to arrange them (together with the former provision for tenancies for the homeless under subsection (6)[6]) under four heads, similar to those under the Rent Acts.

First, there are five exceptions that depend upon the nature of the premises; secondly, four that depend upon some quality in a person interested; thirdly, three that depend upon the terms or status of the tenancy; and fourthly, two that depend on the purpose of the tenancy. Throughout Schedule 1, "tenancy" means "a tenancy under which a dwelling-house is let as a separate dwelling",[7] *i.e.* one that has the potential to be an assured tenancy.

3. List of exceptions

The list of exceptions may accordingly be set out as follows: the paragraph number at the end of each exception refers to its number in Schedule 1 to the Act of 1988. **4–03**

A. NATURE OR STATUS OF THE PREMISES

1. Tenancies of dwelling-houses with high value: paras. 2, 2A.
2. Business tenancies: para. 4.
3. Licensed premises: para. 5.
4. Tenancies of agricultural land: para. 6.
5. Tenancies of agricultural holdings, *etc*.: para. 7.

B. SOME QUALITY IN A PERSON INTERESTED

6. Lettings to students: para. 8.
7. Resident landlords: para. 10.
8. Crown tenancies: para. 11.
9. Local authority tenancies, *etc*.: para. 12.

[5] See Vol. 1, p. 123.
[6] *Supra*.
[7] Act of 1988, s.1(2)(a).

C. TERMS OF THE TENANCY

10. Tenancies entered into before commencement: para. 1.
11. Tenancies at a low rent: paras. 3, 3A, 3B.
12. "Transitional cases" (protected tenancies, housing association tenancies, secure tenancies, and protected occupancies under the Act of 1976): para. 13.

D. PURPOSE OF THE TENANCY

13. Holiday lettings: para. 9.
14. Lettings arranged by local housing authorities for housing the homeless: section 1(6).

Unlike under the Rent Acts,[8] there is no exception for tenancies under which the rent includes payments for board or attendance.

Sect. 1. High Value

1. The exception

4–04 The Act of 1988 excluded larger dwellings from security of tenure under Part I by reference to their high rateable values. On April 1, 1990, domestic rates were replaced by community charges under the Local Government Finance Act 1988, and amending or supplementary provisions were clearly needed for, *inter alia*, this exception of larger dwellings. Provision for the amendment of statutory references to rating was made, in the widest terms, by section 149 of the Local Government and Housing Act 1989,[9] and amendments to the Act of 1988 have been made by the References to Rating (Housing) Regulations 1990 (referred to hereafter as the "Regulations of 1990").[10] In Schedule 1 to the Act of 1988, the complexities of paragraphs 2 and 2A now replace the relative simplicity of the former paragraph 2,[11] which specified two rateable value figures (one for Greater London and another for elsewhere) above which a dwelling-house could not support an assured tenancy. There are now two classes of tenancy for the purposes of this exception: those entered into before, and those entered into on or after, April 1, 1990.

[8] See Vol. 1, pp. 167 *et seq.*

[9] Printed *post*, p. 497.

[10] S.I. 1990 No. 434. For similar amendments to Act of 1977 in relation to tenancies of larger dwellings, see Supplement, annotation to Vol. 1, pp. 118–121.

[11] All printed *post*, p. 438.

2. The changes

So far as practicable, the existing exclusion based on high rateable value has been retained.[12] It has been supplemented, however, by a new exclusion based on a fixed high level of rent.[13] Essentially, the existing exclusion still applies to tenancies entered into before April 1, 1990, and the new exclusion applies to tenancies entered into on or after that date. But there is one exception, and there are some difficult transitional provisions. **4–05**

(a) Pre-April 1990 tenancies

Where a tenancy was entered into before April 1, 1990, the existing exception based on rateable value still applies, subject to one amendment[14] under which the rateable value on a fixed date is taken, in contrast with the original provision for taking the rateable value "for the time being".[15] Thus, the tenancy cannot be an assured tenancy if the rateable value of the dwelling-house on March 31, 1990 exceeded £1,500 (for a dwelling-house in Greater London) or £750 (for a dwelling-house elsewhere). Provision has been made for determining the rateable value of a dwelling-house where, immediately before April 1, 1990, no such value was assigned to it.[16] Where the dwelling-house forms part only of a hereditament for which a rateable value was shown in the list on March 31, 1990, or where the dwelling-house consists, or forms part, of more than one such hereditament, its rateable value must be ascertained by a proper apportionment or aggregation of the rateable values thus shown,[17] or by both, as where the dwelling forms part of two or more such hereditaments. Any question arising under this head as to the proper apportionment or aggregation of any value or values is to be determined by the county court, and the decision of that court is final.[18] **4–06**

(b) Post-March 1990 tenancies

A tenancy entered into on or after April 1, 1990 cannot be an assured tenancy if, under it, "the rent payable for the time being is payable at a rate exceeding £25,000 a year".[19] The words "for the time being" clearly show that a tenancy can become assured or cease to be assured in consequence of a reduction or increase in the rent payable under it, including an increase in rent above the rate **4–07**

[12] Act of 1988, Sched. 1, Pt. I, para. 2A, inserted by Regulations of 1990, Sched., para. 29.
[13] Act of 1988, Sched. 1, Pt. I, para. 2, as substituted by Regulations of 1990, Sched., para. 29.
[14] Act of 1988, Sched. 1, Pt. I, para. 2A.
[15] For the original provision, see the first edition (1989) of this book, p. 34.
[16] See *infra*, "Transitional provisions".
[17] Act of 1988, Sched. 1, Pt. II, para. 14(1).
[18] *ibid.*, para. 14(2). For "final", see Vol. 1, p. 346.
[19] Act of 1988, Sched. 1, Pt. I, para. 2(1), inserted by Regulations of 1990, Sched., para. 29. The amount of £25,000 may be replaced by a sum specified by the Secretary of State by statutory instrument, subject to a negative resolution of either House of Parliament: Act of 1988, s.1(2A), inserted by Regulations of 1990, Sched., para. 27.

of £25,000 a year determined by a rent assessment committee under the Act of 1988.[20]

(i) "RENT". Subject to the exclusion considered below, "rent" appears to bear the same meaning as under the Rent Acts, *i.e.* the total sum of money which on the date in question is lawfully payable to the landlord in money.[21]

(ii) EXCLUSION. For the purposes of this provision, there is excluded from "rent" "any sum payable by the tenant as is expressed (in whatever terms) to be payable in respect of rates, council tax, services, management, repairs, maintenance or insurance, unless it could not have been regarded by the parties to the tenancy as a sum so payable".[22] Except for the insertion of "management", this provision is in substance identical with the provision in the Rent Acts for defining long tenancies at a low rent.[23]

(c) The exception

4–08 For these purposes, a tenancy entered into on or after April 1, 1990 in pursuance of a contract made before that date is treated as a pre-April 1990 tenancy, provided that the dwelling-house had a rateable value on March 31, 1990.[24] The existing exclusion based on high rateable value will therefore apply to it, and the new "high rent" exclusion will not.

3. Transitional provisions

(a) Effect of abolition of domestic rates

4–09 *Prima facie*, the abolition of domestic rates on April 1, 1990 meant that a dwelling which was not by that date entered on the valuation list would not thereafter be entered. But in some circumstances, subsequent ascertainment of rateable value would be essential;[25] in others, convenient at least. Provision was therefore

[20] *R. v. London Rent Assessment Panel, ex p. Cadogan Estates Limited* [1998] Q.B. 398, QB, deciding that a rent assessment committee must not artificially limit its determination of the increase in rent to keep the tenancy an assured tenancy.

[21] See Vol. 1, pp. 161, 162.

[22] Act of 1988, Sched. 1, Pt. I, para. 2(2), inserted by Regulations of 1990, Sched., para. 29, and amended subsequently (as to council tax) by Local Government Finance (Housing) (Consequential Amendments) Order 1993 (S.I. 1993 No. 651), art. 2(1), Sched. 1, para. 19.

[23] Act of 1977, s.5(4), as amended by Local Government Finance (Housing) (Consequential Amendments) Order 1993 (S.I. 1993 No. 651), art. 2(1), Sched. 1, para. 4. See Vol. 1, p. 162.

[24] Act of 1988, Sched. 1, Pt. I, paras. 2(1)(a), 2A, as inserted by Regulations of 1990, Sched., para. 29.

[25] *e.g.*, a tenancy entered into before April 1, 1990 of a dwelling-house with no rateable value; *supra*.

made, notwithstanding the repeal of the relevant parts of the General Rate Act 1967,[26] for rateable values to be determined after April 1, 1990. Different provisions apply according to whether or not a proposal to enter the dwelling in a valuation list was made before April 1, 1990.

(b) The provisions

(i) PROPOSAL FOR VALUATION OUTSTANDING. Where a proposal to enter the dwelling in a valuation list was made before April 1, 1990, but no effect had been given to the proposal by that date, the provisions of the General Rate Act 1967 continue to have effect (despite the repeal) for the purposes of altering the valuation list pursuant to the proposal made.[27] When made, the alteration is effective from the beginning of the rating period in which the proposal was made[28] **4–10**

(ii) NO OUTSTANDING PROPOSAL FOR VALUATION. Where either no proposal to enter the dwelling in a valuation list had been made before April 1, 1990 or an entry in a valuation list then existed but no proposal to alter it (in consequence of structural alterations completed by April 1, 1990) had been made before that date, the landlord or the tenant under a tenancy entered into before April 1, 1990 can each apply to the valuation officer for a certificate. The officer must certify the amount that, but for the repeal of the General Rate Act 1967, he would have proposed as the rateable value of the dwelling.[29] The amount certified is treated as being the rateable value of the dwelling on March 31, 1990.[30] **4–11**

(c) Effect of provisions

The transitional provisions do not have any unexpected effect so far as tenancies falling within category (a) above (pre-April 1990 tenancies) are concerned. The entry on the valuation list, or the issue of the certificate (as the case may be), identifies the all-important rateable value on March 31, 1990. But one type of tenancy falling initially within category (b) above (post-March 1990 tenancies) might, in consequence of the effect of the transitional provisions, be brought within category (a) above. As stated, a tenancy entered into on or after April 1, 1990 in pursuance of a contract made before that date falls within category (b) above if the dwelling-house did not have a rateable value on March 31, 1990. **4–12**

[26] By Local Government Finance Act 1988, s.117(1), Sched. 13, Pt. I.

[27] General Rate Act 1967 and Related Provisions (Savings and Consequential Provision) Regulations 1990 (S.I. 1990 No. 777), reg. 3(1)(c).

[28] General Rate Act 1967, s.79.

[29] Local Government Finance (Repeals, Savings and Consequential Amendments) Order 1990 (S.I. 1990 No. 776), art. 5.

[30] *ibid.*

If, in consequence of a subsequent entry in the valuation list the dwelling then has a rateable value on March 31, 1990, it is arguable that the tenancy then satisfied the conditions of category (a) above, and no longer category (b).[31]

Sect. 2. Business Tenancies

4–13 ''A tenancy to which Part II of the Landlord and Tenant Act 1954 applies'' cannot be an assured tenancy.[32] Where there is a mixed business and residential use of premises, the question whether a tenancy that otherwise could be an assured tenancy[33] is such a tenancy will depend solely on whether at the time in question it is within Part II of that Act;[34] and this may accordingly vary from time to time.[35] But if the dwelling-house was let ''as'' something else, *e.g.*, as business premises, the tenancy cannot become an assured tenancy within the Act of 1988 by a mere unilateral abandonment of all business use.[36] Thus, where a lease of premises as ''a sculptors or artists residential studio'' created a business tenancy within Part II from its commencement, it did not become a regulated tenancy under the Rent Acts when the tenant, without the landlord's agreement, began to use the premises solely as a residence.[37]

The nature of the premises demised and the question of what the premises were let ''as'' are different questions from whether Part II of the Act of 1954 applies from time to time. So, if a dwelling-house was let as a separate dwelling, and subsequently the tenant lawfully[38] used the premises for a substantial business purpose as well as for residential purposes, the tenancy can become protected by Part II of the Act of 1954 and will thereupon cease to be an assured tenancy. The courts have recently proved themselves reluctant, however, to

[31] The argument turns on the construction of the words ''had a rateable value on 31st March 1990'' in Act of 1988, Sched. 1, Pt. I, paras. 2(1)(a), 2A(b): they could be directed to a question of fact (judged on March 31, 1990) or a question of law (judged in retrospect). The better view is that the tenancy does indeed change category, otherwise a tenancy entered into *before* April 1, 1990 with no rateable value could never fall within either category for the purpose of applying the exclusion.

[32] Act of 1988, Sched. 1, para. 4.

[33] Because the demised premises are a dwelling-house which was let as a separate dwelling within Act of 1988, s.1(1).

[34] *i.e.*, on whether the demised premises are wholly or in part ''occupied by the tenant . . . for the purposes of a business carried on by him or for those and other purposes'' within Landlord and Tenant Act 1954, s.23(1). For Part II of the Act of 1954 to apply, the business use must be *a* (but not necessarily *the*) substantial use of the premises: *Cheryl Investments Ltd. v. Saldanha* [1978] 1 W.L.R. 1379, CA.

[35] The Act of 1988 therefore works in the same way as the Act of 1977: see *ibid.*, s.24(3) and the cases cited *infra*.

[36] See *Russell v. Booker* (1982) 5 H.L.R. 10, CA; *Pulleng v. Curran* (1982) 44 P. & C.R. 58, CA.

[37] *Wagle v. Trustees of Henry Smith's Charity Kensington Estate* [1990] 1 Q.B. 42, CA; *Webb v. L. B. of Barnet* (1988) 21 H.L.R. 228, CA (secure tenancy: residence and workshop; cesser of use as workshop).

[38] See Act of 1954, s.23(4).

accept that a business use of a residence is a sufficiently substantial use to fall within Part II.[39]

Sect. 3. Licensed Premises

"A tenancy under which the dwelling-house consists of or comprises premises licensed for the sale of intoxicating liquors for consumption on the premises" cannot be an assured tenancy.[40] This language is substantially the same as that in the Rent Acts.[41] "Off-licences" are not within this exclusion, but may fall within the business tenancies exclusion.[42] **4–14**

Sect. 4. Tenancies of Agricultural Land

"A tenancy under which agricultural land, exceeding two acres, is let together with the dwelling-house" cannot be an assured tenancy.[43] "Agricultural land" has the same meaning as under the Rent Acts,[44] namely "any land used as arable meadow or pasture ground only, land used for a plantation or a wood or for the growth of saleable underwood, land exceeding one quarter of an acre used for the purpose of poultry farming, cottage gardens exceeding one quarter of an acre, market gardens, nursery grounds, orchards or allotments, including allotment gardens within the meaning of the Allotments Act 1922".[45] **4–15**

The phrase "let together with" has already been considered in connection with the general rule concerning a dwelling-house that is "let together with" other land.[46] Put shortly, the general rule is that if and so long as the main purpose of the letting is to provide a home for the tenant, the land will be treated as part of the dwelling-house, but otherwise the dwelling-house will be treated as not being let as a separate dwelling, and so the tenancy will not be an assured

[39] See *Gurton v. Parrott* (1990) 23 H.L.R. 418, CA; *Wright v. Mortimer* (1996) 28 H.L.R. 719, CA. And compare the minimal business use in *Pulleng v. Curran, supra.*

[40] Act of 1988, Sched. 1, para. 5.

[41] Act of 1977, s.11; Vol. 1, p. 138.

[42] Off-licences were never within the exclusion from protection of Act of 1954, s.43(1)(d), now itself repealed (with transitional provisions) by Landlord and Tenant (Licensed Premises) Act 1990, ss.1, 2.

[43] Act of 1988, Sched. 1, para. 6(1).

[44] *ibid.*, para. 6(2).

[45] General Rate Act 1967, s.26(3)(a), which continues to have effect after March 31, 1990 for the purposes of *inter alia* Act of 1988, Sched. 1, para. 6 notwithstanding its repeal from that date by Local Government Finance Act 1988, s.117(1), Sched. 13, Pt. I: Reference to Rating (Housing) Regulations 1990 (S.I. 1990 No. 434), reg. 3.

[46] *Ante*, para. 3–13. See also *Farmer (Valuation Officer) v. Buxted Poultry Ltd.* [1993] A.C. 369 (building not occupied "together with" agricultural land for valuation purposes unless land and building formed a single agricultural unit).

tenancy. But where, as this exception provides, it is agricultural land of over two acres that is "let together with" the dwelling-house, there can be no assured tenancy, even if the object is to provide a home for the tenant.

Sect. 5. Tenancies of Agricultural Holdings, etc.

4–16 A tenancy cannot be an assured tenancy if the dwelling-house not only is "comprised in an agricultural holding" but also is "occupied by the person responsible for the control ... of the farming of the holding".[47] This substantially repeats the corresponding provision in the Rent Acts.[48] "Agricultural holding" means any agricultural holding within the meaning of the Agricultural Holdings Act 1986 held under a tenancy in relation to which that Act applies;[49] and it does not matter whether the occupier responsible for the control of the farming is the tenant or a servant or agent of his.[50] A dwelling does not cease to be "comprised in" an agricultural holding merely because, without the landlord's consent, the holding is partitioned between the two tenants, one taking the dwelling and the other the land.[51] Similarly, premises let as an agricultural holding do not become premises protected by the Act of 1988 by a unilateral abandonment by the tenant of the agricultural use.[52]

4–17 As from September 1, 1995, the agricultural holdings regime was replaced (for the future) by a new regime of farm business tenancies under the Agricultural Tenancies Act 1995. A similar exclusion was provided, by amendment, for such tenancies. Under it, a tenancy cannot be an assured tenancy if the dwelling-house is both "comprised in the holding held under a farm business tenancy" and "occupied by the person responsible for the control of the management of the holding".[53] "Farm business tenancy" and "holding", in relation to such a tenancy, have the same meanings as in the Agricultural Tenancies Act 1995.[54] Again, it does not matter whether the occupier responsible for the control of the management of the holding is the tenant or his servant or agent.[55]

[47] Act of 1988, Sched. 1, para. 7(1), substituted with effect from September 1, 1995 by Agricultural Tenancies Act 1995, ss.40, 41(2), Sched., para. 34. The substitution made no difference to the wording of the exception based on the Agricultural Holdings Act 1986, but added an equivalent exception for farm business tenancies under the new Act of 1995.

[48] Act of 1977, s.10, as substituted with effect from September 1, 1995 by Agricultural Tenancies Act 1995, ss.40, 41(2), Sched., para. 27. See n. 47, *supra*.

[49] Act of 1988, Sched. 1, para. 7(3), substituted by Agricultural Tenancies Act 1995, ss.40, 41(2), Sched., para. 34.

[50] Act of 1988, para. 7(1)(b).

[51] *Lester v. Ridd* [1990] 2 Q.B. 430, CA.

[52] *Russell v. Booker* (1982) 5 H.L.R. 10, CA (a case decided under the Rent Acts).

[53] Act of 1988, Sched. 1, para. 7(2), substituted with effect from September 1, 1995 by Agricultural Tenancies Act 1995, ss.40, 41(2), Sched., para. 34.

[54] Act of 1988, para. 7(3).

[55] *ibid.*, para. 7(2)(b).

Sect. 6. Lettings to Students

1. The exception

A tenancy cannot be an assured tenancy if— **4–18**

(a) it "is granted to a person who is pursuing, or intends to pursue, a course of study provided by a specified educational institution", and
(b) it "is so granted either by that institution or by another specified institution or body of persons".[56]

Here too the language is almost identical with that in the Rent Acts;[57] and a tenancy granted by a non-specified institution or body will not fall within this exception, even if it is granted to a student who is pursuing a course of study provided by a specified educational institution. "Specified" similarly means specified (or of a class specified) for this purpose by regulations made by the Secretary of State by statutory instrument, subject to annulment pursuant to a resolution of either House of Parliament.[58] Under the corresponding provisions in the Rent Acts many institutions and classes of institution were specified, and the same course has been followed under the Act of 1988. Since 1988 there has been one set of regulations for the purposes of both the Rent Acts and the Act of 1988.[59] With effect from September 1, 1998, the 1988 Regulations were revoked by the Assured and Protected Tenancies (Lettings to Students) Regulations 1998[60] ("the 1998 Regulations"), which consolidated them and the many amendment regulations[61] as the 1998 Regulations.

Under these, a substantial number of educational institutions and bodies have been specified. Whereas under the 1988 Regulations as originally made,[62] institutions and bodies specified were specified under the Rent Acts and the Act of 1988 alike, since 1989 the amended 1988 Regulations, and now the 1998 Regulations, have included a number of institutions and bodies which are only specified for the purposes of the Act of 1988.[63] These include all registered housing associations within the meaning of section 1 of the Housing Associations Act 1985 which are not already specified in the Regulations for the purposes of both the Rent Acts and the Act of 1988.[64]

[56] Act of 1988, Sched. 1, para. 8(1).
[57] Act of 1977, s.8(1); see Vol. 1, pp. 157, 158.
[58] Act of 1988, Sched. 1, para. 8(2), (3).
[59] Assured and Protected Tenancies (Lettings to Students) Regulations 1988 (S.I. 1988 No. 2236) ("the 1988 Regulations"), as amended successively by Assured and Protected Tenancies (Lettings to Students) (Amendment) Regulations of 1989 (S.I. 1989 No. 1628), 1990 (S.I. 1990 No. 1825), 1991 (S.I. 1991 No. 233), 1992 (S.I. 1992 No. 515), 1993 (S.I. 1993 No. 2390), 1996 (S.I. 1996 No. 458) and by Assured and Protected Tenancies (Lettings to Students) (Amendment) (No. 2) Regulations 1996 (S.I. 1996 No. 2198). A further amendment was made with effect from April 1, 1993 by the Further and Higher Education Act 1992 (Consequential Amendments) Regulations 1993 (S.I. 1993 No. 559), reg. 6.
[60] S.I. 1998 No. 1967, reg. 6.
[61] n. 59, *supra*.
[62] S.I. 1988 No. 2236, *supra*.
[63] These are listed in Sched. 2 to the 1998 Regulations (S.I. 1998 No. 1967) printed *post*, p. 672.
[64] S.I. 1998 No. 1967, reg. 5(a).

2. Specified educational institutions

4–19 The specified educational institutions consist of any university or university college; any constituent college, school or hall or other institution of a university; any other publicly funded institution which provides further education or higher education, or both; and the David Game Tutorial College, London.[65] "Higher education" means education by means of a course of any description mentioned in Schedule 6 to the Education Reform Act 1988.[66] "Further education" has the meaning assigned to it by subsections (3) and (5) of section 2 of the Education Act 1996.[67] There are four categories of "publicly funded" institution.[68] First, one that is provided or assisted[69] by a local education authority. Secondly, one in receipt of grant under regulations made under section 485 of the Education Act 1996. Thirdly, an institution (not being a university) within the higher education sector.[70] Fourthly, one within the further education sector.[71]

3. Specified bodies

4–20 The specified bodies for the purposes of the Act of 1988 consist of the following bodies of persons (whether corporate or not), namely: the governing body of any of the specified educational institutions; the body (not being a local education authority) that provides any such educational institution; a housing association registered under and within the meaning of the Housing Associations Act 1985; and twenty-three bodies individually named in Schedules 1 and 2 to the 1998 Regulations.[72]

Sect. 7. Resident Landlords

4–21 The concept of the "resident landlord", namely a landlord resident in the same building as his tenant, was introduced by the Rent Act 1974 as a transitional provision relating to changes in the protection afforded to tenants under furnished lettings and those who shared accommodation with their landlords.[73] The new provisions were consolidated in the Act of 1977, as subsequently amended by the Housing Act 1980,[74] and in broad terms, the same principles (with all

[65] 1998 Regulations, reg. 3.
[66] 1998 Regulations, reg. 2.
[67] *ibid.*
[68] *ibid.*
[69] As defined in Education Act 1996, s.579(5), (6).
[70] Within the meaning of Further and Higher Education Act 1992, s.91(5).
[71] Within the meaning of *ibid.*, s.91(3).
[72] 1998 Regulations, regs. 4, 5. The named bodies are set out in the 1998 Regulations, printed *post*, pp. 671, 672.
[73] Rent Act 1974, s.16(1), Sched. 3. For a detailed analysis, see Vol. 1, p. 189.
[74] Act of 1977, s.12, Scheds. 2, 24, para. 6, as amended.

their complexities[75]) have been continued under the Act of 1988 in relation to assured tenancies. Where the resident landlord requirements were satisfied, the Act of 1977 prevented the tenancy from being a protected tenancy, but made it a restricted contract instead.[76] Under the Act of 1988, there is no equivalent to the restricted contract status under the Act of 1977: if the resident landlord requirements are satisfied, the tenancy is prevented from being an assured tenancy.[77]

A tenancy will be within the resident landlord category under the Act of 1988 if four conditions are satisfied.[78]

1. THE FOUR CONDITIONS

1. Part of a building

The first condition is that "the dwelling-house forms part only of a building and, except in a case where the dwelling-house also forms part of a flat, the building is not a purpose-built block of flats".[79] For these purposes, a building is a purpose-built block of flats if, as constructed, it contained, and it contains, two or more flats.[80] "Flat" here means a dwelling-house which forms part only of a building and is separated horizontally from another dwelling-house which forms part of the same building.[81] These definitions of the Act of 1988 are identical with the Act of 1977. "Building" is clearly a word with a very wide meaning, but here the building in question must necessarily include at least two dwelling-houses, otherwise the resident landlord issue will not arise.[82] The context of the exception must exclude the usual rule[83] that the singular includes the plural: two or more "buildings" will not satisfy the condition. But whether two dwelling-houses are each part of the same building can be a marginal and difficult question.[84] The meaning of "separated horizontally" must denote separation by a horizontal division or structure, as opposed to by a vertical wall. The definition of purpose-built block of flats requires one to consider the block both at the time of its construction and when the issue arises; but a building may constitute a newly-constructed building if it is completely rebuilt inside.[85] 4–22

[75] See Vol. 1, pp. 189–209. Parliament did not feel the same way about the complexities of "deeming" and "disregarding" that the authors of Vol. 1 did: see *ibid.*, pp. 210, 211.

[76] Vol. 1, p. 190.

[77] Act of 1988, Sched. 1, para. 10.

[78] *ibid.*, as supplemented by paras. 17–22 (Sched. 1, Pt. III), given legislative effect by s.1(2)(c).

[79] *ibid.*, para. 10(1)(a).

[80] *ibid.*, para. 22.

[81] *ibid.*

[82] See condition 3, *infra*.

[83] Interpretation Act 1978, s.6.

[84] See *Wolff v. Waddington* (1989) 22 H.L.R. 72, CA; *Lewis-Graham v. Conacher* (1991) 24 H.L.R. 132, CA; and the further cases cited in Vol. 1, p. 195.

[85] See *Barnes v. Gorsuch* (1981) 43 P. & C.R. 294 at 297, CA (decided under the Rent Acts).

2. Grant not made to existing assured tenant

4–23 Unlike the Rent Acts, the Act of 1988 does not expressly require that the tenancy should have been granted after any particular date.[86] But part of the provision under the Rent Acts, relating to grants to an existing tenant, is in effect repeated in the Act of 1988, for grants to an existing assured tenant cannot fall within this exclusion and will (subject to not otherwise being excluded from protection) create assured tenancies even if the resident landlord conditions are otherwise satisfied. A tenancy does not satisfy this second condition if—

(a) it is granted to a person (either alone, or jointly with others) who, immediately before it was granted, was a tenant under an assured tenancy of the same dwelling-house, or of another dwelling-house which forms part of the building; and
(b) the same person is the landlord under both tenancies (or is one of the landlords under both tenancies, if either was granted by two or more persons jointly).[87]

Although not expressly stated, it obviously suffices that the person to whom the new tenancy is granted was one of two or more joint tenants of the dwelling-house or other dwelling-house in the building under the former tenancy. This condition prevents a non-resident landlord from depriving a tenant of his assured tenancy by becoming resident and then inducing the tenant to take a new tenancy of his existing dwelling or of another dwelling in the same building.

3. Grant by resident landlord

4–24 The third condition is that ''the tenancy was granted by an individual who, at the time when the tenancy was granted, occupied as his only or principal home another dwelling-house, and that, where the tenant's dwelling-house is part of a flat, the landlord's dwelling-house ''also forms part of the flat'' , or, where the tenant's dwelling-house is not part of a flat, the landlord's dwelling-house ''also forms part of the building'' and ''the building is not a purpose-built block of flats''.[88] This is substantially the same condition as under the Act of 1977,[89] and it focuses on the moment of time when the tenancy was granted.[90] There are, however, two differences from the Act of 1977. The substitution of ''individual''[91] for ''person'' appears to make no difference, for in any case a corpor-

[86] Vol. 1, p. 191.
[87] Act of 1988, Sched. 1, para. 10(1)(d), (3).
[88] *ibid.*, para. 10(1)(b), read together with para. 10(1)(a).
[89] Act of 1977, s.12(1)(b).
[90] Perhaps not very precisely: see *Barnett v. O'Sullivan* [1994] 1 W.L.R. 1667, CA (tenant moved house with his landlords and their family, but tenant occupied the new property for a week or so before landlords moved in: resident landlord condition satisfied at time of grant of new tenancy).
[91] For ''individual'', see *ante*, para. 3–23.

ate landlord could not occupy a dwelling-house as a residence;[92] and when a tenancy is granted by two or more persons jointly, "individual" here means any one of them.[93] But the substitution of "only or principal home"[94] for "residence" tightens the requirement by preventing a landlord from being a resident landlord in more buildings than one. A "two-homes landlord" might even be a "resident landlord" in neither building if the homes are of equal significance to him and so neither is his "principal" home.

A landlord who lets part of his dwelling-house to another tenant must be able to show that the part that he retains constitutes a dwelling-house in itself.[95] And a landlord who carries on some essential living functions elsewhere may not be occupying the dwelling-house as a home.[96]

4. Continuous residence

The fourth condition is that "at all times since the tenancy was granted the interest of the landlord under the tenancy has belonged to an individual who, at the time he owned that interest, occupied as his only or principal home another dwelling-house" which also formed part of the building or flat in accordance with the first condition above[97]. Apart from "individual" and "only or principal home", considered above, this is substantially the same as the provision under the Act of 1977.[98] Here again, if the landlord's interest is for the time being held by two or more persons jointly, occupation by any one of them suffices.[99] **4–25**

This fourth condition creates for the Act of 1988 a requirement that is substantially the same as the notoriously complex condition of "continuous residence" (as it has been called) under the Act of 1977. In particular, the provisions for "deeming" and "disregarding" are in substance repeated, preventing certain breaks in fact in the continuity of residence from being treated as a matter of law from having broken it. Whereas the "deeming" provisions have the effect that the continuous residence requirement is fulfilled in law during a time when in fact it is not, the "disregard" provisions remove the time in question from consideration. Both therefore operate to preserve the benefit of resident landlord status during the time when they are running.[1] These provisions fall under four heads, and will be considered in turn.

[92] Though see *Mortgage Corp. Ltd. v. Ubah* (1996) 73 P. & C.R. 580, CA (dwelling-house did not become "separate" when reversion on tenancy providing for sharing with landlord became vested in corporation).

[93] Act of 1988, Sched. 1, para. 10(2), making explicit what was implicit under Act of 1977: see Vol. 1, p. 194.

[94] Considered *ante*, paras. 3–24 *et seq.*

[95] *Lyons v. Caffery* (1982) 5 H.L.R. 63, CA.

[96] See *Cliffe v. Standard* (1981) 132 New L.J. 186, CA.

[97] Act of 1988, Sched. 1, para. 10(1)(c).

[98] Act of 1977, s.12(1)(c); for a discussion of the phrases "at all times" and "has belonged to", see Vol. 1, pp. 195, 196.

[99] Act of 1988, Sched. 1, para. 10(2).

[1] For their difference, see *post*, para. 4–35.

(a) Trustees and resident beneficiary: deeming

4–26 The requirement of continuous residence is "deemed to be fulfilled" during "any period when—

(a) the interest of the landlord under the tenancy . . . is vested in trustees as such, and
(b) that interest is held on trust for any person who . . . occupies as his only or principal home a dwelling-house which forms part" of the requisite building or flat.[2]

This provision very largely repeats the corresponding provision under the Rent Acts,[3] and like it this provision operates without any limit of time. It is uncertain whether the beneficiary must be occupying by right of an interest in possession, or whether a beneficiary contingently interested, or a discretionary beneficiary, suffices. Four differences from the provision under the Act of 1977 must be mentioned. First, where the trust is for two or more persons, it is now provided that it suffices if at least one of them occupies the dwelling-house in the requisite way;[4] yet this seems only to have made explicit what appeared to be implicit in the Act of 1977. Secondly, the more stringent phrase "his only or principal home"[5] replaces the less demanding words "his residence". Thirdly, on the death of a resident beneficiary, the deeming under the Act of 1977 ended,[6] whereas under the Act of 1988 it is in effect prolonged while the landlord's interest remains vested in the trustees as such, for up to two years, by disregarding the period from the death until the condition of continuous residence is again deemed to be fulfilled under this head.[7] The fourth difference relates to the satisfaction of condition 3 above (grant by resident landlord) at a time when the interest of the landlord is vested in trustees as such. If a tenancy comes to an end while there is a deeming under this head, and the trustees grant a new tenancy of the same (or substantially the same) dwelling-house to a person who was the tenant, or one of the tenants, under the previous tenancy, the third condition, relating to a grant made by a resident landlord, is deemed to be fulfilled for the new tenancy.[8]

(b) Personal representatives: deeming

4–27 Where there is a resident landlord, and "the interest of the landlord under the tenancy becomes vested in the personal representatives of a deceased person acting in that capacity", the requirement of continuous residence is "deemed to

[2] Act of 1988, Sched. 1, para. 18(1), as amended with effect from January 1, 1997 by Trusts of Land and Appointment of Trustees Act 1996, ss.25(2), 27(2), Sched. 4; S.I. 1996 No. 2974.
[3] Act of 1977, Sched. 2, para. 2, as amended; Vol. 1, p. 198.
[4] Act of 1988, Sched. 1, para. 18(1).
[5] Considered *ante*, para. 4–24.
[6] See Vol. 1, p. 199.
[7] Act of 1988, Sched. 1, para. 18(2).
[8] *ibid.*, para. 19. *Ante*, para. 4–24.

be fulfilled for any period, beginning with the date on which the interest becomes vested in the personal representatives and not exceeding two years, during which the interest of the landlord remains so vested''.[9] Where the landlord dies intestate, the date in question is the date on which letters of administration are granted; if the reversion is disposed of under the will of the landlord, the date is the date of his death. This is the same as under the Act of 1977, preserving the benefit of the resident landlord status of the deceased for his estate while it is being administered. Thus, if before the end of the two years the personal representatives dispose of the reversion to a person who is himself resident in another dwelling-house in the same building, that person is enabled to take full advantage of the exception. Equally, if the personal representatives terminate the tenancy (by notice to quit, or by exercise of a break notice or forfeiture, if available) whilst the landlord's interest is vested in them as such and before the end of the two year period, the tenant will have no defence to a claim for possession on the basis that he is an assured tenant.

Where the landlord dies intestate or without appointing executors, the period of two years' deemed fulfilment of the residence condition can follow the period of disregard next considered.

(c) Trustees, Probate Judge or Public Trustee: disregard

In determining whether the requirement of continuous residence ''is at any time fulfilled with respect to a tenancy, there shall be disregarded . . . any period of not more than two years beginning with the date on which the interest of the landlord under the tenancy becomes, and during which it remains, vested— **4–28**

(i) in trustees as such; or
(ii) by virtue of section 9 of the Administration of Estates Act 1925, in the Probate Judge, or the Public Trustee''.[10]

This is the same disregard as under the Act of 1977, as amended.[11] It preserves the benefit of being a resident landlord while the landlord's interest is vested in the inert hands of the Probate Judge or Public Trustee,[12] or in the hands of trustees, who may need time to administer the trust property. Trustees are ''trustees as such'' whether the trust arises *inter vivos* or under a will or upon intestacy.[13]

[9] Act of 1988, Sched. 1, para. 20.
[10] Act of 1988, Sched. 1, para. 17(1)(c), as amended from July 1, 1995 by Law of Property (Miscellaneous Provisions) Act 1994, ss.21(1), 23(1), Sched. 1, para. 11; S.I. 1995 No. 1317.
[11] See Vol. 1, p. 202 and Law of Property (Miscellaneous Provisions) Act 1994, ss.21(1), 23(1), Sched. 1, para. 8; S.I. 1995 No. 1317.
[12] As from July 1, 1995, the property of intestates vests in the Public Trustee pending the filing of letters of administration, as does the property of a testator where there is no executor with power to obtain probate: Law of Property (Miscellaneous Provisions) Act 1994, s.14(1), substituting new Administration of Estates Act 1925, s.9. See *Practice Direction (Probate: Notice to Quit)* [1995] 1 W.L.R. 1120, Fam. (notices to quit to be served on Public Trustee at Public Trust Office in London).
[13] See *Williams v. Mate* (1982) 46 P. & C.R. 43 at 51, CA.

(d) Transfers: disregard

4–29 For cases where a resident landlord's interest is sold or otherwise disposed of, the Act of 1988 prevents the loss of resident landlord status merely because there is an interval between the outgoing landlord ceasing to be resident and the incoming landlord becoming resident. The provisions are twofold, and mirror the provisions under the Act of 1977. First, there is an automatic period of not more than 28 days; and secondly, there is an extension of this period to not more than six months if the landlord gives due notice to the tenant (*e.g.*, so as to allow the new landlord to arrange for redecoration and repairs).

4–30 (i) THE AUTOMATIC 28 DAYS. In determining whether the requirement of continuous residence is fulfilled with respect to a tenancy, there must be disregarded "any period of not more than twenty-eight days, beginning with the date on which the interest of the landlord under the tenancy becomes vested at law and in equity in an individual who, during that period, does not occupy as his only or principal home another dwelling-house which forms part of the building or, as the case may be, flat concerned".[14] This repeats the corresponding provision in the Rent Acts,[15] save that again "only or principal home" replaces the less stringent "residence". Further, there is now express provision[16] for cases where the landlord's interest becomes vested in two or more persons jointly and at least one of them is an individual.[17] In that case the 28 day provision applies only if none of the joint landlords occupies the other dwelling-house under this provision.[18] If the landlord or landlords hold the reversion on trust for others beside themselves, this provision cannot apply because there is no "individual" in whom the reversion is vested at law and in equity.

4–31 (ii) THE CONDITIONAL SIX MONTHS. The automatic 28 days may be extended to six months if within the 28 days "the individual concerned notifies the tenant in writing of his intention to occupy as his only or principal home another dwelling-house in the building or, as the case may be, flat concerned".[19] Once again there is express provision for the case where there are joint landlords. If the landlord's interest becomes vested at law and in equity in two or more persons jointly and at least one of them is an individual,[20] the notice to the tenant may be given by any of the joint landlords.[21] Apart from replacing "residence" by "only or principal home", this repeats the provision in the Rent Acts.[22] Probably there must be strict compliance with the time limits, and so if the purchasers are a day late with the written notice and do not upon the expiry

[14] Act of 1988, Sched. 1, para. 17(1)(a).
[15] Act of 1977, Sched. 2, para. 1(a), as amended; see Vol. 1, p. 203.
[16] Corresponding to the definition of the resident landlord: *ante*, para. 4–24.
[17] Under the Rent Acts, all had to be individuals: Vol. 1, p. 203.
[18] Act of 1988, Sched.1, para. 17(2). Because the occupation by one as his only or principal home suffices: *ibid.*, para. 10(2); *ante*, para. 4–25.
[19] *ibid.*, para. 17(1)(b).
[20] See *supra*.
[21] Act of 1988, Sched. 1, para. 17(2)(b).
[22] Act of 1977, Sched. 2, para. 1(b), as amended; Vol. 1, p. 204.

of 28 days actually satisfy the residence condition, the tenancy, will become assured. The effect of the notice is that in determining whether the requirement of continuous residence is fulfilled with respect to the tenancy, a period of up to six months is disregarded. The period begins with the date on which the interest of the landlord under the tenancy became vested in the individual, or in the joint landlords as the case may be, at law and in equity. The period ends on the earliest of three possible times, two of which are straightforward and the third of which is more complex. First, the expiry of the period of six months beginning on that date. Secondly, the date on which the interest of the landlord ceases to be so vested in that individual or those joint landlords. Thirdly, the date on which the landlord's interest becomes again vested in an individual landlord (or in the case of joint landlords, one of them who is an individual) who actually satisfies the residence condition,[23] or the date on which that condition is deemed to be fulfilled by virtue of the two deeming provisions considered above.[24]

The effect of these provisions is that if, before the six months has expired, the landlord ceases to be the owner of the reversion both at law and in equity, the time following that change is no longer to be disregarded. Here, in the case of joint landlords, it appears to suffice if one of them is no longer an owner at law and in equity, even if the others remain such. The period of disregard will also come to an end before the six months expire as soon as the continuous residence condition is again actually satisfied; there is then no need for it. But it will also come to an end if it is supplanted, as it were, by a period of deemed fulfilment: the deeming outweighs the disregard. **4–32**

This provision closely follows the corresponding provision in the Rent Acts, but two changes must be noted. First, in providing for the length of the extended period of disregard, instead of speaking as the Act of 1977 does in terms of "the condition . . . again applies" (referring to the condition for being a resident landlord), the Act of 1988 makes it explicit that the six months' period will end not only when the condition for being a resident landlord is again actually satisfied but also when it is deemed to be satisfied. Secondly, express provision is made for cases where the landlord's interest becomes vested in two or more persons jointly, at least one of whom is an individual.

2. OPERATION OF THE PROVISIONS

In general, the operation of the resident landlord provisions of the Act of 1988 is the same as that of the corresponding provisions of the Rent Acts.[25] Two aspects are of particular importance. **4–33**

[23] *i.e.* the condition in para. 10(1)(c).
[24] Act of 1988, para. 17(1)(b).
[25] See Vol. 1, pp. 205–209.

1. Cumulative periods

4–34 There is no reason why one period of deeming or disregard should not be added to another period of deeming or disregard. Thus, for example, if personal representatives vest the landlord's interest in trustees within the two-year period of deemed fulfilment, and there is from that time a resident beneficiary under the trusts, the unlimited period of deemed fulfilment for the beneficiary's occupation may succeed the limited period of deeming enjoyed while the landlord's interest was vested in the personal representatives.

2. Deeming and disregarding

4–35 Deeming and disregarding both operate to preserve the benefit of resident landlord status while the periods are running; but they differ in an important way. During any period of disregard,[26] as distinct from a period of deeming, no order for possession of the dwelling-house can be made except an order which might be made if the tenancy were (or had been) an assured tenancy.[27] During a period of deemed fulfilment, on the other hand, there is no bar to the landlord recovering possession if, at common law,[28] he is entitled to do so. This corresponds to the provision under the Rent Acts relating to regulated tenancies, and its rationale rests in a similar, unexplained obscurity.[29]

Sect. 8. Crown Tenancies

1. The exception

4–36 The general rule is that the Act of 1988 binds the Crown,[30] but a tenancy under which the interest of the landlord—

(1) "belongs to Her Majesty in right of the Crown", or
(2) "belongs . . . to a government department", or
(3) "is held in trust for Her Majesty for the purposes of a government department"

cannot be an assured tenancy.[31] These are all cases of sovereignty or governmental ownership, as distinct from private or personal ownership.

[26] *i.e.* under either para. 17 or para. 18(2) of Act of 1988, Sched. 1.
[27] *ibid.*, para. 21.
[28] And subject to the Protection from Eviction Act 1977.
[29] Vol. 1, pp. 205, 206.
[30] See *ante*, p. 16.
[31] Act of 1988, Sched. 1, para. 11(1).

2. Limits to the exception

The exception does not apply where the interest of the landlord belongs to Her Majesty in right of the Crown and "that interest is under the management of the Crown Estate Commissioners or is held by the Secretary of State as the result of the exercise by him of functions under Part III of the Housing Associations Act 1985".[32] Further, where an interest belongs to Her Majesty in right of the Duchy of Lancaster, the Chancellor of the Duchy of Lancaster is deemed to be the owner of the interest,[33] so that it will be outside the exception. No express provision is made for the Duchy of Cornwall,[34] but as the Duchy property does not belong to Her Majesty, it too is outside the exception. As under the Rent Acts,[35] the exception applies only to direct Crown tenants, and so sub-tenants of Crown tenants are not within it. **4–37**

Further limits were introduced[36] with effect from April 1, 1991 in relation to health service land. In three categories of case, tenancies held of certain landlords will no longer enjoy Crown exemption, subject to transitional provisions.[37] **4–38**

(a) The three categories

All three turn on the ownership, control or use by a "health service body", rather than on the identity of the landlord as such.

(i) OWNERSHIP OF HEALTH SERVICE BODY. The exemption is lost where the interest of the landlord is vested in a "health service body".[38] This is because from April 1, 1991 no health service body is regarded as the servant or agent of the Crown. The following are health service bodies for these purposes: **4–39**

(1) a health authority within the meaning of the National Health Service Act 1977;
(2) a Health Board or Special Health Board constituted under section 2 of the National Health Service (Scotland) Act 1978;
(3) a State Hospital Management Committee constituted under section 91 of the Mental Health (Scotland) Act 1984;
(4) a Family Health Services Authority;
(5) the Common Services Agency for the Scottish Health Service;

[32] Act of 1988, Sched. 1, para. 11(2), as amended on January 15, 1999 by Government of Wales Act 1998 (Housing) (Amendments) Order 1999 (S.I. 1999 No. 61), art: 2, Sched., para. 3(4). The "functions" in question were exercised by Housing for Wales prior to the transfer of its interests on November 1, 1998 to the Secretary of State: see Government of Wales Act 1998, s.140.

[33] Act of 1988, s.44(4). This deeming applies to ss.1–33 of the Act, and as it is s.1 that gives effect to the list in Sched. 1, presumably it also applies to that Schedule.

[34] Yet the Rent Acts expressly dealt with it: Vol. 1, p. 146.

[35] See Vol. 1, p. 146.

[36] By National Health Service and Community Care Act 1990, s.60 and National Health Service and Community Care Act (Commencement No. 1) Order 1990 (S.I. 1990 No. 1329).

[37] Considered *infra*.

[38] As defined by National Health Service and Community Care Act 1990, s.60(7); *ibid*., s.60(1).

(6) the Dental Practice Board;
(7) the Scottish Dental Practice Board, and
(8) the Public Health Laboratory Service Board.

4–40 (ii) CONTROL OF HEALTH SERVICE BODY. Tenancies will no longer enjoy Crown exemption where the interest of the landlord is vested in the Secretary of State for Health and, by virtue of directions made under any provision of the National Health Service Act 1977, the Mental Health (Scotland) Act 1984 or the Health and Medicines Act 1988, or by virtue of orders made under section 2 or section 10 of the National Health Service (Scotland) Act 1978, powers of disposal or management ("the statutory powers") with respect to the land are conferred on a "health service body".[39] At any time when the statutory powers are so conferred, the land is treated for the purposes of any enactment or rule of law relating to Crown land or interests as if it were held otherwise than by the Secretary of State or any other emanation of the Crown.[40] This is clearly wide enough to include paragraph 11 of Schedule 1 to the Act of 1988.

4–41 (iii) HELD, USED OR OCCUPIED BY HEALTH SERVICE BODY. The exemption is lost where the landlord is the Secretary of State for Health and the land is otherwise held, used or occupied by a health service body.[41] At any time when the land is so held, used or occupied, the land is treated for the purposes of any enactment or rule of law relating to Crown land or interests as if it were held otherwise than by the Secretary of State or any other emanation of the Crown.[42] Once again, this must include the exclusionary paragraph of the Act of 1988.

(b) Transitional provisions

4–42 Where a tenancy was entered into before April 1, 1991 and is of land in England and Wales which immediately before that date was subject to "the statutory powers" in the hands of a health service body, or was otherwise held, used or occupied by a health service body, the following transitional provision applies for the purposes of the Crown exemption provision of the Act of 1988.[43] If and so long as the interest of the landlord under such a tenancy continues on and after April 1, 1991 to belong in fact either to the Secretary of State for Health or to an NHS trust,[44] it is taken to belong to a government department and therefore Crown exemption is continued.[45]

[39] National Health Service and Community Care Act 1990, s.60(1)(a).
[40] *ibid.*, s.60(1).
[41] *ibid.*, s.60(1)(b).
[42] *ibid.*, s.60(1).
[43] And of the Act of 1977 alike.
[44] *i.e.* a trust established under the National Health Service and Community Care Act 1990, Pt. I, or under the National Health Service (Scotland) Act 1978: National Health Service and Community Care Act 1990, Sched. 8, para. 12(d).
[45] National Health Service and Community Care Act 1990, Sched. 8, para. 19.

Sect. 9. Local Authorities and Other Exempted Bodies

1. The exemption

A tenancy cannot be an assured tenancy if the interest of the landlord belongs to a local authority or to one of certain other bodies with local or housing functions.[46] There is no limitation by reference to the purpose for which the landlord's interest *belongs* to such a body, and therefore a house held by such a body outside its area of housing functions or responsibilities falls within this exception. But it does not include houses in respect of which a "control order" has been made by a local authority.[47] These exempted bodies may be grouped under three heads. **4–43**

(a) Local authorities

First, there are bodies that are generally regarded as being local authorities.[48] These are the council of a county, county borough,[49] district or London borough; the Common Council of the City of London; the Council of the Isles of Scilly; the Broads Authority; a National Park authority;[50] the Inner London Education Authority; a joint authority within the meaning of the Local Government Act 1985; and various police authorities.[51] **4–44**

(b) Authorities with local functions

Secondly, there are various bodies which discharge certain local functions.[52] These are the Commission for the New Towns; the Development Board for Rural Wales[52a]; an urban development corporation;[53] a development corporation;[54] a waste disposal authority;[55] a residuary body;[56] and specifically the Residuary Body for Wales (Corff Gwenddilliol Cymru).[57] **4–45**

[46] Act of 1988, Sched. 1, para. 12.
[47] Housing Act 1985, s.382(2), (3).
[48] Act of 1988, Sched. 1, para. 12(1)(a), (2).
[49] Inserted by Local Government (Wales) Act 1994, ss.22(2), 66(3), Sched. 8, para. 9(2); S.I. 1996 No. 396.
[50] Added by the Environment Act 1995.
[51] Added by the Police and Magistrates' Courts Act 1994, the Police Act 1996 and the Police Act 1997. Act of 1988, Sched. 1, para. 12(2)(g).
[52] Act of 1988, Sched. 1, para. 12(1)(b)–(g).
[52a] Before its functions ceased to exist on October 1, 1998: Government of Wales Act 1998, ss.129(1), 152, 158(1), Sched. 18, Pt. IV; S.I. 1998 No. 2244, art. 4.
[53] *i.e.* one established by an order made under Local Government, Planning and Land Act 1980, s.135.
[54] Within the meaning of the New Towns Act 1981.
[55] *i.e.* an authority established under Local Government Act 1985, s.10.
[56] Within the meaning of the Local Government Act 1985.
[57] Established by the Local Government (Wales) Act 1994, s.39(1).

(c) Housing bodies

4–46 Thirdly, there are two classes of bodies established for housing purposes.[58] They are a fully mutual housing association;[59] and a housing action trust.[60]

2. Introductory tenancies

4–47 Under Part V of the Housing Act 1996,[61] a local housing authority or a housing action trust may elect to operate an "introductory tenancy" regime.[62] Where such an election is in force, every periodic tenancy of a dwelling-house entered into or adopted by that authority or trust after the date of the election will, subject to three exceptions be an "introductory tenancy" if it would otherwise have been a secure tenancy.[63] "Adopted" for these purposes means no more than that the authority or trust becomes landlord, whether on a disposal or surrender of the interest of the former landlord.[64] The three exceptions are: first, where the tenancy is entered into or adopted in pursuance of a contract made before the date of the election; secondly, if immediately before the tenancy was entered into or adopted the tenant (or in the case of joint tenants, one or more of them) was a secure tenant of the same or another dwelling-house; thirdly, if immediately before the tenancy was entered into or adopted the tenant (or in the case of joint tenants, one or more of them) was an assured tenant (other than an assured shorthold tenant) of a registered social landlord[65] in respect of the same or another dwelling-house.[66] This new regime did not require any further exceptions from assured tenancies under the Act of 1988 because introductory tenancies can only be granted by exempted bodies falling within this Section.

Sect. 10. Tenancies Entered into before Commencement

4–48 A tenancy cannot be an assured tenancy if it was "entered into before, or pursuant to a contract made before, the commencement of this Act".[67] Such a tenancy will generally be protected by the Rent Acts if it would have been an assured tenancy but for this exception. The exception is reinforced by the provision for "Transitional Cases" in Section 12 below.[68] It is also subject to certain provisions for the conversion of tenancies. Under these, "old" assured tenancies

[58] Act of 1988, Sched. 1, para. 12(1)(h), (i).
[59] See Housing Associations Act 1985, s.1.
[60] *i.e.* one established under Act of 1988, Pt. III.
[61] Effective from February 12, 1997: Housing Act 1996, ss.124, 232(3); S.I. 1997 No. 66.
[62] Housing Act 1996, s.124(1).
[63] *ibid.*, s.124(2).
[64] *ibid.*, s.124(4).
[65] Under Housing Act 1996, Pt. I, Chap. I; see *post*, paras. 5–36 *et seq.*
[66] *ibid.*, s.124(2).
[67] Act of 1988, Sched. 1, para. 1.
[68] See *post*, p. 60.

become assured tenancies under the Act of 1988,[69] and other tenancies may also become assured tenancies upon a change of landlord,[70] even though they were entered into before, or pursuant to a contract made before, the commencement.

1. "The commencement of this Act"

The Act of 1988 provides for different Parts and sections of the Act to be brought into force by the Secretary of State by order made by statutory instrument; and different days may be appointed for different provisions or for different purposes, and such transitional provisions may be made as appear to him to be necessary or expedient in connection with the provisions brought into force by the order.[71] But for the purposes of Part I of the Act, references to the commencement of the Act are to be construed as being references to the coming into force of Part I of the Act, and this was on January 15, 1989.[72] **4–49**

2. "Before"

(a) Not assured

A tenancy cannot be an assured tenancy if it was— **4–50**

(1) "entered into before" January 15, 1989, or
(2) "entered into . . . pursuant to a contract made before" January 15, 1989.[73]

A tenancy entered into before that date cannot be an assured tenancy, it seems, even if it provided for the term to commence on or after that date; for the Act is phrased in terms of when the tenancy was entered into, and not when the term commences. Where the tenancy was entered into in pursuance of a contract, the test is when the contract was made, and not when the tenancy is to be granted or the term is to commence. For these purposes, a contract to grant a tenancy is essential; a mere agreement as to its terms if it is granted is not enough.[74]

(b) Assured

Where a tenancy is not within paragraph (a) above, it will be capable of being an assured tenancy, subject to satisfying the other requirements of the Act. This **4–51**

[69] See *post*, paras. 5–02 *et seq.*
[70] See *post*, paras. 5–44 *et seq.*
[71] Act of 1988, s.141(2), (4).
[72] *ibid.*, s.141(2), (3).
[73] *Supra*. Compare *post*, para. 5–08.
[74] See *Proma Ltd. v. Curtis* (1989) 59 P. & C.R. 242, CA (on Leasehold Reform Act 1967, s.3(1) and Housing Act 1980, Sched. 21, para. 3).

appears to be the case even if the tenancy provides for the term to commence from a date prior to January 15, 1989; for the term cannot begin until the tenancy has been granted, and the expressed commencement date will merely provide a means of calculating the length of the term at the date of the grant, or imposing contractual obligations by reference to the period before grant, or both.[75]

3. "Entered into" or "made"

4–52 It does not appear why "entered into" was used instead of the more normal "granted"; but probably no distinction was intended. It seems that for this purpose a contract may be "made" even if it is unenforceable by action for lack of sufficient evidence in writing or part performance. A contract is still a contract even if it is unenforceable by action, and in any case subsequent evidence in writing or part performance may make it enforceable by action,[76] unless it is made on or after September 27, 1989.[77]

Sect. 11. Tenancies at a Low Rent

1. The exception

4–53 The "low rent" exclusion, which was solely determined by reference to the rateable value of the dwelling-house,[78] was amended on April 1, 1990 by the References to Rating (Housing) Regulations 1990[79] ("Regulations of 1990"). As with tenancies at a high rent,[80] the amendment was necessitated by the abolition of domestic rates.[81] Accordingly, the relatively simple paragraph in Schedule 1 to the Act of 1988, which prevented a tenancy at a low rent from being an assured tenancy, has been replaced by three new paragraphs designed to cater for dwelling-houses without rateable values. There are now three separate paragraphs in the Schedule. The new paragraph 3 merely excludes rent-free tenancies; but the effect of paragraphs 3A and 3B is essentially to divide tenancies into two classes, namely those granted before April 1, 1990, and those

[75] See, *e.g.*, *Bradshaw v. Pawley* [1980] 1 W.L.R. 10, Ch.

[76] See, *e.g.*, Megarry & Wade, *The Law of Real Property* (5th ed. 1984) pp. 572–576, 587 *et seq.*, 637–640. An imperfect tenancy may be treated as a contract; but there are difficulties here.

[77] When such contracts must be made in writing (unless a contract for a "short lease" within Law of Property Act 1925, s.54(2)), and Law of Property Act 1925, s.40 was repealed, with no saving for part performance: Law of Property (Miscellaneous Provisions) Act 1989, ss. 2, 4, 5, Sched. 2. And see *Spiro v. Glencrown Properties Ltd.* [1991] Ch. 537, Ch., where the Act of 1989 was satisfied by the grant but not by the exercise of an option. Of course, any contract made before January 15, 1989 must have been governed by the old regime.

[78] The repealed provisions are set out *post*, p. 439

[79] S.I. 1990 No. 434.

[80] See *ante*, paras. 4–04 *et seq.*

[81] By Local Government Finance Act 1988, s. 117(1), Sched. 13, Pt. I; and see *ante*, para. 4–04.

granted on or after that date.[82] It is therefore necessary to examine in detail the amendments that were made, and the two classes.

2. The amendments

4–54 So far as practicable, the original low rent exclusion (''rent . . . less than two-thirds of the rateable value of the dwelling-house for the time being'') has been retained.[83] It has been supplemented, however, by a new exclusion based on a fixed low level of rent.[84] Essentially, the existing exclusion still applies to tenancies entered into before April 1, 1990, and the new exclusion applies to tenancies entered into on or after that date. But there is one exception, and some difficult transitional provisions. These exclusions affect only the tenancy in question; they do not prevent any sub-tenancies from being assured tenancies, unless the sub-tenancies too fall within these exclusions.[85]

(a) Pre-April 1990 tenancies

4–55 Where a tenancy is entered into[86] before April 1, 1990, the existing exemption still applies,[87] subject to one amendment. The tenancy cannot be an assured tenancy if ''for the time being'' either no rent is payable, or the rent is less than two-thirds of the rateable value of the dwelling-house on March 31, 1990.[88] The amendment thus provides for a fixed date for identification of the rateable value, in place of the original provision for taking the rateable value of the dwelling-house ''for the time being''. Provision has been made for determining the rateable value of a dwelling-house where, immediately before April 1, 1990, no such value was assigned to it.[89]

4–56 (i) RENT. Subject to the disregards considered below, ''rent'' appears to bear the same meaning as under the Rent Acts, *i.e.* the total sum of money which on the date in question is lawfully payable to the landlord as rent.[90] The burden of proving that the rent is enough to exclude this provision appears to lie on the tenant.[91]

4–57 (ii) DISREGARDS. For the purpose of this provision, part of the rent is to be disregarded. This is ''any sum payable by the tenant as is expressed (in whatever

[82] Regulations of 1990, Sched., para. 30. A new para. 3C is added, but it is merely ancillary.
[83] Act of 1988, Sched. 1, para. 3B.
[84] *ibid.*, para. 3A.
[85] For the position of sub-tenants, see *post*, paras. 11–10 *et seq.*
[86] See *ante*, para. 4–52, for ''entered into''.
[87] Act of 1988, Sched. 1, paras. 3, 3B.
[88] *ibid.*
[89] *Infra*, ''The transitional provisions''.
[90] See Vol. 1, p. 161.
[91] See *Ford v. Langford* [1949] L.J.R. 586, CA (decided under the Rent Acts).

terms) to be payable in respect of rates, council tax,[92] services, management, repairs, maintenance or insurance, unless it could not have been regarded by the parties to the tenancy as a sum so payable''.[93] Except for the insertion of ''management'', this provision is substantially identical with the provision in the Rent Acts for determining whether ''long tenancies'' are at a low rent.[94]

(b) Post-March 1990 tenancies

4–58 A tenancy entered into on or after April 1, 1990 cannot be an assured tenancy if, under it, ''for the time being'' either no rent is payable,[95] or the rent is payable at a rate of £1,000 a year or less if the dwelling-house is in Greater London, and £250 a year or less if it is elsewhere.[96] The words ''for the time being'' clearly show that a tenancy can become assured or cease to be assured in consequence of an increase or a reduction in the rent payable under it.[97] What is said above under the headings of ''RENT'' and ''DISREGARDS'' applies equally to this class of tenancy.

(c) The exception

4–59 For these purposes, a tenancy entered into on or after April 1, 1990 in pursuance of a contract made before that date is treated as a pre-April 1990 tenancy, provided that the dwelling-house had a rateable value on March 31, 1990.[98] The exclusion based on rateable value[99] will therefore apply to it, and the new ''fixed low rent'' exclusion will not. The contract must be a contract for the grant of a tenancy, and not merely an agreement as to the terms of the tenancy if one is granted. Arguably, a contract would suffice even though unenforceable at law;[1] but after September 26, 1989, a contract for the grant of a lease (other than a ''short lease'' falling within section 54(2) of the Law of Property Act 1925[2])

[92] As from April 1, 1993, the unpopular and short-lived community charge, the implementation of which was the reason for abolition of domestic rates, was itself replaced by the council tax. Mercifully, further complicated amendments to the Act of 1988 were not needed.

[93] Act of 1988, Sched. 1, paras. 2(2), 3C, as amended by Regulations of 1990, Sched., para. 30 and by Local Government Finance (Housing) (Consequential Amendments) Order 1993 (S.I. 1993 No. 651), art. 2(1), Sched. 1, para. 19.

[94] Act of 1977, s.5(4), as amended by Local Government Finance (Housing) (Consequential Amendments) Order 1993 (S.I. 1993 No. 651), art. 2(1), Sched. 1, para. 4 (insertion of ''council tax'').

[95] Act of 1988, Sched. 1, para. 3, as amended by Regulations of 1990, Sched., para. 30.

[96] *ibid.*, para. 3A. The amounts of £1,000 and £250 may be replaced by sums specified by the Secretary of State by statutory instrument, subject to a negative resolution of either House of Parliament: Act of 1988, s.1(2A), inserted by Regulations of 1990, Sched., para. 27.

[97] See, by analogy, *R. v. London Rent Assessment Panel, ex. p. Cadogan Estates Ltd.* [1998] Q.B. 398, QB.

[98] Act of 1988, Sched. 1, paras. 3A(a), 3B(a). If it did not, then *prima facie* the tenancy falls within class (b), though the transitional provisions, *infra*, might apply.

[99] *i.e.* class (a), *supra*.

[1] See *ante*, para. 4–52.

[2] As to which, consider *Long v. Tower Hamlets L.B.C.* [1998] Ch. 197, CA.

must be made in writing and signed by or on behalf of each party to the contract.[3]

3. The transitional provisions

(a) Effect of abolition of domestic rates

Prima facie, the abolition of domestic rates on April 1, 1990 meant that a dwelling which was not by that date entered in the valuation list would not thereafter be entered. But in some circumstances, subsequent ascertainment of rateable value would be essential;[4] in others, convenient at least. Provision was therefore made, notwithstanding the repeal of the relevant parts of the General Rate Act 1967,[5] for rateable values to be determined after April 1, 1990. Different provisions apply according to whether or not a proposal to enter the dwelling in a valuation list was made before April 1, 1990. **4–60**

(b) The provisions

(i) PROPOSAL FOR VALUATION OUTSTANDING. Where a proposal to enter the dwelling in a valuation list was made before April 1, 1990, but no effect had been given to the proposal by that date, the provisions of the General Rate Act 1967 continue to have effect (despite the repeal) for the purposes of altering the valuation list pursuant to the proposal made.[6] When made, the alteration is effective from the beginning of the rating period in which the proposal was made.[7] **4–61**

(ii) NO OUTSTANDING PROPOSAL FOR VALUATION. Where either no proposal to enter the dwelling in a valuation list had been made before April 1, 1990 or an entry in a valuation list then existed but no proposal to alter it (in consequence of structural alterations completed by April 1, 1990) had been made before that date, the landlord or tenant under a tenancy entered into before April 1, 1990 can each apply to the valuation officer for a certificate. The officer must certify the amount that, but for the repeal of the General Rate Act 1967, he would have proposed as the rateable value of the dwelling.[8] The amount certified is treated as being the rateable value of the dwelling on March 31, 1990.[9] **4–62**

[3] Law of Property (Miscellaneous Provisions) Act 1989, s.2(1), (3). Failure to comply with these requirements means that no contract exists, and not that it is merely unenforceable as was the case under Law of Property Act 1925, s.40.

[4] *e.g.*, a tenancy entered into before April 1, 1990 relating to a dwelling-house with no rateable value; *supra*.

[5] By Local Government Finance Act 1988, s.117(1), Sched. 13, Pt. I.

[6] General Rate Act 1967 and Related Provisions (Savings and Consequential Provision) Regulations 1990 (S.I. 1990 No. 777), reg. 3(1)(c).

[7] General Rate Act 1967, s.79.

[8] Local Government Finance (Repeals, Savings and Consequential Amendments) Order 1990 (S.I. 1990 No. 776), art. 5.

[9] *ibid.*

(c) Effect of provisions

4–63 The transitional provisions do not have any unexpected effect so far as tenancies falling within category (a) above (pre-April 1990 tenancies) are concerned. The entry in the valuation list, or the issue of the certificate (as the case may be), identifies the all-important rateable value on March 31, 1990. But one type of tenancy falling initially within category (b) above (post-March 1990 tenancies) might, in consequence of the effect of the transitional provisions, be brought within category (a) above. As stated, a tenancy entered into on or after April 1, 1990 in pursuance of a contract made before that date falls within category (b) above if the dwelling-house did not have a rateable value on March 31, 1990. If, in consequence of a subsequent entry in the valuation list the dwelling then has a rateable value on March 31, 1990, it is arguable that the tenancy then satisfied the conditions of category (a) above, and no longer category (b).[10]

Sect. 12. Transitional Cases

4–64 The statutory heading ''Transitional cases'' may be a little misleading, for there is nothing in the provisions of this paragraph[11] that is transitional in the ordinary sense. It does not apply the statutory provisions in a variant form to pre-existing cases, but merely excludes four categories of tenancy from being assured tenancies. The four categories are—

(1) ''A protected tenancy within the meaning of the Rent Act 1977'';[12]
(2) ''A housing association tenancy'' within the meaning of Part VI of the Rent Act;[13]
(3) ''A secure tenancy'',[14] and
(4) The relevant tenancy (within the meaning of the Rent (Agriculture) Act 1976) by virtue of which a protected occupier of a dwelling-house (within the meaning of that Act) occupies it.[15]

In many cases this provision will merely make exclusion doubly sure by excluding from the ranks of assured tenancies various tenancies that are already excluded under other provisions of the Act. Thus, most protected tenancies were granted before January 15, 1989, and so the date of grant will of itself prevent

[10] The argument turns on the construction of the words ''had a rateable value on March 31, 1990'' in Act of 1988, Sched. 1, Pt. I, paras. 3A(a), 3B(a): they could be directed to a question of fact (judged on March 31, 1990) or a question of law (judged in retrospect). The better view is that the tenancy does indeed change category, otherwise a tenancy entered into *before* April 1, 1990 with no rateable value could never fall within either category for the purpose of applying the exclusion.
[11] Act of 1988, Sched. 1, para. 13.
[12] See Act of 1977, s.1.
[13] *ibid.*, s.86, as amended by Act of 1988, Sched. 17, para. 100.
[14] *i.e.* within the meaning of Housing Act 1985, s.79: Act of 1988, s.45(1).
[15] See Vol. 1, p. 300.

the tenancy from being an assured tenancy.[16] On the other hand, secure tenancies both ante- and post-date January 15, 1989, and so this exclusion performs a useful service by ensuring that, although different statutory provisions for protecting tenants do not necessarily exclude each other,[17] the tenancies specified here and assured tenancies are mutually exclusive.

Sect. 13. Holiday Lettings

1. The exception

"A tenancy the purpose of which is to confer on the tenant the right to occupy the dwelling-house for a holiday" cannot be an assured tenancy.[18] This provision is in virtually the same terms as the corresponding exception from the Rent Acts.[19] This exclusion is based on the purpose of the tenancy, rather than the actual use made of the dwelling-house, and will usually be determined by the terms of the tenancy agreement, unless it can be proved that the terms in this regard are a sham.[20] **4–65**

2. Holiday

There is no applicable definition of "holiday" under the Act of 1988, but the better view is that a "period of cessation of work, or period of recreation" is a good working meaning, provided that the word "recreation" is not too narrowly construed.[21] Perhaps a working holiday is a "holiday" within this exception, although a rent tribunal has once considered that a 188 day "short (working holiday) let" was not within the equivalent provision of the Rent Acts.[22] Some assistance may possibly be obtained from the wording of the mandatory ground for possession, Ground 3,[23] which is clearly intended to be complementary to this exclusion. That Ground requires the term of the assured tenancy to be no more that eight months. **4–66**

[16] See *ante*, para. 4–48. But there are four cases, based on circumstances existing before that date, where a tenancy may be a protected tenancy even though it was entered into on or after that date: Act of 1988, s.34(1), as amended; *post*, paras. 5–09 *et seq.*

[17] See, *e.g.*, *Lambeth L.B.C. v. Udechuku* (1980) 41 P. & C.R. 200, CA.

[18] Act of 1988, Sched. 1, para. 9.

[19] Act of 1977, s.9; the differences are merely grammatical.

[20] *Buchmann v. May* [1978] 2 All E.R. 993, CA; *R. v. Rent Officer for London Borough of Camden, ex p. Plant* (1980) 7 H.L.R. 15, Q.B. On shams generally, see *Antoniades v. Villiers* [1990] A.C. 417. These cases were decided under the Rent Acts, but the applicable principle is the same.

[21] *Buchmann v. May*, *supra*, in relation to the definition in the Shorter Oxford English Dictionary.

[22] Recorded in *R. v. Croydon and South West London Rent Tribunal, ex p. Ryzewska* [1977] Q.B. 876, D.C.

[23] Act of 1988, Sched. 2, Pt. I, Ground 3; *post*, paras. 14–35 *et seq.*

Sect. 14. Lettings Arranged by Local Housing Authorities for Housing the Homeless

4–67 A tenancy cannot be an assured tenancy if it is granted by a person under arrangements made by a local housing authority, in discharge of certain temporary or interim housing duties which the authority had, upon an application to the authority for accommmodation or for assistance in obtaining accommodation. These duties are, essentially, to provide accommodation for the homeless while it is being determined whether, or in respect of which authority, there is a duty to provide permanent accommodation.[24] This exclusion from being an assured tenancy matches the duty in that (unlike the other exceptions) it takes effect for only a limited period. But it might be unnecessary in most cases in that a homeless person, who is housed temporarily pending the local authority's determination of whether it is obliged to house him permanently, is most likely living in a hostel room or bed-sit which is not a dwelling-house, and even if it is he is probably not occupying the dwelling as a home.[25] Nevertheless, the provisions have been renewed in Part VII of the Housing Act 1996,[26] and it is to those sections that reference is made hereafter.

1. The duty

4–68 The exception applies only if the local housing authority are acting in pursuance of any of their housing functions under Part VII of the Housing Act 1996 to "secure that accommodation is made available for his occupation"[27] (which may be abbreviated to "secure housing for him") under one of four provisions in the Housing Act 1996. These are—

(a) under section 188, where the authority have reason to believe that the applicant "may be homeless, eligible for assistance and have a priority need":[28] here, their duty is to secure housing for him pending a decision as to the duty owed to him (if any) under the Act;
(b) under section 190, where the authority are satisfied that the applicant is homeless and is eligible for assistance "but are also satisfied that he became homeless intentionally":[29] here, their duty is to secure housing

[24] Act of 1988, s.1(6), (7). These two subsections were repealed on January 20, 1997 by Housing Act 1996, ss.227, 232(3), Sched. 19, Pt. VIII, but the repeal did not apply in relation to an applicant whose application for accommodation or assistance was made before that date: Housing Act 1996 (Commencement No. 5 and Transitional Provisions) Order 1996 (S.I. 1996 No. 2959), art. 2, Sched., para. 1. The subsections are replaced by provisions to substantially the same effect in Housing Act 1996, s. 209, which came into effect on January 20, 1997: S.I. 1996 No. 2959, art. 2.
[25] See *Mohamed v. Manek* (1995) 27 H.L.R. 439 at 447–450, CA, *per* Auld L.J.
[26] Section 209. Housing Act 1996, Pt. VII ("Homelessness") repealed and replaced Housing Act 1985, Pt. III on January 20, 1997: S.I. 1996 No. 2959.
[27] Housing Act 1996, ss.188(1), 190(2)(a), 200(1).
[28] For "homeless" and "priority need", see Housing Act 1996, ss.175, 189.
[29] For becoming homeless "intentionally", see Housing Act 1996, s.191.

for him for such period as they consider will give him a reasonable opportunity for securing accommodation for his occupation;

(c) under section 200, where the authority are satisfied that the applicant is homeless and has a priority need, and are satisfied that he did not become homeless intentionally, but are of opinion that the conditions for the application to be referred to another housing authority[30] (*e.g.*, because of the applicant's local connections) are met: here, their duty is to secure housing for him until he is notified of the decision whether the conditions for referral are met; and

(d) under section 204(4), where the authority was under a duty under one of (a), (b) and (c) above, they *may* continue to secure housing for the applicant during the period for appealing any decision of the authority[31] and, if an appeal is brought, until the appeal (and any further appeal) is finally determined.

Under the Housing Act 1996, ''local housing authority'' means ''a district council, a London borough council, the Common Council of the City of London, a Welsh county council or county borough council, or the Council of the Isles of Scilly''.[32]

2. Tenancy pursuant to arrangements

The exception applies where, in discharge of any of their housing functions set out above, the authority have made ''arrangements with a private landlord to provide accommodation''[33] and a tenancy has been ''granted in pursuance of the arrangements to a person specified by the authority''.[34] **4–69**

3. Duration of exception

Where these conditions are satisfied, the tenancy ''cannot be an assured tenancy before the end of the period of twelve months beginning with'' a specified date ''unless, before or during that period, the tenant is notified by the landlord (or, in the case of joint landlords, at least one of them) that the tenancy is to be regarded as an assured shorthold tenancy or an assured tenancy other than an assured shorthold tenancy''.[35] There is one significant change here from the previous provisions of the Act of 1988.[35a] On and after February 28, 1997, the grant of an assured tenancy will in most cases create an assured shorthold ten- **4–70**

30 See Housing Act 1996, s.198.
31 21 days: s.202(2).
32 Housing Act 1996, s.230, by reference to Housing Act 1985, s.1, as amended by Local Government (Wales) Act 1994, ss.22(2), 66(3), Sched. 8, para. 5(1); S.I. 1996 No. 396 (effective April 1, 1996).
33 Housing Act 1996, s.209(1). A ''private landlord'' for these purposes is a landlord who does not satisfy the ''landlord condition'' for secure tenancies in Housing Act 1985, s.80(1).
34 Housing Act 1996, s.209(2).
35 *ibid.*
35a Act of 1988, s.1(6), (7).

ancy without the need for any shorthold notice or other formality.[36] But the landlord can make the shorthold tenancy into a full assured tenancy by giving notice at any time during the tenancy.[37] Accordingly, it is provided here that the landlord's notice may state that the tenancy is to be regarded as either an assured shorthold tenancy, or as a ''full'' assured tenancy.

The specified date from which the period of 12 months starts to run is, in the case of a decision on homelessness or referral to another local housing authority, the date on which the applicant was notified of the authority's decision.[38] In the case of a review of that decision made by the authority upon request made by the applicant[39] or of an appeal to the court,[40] it is the date on which the applicant is notified of a decision on review or of the date on which the appeal is finally determined, as the case may be.[41] Once the authority have completed their inquiries, they are not entitled to delay either their decision (*e.g.,* so as to be assured that the position will not change),[42] or their notification of it.[43]

4. Cessation of exception

4–71 As soon as the period of exception expires, the tenancy will become an assured tenancy, if otherwise capable of doing so. This will be so, it seems, even if a valid notice to quit is still running then, but not if it has previously taken effect and so has left no tenancy in existence that could become assured.

[36] See *post*, para. 8–46.
[37] Act of 1988, s.19A, Sched. 2A, para. 2, inserted on February 28, 1997 by Housing Act 1996, ss.96, 232(3), Sched. 7; S.I. 1997 No. 225. See *post*, para. 8–06
[38] Housing Act 1996, s.209(2)(a).
[39] Under *ibid.*, s.202.
[40] Under *ibid.*, s.204.
[41] *ibid.*, s.209(2)(b).
[42] See *R. v. London Borough of Ealing, ex p. Sidhu* (1982) 2 H.L.R. 45, Q.B. (on earlier legislation).
[43] See *Family Housing Association v. Miah* (1982) 5 H.L.R. 94 at 103, CA (on different language in an earlier Act), recording an argument that the period of exception can begin when the notification ought to have been received by the tenant.

Chapter 5

Assured Tenancies in relation to Other Tenancies

The Act of 1988 contains many complex provisions which relate to tenancies that are not assured tenancies, the relationship between them and assured tenancies, and the circumstances in which non-assured tenancies may become assured tenancies, and *vice versa*. By the date of this edition, there are probably tens of thousands of regular, assured tenancies in existence, almost all of which were granted after January 15, 1989, and which satisfy the requirements already considered;[1] but there are some tenancies granted before that date which the Act of 1988 has converted into assured tenancies. The provisions relating to such tenancies will be considered under the following heads: **5–01**

(1) Old assured tenancies.
(2) Protected tenancies.
(3) Restricted contracts.
(4) Housing association tenancies.
(5) Long tenancies.
(6) Secure tenancies: change of landlord.

Sect. 1. Old Assured Tenancies

It is convenient to use the term "old assured tenancy" to describe an assured tenancy under the Housing Act 1980, and the term "assured tenancy", *simpliciter*, for the new (and very different) assured tenancy under the Act of 1988. One of the objects of the Act of 1988 was to replace old assured tenancies with the much broader provisions for assured tenancies under the Act of 1988; and this it has done. Although the name "assured" is used for both types of tenancy, this must not be allowed to obscure the differences between the two, nor to suggest that they are closely related as concepts. The Act of 1988 converts existing old assured tenancies and prohibits the creation of any new ones. **5–02**

[1] *Ante*, Chaps. 3, 4, pp. 18–64.

1. Prohibition

5–03 No tenancy entered into on or after January 15, 1989 can be an old assured tenancy.[2]

2. Conversion

5–04 On January 15, 1989, every tenancy—

(a) "under which a dwelling-house was then let as a separate dwelling", and
(b) which immediately before that date was an old assured tenancy (*i.e.* "an assured tenancy for the purposes of sections 56 to 58 of the Housing Act 1980")

became an assured tenancy for the purposes of the Act of 1988,[3] freed from the provisions governing old assured tenancies.[4] On these provisions for prohibition and conversion, however, three further points must be considered.

3. Pending applications

5–05 First, the provision for automatic conversion did not apply if on January 15, 1989 an application to the court for the grant of a new tenancy had been made by the tenant under an old assured tenancy, and by statute[5] that tenancy was still continuing.[6] In such cases the tenancy remains an old assured tenancy, though only temporarily. For if the court makes an order for the grant of a new tenancy,[7] the tenancy so granted will not be an old assured tenancy but an assured tenancy under the Act of 1988;[8] and if an order is refused the tenancy will determine when the statutory period of continuation[9] expires.

4. Subsisting contract

5–06 Secondly, where on January 15, 1989 a contract to grant an old assured tenancy subsisted but no tenancy had been granted, the usual rule of treating the tenancy as if it had been granted before that date does not apply. Instead, statute alters

[2] Act of 1988, s.37(1).
[3] *ibid.*, s.1(3).
[4] *ibid.*, s.1(4)(b).
[5] *i.e.* under Landlord and Tenant Act 1954, s.24, or *ibid.*, Pt. IV, as applied by Housing Act 1980, s.58: Act of 1988, s.37(6).
[6] Act of 1988, s.37(2).
[7] Under Landlord and Tenant Act 1954, s.29, as applied by Housing Act 1980, s.58: Act of 1988, s.37(6).
[8] Act of 1988, s.37(3).
[9] Under Landlord and Tenant Act 1954, ss.24(1), 64, as applied by Housing Act 1980, s.58.

the contract by providing that it will take effect as a contract for the grant of an assured tenancy under the Act of 1988,[10] and not an old assured tenancy.

5. Reduction of exceptions

Thirdly, tenancies which arise under the foregoing provisions of conversion, pursuant to a court order for the grant of a new tenancy or pursuant to a contract for an old assured tenancy, are freed from most of the exceptions which prevent a tenancy from being an assured tenancy. Such tenancies are subject to none of the 13 exceptions in Schedule 1 to the Act of 1988[11] except those under paragraph 11 (Crown tenancies) and paragraph 12 (where the landlord is a local authority or other exempted body).[12] Further, if a "fully mutual housing association" (*i.e.* one which confines membership and tenancies to its tenants or prospective tenants[13]) was the landlord on January 15, 1989 (in the case of conversion of existing tenancies), or granted the tenancy (in the cases where new tenancies were granted after that date), then as long as that association remains the landlord under that tenancy (or under any statutory periodic tenancy that arises when it comes to an end[14]), paragraph 12 of Schedule 1 is to be read as if the words "a fully mutual housing association" were omitted,[15] thereby preserving the status of the tenancy as an assured tenancy. **5–07**

Sect. 2. Protected Tenancies

The relationship between protected tenancies under the Rent Acts and assured tenancies is subject to two general rules: **5–08**

(1) a tenancy entered into on or after January 15, 1989 cannot be a protected tenancy;[16] and
(2) a protected tenancy cannot be an assured tenancy.[17]

The first of these rules plainly does not affect any tenancy that had come into existence before January 15, 1989. If such tenancies are protected tenancies under the Act of 1977, they cannot be assured tenancies. But even in relation to tenancies entered into after that date, the general rule is subject to four important exceptions. These will now be considered in turn.

[10] Act of 1988, s.37(4). Contrast, *e.g.*, new assured tenancies (*ante*, para. 4–48), and protected tenancies (*post*, para. 5–09).
[11] See *ante*, para. 4–01 *et seq.*
[12] Act of 1988, ss.1(4)(a), 37(5).
[13] See Housing Associations Act 1985, s.1(2): Act of 1988, s.45(1); and see *post*, para. 5–26.
[14] *Post*, paras. 7–01 *et seq.*
[15] Act of 1988, ss.1(5), 37(5).
[16] *ibid.*, s.34(1).
[17] *ibid.*, Sched. 1, para. 13(1); *ante*, para. 4–64.

1. Prior contract

5–09 The first exception is that a tenancy entered into on or after January 15, 1989 can be a protected tenancy if it was "entered into in pursuance of a contract made before" that date.[18] This provision is in substantially[19] the same terms as the exception for tenancies entered into before commencement of the Act of 1988.[20] As with it, the critical issue is when the contract was made, not when the term of the lease commences. A contract is essential; a mere agreement as to its terms if it is granted is not enough.[21] But a contract may be made even if it is unenforceable by action for lack of sufficient evidence in writing or part performance.[22] It is important to note that this exception does not mean that a tenancy entered into in these circumstances *is* without more a protected tenancy. The provision merely removes one obstacle to the tenancy being a protected tenancy, and does not affect the need for it to comply with the other requirements of the Rent Acts.

2. Grant to sitting tenant

(a) The provision

5–10 Secondly, the rule that a tenancy entered into on or after January 15, 1989 cannot be a protected tenancy does not apply if the tenancy—

(1) "is granted to a person (alone or jointly with others) who, immediately before the tenancy was granted, was a protected or statutory tenant", and
(2) "is so granted by the person who at that time was the landlord (or one of the joint landlords) under the protected or statutory tenancy".[23]

This provision is designed to prevent a protected or statutory tenant from losing the protection of the Rent Acts by accepting a new tenancy of the dwelling. But this provision is not in terms confined to a case where both tenancies are of the same dwelling-house, so that it can apply where the parties agree to a substitute for the existing dwelling-house.[24] Corresponding provisions apply to the Act of 1976: a tenancy or licence entered into on or after January 15, 1989 and not under a prior contract cannot be a "relevant tenancy" or "relevant licence"[25]

[18] Act of 1988, s.34(1)(a).
[19] "In pursuance of" replaces "pursuant to", and of course one is "before" and the other "on or after".
[20] Considered *ante*, para. 4–48.
[21] See *ante*, para. 4–50, n. 74.
[22] *i.e.* not such as to satisfy Law of Property Act 1925, s.40. The law changed with effect from September 27, 1989 (Law of Property (Miscellaneous Provisions) Act 1989, s.2), but this change could not of course affect contracts made before January 15, 1989.
[23] Act of 1988, s.34(1)(b).
[24] And see Act of 1988, s.34(3)(b).
[25] See *post*, para. 9–09.

under the Act unless granted to a sitting tenant.[26] Once again, however, the effect of the provision is not that the re-granted tenancy *is* a protected tenancy or occupancy; it may be, but that depends on the fulfilment of the other requirements of the Act of 1977, or the Act of 1976, as the case may be. A statutory tenancy which arises by dint of statute[27] upon the termination after January 15, 1989 of a protected tenancy is not a tenancy "granted to" the protected tenant within the meaning of the provision, and accordingly no assured tenancy comes into existence.[28] And this provision does not apply where an order for possession has been made on the ground of suitable alternative accommodation to be let by the landlord to the previously protected tenant without the court directing that the new tenancy is to be a protected tenancy.[28a]

(b) "Alone or jointly with others"

The statutory requirement is clearly satisfied where the new tenancy is granted to two or more persons who include the sole protected or statutory tenant, or to all of them where there are joint protected or statutory tenants; for references to "the tenant" are references to all the persons who jointly constitute the tenant.[29] What is not made clear is whether it suffices if the new tenancy is granted to persons who include only one of two or more joint protected or statutory tenants. Probably it does; for even though he is not *the* tenant he can properly be described as being "a" protected tenant,[30] and under the Rent Acts the courts have adopted a somewhat relaxed attitude towards the technicalities of joint tenancy.[31] Further, the statute plainly accepts a measure of dilution, in that it does not demand that the new tenants and the old should be identical. **5–11**

(c) "Protected or statutory tenant"

The term "protected or statutory tenant" does not here include a tenant under a protected shorthold tenancy.[32] Nor does it include a protected or statutory tenant of a dwelling-house under a protected shorthold tenancy which ended before January 15, 1989, if by that date either no grant of a further tenancy had been made, or else a grant had been made to the person who, immediately before the grant, was in possession of the dwelling-house as a protected or statutory tenant.[33] The effect is to exclude not just re-grants to tenants under subsisting protected shorthold tenancies, but also tenants whose tenure, whether as a statutory or a protected tenant, remained subject to the mandatory protected shorthold **5–12**

[26] Act of 1988, s.34(4); *post*, para. 9–09.
[27] Act of 1977, s.2(1)(a).
[28] *Ridehalgh v. Horsefield* (1992) 24 H.L.R. 453, CA.
[28a] *Laimond Properties Ltd. v. Al-Shakarchi* (1998) 30 H.L.R. 1099, C.A. For the suitable alternative accommodation exception, see *post*, para. 5–15.
[29] Act of 1988, s.45(3).
[30] Which is the language used by the subsection.
[31] See *Lloyd v. Sadler* [1978] Q.B. 774, CA; Vol. 1, pp. 229, 230; and see p. 281.
[32] Act of 1988, s.34(2)(a). For such tenancies, see Vol. 1, pp. 212–217.
[33] *ibid.*, s.34(2)(b).

ground for possession.[34] And for these purposes "protected shorthold tenancy" includes a tenancy which in proceedings for possession under Case 19 of the Rent Act 1977 is treated as being a protected shorthold tenancy.[35] Thus, protected shorthold tenants who were at risk of mandatory possession proceedings do not get the greater degree of protection of a protected tenancy upon a re-grant; but neither do they get an assured tenancy. The Act of 1988 provides that the new tenancy is an assured shorthold tenancy.[36]

(d) "The landlord (or one of the joint landlords)"

5–13 The statute expressly includes a tenancy granted by a sole landlord or by one or more of the joint landlords under the protected or statutory tenancy.[37] It might also include the case where the sole landlord under the protected or statutory tenancy, or one or more such joint landlords, joins with another or others to re-grant the new tenancy. On the one hand, it would be argued that the former landlord is not prevented from "granting" a tenancy within the meaning of the Act of 1988 merely because he does so in conjunction with others.[38] On the other hand, it might not be accurate to describe a tenancy so granted as having been granted by "the person ... who was the landlord (or one of the joint landlords)", because it was granted by that person and others.

(e) Time of grant

5–14 The time at which these requirements must be satisfied is "immediately before the tenancy is granted" both for the landlord and for the tenant.[39] A short period of time, perhaps a matter of hours only, may suffice for the time not to be "immediately before" the new tenancy is granted. Accordingly, where the tenant under a protected tenancy agreed to and did vacate the dwelling for at least twenty-four hours, handing back the keys for the purpose of effecting a surrender by operation of law, and then took a new tenancy after the expiry of that period, he was not a protected tenant "immediately before it was granted",[40] and accordingly the new tenancy was a protected shorthold tenancy.[41]

3. Suitable alternative accommodation

5–15 Thirdly, the rule that a tenancy entered into on or after January 15, 1989 cannot be a protected tenancy does not apply to certain cases in which an order for

[34] See Act of 1977, Sched. 15, Case 19, para. (a); Vol. 1, p. 484.
[35] *ibid.* See Vol. 1, p. 483, referring to the court's power to treat a tenancy as being a protected shorthold, notwithstanding the failure to give a protected shorthold notice, where it is just and equitable to make an order for possession.
[36] Act of 1988, s.34(3).
[37] *ibid.*, ss.34(1)(b), 45(3).
[38] See *Cooper v. Tait* (1984) 48 P. & C.R. 460, CA, as cited in Vol. 1, p. 194.
[39] Act of 1988, s.34(1)(b) ("at that time").
[40] Within the meaning of Housing Act 1980, s.52(2) (protected shorthold tenancies).
[41] *Bolnore Properties Ltd. v. Cobb* (1996) 29 H.L.R. 202, CA.

possession is made against a statutory tenant under the Act of 1977, or under the Rent (Agriculture) Act 1976, on the ground of suitable alternative accommodation being available, and the tenancy is a tenancy of that alternative accommodation. There are five requirements.[42]

(a) The requirements

(1) "Prior to the grant of the tenancy" to the tenant, "an order for possession of a dwelling-house was made against him (alone or jointly with others)". This wording means that the first requirement will not be satisfied if, although the tenant was a statutory tenant of the dwelling-house, the order for possession was not in fact made against him.[43] **5–16**
(2) The order was made "on the court being satisfied" that "suitable alternative accommodation" was available for the tenant.[44]
(3) The tenancy is granted to him, whether alone or jointly with others.
(4) The tenancy is "of the premises which constitute the suitable alternative accommodation as to which the court was so satisfied".
(5) "In the proceedings for possession the court considered that, in the circumstances, the grant of an assured tenancy would not afford the required security and, accordingly, directed that the tenancy would be a protected tenancy".

If these requirements are satisfied, the new tenancy granted pursuant to the court order will not be prevented from being a protected tenancy merely because it was granted on or after January 15, 1989. Once again, though, there is nothing to absolve it from complying with the other statutory requirements for a protected tenancy.

(b) Limits to requirements

There is no requirement that the same person should be the landlord under each tenancy. Further, where there are joint tenants, it suffices if one of those against whom the order for possession was made is also one of those to whom the tenancy is granted. But an order for possession is essential, and accordingly it would seem that two or more joint tenants under the previous statutory tenancy would each have to be provided with suitable alternative accommodation to the satisfaction of the court before an order for possession could be made against any of them on this ground. A mere agreement between the parties is no substitute for an order for possession. If the parties wish to obtain a consent order, it is not enough for them merely to consent to the order. Instead, there must be **5–17**

[42] Act of 1988, s.34(1)(c). For a similar provision for housing association tenancies, see *post*, para. 5–33.
[43] Although it might be argued that an order for possession, taking effect *in rem*, is "made against" any person in occupation of the dwelling-house.
[44] Under Act of 1977, s.98(1)(a), or under Sched. 16, "Case 1"; or under Act of 1976, Sched. 4, "Case 1". (Each reference should have been to "Case I").

admissions as to specific facts which establish the ground for possession and which show that it is reasonable to make the order.[45]

(c) Direction by the court

5–18 The direction by the court is essential. It can be given only if the court considers that "in the circumstances, the grant of an assured tenancy would not afford the required security". If satisfied that an assured tenancy would in the circumstances afford the tenant the required security of tenure, the court was not bound to make the direction;[46] indeed *semble* the court would be bound not to. For alternative accommodation to be "suitable", it must afford the tenant "security of tenure reasonably equivalent" to that of a protected tenancy which is not subject to mandatory grounds for possession,[47] and this must depend upon the facts. It is not certain that the direction of the court must be contained in the formal order for possession,[48] though no doubt it is good practice for it to be so. If no direction appears in the order, it may be possible, despite the words "in the proceedings for possession", to have it inserted on a subsequent application, either under the "slip rule"[49] (if this applies) or on an application under the court's wide powers over orders for possession.[50]

4. New Town tenancies

5–19 Fourthly, the rule that a tenancy entered into on or after January 15, 1989 cannot be a protected tenancy is modified where the interest of the landlord at the time the tenancy was granted was held by a New Town corporation.[51] In such cases, if before January 15, 1991[52] that interest ceased to be so held by virtue of a disposal by the Commission for the New Towns,[53] the tenancy can be a protected tenancy. If it is disposed of on or after January 15, 1991, the tenancy is not capable of being a protected tenancy.[54] There is accordingly a two year window during which a tenancy created by a new town corporation, and subsequently disposed of to a person capable of being the landlord of a protected tenant, may

[45] See Vol. 1, p. 369; and see *R. v. Newcastle Upon Tyne County Court, ex p. Thompson* (1988) 20 H.L.R. 430 at 437, QB.
[46] *Laimond Properties Ltd. v. Al-Shakarchi* (1998) 30 H.L.R. 1099, CA.
[47] See Act of 1977, Sched. 15, Pt. IV, para. 4(1)(b); Vol. 1, p. 445.
[48] The language used is "... in the proceedings for possession the court considered that ... and directed that ..".
[49] C.C.R. Order 16, r. 5.
[50] See Act of 1977, s.100; Vol. 1, pp. 373–379; and consider the comments in *Victoria Square Property Co. Ltd. v. Southwark L.B.C.* [1978] 1 W.L.R. 463 at 468, 476, CA (on a statutory requirement for the judge to include a finding "in his judgment").
[51] Within the meaning of Housing Act 1985, s.80: Act of 1988, s.34(1)(d), as substituted on November 16, 1989 by Local Government and Housing Act 1989, s.194(1), Sched. 11, para. 104.
[52] *i.e.* two years after the commencement of the Act of 1988. The Secretary of State did not specify any other date by order before the expiry of the two years: Act of 1988, s.38(4)(b).
[53] Made pursuant to a direction under New Towns Act 1981, s.37.
[54] Act of 1988, s.38(1), (3), (4), as amended on November 16, 1989 by Local Government and Housing Act 1989, s.194(1), Sched. 11, para. 106. See further, *post*, para. 5–60.

become a protected tenancy notwithstanding that the tenancy was granted after the Act of 1988 came into force.

Sect. 3. Restricted Contracts

Under the Rent Acts, restricted contracts (which include both tenancies and licences) are subject to the jurisdiction of rent tribunals in fixing the rent,[55] and they receive (to a diminishing extent) a limited and unsatisfactory degree of security of tenure.[56] The Act of 1988 has not abolished this law, but it has provided no counterpart, and it has prevented the creation of any new restricted contracts. The jurisdiction will thus gradually shrink as the pre-existing contracts come to an end, and finally it will disappear. **5–20**

1. No new restricted contracts

''A tenancy or other contract entered into'' on or after January 15, 1989 ''cannot be a restricted contract for the purposes of the Rent Act 1977''.[57] This, however, does not apply to a tenancy or other contract that ''is entered into in pursuance of a contract made'' before January 15, 1989.[58] This provision corresponds to the provisions relating to assured and protected tenancies,[59] and in general the same comments apply. **5–21**

2. Variation of restricted contracts

(a) Variations not affecting rent

If the terms of a restricted contract are varied on or after January 15, 1989, but the variations do not affect the amount of rent[60] payable under the contract for the dwelling, any question whether the variations have brought a new contract into being in place of the old must be determined according to the general law; for the Act of 1988 does not affect this issue.[61] Thus, variations in the terms of a tenancy may be so substantial as to result in the creation of a new tenancy by surrender and re-grant, or they may merely leave the existing tenancy to continue **5–22**

[55] Although the power of local authorities to refer restricted contracts to a rent tribunal and to refer a case for reconsideration of the registered rent has been abrogated: see Supplement, annotation to Vol. 1, p. 764.

[56] For this, see Vol. 1, pp. 741–803.

[57] Act of 1988, s.36(1).

[58] *ibid*. For ''in pursuance of'', see *Proma Ltd. v. Curtis* (1989) 59 P. & C.R. 242, CA; *ante*, para. 4–50.

[59] *Ante*, paras. 4–50, 5–09 (though of course one is''before'' and the other ''on or after'').

[60] ''Rent'' here has the same meaning as in Act of 1977, Pt. V: Act of 1988, s.36(5). For this, see Vol. 1, p. 754.

[61] See Act of 1988, s.36(2)(b).

in varied form. In two cases, the variation in the terms of a tenancy result, of necessity, in the surrender of the existing tenancy and the re-grant of a new tenancy on the varied terms: these are where the length of the term granted by, or the premises comprised in, the tenancy is or are extended.[62] This takes effect even if the parties do not intend it. Subject to these cases, whether or not there is a surrender and re-grant, or whether the existing tenancy continues as varied, is a question of the intention of the parties, judged objectively from the language of the variation and the circumstances.[63]

(b) Variations affecting rent

5–23 Where any variation made on or after January 15, 1989 affects the amount of the rent payable under the contract for the dwelling, the rule is that the contract must be treated as a new contract entered into at the time of the variation.[64] It therefore cannot be a restricted contract. But this rule does not apply to—

(1) a reduction or increase in the rent effected[65] by a rent tribunal,[66] nor
(2) a variation made by the parties which has the effect of making the rent expressed to be payable under the contract the same as the registered[67] rent.[68]

In these two cases, the ordinary law applies.[69]

Sect. 4. Housing Association Tenancies

5–24 As has been seen,[70] a tenancy cannot be an assured tenancy if it is a housing association tenancy. The Act of 1988 severely restricted the creation of new housing association tenancies after January 15, 1989. The definition of these tenancies, and the extent of these restrictions, will be considered in turn.

[62] See *Friends Provident Life Office v. British Railways Board* [1996] 1 All E.R. 336, CA.
[63] *J. W. Childers Trustees v. Anker* [1996] 1 E.G.L.R. 1, CA.
[64] Act of 1988, s.36(2)(a).
[65] Under Act of 1977, s.78.
[66] Act of 1988, s.36(3)(a).
[67] *i.e.* registered under Act of 1977, s.79: see Vol. 1, p. 779.
[68] Act of 1988, s.36(3)(b).
[69] And therefore, absent a clear intention to surrender and re-grant, no new contract will be made. See *post*, para. 16–42, where the similar provisions of Protection from Eviction Act 1977, s.8(5), (6) (inserted by Act of 1988, s.33(3)) are considered.
[70] *Ante*, para. 4–64.

1. Housing association tenancy

A "housing association tenancy" is a tenancy where the interest of the landlord under the tenancy belongs to a housing association, a charitable housing trust, the Housing Corporation, or Housing for Wales, and the tenancy would be a protected tenancy but for the exclusion from the Rent Acts[71] of tenancies held from one of these bodies.[72] Two types of tenancy are, however, excluded from being a housing association tenancy. 5–25

(a) Housing association

A housing association is "a society, body of trustees or company" which satisfies two requirements, each of which has two alternatives.[73] These are that— 5–26

(1) either (i) it is established for the purpose of "providing, constructing, improving or managing" housing accommodation, or of "facilitating or encouraging the construction or improvement" of such accommodation, or (ii) these housing purposes are included amongst its objects or powers; and
(2) either (i) it "does not trade for profit", or (ii) its "constitution or rules prohibit the issue of capital with interest or dividend exceeding such rate as may be prescribed by the Treasury, whether with or without differentiation as between share and loan capital".

By virtue of the requirement that the tenancy would otherwise have been a protected tenancy,[74] a housing association can be the landlord under a housing association tenancy only if it is a registered social landlord within the meaning of the Housing Act 1985,[75] or if it is a co-operative housing association within the meaning of the Housing Associations Act 1985.[76] A "co-operative housing association" is a "fully mutual housing association which is a society registered under the Industrial and Provident Societies Act 1965";[77] and a housing association is "fully mutual" if its rules not only "restrict membership to persons

[71] Act of 1977, ss.15, 16.
[72] Act of 1988, s.35(1), applying Act of 1977, s.86, as amended by Act of 1988, Sched. 17, para. 100.
[73] Housing Associations Act 1985, s.1, applied by Act of 1977, s.86(3) and Act of 1988, s.35(1). See the definition in Vol. 1, pp. 148, 149. Registration under Housing Associations Act 1985, Pt. I, is after October 1, 1996 to be equated with registration as a social landlord under Housing Act 1996, Pt. I: Housing Act (Consequential Provisions) Order 1996 (S.I. 1996 No. 2325), art. 3.; and all housing associations that were registered under the 1985 Act on that date are automatically registered social landlords under Housing Act 1996, Pt. I.
[74] *Supra.*
[75] See Housing Act 1985, s.5(4), (5).
[76] Act of 1977, s.15(3), as amended on October 1, 1996 by Housing Act 1996 (Consequential Provisions) Order 1996 (S.I. 1996 No. 2325), art. 5(1), Sched. 2, para. 6. Formerly, housing associations were registered under the Housing Associations Act 1985.
[77] Housing Associations Act 1985, s.1(2): Act of 1988, s.45(1).

who are tenants or prospective tenants of the association'' but also ''preclude the granting or assignment of tenancies to persons other than members''.[78]

(b) Charitable housing trust

5–27 A charitable housing trust is a corporation or body of persons which satisfies two requirements[79]—

(1) It is a charity within the meaning of the Charities Act 1993; and
(2) Either—
 (a) it is required by the terms of its constituent instrument to use the whole of its funds (including any surplus which may arise from its operations) for the purpose of providing housing accommodation; or
 (b) it is required by the terms of its constituent instrument to devote the whole (or substantially the whole) of its funds to charitable purposes, and it in fact uses the whole (or substantially the whole) of its funds for the purpose of providing housing accommodation.[80]

(c) The Housing Corporation and Housing for Wales

5–28 The Housing Corporation and Housing for Wales are bodies corporate, with their members appointed by the Secretary of State. Their functions include assisting and supervising registered housing associations.[81] The functions, property, rights and liabilities of Housing for Wales were transferred to the Secretary of State for Wales on November 1, 1998.[81a]

(d) Excluded tenancies

5–29 The tenancy cannot be a housing association tenancy if it is either a business tenancy within Part II of the Landlord and Tenant Act 1954 or a co-ownership tenancy.[82] A tenancy is a co-ownership tenancy if two requirements are satisfied. First, that the tenancy was granted by a co-operative housing association;[83] and secondly, that on ceasing to be a member of the association, the tenant or his personal representatives will, under the terms of the tenancy agreement or of

[78] *ibid.*
[79] Act of 1977, ss.15(2), (5), 86(4).
[80] Housing Act 1985, s.6. See *Hounslow L.B.C. v. Hare* (1990) 24 H.L.R. 9, Ch.
[81] Housing Associations Act 1985, ss.74, 75, Sched. 6, as amended (as from April 1, 1989: S.I. 1988 No. 2152; S.I. 1989 No. 404) by Act of 1988, s.59, Sched. 6, paras. 31, 32, 37.
[81a] Government of Wales Act 1998, ss. 140(1),(2), 158(1), Sched. 16; S.I. 1998 No. 2244, art. 5.
[82] Act of 1988, s.35(1), applying Act of 1977, s.86, as amended by Act of 1988, Sched. 17, para. 100.
[83] *Supra.*

the agreement under which he became a member, be entitled (subject to any conditions stated in either agreement) to a sum calculated by reference directly or indirectly to the value of the dwelling-house.[84]

2. Restrictions on creation of housing association tenancies

Housing association tenancies that were entered into before January 15, 1989 are not affected. But the general rule is that a tenancy that is entered into on or after that date cannot be a housing association tenancy.[85] To this rule there are five exceptions. **5–30**

(a) Prior contract

The first exception is a tenancy which is entered into in pursuance of a contract made before January 15, 1989.[86] This is the same as for protected tenancies.[87] **5–31**

(b) Grant to sitting tenant

The second exception is a tenancy which— **5–32**

(1) "is granted to a person (alone or jointly with others) who, immediately before the tenancy was granted, was a tenant under a housing association tenancy", and
(2) "is so granted by the person who at that time was the landlord under that housing association tenancy".[88]

This, too, is the same as for protected tenancies,[89] save that there is understandably no reference to joint landlords.

(c) Suitable alternative accommodation

The third exception is of certain cases in which an order for possession is made on the ground of suitable alternative accommodation being available, and the tenancy is a tenancy of that alternative accommodation. There are five requirements:[90] **5–33**

[84] Act of 1977, s.86(3A).
[85] Act of 1988, s.35(2), as amended by Local Government and Housing Act 1989, s.194, Sched. 11, para. 105.
[86] Act of 1988, s.35(2)(a).
[87] See *ante*, para. 5–09.
[88] Act of 1988, s.35(2)(b).
[89] See *ante*, para. 5–10.
[90] Act of 1988, s.35(2)(c).

(1) "Prior to the grant of the tenancy" to a person "an order for possession of a dwelling-house was made against him (alone or jointly with others)".
(2) The order was made "on the court being satisfied" that certain grounds for possession were established. These grounds are that suitable alternative accommodation will be available when the order takes effect, and either that the case falls within one or more of Grounds 9 to 11 under the Housing Act 1985, or else that it is reasonable to make the order and the case falls within one or more of Grounds 12 to 16 under that Act.[91]
(3) The tenancy is granted to that person, whether alone or jointly with others.
(4) The tenancy is "of the premises which constitute the suitable accommodation as to which the court was so satisfied".
(5) "In the proceedings for possession the court directed that the tenancy would be a housing association tenancy".

This provision corresponds to the similar provision made for protected tenancies,[92] though here the court, in giving a direction, is not required to consider whether the grant of an assured tenancy would afford the required security. Indeed, in the absence of any such provision, it is unclear on what basis the court should exercise the discretion that it is apparently given.[93]

(d) New Town tenancies

5–34 As in the case of protected tenancies,[94] there is a temporary exception to the rule where the interest of the landlord is held by a New Town corporation. If the interest of the landlord at the time a tenancy was granted was held by a New Town corporation,[95] and before January 15, 1991[96] that interest ceased to be so held by virtue of a disposal by the Commission for the New Towns,[97] the tenancy can be a protected tenancy notwithstanding its being granted on or after that date. If it is disposed of on or after January 15, 1991, the tenancy is not

[91] Housing Act 1985, s.84(2)(b), (c). The grounds appear in Sched. 2, Pts. II, III, and suitability in Pt. IV. For Grounds 9–11 there is no statutory requirement of reasonableness. The titles to Pts. II and III refer to "suitable alternative accommodation", but elsewhere (*e.g.*, in s.84) the phrase is merely "suitable accommodation".
[92] *Ante*, paras. 5–15 *et seq*.
[93] See also *post*, para. 5–47, for the removal of the housing association group from the list of landlords capable of satisfying the landlord condition under Housing Act 1985, Pt. IV for the grant of secure tenancies.
[94] *Ante*, para. 5–19.
[95] Within the meaning of Housing Act 1985, s.80: Act of 1988, s.34(1)(d), as substituted on November 16, 1989 by Local Government and Housing Act 1989, s.194(1), Sched. 11, para. 104.
[96] *i.e.* two years after the commencement of the Act of 1988. The Secretary of State did not specify any other date by order before the expiry of the two years: Act of 1988, s.38(4)(b).
[97] Made pursuant to a direction under New Towns Act 1981, s.37.

capable of being a housing association tenancy.[98] The effect of this provision is dealt with later in considering changes of landlord.[99]

(e) Tenancy of repurchased defective dwelling

Certain classes of dwellings that are defective "by reason of their design or construction" and have had their value "substantially reduced" by reason of this "having become generally known" may be designated as "defective dwellings".[1] This category mainly comprises some so-called "system-built" dwellings. A purchaser of such a dwelling from an authority in the public sector may usually require the vendor to repurchase it, and to grant him a tenancy of it.[2] Where the repurchaser is a registered social landlord,[3] and the purchaser, before his purchase, was a secure tenant, the tenancy to be granted by the social landlord to him (or to his spouse, former spouse, widow or widower, or if he is dead, to a qualifying member of the family, who was residing with him when he died, and for the previous year) is to be a secure tenancy,[4] and not a protected or assured tenancy. In such a case, it is to be assumed for this purpose that the tenancy was granted before January 15, 1989,[5] and so it will not be precluded from being a housing association tenancy. **5–35**

Where the interest of a landlord under a housing association tenancy which was entered into or contracted before January 15, 1989 is transferred to another body or person after that date, the tenancy may remain a housing association tenancy, or become an assured tenancy, or become a secure tenancy. These circumstances are addressed in Section 6 below.[6]

3. Registered social landlords

The effect of the reforms introduced by the Act of 1988 was that, subject to transitional provisions, tenancies granted by housing associations and charitable housing trusts could no longer be secure tenancies,[7] whereas many[8] would be assured tenancies. The Housing Act 1996 created, with effect from October 1, 1996, a new class of "social landlords" capable of registration as such, regu- **5–36**

[98] Act of 1988, ss.35(2)(d) (as substituted by Local Government and Housing Act 1989, s.194(1), Sched. 11, para. 105), 38(4) (as amended by Local Government and Housing Act 1989, s.194(1), Sched. 11, para. 106). See further, *post*, para. 5–60.

[99] *Post*, para. 5–60.

[1] Housing Act 1985, ss.528(1), 559(1).

[2] *ibid.*, ss.547–554, Sched. 20. The text above merely gives a general indication of these complex provisions, so far as is necessary for present purposes.

[3] Formerly, a registered housing association; see *infra*, and Housing Act 1996 (Consequential Provisions) Order 1996 (S.I. 1996 No. 2325), art. 5(1), Sched. 2, para. 14(28).

[4] Housing Act 1985, s.554, as amended by Act of 1988, Sched. 17, para. 61 and by S.I. 1996 No. 2325, art. 5, Sched. 2, para. 14; and see Housing Act 1985, s.186, for member of family.

[5] Act of 1988, s.35(3), applying Act of 1977, ss.15, 16, 86(2)(b).

[6] *Post*, paras. 5–62 *et seq.*

[7] See *post*, paras. 5–47 to 5–49.

[8] With the exception of fully mutual housing associations: Act of 1988, Sched. 1, para. 12(1)(h).

lated by and eligible for housing grants from the Housing Corporation or Housing for Wales.[9] The detail of this is beyond the scope of this book, but a summary of the main aspects as they affect the former housing association group and assured tenancies follows.

5–37 The bodies eligible for registration include registered charities which are housing associations, societies registered under the Industrial and Provident Societies Act 1965 which are non-profit making and concerned with housing, and limited companies registered under the Companies Act 1985 which are similarly non-profit making and concerned with housing.[10] All housing associations which immediately before October 1, 1996 were registered housing associations under Part I of the Housing Associations Act 1985 became registered as social landlords on that date.[11]

5–38 On April 1, 1997, tenants of social landlords were given rights similar to those enjoyed by secure tenants under Part V of the Housing Act 1985 to acquire the dwellings of which they are tenants.[12] For the first time, such rights have been given to some assured tenants as well as to secure tenants. An assured tenant has the right to acquire the freehold or a lease of his dwelling if three conditions are satisfied in addition to his landlord being a registered social landlord. First, the tenancy must not be an assured shorthold tenancy or a long tenancy.[13] Most assured tenancies granted after February 28, 1997 will be assured shorthold tenancies.[14] Secondly, the dwelling must have been provided with public money and remained in the social rented sector.[15] Thirdly, the tenant must satisfy qualifying conditions under Part V of the Housing Act 1985 as they apply in relation to the right to acquire under Part I of the Housing Act 1996.[16] These include a qualifying period of two years' occupation of the dwelling.[17] A tenant of a co-operative housing asociation does not have the right to acquire his dwelling.[18] There is no preservation of the right to acquire upon a transfer of the landlord's interest from a registered social landlord to the private sector;[19] but the right of a social landlord to dispose of any of its housing stock is, with exceptions, subject to the consent of the Corporation,[20] and is therefore unlikely to occur where tenants are entitled to acquire the freehold or a lease of their dwellings.

[9] Housing Act 1996, Pt. I, Chaps. I, III; S.I. 1996 No. 2402.
[10] Housing Act 1996, s.2(1), (2).
[11] *ibid.*, s.1(2).
[12] *ibid.*, ss.16. 232(3); S.I. 1997 No. 618.
[13] Housing Act 1996, s.16(1)(a). "Long tenancy" has the same meaning as under Housing Act 1985, s.187: see *ibid.*, s.63(1).
[14] See *post*, para. 8–02.
[15] Housing Act 1996, s.16(1)(b), (2), (3), (4).
[16] *ibid.*, s.16(1)(c). Regulations were made under *ibid.*, s.17 to adapt the terms of Housing Act 1985, Pt. V (right to buy) to the right to acquire from social landlords, and these Regs. print Pt. V as it applies to such acquisitions: Housing (Right to Acquire) Regulations 1997 (S.I. 1997 No. 619), in force on April 1, 1997.
[17] Housing (Right to Acquire) Regulations 1997 (S.I. 1997 No. 619), reg. 2(2), Sched. 2, para. 119(1), Sched. 4.
[18] *ibid.*, Sched. 5, para. 2.
[19] *ibid.*, reg. 2(1), Sched. 1, para. 27.
[20] Housing Act 1996, ss. 8–10.

Sect. 5. Long Tenancies

Under the Act of 1988, the position of long tenancies depends on whether or not the rent is a "low" rent. If they are at a low rent, they will not enjoy the protection of the Act of 1988 until their termination;[21] if they are not at a low rent, they will (if they otherwise satisfy the requirements of the Act for assured tenancies) be assured tenancies regardless of the length of the term granted. After January 15, 1999, almost all long tenancies at low rents which had not by then terminated became subject to a regime under which, in due course, the tenant will be entitled to remain in occupation as an assured tenant at the end of the term. These complex provisions are considered elsewhere.[22] A summary of the way in which long tenancies relate to assured tenancies is given here. **5–39**

1. Low rent

Most long tenancies at a low rent are protected under either Part I of the Landlord and Tenant Act 1954 ("Part I") or Schedule 10 to the Local Government and Housing Act 1989 ("Schedule 10"). On January 15, 1999, a long tenancy which was in existence then, and which immediately before April 1, 1990 was (or was deemed to be) a long tenancy at a low rent for the purposes of Part I, was deemed to be a long tenancy at a low rent for the purposes of Schedule 10, and that Schedule applies to the tenancy instead of Part I.[23] After that date, therefore, Part I only continues to apply to those long tenancies where both the contractual term date of the long tenancy fell before January 15, 1999 and a notice of termination under Part I specifying a date of termination before that date had been served.[24] It seems unlikely that landlords under Part I long tenancies will have been rushing to serve notices expiring before January 15, 1999. Mysteriously, there still appears to be a category of long tenancies protected by neither Part I nor Schedule 10.[25] **5–40**

In essence, the protection under Schedule 10 consists of giving the tenant the right to an assured tenancy when the term expires, and of prolonging the long tenancy until the terms of the assured periodic tenancy have been settled.[26] The "qualifying condition" which "for the time being" must be fulfilled in order to obtain this protection is that if the tenancy had not been at a low rent, the circumstances are such that the tenancy would have been an assured tenancy.[27] In short, the low rent must be the only reason for the exclusion of Part I of the Act of 1988. **5–41**

In consequence of the abolition of domestic rates on April 1, 1990, the cri-

[21] See *ante*, paras. 4–53 *et seq.*

[22] *Post*, Chap. 10, pp. 142 *et seq.*

[23] Local Government and Housing Act 1989, s.186(2), (3), (6).

[24] *ibid.*, s.186(3), Sched. 10, paras. 3(2), 21. For a full treatment of the transitional provisions, as well as of the provisions of Sched. 10, see *post*, Chap. 10, pp. 142 *et seq.* For a case where an issue arose as to the validity of notices to terminate under Part I, see *St. Ermins Property Co. Ltd. v. Patel* (1997) 30 H.L.R. 462, CA.

[25] *Post*, para. 10–17.

[26] See *post*, paras. 10–18 *et seq.*

[27] Local Government and Housing Act 1989, Sched. 10, para. 1(1).

terion for identifying a tenancy at a low rent has been amended. Broadly, the established criterion ("rent . . . less than two-thirds of the rateable value") remains applicable to tenancies entered into before April 1, 1990, and a new criterion of a fixed maximum rent applies to tenancies entered into on or after that date. There is, however, one exception; and transitional provisions apply, and these are considered in detail in Chapter 4.[28]

5–42 If a long tenancy at a low rent was entered into before January 15, 1989, or on or after that date in pursuance of a contract made before it, there is nothing in the Act of 1988 to prevent the "qualifying condition" in Part I from being satisfied. Accordingly, such a tenancy remained within Part I until January 15, 1999 unless it was terminated before that date, and Schedule 10 applied to it on and with effect from that date.[29] At the end of the term, therefore, the tenant may become an assured tenant.

A long tenancy at a low rent entered into on or after April 1, 1990 will normally be a Schedule 10 tenancy, unless entered into pursuant to a contract made before that date. The "qualifying condition" in Schedule 10 will be satisfied if the low rent is the only reason why the tenancy is not an assured tenancy. But most tenancies entered into between January 15, 1989 and April 1, 1990, together with those entered into on or after April 1, 1990 pursuant to a contract made between those two dates, appear to enjoy the protection of neither Part I nor Schedule 10.[30] Nor will they be assured tenancies, being tenancies at a low rent.[31] But those tenancies may be able to satisfy the requirements of the Leasehold Reform Act 1967[32] if they are tenancies of houses, or of the Leasehold Reform, Housing and Urban Development Act 1993[33] if they are tenancies of flats, and if they do the tenants will have rights of enfranchisement and extension.

2. Rent not low

5–43 Where the rent under a long tenancy is not low and the requisite conditions are satisfied, the tenancy will be a protected tenancy within the Rent Acts if it was entered into before January 15, 1989.[34] If the tenancy is a protected tenancy it cannot be an assured tenancy under the Act of 1988.[35] But if the tenancy was entered into on or after that date, it will normally[36] be an assured tenancy.

Sect. 6. Secure Tenancies: Change of Landlord

5–44 A change of landlord may alter the status of a tenancy, as where a landlord in

[28] *Ante*, paras. 4–59 *et seq.*
[29] Local Government and Housing Act 1989, s.186(3).
[30] See *post*, paras. 10–17.
[31] See *ante*, paras. 4–53 *et seq.*
[32] Sections 1–4A, as amended by Leasehold Reform, Housing and Urban Development Act 1993, ss. 63–65, and Housing Act 1996, ss. 105, 106, 114, 115.
[33] Chaps I, II.
[34] See *ante*, para. 5–08.
[35] Act of 1988, Sched. 1, Pt. I, para. 13(1); *ante*, para. 4–64.
[36] Subject to the transitional provisions of Act of 1988, s.34: *ante*, paras. 5–09 *et seq.*

the public sector is replaced by a landlord in the private sector, and *vice versa*. The Act of 1988 accentuated the legislative policy of the previous eight years[37] in reducing the substantial stock of housing owned by local authorities. Part III of the Act provided for the Secretary of State to designate housing action trust areas and to establish or specify housing action trusts.[38] These trusts may take over and improve local authority housing and then dispose of it,[39] either within the public sector or into the private sector.[40] Similarly, "approved landlords" were given the right to acquire local authority and other public sector housing stock.[41] The Act has also reduced the ambit of secure tenancies by excluding the housing association group from the list of those who can be landlords under secure tenancies.[42]

Before considering the effect of a change of landlord, something must be said about secure tenancies; for although they are outside the scope of this book, they play a substantial part in the process of changes of landlord.

A. SECURE TENANCIES

1. Nature

Secure tenancies were introduced by the Housing Act 1980. They give the tenant security of tenure on lines broadly similar to the Rent Acts (though with many differences), but confer no protection as to rent unless the landlord is a housing association, housing trust or the Housing Corporation; and subject to certain conditions, many secure tenants also have a right to buy their dwellings at discounted prices.[43] **5–45**

2. Requirements

Where a dwelling-house is "let as a separate dwelling", the tenancy will be a secure tenancy at any time when the "landlord condition" and the "tenant condition" are both satisfied; and a licence to occupy a dwelling-house is also included unless it was granted as a temporary expedient to a person who entered as a trespasser.[44] The "landlord condition" is that the interest of the landlord belongs to one of certain bodies in the public sector set out below.[45] The "tenant **5–46**

[37] See Housing Act 1980; Housing and Building Control Act 1984; Housing Act 1985; Housing and Planning Act 1986.

[38] Act of 1988, ss.60, 62.

[39] *ibid.*, ss.63–65, 72–75, 79.

[40] *ibid.*, s.79.

[41] Act of 1988, Pt. IV, later repealed with effect from October 1, 1996 by Housing Act 1996, ss.227, 232(3), Sched. 19, Pt. IX; S.I. 1996 No. 2402. Before the repeal, large tracts of council-owned housing were purchased by approved landlords, sometimes at negative prices reflecting the poor condition of the housing stock.

[42] *Infra.*

[43] Now under Housing Act 1985, Pt. V.

[44] *ibid.*, s.79.

[45] *ibid.*, s.80.

condition'' is that the tenant is an individual, and occupies the dwelling-house as his only or principal home, or, if there are joint tenants, each is an individual and at least one of them occupies the dwelling-house as his only or principal home.[46]

5–47 Under the Housing Act 1985, as now amended, the following bodies can all satisfy the landlord condition:[47]

(1) a local authority;
(2) a New Town corporation;
(3) an urban development corporation;
(4) a housing action trust;
(5) The Development Board for Rural Wales[47a]; and
(6) a housing co-operative, if the tenancy or licence is of a dwelling-house comprised in a housing co-operative agreement with a local housing authority.

The Act of 1988[48] inserted housing action trusts into the list, but it also deleted four bodies that had previously been included, namely the Housing Corporation, a charitable housing trust, a registered housing association (other than a co-operative housing association) (now called a ''registered social landlord'' under Part I of the Housing Act 1996), and a co-operative housing association which is not a registered housing association (or registered social landlord).[49] The removal of this housing association group (as it may conveniently be called) substantially reduces the number of tenancies which can be secure tenancies.

3. New secure tenancies

5–48 A tenancy or licence entered into on or after January 15, 1989 can be a secure tenancy only if it falls within one of the following categories:[50]

(a) Public body

5–49 The interest of the landlord under the tenancy or licence belongs to one of the public bodies in the list set out above.[51] This head now constitutes the main source of new secure tenancies; but local authorities and housing action trusts

[46] Housing Act 1985, s.81.
[47] Housing Act 1985, ss.4, 27, 80; Housing and Planning Act 1986, s.10, Sched. 5, para. 26; Act of 1988, s.83(2), Sched. 18.
[47a] On October 1, 1998, the functions of the Development Board for Rural Wales ceased to exist, and its property, rights and liabilities thereupon vested in the Welsh Development Agency: Government of Wales Act 1998, ss. 129, 130(1), 158(1), Sched. 15; S.I. 1998 No. 2244, art. 4.
[48] S. 83(2).
[49] Act of 1988, Sched. 18, deleting those bodies from Housing Act 1985, s.80.
[50] Act of 1988, s.35(4).
[51] *ibid.*, s.35(4)(a), (b).

can now[52] elect to grant "introductory tenancies", being periodic licences or tenancies which are not assured tenancies and which do not become secure tenancies until after the expiry of a trial period, which is generally one year from grant.[53] Where such an election is made, all periodic licences or tenancies granted or adopted by that body before the election is revoked which would otherwise be secure tenancies are introductory tenancies.[54] An introductory tenancy cannot be granted to a person who was the secure tenant, or one of the secure tenants, of the same or another dwelling-house immediately before the tenancy was granted or adopted.[55]

Ordinarily, a secure tenancy granted after January 15, 1989 will only remain a secure tenancy for so long as the interest of the landlord is vested in any of the public bodies listed above. But where a tenancy was granted by a New Town corporation, and before January 15, 1991 the interest of the landlord ceased to be so held by virtue of a disposal by the Commission for the New Towns[56] to a registered housing association, the tenancy will remain a secure tenancy for so long as the landlord's interest is held by a housing association, housing trust, the Housing Corporation, Housing for Wales[56a] or any of the other public bodies listed above.[57] **5–50**

The removal of the housing association group from the list of public bodies[58] does not have effect in relation to a tenancy while it is a housing association tenancy.[59] So if a new tenancy granted after January 15, 1989 is a housing association tenancy,[60] it will also be a secure tenancy.

(b) Prior contract

The tenancy or licence is entered into in pursuance of a contract made before January 15, 1989.[61] **5–51**

(c) Existing secure tenancy

The tenancy or licence is granted to a person (either alone or jointly with others) who, immediately before it was entered into, was a secure tenant, and it is so **5–52**

[52] On and after February 12, 1997.
[53] Housing Act 1996, Pt. V, ss.124–126; *ante*, para. 4–47.
[54] *ibid.*, s.124(2), (4), (5).
[55] *ibid.*, s.124(2).
[56] Made pursuant to a direction under New Towns Act 1981, s.37: Act of 1988, s.38(4), as amended by Local Government and Housing Act 1989, s.194(1), Sched. 11, para. 106.
[56a] The functions, property, rights and liabilities of Housing for Wales were transferred to the Secretary of State for Wales on November 1, 1998: Government of Wales Act 1998, ss. 140(1), (2), 158(1), Sched. 16; S.I. 1998 No. 2244, Art. 5.
[57] Act of 1988, s.38(4A), inserted by Local Government and Housing Act 1989, s.194(1), Sched. 11, para. 106(3).
[58] In Housing Act 1985, s.80.
[59] Act of 1988, Sched. 18, n.(4)(c), inserted by Local Government and Housing Act 1989, ss.194(1), 195(2), Sched. 11, para. 112; S.I. 1989 No. 2445.
[60] As to which, see *ante*, paras. 5–30 *et seq*.
[61] Act of 1988, s.35(4)(c); cp. *ante*, paras. 4–50, 5–09.

granted by the body which then was the landlord or licensor under the same tenancy.[62]

(d) Suitable alternative accommodation

5–53 The tenancy or licence is granted to a person (alone or jointly with others) where, prior to the grant, an order for possession of the dwelling-house was made against him (either alone or jointly with others) on the court being satisfied that suitable alternative accommodation was available for him,[63] and the tenancy or licence was of that alternative accommodation; and in addition, in the proceedings for possession, the court, considering that in the circumstances the grant of an assured tenancy would not afford the required security, directed that the tenancy or licence would be a secure tenancy.[64]

(e) Defective system-built dwelling

5–54 The tenancy or licence is granted pursuant to an obligation under the provisions for the grant of tenancies by the repurchaser of a defective dwelling in the circumstances already considered in relation to housing association tenancies.[65]

5–55 For the purposes of paragraphs (b) to (e) above, the removal of the housing association group from the list of landlords[66] who can satisfy the landlord condition has no effect.[67]

B. CONVERSION OF TENANCIES

When there is a change of landlord, any protected or statutory tenancies, secure tenancies, and housing association tenancies may be converted into other types of tenancy, as may tenancies held of the Crown. These tenancies will be considered in turn.

1. Protected and statutory tenancies

5–56 If on or after January 15, 1989 the landlord's interest in a protected or statutory tenancy becomes vested in one of the bodies which can satisfy the "landlord

[62] Act of 1988, s.35(4)(d); cp. *ante*, paras. 5–10 *et seq.*
[63] Under Housing Act 1985, s.84(2)(b), (c); see *ante*, para. 5–33.
[64] Act of 1988, s.35(4)(e); cp. *ante*, paras. 5–15 *et seq*, 5–33.
[65] *ibid.*, s.35(4)(f); see *ante*, para. 5–35.
[66] In Housing Act 1985, s.80.
[67] Act of 1988, Sched. 18, n.4(b).

condition'',[68] it will cease to be a protected or statutory tenancy and become instead a secure tenancy, as it did before the Act of 1988.[69] For this purpose, the removal of the housing association group from the list of the bodies which satisfy the landlord condition is to be ignored,[70–71] so that if one of the bodies in the group becomes the landlord, the tenancy will become a secure tenancy; and it will also become a housing association tenancy.[72]

2. Crown tenancies

Where the Crown is the landlord, tenancies normally cannot be protected, statutory, assured or secure.[73] But if the Crown interest is under the management of the Crown Estate Commissioners, a tenancy may be a protected or statutory tenancy, or an assured tenancy, though it cannot be a secure tenancy.[74] If such a protected tenancy was entered into before January 15, 1989 (or pursuant to a contract made before then), and after that date the Crown's interest is transferred, the tenancy will become either a secure tenancy or an assured tenancy. It will be a secure tenancy if the new landlord satisfies the ''landlord condition'',[75] and for these purposes the housing association group is not included. Otherwise it may be an assured tenancy if it satisfies the requirements of the Act of 1988, even though it was granted before January 15, 1989 (or pursuant to a contract made before then), and so could normally not be assured.[76] Thereafter, the tenancy cannot again become a protected tenancy or a housing association tenancy, though it may become or remain a secure tenancy if and whenever the landlord condition is satisfied.[77] **5–57**

In cases where the interest of the Crown is not under the management of the Commissioners, the tenancy could not have been a protected or statutory tenancy.[78] If the Crown disposes of the interest of the landlord under such a tenancy, the tenancy will become secure if the landlord condition is satisfied, and assured if the requirements of the Act of 1988[79] are satisfied.[80]

[68] See *ante*, para. 5–47.

[69] See Vol. 1, pp. 153, 363.

[70–71] Act of 1988, s.35(5). In this, ''housing association'' and ''housing trust'' have the same meaning as in Housing Act 1985: Act of 1988, s.35(6).

[72] Act of 1988, s.35(5). Before November 1, 1998, the list included Housing for Wales: Act of 1998, ss. 35(5), 46, 47; but see n. 56a, *supra*. With effect from January 15, 1999, if the interest of the landlord becomes held by the Secretary of State as a result of the exercise by him of functions under Housing Associations Act 1985, Pt. III, the tenancy will similarly become a secure tenancy and a housing association tenancy: Government of Wales Act 1998 (Housing) (Amendments) Order 1999 (S.I. 1999 No. 61), art. 2, Sched., para. 3(2).

[73] See Vol. 1, pp. 143–146; Act of 1988, Sched. 1, paras. 11 (*ante*, paras. 4–36 *et seq.*); Housing Act 1985, s.80 (omitting the Crown from the bodies which can satisfy the ''landlord condition'').

[74] *ibid.*

[75] *Ante*, para. 5–47; Act of 1988, s.38(1), (3)(b), (5) (''public body'').

[76] Act of 1988, s.38(3)(a), (c), excluding Sched. 1, para. 1 for these purposes.

[77] *ibid.*, s.38(3)(a), (b).

[78] *Supra.*

[79] Other than being granted on or after January 15, 1989.

[80] Act of 1988, s.38(1), (3), (5).

3. Secure tenancies

(a) Remaining secure

5–58 If on or after January 15, 1989 the landlord's interest in a secure tenancy becomes vested in another of the bodies which can satisfy the "landlord condition",[81] the tenancy will remain a secure tenancy.[82] In a case where the interest of the landlord or licensor was held immediately before January 15, 1989 by a body in the housing association group which thereafter was unable to satisfy the landlord condition, the repeal of the housing association group has no effect in relation to the tenancy or licence in question. Accordingly, if after that date the interest of the landlord or licensor is assigned to another body in the housing association group, the tenancy remains a secure tenancy,[83] just as it would if the interest were assigned to a landlord would could satisfy the landlord condition. The same applies where, by virtue of a disposal made by the Secretary of State under Part III of the Housing Associations Act 1985 in the exercise of functions exercised before November 1, 1998, by Housing for Wales the interest of a landlord under a secure tenancy passes to a registered social landlord.[83a]

(b) Becoming assured

5–59 If instead the landlord's interest ceases to be held by one of the bodies capable of satisfying the landlord condition,[84] the tenancy will normally become an assured tenancy, even though it was granted before January 15, 1989 (or pursuant to a contract made before then) and so normally could not be an assured tenancy.[85] If the tenancy then becomes vested in one of the bodies that can now satisfy the "landlord condition",[86] it will become a secure tenancy once again.[87] But the tenancy cannot ever become a protected tenancy, a protected occupancy, or a housing association tenancy.[88] There will be no statutory protection if the landlord's interest vests in a landlord whose tenants can be neither assured nor secure, such as the Crown where the Crown interest is not managed by the Crown Estate Commissioners.[89]

[81] See *ante*, para. 5–47.
[82] Act of 1988, s.38(1), (3)(b).
[83] Act of 1988, Sched. 18, n.4(a).
[83a] *ibid.*, s. 38(4B), inserted on January 15, 1999 by Government of Wales Act 1998 (Housing) (Amendments) Order 1999 (S.I. 1999 No. 61), art. 2, Sched., para. 3(3); and see *ante*, n. 56a. The tenancy is capable of being a housing association tenancy.
[84] As opposed to one of the bodies in the housing association group. For these, see *post*, paras. 5–62 *et seq.*
[85] Act of 1988, s.38(1), (3)(c), excluding Sched. 1, para. 1.
[86] See *ante*, para. 5–47; the housing association group is thus not included here.
[87] Act of 1988, s.38(3)(b), (5).
[88] *ibid.*, s.38(3)(a).
[89] See, *e.g.*, Act of 1988, Sched. 1, para. 11, *ante*, para. 5–57; and compare Act of 1988, s.38(5)(d) where the landlord's interest is held by the Crown on January 15, 1989.

(c) New Town tenants

If the interest of the landlord is held by a New Town corporation, the above provisions are varied to enable housing association tenancies to be "created" by a disposal by the New Towns Commission made before January 15, 1991. A New Town corporation is a development corporation established by order made under the New Towns Act 1981, or having effect as if so made.[90] So, where on January 15, 1989 or, if later, the date on which the tenancy is entered into, the interest of the landlord under the tenancy is held by a New Town corporation, and that interest is disposed of before January 15, 1991 by the Commission to a registered housing association pursuant to a direction made under section 37 of the New Towns Act 1981, then so long as the interest of the landlord is held by a member of the housing association group, the tenancy continues to be a secure tenancy and to be capable of being a housing association tenancy.[91] If the interest of the landlord is disposed of *on or after* January 15, 1991, then the same consequences ensue as for secure tenancies, and the tenancy will either remain secure or become assured,[92] depending on the identity of the transferee; but the tenancy will never become a housing association tenancy. **5–60**

(d) Preservation of right to buy

In most cases a secure tenant has a right to buy his dwelling-house, a right which includes the right to take a long lease of it.[93] This right is outside the scope of this volume, but something must be said about the position if the dwelling-house moves from the public sector to the private sector upon the landlord's interest ceasing to be held by a body that satisfies the landlord condition.[94] In such a case before January 15, 1989, the tenancy usually became a protected tenancy; but under the Act of 1988 it now normally becomes an assured tenancy. There are provisions[95] which in each case will usually preserve the tenant's right to buy, despite the transfer and the change of status of the tenancy. The Act of 1988 has made various amendments to these provisions so as to adapt them to the Act. These relate to the "qualifying successor"[96] to the **5–61**

[90] Housing Act 1985, s.4(c), 80; Act of 1988, s.38(4).

[91] Act of 1988, s.38(4), (4A), amended and inserted respectively by Local Government and Housing Act 1989, s.194(1), Sched. 11, para. 106.

[92] Or possibly not be subject to any statutory regime, *e.g.* if it is transferred to Her Majesty in right of the Crown.

[93] Housing Act 1985, Pt. V (ss.118–188), replacing earlier provisions which are summarised in Megarry & Wade's *Law of Real Property* (5th ed. 1984) pp. 1137–1144.

[94] For this, see *ante*, para. 5–47.

[95] Housing Act 1985, ss.171A–171H, inserted by Housing and Planning Act 1986, s.8. These came into force on April 5, 1989 (not January 7, 1987, as wrongly stated in Vol. 1, p. 361, n.56): Housing and Planning Act 1986 (Commencement No. 13) Order 1989 (S.I. 1989 No. 430). The provisions have been amended successively by Act of 1988, ss.127(1), 140(1), Sched. 17, para. 42; Leasehold Reform, Housing and Urban Development Act 1993, Sched. 21, para. 19, Sched. 22; Family Law Act 1996, s.66(1), Sched. 8, paras. 34, 56; and by Housing Act 1996, ss.222, 232(2), (3), Sched. 18, paras. 16, 26 (S.I. 1996 No. 2402).

[96] See Vol. 1, p. 361.

right to buy,[97] and to the case where an order for possession against the tenant is made on the ground that suitable alternative accommodation is available.[98] The rights of some assured and secure tenants of registered social landlords[99] after April 1, 1997 to acquire the dwellings of which they are tenants in some circumstances are not subject to any such preservation of rights in the event of a transfer of the landlord's interest to the private sector.[1]

It might be added that the "right of first refusal" which many tenants of flats enjoy under Part I of the Landlord and Tenant Act 1987 is not given to assured tenants.[2]

3. Housing association tenancies

5–62 If a tenancy was entered into before January 15, 1989 (or pursuant to a contract made before then), and it was then a housing association tenancy, the effect of the subsequent transfer of the interest of the landlord depends on the identity of the new landlord.

(a) Remaining housing association tenancy

5–63 If the new landlord is in the housing association group, so that the tenancy can still be a housing association tenancy,[3] it will remain a housing association tenancy.[4]

(b) Remaining secure tenancy

5–64 After January 15, 1989, for so long as the interest of the landlord remained vested in the landlord in the housing association group, the tenancy remained both a housing association tenancy and a secure tenancy.[5] If, at a later time, the interest is transferred to a landlord capable of satisfying the "landlord condition",[6] the tenancy remains secure, but ceases to be a housing association tenancy, and cannot thereafter become a housing association tenancy again.[7]

[97] Act of 1988, s.127, amending Housing Act 1985, ss.171B(4), 171C(2)(a), and inserting s.171C(5). Housing Act 1985, s.171B(4) was further amended with effect from October 1, 1997 by Family Law Act 1996, s.66(1), Sched. 8, para. 56; S.I. 1997 No. 1892.

[98] Act of 1988, Sched. 17, para. 42, extending Housing Act 1985, s.171F (see Vol. 1, p. 362) to alternative accommodation under Act of 1988, Sched. 2, Ground 9; *post*, paras. 15–06 *et seq.*

[99] Under Housing Act 1996, Pt. I, Chap. I.

[1] Housing Act 1996, ss.16(1), 17(2), 232(3); S.I. 1997 No. 618; Housing (Right to Acquire) Regulations 1997 (S.I. 1997 No. 619), reg. 2(1), Sched. 1, para. 27.

[2] Act of 1988, Sched. 13, para. 2(1), excluding assured tenancies and assured agricultural occupancies by adding para. (d) to Landlord and Tenant Act 1987, s.3(1).

[3] *Ante*, para. 5–25.

[4] For under Act of 1988, s.38(2)(b), it has not ceased to be a housing association tenancy, and so s.38(3) does not apply. "Housing association tenancy" here means a tenancy to which Act of 1977, Pt. VI, applies: Act of 1988, s.38(6). See *ante*, para. 5–58, for a further case in which a tenancy can remain a housing association tenancy.

[5] Act of 1988, Sched. 18, n.4(a).

[6] In Housing Act 1985, s.80, as amended to exclude the housing association group.

[7] Act of 1988, s.38(2), (3)(b).

(c) Becoming assured tenancy

5–65 If the new landlord is not in the housing association group nor capable of satisfying the landlord condition, the tenancy will cease to be a housing association tenancy, and will normally become an assured tenancy, even though it was granted before January 15, 1989.[8] Such a tenancy can never become a protected tenancy, a protected occupancy, or become a housing association tenancy again; and it can become a secure tenancy only if (and while) the interest of the landlord is held by a public body, as defined.[9]

[8] Act of 1988, s.38(2), (3)(c), excluding Sched. 1, para. 1.
[9] *ibid.*, s.38(3), (5), defining "public body" for these purposes.

Chapter 6

Assured Tenancies

The detailed provisions relating to assured tenancies are discussed in their appropriate places in this book. This Chapter serves as an outline of the nature of assured tenancies, their creation, their terms, and their termination.

Sect. 1. Nature

1. Contractual

6–01 It is of the essence of assured tenancies that they are contractual tenancies. Subject to those provisions of the Act of 1988 which give assured tenants a limited but important measure of protection, both at law and in equity an assured tenancy is an ordinary tenancy that is governed by the ordinary law of landlord and tenant, and it is held upon whatever terms the parties have agreed. A tenancy by estoppel is capable of being an assured tenancy.[1] The concept of the statutory tenancy under the Rent Acts plays no part in assured tenancies. There is indeed what is known as a "statutory periodic tenancy" which generally arises at the end of an assured tenancy for a fixed term; but notwithstanding its name, this too is a contractual tenancy, despite having been brought into being by statute deeming it to have been granted. It is considered in the next Chapter.[2]

2. Assured tenancies and assured shorthold tenancies

(a) Assured tenancies: fixed term or periodic

6–02 Assured tenancies are either fixed term tenancies or periodic tenancies. A "fixed term tenancy" is "any tenancy other than a periodic tenancy".[3] For this purpose

[1] But no estoppel arises where the parties expressly grant a licence, knowing that the licensor does not have a legal estate out of which to grant a tenancy: *Bruton v. London & Quadrant Housing Trust* [1998] Q.B. 834, CA. An appeal to the House of Lords is pending.

[2] *Post*, Chap. 7, pp. 100 *et seq*.

[3] Act of 1988, s.45(1).

a tenancy at will or a tenancy at sufferance[4] is accordingly a fixed term tenancy; but a tenancy by estoppel may be either a periodic tenancy or a fixed term tenancy, according to its nature. A tenancy for a fixed term and thereafter from year to year is therefore probably a fixed term tenancy, though once the fixed term has expired it is better regarded as a periodic tenancy. The Act of 1988 treats fixed term tenancies and periodic tenancies differently in certain respects, but most of the provisions apply to each of them.

(b) Assured shorthold tenancies

An assured shorthold tenancy used to be a fixed term tenancy granted for a term of not less than six months which complied with certain preconditions when it was granted. But now most assured tenancies[5] are assured shorthold tenancies, regardless of whether they are fixed term or periodic, and there are no preconditions to their grant. An assured shorthold tenancy is an ordinary assured tenancy that is subject to some special provisions, including a mandatory ground for possession and a measure of rent control. If when a shorthold tenancy ends it is replaced by a further tenancy of the same premises between the same parties, the new tenancy will also be an assured shorthold tenancy. Now that there are no preconditions to the grant of an assured shorthold tenancy, however, the distinction between "original" assured shorthold tenancies and "derivative"[6] assured shorthold tenancies is less important. But the change in the law relating to the creation of assured shorthold tenancies has given rise to a further distinction of some importance between "new" assured shorthold tenancies[7] and "old" assured shorthold tenancies.[8] **6–03**

(c) Comparative merits

From the point of view of the landlord (who normally will decide what form of tenancy is to be granted), there are two major points of contrast between assured tenancies and assured shorthold tenancies. First, under an assured tenancy the landlord can normally recover possession of the dwelling only on the grounds for possession specified in the Act of 1988.[9] On the other hand, under an assured shorthold tenancy the landlord, subject to giving due notice in writing, is entitled to possession as of right at the end of the fixed term or, if the tenancy is periodic, when a notice to quit would have expired.[10] Secondly, under an assured tenancy **6–04**

[4] See *ante*, para. 3–01.

[5] Tenancies entered into on or after February 28, 1997, other than pursuant to a contract made before that day, save for certain excluded tenancies: Act of 1988, s.19A, inserted by Housing Act 1996, ss.96, 232(3); S.I. 1997 No. 225. For a detailed treatment, see *post*, Chap. 8, pp. 110 *et seq.*

[6] *i.e.* those that follow on from "original" tenancies.

[7] *i.e.* those entered into on or after February 28, 1997 otherwise than pursuant to a contract made before that date, and those statutory periodic assured shorthold tenancies which come into being under Act of 1988, s.5 on the coming of an end of a "new" shorthold tenancy: Act of 1988, s.19A.

[8] *i.e.* assured shorthold tenancies other than "new" assured shorthold tenancies.

[9] See *post*, para. 13–40.

[10] See *post*, paras. 14–78 *et seq.*

the tenant initially has no right to refer the rent to a rent assessment committee or any other body;[11] and although the tenant may refer the rent to the rent assessment committee if the tenancy is a periodic tenancy and the landlord seeks to exercise his statutory power to increase the rent,[12] the rent fixed by the committee will not be lower than the open market rent.[13] Under an original old assured shorthold tenancy (as distinct from a derivative old or a new assured shorthold tenancy) the tenant may at any time refer the rent to a rent assessment committee. Under a new assured shorthold tenancy, the tenant may refer the rent to a rent assessment committee at any time before six months from the beginning of the original shorthold tenancy have expired. However, unless the rent is "significantly higher" than the rent reasonably obtainable for the dwelling-house (having regard to other assured shorthold tenancies in the locality), and there is a sufficiency of "comparables", the committee must not make any determination.[14]

6–05 With the absence of any restriction under the Act of 1988 to "fair rents", the main burden of possible proceedings before a rent assessment committee probably lies in the cost and inconvenience of being required to take part in them; and that is generally regarded a small price to pay for the certainty of obtaining possession. Certainly, the practice during the first 10 years of existence of assured tenancies was that the vast majority of such tenancies created were assured shorthold tenancies, and that occasions when the rent agreed was reduced by a rent assessment committee were very few. Parliament has reflected the practice of creating shorthold tenancies in the Housing Act 1996, which introduced new assured shorthold tenancies; and under the Rent Acts the primacy of open market rental evidence has been established as the necessary starting point for consideration of fair rents under those Acts. In the light of these developments, the primacy of assured shorthold tenancies is highly likely to continue.

3. Mutability of status

6–06 An assured tenancy is an assured tenancy only "if and so long as"[15] it satisfies the requirements of the Act of 1988. These requirements have already been considered: there must be a "tenancy" of a "dwelling-house" which is "let as a separate dwelling" to an "individual" who occupies it as "his only or principal home", and the tenancy also must not fall within any of the statutory exceptions. The importance of the phrase "if and so long as" has already been stressed.[16] It makes it clear that a tenancy may from time to time move into and out of the status of being an assured tenancy as frequently as the statutory requirements are satisfied and cease to be satisfied, for example where the

[11] See *post*, paras. 17–01.
[12] No increase can be made before the end of the first year of the tenancy.
[13] See *post*, paras. 17–30.
[14] See *post*, paras. 18–11, 18–12.
[15] Act of 1988, s.1(1); see *ante*, p. 16.
[16] *Ante*, p. 16.

amount of the rent is varied,[17] or the tenancy becomes a business tenancy and then ceases to be such.[18] No doubt few tenancies will shuttle in and out of the status of assured tenancy from day to day, but it is important to realise that although a tenancy may continue in being, its status as an assured tenancy is far from being immutably attached to it. The question whether or not a tenancy is an assured tenancy must be determined as at whatever is the relevant time for the purpose in point, *e.g.*, whether a proposed increase in rent can be referred to a rent assessment committee, or whether an order for possession can be made against the tenant.[19]

Sect. 2. Creation

Although an assured tenancy is a contractual tenancy, a new assured tenancy may arise in various ways, of which express agreement is only one. These are each considered elsewhere in this volume, but they may be summarised here. They are: **6–07**

(1) By the grant of a tenancy on or after January 15, 1989 (other than pursuant to a contract made before then) which complies with the statutory requirements for an assured tenancy.[20]
(2) By the automatic conversion of old assured tenancies under previous legislation into assured tenancies under the Act of 1988. Except in two instances, this takes place even for tenancies which fall within the list of statutory exceptions from being an assured tenancy.[21]
(3) By a change of landlord which transfers a tenancy from the public sector to the private sector, and thereby normally converts the tenancy into an assured tenancy.[22]
(4) On a transmission on death under the Acts of 1976 or 1977, as now amended.[23]
(5) By the statutory, deemed grant of a periodic tenancy upon expiry of a fixed term assured tenancy.[23a]

Sect. 3. Terms

In general, the terms of an assured tenancy are whatever terms the parties have **6–08**

[17] *R. v. London Rent Assessment Panel, ex p. Cadogan Estates Ltd.* [1998] Q.B. 398, QB. See *ante*, paras. 14–07, 4–58.
[18] According to whether the conditions of Landlord and Tenant Act 1954, s.23(1) are satisfied: see *ante*, para. 4–13.
[19] See *post*, Chaps. 13, 17.
[20] See *ante*, pp. 15 *et seq.*
[21] See *ante*, paras. 5–02 *et seq.*
[22] See *ante*, paras. 5–59, 5–65.
[23] See *post*, paras. 12–18 *et seq.*, 12–30 *et seq.*
[23a] Under Act of 1988, s.5(2); post, paras. 7–02 *et seq.*

agreed, whether as to rent or any other matter. But this is subject to the provisions of the Act of 1988, which in a number of respects modify the agreed terms either by varying or invalidating them or by inserting implied terms into the tenancy. These provisions will be considered in their appropriate places in this volume, and only their general nature will be indicated here. An assured tenancy is subject to the following:

(1) Provisions giving security of tenure.[24] These essentially prevent termination of the tenancy except on limited grounds, or in such a way as to give rise to the implied grant of a new tenancy.
(2) The invalidation of terms for terminating or modifying the tenant's right to share the use of living accommodation.[25]
(3) For certain periodic tenancies, implied terms prohibiting the tenant from assigning, sub-letting or parting with possession of the dwelling-house or any part of it.[26]
(4) For periodic tenancies, a provision that on the death of the tenant the tenancy will vest in his or her surviving spouse and not devolve under the will or intestacy.[27]
(5) A right for the tenant under a periodic assured tenancy which makes no contractual provision for increasing the rent to refer a landlord's statutory notice of increase to the rent assessment committee.[28]
(6) For statutory periodic tenancies, a power for the rent assessment committee to vary the terms of the tenancy.[29]

In addition, it is an implied term of every assured tenancy that the tenant will "afford to the landlord access to the dwelling-house let on the tenancy and all reasonable facilities for executing thereon any repairs which the landlord is entitled to execute".[30] Like the corresponding provision for statutory tenants,[31] this is confined to "repairs" which the landlord is "entitled" to execute, and so does not embrace "improvements" that he merely "wishes" to effect. An assured tenancy for a term of less than seven years will, like a protected tenancy of similar length or a secure tenancy, be subject to the landlord's statutorily implied repairing obligations.[32] And assured tenancies like other tenancies will be subject to terms implied at common law, such as the landlord's obligation not to derogate from grant and the tenant's obligation to use the dwelling-house in a tenant-like manner.

[24] *Post*, pp. 204–302.
[25] *Ante*, para. 3–21.
[26] *Post*, pp. 174 *et seq.*
[27] *Post*, paras. 12–02 to 12–09 *et seq.*
[28] *Post*, paras. 17–16 *et seq.*
[29] *Post*, paras. 7–14 *et seq.*
[30] Act of 1988, s.16.
[31] Act of 1977, s.3(2), discussed in Vol. 1, p. 264. Access and occupation should be limited to what is necessary: see *McGreal v. Wake* (1984) 13 H.L.R. 107, CA.
[32] Under Landlord and Tenant Act 1985, ss.11–14.

Sect. 4. Determination

In the Act of 1988, the basic provision that confers security of tenure on assured tenants is that "an assured tenancy cannot be brought to an end by the landlord except by obtaining an order of the court"[33] in accordance with Chapters I and II of the Act.[34] This provision applies only to the landlord: it does not affect determination of the tenancy by the tenant, and he remains free to terminate the tenancy in accordance with the common law,[35] as by a notice to quit[36] or by surrender.[37] A tenant who does so will be protected neither by contract nor by statute.[38] **6–09**

1. Periodic tenancies

For periodic assured tenancies, the basic provision operates without qualification. It is emphasised by the addition of an express provision that "accordingly, the service by the landlord of a notice to quit shall be of no effect in relation to a periodic assured tenancy".[39] Security of tenure is thus provided by the statutory prolongation of the contract of tenancy, notwithstanding the service of an otherwise valid notice to quit by the landlord. This concept has some similarity to the provisions previously made for security of tenure under "old" restricted contracts,[40] under business tenancies pending the grant of a new tenancy,[41] and for long tenancies under Part I of the Landlord and Tenant Act 1954 or Schedule 10 to the Local Government and Housing Act 1989.[42] For periodic tenancies (unlike fixed term tenancies[43]) there is nothing that in terms applies to a power for the landlord "to determine the tenancy in certain circumstances" (for example under a break clause). Such powers have hitherto been rare in periodic tenancies, but landlords would gain little from introducing them now; for even **6–10**

[33] Act of 1988, s.5(1).
[34] *i.e.* ss.6–12 and 21 in particular.
[35] See *Greenwich L.B.C. v. McGrady* (1982) 46 P. & C.R. 223 at 224, CA; *R. v. L. B. Croydon, ex p. Toth* (1986) 18 H.L.R. 493 at 499, QB (affirmed (1987) 20 H.L.R. 576, CA) on secure tenancies under the similar wording of Housing Act 1980, s.32(1), now replaced by Housing Act 1985, s.82(1).
[36] For notices to quit, see Vol. 1, pp. 232, 411.
[37] In theory, it is the landlord who brings the tenancy to an end by accepting the surrender: but the substance is the surrender by the tenant, as Act of 1988, s.5(2) assumes; and see the *ex p. Toth* case, *supra*. In recent years, surrender by operation of law has been frequently invoked as the basis for the termination of a tenancy (see *Chamberlain v. Scalley* (1992) 26 H.L.R. 26, CA, *Camden L.B.C. v. Alexandrou* (1997) 30 H.L.R. 534, CA, and *Mattey Securities Ltd. v. Ervin* (1998) 77 P. & C. R. 160, CA in the residential arena), and the doctrine certainly applies in principle to an assured tenancy.
[38] Contrast Case 5 under the Rent Acts, where a notice to quit would only terminate the contractual tenancy, leaving the statutory tenancy and a discretionary ground for possession: Vol. 1, pp. 410–412.
[39] Act of 1988, s.5(1).
[40] See Vol. 1, pp. 797–801; but there the protection is tied to notices to quit, and is not general.
[41] Landlord and Tenant Act 1954, ss. 24, 64; see *Bowes-Lyon v. Green* [1963] A.C. 420 at 434.
[42] *Ante*, para. 5–41.
[43] *Infra.*

if the exercise of such a power is not a notice to quit,[44] it would still be subject to the general prohibition against the tenancy being brought to an end by the landlord.

2. Fixed term tenancies

6–11 For assured tenancies for a fixed term, there is a limited alternative in the operation of the basic statutory provision. Such a tenancy "cannot be brought to an end by the landlord except"—

(a) "by obtaining an order of the court", or
(b) "in the case of a fixed term tenancy which contains power for the landlord to determine the tenancy in certain circumstances, by the exercise of that power".[45]

The power under (b) above is expressed generally, and it would plainly include a "break" clause in a tenancy. But for the avoidance of doubt the Act of 1988 declares that this expression "does not include a reference to a power of re-entry or forfeiture for breach of any term or condition of the tenancy".[46] Accordingly, an attempted forfeiture by the landlord for non-payment of rent or breach of covenant will not bring the tenancy to an end[46a]; instead, the landlord will have to seek an order of the court, and this may be made on various mandatory or discretionary grounds.[47] For other powers,[48] however, the landlord may still bring the tenancy to an end by exercising the power. Yet if he does this, the tenant will thereupon become entitled to remain in possession under a "statutory periodic tenancy",[49] and so the landlord will only have brought about the substitution of one tenancy for another.

6–12 As stated above,[50] these provisions of the Act of 1988 apply only to determination by the landlord. They do not prevent the tenancy from coming to an end in any other way, as by effluxion of time or by an act of the tenant such as operating a break clause or surrendering the tenancy. But in these cases, unless the tenancy is brought to an end by the tenant or by the court, the tenant will again be entitled to remain in possession under a statutory periodic tenancy;[51] and this will therefore be so if the tenancy terminates by effluxion of time.

[44] As it may be (see Vol. 1, p. 791); yet in Act of 1988, s.5(1), the contrast between "the exercise of that power" and "service . . . of a notice to quit" is sharp.
[45] Act of 1988, s.5(1).
[46] *ibid.*, s.45(4). For difficulties in this provision, see *post*, paras. 13–10 *et seq*.
[46a] *Artesian Residential Investments Ltd. v. Beck* [1999] E.G.C.S. 46, CA.
[47] See, *e.g.*, Ground 8 (mandatory: two months' arrears of rent), Ground 10 (discretionary: arrears of rent); Ground 11 (discretionary: persistent delays in payment of rent); Ground 12 (discretionary: breach or non-performance of obligation of tenancy other than for rent); *post*, paras. 14–70, 15–17, 15–20, 15–21.
[48] Probably including a power to determine a tenancy at will, for such a power is intrinsic, and so a tenancy at will probably "contains" it.
[49] Act of 1988, s.5(2); *post*, paras. 7–02 *et seq*.
[50] *Ante*, para. 6–09.
[51] *Supra*, and *post*, para. 7–04.

3. Curb on evasion

Landlords might exploit the tenant's unrestricted ability to terminate the tenancy by refusing to grant a tenancy unless the tenant first undertook to terminate it in certain events, or signed documents that could be used to terminate it. The Act of 1988 accordingly provides that if, on or before the date on which the tenancy is entered into (or, for a statutory periodic tenancy, is deemed to be granted), the tenant enters into ''an obligation to do any act'' which ''will cause the tenancy to come to an end'' while it is an assured tenancy, or ''executes, signs or gives any surrender, notice to quit or other document'' which would have the effect of doing this, the obligation will be unenforceable, and the document will be of no effect.[52] **6–13**

It is not clear whether ''obligation'' here includes a contingent or conditional obligation. For example, a lease might provide that if the tenant wishes to assign it he must first offer to surrender it to the landlord.[53] There, the tenant comes under no obligation to do an act that will cause the tenancy to come to an end unless he seeks to assign it, and so probably the obligation is valid.[54] But even if this does invoke the statute, an inducement is not an obligation, so that the statute would not apply if the lease provides for a progressive rent,[55] or for the tenant to be subject to some additional burden such as repairs at some future date, so that when the time comes this will persuade the tenant to exercise an option to surrender the tenancy. Nor does the statute apply to any obligation entered into or document signed after the date when the tenancy was entered into or was deemed to be granted; and it is directed solely to the tenancy coming to an end, and not to its ceasing to be assured.

[52] Act of 1988, s.5(5).

[53] See *Bocardo S.A. v. S. & M. Hotels Ltd.* [1980] 1 W.L.R. 17, CA.

[54] On the basis that the tenant is not under any *obligation* to do the act which *apart from the subsection* will cause the tenancy to end, nor has he signed any *other* document which has that effect.

[55] *i.e.* a rent which automatically rises during the tenancy, whether at fixed dates or on contingencies happening: see *Wheeler v. Wirral Estates Ltd.* [1935] 1 K.B. 294 at 300, CA; *Bryanston Property Co. Ltd. v. Edwards* [1944] K.B. 32 at 36, CA.

Chapter 7

Statutory Periodic Tenancies

7–01 If an assured tenancy which is a fixed term tenancy is terminated by order of the court, or by surrender or other action by the tenant, the tenancy ends, and no statutory periodic tenancy arises. But if the tenancy expires by effluxion of time, or is determined by the landlord without any order of the court, in most cases a "statutory periodic tenancy" arises under the Act of 1988. These tenancies have already been briefly mentioned,[1] and they will now be examined in greater detail.

Sect. 1. Creation

7–02 A statutory periodic tenancy is "deemed to have been granted"[2] if three conditions are satisfied. The tenancy arises automatically by virtue of the Act of 1988,[3] without any actual grant or other act. The conditions are the following.

1. Assured fixed term tenancy

7–03 There must be "an assured tenancy which is a fixed term tenancy".[4] As has been seen, every tenancy is a fixed term tenancy if it is not a periodic tenancy.[5] The tenancy will be an assured tenancy on its determination only if the requirements for such tenancies[6] are all satisfied then.

[1] *Ante*, para. 6–01.
[2] Act of 1988, s.5(3)(b). References to a "statutory periodic tenancy" in Act of 1988, Pt. I are to a periodic tenancy arising under s.5: ss.5(7), 45(1).
[3] *ibid.*, s.5(2).
[4] *ibid.*
[5] *ibid.*, s.45(1); *ante*, para. 6–02.
[6] *Ante*, pp. 23–64.

2. Tenancy terminated

The assured term tenancy must have come to an end otherwise than by virtue of "an order of the court" or "a surrender or other action on the part of the tenant".[7] Thus this requirement will be satisfied by the tenancy ending on the expiration of the fixed term, or by its being terminated by the landlord under a power of a determination which is not a provision for forfeiture or re-entry.[8] **7–04**

3. No new tenancy

No statutory periodic tenancy will arise if at the end of the fixed term tenancy the tenant is entitled under another tenancy to possession of the same dwelling-house (or substantially the same) as was let to him under the fixed term tenancy.[9] So, if the tenant was granted a reversionary tenancy before the end of the fixed term tenancy, his interest in the dwelling-house upon the termination of the fixed term will be under that reversionary tenancy, and not under a statutory periodic tenancy. But unless the reversionary tenancy is made in writing at least, containing all the terms agreed and signed by the parties or their lawfully authorised agents, the reversionary tenancy will be an interest at will only, and not a tenancy;[10] and in such a case the statutory periodic tenancy would prevail. **7–05**

Sect. 2. Nature

1. "Grant"

A statutory periodic tenancy is a periodic tenancy which by statute is "deemed to have been granted" by the landlord to the tenant at the end of the fixed term tenancy.[11] It is therefore a contractual interest and an estate in land, and very different from a statutory tenancy under the Rent Acts, for that is not a true tenancy but merely a personal right of occupation, or a status of irremovability.[12] Nor is it a statutory prolongation of the previous tenancy, as is the case with business tenancies pending the grant of a new tenancy,[13] restricted contracts, where periodic tenancies are prolonged by notices to quit being made temporar- **7–06**

[7] Act of 1988, s.5(2); compare Housing Act 1985, s.86.
[8] *ibid.*, ss.5(1), (2), 45(4); *ante*, para. 6–11; *post*, paras. 13–10 *et seq.*
[9] Act of 1988, s.5(4).
[10] Law of Property Act 1925, s.54(1), the exception in *ibid.*, s.54(2) not applying to reversionary tenancies: see *Long v. Tower Hamlets L.B.C.* [1998] Ch. 197, CA. In such circumstances, the lack of a deed will not prevent there being an enforceable agreement for a lease, which is a tenancy for these purposes: Law of Property Act 1925, s.52(1); Law of Property (Miscellaneous Provisions) Act 1989, s.2; Act of 1988, ss.5(4), 45(1).
[11] Act of 1988, s.5(3)(b).
[12] See Vol. 1, pp. 252–255.
[13] Landlord and Tenant Act 1954, ss. 24, 64; see *Bowes-Lyon v. Green* [1963] A.C. 420 at 434.

ily ineffective,[14] or with periodic assured tenancies under the Act of 1988 itself.[15] A statutory periodic tenancy is a new tenancy, deemed by statute to have been created by grant; and like other tenancies created by grant, it is a contractual tenancy.

2. Assured or not

7–07 Initially, a statutory periodic tenancy will be an assured tenancy, since the fixed term tenancy out of which it arose was necessarily an assured tenancy upon its termination.[16] Thereafter, the statutory periodic tenancy will only be an assured tenancy "if and so long as" it satisfies the statutory requirements for assured tenancies.[17] But in some cases these requirements are reduced. If the fixed term tenancy was an old assured tenancy which became an assured tenancy under the Act of 1988, or was a new tenancy granted by the court to an old assured tenant,[18] the fixed term tenancy was subject to only two of the exceptions from being an assured tenancy, namely Crown tenancies and tenancies held from local authorities or other exempted bodies.[19] In such cases, the statutory periodic tenancy is similarly subject only to the same two exceptions.[20] The mutable nature of statutory periodic tenancies is recognised by certain provisions of the Act of 1988 for statutory periodic tenancies which are not to have effect "while the tenancy remains an assured tenancy",[21] or are not to apply to a statutory periodic tenancy "at a time when . . . it cannot be an assured tenancy".[22] A statutory periodic tenancy does not come to an end merely because it ceases to be assured, and it will continue until properly determined.

Sect. 3. Terms

The terms of a statutory periodic tenancy are laid down by the Act of 1988.[23]

1. Parties

7–08 The tenancy is "deemed to have been granted by the person who was the landlord under the fixed term tenancy immediately before it came to an end to the

[14] See Vol. 1, pp. 797–801, applicable only to "old" restricted contracts.
[15] See *ante*, para. 6–10.
[16] Act of 1988, s.5(2); *ante*, para. 7–03.
[17] *Ante*, p. 16.
[18] Act of 1988, ss.1(3), 37(3).
[19] *ibid*., ss.1(4)(a), 37(5); and see *ante*, pp. 50–54.
[20] *ibid*., s.5(6).
[21] *ibid*., s.5(3)(e); see *post*, para. 7–12.
[22] *ibid*., s.6(1); see *post*, para. 7–15.
[23] *ibid*., s.5(3).

person who was then the tenant under that tenancy''.[24] ''Landlord'' is widely defined,[25] but here there is no scope for ambiguity because there cannot be a change between the end of the fixed term tenancy and the moment of grant of the statutory periodic tenancy.[26] Where there are joint landlords or joint tenants, ''landlord'' means all the joint landlords, and ''tenant'' means all the joint tenants.[27]

2. Premises

The premises let under the statutory periodic tenancy are the same dwelling-house as ''was let'' under the fixed term tenancy.[28] This seems to refer to the dwelling-house as it was at the end of the fixed term tenancy, and not as it was when it was initially let under it. **7–09**

3. Commencement

The tenancy takes effect immediately on the coming to an end of the fixed term tenancy.[29] **7–10**

4. Periods

The periods of the tenancy will be ''the same as those for which rent was last payable under the fixed term tenancy''.[30] Thus, where the fixed term tenancy was held at a yearly rent payable by quarterly instalments, the statutory periodic tenancy will be a quarterly tenancy and not a yearly tenancy. **7–11**

5. Other terms

All the other terms of the tenancy will be ''the same as those of the fixed term tenancy immediately before it came to an end''.[31] Thus, if the terms of the fixed term tenancy have been varied, it is the terms as varied that will be carried into the statutory periodic tenancy. Terms as to rent are included in this provision,[32] but there may be some difficulty about covenants to do acts at a particular time or within a stated period, *e.g.*, to decorate the premises between December 1 **7–12**

[24] Act of 1988, s.5(3)(b).
[25] *ibid.*, s.45(1) (any person from time to time deriving title under the original landlord, and any person who is or would be entitled to possession but for the tenant's interest).
[26] *Infra.*
[27] Act of 1988, s.45(3).
[28] *ibid.*, s.5(3)(c).
[29] *ibid.*, s.5(3)(a).
[30] *ibid.*, s.5(3)(d).
[31] *ibid.*, s.5(3)(e).
[32] This seems a necessary inference from Act of 1988, s.6(1)(b), but is subject to the express provision of the Act about periods for payment of rent, *supra.*

and December 31, 1995, or to paint the interior in every fourth year of the term. "Any term which makes provision for determination by the landlord or the tenant"[33] (not being a power of re-entry or forfeiture for breach of any term or condition of the tenancy[34]) is subject to a special rule. Such a term does not "have effect while the tenancy remains an assured tenancy".[35] This wording suggests that although the term will be included in the statutory periodic tenancy, it will be inoperative as long as that tenancy is an assured tenancy, but that thereafter it will be effective at least until the tenancy again becomes an assured tenancy.

7–13 This provision for incorporating the terms of the fixed term tenancy takes effect subject to certain other provisions.[36] This allows the tenancy to be subject to the statutory provisions, applicable to all statutory periodic tenancies, which prohibit any assignment or sub-letting without the landlord's consent. These provisions will be considered later.[37] This provision also appears to prevent any clause for increasing the rent being included so as to oust the statutory provisions for this purpose. This also will be considered later.[38]

Sect. 4. Variation of Terms

7–14 At any time within a year of a statutory periodic tenancy being deemed to be granted, either party may seek to have the terms of the tenancy varied under a statutory procedure.

1. Tenancies

7–15 With two exceptions, the statutory procedure applies to all statutory periodic tenancies, whether or not they are assured tenancies.[39] The exceptions are tenancies which for the time being cannot be assured tenancies by virtue of being either Crown tenancies or tenancies held from local authorities or other exempted bodies.[40]

2. Terms within the procedure

7–16 The statutory procedure does not apply to the provisions relating to the commencement of the tenancy, the parties, the premises demised, the periods of the

[33] Act of 1988, s.5(3)(e).
[34] *ibid.*, s.45(4).
[35] *ibid.*, s.5(3)(e).
[36] "Subject to the following provisions of this Part of this Act" (*i.e.* Part I of the Act of 1988), namely ss.5(4)–45: s.5(3)(e).
[37] *Post*, Chap. 10, pp. 174 *et seq.*
[38] *Post*, para. 17–06
[39] Act of 1988, s.6(1), assuming the proposition without expressly stating it.
[40] *ibid.*, applying Sched. 1, paras. 11, 12; *ante*, pp. 50–54.

tenancy, or (with important qualifications) the amount of the rent.[41] But it does apply to all the other implied terms which are imported from the previous fixed term tenancy into the statutory periodic tenancy on its creation.[42]

3. Procedure

(a) Notice of variation

The first step for the party seeking a variation is for him to serve a notice on the other "proposing terms of the statutory periodic tenancy different from the implied terms"; and if the party serving the notice considers it appropriate, the notice may also propose "an adjustment of the amount of the rent to take account of the proposed terms".[43] An application to vary the amount of the rent must normally be made under different procedures,[44] but it can be made under this head if it is merely ancillary to an application to vary other implied terms of the tenancy. **7–17**

Any notice of variation must be served not later than the "first anniversary of the day on which the former tenancy came to an end".[45] The notice must be in the prescribed form,[46] and must specify a date from which the proposed terms are to take effect.[47] The prescribed form is Form No. 1 contained in the Schedule to the 1997 Forms Regulations,[48] or a form substantially to the same effect.[49] Where there are joint landlords or joint tenants, the form must be signed by or on behalf of all of them, or by one of them on behalf of the others[50] with their agreement.[51] There is nothing that prevents a person served with such a notice **7–18**

[41] Act of 1988, s.6(1)(b); see *infra*.

[42] *i.e.* those imported by Act of 1988, s.5(3)(e); *ante*, para. 7–12. In s.6, "the former tenancy" means the fixed term tenancy which, on ending, gave rise to the statutory periodic tenancy: s.6(1)(a).

[43] Act of 1988, s.6(2).

[44] *Post*, paras. 17–16 *et seq.*, 18–04 *et seq.*

[45] Act of 1988, s.6(2). Being statutory, the time limits cannot be extended: see *Donegal Tweed Co. v. Stephenson* (1929) 98 L.J.K.B. 657, DC.

[46] Act of 1988, s.6(2); Assured Tenancies and Agricultural Occupancies (Forms) Regulations 1997 (S.I. 1997 No. 194), reg. 3(a), Sched., Form No. 1. In Part I of the Act of 1988, "prescribed" means prescribed by regulations made by the Secretary of State by statutory instrument; and such regulations may make different provision with respect to different cases or descriptions of case, including different provision for different areas: s.45(1), (5).

[47] *ibid.*; Act of 1988, s.6(3)(b).

[48] S.I. 1997 No. 194, *supra*.

[49] *ibid.*, reg. 2. The change in the prescribed forms with effect from February 28, 1997—the 1997 Forms Regulations replaced and revoked for the future the Assured Tenancies and Agricultural Occupancies (Forms) Regulations 1988 ("the 1988 Forms Regulations"), as amended—has given rise to predictable litigation over whether a corresponding form under the 1988 Forms Regulations is to substantially the same effect as the correct form in the 1997 Forms Regulations. In relation to other such forms changes, the courts have shown themselves predisposed to accept, where possible, the previous corresponding form: see, *e.g.*, *Beckerman v. Durling* (1981) 6 H.L.R. 87, CA (notice to quit prescribed information); *Sun Alliance and London Insurance Co. Ltd. v. Hayman* [1975] 1 W.L.R. 177, CA; *Morris v. Patel* [1987] 1 E.G.L.R. 75, CA (business tenancy notices to terminate).

[50] And presumably of himself as well.

[51] Act of 1988, s.45(3); Form No. 1, *supra*.

from himself serving such a notice on the other party, proposing different variations of the terms of the tenancy. Nor, if still within time, does there seem to be anything to prevent a party who has served one notice from serving another if, for example, he has become dissatisfied with the terms proposed in the first notice.

(b) Response

7–19 (i) REFERENCE. Within three months of the date of service, the party served may refer the notice to a rent assessment committee.[52] This must be done by an application made in the prescribed form.[53]

7–20 (ii) VARIATION. If no such reference is made, the terms proposed in the notice will become terms of the tenancy in substitution for any of the implied terms dealing with the same subject matter, and the amount of the rent will be varied in accordance with the proposed adjustment.[54] These changes take effect from the date specified in the notice, which must be at least three months after the notice is served.[55] If landlord and tenant serve notices on each other, and neither notice is referred to the rent assessment committee within the three months, each notice will apparently vary the terms of the tenancy on the date specified in the notice, so that the variations made on the earlier date will soon be ousted by the variations made on the later date.

4. Rent assessment committee

(a) Consideration

7–21 Where a notice has been referred to a rent assessment committee, the committee must serve a notice on each party, providing an opportunity of making representations in writing or seeking an oral hearing; and the committee may also require each party to provide information.[56] The committee will usually then consider the terms proposed in the notice and duly determine the matter.[57] But if the tenancy has come to an end, or if the parties have given notice in writing that they no longer require such a determination, nothing in the relevant provisions[58] "requires" the committee to continue with a determination.[59] Such a withdrawal will usually terminate the proceedings; but probably it does not

[52] Act of 1988, s.6(3)(a).
[53] *ibid.*; 1997 Forms Regulations (S.I. 1997 No. 194), reg. 3(b), Sched., Form No. 2, or a form substantially to the same effect. The requirements for signature are the same as for the initial notice; and the time limit cannot be extended: *supra*.
[54] Act of 1988, s.6(3)(b).
[55] *ibid.*, and see Form No. 1, *supra*.
[56] For the details, see *post*, para. 17–17.
[57] Act of 1988, s.6(4).
[58] *i.e.* those of Act of 1988, s.6.
[59] *ibid.*, s.6(8).

deprive the committee of jurisdiction, so that they might nevertheless proceed, for instance if it appeared that the agreement was procured by undue pressure.[60]

(b) Determination of terms

The Act requires the committee to consider the terms proposed in the notice,[61] and then to determine whether those terms, or some other terms that deal with the same subject matter as the terms, satisfy certain criteria. The committee must determine whether the terms are such as, in the committee's opinion, "might reasonably be expected to be found in an assured periodic tenancy of the dwelling-house concerned", that tenancy being one which— **7–22**

(1) began when the former tenancy ended;
(2) is granted by a willing landlord; and
(3) is granted on all the terms of the statutory periodic tenancy as they are at the time of the committee's consideration except so far as they relate to the subject matter of the proposed terms.[62]

In doing this, the committee must disregard any effect on the terms attributable to the granting of a tenancy to a sitting tenant.[63] It is on this basis that the committee must determine what the terms of the tenancy are to be.[64]

Before the terms of any substantial body of assured periodic tenancies became known, committees had to exercise a lively imagination. The subject-matter of the reference is directed not at what the committees consider to be fair or just or reasonable in the abstract, but at what they consider might reasonably be "expected" to be "found" in an assured periodic tenancy of the particular dwelling-house, situated where it is in the district and population as they exist, granted when it was deemed to have been granted (*i.e.* at the end of the fixed term tenancy), and including all the other terms of the tenancy which do not deal with the same subject-matter as any of the terms proposed. There is no roving jurisdiction over all the terms of the tenancy, but merely jurisdiction over the terms proposed in the notice. Yet in considering those terms, committees are free to put forward and consider any new terms or amendments that deal with the same subject matter. By now, however, experience of assured tenancies is widespread, though perhaps the jurisdiction to determine the terms of a statutory tenancy is not frequently exercised. **7–23**

Shared accommodation is not expressly dealt with, apart from making the provi- **7–24**

[60] Consider Vol. 1, p. 622, though the element of public interest was greater there: and see *post*, paras. 7–23 *et seq.*
[61] Act of 1988, s.6(4).
[62] *ibid.*
[63] *ibid.*, s.6(6).
[64] The Act is curiously indirect: s.6(4) merely requires the committee to determine "whether" the terms satisfy the criteria, yet s.6(5), (7) assume that the committee will "determine" the "terms" of the tenancy.

sions for variation subject to the same principle as governs the court's power to make an order for possession of shared accommodation.[65]

(c) Rent

7–25 Where the committee determine the terms of the tenancy, they must, if they consider it appropriate, specify an adjustment of the rent so as "to take account of the terms so determined".[66] This must be done whether or not the notice of variation proposed any adjustment of the amount of the rent.[67] Thus a change in the burdens of the repairing obligations might justify a substantial variation in the amount of the rent. But here too, any effect on the amount of rent attributable to the granting of a tenancy to a sitting tenant must be disregarded.[68] If the committee have before them at the same time both a reference for the variation of terms under this head and a reference by the tenant of a notice of increase of rent, and the committee propose to hear the two references together, then the following order must be observed. If the date specified for the variation is not later than the first day of the period specified for the new rent to take effect, the reference for the variation (and any adjustment of rent) must be determined before determining the reference of the rent.[69]

5. Effect of committee's decision

7–26 Unless the landlord and the tenant otherwise agree, any terms determined by the committee become terms of the statutory periodic tenancy in substitution for any of the implied terms dealing with the same subject matter; and the amount of any rent under the tenancy must also be altered so as to accord with any adjustment specified by the committee.[70] These changes take effect from such date as the committee may direct, though that date cannot be earlier than the date specified in the notice of variation as the date from which the changes are to take effect.[71] No limit is placed on the power of the parties to agree, so that they could no doubt vary the date for the variation or adjustment, or the terms of the tenancy or the amount of the rent, or indeed agree to leave the terms of the tenancy unchanged.

[65] Under Act of 1988, s.10(2) (order for possession: see *ante*, para. 3–20), s.6 "shall have effect accordingly", *i.e.* according to s.10(2); but s.10(3) (termination or modification of rights) is not so expressed. The drafting is puzzling and the effect obscure.
[66] Act of 1988, s.6(5).
[67] *ibid.*
[68] *ibid.*, s.6(6).
[69] *ibid.*, s.14(6); for increase of rent, see *post*, paras. 17–30 *et seq.*
[70] *ibid.*, s.6(7).
[71] *ibid.*

Sect. 5. Determination

If a statutory periodic tenancy is an assured tenancy, it can be brought to an end only in accordance with the law governing assured tenancies;[72] and the curb on evasion for such tenancies will also apply.[73] If the tenancy is not an assured tenancy, there is nothing to prevent its being determined under the general law. 7–27

[72] *Ante*, paras. 6–09 *et seq.*
[73] *Ante*, paras. 6–13.

Chapter 8

Assured Shorthold Tenancies

8–01 The assured shorthold tenancy has its origins in the protected shorthold tenancy provisions of the Housing Act 1980.[1] These relaxed the security of tenure provisions of the Rent Act by providing a new mandatory ground for recovering possession from tenants of some fixed term tenancies who had been warned, prior to grant, that possession of their homes might be recovered on this mandatory ground. The political and economic imperatives which led to the protected shorthold tenancy provisions, with a view to providing the property market with a larger supply of rented accommodation, still applied when Parliament passed the Housing Act 1988. Accordingly, the Act of 1988 provided for the grant of assured shorthold tenancies where a fixed term of six months or more was granted and notice of the shorthold status of the tenancy was given to the tenant before the tenancy was entered into. Assured shorthold tenancies are also subject to a mandatory ground for recovery of possession and, unlike protected shorthold tenancies, which were subject to full rent control under the Rent Acts, they have their own limited system of rent control. It is important to recognise that, apart from these special features, assured shorthold tenancies are merely assured tenancies. For reasons explained in the next paragraph, it is necessary to distinguish assured shorthold tenancies granted under the original regime of the Act of 1988 from those granted on or after February 28, 1997 under the amendments introduced by the Housing Act 1996. In this Chapter, the former will be called "old" assured shorthold tenancies and the latter will be called "new" assured shorthold tenancies.

8–02 In practice, the availability of the old assured shorthold tenancy transformed the private rented sector of the property market, and the substantial majority of private residential tenancies granted after January 15, 1989 were old assured shorthold tenancies. The attractions for the landlord were the certainty of recovering possession, the relative[2] simplicity of the notice system for creating such tenancies and then recovering possession, and the minimal effect in practice

[1] See Vol. 1, pp. 212–217.

[2] As compared with the complexities of the notice procedure for granting and terminating protected shorthold tenancies: see *ibid*.

of the rent control system applicable to them.[3] Partly because of the great preponderance of old assured shorthold tenancies, and partly because the notice requirement was still seen as a possible trap for unwary landlords, the Housing Act 1996 has reformed the shorthold tenancy provisions of the Act of 1988. As from February 28, 1997,[4] all assured tenancies expressly granted which do not fall within categories of tenancy excluded from being shorthold tenancies are new assured shorthold tenancies, without any requirement of prior notice, and without any limitation on the type or length of term granted. There are many attributes which old and new assured shorthold tenancies have in common, in particular both are assured tenancies;[5] but there are also many significant differences between them, and accordingly it is important to distinguish them at all times.

Sect. 1. "Old" and "New" Assured Shorthold Tenancies

In seeking to identify whether an assured tenancy is an old or a new assured shorthold tenancy, it is necessary to consider first the date of grant of the tenancy, and secondly whether the tenancy is excluded from being a new assured shorthold tenancy. **8–03**

1. Date of grant

An assured tenancy which is entered into prior to February 28, 1997 cannot be a new assured shorthold tenancy; it will be an old assured shorthold tenancy if it complies with the requirements[6] for the creation of such a tenancy. In the case of an assured tenancy entered into on or after February 28, 1997 but pursuant to a contract made before that date, the tenancy will be an old assured shorthold tenancy if it complies with those requirements. **8–04**

2. Exclusion from being a "new" assured shorthold tenancy

An assured tenancy entered into on or after February 28, 1997 otherwise than pursuant to a contract made before that date can be an old assured shorthold tenancy only if it is not a tenancy to which section 19A of the Housing Act 1988[7] (which contains the provisions for, and refers to the exclusions from being, a **8–05**

[3] See *post*, paras. 18–10 *et seq.*

[4] The date on which Housing Act 1996, s.96 came into force: *ibid.*, s.232(3); Housing Act 1996 (Commencement No. 7 and Savings) Order 1997 (S.I. 1997 No. 225), arts. 1(2), 2.

[5] Accordingly, if by virtue of any provision of Act of 1988, ss.1–4 and Sched. 1 a tenancy is at any time precluded from being an assured tenancy, it cannot at that time be either an old or a new assured shorthold tenancy.

[6] See Sect. 2, *post*, p. 120.

[7] Inserted by Housing Act 1996, ss.96(1), 232(3); S.I. 1997 No. 225.

new assured shorthold tenancy) applies.[8] It is therefore necessary to look first at these exclusions. If none of them applies, the tenancy is a new assured shorthold tenancy; if any of the exclusions does apply, the tenancy can be an old assured shorthold tenancy provided that the requirements for creation of such a tenancy have been complied with.[9]

3. The exclusions

There are seven categories of exclusion.[10]

(a) Exclusion by notice

8–06 An assured tenancy will not be a new assured shorthold tenancy if the landlord, either before or after the assured tenancy is entered into, serves notice on the tenant stating that the assured tenancy to which it relates is not to be, or is no longer (as the case might be), an assured shorthold tenancy.[11] In effect, therefore, the landlord alone is given the option at any time to forgo the advantage of being able to recover possession from the tenant on a mandatory ground. It is implicit, though nowhere expressly stated, that the landlord cannot change his mind subsequently to the service of the notice and make the tenancy once again a new assured shorthold tenancy. There is, however, no time restriction on service of such a notice before the assured tenancy is entered into; and it is considered that a landlord can escape from the consequences of having served such a notice by granting a different tenancy from that to which the notice relates.[12] Once the tenancy has been entered into, it seems that a notice stating that it is no longer an assured shorthold tenancy must be served (if at all) before the contractual term date of the tenancy, otherwise the landlord and tenant will no longer be landlord and tenant respectively under that tenancy, but under a statutory periodic assured shorthold tenancy arising by law upon the expiry of the tenancy granted.[13] There is no form prescribed for such notices, but the use of the words ''served'' and ''states'' indicates that they must be in writing. In the case of joint landlords or joint tenants, a notice served after the tenancy has commenced must be served by or on each of them, as the case may be;[14] the same is probably also true of a notice given before the tenancy has been entered into.

[8] Act of 1988, s.20(1), as substituted by Housing Act 1996, ss.104, 232(3), Sched. 8, para. 3; S.I. 1997 No. 225.

[9] As to which, see Sect. 2, *post*, and especially at para. 8–26.

[10] Act of 1988, Sched. 2A, inserted by Housing Act 1996. ss.96(2), 232(3); S.I. 1997 No. 225.

[11] Act of 1988, Sched. 2A, paras. 1, 2.

[12] A change in the length of term granted or of the demised premises must suffice, but whether or not a variation in any of the other agreed terms of the tenancy would suffice must be a question of fact and degree: is the tenancy granted the same tenancy as that to which the notice related? The tenancy might well have been agreed orally, of course, and in such cases it might be difficult for the landlord to argue that a different tenancy was ultimately granted.

[13] See *post*, para. 8–48.

[14] Act of 1988, s.45(3).

8–07 Where the notice has been served after the assured tenancy has been entered into, the tenancy will (unless otherwise excluded) have taken effect as a new assured shorthold tenancy, and it is inherently unlikely that the requirements for the valid grant of an old assured shorthold tenancy were complied with.[15] The effect of the landlord's notice will thus be to exclude the tenancy from being a shorthold, and the tenancy will thenceforth be an assured tenancy simpliciter. Where the notice is served before the assured tenancy is entered into, with the effect that the tenancy when granted is not a new assured shorthold tenancy within section 19A,[16] the landlord probably cannot then serve the requisite notice for an old shorthold tenancy[17] with the result that the tenancy when entered into will (provided it satisfies the other requirements) take effect as such.[18] It appears that even if the tenancy agreement contains an express provision that the tenancy is to be an assured shorthold tenancy, a prior notice given by the landlord to the contrary effect will mean that the tenancy is not a shorthold.[19]

(b) Exclusionary provision in tenancy

8–08 An assured tenancy will not be a new assured shorthold tenancy if the tenancy contains a provision to the effect that the tenancy is not an assured shorthold tenancy.[20] Again, it is probably implicit that it is a written tenancy agreement or lease which must contain the negative provision, and accordingly an oral tenancy agreement cannot be excluded from being a new assured shorthold tenancy on this ground. Unlike ground (a) above, this ground requires the agreement of both parties to the tenancy agreement or lease before the shorthold is excluded. The tenant might not wish to agree if he has it in mind to challenge at a rent assessment committee[21] the rent which he has had to agree in order to obtain the grant of a tenancy; but the landlord has the remedy in his own hands:

[15] Even if they were, the tenancy will still have commenced as a new assured shorthold tenancy, and it is considered that in view of the terms of the notice served, the tenancy could not become an old assured shorthold tenancy.

[16] Act of 1988, s.19A. See n. 7, *supra*.

[17] Required by *ibid*., s.20(1)(c), as amended.

[18] As from February 28, 1997, the prescribed form of shorthold notice was revoked (by Assured Tenancies and Agricultural Occupancies (Forms) Regulations 1997 (S.I. 1997 No. 194), reg. 4), and no new form was prescribed. Accordingly, the notice required by Housing Act 1988, s.20(1)(c) need only state that the assured tenancy to which it relates is to be a shorthold tenancy. The landlord will, however, already have served on the tenant notice stating that the assured tenancy is not to be an assured shorthold tenancy. Any landlord who tried to serve both notices prior to the grant of the tenancy would probably find that he had not served a notice under Act of 1988, Sched. 2A, para. 1 effective to exclude the tenancy from the new assured shorthold tenancy regime.

[19] The wording of Act of 1988, s.19A appears to be mandatory. The only contrary argument is that the effect of the agreement in the tenancy agreement itself could estop the landlord from relying on the notice, though estoppels in the context of the Rent Acts are notoriously difficult to establish: see *ante*, para. 1–14. The circumstances in which the landlord would be arguing for increased security of tenure and the tenant for less would be far from commonplace, however: see, in a similar vein, the bizarre litigation noted in the Preface to *The Rent Acts* (5th ed.), printed in 10th ed. at pp. xxvi, xxvii.

[20] Act of 1988, Sched. 2A, para. 3.

[21] See *post*, para. 18–27.

he can serve a notice under (a) above once the tenancy has commenced and before the tenant has applied to the rent assessment committee[21a].

(c) Statutory succession tenancies

8–09 An assured tenancy will not be a new assured shorthold tenancy if it arises by virtue of the statutory succession provisions of the Rent Act 1977 or the Rent (Agriculture) Act 1976.[22] There is one exception to this exclusion: where, immediately before the death of the person on whose death the successor became entitled to an assured tenancy, the landlord might have recovered possession of the dwelling-house under the Rent Act on the mandatory shorthold ground.[23] In such a case, the succession provisions state that the succession tenancy shall be an assured shorthold tenancy,[24] and the exclusion respects this provision by taking such a case outside its scope. Accordingly, in such circumstances, the successor becomes entitled to a new assured shorthold tenancy.

(d) Former secure tenancies

8–10 Where a tenancy which was immediately previously a secure tenancy[25] becomes an assured tenancy (generally upon transfer of the landlord's interest from a public sector landlord to a private landlord), the tenancy is an assured tenancy and not a new assured shorthold tenancy.[26]

(e) Assured tenancies arising on termination of long tenancies at low rents

8–11 An assured tenancy will not be a new assured shorthold tenancy if it arises by virtue of Schedule 10 to the Local Government and Housing Act 1989 (here called "Schedule 10" *simpliciter*).[27] Schedule 10 is a replacement regime for Part I of the Landlord and Tenant Act 1954, and makes provision for the rights of long lessees of dwelling-houses at low rents to be entitled to remain in possession pursuant to assured tenancies (rather than statutory tenancies under the Rent Acts, as provided by the Act of 1954) at the expiry of the term of the lease.[28] Under Schedule 10, long leases granted on or after April 1, 1990 are governed by the new provisions from their commencement (though of course such tenancies cannot expire by effluxion of time until April 1, 2011 at the earliest). Long leases which were already in existence on April 1, 1990 continued to be gov-

[21a] See *post*, para. 18–29.

[22] As amended by Act of 1988, s.39, Sched. 4, Pts. I, II, which made provision for certain categories of successor to be entitled to an assured tenancy under the Act of 1988 rather than a statutory tenancy under the Rent Acts.

[23] *i.e.* under Rent Act 1977, Sched. 15, Case 19.

[24] *Post*, para. 12–24.

[25] *i.e.* within the meaning of Housing Act 1985, Pt. IV.

[26] Act of 1988, Sched. 2A, para. 5.

[27] *ibid.*, para. 6.

[28] A detailed treatment of Sched. 10 is contained in Chap. 10, *post*.

erned by Part I of the Act of 1954; but under transitional provisions, such leases which were still in existence on January 15, 1999[29] are thenceforth governed by Schedule 10;[30] and accordingly assured tenancies may arise by virtue of Schedule 10 at any time after January 15, 1999. Any such assured tenancies will not be new assured shorthold tenancies.

(f) Re-grants to assured tenants

An assured tenancy will not be a new assured shorthold tenancy if it is in substance a re-grant by a landlord to an assured tenant of his who is not a shorthold tenant under the existing tenancy.[31] But the tenant may in such a case elect by notice in writing served on the landlord to have it be a shorthold tenancy. The clear legislative purpose underlying this exclusion is to prevent landlords from removing the security of tenure enjoyed by assured tenants by offering to renew their tenancies. It seems clear that a tenant under an "old" assured shorthold tenancy is a shorthold tenant for these purposes as much as is a "new" assured shorthold tenant. For the exclusion to apply, the following conditions must be satisfied. **8–12**

(i) RE-GRANT: the new tenancy must be granted to a person, either alone or jointly with others, who, immediately before the grant, was the tenant (or one of two or more joint tenants) under an assured tenancy other than a shorthold tenancy ("the old tenancy").[32] There is no requirement that the old tenancy and the new tenancy be of the same premises, or substantially the same premises. So one of four joint tenants under an assured tenancy of one house will retain his full assured status if he takes an assured tenancy jointly with three other, different persons of another house. But the tenant must have been an assured tenant *immediately before* the grant of the new tenancy. What is immediate in this context will be a question of fact and degree in each case; but where a previous statutory tenancy had been surrendered and possession of the premises vacated for at least 24 hours before the grant of a protected shorthold tenancy, the tenant was held not to have been a protected or statutory tenant "immediately before" the grant of the new tenancy.[33] **8–13**

(ii) BY THE SAME LANDLORD: the new tenancy must be granted alone or jointly with others by a person who, immediately before the grant, was the landlord (or one of the joint landlords) under the old tenancy.[34] So a landlord cannot jointly with his wife grant a shorthold tenancy of their house to a person who was **8–14**

[29] *i.e.* 10 years after the assured tenancy provisions of Act of 1988 came into force.
[30] Local Government and Housing Act 1989, s.186(3).
[31] Act of 1988, Sched. 2A, para. 7.
[32] *ibid.*, para. 7(1)(a).
[33] *Bolnore Properties Ltd. v. Cobb* (1996) 29 H.L.R. 202, CA, a decision on similar wording in Housing Act 1980, s.52(2); for it, see Vol. 1, p. 213. See also *Dibbs v. Campbell* (1988) 20 H.L.R. 374, CA.
[34] Housing Act 1988, Sched. 2A, para. 7(1)(b).

immediately prior to the grant the assured tenant of another house owned jointly by the landlord and his mistress.

8–15 (iii) NO NOTICE BY TENANT: the new assured tenancy will be a new assured shorthold tenancy if, before the new tenancy is entered into, the tenant under that tenancy serves on the person who is to be the landlord under that tenancy (or, in the case of joint landlords, on at least one of them) a notice in the prescribed form stating that the assured tenancy to which it relates[35] is to be a shorthold tenancy.[36] Although service on one of two or more joint landlords suffices, service by fewer than all the joint tenants under the new tenancy will not be a valid notice for these purposes;[37] so the landlord cannot prevail upon one only, even if, *semble*, he is the only one of the joint tenants who was previously an assured tenant of the landlord.[38] This form of notice is prescribed, doubtless, so as to ensure that warning notes as to the entitlement of the tenant not to give notice, and as to the consequences of giving up security of tenure, are brought to the tenant's attention prior to his giving the notice. The form prescribed for the tenant's notice is Form No.8 in the Schedule to the Assured Tenancies and Agricultural Occupancies (Forms) Regulations 1997.[39] In the Form, the tenant proposes that the assured tenancy to which the notice relates should be ''replaced by'' a shorthold tenancy, which appears to be a misreading of the statutory provision: the assured tenancy to which the notice must ''relate'' is the new assured tenancy proposed to be granted, not the ''old tenancy''. Nevertheless, the Form only requires particulars of the commencement date of the new tenancy to be inserted by the tenant, and so the inaccuracy may not much matter. On the other hand, if the tenant serves the notice and then regrets it, he can preserve his assured status in relation to the old tenancy by not entering into the new tenancy. If, instead, he renegotiates the terms of a new tenancy and enters into it subsequently without serving a fresh notice, it may well be arguable that the new tenancy is not a shorthold on the basis that the notice served did not ''relate to'' the assured tenancy eventually granted.[40]

(g) Statutory periodic tenancies

8–16 If, on or after February 28, 1997, a statutory periodic tenancy comes into being[41]

[35] *i.e.* the new tenancy. For the form, see *infra*.

[36] Act of 1988, Sched. 2A, para. 7(1)(c), (2).

[37] *ibid.*, s.45(3).

[38] The contrary is certainly arguable on the basis that ''the person who is to be the tenant'' in Act of 1988, Sched. 2A, para. 7(2)(c) is to be equated with ''a person'' in *ibid.*, para. 7(1)(a); but the contrast with the specific provision in para. 7(2)(c) for service on ''one of the persons who are to be joint landlords'' is marked, and there do seem to be good policy reasons for requiring all joint tenants to agree to give up their security of tenure. The draftsman of the prescribed form seems to have proceeded on this understanding: see *infra*.

[39] S.I. 1997 No. 194, regs. 2, 3(h), Sched.; printed *post*, pp. 621, 622, 637. These Regulations were made by the Secretary of State pursuant to Act of 1988, s.45(1), (5) on January 29, 1997, and came into force on February 28, 1997. Act of 1988, Sched. 2A, para. 7(2)(a) was brought into force on August 23, 1996 for the purpose only of empowering the Secretary of State to make such regulations, etc.: Housing Act 1996 (Commencement No. 2 and Savings) Order 1996 (S.I. 1996 No. 2212), art. 2(1).

[40] This is a similar argument to that which a landlord may deploy in relation to exclusion (a); *ante*, para. 8–06.

[41] Pursuant to Act of 1988, s.5(2). See *ante*, para. 7–06.

on the coming to an end of an assured tenancy which is not a shorthold tenancy, that statutory periodic tenancy is not a new assured shorthold tenancy.[42] It seems clear that an "old" assured shorthold tenancy which comes to an end is a shorthold tenancy for these purposes as much as is a "new" assured shorthold tenancy. So, as with an express re-grant, the deemed grant of a new assured tenancy by operation of the Act of 1988 does not take away the full assured status of the tenant. But where the statutory periodic tenancy comes into being on or after February 28, 1997 on the coming to an end of a shorthold tenancy, there is, as one would expect, no specific exclusion to prevent the statutory periodic tenancy being an assured shorthold tenancy. Where the expired tenancy is an old assured shorthold tenancy, the position is governed by the original[43] provisions of the Act of 1988. Unless before the statutory periodic tenancy takes effect in possession the landlord serves notice on the tenant that the new tenancy is not to be a shorthold tenancy, the new tenancy is an assured shorthold tenancy if and so long as it is an assured tenancy whether or not it fulfils the statutory requirements for the effectual grant of an old assured shorthold tenancy.[44] These original provisions of the Act of 1988 do not apply where the new tenancy is one to which section 19A of the Act of 1988 applies.[45] Apart from a new tenancy expressly entered into on or after February 28, 1997, section 19A applies to an assured tenancy which comes into being by virtue of section 5 of the Housing Act 1988 on the coming to an end of an assured tenancy which *was* expressly entered into on or after February 28, 1997. Thus, where the expired tenancy is a new assured shorthold tenancy, the statutory periodic tenancy which comes into being will also be a new assured shorthold tenancy unless one of the exclusions applies.[46] So it seems that an old assured shorthold tenancy will remain such unless and until there is an express grant of a new tenancy on or after February 28, 1997, whereupon the new tenancy will be a new assured shorthold tenancy unless one of the exclusions applies.[47]

(h) Assured agricultural occupancies

An assured tenancy will not be a new assured shorthold tenancy at any time when the tenancy is an assured agricultural occupancy as well as being an actual (as opposed to deemed[48]) assured tenancy.[49] This exclusion is itself subject to **8–17**

[42] Act of 1988, Sched. 2A, para. 8.
[43] *i.e.* s.20(4), unaffected by the amendments introduced by Housing Act 1996.
[44] Act of 1988, s.20(4), (5).
[45] *ibid.*, s.20(5A), inserted on February 28, 1997 by Housing Act 1996, ss.104, 232(3), Sched. 8, para. 2(4); S.I. 1997 No. 225.
[46] Act of 1988, s.19A(b). Of these exclusions, only notice given by the landlord is likely to be of relevance.
[47] *ibid.*, s.19A(a).
[48] By Act of 1988, s.24(3), every assured agricultural occupancy which is not an assured tenancy is treated as if it were for the purposes of Chap. I of the Act ("Assured Tenancies") and of Chap. III ("Assured Agricultural Occupancies"). But this deeming provision does not apply for the purposes of Chap. II ("Assured Shorthold Tenancies"); and so for the purposes of *inter alia* s.19A and Sched. 2A, only true assured tenancies and not deemed assured tenancies are affected.
[49] Pursuant to Act of 1988, s.24(1), (2)(a).

two exceptions, and when these apply the assured tenancy can be a new assured shorthold tenancy.

8–18 (i) THE EXCLUSION: where the agricultural worker condition is, by virtue of any provision of Schedule 3 to the Act of 1988, for the time being fulfilled with respect to the dwelling-house subject to the tenancy.[50] This exclusion differs from the others in that the status of the tenancy, shorthold or not, is not determined at the commencement of the term or when it becomes an assured tenancy, or even once and for all when a notice is served;[51] but it may be a shorthold whenever the agricultural worker condition is not satisfied, and then revert to being a non-shorthold assured tenancy when the condition is satisfied again. The agricultural worker condition and the terms of Schedule 3 are considered in detail in the following Chapter.[52]

8–19 (ii) THE TWO EXCEPTIONS: the exclusion does not apply, and the tenancy is accordingly a new assured shorthold tenancy, in either of the following sets of circumstances—

(1) If the tenancy is not an "excepted tenancy" and, before it is entered into, the landlord serves on the tenant a notice in the prescribed form stating that the tenancy is to be a shorthold tenancy.[53] An assured tenancy is an "excepted tenancy" if—

(a) the tenant or, where there are joint tenants, at least one of them was, immediately before it is granted, a tenant or licensee under an assured agricultural occupancy, and
(b) the landlord or, where there are joint landlords, at least one of them was, immediately before it is granted, a landlord or licensor under that assured agricultural occupancy.[54]

There is thus no requirement that the old assured agricultural occupancy and the new tenancy be of the same premises, or substantially the same premises. But the tenant must have been a tenant or licensee under an assured agricultural occupancy *immediately before* the grant of the new tenancy. What is immediate in this context will be a question of fact and degree in each case; but where a previous statutory tenancy had been surrendered and possession of the premises vacated for at least 24 hours before the grant of a protected shorthold tenancy, the tenant was held not to have been a protected or statutory tenant "immediately before" the grant of the new tenancy.[55]

The written notice must be served by the landlord under the new

[50] Act of 1988, Sched. 2A, para. 9(1)(a).
[51] As with *ibid.*, para. 2.
[52] In particular, at paras, 9–07 and 9–11 *et seq.*
[53] Act of 1988, Sched. 2A, para. 9(2).
[54] *ibid.*, para. 9(1)(b), (2)(b), (3).
[55] *Bolnore Properties Ltd. v. Cobb* (1996) 29 H.L.R. 202, CA, a decision on similar wording in Housing Act 1980, s.52(2); for it, see Vol. 1, p. 213. See also *Dibbs v. Campbell* (1988) 20 H.L.R. 374, CA.

tenancy on the tenant, before the new tenancy is entered into, in the prescribed form, stating that the tenancy is to be a shorthold tenancy.[56] Here, service by *the* person who is to be the landlord on *the* person who is to be the tenant is required: there seems to be no room for argument that service by or on behalf of some only of the landlords or on fewer than all the joint tenants suffices.[57] The form prescribed for the tenant's notice is Form No.9 in the Schedule to the Assured Tenancies and Agricultural Occupancies (Forms) Regulations 1997.[58] In the Form, the landlord identifies the address of the premises to be let, the commencement date of the tenancy, and informs the tenant of the limited security of tenure such tenancy will give him and of his right to apply to a rent assessment committee within six months of the beginning of the tenancy.

The effect of this complex drafting is that, provided the tenancy is not in substance a re-grant by a landlord or licensor to the tenant or licensee under an existing assured agricultural occupancy, and provided that written notice is given to the tenant prior to the grant of the new tenancy, the new tenancy can take effect as a new assured shorthold tenancy even though the agricultural worker condition is satisfied. Before February 28, 1997, an old shorthold tenancy could not be an assured agricultural occupancy[59] and, except in the case of a re-grant of an assured agricultural occupancy which was a true (as opposed to deemed) assured tenancy, a landlord could always ensure that his assured tenancy was a shorthold. So, on or after that date, a landlord can still create a shorthold rather than an assured agricultural occupancy by serving an appropriate notice, but that ability has been taken away in the cases of re-grants of assured agricultural occupancies which were either tenancies other than assured tenancies or licences.[60]

(2) If the assured tenancy comes into being by operation of law[61] upon the coming to an end of a tenancy, other than an "excepted tenancy",[62] in respect of which the landlord served the prescribed form notice[63] stating that the tenancy was to be a shorthold tenancy.[64] Thus, once the landlord has validly elected to make the tenancy a shorthold tenancy, **8–20**

[56] Act of 1988, Sched. 2A, para. 7(1)(c), (2).

[57] Although the express provision in Act of 1988, s.45(3) does not strictly apply because the reference here is not to "the landlord" or "the tenant".

[58] S.I. 1997 No. 194, regs. 2, 3(h), Sched: printed *post*, pp. 621, 622, 638. These Regulations were made by the Secretary of State pursuant to Act of 1988, s.45(1), (5) on January 29, 1997, and came into force on February 28, 1997. Act of 1988, Sched. 2A, para. 9(2)(a) was brought into force on August 23, 1996 for the purpose only of empowering the Secretary of State to make such regulations, etc.: Housing Act 1996 (Commencement No. 2 and Savings) Order 1996 (S.I. 1996 No. 2212), art. 2(1).

[59] See Act of 1988, s.24(2)(a).

[60] It is unclear whether Parliament intended this effect, or whether the absence of any deeming provision under Act of 1988, s.24(3) in relation to Chap. II of that Act was overlooked.

[61] Pursuant to Act of 1988, s.5(2).

[62] See (1), *supra*.

[63] *Supra*.

[64] Act of 1988, Sched. 2A, para. 9(1)(b), (4).

the statutory periodic tenancy which arises upon its termination will also be a shorthold without the need for the service of a further notice.

4. Derivative shorthold tenancies

8–21 Both "old" assured shorthold tenancies and "new" assured shorthold tenancies, being assured tenancies, will upon the expiry of their fixed terms[65] give rise to statutory periodic tenancies provided that at the end of the term the tenancy is still an assured tenancy. In the case of an "old" assured shorthold tenancy which expires, the statutory periodic tenancy will be an assured shorthold tenancy regardless of the preconditions for the express grant of such an "old" shorthold.[66] But in the case of "new" assured shorthold tenancies which expire, the statutory tenancy is only a shorthold provided that none of the exclusions set out above apply to it.[67–68]

8–22 It is often necessary to distinguish original, expressly-granted shortholds which comply with the conditions for creation of shorthold tenancies from subsequent, derivative shortholds which do not, as well as between "old" and "new" shortholds, and the terms "original" and "derivative" will be used in this Chapter for this purpose.

A. "OLD" ASSURED SHORTHOLD TENANCIES

In this Part, for brevity, the terms "shorthold" or "assured shorthold tenancy" denote an "old" assured shorthold tenancy; where a "new" assured shorthold tenancy is intended to be referred to, that terminology will be specifically used.

Sect. 2. Creation of Original Old Assured Shorthold Tenancies

8–23 A tenancy cannot be an original assured shorthold tenancy unless it complies with the requirements for being an assured tenancy.[69] As explained in Section 1, above, a tenancy cannot be an assured shorthold tenancy if it is a new assured shorthold tenancy; and most original tenancies granted on or after February 28, 1997 will fall into this class.[70] Subject to that, an original assured shorthold

[65] Note that after February 28, 1997 an expressly granted periodic tenancy can be a "new" assured shorthold tenancy, notwithstanding the lack of a term certain; "old" assured shorthold tenancies which are expressly granted, must have a fixed term of at least six months: see *post*, para. 8–24.

[66] Act of 1988, s.20(4). The landlord can prevent this occurring by serving an appropriate notice on the tenant before the statutory tenancy takes effect in possession: *ibid.*, s.20(5).

[67–68] Act of 1988, s.19A(b). See *ante*, n. 46.

[69] See *ante*, pp. 23–64.

[70] See *supra*.

tenancy must comply with three other conditions. There is nothing in the Act of 1988 which requires a shorthold tenancy to be made in writing;[71] and so a shorthold tenancy taking effect in possession for a term not exceeding three years and at the best rent which can reasonably be obtained without taking a fine[72] can be created orally.

1. Fixed term of six months or more

The tenancy must be "a fixed term tenancy granted for a term certain of not less than six months".[73] Fractions of a day are included in calculating the six months.[74] The term of a tenancy does not include any period expressed to be part of the term but antedating the date of grant.[75] But, in an appropriate case,[76] a tenancy agreement or lease may be rectified and thereby satisfy the six months condition.[77] There must also be no power for the landlord to determine the tenancy at any time earlier than six months from the beginning of the tenancy,[78] that is to say from the day on which the tenancy is entered into or, if later, the day on which, under the terms of "any lease, agreement or other document", the tenant is entitled to possession under the tenancy.[79] But a power of re-entry or forfeiture for breach of any term or condition of the tenancy is not "a power . . . to determine the tenancy" for these purposes.[80] So the inclusion of a standard form proviso for re-entry will not prevent the tenancy from being a shorthold tenancy; and the landlord can, in an appropriate case, terminate the tenancy before the expiry of the six months under the Chapter I procedure for claiming possession from assured tenants.[81] **8–24**

2. Shorthold notice duly served

The second condition is that a shorthold notice must have been duly served.[82] **8–25**
The notice must be in the prescribed form,[83] or in a form substantially to the

[71] As opposed to the previous giving of a written shorthold notice: see *infra*.
[72] Law of Property Act 1925, s.54(2). For an interesting case on the exact meaning of this well-known formula, see *Long v. Tower Hamlets L.B.C.* [1998] Ch. 197, CA.
[73] Act of 1988, s.20(1)(a), amended by Housing Act 1996, ss.104, 232(3), Sched. 8, para. 2(3); S.I. 1997 No. 225; but not affecting this requirement.
[74] Thus, where the term was in fact less than six months exactly because the tenancy was not signed until the afternoon of the first day, it was an assured shorthold tenancy: *Bedding v. McCarthy* [1994] 2 E.G.L.R. 40, CA.
[75] The term of a lease does not commence until the day on which the lease is made or, if later, the expressed commencement date: *Bradshaw v. Pawley* [1980] 1 W.L.R. 10, Ch.
[76] *i.e.* subject to proving common or unilateral mistake as to the contents of the lease and to the exercise of the court's discretion in favour of rectification.
[77] *Mundy v. Hook* [1997] E.G.C.S. 119, CA (term mistakenly granted for five, not six, months).
[78] Act of 1988, s.20(1)(b).
[79] *ibid.*, s.45(2).
[80] *ibid.*, s.45(4).
[81] More specifically, the proviso for re-entry serves the function of a provision for the tenancy to be brought to an end within the meaning of Act of 1988, s.7(6)(b): see *post*, para. 13–42.
[82] Act of 1988, s.20(1)(c).
[83] *ibid.*, s.20(2)(a); Assured Tenancies and Agricultural Occupancies (Forms) Regulations 1988 (S.I. 1988 No. 2203), reg. 3(7), Sched., Form No. 7, as amended successively by Assured Tenancies

same effect,[84] and must state that "the assured tenancy to which it relates is to be a shorthold tenancy".[85] This notice must be served before the tenancy is entered into,[86] and it must be served by the person who is to be the landlord under the tenancy on the person who is to be the tenant under it.[87] Where there are to be joint landlords or joint tenants, all the joint tenants must be served;[88] but service by one of the joint landlords suffices.[89] In contrast with protected shorthold tenancies,[90] the court is given no power to dispense with service of a shorthold notice. Although the shorthold notice is therefore of great importance,[91] obvious mistakes in the notice have been held not to invalidate it, at least where they did not matter or it was obvious what was really meant.[92]

8–26 When the new assured shorthold tenancy regime introduced by the Housing Act 1996 came into force on February 28, 1997, the prescribed form for service of a shorthold notice was revoked,[93] and no new form for a shorthold notice was prescribed. But the revocation does not affect the validity of any shorthold notice served in the then prescribed form before February 28, 1997.[94] It is difficult, though not impossible, to envisage circumstances in which an original assured tenancy could be granted on or after February 28, 1997 which would not be a "new" assured shorthold tenancy[95] and which therefore could theoretically be an "old" shorthold. In such cases, although a shorthold notice would be required to create such a tenancy, there being no longer a prescribed form the notice need only state that the assured tenancy to which it relates is to be a shorthold tenancy. In the case of a derivative assured shorthold tenancy, there is no requirement of a shorthold notice.[96]

3. Tenant not previously an assured or protected tenant

8–27 The third condition is that the tenancy is not in substance a re-grant to an assured

and Agricultural Occupancies (Forms) (Amendment) Regulations 1990 (S.I. 1990 No. 1532), reg. 2(b) and by Assured Tenancies and Agricultural Occupancies (Forms) (Amendment) Regulations 1993 (S.I. 1993 No. 654), reg. 2(f).

84 Assured Tenancies and Agricultural Occupancies (Forms) Regulations 1988 (S.I. 1988 No. 2203), reg. 2.

85 Act of 1988, s.20(2)(d).

86 *ibid.*, s.20(2)(b).

87 *ibid.*, s.20(2)(c).

88 *ibid.*, s.45(3).

89 *ibid.*, s.20(6)(a).

90 See Vol. 1, pp. 483, 484.

91 In one case where a shorthold notice was given, the court was prepared to hold a tenancy agreement made even though the agreement itself was not signed: *York v. Casey* [1998] 2 E.G.L.R. 25, CA.

92 See *Brewer v. Andrews* [1997] E.G.C.S. 19, CA and *York v. Casey*, *supra*, applying the principles enunciated by the House of Lords in *Mannai Investment Co. Ltd. v. Eagle Star Life Assurance Co. Ltd.* [1997] A.C. 749. Compare *Panayi v. Roberts* (1993) 25 H.L.R. 421, CA and *Clickex Ltd. v. McCann* [1999] E.G.C.S. 73, CA, and decisions in other fields of landlord and tenant law where the missing part of the defective notice was either material (*Sabella Ltd. v. Montgomery* [1998] 1 E.G.L.R. 65, CA) or specifically required by statute (*Free Grammar School of John Lyon v. Mayhew* (1996) 29 H.L.R. 719, CA).

93 By Assured Tenancies and Agricultural Occupancies (Forms) Regulations 1997 (S.I. 1997 No. 194), reg. 4(1).

94 *ibid.*, reg. 4(2).

95 By reason of one of the exclusions applying: see *ante*, paras. 8–06 *et seq*.

96 See *post*, para. 8–40.

tenant who is not a shorthold tenant, or to a protected or statutory tenant. There are two different cases here.

(a) Previous assured tenancy

First, a tenancy cannot normally be a shorthold if it is granted to a tenant who was previously an ordinary assured tenant of the same landlord, and not an assured shorthold tenant. This exclusion applies only if two conditions are satisfied. **8–28**

(i) RE-GRANT: immediately before the new tenancy is granted, the person to whom it is granted was a tenant under an assured tenancy which was not a shorthold tenancy.[97] Where the new tenancy is granted to joint tenants, this condition is satisfied if at least one of them was a tenant under the former assured tenancy.[98] What amounts to "immediately" in this context will be a question of fact and degree in each case; but where a previous statutory tenancy had been surrendered, and possession of the premises vacated for at least 24 hours before the grant of a protected shorthold tenancy, the tenant was held not to have been a protected or statutory tenant "immediately before" the grant of the new tenancy.[99] **8–29**

(ii) BY THE SAME LANDLORD: the new tenancy is granted by the person who, immediately before it began, was the landlord under the former assured tenancy.[1] In the case of joint landlords under the new tenancy, this condition seems to be satisfied only if *all* of them were the landlord under the former tenancy.[2] The former prescribed form shorthold notice stated: "If you have an assured tenancy which is not a shorthold under the Housing Act 1988, you cannot be offered an assured shorthold tenancy of the same or other accommodation by the same landlord". It is suggested that the difference between the provision in this regard for excluding "new" assured shorthold tenancies and this exclusion cannot have been intentional. **8–30**

In contrast with protected shorthold tenancies,[3] there is no requirement here that the premises comprised in the two tenancies should be the same or even substantially the same;[4] and so a tenancy of wholly different premises will be **8–31**

[97] Act of 1988, s.20(3)(a).
[98] *ibid.*
[99] *Bolnore Properties Ltd. v. Cobb* (1996) 29 H.L.R. 202, CA, a decision on the equivalent provision in relation to protected shorthold tenancies under Housing Act 1980, s.52(2); for it, see Vol. 1, p. 213. See also *Dibbs v. Campbell* (1988) 20 H.L.R. 374, CA.
[1] Act of 1988, s.20(3)(b).
[2] *ibid.*, s.45(3). Section 20(6), which makes provision for one of two or more joint landlords to suffice in some respects, conspicuously omits any reference to s.20(3)(b). Contrast the equivalent provisions in Sched. 2A, para. 7(1)(b) (exclusion of new assured shorthold tenancy) and in s.34(1)(b) (re-grant to protected or statutory tenant).
[3] Housing Act 1980, s.52(2); Vol. 1, pp. 213, 214.
[4] Contrast Act of 1988, s.20(4); *post*, para. 8–38.

an assured tenancy and not a shorthold provided that the identity of the parties is the same.

(b) Protected or statutory tenant

8–32 Secondly, there are provisions which apply when a tenancy is granted on or after January 15, 1989 to a protected or statutory tenant. These provisions have already been considered.[5] They operate under two heads, depending on whether or not the tenant was a protected shorthold tenant.

8–33 (i) PROTECTED OR STATUTORY TENANT, NOT SHORTHOLD. Put shortly, if a tenancy is granted by a landlord to a person who is a protected or statutory tenant of his, but not a shorthold tenant within head (ii) below, then whether the premises are the same or different, the tenancy cannot be an assured tenancy but will usually be a protected tenancy.[6]

8–34 (ii) PROTECTED SHORTHOLD. The previous head does not apply where the tenant is a protected shorthold tenant. For these purposes, ''protected shorthold'' is used in an extended sense as including both tenancies which are protected shortholds and those which in possession proceedings are treated as protected shortholds.[7] Where the requirements of the previous head are satisfied in all respects save that the tenancy is a protected shorthold, and the landlord and the tenant under the new tenancy are the same[8] as at the end of the former tenancy, the new tenancy will be an assured shorthold tenancy, even if it fulfils none of the requirements for such a tenancy.[9] The landlord, however, can prevent this result if, before the new tenancy is entered into, he serves notice on the tenant that it is not to be a shorthold tenancy.[10] If he does this, the tenancy will be an ordinary assured tenancy, and not an assured shorthold tenancy. The word ''serves'' indicates that the notice must be in writing, but there is no requirement for it to be in any particular form.

Sect. 3. Continuance: Derivative Old Assured Shorthold Tenancy

8–35 It is necessary, in connection with the right to refer rents to the rent assessment committee and with termination notices, to distinguish original shortholds from derivative shortholds. Derivative shortholds are those which come into existence

[5] *Ante*, paras. 5–10 *et seq.*
[6] Act of 1988, s.34(1)(b). For the details, see *ante*, paras. 5–10 *et seq.*
[7] See *ante*, para. 5–12, and *Thalmann v. Evans* [1996] 8 C.L. 420, C.C.
[8] This seems to be a requirement of complete identity: compare Act of 1988, s.34(3)(c) with s.34(1)(b).
[9] *ibid.*, s.34(3), referring to the requirements in s.20(1).
[10] *ibid.*

upon the termination of the original shorthold. They may arise either expressly, or pursuant to the Act of 1988.

1. Conditions for continuance

Once an assured shorthold tenancy has been created, any further tenancy of the same premises between the same parties will normally also be an assured shorthold tenancy, provided that four conditions are satisfied. **8–36**

(a) New tenancy

On the assured shorthold tenancy coming to an end, a further assured tenancy must have come into being.[11] It is immaterial whether the prior tenancy had ceased to be assured before it came to an end, provided that it was a shorthold at some time and that the new tenancy is an assured tenancy.[12] It is also immaterial whether the new tenancy is expressly granted or a statutory periodic tenancy which comes into being under the Act of 1988.[13] **8–37**

(b) Same premises

The premises under the two tenancies must be the same, or substantially the same.[14] **8–38**

(c) Same parties

The landlord and the tenant must be the same under the new tenancy as at the coming to an end of the earlier tenancy.[15] Where there are joint landlords or joint tenants, the words "landlord" and "tenant" refer to "all the persons who jointly constitute the landlord or the tenant".[16] Where the new tenancy is a statutory periodic tenancy, no difficulty is likely to arise as the new tenancy is impliedly granted *eo instante* as the ending of the original shorthold tenancy. But in the case of an expressly granted derivative tenancy, the grant may be made before the expiry of the original tenancy, to take effect upon its termination. In such a case, the critical time is the coming to an end of the original shorthold tenancy, and so it is the identity of the landlords under the new tenancy *at that time* which is important, not the identity of the lessors at the date of grant. **8–39**

[11] Act of 1988, s.20(4).
[12] *ibid.*; see *ante*, p. 16 ("if and so long as").
[13] See *ante*, paras. 7–02 *et seq.*
[14] Act of 1988, s.20(4).
[15] *ibid.*
[16] *ibid.*, s.45(3).

2. The tenancy

8–40 Where these conditions are satisfied, the new tenancy will, if and so long as it is an assured tenancy, be an assured shorthold tenancy, whether or not it otherwise satisfies the requirements[17] for such a tenancy.[18] Thus it may be a periodic tenancy, a fixed term tenancy for less than six months, or a tenancy for which no shorthold notice was given before it began. However, if the landlord (or, where there are joint landlords, one of them[19]) serves notice on the tenant that the new tenancy is not to be a shorthold tenancy, and he does this before the tenancy is entered into (or before it takes effect in possession, if it is a statutory periodic tenancy), the tenancy will be an ordinary assured tenancy and not a shorthold tenancy.[20]

3. Repeated continuance

8–41 There is no limit to the number of times that these derivative shorthold tenancy provisions can operate.[21] So, for example, if before the termination of the original shorthold a new assured tenancy is expressly granted to take effect upon termination, and six months after expiry of that new tenancy a further new assured tenancy is expressly granted, both expressly granted tenancies and the intervening statutory periodic assured tenancy are assured shorthold tenancies.

Sect. 4. Nature of Old Assured Shorthold Tenancies

1. Rights of assured shorthold tenants

(a) Assured tenants

8–42 In all repects save as to termination and references to rent assessment committees, assured shorthold tenants have the same rights and protection, and are subject to the same obligations and liabilities, as assured tenants. So, for example, even a 12 months fixed term shorthold tenancy can be terminated by a possession order on any of the grounds (subject to the same preconditions and restrictions) as a 12 months fixed term assured tenancy could be.[22]

[17] *i.e.* those in Act of 1988, s.20(1).
[18] Act of 1988, s.20(4).
[19] *ibid.*, s.20(6)(b).
[20] *ibid.*, s.20(5).
[21] *Lower Street Properties Ltd. v. Jones* [1996] 2 E.G.L.R. 67, CA.
[22] Act of 1988, ss.7(6), 21(1), Sched. 2, Grounds 2, 8, 10, 11, 12, 13, 14, 14A, 15 and 17: see *post*, para. 13–42.

(b) Rent assessment committees

Unlike assured tenants, who only have the right to challenge a notice served by their landlord proposing an increased rent under a statutory periodic tenancy,[23] original assured shorthold tenants have the right to apply to a rent assessment committee for a determination of the rent which the landlord might reasonably be expected to obtain under the tenancy.[24] This right is not to be equated with the right of a protected tenant to refer the rent payable to a rent officer. Under the Act of 1988, the rent assessment committee will only make a determination if they consider that the rent payable under the shorthold tenancy is "significantly higher" than the landlord might reasonably have been expected to obtain having regard to the level of rents under assured tenancies in the area.[25] There is little evidence to suggest that rent assessment committees have been very active in exercising this jurisdiction. But it may be of some comfort to a prospective tenant in a strong letting market, who has to offer to pay "over the odds" in order to obtain the tenancy. The limited rent control was presumably regarded by Parliament as the "price" to be paid by the landlord for the benefit of excluding security of tenure. Parliament was still of essentially the same view when it came to pass the Housing Act 1996.[26] **8–43**

Tenants under derivative assured shortholds, on the other hand, have no right as such to refer the rent to a rent assessment committee.[27] But if the tenancy is periodic, and not for a fixed term, the tenant has the right, in common with other periodic assured tenants, to refer the rent to the committee if the landlord serves a notice of increase.[28] **8–44**

2. Mandatory ground for possession

Assured shorthold tenancies, like protected shorthold tenancies before them, are subject to a special mandatory ground for possession. For these purposes, the classification is different, namely fixed term and periodic tenancies. All original assured shortholds are necessarily for a fixed term, but derivative assured shortholds may be either fixed term (if expressly granted) or periodic (if statutory periodic tenancies). One statutory provision applies to claims to possession of a dwelling-house let on a fixed term shorthold tenancy; another applies where the shorthold is a periodic tenancy. The provisions of this special mandatory ground for possession are considered in detail in Chapter 14, "Mandatory Grounds for Possession".[29–30] **8–45**

[23] For the details, see *post*, para. 17–16.
[24] Act of 1988, s.22(1). For the details, see *post*, paras. 18–04 *et seq.*
[25] *ibid.*, s.22(3).
[26] See *post*, para. 8–57.
[27] Act of 1988, s.22(2)(b).
[28] *Post*, paras. 17–16 *et seq.*
[29–30] *Post*, paras. 14–78 *et seq.*

B. "NEW" ASSURED SHORTHOLD TENANCIES

In this Part, for brevity, the terms "shorthold" or "assured shorthold tenancy" denote a "new" assured shorthold tenancy; where an "old" assured shorthold tenancy is intended to be referred to, that terminology will be specifically used.

Sect. 5. Creation of New Assured Shorthold Tenancies

8–46 A tenancy cannot be a "new" assured shorthold tenancy unless it is entered into on or after February 28, 1997 and it complies with the requirements for being an assured tenancy.[31] Subject to those conditions, the tenancy is *ipso facto* an assured shorthold tenancy unless it falls within any of the excluded categories discussed in Section 1 above.[32] There is therefore no requirement that any notice be given to the tenant stating that the tenancy is to be a shorthold tenancy; nor is there any restriction on the length or type of term to be granted, or on the terms of the tenancy as to termination.[33] In effect, one of the "conditions" of creation of a shorthold tenancy is the same as that which applied in the case of "old" shorthold tenancies because one of the categories of exclusion is where the tenant has previously been a tenant of the same landlord under a non-shorthold assured tenancy.[34] Similarly, a re-grant to a protected or statutory tenant (but not to a protected shorthold tenant or a "deemed" protected shorthold tenant) will create a protected tenancy, and not an assured tenancy at all.[35]

8–47 It follows that a weekly periodic tenancy can be an original assured shorthold tenancy, as can a fixed term tenancy of less than six months. As with "old" assured shorthold tenancies, there is nothing in the Act of 1988 which requires a shorthold tenancy to be made in writing; and so a tenancy taking effect in possession for a term not exceeding three years and at the best rent which can reasonably be obtained without taking a fine[36] can be created orally.

[31] See *ante*, pp. 23–64.
[32] Act of 1988, s.19A, inserted by Housing Act 1996, ss.96(1), 232(3); S.I. 1997 No. 225. The excluded categories are those in Act of 1988, Sched. 2A, similarly inserted pursuant to *ibid.*, s.96(2): see *ante*, paras. 8–05 *et seq.*
[33] Some measure of security, a minimum of 6 months, is conferred by the provisions as to recovery of possession from an assured shorthold tenant: see *post*, para. 14–102.
[34] Act of 1988, Sched. 2A, para. 7; *ante*, paras. 8–12 *et seq.*
[35] In this respect, the effect is the same as that considered at para. 8–32, *ante*, in relation to "old" assured shorthold tenancies.
[36] Law of Property Act 1925, s.54(2). For an interesting case on the exact meaning of this well-known formula, see *Long v. Tower Hamlets L.B.C.* [1998] Ch. 197, CA.

Sect. 6. Continuance: Derivative New Assured Shorthold Tenancy

Derivative shortholds are those which come into existence upon the termination of the original shorthold. They may arise either expressly, or pursuant to the Act of 1988. In the new provisions of the Act of 1988 relating to assured shorthold tenancies,[37] derivative shortholds, regardless of whether they are expressly granted or statutory, are referred to as "replacement" tenancies and that terminology will be used in this Part to assist in distinguishing "new" shortholds from "old" shortholds. 8–48

The provisions relating to derivative "old" assured shorthold tenancies do not apply;[38] they do not need to because, subject to the exclusions, any assured tenancy entered into on or after February 28, 1997 will be a shorthold, regardless of length of term, shorthold notices, and termination provisions.[39] Instead, the Act of 1988 makes clear that any assured statutory periodic tenancy coming into being under section 5 of the Act on the termination of an assured shorthold tenancy is, subject to the exclusions, an assured shorthold tenancy.[40] Equally, any expressly-granted replacement tenancy will, subject to the exclusions, be an assured shorthold tenancy in its own right.[41] There are not, and do not need to be, any provisions as to the identity of the tenant and the landlord being the same under the replacement tenancy. If, on the other hand, the existing assured tenancy is not a shorthold tenancy, a re-grant by at least one of the landlords to at least one of the tenants under that tenancy is not a shorthold unless the tenant elects by notice to have it so.[42]

Sect. 7. Nature of New Assured Shorthold Tenancies

(a) Assured tenants

Like "old" assured shorthold tenancies, "new" shortholds are assured tenancies and so, save as otherwise stated in this section, are subject to the same incidents, rights and obligations as normal assured tenancies. There are three main differences: the right of a shorthold tenant in certain circumstances to require his landlord to provide him with a written statement of terms of the tenancy;[43] his right to refer the rent payable under the shorthold to a rent assess- 8–49

[37] Inserted on February 28, 1997 by Housing Act 1996, ss.96–100, 104, Scheds. 7, 8; S.I. 1997 No. 225.
[38] Act of 1988, s.20(5A), inserted by Housing Act 1996, ss.104, 232(3), Sched. 8, para. 2(4); S.I. 1997 No. 225.
[39] Act of 1988, s.19A(a).
[40] *ibid.*, s.19(A)(b).
[41] *ibid.*, s.19A(a).
[42] *ibid.*, s.19A, Sched. 2A, para. 7.
[43] *Ibid.*, s.20A; see *infra*.

ment committee; and the special mandatory ground for possession. These will be considered in turn.

(b) Statement of terms of tenancy

8–50 The effect of the changes made by the Housing Act 1996 to the shorthold tenancy provisions of the Act of 1988 is that a shorthold tenancy can now be created without any formality at all: neither a written shorthold notice, nor even (in the case of a short lease) a written agreement.[44] A short assured tenancy has always been capable of creation orally, but in such a case the tenant at least has security of tenure, and probably knows full well the amount of the rent agreed. Where a shorthold is concerned, the length of the term granted and the commencement date may be of greater importance in relation to the landlord's entitlement to recover possession six months after the beginning of the original shorthold.[45] Accordingly, a new section[46] has been introduced[47] into the Act of 1988 which, in certain circumstances, entitles a tenant under an assured shorthold tenancy to serve a notice requiring his landlord, upon pain of committing a criminal offence, to provide a written statement of certain terms of the tenancy.

8–51 (i) THE ENTITLEMENT: at any time, in relation to a permitted term,[48] if the term in question is not evidenced in writing,[49] and provided that the landlord has not previously given a written statement of that term in response to an earlier notice served by the tenant, the term in question being unchanged since the date when that statement was provided.[50] The landlord here is "the landlord under the tenancy", and so a statement given by the landlord's predecessor in relation to a term will, provided that the term has not since been varied, preclude the tenant from serving a further notice on the successor landlord. Equally, it appears that if "the tenant under the tenancy" has already given a written notice in relation to a permitted term and that term has not been varied since the previous written statement in response, the tenant cannot serve a further notice, even if the earlier notice was given by his predecessor in title. It is specifically provided[51] that a notice given by one or more joint tenants to one or more joint landlords is permitted;[52] accordingly, one joint tenant will not be entitled to serve a notice on one joint landlord if his co-tenant has previously served notice

[44] Even under the "old" shorthold system, there was no need for a written tenancy agreement if the lease was a short lease, but at least the mandatory shorthold notice fully identified the parties and their addresses (and the landlord's agent), the dwelling-house, and the term and commencement date of the tenancy.

[45] *Post*, paras. 14–102 *et seq*.; and equally in relation to the tenant's right to refer the rent: *post*, para. 18–27.

[46] Act of 1988, s.20A.

[47] By Housing Act 1996, ss.97, 232(3); S.I. 1997 No. 225.

[48] Act of 1988, s.20A(1)(a).

[49] At first blush, the use of the phrase "evidenced in writing" is odd, but it appears to be consciously designed to cover the case where there is a written tenancy agreement but the document is silent as to one of the terms in question, such as the commencement date.

[50] *ibid*., s.20A(3).

[51] Thereby ousting the contrary general provision in Act of 1988, s.45(3).

[52] *ibid*., s.20A(7).

on and received a written statement relating to the same (unvaried) term from another joint landlord, or even from a previous landlord. If the term in question is varied subsequently to a written response, the tenant is entitled to serve a further notice.

Where a term of a statutory periodic tenancy became such by virtue of its being a term of the previous fixed term tenancy,[53] and that term in that tenancy was evidenced in writing, the tenant is not entitled to serve a notice under the statutory periodic tenancy in relation to that term.[54] Similarly, where a term of a succession assured shorthold tenancy[55] became such by virtue of its being a term of the previous actual or deemed protected shorthold tenancy vested in the deceased,[56] and that term in that tenancy was evidenced in writing, the tenant is not entitled to serve a notice under the statutory periodic assured shorthold tenancy in relation to that term.[57] **8–52**

(ii) THE PERMITTED TERMS: there are four categories of terms in respect of which the tenant is entitled to serve a notice: **8–53**

(1) the date on which the tenancy began or, if it is a statutory periodic tenancy or an assured shorthold tenancy to which the tenant succeeded on the death of his predecessor,[58] the date on which the tenancy came into being;[59]
(2) the rent payable under the tenancy and the dates on which that rent is payable;[60]
(3) any term providing for a review of the rent payable under the tenancy,[61] and
(4) in the case of a fixed term tenancy only, the length of the fixed term.[62]

(iii) THE NOTICE: there is no form prescribed for such a written notice, and accordingly it need only state that the landlord is required to provide the giver of the notice with a written statement of the permitted term or terms (which the notice identifies) of the shorthold tenancy. Where there are joint tenants, the notice may be given by any one or more of them, and it may be given to any one or more of joint landlords.[63] **8–54**

(iv) THE SANCTION: if a landlord fails, without reasonable excuse, to comply with a written notice by a tenant within the period of 28 days beginning with **8–55**

[53] Pursuant to Act of 1988, s.5(3)(e).
[54] Act of 1988, s.20A(6)(a).
[55] Arising in the circumstances identified *post*, at para. 12–24.
[56] *i.e.* pursuant to *ibid.*, s.39(6)(e).
[57] *ibid.*, s.20A(6)(b).
[58] Pursuant to Act of 1988, s.39(7). Of the many possible categories of succession to an assured tenancy, this is the only one where the successor becomes entitled to an assured shorthold tenancy: *ibid.*, Sched. 2A, para. 4.
[59] *ibid.*, s.20A(2)(a).
[60] *ibid.*, s.20A(2)(b).
[61] *ibid.*, s.20A(2)(c).
[62] *ibid.*, s.20A(2)(d).
[63] *ibid.*, s.20A(7), ousting the general provision in *ibid.*, s.45(3) to the contrary.

the date on which he received the notice, he is liable on summary conviction to a fine not exceeding level 4[64] on the standard scale.[65] The Act states that in certain circumstances[66] no notice may be given by the tenant; it also states that a notice may be given in relation to certain terms only[67] which are not evidenced in writing. It seems that the *actus reus* of the offence is not made out if the landlord fails timeously to respond to a notice given by the tenant when he (the tenant) is not entitled to do so, or to a notice in relation to a non-permitted term, or to a notice in relation to a term evidenced in writing,[68] and the landlord in those circumstances will not have to discharge the onus of proving a reasonable excuse within the meaning of the Act. To comply, *semble* the landlord must provide the tenant with the written statement of the term no later than the twenty-seventh day after the day on which he received the notice. Whether such written statement is ''provided'' to the tenant if it is left for him at the dwelling-house, as opposed to handed to him, is not clear.

8–56 (v) EVIDENTIAL VALUE OF WRITTEN STATEMENT: it is not regarded as conclusive evidence of what was agreed by the parties to the tenancy in question.[69] In the two cases identified in (i) above,[70] the tenancy in question must be taken to be the previous fixed term or protected shorthold tenancy, as the case may be.

(c) Rent assessment committees

8–57 Unlike assured tenants, who only have the right to challenge a notice served by their landlord proposing an increased rent under a statutory periodic tenancy,[71] original assured shorthold tenants have the right to apply to a rent assessment committee for a determination of the rent which the landlord might reasonably be expected to obtain under the tenancy.[72] This right is not to be equated with the right of a protected tenant to refer the rent payable to a Rent Officer. Under the Act of 1988, the rent assessment committee will only make a determination if they consider that the rent payable under the shorthold tenancy is ''significantly higher'' than the landlord might reasonably have been expected to obtain having regard to the level of rents under assured tenancies in the area.[73] There is little evidence to suggest that rent assessment committees have been very active in exercising this jurisdiction. But it may be of some comfort to a prospective tenant in a strong letting market, who has to offer to pay ''over the odds'' in order to obtain the tenancy. The limited rent control was presumably

[64] Currently £2,500.
[65] Act of 1988, s.20A(4).
[66] See (i) THE ENTITLEMENT, *supra*.
[67] *Supra*.
[68] Because the offence is failing to comply with a notice ''under subsection (1) above'' and all three such notices would not be in accordance with paras. (a) and (b) of s.20(A)(1).
[69] Act of 1988, s.20A(5).
[70] Statutory periodic tenancy and succession assured shorthold tenancy: *ante*, para. 8–52.
[71] For the details, see *post*, paras. 17–16 *et seq.*
[72] Act of 1988, s.22(1). For the details, see *post*, paras. 18–26 *et seq.*
[73] *ibid.*, s.22(3).

regarded by Parliament as the "price" to be paid by the landlord for the benefit of excluding security of tenure.

Tenants under "replacement", assured shortholds have no right as such to refer the rent to a rent assessment committee once six months have elapsed since the beginning of the original tenancy.[74] But if the tenancy is periodic, and not for a fixed term, the tenant has the right, in common with other periodic assured tenants, to refer the rent to the committee if the landlord serves a notice of increase.[75] **8–58**

(d) Mandatory ground for possession

The provisions of the special mandatory ground for possession are considered in detail in Chapter 14, "Mandatory Grounds for Possession".[76] **8–59**

[74] Act of 1988, s.22(2)(aa).
[75] *Post*, paras. 17–16 *et seq.*
[76] *Post*, paras. 14–101 *et seq.*

Chapter 9

Assured Agricultural Occupancies

9–01 Workers in agriculture and forestry often occupied their homes on terms which formerly left them outside the Rent Acts. Some were mere service occupiers or other licensees, and so held no tenancy; others, although tenants, were outside the Rent Acts because they paid little or no rent, or because they received meals, so that their rent included payment for "board".[1] The Rent (Agriculture) Act 1976 gave such workers the status of being "protected occupiers", with a form of protection that was similar to that given by the Rent Acts, including a somewhat modified form of statutory tenancy.[2] At the same time, the Act of 1976 varied the Rent Acts so that the protection given to such of these workers as fell within the Rent Acts was the same as the protection that was given to those who did not. The Act of 1988, with its new regime of assured tenancies, continued this uniformity of treatment, and uses the term "assured agricultural occupancy" to include both tenancies and licences where the agricultural worker condition is for the time being fulfilled. "Protected occupiers" continue as before under the Rent (Agriculture) Act 1976, but (subject to transitional provisions) no new protected occupancies under that Act can be created after January 15, 1989.

Sect. 1. Assured Agricultural Occupancies Defined

1. Definition

9–02 A tenancy or licence of a dwelling-house will be an assured agricultural occupancy if it satisfies three requirements.

[1] See Vol. 1, pp. 67–80, 160–164, 167–173. For the final say on the meaning of "board", see *Otter v. Norman* [1989] A.C. 129.
[2] Vol. 1, p. 300.

(a) Type of tenancy or licence

In order to be an assured agricultural occupancy, a tenancy or licence must fall within one of the three following categories.

(i) ASSURED TENANCY. "An assured tenancy which is not an assured shorthold tenancy".[3] This imports the conditions for being an assured tenancy and an assured shorthold tenancy that have already been considered.[4] For these purposes, there is no distinction between a "new" and an "old" assured shorthold tenancy.[5] An assured tenancy in respect of which the agricultural worker condition[6] is for the time being fulfilled with regard to the dwelling-house subject to the tenancy cannot generally be a "new" assured shorthold tenancy.[7] But it may be a "new" assured shorthold tenancy if in certain circumstances, prior to entering into the tenancy, the landlord serves on the tenant a notice in the prescribed form stating that the tenancy is to be an assured shorthold tenancy.[8] These circumstances do not include the case where the tenancy is to be granted to the tenant or licensee (or, where there are joint tenants or licensees, at least one of them) by the landlord or licensor (or at least one of joint landlords or licensors) under an assured agricultural occupancy which existed immediately before the grant of the tenancy;[9] but they do include the case of a statutory periodic tenancy arising[10] upon the termination of an assured shorthold tenancy in respect of which the prescribed form notice was served.[11] **9–03**

(ii) EXCEPTED TENANCIES. A tenancy other than a tenancy of an agricultural holding[12] or a farm business tenancy[13] that is not an assured tenancy for one or both of two reasons. First, because the rent is low, or no rent is payable; secondly, because the dwelling-house is comprised in an agricultural holding or in the holding held under a farm business tenancy, and in either case is occupied by the person responsible for the control of the farming or management of the holding.[14] Thus, dwellings comprised in agricultural holdings or holdings under new farm business tenancies are excluded from being assured agricultural occupancies where the tenant under such a holding or tenancy occupies them; but **9–04**

[3] Act of 1988, s.24(1)(a), (2)(a).
[4] See *ante*, pp. 18–64 (assured tenancy), 110 *et seq.* (assured shorthold tenancy).
[5] For these, see *ante*, paras. 8–01, 8–02.
[6] See *infra*.
[7] Act of 1988, s.19A, Sched. 2A, para. 9(1), inserted with effect from February 28, 1997 by Housing Act 1996, ss. 96, 232(3), Sched. 7; S.I. 1997 No. 225.
[8] Act of 1988, Sched. 2A, para. 9(2); Assured Tenancies and Agricultural Occupancies (Forms) Regulations 1997 (S.I. 1997 No. 194), reg. 3(i), Sched., Form No. 9.
[9] Act of 1988, Sched. 2A, para. 9(2)(b), (3).
[10] *i.e.* under *ibid.*, s.5.
[11] *ibid.*, Sched. 2A, para. 9(4).
[12] Within the meaning of the Agricultural Holdings Act 1986, and to which that Act applies.
[13] Within the meaning of the Agricultural Tenancies Act 1995.
[14] Act of 1988, s.24(1)(a), (2)(b), as amended successively by References to Rating (Housing) Regulations 1990 (S.I. 1990 No. 434), Sched., para. 28 (applying the three new paragraphs of Act of 1988, Sched. 1 relating to the low rent test instead of the one previous paragraph based on rateable value: see *ante*, paras. 4–53 *et seq.*), and by Housing Act 1996, ss.103, 232(3); S.I. 1997 No. 225 (adding the exclusion of tenancies of agricultural holdings and farm business tenancies).

they are not excluded if they are occupied by some other person responsible for the control of the farming or management of the holding.

9–05 (iii) LICENCES. A licence under which a person has the exclusive occupation of a dwelling-house as a separate dwelling, and which, if it conferred a sufficient interest in land to be a tenancy, would be a tenancy falling within categories (i) or (ii) above.[15] The terms "licence", "exclusive occupation", "dwelling-house" and "as a separate dwelling" have all been considered above.[16]

9–06 A tenancy or licence which falls within one of the three heads above is called a "relevant tenancy or licence",[17] and the tenant or licensee under it, and the dwelling-house let or occupied under it, are called "the occupier" and "the dwelling-house" respectively.[18]

(b) Agricultural worker condition

9–07 The second requirement of an assured agricultural occupancy is that the "agricultural worker condition" must be "for the time being fulfilled with respect to the dwelling-house subject to the tenancy or licence".[19] The "agricultural worker condition" is a very complex concept that depends upon the terms "agriculture", "qualifying ownership", "a qualifying worker" and "a qualifying injury or disease".[20] The agricultural worker condition is fulfilled if at any time during the subsistence of the tenancy or licence (whether or not it was at that time a "relevant tenancy or licence")—

(1) the dwelling-house is or has been in qualifying ownership, and
(2) the occupier (or one of them, if there are joint occupiers) is or has been a qualifying worker.[21]

An alternative to (2) is that the occupier (or one of them, if there are joint occupiers) is incapable of whole-time work in agriculture (or work in agriculture as a permit worker) in consequence of a qualifying injury or disease, and became incapable while thus employed in agriculture.[22]

The Act of 1988[23] gives these terms the same meaning as the Rent (Agriculture) Act 1976 gave them.[24] Put shortly, "agriculture" includes dairy-farming, livestock keeping and breeding, the production of consumable produce for trade or business or for any other undertaking, the use of land as grazing, meadow, pasture or orchard land, or for market gardens or nursery grounds, and

[15] Act of 1988, s.24(1)(a), (2)(c).
[16] *Ante*, paras. 3–02 *et seq*, 3–09, 3–15.
[17] Act of 1988, Sched. 3, para. 1(1).
[18] *ibid*., para. 1(2).
[19] *ibid*., s.24(1)(b), Sched. 3.
[20] See *infra* for these, and the Act for full details.
[21] Act of 1988, Sched. 3, para. 2(a), (b).
[22] *ibid*., para. 2(b)(ii). See also the extensions of the condition considered *post*, p. 138.
[23] See Act of 1988, Sched. 3, para. 1(1), (3), applying Act of 1976, s.1(1), Sched. 3, paras. 1–3.
[24] See Vol. 1, p. 301.

forestry.[25] A dwelling-house is in "qualifying ownership" if the occupier is employed in agriculture, and his employer in agriculture (or one of his employers) either owns the dwelling-house and is the occupier's immediate landlord or licensor, or else has made arrangements with a landlord or licensor for the dwelling-house to be used as living accommodation for persons employed by him in agriculture.[26] A person is a "qualifying worker" if at the time he has worked in agriculture whole-time (or as a permit worker) for not less than 91 out of the 104 previous weeks.[27] In broad terms, a "qualifying injury or disease" is one that arose out of employment in agriculture.[28]

(c) Grant on or after January 15, 1989

As an assured agricultural occupancy is treated as if it were an assured tenancy,[29] it is subject to the list of exceptions from being an assured tenancy,[30] and in particular to the exception of having been entered into before January 15, 1989, or pursuant to a contract made before then.[31] A tenancy or licence can therefore be an assured agricultural occupancy only if it was entered into on or after that date, and not pursuant to a contract made before then. Existing protected occupiers or statutory tenants under the Act of 1976 accordingly continue as such.[32] **9–08**

There are also two cases[33] in which a person will be a protected occupier even if the licence or tenancy is entered into on or after January 15, 1989. They are as follows. **9–09**

(i) PRIOR CONTRACT: where the licence or tenancy is entered into pursuant to a contract made before that date.[34]

(ii) GRANT TO SITTING TENANT: where the licence or tenancy is granted to a person (either alone or jointly with others) who immediately before was a protected occupier or statutory tenant under the Rent (Agriculture) Act 1976, and it is granted by the person who is then the licensor or landlord under the protected occupancy or statutory tenancy, or one of the joint licensors or landlords.[35]

The provisions for the conversion of tenancies on a change of landlord that have already been considered also apply to protected occupancies or statutory tenancies under the Act of 1976.[36] Accordingly, if on January 15, 1989 the interest **9–10**

[25] Act of 1976, s.1(1); and see s.1(2).
[26] *ibid.*, Sched. 3, para. 3.
[27] *ibid.*, para. 1.
[28] *ibid.*, para. 2.
[29] *Post*, para. 9–17.
[30] *Ante*, para. 4–03.
[31] *Ante*, paras. 4–48 *et seq.*
[32] For them, see Vol. 1, pp. 299–303, 677–680.
[33] Corresponding to similar transitional provisions for protected tenancies: *ante*, paras. 5–09, 5–10.
[34] Act of 1988, s.34(4)(a).
[35] *ibid.*, s.34(4)(b).
[36] *ibid.*, s.38; see *ante*, paras. 5–56, 5–59.

of the landlord under the tenancy was held by a "public body"[37] or the tenancy was then a housing association tenancy, and (in either case) the interest of the landlord is transferred to a private owner, the tenancy cannot thereupon (or at any time thereafter) become a protected occupancy under the Act of 1976, but subject to satisfaction of the statutory requirements other than the one as to date of grant,[38] the tenancy may be an assured tenancy and, accordingly, may be an assured agricultural occupancy.[39] There is a separate provision for interests held by a New Town corporation,[40] but this is most unlikely to give rise to either a protected occupancy or an assured agricultural occupancy.

2. Extensions of agricultural worker condition

9–11 The "agricultural worker condition" is extended so as to include three other cases.[41]

(a) Transmission on death

9–12 If the agricultural worker condition is fulfilled, but the occupier dies, provision is made whereby that condition will be fulfilled so that his or her "qualifying widow or widower", or the "qualifying member" of his or her family, will be the occupier within the Act of 1988.[42] This is considered later.[43]

(b) Change of dwelling-house

9–13 Provision is made for the agricultural worker condition to be fulfilled despite the occupier moving from one dwelling-house to another. If the new dwelling-house is to be subject to a relevant tenancy or licence, the agricultural worker condition is fulfilled if two requirements are satisfied:

(1) that the tenancy or licence is granted to the occupier in consideration of his giving up possession of another dwelling-house of which he was the occupier under another relevant tenancy or licence.[44] Where the grant is made to joint occupiers, it suffices if it is made in consideration of one of them giving up possession of the other dwelling-house either as occupier or as one of the occupiers.[45]
(2) that as a result of the occupier's occupation, immediately before pos-

[37] As defined in *ibid.*, s.38(5), and including the Crown.
[38] *ibid.*, Sched. 1, para. 1, excluded by s.38(3)(c).
[39] *ibid.*, s.38(3).
[40] *Ante*, para. 5–60.
[41] For the corresponding provision under the Act of 1976, see Vol. 1, p. 301.
[42] Act of 1988, Sched. 3, para. 3.
[43] *Post*, paras. 12–13 *et seq.*
[44] Act of 1988, Sched. 3, para. 4(a).
[45] *ibid.*

session of the other dwelling-house was given up, the agricultural worker condition was fulfilled with respect to it.[46]

(c) New occupancy of same dwelling-house

Provision is also made for the fulfilment of the agricultural worker condition on the grant of a new tenancy or licence of the same dwelling-house. There are two requirements: **9–14**

(1) the agricultural worker condition must be fulfilled with respect to a dwelling-house that is subject to a relevant tenancy or licence ("the earlier tenancy or licence");[47]
(2) another relevant tenancy or licence of the same dwelling-house ("the later tenancy or licence") must have been granted to the person who, immediately before the grant, was the occupier (or one of joint occupiers) under the earlier tenancy or licence, and it must have been as a result of his occupation that the agricultural worker condition was fulfilled under (1) above.[48]

In these cases, so long as the person whose occupation caused the agricultural worker condition to be fulfilled under the earlier tenancy or licence continues to be the occupier (or one of joint occupiers) under the later tenancy or licence, the agricultural worker condition will be fulfilled.[49]

Where the agricultural worker condition is fulfilled under any of these three extensions, it is to be treated as being fulfilled under the same extension for any later tenancy of licence.[50] **9–15**

Sect. 2. Statutory Periodic Tenancies

If an assured agricultural occupancy is a fixed term tenancy, then as in the case of other fixed term assured tenancies a statutory periodic tenancy may arise when the fixed term tenancy ends.[51] That statutory periodic tenancy will itself be an assured agricultural occupancy as long as the agricultural worker condition is for the time being fulfilled with respect to the dwelling-house in question;[52] one assured agricultural occupancy will thus replace another. Where no rent was payable under the fixed term tenancy, and so there is nothing to determine what **9–16**

[46] *ibid.*, para. 4(b), applying to fulfilment under paras. 2, 3 or 4.
[47] *ibid.*, para. 5(1)(a), applying to fulfilment under paras. 2, 3 or 4.
[48] *ibid.*, para. 5(1)(b).
[49] *ibid.*, para. 5(2).
[50] *ibid.*, para. 5(3).
[51] *ibid.*, ss.5(2), 25(1). See *ante*, pp. 100 *et seq.* for statutory periodic tenancies.
[52] *ibid.*, s.25(1)(a).

the periods of the statutory periodic tenancy are to be,[53] the periods will be monthly, beginning on the day following the coming to an end of the fixed term tenancy.[54]

Sect. 3. Nature of Assured Agricultural Occupancies

1. Treatment as assured tenancy

9–17 "Every assured agricultural occupancy which is not an assured tenancy shall be treated as if it were such a tenancy".[55] For this purpose, any reference to a tenant, a landlord or any other expression appropriate to a tenancy is to be construed accordingly.[56] The provisions relating to assured tenancies[57] have effect, however, subject to the provisions[58] relating to assured agricultural occupancies,[59] though there are few of these. They are considered below.

2. Special treatment

9–18 In four cases, assured agricultural occupancies are treated differently from assured tenancies, or have special rules.

(a) Open market rent

9–19 In considering the open market rent for a dwelling-house, a rent assessment committee must, for these occupancies, consider a letting under an assured agricultural occupancy instead of under an assured tenancy.[60] This is considered later.[61]

(b) Notice to quit

9–20 If the tenant under an assured agricultural occupancy gives notice to terminate his employment, the notice is not to constitute a notice to quit as respects the occupancy, notwithstanding anything in any agreement or otherwise.[62] But this

53 See *ante*, para. 7–11.
54 Act of 1988, s.5(3)(d), as varied by s.25(1)(b).
55 *ibid.*, s.24(3), applying ss.1–19, 24–26.
56 *ibid.*
57 *i.e.* Act of 1988, Chap. I (ss.1–19).
58 *i.e.* Act of 1988, Chap. III (ss.24–26).
59 *ibid.*, s.24(3).
60 *ibid.*, s.14(1), as modified by s.24(4).
61 *Post*, para. 17–51.
62 Act of 1988, s.25(4).

does not affect the operation of any actual notice to quit given in respect of the occupancy.[63]

(c) Grounds for possession

There is one ground for possession which does not apply to assured agricultural occupancies.[64] That is Ground 16, which applies where a dwelling-house has been let to the tenant in consequence of his employment by the landlord or a previous landlord, and he has ceased to be in that employment.[65] In addition, in considering alternative accommodation[66] in respect of these occupancies, premises which are capable of constituting suitable alternative accommodation include those that are to be let on an assured agricultural occupancy as well as those to be let on an assured tenancy.[67] The grounds for possession applicable to an assured tenancy are considered later.[68] **9–21**

(d) Transmission on death

There are certain differences between the provisions for succession to an assured tenancy on the death of the tenant, and the provisions for succession to an assured agricultural occupancy on the death of the occupier. These are considered later.[69] **9–22**

[63] Act of 1988, s.25(5).
[64] *ibid.*, s.25(2).
[65] *ibid.*, Sched. 2, Ground 16; *post*, para. 15–39.
[66] *ibid.*, Sched. 2, Ground 9; Pt. III.
[67] *ibid.*, s.25(3).
[68] *Post*, pp. 240–302.
[69] *Post*, paras. 12–02 *et seq.*, 12–13 *et seq.*

Chapter 10

Long Tenancies at a Low Rent

INTRODUCTION

10–01 Important and complex changes have been made in the law governing long tenancies at a low rent under Part I of the Landlord and Tenant Act 1954: for brevity, this will usually be called ''Part I'' *simpliciter*. These changes were made by the Local Government and Housing Act 1989[1] (''Act of 1989''), and by the References to Rating (Housing) Regulations 1990[2] (''Regulations of 1990'') that were made under it. Before January 15, 1989, long tenancies at a low rent were not protected tenancies under the Rent Acts by virtue of their low rent; but upon expiry of the contractual term of the long tenancy, the tenant might obtain security of tenure under the Rent Acts. The changes are threefold; but the most significant is the transfer of security of tenure for such tenants from the Rent Acts to the Act of 1988 and assured tenancies.

1. The changes

The changes fall under three heads.

(a) Rateable value

10–02 The protection conferred by Part I depended on the tenancy being a tenancy ''at a low rent'', and also on the ''qualifying condition'' being satisfied. Each of these requirements depended upon the rateable value of the dwelling. A ''low rent'' was a rent that was ''less than two-thirds of the rateable value of the property comprised in the tenancy''. The ''qualifying condition'' (put shortly)

[1] See s.186, Sched. 10, brought into force on April 1, 1990, by Local Government and Housing Act 1989 (Commencement No. 5 and Transitional Provisions) Order 1990 (S.I. 1990 No. 431).

[2] S.I. 1990 No. 434. The first print of these Regulations contained errors that were corrected in a revised printing.

required that if the tenancy had not been "at a low rent" it would have been protected by the Rent Acts, and this in turn meant that the rateable value of the dwelling must not exceed the specified figures.[3] With the abolition of the domestic rating system on April 1, 1990, and its replacement by the new system of community charges,[4] some provision was needed to supplement the tests of rateable value.

(b) Exclusion of new tenancies from the Rent Acts

Under the Act of 1988, a tenancy entered into on or after January 15, 1989 normally cannot be protected by the Rent Acts; at most it will be an assured tenancy under the Act of 1988.[5] One consequence of this is that however low the rent and however long the tenancy, a tenancy entered into on or after that date could not be protected by Part I. For under Part I, the "qualifying condition" required that the only reason for the Rent Acts being excluded should be that the rent was a "low rent", and this requirement could not be satisfied where the Rent Acts were also excluded by the date on which the tenancy was granted. This was recognised as being anomalous,[6] and provision was needed to cure the oversight. **10–03**

(c) Assured tenancies in place of statutory tenancies

Part I provided that when a long tenancy at a low rent was due to expire, the tenant should receive a statutory tenancy under the Rent Acts unless the landlord obtained possession.[7] The continuation of this system would have been inconsistent with the scheme of the Act of 1988, and so the Act of 1989 provided for the tenant to receive an assured periodic tenancy under the Act of 1988 in lieu of a statutory tenancy under the Rent Acts. Instead of merely amending Part I, the Act of 1989 enacted a comprehensive new code. This applies to most tenancies granted on or after April 1, 1990; and with effect from January 15, 1999 transitional provisions applied it to nearly all tenancies then still within Part I.[8] **10–04**

2. Categories of tenancy

It is convenient to divide long tenancies at a low rent into three categories, mainly based on the date when the tenancy was entered into. The categories are as follows. **10–05**

[3] See Vol. 1, pp. 118, 119, 305, 306.
[4] Under the Local Government Finance Act 1988.
[5] See *ante* pp. 67–73.
[6] See *ante* para. 5–40 and First Supplement (1989), p. 20.
[7] See Vol. 1, pp. 308–314.
[8] See *post*, paras. 10–63 *et seq.*

(a) Old tenancies

10–06 In general, an ''old'' tenancy is a tenancy entered into before January 15, 1989. Such tenancies stand outside the provision that a tenancy entered into on or after January 15, 1989 cannot be a protected tenancy.[9] The low rent is thus capable of being the only reason why the Rent Acts are excluded, and so the qualifying condition under Part I can be satisfied. In addition, certain tenancies entered into on or after January 15, 1989 are expressly excluded from the provision preventing such tenancies from being protected tenancies, and so these too will be treated as being ''old'' tenancies. These tenancies are[10]—

10–07 (i) PRIOR CONTRACT: a tenancy entered into in pursuance of[11] a contract made before January 15, 1989; and

10–08 (ii) GRANT TO SITTING TENANT: a tenancy granted to a person (alone or jointly with others) who, immediately before the tenancy was granted, was a protected or statutory tenant, where the tenancy is so granted by the person who was the landlord (or one of the joint landlords) under the protected or statutory tenancy.[12]

Yet ''old'' tenancies did not all remain old. Those that still existed on January 15, 1999 were subject to transitional provisions that brought them within the system that applies to ''new'' tenancies.[13]

(b) Omitted tenancies

10–09 Some tenancies are neither old tenancies within para. (a) above nor new tenancies within para. (c) below. Such tenancies appear to have been omitted from the protection both of Part I and of the Act of 1989, and so they may be called ''omitted'' tenancies. Most tenancies granted on or after January 15, 1989, but before April 1, 1990, fall into this category.

(c) New tenancies

10–10 A tenancy will be subject to the new code introduced by the Act of 1989 if it was entered into on or after April 1, 1990, otherwise than in pursuance of a contract made before that day.[14] Such tenancies are here called ''new'' tenancies.

These three categories will be considered in turn.

[9] See *ante* pp. 67–73.
[10] Act of 1988, s.34(1).
[11] *i.e.* where the contract requires the tenancy to be granted, and does not merely provide for its terms if granted: see *Proma Ltd. v. Curtis* (1989) 59 P. & C.R. 242, CA (on Leasehold Reform Act 1967, s.3(1), as amended).
[12] For two other instances, of very limited application (relating to orders for possession based on suitable alternative accommodation, and to New Towns), see *ante* paras. 5–15 to 5–19.
[13] See *post*, paras. 10–63 *et seq.*
[14] Act of 1989, s.186(2).

A. OLD TENANCIES

In general, "old" tenancies continued to be governed by Part I until they were terminated or until January 15, 1999, whichever was the sooner. Until that time, Part I applied as set out in Volume 1,[15] but as amended by the Act of 1989 and the Regulations of 1990 as set out below.

1. "Low rent"

(a) Less than two-thirds of the rateable value

As far as possible, the existing test of whether the rent "is less than . . . two-thirds of the rateable value of the property" on the appropriate day[16] has been retained; and this includes the provision that where there is a progressive rent, "rent" means the maximum rent.[17–18] This test continued to apply in two categories of tenancy. 10–11

(i) PRE-APRIL 1990 TENANCY. The first category is where the tenancy was entered into before April 1, 1990. Here, the dwelling will normally have a rateable value on the appropriate day. If it does not, but a rateable value is subsequently entered in the list, provision has been made for that rateable value, when entered, to apply for these purposes.[19] 10–12

(ii) PRE-APRIL 1990 CONTRACT. The second category is where the tenancy was entered into on or after April 1, 1990 in pursuance of a contract made before that date, but the dwelling had a rateable value on March 31, 1990. It is arguable that this category includes cases where a rateable value for the dwelling is subsequently entered in the list if that was pursuant to a proposal made before April 1, 1990.[20]

(b) Not more than fixed sums

Where the tenancy was entered into on or after April 1, 1990, and it does not fall within category (a)(ii) above, the test is whether the rent is £1,000 a year or less for property in Greater London, or £250 a year or less elsewhere.[21] This is 10–13

15 pp. 304–317.
16 Act of 1954, s.2(5), substituted by Regulations of 1990, Sched., para. 3; Act of 1977, s.5(1).
17–18 *ibid.*
19 See Local Government Finance (Repeals, Savings and Consequential Amendments) Order 1990 (S.I. 1990 No. 776) and General Rate Act 1967 and Related Provisions (Savings and Consequential Provision) Regulations 1990 (S.I. 1990 No. 777); *ante*, paras. 4–09 *et seq.*
20 See *ante*, para. 4–12.
21 Act of 1954, s.2(5), substituted by Regulations of 1990, Sched., para. 3. The grammar of s.2(5)(b) is curious: ". . . the rent . . . is less than . . . is payable at the rate of, — (i) £1,000 or less a year [London] and (ii) £250 or less a year [elsewhere]".

the test that applies to new tenancies as well; it is considered below.[22] The Secretary of State may alter these figures by a statutory instrument, subject to a negative resolution by either House of Parliament.[23]

2. Qualifying condition

As stated above,[24] certain tenancies entered into on or after April 1, 1990 will nevertheless rank as "old" tenancies. For the purposes of the "qualifying condition" they fall into two categories.

(a) Prior contract and rateable value

10–14 Where the tenancy was entered into in pursuance of a contract made before April 1, 1990, and the dwelling comprised in the tenancy also had a rateable value on March 31, 1990, the qualifying condition under the Act of 1954[25] continued to apply.

(b) Other tenancies

10–15 In all other cases, provision was made for in effect decapitalising any premium paid for the grant of the tenancy. This provision is complementary to an amended provision which prevents a tenancy under this head from being a protected tenancy if the rent for the time being is payable at a rate exceeding £25,000 a year.[26] Where a premium has been paid, a complex formula has to be applied for the sole purpose of determining whether the qualifying condition is satisfied. The tenancy cannot be a protected tenancy (and so the qualifying condition cannot be satisfied) if—

> "on the date the contract for the grant of the tenancy was made . . . R exceeded £25,000 under the formula—
>
> $$R = \frac{P \times I}{1 - (1 + I)^{-T}}$$
>
> where—
>
> P is the premium payable as a condition of the grant of the tenancy (and includes a payment of money's worth) or, where no premium is so payable, zero,
> I is 0.06, and
> T is the term, expressed in years, granted by the tenancy (disregarding any

[22] *Post*, para. 10–22.
[23] Act of 1954, s.2(8), inserted by Regulations of 1990, Sched., para. 4.
[24] *Ante*, paras. 10–07, 10–08.
[25] Act of 1954, s.2(1); Vol. 1, pp. 306, 307.
[26] Act of 1977, s.4(4), inserted by Regulations of 1990, Sched., para. 16.

right to terminate the tenancy before the end of the term or to extend the tenancy)''.[27]

In considering this deplorable formula, the first step is to eliminate the ''–T''. This may be done by rewriting the formula as—

$$R = \frac{P \times I}{1 - \frac{1}{(1 + I)^T}}$$

Few will wish, or be able, to proceed further without the aid of a calculator. But two examples may be given to show how the formula operates. **10–16**

(a) 99-year lease, premium £80,000

$$R = \frac{80{,}000 \times 0.06}{1 - \frac{1}{(1.06)^{99}}} = \frac{4800}{1 - \frac{1}{320.1}} = \frac{4800}{0.997} = £4{,}814.44$$

As R does not exceed £25,000, the tenancy is not prevented from being a protected tenancy on this ground.

(b) 50-year lease, premium £395,000

$$R = \frac{395{,}000 \times 0.06}{1 - \frac{1}{(1.06)^{50}}} = \frac{23{,}700}{1 - \frac{1}{18.42}} = \frac{23{,}700}{0.9457} = £25{,}060.80$$

As R exceeds £25,000 the tenancy cannot be a protected tenancy.

In view of the many possible combinations of rent and premium it seems a little surprising that no provision appears to have been made for adding any rent to R, even if the rent is substantial enough to be near the limit for a ''low'' rent.

B. OMITTED TENANCIES

A long tenancy at a low rent entered into on or after January 15, 1989 and before April 1, 1990 will usually qualify neither as an ''old'' tenancy nor as a ''new'' tenancy. The principal exceptions (prior contracts, and grants to sitting tenants) have already been considered;[28] but apart from these, long tenancies at a low rent which were granted during this period of over 14 months appear to receive the benefits neither of Part I nor of the Act of 1989. The same applies **10–17**

[27] Landlord and Tenant Act 1954, s.2(1A), inserted by Regulations of 1990, Sched., para. 2.
[28] *Ante.*, paras. 10–07, 10–08.

to a tenancy entered into after April 1, 1990 in pursuance of a contract made on or after January 15, 1989 but before April 1, 1990. Such tenancies cannot satisfy the qualifying condition in Part I, because the low rent is not the only reason why the tenancy is not a protected tenancy under the Rent Acts: the date on which the tenancy was granted prevents the tenancy being a protected tenancy. Nor will the tenancy receive the benefits of the Act of 1989, for these are confined to tenancies entered into on or after April 1, 1990 otherwise than in pursuance of a contract made before that day.[29] Tenancies in this category seem to have been simply omitted from the legislation.

It is very difficult to see any good reason for denying protection to this category of tenancy. It is possible that such tenancies were intended to continue within the protection of Part I until the new system under the Act of 1989 came into operation, but that the effect of the Act of 1988 on the qualifying condition was not realised. However, unless forensic ingenuity can detect a means of producing this result, or amending legislation is enacted, the position seems to be as stated above.[30] In one sense there is no immediate problem. A tenancy can be a "long" tenancy only if it is granted for a term certain exceeding 21 years,[31] and if such a term is granted on or after January 15, 1989, it cannot expire before January 16, 2010. But in the interim the marketability of such tenancies may well be affected, and problems may arise in relation to applications for declarations and questions of forfeiture.

C. NEW TENANCIES

Sect. 1. Introductory

10–18 The term "new" tenancy is here used to describe a long tenancy at a low rent that is entered into on or after April 1, 1990, otherwise than in pursuance of a contract made before that date.[32] Such tenancies are governed by the provisions of Schedule 10 to the Act of 1989; for brevity, this will usually be called "Schedule 10" *simpliciter*. In general, Schedule 10 confers on tenants under a new tenancy a form of security of tenure that is substantially the same as that formerly conferred by Part I of the Act of 1954, though there are many alterations of detail, and two important changes that should be mentioned here. These are—

(i) Assured not statutory. If at the end of the term the landlord cannot or does not establish a ground for possession, the tenant can no longer obtain a statutory tenancy but instead is entitled to an assured tenancy.

[29] Act of 1989, s.186(2).
[30] Surprisingly, almost ten years on, the omission still has not been corrected.
[31] See Vol. 1, p. 305.
[32] Act of 1989, s.186(2).

(ii) Interim rent. There is now provision for an interim rent to be payable until the rent under the assured tenancy becomes payable.

The detailed provisions of Schedule 10 will be considered under the same headings used in Volume 1 for Part I tenancies,[33] with an additional section dealing with the transitional provisions of the Act of 1989. Under these, on January 15, 1999, long tenancies at low rent that were still within Part I and in respect of which no notice of termination expiring before that date had been served, were transferred from the provisions of Part I to those of Schedule 10.[34] **10–19**

Schedule 10 takes effect notwithstanding any agreement to the contrary.[35]

Sect. 2. Conditions to be Satisfied

Schedule 10 to the Act of 1989 applies to tenancies entered into on or after April 1, 1990 otherwise than in pursuance of a contract made before that date[36–37] only if three conditions are satisfied. Schedule 10 refers to a tenancy which satisfies the three conditions as "a long residential tenancy".[38] **10–20**

1. Long tenancy

The tenancy must be a "long tenancy",[39] *i.e.* "a tenancy granted for a term of years certain exceeding 21 years, whether or not subsequently extended by act of the parties or by any enactment, but excluding any tenancy which is, or may become, terminable before the end of the term by notice given to the tenant".[40] Where at the end of a long tenancy at a low rent a new tenancy of any or all of the premises is expressly or impliedly granted at a low rent, the new tenancy is deemed to be a long tenancy, however short it is, and even if it is a periodic tenancy, though it is subject to certain special provisions.[41] **10–21**

2. Low rent

The tenancy must also be "at a low rent".[42] For these purposes, a "new" tenancy is at a low rent if under the tenancy— **10–22**

(i) no rent is payable, or

[33] Vol. 1, pp. 304–317.
[34] Act of 1989, s.186(3); see *post*, paras. 10–63 *et seq*.
[35] Act of 1989, s.186(4).
[36–37] *ibid.*, ss.186(2)(b), 195(2); S.I. 1990 No. 431.
[38] Act of 1989, Sched. 10, para. 1(5).
[39] *ibid.*, para. 1(1).
[40] *ibid.*, para. 2(3).
[41] *ibid.*, para. 16(1); and see para. 16(2)–(6).
[42] *ibid.*, para. 1(1).

(ii) "the maximum rent payable at any time" is payable at a rate of £1,000 a year or less if the dwelling is in Greater London, or £250 a year or less if it is elsewhere.[43]

For these purposes, "rent" does not include any sum payable by the tenant as is expressed (in whatever terms) to be payable in respect of rates, council tax, services, management, repairs, maintenance or insurance unless it could not have been regarded by the parties to the tenancy as a sum so payable.[44] There is now no express reference to progressive rents,[45] but the words "payable at any time" are wide enough to include them.

3. Qualifying condition

10–23 The "qualifying condition" must for the time being be fulfilled.[46]

(a) The condition

10–24 The "qualifying condition" is that "the circumstances (as respects the property let under the tenancy, the use of that property and all other relevant matters) are such that, if the tenancy were not at a low rent, it would at that time be an assured tenancy within the meaning of Part I of the Housing Act 1988".[47] Capacity for being an assured tenancy under the Act of 1988 thus replaces capacity for entitlement to retain possession under the Rent Acts, but in other respects the qualifying condition is in substance unchanged.[48] As before,[49] the low rent must be the only reason why the tenancy could not receive the statutory protection. Thus the qualifying condition cannot be fulfilled where the Act of 1988 is excluded by the resident landlord provision.[50] Many of the other grounds on which tenancies cannot be assured tenancies within the Act of 1988[51] are unlikely to be applicable to long tenancies at a low rent, and the Act of 1989 has specifically provided that in determining whether the qualifying condition is fulfilled the exclusion of tenancies entered into before January 15, 1989 (or pursuant to contracts made before then) is to be omitted.[52]

[43] *ibid.*, para. 2(4), as substituted by Regulations of 1990, Sched., para. 33.
[44] Act of 1988, Sched. 1, para. 2(2) (inserted by Regulations of 1990, Sched., para. 29, in place of para. 3(2)), as amended by S.I. 1993 No. 651, art. 2(1), Sched. 1, para. 19, as applied by Act of 1989, Sched. 10, para. 2(5).
[45] See Vol. 1, p. 305.
[46] Sched. 10, para. 1(1).
[47] *ibid.*; and see para. 1(3), (4), for proleptic applications.
[48] See Vol. 1, p. 306; *ante*, paras. 5–40, 5–41.
[49] *ibid.*
[50] See *ante*, paras. 4–21 *et seq*.
[51] Act of 1988, Sched. 1; see *ante*, Chap. 4.
[52] Act of 1989, Sched. 10, para. 1(2).

(b) High value

An important ground on which a tenancy could not be an assured tenancy was that the dwelling had a high value. Under the unamended Act of 1988, the test was whether the dwelling had for the time being a rateable value that exceeded £1,500 in Greater London and £750 elsewhere.[53] When domestic rates were abolished[54] and rateable values would no longer be fixed for new dwellings, this test was continued for dwellings which already had a rateable value; but for other dwellings the test was whether for the time being the rent was payable at a rate exceeding £25,000 a year.[55] This plainly would not apply to tenancies at a low rent, for which a premium was usually payable. What was required was a provision based on the rental equivalent of the premium that would correspond to a rent of £25,000 a year, and this was provided by means of a statutory formula. **10–25**

This formula applies only for the purpose of determining whether the qualifying condition is fulfilled for a tenancy that is entered into on or after April 1, 1990; and even then it does not apply if the tenancy was entered into pursuant to a contract made before that date, provided the dwelling had a rateable value on March 31, 1990.[56] The formula is virtually[57] identical with the formula already considered in relation to old tenancies.[58] For the purposes of the qualifying condition, a tenancy to which the formula applies cannot be an assured tenancy—

> ''where (on the date the contract for the grant of the tenancy was made or, if there was no such contract, on the date the tenancy was entered into) R exceeded £25,000 under the formula—
>
> $$R=\frac{P \times I}{1-(1+I)^{-T}}$$
>
> where—
>
> P is the premium payable as a condition of the grant of the tenancy (and includes a payment of money's worth) or, where no premium is so payable, zero,
> I is 0.06,
> T is the term, expressed in years, granted by the tenancy (disregarding any right to terminate the tenancy before the end of the term or to extend the tenancy)''.[59]

53 Act of 1988, Sched. 1, para. 2; *ante*, para. 4–06.
54 By Local Government Finance Act 1988, taking effect on April 1, 1990.
55 See Act of 1988, Sched. 1, para. 2, as substituted by Regulations of 1990, Sched., para. 29.
56 Act of 1989, Sched. 10, para. 1(2A), inserted by Regulations of 1990, Sched., para. 31, replacing Act of 1988, Sched. 1, para. 2(1)(b), (2).
57 For old tenancies, ''0.06'', is followed by the word ''and''; not so for new tenancies.
58 *Ante*, para. 10–15.
59 Act of 1989, Sched. 10, para. 1(2A), inserted by Regulations of 1990, Sched., para. 31, replacing Act of 1988, Sched. 1, para. 2(1)(b), (2).

The examples of the operation of this formula that have been given for old tenancies[60] are equally applicable here.

(c) Nature and purpose

10–26 In determining whether the property comprised in the tenancy was ''let as a separate dwelling'', ''the nature of the property'' when the tenancy was created is ''deemed to have been the same as its nature'' when the question arises; and ''the purpose for which it was let under the tenancy'' is to be ''deemed to have been the same as the purpose for which it is or was used'' when the question arises.[61] What is important is the *de facto* state of affairs, both as to user and the nature of the property, when the question arises, and not the terms of the tenancy or the nature of the property at the date of the grant. But these provisions relate only to ''nature'' and ''purpose'', and not to extent; and a tenant may satisfy the ''qualifying condition'' at any time, however short the period, and even if he occupies only part of the dwelling.[62]

Sect. 3. Continuance

10–27 If, immediately before the term date (*i.e.* the date of expiry of the term of a term of years certain[63]), a tenancy is a ''long residential tenancy'', it does not come to an end on that date but continues until it is terminated under the provisions of Schedule 10.[64] While it continues it is deemed to be a ''long residential tenancy'' notwithstanding any change in circumstances;[65] and a tenancy thus continuing does so ''at the same rent and in other respects on the same terms[66] as before the term date''.[67]

Sect. 4. Determination

10–28 A ''long residential tenancy'' can be terminated on or after the term date only in accordance with the provisions of Schedule 10.[68] This may be done by a notice in writing given in accordance with Schedule 10 either by the landlord[69]

[60] *Ante*, para. 10–16.
[61] Act of 1989, Sched. 10, para. 1(7); and see Vol. 1, pp. 306, 307. See, on the limits of this deeming provision, *Grosvenor Estates Belgravia v. Cochran*, (1991) 24 H.L.R. 98, CA (a decision on the equivalent deeming provision in Landlord and Tenant Act 1954, Pt. I).
[62] See Vol. 1, pp. 306, 307.
[63] Sched. 10, para. 2(6).
[64] *ibid.*, para. 3(1).
[65] *ibid.*
[66] For these words, see Vol. 1, p. 308.
[67] Sched. 10, para. 3(3).
[68] *ibid.*, para. 3(1).
[69] *ibid.*, para. 4(1); for the definition of ''landlord'' (who may not be the immediate landlord), see para. 19(1) (*post*, para. 10–59) which incorporates Act of 1954, s.21, substantially unamended.

or by the tenant,[70] or by an agreement for the grant of a new tenancy not at a low rent.[71]

1. Landlord's notice: requirements

A landlord's notice must comply with certain requirements. These depend on whether the notice is a "landlord's notice proposing an assured tenancy" or is a "landlord's notice to resume possession".[72] These separate requirements and their operation will be considered after setting out the general requirements for landlords' notices. **10–29**

A landlord's notice— **10–30**

(i) must be in the prescribed form;[73]

(ii) must specify as the date at which the tenancy is to come to an end either the term date or a later date;[74] the date so specified is called the "specified date of termination";[75]

(iii) must be served on the tenant not more than twelve nor less than six months before the specified date of termination;[76]

(iv) must either propose an assured monthly periodic tenancy,[77] or else give notice that if the tenant is not willing to give up possession at "the date of termination" (as defined below), the landlord proposes to apply to the court for possession on one or more grounds which are stated in the notice.[78] In the former case the notice is a "landlord's notice proposing an assured tenancy" and in the latter case it is a "landlord's notice to resume possession";[79]

(v) must invite the tenant, within two months of the service of the notice, to notify the landlord in writing, in the case of a landlord's notice proposing an assured tenancy, whether he wishes to remain in possession, and in the case of a landlord's notice to resume possession, whether he is willing to give up possession at the date of termination. Notification by the tenant that he wishes to remain in possession or, as the case may be, that he is not willing to give up possession, is known as "an election by the tenant to retain possession";[80]

[70] Sched. 10, para. 8.
[71] *ibid.*, para. 17; *post*, para. 10–56.
[72] *ibid.*, paras. 2(6), 4(5). See para. (iv), *infra*.
[73] *ibid.*, para. 4(1). Unsurprisingly, different forms have been prescribed for notices proposing an assured tenancy and for notices to resume possession. For the former, the form prescribed is Form 1 in the Long Residential Tenancies (Principal Forms) Regulations 1997 (S.I. 1997 No. 3008), Sched., or a form substantially to the same effect: *ibid.*, r.2. For the latter, the form prescribed is Form 2 in the Schedule to the same Regulations, or a form substantially to the same effect.
[74] Sched. 10, para. 4(1)(a).
[75] *ibid.*, para. 2(6).
[76] *ibid.*, para. 4(1)(b).
[77] *ibid.*, para. 4(5)(a).
[78] *ibid.*, para. 4(5)(b).
[79] *ibid.*, para. 2(6).
[80] *ibid.*, para. 4(7).

(vi) must state (if no previous notice terminating the tenancy has been given under Schedule 10 or under the Act of 1954[81])—

(1) that if the tenant has a right to acquire the freehold or an extended lease of the property comprised in the tenancy under the Leasehold Reform Act 1967, notice of his desire to have the freehold or an extended lease cannot be given more than two months after service of the landlord's notice;

(2) that if the tenant has that right and gives such notice within those two months, the landlord's notice will not operate; and

(3) that if the tenant gives such notice within those two months the landlord will be entitled to apply to the court under section 17 (redevelopment rights) or section 18 (residential rights) of the Leasehold Reform Act 1967 and proposes to do so or (as the case may be) will not be entitled or does not propose to do so.[82]

10–31 The "date of termination" mentioned in paragraph (iv) above is the same as the "specified date of termination" appearing in the landlord's notice unless it is postponed as follows.[83] Where an application is made to the court or a rent assessment committee under Schedule 10, and it is not merely an application for an interim rent to be fixed,[84] a notice that would otherwise terminate the tenancy before the expiration of the period of three months from the date on which the application "is finally disposed of" will terminate the tenancy at the expiry of that period and not at any other time.[85] An application is "finally disposed of" on the earliest date when the proceedings on the application (including any proceedings on or in consequence of an appeal) have been determined and any time for appealing or further appealing has expired, or when the application is withdrawn or the appeal abandoned.[86]

2. Landlord's notice proposing an assured tenancy

(a) Contents of notice

10–32 A landlord's notice proposing an assured tenancy—

(i) must be in Form 1 in the Schedule to the Long Residential Tenancies

[81] *i.e.* under either s.4 or s.25 of the Act of 1954.

[82] Leasehold Reform Act 1967, s.22, Sched. 3, para. 10, as amended by Act of 1989, s.194(1), Sched. 11, para. 13(5).

[83] Sched. 10, para. 4(2), (4).

[84] See *post*, paras. 10–41 *et seq.*

[85] Sched. 10, para. 4(2).

[86] *ibid.*, para. 4(3); and see para. 15(5), which is to the same effect. These provisions are similar to those of Act of 1954, s.64, which are familiar in relation to business tenancies. The cases on s.64 (see Woodfall's *Law of Landlord and Tenant* (28th (looseleaf) ed.), paras. 22.095, 22.096) are thus likely to be relevant here.

(Principal Forms) Regulations 1997, or in a form substantially to the same effect;[87]

(ii) must propose an assured monthly periodic tenancy of the dwelling-house;[88]

(iii) must propose a rent for that tenancy such that it would not be a tenancy at a low rent;[89]

(iv) must state that the other terms of the tenancy will be the same as those of the long residential tenancy immediately before it is terminated (which are called "the implied terms").[90] But this is subject to the right of the landlord to propose in his notice terms of the tenancy that are different from the implied terms; and references to the terms of the tenancy specified in the landlord's notice are to the implied terms as so varied;[91]

(v) must invite the tenant, within two months of the service of the notice, to notify the landlord in writing whether he wishes to remain in possession, *i.e.* whether he elects to retain possession.[92]

(b) Consequences of notice

(i) POSSESSION. In general, the effect of a landlord's notice proposing an assured tenancy is that the tenant is entitled to remain in possession under the proposed tenancy. But this is subject to important qualifications. **10–33**

(1) If within two months after service of the notice the tenant makes a valid claim under the Leasehold Reform Act 1967 to the freehold or an extended lease, the landlord's notice ceases to have effect.[93]

(2) If two months after service of the landlord's notice the qualifying condition is not fulfilled and the tenant has not also elected to retain possession, the tenant is not entitled to remain in possession after the specified date of termination.[94]

(3) If at the specified date of termination the qualifying condition is not fulfilled, the tenant is not entitled to remain in possession, even if he has elected to retain possession.[95]

(ii) ASSURED TENANCY. Apart from these three cases, the effect of the landlord's notice is that the tenant is entitled to remain in possession of the dwelling under an assured periodic tenancy.[96] That tenancy takes effect in possession on

[87] S.I. 1997 No. 3008, regs. 2, 3(a).
[88] Sched. 10, para. 4(5).
[89] *ibid.*
[90] *ibid.*
[91] *ibid.*, para. 4(6).
[92] *ibid.*, para. 4(7).
[93] Leasehold Reform Act 1967, Sched. 3, para. 2(2), as amended by Act of 1989, s.194(1), Sched. 11, para. 13; and see Vol. 1, p. 311, n. 56.
[94] Sched. 10, para. 9(3).
[95] *ibid.*
[96] *ibid.*, para. 9(1).

the day following the date of termination. It is a tenancy of the dwelling that is deemed to have been granted by the person who was the landlord under the former tenancy on the date of termination to the person who was then the tenant under it. The periods of the tenancy, and the intervals at which rent is to be paid, are monthly, beginning on the day after the date of termination.[97]

(c) Rent and terms of tenancy

10–34 (i) INITIAL PROPOSALS. As from the date when the assured periodic tenancy takes effect in possession, the rent and the terms of the tenancy will be those proposed in the landlord's notice unless within two months after service of that notice the tenant serves on the landlord a "tenant's notice" in the prescribed form proposing a different rent or different terms, or both[98]; but this is subject to any different rent or terms (or both) that the landlord and tenant may agree.[99] If the tenant serves such a notice, the landlord may, within two months after service of the tenant's notice, refer the notice to a rent assessment committee by making an application in the prescribed form.[1] If there is no such application, then as from the date when the assured periodic tenancy takes effect in possession the rent will be the rent proposed in the tenant's notice (or, if none, the rent proposed in the landlord's notice), while the other terms of the tenancy will be those (if any) proposed in the tenant's notice, together with those specified in the landlord's notice so far as they do not conflict with those proposed in the tenant's notice.[2]

10–35 (ii) REFERENCE TO RENT ASSESSMENT COMMITTEE. Where a tenant's notice is referred to a rent assessment committee, the committee must first decide, having regard only to the contents of the landlord's notice and the tenant's notice, whether there is any dispute as to the terms of the assured periodic tenancy (apart from rent) and what the "disputed terms" are, and also whether there is any dispute as to rent under the tenancy.[3] (References to "undisputed terms" are to terms proposed in the landlord's notice or the tenant's notice which are not "disputed terms" and do not relate to rent.[4]) If the committee decide that there are no disputed terms and that there is no dispute as to the rent, the terms and the rent under the tenancy will be the same as if the tenant's notice had not been referred to the committee.[5] The same will apply if the landlord serves notice on the committee that he no longer requires a determination by them.[6] If

[97] Sched. 10, para. 9(2).

[98] *ibid.*, para. 10(1). The form prescribed is Form 4 in the Long Residential Tenancies (Principal Forms) Regulations 1997 (S.I. 1997 No. 3008), Sched., or a form substantially to the same effect: *ibid.*, reg. 2.

[99] See *post*, para. 10–56.

[1] Sched. 10, para. 10(2). The form prescribed is Form 5 in the Long Residential Tenancies (Principal Forms) Regulations 1997 (S.I. 1997 No. 3008), Sched., or a form substantially to the same effect: *ibid.*, reg. 2.

[2] Sched. 10, para. 10(2).

[3] *ibid.*, para. 11(1).

[4] *ibid.*, para. 11(2).

[5] *ibid.*, para. 11(8)(a); see *supra*.

[6] *ibid.*, para. 12(3).

he does this, or if the long residential tenancy has come to an end, the committee is not required to proceed with a determination.[7] But otherwise, if there is a dispute under either head (or under both heads), the committee will determine the matters in dispute.[8] Where the terms and the rent are both disputed, the committee must determine the terms of the tenancy before determining the rent payable under it.[9]

(iii) DISPUTED TERMS OF TENANCY. Where there are disputed terms of the tenancy, the committee are to determine whether the terms in the landlord's notice, the terms in the tenant's notice, or some other terms dealing with the same subject matter as the disputed terms, are such as might, in the committee's opinion, "reasonably be expected to be found" in an assured monthly periodic tenancy of the dwelling on certain assumptions.[10] These assumptions are that the tenancy is not an assured shorthold tenancy; that it begins on the day following the date of termination; that it is granted by a willing landlord on the undisputed terms, except so far as they relate to the subject matter of the disputed terms; and that possession is not recoverable on mandatory grounds Nos. 1 to 5[11] in the Act of 1988.[12] The committee must also, if they consider it appropriate, specify an adjustment of the undisputed terms to take account of the terms so determined, and also specify an adjustment of rent to take account of the terms so determined and (if applicable) so adjusted.[13] In making these determinations and adjustments, the committee must disregard any effect on the terms or the amount of rent that is attributable to granting a tenancy to a sitting tenant.[14] **10–36**

(iv) DISPUTED RENT. Where there is a dispute as to the rent, the committee must determine the monthly rent at which they consider the dwelling "might reasonably be expected to be let in the open market by a willing landlord under an assured tenancy"[15] on certain assumptions.[16] These assumptions are that the tenancy is not an assured shorthold tenancy; that it begins on the day following the date of termination; that possession cannot be recovered on mandatory grounds Nos. 1 to 5 in the Act of 1988;[17] and that the terms of the tenancy (apart from those relating to the amount of rent) are the same as the undisputed terms, or, where the committee have made a determination of the terms in respect of disputed terms, the terms so determined and the undisputed terms, as adjusted (if at all) by the committee.[18] **10–37**

In determining the rent, the committee must disregard certain matters. These matters are any effect on the rent attributable to the tenancy being granted to a

[7] Sched. 10, para. 12(3).
[8] *ibid.*, para. 11(3), (5); and see *infra*.
[9] *ibid.*, para. 11(1).
[10] *ibid.*, para. 11(3).
[11] For these, see *post* pp. 240–250. Shortly, they are: landlord's only or principal home; sale by mortgagee; holiday accommodation; student accommodation; and minister of religion.
[12] Sched. 10, para. 11(3).
[13] *ibid.*
[14] *ibid.*, para. 11(4).
[15] The language is the same as that in Act of 1988, s.14(1); see *post*, paras. 17–47 *et seq.*
[16] Sched. 10, para. 11(5).
[17] See n. 11 *supra.*
[18] Sched. 10, para. 11(5).

sitting tenant; any increase in the value of the dwelling attributable to certain improvements carried out by the tenant under the long residential tenancy; and any reduction in the value of the dwelling attributable to a failure by the tenant to comply with the terms of the long residential tenancy.[19] In these provisions, "rent" bears the same meaning as it does under similar provisions of the Act of 1988 (subject to certain consequential amendments), and so it excluded rates (when these were payable) but includes payments for the use of furniture, in respect of council tax, and for service charge matters.[20]

10–38 (v) AGREEMENT OF PARTIES. These provisions do not affect the right of the landlord and the tenant to agree any terms of the assured periodic tenancy (including terms relating to rent) before the tenancy takes effect in possession.[21] Such "expressly agreed terms" become terms of the tenancy in substitution for any terms dealing with the same subject matter that would otherwise be terms of the tenancy by virtue of the landlord's notice, the tenant's notice, or a determination of the committee.[22] Where a reference to the committee has been made but not determined, the committee must have regard to the expressly agreed terms, as notified to them by the landlord and the tenant, in deciding what the disputed terms are and whether there is any dispute as to the rent; and the committee cannot make any adjustment to the terms thus notified.[23] In addition, after the tenancy has taken effect in possession, the Act preserves the right of the landlord and the tenant to vary by agreement any term of the tenancy, including a term relating to rent.[24]

10–39 (vi) INFORMATION REQUIRED BY THE COMMITTEE. Rent assessment committees acting under these provisions have the same powers of obtaining information from landlords and tenants as they have on references made to them under the Act of 1988.[25]

10–40 (vii) EFFECT OF DETERMINATION BY COMMITTEE. Where there are disputed terms of the tenancy, the terms determined by the committee will be terms of the tenancy so far as their subject matter is concerned, together with the undisputed terms as adjusted (if at all) by the committee.[26] Where the dispute is as to the terms of the tenancy alone, and not as to the rent, the rent specified in the landlord's notice or, as the case may be, in the tenant's notice will be the rent under the assured tenancy, subject to any adjustment of the rent specified by the committee to take account of terms determined by them, and also any terms

[19] Sched. 10, para. 11(6), (7), applying Act of 1988, s.14(2), with variations; see *post*, pp. 358–360.
[20] Sched. 10, para. 11(6), as amended by S.I. 1993 No. 651, art. 2(1), Sched. 1, para. 20 (inserting "council tax"), applying Act of 1988, s.14(4), (5); see *post*, pp. 360–363.
[21] Sched. 10, para. 12(2).
[22] *ibid.*, para. 12(2)(a).
[23] *ibid.*, para. 12(2)(b).
[24] *ibid.*, para. 11(9).
[25] *ibid.*, para. 12(1), applying Act of 1988, s.41(2)–(4); see *post*, para. 17–18. A form has been prescribed for this purpose: the Long Residential Tenancies (Principal Forms) Regulations 1997 (S.I. 1997 No. 3008), Sched., Form 6, or a form substantially to the same effect: *ibid.*, reg. 2.
[26] Sched. 10, para. 11(8)(c); for adjustment, see *ante*, paras. 10–36, 10–37, and *infra*.

adjusted by them.[27] Where there is also a dispute as to rent, the rent determined by the committee will be the rent under the assured tenancy.[28]

(d) Interim rent

(i) INTERIM RENT NOTICE. When serving a landlord's notice proposing an assured tenancy, or at any time between that date and the date of termination, the landlord may serve on the tenant a notice in the prescribed form proposing an interim monthly rent, the rent to take effect from a date specified in the notice (not being earlier than the date of termination specified in the landlord's notice proposing an assured tenancy) and to continue while the tenancy is being continued under Schedule 10.[29] Within two months after service of this interim rent notice the tenant may refer the rent proposed in it to a rent assessment committee.[30] If he does not do so, the rent proposed in the notice becomes payable as the rent under the tenancy from the date specified in the landlord's interim rent notice or two months after the service of that notice on the tenant, whichever is the later.[31] **10–41**

(ii) RENT ASSESSMENT COMMITTEE. Where the proposed interim rent is duly referred to a rent assessment committee, the committee must determine the monthly rent at which they consider the dwelling "might reasonably be expected to be let on the open market by a willing landlord under a monthly periodic tenancy" on certain terms.[32] These terms, which are closely similar to those that apply where there is a disputed rent,[33] are that the tenancy begins on the day following the specified date of termination; that the other terms of the tenancy are the same as those of the existing tenancy were when the landlord gave notice proposing an assured tenancy; and that the tenancy affords the tenant security of tenure equivalent to that afforded by an assured tenancy[34] (not being an assured shorthold tenancy) in respect of which possession cannot be recovered under mandatory grounds Nos. 1 to 5 in the Act of 1988.[35] In addition, there are the same disregards and matters to be included in the rent as for disputed rents.[36] The committee are not required to continue with the determination of an interim rent if the tenant gives written notice that he no longer requires such a determina- **10–42**

[27] Sched. 10, para. 11(8)(b).
[28] *ibid.*, para. 11(8)(b).
[29] Sched. 10, para. 6(1); for continuance, see *ante*, para. 10–27. The form prescribed is Form 3 in the Long Residential Tenancies (Principal Forms) Regulations 1997 (S.I. 1997 No. 3008), Sched., or a form substantially to the same effect: *ibid.*, reg. 2.
[30] *ibid.*, para. 6(2)(a).
[31] *ibid.*, para. 6(2)(b).
[32] *ibid.*, para. 6(3).
[33] See *ante*, para. 10–37.
[34] *i.e.* under Act of 1988, Pt. I, Chap. I.
[35] Sched. 10, para. 6(3), referring to Act of 1988, Sched. 2, Pt. I. For these grounds, see *post*, pp. 240–250.
[36] Sched. 10, para. 6(4), (5), the former as amended by S.I. 1993 No. 651, art. 2(1), Sched. 1, para. 20 (inserting "council tax"); *ante*, para. 10–37.

tion, or if the long residential tenancy ends on or before the specified date of termination.[37]

10–43 (iii) Effect of determination. Where the committee have determined an interim rent, that rent becomes the rent under the tenancy with effect from the date specified in the landlord's interim rent notice, or two months after the service of that notice on the tenant, whichever is the later.[38] The landlord and the tenant may agree the interim monthly rent, and the date from which it is to take effect, and if they do this, the agreed rent becomes the rent for the tenancy from the agreed date, and no steps (or no further steps) can be taken in the reference to the rent assessment committee.[39] The interim rent, whether agreed or determined by the committee, will normally not be a "low" rent, yet despite this the tenancy will not be an assured tenancy but will be regarded as still being a tenancy at a low rent, and thus a long residential tenancy.[40]

3. Landlord's notice to resume possession

(a) Contents of notice

10–44 Instead of serving a landlord's notice proposing an assured tenancy, the landlord may serve a "landlord's notice to resume possession".[41] Such a notice—

(i) must be in Form 2 in the Schedule to the Long Residential Tenancies (Principal Forms) Regulations 1997, or a form substantially to the same effect.[42]

(ii) must give the tenant notice that if he is not willing to give up possession at the date of termination, the landlord proposes to apply to the court for possession of the property let under the tenancy on one or more of certain specified grounds, stating which;[43] and

(iii) must invite the tenant, within two months from the service of the notice, to notify the landlord in writing whether he is willing to give up possession at the date of termination, *i.e.* whether he elects to retain possession.[44]

10–45 The landlord may withdraw the notice at any time by a notice in writing served on the tenant; but if this is done after the landlord has applied to the court for possession, the court's power to make an order as to costs is not prejudiced.[45] Within one month of withdrawing his notice, the landlord may serve on the

37 Sched. 10, para. 7(2).
38 *ibid.*, para. 6(6).
39 *ibid.*, para. 7(1).
40 *ibid.*, para. 7(3).
41 *ibid.*, paras. 2(6), 4(5).
42 S.I. 1997 No. 3008, regs. 2, 3(b).
43 Sched. 10, paras. 2(6), 4(5).
44 *ibid.*, para. 4(7).
45 *ibid.*, para. 15(6).

tenant a new notice proposing an assured tenancy. In such cases, provision is made for the earliest date that may be specified in that notice as the date of termination. That date is the day after the lapse of four months from service of that notice, or the day after the lapse of six months from service of the withdrawn notice, whichever is the later.[46]

(b) Application to court

If the tenant elects to retain possession, or if the qualifying condition is fulfilled at the end of two months after service of the landlord's notice to resume possession, the landlord may apply to the court for an order for possession on such of the grounds for possession as he specified in his notice to resume possession.[47] The county court has exclusive jurisdiction under Schedule 10.[48] Such an application must be made within two months of the tenant's election to retain possession, or, if there is no such election, within four months of the service of the landlord's notice.[49] If the landlord fails to make his application within this time, the court "shall not entertain" it, and the notice, and anything done in pursuance of it, cease to have effect.[50] It therefore seems clear that once time has expired there is an absolute jurisdictional bar to proceedings under this head.[51] **10–46**

(c) Grounds for possession

There are ten grounds for recovering possession under this head, two mandatory and the rest discretionary.[52] Eight of the grounds are substantially the same as grounds for assured tenancies under the Act of 1988, and two are new. The ten grounds are as follows. **10–47**

(i) DEMOLITION, RECONSTRUCTION OR SUBSTANTIAL WORKS: the landlord intends to demolish or reconstruct the whole or a substantial part of the dwelling-house, or to carry out substantial works on it or any part of it or any building of which it forms part.[53] This mandatory ground is the same as mandatory ground No. 6 under the Act of 1988,[54] and it similarly does not apply to assured **10–48**

[46] Sched. 10, para. 15(7).
[47] *ibid.*, para. 13(1).
[48] *ibid.*, para. 20(3), applying Act of 1954, s.63(1).
[49] Sched. 10, para. 13(2).
[50] *ibid.*, paras. 13(2), 15(2).
[51] The language of Sched. 10, para. 15(2) excludes *Kammins Ballrooms Co. Ltd. v. Zenith Investments (Torquay) Ltd.* [1971] A.C. 850, holding that under Landlord and Tenant Act 1954, s.29(3) the time limits for application to the court could be waived.
[52] Sched. 10, paras. 5(1), 13(3), (4), (7). The new grounds added to Act of 1988, Sched. 2 on February 28, 1997 by Housing Act 1996, ss.102, 148, 149, 232(3), S.I. 1997 No. 225, do not seem to have been carried forward into Sched. 10 except, presumably, to the extent that the new Ground 14 replaces the old Ground 14.
[53] Sched. 10, para. 13(3), applying Act of 1988, Sched. 2, Pt. I, Ground 6.
[54] See *post*, paras. 14–49 *et seq.*

tenancies by transmission.[55] But there are certain amendments. The ground does not apply to former 1954 Act tenancies,[56] nor do the provisions under the Act of 1988 relating to the landlord paying the tenant's removal expenses[57] appear to apply. Where this is the ground, or one of the grounds, specified in the landlord's notice to resume possession, and the court is satisfied that the landlord has established that ground, the court must order the tenant to give up possession of the property then let under the tenancy on the date of termination.[58]

10–49 (ii) DEMOLITION OR RECONSTRUCTION FOR REDEVELOPMENT: "for the purposes of redevelopment after the termination of the tenancy, the landlord proposes to demolish or reconstruct the whole or a substantial part of the premises".[59] This mandatory ground, which is new, is narrowly confined.[60] The only landlords which can specify this ground in a notice to resume possession are certain public bodies, and then only if they require the premises for "relevant development", as defined.[61] If the court is satisfied that such a landlord has established this ground, that possession will be required by the landlord on the date of termination, and that the landlord has made such preparations for proceeding with the redevelopment as are reasonable in the circumstances, the court must order the tenant to give up possession of the property then let under the tenancy at the date of termination.[62] The "preparations" mentioned include obtaining any requisite possession or consent for the redevelopment, whether from any authority whose permission or consent is required under any enactment, or from the owner of any interest in any property.[63] If it is not reasonably practicable to obtain the permission or consent, preparations relating to obtaining it may suffice.[64]

Where the court is not satisfied that this ground for possession has been established, but would be satisfied if the date of termination had been a date not more than one year later ("the postponed date"), the court must, if the landlord so requires, make an order specifying the postponed date.[65] In doing this, the court must also order that the tenancy of the whole of the property let under the tenancy is to continue after the date of termination at the same rent and on the same terms, but that unless the tenancy comes to an end before the postponed date, the tenant must on that date give up possession of the property then let under the tenancy.[66] Such an order does not prejudice the power of the tenant to terminate the tenancy sooner.[67]

10–50 The other eight grounds are all discretionary. In each case the court must order

[55] Sched. 10, para. 5(2), excluding para. (c) of Ground 6. For such tenancies, see *post*, para. 14–61.
[56] *i.e.* tenancies to which Sched. 10 applies on and after January 15, 1999, by virtue of Act of 1989, s.186(3) (see *post*, paras. 10–63 *et seq.*): Sched. 10, para. 5(2).
[57] See *post*, paras. 14–62 *et seq.*
[58] Sched. 10, para. 13(3).
[59] *ibid.*, para. 5(1)(b).
[60] By Sched. 10, para. 5(4).
[61] Leasehold Reform Act 1967, s.28: see subs. (5), (6).
[62] Sched. 10, para. 13(7).
[63] *ibid.*
[64] *ibid.*
[65] *ibid.*, para. 14(1), (2).
[66] *ibid.*, para. 14(2).
[67] *ibid.*, para. 14(4); see *post*, para. 10–55.

the tenant to give up possession of the property then let under the tenancy on the date of termination only if the court is satisfied that the landlord has established not only the ground for possession but also "that it is reasonable that the landlord should be granted possession".[68] These grounds are as follows.

(iii) SUITABLE ALTERNATIVE ACCOMMODATION. Ground 9,[69] a discretionary ground, applies without any significant alteration.[70]

(iv) UNPAID RENT. Ground 10,[71] a discretionary ground, applies with only minor adaptations.[72] The rent must be in arrears at the date of the landlord's notice to resume possession (instead of at the date of the possession notice required under the Act of 1988[73]), and the reference to the court's power to dispense with a possession notice is deleted.[74]

(v) PERSISTENT DELAYS IN PAYING RENT: Ground 11.

(vi) BREACH OF OBLIGATION: Ground 12.

(vii) DETERIORATION OF PREMISES BY WASTE OR NEGLECT: Ground 13.

(viii) NUISANCE OR ILLEGAL USER: Ground 14.[75]

(ix) DETERIORATION OF FURNITURE FROM ILL-TREATMENT: Ground 15.

The above five discretionary grounds[76] all apply without alteration.[77]

(x) REQUIRED FOR LANDLORD OR FAMILY: This discretionary ground is new,[78] **10–51**
though it has features in common with Case 9 in the Act of 1977 and Ground 1 in the Act of 1988.[79] The ground has four conditions that must be specified in the landlord's notice,[80] and there is a fifth that must be satisfied as well if an order for possession is to be made.[81] These requirements are as follows.[82]

[68] Sched. 10, para. 13(4). For reasonableness, see Vol. 1, pp. 387–393 and *post*, paras. 15–04. *et seq*.
[69] *i.e.* Act of 1988, Sched. 2, Pt. II, Ground 9, Pt. III. See *post*, pp. 282–288.
[70] Sched. 10, paras. 5(1), 13(4), (5), substituting "long residential tenancy" for "assured tenancy" in the concluding words of Act of 1988, Sched. 2, Pt. III, para. 3(1).
[71] Act of 1988, Sched. 2, Pt. II, Ground 10. See *post*, pp. 288, 289.
[72] Sched. 10, paras. 5(1), 13(4).
[73] See *post*, paras. 13–20, 15–19.
[74] Sched. 10, para. 5(3).
[75] This Ground was replaced by a new, wider Ground 14 with effect from February 28, 1997, but the change did not have effect where a possession notice under Act of 1988 had been served before that date, or where possession proceedings were started before that date and the court dispensed with the requirement of such a notice: S.I. 1997 No. 225, art. 2, Sched., para. 1.
[76] Under Act of 1988, Sched. 2, Pt. II; see *post*, pp. 289–294, 298, 299.
[77] Sched. 10, para. 5(1)(a), 13(4).
[78] *ibid.*, paras. 5(1)(c), 13(4).
[79] See Vol. 1, pp. 423–439; *post*, paras. 14–22 *et seq.*
[80] Sched. 10, paras. 4(5)(b), 5(1)(c).
[81] *ibid.*, para. 13(6).
[82] *ibid.*, paras. 5(1)(c) (for Nos. 1 to 3), 5(5) (for No. 4), 13(6) (for No. 5).

(1) "The premises or part of them are reasonably required by the landlord for occupation as a residence" by any of certain persons.
(2) Those persons are himself; any son or daughter of his over 18 years old; and his or his spouse's father or mother.
(3) The landlord, if not the immediate landlord, will be the immediate landlord at the specified date of termination.
(4) The interest of the landlord (or an interest which is merged in it, and but for the merger would be the interest of the landlord) was not "purchased or created" after February 18, 1966. This wording may be contrasted with that under previous Acts, such as "become landlord by purchasing" and "acquiring the reversion . . . for money or money's worth".[83]
(5) Having regard to all the circumstances of the case, including whether other accommodation is available for the landlord or the tenant, the court is not satisfied that "greater hardship" would be caused by making the order than by refusing to make it.[84] The onus of establishing greater hardship clearly appears to lie on the tenant, as under the Act of 1977.[85]

(d) Qualifying condition unfulfilled

10–52 There is one case in which a landlord may still obtain an order for possession even if he fails to establish any of the statutory grounds for possession. This will occur if at the hearing the court is satisfied that the qualifying condition is not fulfilled as respects the tenancy. In such a case the court must order the tenant to give up possession of the property then let under the tenancy on the date of termination, notwithstanding any election by the tenant to retain possession.[86]

(e) Compensation for misrepresentation

10–53 Where an order for possession is made under Part I of the Act of 1954 or under Schedule 10 to the Act of 1989, and it is subsequently made to appear that the order was obtained by misrepresentation or the concealment of material facts, the court may order the landlord to pay to the tenant such sum as appears sufficient compensation for damage or loss sustained by the tenant as a result of the order.[87] This is closely similar to provisions made by the Rent Acts for Cases 8 and 9 and by the Act of 1988 for assured tenancies.[88] For these purposes,

[83] See Vol. 1, p. 423; *post*, para. 14–26.
[84] Sched. 10, para. 13(6). For greater hardship under Case 9, see Vol. 1, pp. 435–440.
[85] See Vol. 1, p. 435.
[86] Sched. 10, para. 14(3).
[87] Act of 1954, s.55(1), applied by Act of 1989, Sched. 10, para. 20(2).
[88] See Vol. 1, pp. 440–442; *post*, para. 13–57.

''landlord'' means the person applying for possession, and ''tenant'' means the person against whom the order for possession was made.[89]

(f) Refusal of order

Where the landlord has duly applied for an order for possession, but no order has been made by the time his application is finally disposed of,[90] his notice to resume possession ceases to have effect.[91] Where this has occurred, the landlord may, within one month from the date on which the application was finally disposed of, serve on the tenant a new notice proposing an assured tenancy. In such cases, provision is made for the earliest date that may be specified in that notice as the date of termination. That date is the day after the lapse of four months from service of that notice.[92] **10–54**

4. Tenant's notice of termination

A long residential tenancy may be brought to an end at the term date by not less than one month's notice in writing given by the tenant to his immediate landlord.[93] A tenancy continuing after the term date under the statute[94] may be brought to an end at any time in the same way, whether the notice is given before or after[95] the term date.[96] These provisions apply even if the landlord has already served a landlord's notice, or the tenant has elected to retain possession, or the court has made an order for possession: these matters do not prevent the tenant from terminating the tenancy at a date earlier than the specified date of termination or the date in the order for possession.[97] **10–55**

5. Agreement for a new tenancy; and surrender

A long residential tenancy can be brought to an end by an agreement for the grant of a new tenancy.[98] This applies where— **10–56**

(1) the landlord and the tenant, prior to the date of termination of the long residential tenancy, agree for the grant to the tenant of a future tenancy from a date specified in the agreement;
(2) the future tenancy is a tenancy of the whole or part of the property let under the tenancy;

[89] Act of 1954, s.55(2), applied by Act of 1989, Sched. 10, para. 20(2).
[90] For this, see Sched. 10, para. 15(5); *ante*, para. 10–31.
[91] Sched. 10, para. 15(3).
[92] *ibid.*, para. 15(4).
[93] *ibid.*, para. 8(1).
[94] *ibid.*, para. 3; *ante*, para. 10–27.
[95] Or presumably on it.
[96] Sched. 10, para. 8(2).
[97] *ibid.*, paras. 8(3), 14(4).
[98] *ibid.*, para. 17.

(3) the rent agreed for the future tenancy is not a low rent;[99] and
(4) the agreement specifies the terms of the future tenancy.[1]

The effect of such an agreement is that the long residential tenancy will continue until the specified date, but no longer, and that the provisions of Schedule 10 will cease to apply to the tenancy with effect from the date of the agreement or identical part and counterpart, each signed by one of the parties.[2] Any such agreement must now be made in writing, with all the expressly agreed terms in a single signed document or in identical part and counterpart.[3]

Apart from this provision, there is nothing to prevent a tenancy from being brought to an end by a surrender.[4]

6. Protection against forfeiture

10–57 The provisions of the Act of 1954 which provide protection against the forfeiture of long tenancies at a low rent[5] apply equally to long residential tenancies under Schedule 10 to the Act of 1989.[6] The tenant may thus obtain relief against forfeiture at the price of accelerating the term date and so the service of a landlord's notice.

Sect. 5. General Provisions

1. Future questions

10–58 Provision is made for cases where under Schedule 10 any question falls to be determined by the court or a rent assessment committee by reference to circumstances at a future date. In such a case, the court or committee—

(1) must have regard to all rights, interests and obligations under or relating to the tenancy as they subsist at the time of the determination;
(2) must have regard to all the relevant circumstances as they then subsist; and
(3) must assume, "except so far as the contrary is shown", that those rights, interests, obligations and circumstances will continue to subsist unchanged until that future date.[7]

[99] If the rent is low, the tenancy will be a long tenancy: *ante*, para. 10–21.
[1] Sched. 10, para. 17.
[2] *ibid.*
[3] Law of Property (Miscellaneous Provisions) Act 1989, s.2, excepting (*inter alia*) certain leases for not more than three years.
[4] Act of 1989, s.186(4).
[5] Act of 1954, s.16; Vol. 1, pp. 315–317.
[6] Sched. 10, para. 20(1), making four consequential amendments to Act of 1954, s.16.
[7] Sched. 10, para. 18.

Read literally, the word "shown" suggests that the statutory assumption of continuance is to prevail over mere improbability, even if strong; but common sense is likely to break in.

2. The landlord

The definition of "the landlord" in the Act of 1954[8] is applied to Schedule 10, with the necessary modifications.[9] Acts of the competent landlord in relation to the long residential tenancy bind all other landlords in relation to it;[10] but the competent landlord may find himself liable to pay compensation to other landlords if he gives a notice to terminate a long residential tenancy under Schedule 10, or makes an agreement with the tenant under it to grant him a new tenancy, without the consent of those other landlords.[11] Accordingly, there are provisions for deeming the consent of any such landlords to have been obtained if it is withheld unreasonably, or if no response to a request for consent is given;[12] and for this purpose two forms of notice are prescribed:[13] one for consent to a notice terminating the long residential tenancy;[14] and another for consent to an agreement with the tenant under Schedule 10[15]. Also applied with the necessary modifications are the provisions of the Act of 1954[16] for a mortgagee of the landlord's interest to do anything authorised or required by Schedule 10 if the mortgagee is in possession or if a receiver has been appointed by him or by the court.[17] **10–59**

3. The Crown

Schedule 10 applies where there is an interest belonging— **10–60**

(1) to Her Majesty in right of the Crown, where that interest is under the management of the Crown Estate Commissioners, or
(2) to Her Majesty in right of the Duchy of Lancaster, or
(3) to the Duchy of Cornwall,

as if the interest were not so belonging.[18] For the purposes of the Schedule, the owner of the interest is deemed to be the Chancellor of the Duchy of Lancaster

[8] Act of 1954, s.21. See Vol. 2, pp. 22, 23.
[9] Sched. 10, para. 19(1), (3).
[10] Act of 1954, Sched. 5, para. 2, as applied to long residential tenancies by Sched. 10, para. 19(3).
[11] Act of 1954, Sched. 5, para. 4, as applied to long residential tenancies by Sched. 10, para. 19(3).
[12] Act of 1954, Sched. 5, para. 5, as applied to long residential tenancies by Sched. 10, para. 19(3).
[13] The Long Residential Tenancies (Supplemental Forms) Regulations 1997 (S.I. 1997 No. 3005), regs. 2, 3(b), (c), Sched., Forms 8, 9.
[14] *ibid.*, Form 8.
[15] *ibid.*, Form 9.
[16] Act of 1954, s.67; Vol. 2, p. 30.
[17] Sched. 10, para. 19(2).
[18] *ibid.*, para. 22(1).

under head (2), and such person as is appointed by the Duke of Cornwall (or other possessor of the Duchy for the time being) under head (3).[19]

4. Duty to give information

10–61 The duty of tenants under Part I of the Act of 1954[20] to comply with a landlord's request for certain information applies, with the necessary modifications, to tenants under Schedule 10 of the Act of 1989.[21] A form has been prescribed for such a request for information.[22]

5. Service of notices

10–62 Any notice, request, demand or other instrument under Schedule 10 (or under the Act of 1954) must be in writing; and it may be served on the person to be served either—

(1) personally; or
(2) by leaving it for him at his last known place of abode in England or Wales; or
(3) by sending it through the post in a registered letter, or by recorded delivery,[23] addressed to him there, or, in the case of a local or public authority or a statutory or public utility company, addressed to the secretary or other proper officer at the principal office of such authority or company.[24]

In the case of a notice to a landlord, the person to be served includes any agent of the landlord duly authorised in that behalf.[25] Further, until a tenant has received notice of the name and address of a new landlord, service by him on his last known landlord is deemed to be service on the landlord.[26]

The statutory method of service is merely permissive, so that service in some other way (*e.g.,* by ordinary post to a wrong address) is valid if the notice is in fact received by the intended recipient.[27] Under the statute, service at the intended recipient's last known place of abode in England or Wales suffices, even if he has left it and gone abroad,[28] and perhaps even if his place of abode abroad

[19] *ibid.*, para. 22(2), (3). This repeats Act of 1988, Sched. 1, para. 11 (see *ante* para. 4–37), with drafting improvements.
[20] See s.18: Vol. 2, p. 21.
[21] Act of 1989, s.186(5).
[22] The Long Residential Tenancies (Supplemental Forms) Regulations 1997 (S.I. 1997 No. 3005), regs. 2, 3(a), Sched., Form 7.
[23] Recorded Delivery Service Act 1962, s.1.
[24] Landlord and Tenant Act 1927, s.23(1), applied by Act of 1954, s.66(4), and Act of 1989, Sched. 10, para. 20(5).
[25] *ibid.*
[26] Landlord and Tenant Act 1927, s.23(2), applied by Act of 1954, s.66(4), and Act of 1989, Sched. 10, para. 20(5).
[27] *Stylo Shoes Ltd. v. Prices Tailors Ltd.* [1960] Ch. 396, Ch.
[28] See *R. v. Webb* [1896] 1 Q.B. 487, CA; *Re Follick, ex p. The Trustee* (1907) 97 L.T. 645, QB.

is known;[29] for although that is his last known place of abode,[30] it is not his last known place of abode "in England or Wales". A notice served by "leaving" it at the address must be left there in a manner that is reasonably likely to bring it to the attention of the intended recipient.[31]

The presumptions of due service in Interpretation Act 1978, s.7, will apply to a notice under Schedule 10 sent by post in a properly addressed and prepaid letter. Unless the contrary is proved,[32] the notice is deemed to have been served at the time when the letter would have been delivered in the ordinary course of post.

Sect. 6. Transitional Provisions for 1999

As has been mentioned,[33] provisions have been made for applying Schedule 10 to long tenancies at a low rent which on January 15, 1999 were still within Part I of the Act of 1954. **10–63**

1. Tenancies within the provisions

The transitional provisions apply to a tenancy only if it satisfies the following conditions:[34]

(1) the tenancy is in existence on January 15, 1999;
(2) the tenancy is not a long tenancy at a low rent (as defined in Schedule 10) which was entered into on or after April 1, 1990 otherwise than in pursuance of a contract made before that day; and
(3) immediately before April 1, 1990, the tenancy was, or was deemed to be, a long tenancy at a low rent for the purposes of Part I of the Act of 1954.[35]

A tenancy which satisfies these conditions is called a "former 1954 Act tenancy".[36] If such a tenancy is not within the definition of a long tenancy at a low rent in Schedule 10[37] it is nevertheless deemed to be a long tenancy at a low rent for the purposes of that Schedule.[38]

[29] See *R. v. Farmer* [1892] 1 Q.B. 637, CA.
[30] *ibid.*
[31] *Lord Newborough v. Jones* [1975] Ch. 90, CA (notice pushed under door slips under linoleum and is concealed: service nevertheless good).
[32] For the onus on a party seeking to "prove the contrary", see *Lex Service plc v. Johns* (1989) 59 P. & C.R. 427, CA (contrary not "proved" by intended recipient's mere denial that he received document).
[33] *Ante*, para. 10–19.
[34] Act of 1989, s.186(2), (3).
[35] See Vol. 1, p. 305.
[36] Sched. 10, para. 2(6).
[37] See *ante*, paras. 10–20 *et seq.*
[38] Act of 1989, s.186(6).

2. Effect of the provisions

10–64 If a tenancy satisfies these conditions and so is a former 1954 Act tenancy, the effect is that on and after January 15, 1999—

(i) Part I of the Act of 1954 will ceased to apply to the tenancy, and
(ii) Schedule 10 to the Act of 1989 applies to it instead.[39]

This provision also takes effect so far as concerns a notice specifying a date of termination on or after January 15, 1999, and any steps taken in consequence of it.[40] But the provisions do not apply if before that date the landlord has served a notice (whether to resume possession or proposing a statutory tenancy[41]) which specifies a date of termination that is earlier than January 15, 1999.[42] The landlord under a former 1954 Act tenancy cannot specify Ground 6 (demolition, reconstruction or substantial works)[43] in a landlord's notice to resume possession.[44]

3. Continuing tenancies

10–65 Provision has also been made for cases where—

(i) the term date of a former 1954 Act tenancy falls before January 15, 1999;
(ii) immediately before that date the tenancy is continuing under Part I of the Act of 1954;[45] and
(iii) on that date the qualifying condition under Schedule 10 is fulfilled.[46]

In such a case, the following provisions apply.

(1) The tenancy continues until terminated under the provisions of Schedule 10.[47]
(2) While thus continuing, the tenancy is deemed to be a long residential tenancy notwithstanding any change in circumstances.[48]
(3) While it is thus continuing, the tenancy continues at the same rent and in other respects on the same terms as before the term date.[49]
(4) References in Schedule 10 to the dwelling-house (or the property) let

39 Act of 1989, s.186(6).
40 *ibid.*, s.186(3).
41 See Act of 1954, s.4.
42 Act of 1989, s.186(3).
43 *Ante*, para. 10–48.
44 Sched. 10, para. 5(2); *ante*, para. 10–48.
45 See Vol. 1, pp. 317, 308.
46 Sched. 10, para. 3(2). For the purposes of determining whether the qualifying condition is fulfilled, Act of 1988, Sched. 1, para. 1 (which excludes tenancies entered into before, or pursuant to contracts made before, January 15, 1989) is omitted: Sched. 10, para. 1(2).
47 Sched. 10, para. 3(2).
48 *ibid.*
49 *ibid.*, para. 3(3).

under the tenancy have effect as references to the premises qualifying for protection within the meaning of Part I of the Act of 1954.[50]

(5) Any question of what are the premises qualifying for protection or (in that context) what is the tenancy will for the purposes of Schedule 10 be determined in accordance with Part I of the Act of 1954.[51]

(6) The landlord under such a tenancy cannot specify Ground 6 (demolition, reconstruction or substantial works)[52] in a landlord's notice to resume possession.[53]

[50] Sched. 10, para. 21(1).

[51] *ibid.*, para. 21(2). What premises qualify for protection raises a potentially very difficult issue under Part I and, accordingly, under these provisions: *St. Ermins Property Co. Ltd. v. Patel* (1997) 30 H.L.R. 462, CA.

[52] *Ante*, para. 10–48.

[53] Sched. 10, para. 5(2).

Part Three

DISPOSITIONS

This Part considers the disposition and transfer of assured tenancies. Chapter 11 deals with dispositions *inter vivos*. There are four main heads. First, the Act of 1988 applies a prohibition against assignment or sub-letting without the landlord's consent to all statutory periodic assured tenancies. This also applies to all other periodic assured tenancies if they do not contain their own provisions on the subject, unless a premium is payable on the grant or renewal of the tenancy. These provisions have no application to fixed term assured tenancies. Secondly, a tenant under an assured sub-tenancy will usually hold directly from the landlord if the head tenancy comes to an end, in a manner similar to the Rent Acts. Thirdly, assured tenancies and assured agricultural occupancies are within the same provisions of the Family Law Act 1996 (and were previously within the provisions of the Matrimonial Homes Act 1983) that apply under the Rent Acts on divorce. Fourthly, on bankruptcy, an assured tenancy will usually not vest in the tenant's trustee in bankruptcy if it has little or no realisable commercial value.

Chapter 12 turns to the position when a tenant dies. In addition to laying down rules for assured tenancies and assured agricultural occupancies under the Act of 1988, the Act has made important revisions to the rules for protected and statutory tenancies under the Act of 1977, and protected occupancies and statutory tenancies under the Act of 1976. These four categories will each be considered separately. In broad terms, the Act of 1988 has enlarged the categories of those who can claim as the tenant's or occupant's surviving spouse; it has prevented there being more than one transmission; it has provided for the surviving spouse to take the same rights as the deceased tenant had, though it has much curtailed the rights that members of the tenant's family will take if there is no surviving spouse; and it has increased from six months to two years the period of residence required if a member of the tenant's family is to take.

Chapter 11

Dispositions *Inter Vivos*

11–01 An assured tenancy is an estate or interest in land, and so, like other estates and interests in land, it can be assigned or otherwise disposed of as the tenant wishes; and the tenant may also grant sub-tenancies. But this freedom to make dispositions is subject both to the terms of the tenancy[1] and to statute. Before turning to the protection of sub-tenants and to the effect of divorce and bankruptcy, the effect of the Act of 1988 on the disposition of assured tenancies will be considered under three heads:

(1) fixed term assured tenancies;
(2) ordinary periodic assured tenancies; and
(3) statutory periodic assured tenancies.

Sect. 1. Fixed Term Assured Tenancies

11–02 The Act of 1988 makes no provision which regulates the assignment or other disposition of fixed term assured tenancies, and so the ordinary law applies.[2] Further, in contrast with the Act 1977,[3] the Act of 1988 does not make an unauthorised assignment or sub-letting of the whole of the premises, as such, a ground for possession; but if the disposition is in breach of the terms of the tenancy, the tenant or assignee, as the case might be, will be vulnerable to a claim to possession on that general ground,[4] and any sub-tenant will not have protection against the landlord.[5]

[1] An assignment in breach of the terms of the tenancy is nonetheless effective to vest the estate in the assignee, and the landlord retains his remedies for breach of contract which may, in an appropriate case, entitle him to apply to the court for an order requiring the assignee to re-assign the tenancy: *Old Grovebury Manor Farm v. Seymour Plant Sales & Hire (No. 2)* [1979] 1 W.L.R. 1397, CA; *Hemingway Securities Ltd. v. Dunraven Ltd.* (1994) 71 P. & C. R. 30, Ch.

[2] As to which, see Woodfall's *Law of Landlord and Tenant* (28th (looseleaf) ed.), paras. 11.113 *et seq.*

[3] Sched. 15, Case 6; Vol. 1, pp. 412–416.

[4] *i.e.* Act of 1988, Sched. 2, Part II, Ground 12.

[5] See *post*, para. 11–11.

Sect. 2. Original Periodic Assured Tenancies

1. Implied term against assignment or sub-letting

With two exceptions, considered below, the Act of 1988 implies a term into all periodic assured tenancies, original and statutory. The effect is different for these two types of tenancy, and so statutory periodic assured tenancies are considered separately.[6] The term that is implied into all periodic assured tenancies is that "except with the consent of the landlord, the tenant shall not— **11–03**

(a) assign the tenancy (in whole or in part); or
(b) sub-let or part with possession of the whole or any part of the dwelling-house let on the tenancy".[7]

Provisions to the same or similar effect are common express terms in many tenancies; but the implied term is not so stringent as express terms sometimes are. First, as considered below, the prohibition is not absolute but qualified. Secondly, there is no prohibition against granting licences, or sharing possession, as distinct from parting with it. On the other hand there is no restriction on the landlord's right to withhold consent, even if he is acting unreasonably in so doing.[8] The effect of imposing the prohibition by means of an implied term is that although a prohibited disposition is not made void,[9] even if the landlord's consent was obtained fraudulently,[10] it constitutes a breach of an obligation of the tenancy, and so provides a discretionary ground on which an order for possession can be made.[11] Because such an assignment would be effective to vest the tenancy in the assignee,[12] any possession notice would have to be served on the assignee.[13]

2. Landlord's consent

The implied term prohibits assignments and other dispositions "except with the consent of the landlord". The consent of all joint landlords would be required.[14] Unlike absolute covenants, covenants that are qualified in this way are usually subject to a statutory proviso that the landlord's consent is not to be unreasonably withheld.[15] But this proviso does not apply to the term implied under the **11–04**

[6] Sect. 3., *post*, p. 178.
[7] Act of 1988, s.15(1).
[8] Para. 11–04, *infra*.
[9] See Vol. 1, p. 228, and n.1, *supra*; and see *Pazgate Ltd. v. McGrath* (1984) 17 H.L.R. 127 at 132, CA.
[10] *Sanctuary Housing Association v. Baker* (1997) 30 H.L.R. 809, CA.
[11] Act of 1988, Sched. 2, Pt. II, Ground 12; *post*, para. 15–21.
[12] See n.1, *supra*, and *Sanctuary Housing Association v. Baker*, *supra*.
[13] See Act of 1988, s.8(1), Sched. 2, Ground 12; and, by analogy, *Old Grovebury Manor Farm v. Seymour Plant Sales & Hire (No. 2)* [1979] 1 W.L.R. 1397, CA. For possession notices, see *post*, paras. 13–20 *et seq*.
[14] Act of 1988, s.45(3).
[15] Landlord and Tenant Act 1927, s.19(1).

Act of 1988,[16] and so however unreasonable a landlord's refusal of consent may be, the tenant seems to have no redress. This is one particularly important difference between the statutorily implied term and an express covenant preventing assignment, etc., without the landlord's consent.[17] A landlord may not, however, require the payment of a fine or a sum of money in the nature of a fine for, or in respect of, such consent;[18] if he does so, the tenant may assign, sub-let or part with possession without paying the fine or sum of money.[19]

3. Term not implied

11–05 In two cases the statutory term will not be implied into an original assured periodic tenancy (as distinct from a statutory periodic assured tenancy), and so the tenancy will be subject only to any restrictions that are actually imposed by the tenancy.[20]

(a) Express provision

11–06 The statutory prohibition is not implied into an original periodic assured tenancy if there is ''a provision . . . under which the tenant''—

(1) ''is prohibited . . . from assigning or sub-letting or parting with possession'', or
(2) ''is permitted . . . to assign, sub-let or part with possession''.[21]

This applies whether the tenant is prohibited or permitted either ''absolutely or conditionally'' and whether the provision is ''contained in the tenancy or not''.[22] The effect is that the statutory term is not implied where there is an express provision binding the tenant or the landlord as the case may; and this is so regardless of the extent of the prohibition or permission. There is no place for the statutory implied term where the parties have agreed their own. This is so even if the provision is not contained in the tenancy agreement and, *semble*, even if made subsequently to it, provided that the provision has contractual force.[23] So, where the tenancy itself is silent on these matters, so that the statutory prohibition is implied, and the parties subsequently agree some express provision about them, it seems that the statutory term will thereupon be ousted. There is no requirement for this provision to be in writing. It must be remembered that the whole of the implied term may be excluded by the parties later making a binding agreement, for example a provision in a deed that the tenant

[16] Act of 1988, s.15(2).
[17] See *infra*.
[18] Law of Property Act 1925, s.144.
[19] *Andrew v. Bridgman* [1908] 1 K.B. 596, CA.
[20] Act of 1988, s.15(3).
[21] *ibid.*, s.15(3)(a).
[22] *ibid.*
[23] This is implicit in the use of the words ''prohibited'' and ''permitted''.

may assign the whole of the demised premises if the assignee provides a guarantor for his obligations.

The general object of these provisions seems to be to exclude the statutory implied term whenever the parties have made their own provisions on the same subject matter; but the drafting lacks clarity. First, it is not made explicit whether the whole of the statutory prohibition will be excluded by express provisions that are merely partial, as where they prohibit sub-letting but are silent about assignment. Secondly, it may be questioned whether the entire statutory prohibition will be ousted by an express provision that deals with only part of the dwelling, as where it merely permits sub-letting of part of it. The bare references to assigning or sub-letting or parting with possession, without providing the verbs with an object, contrast with the explicit references to the "whole" or "part" in the statutory prohibition; and a covenant "not to sub-let" *simpliciter* does not apply to the sub-letting of part.[24] No doubt the courts will attempt to make the statute work reasonably; and with some hesitation it is suggested that the result would be as follows— **11–07**

(1) the statutory prohibition will either be implied as a whole or else be totally excluded;
(2) the statutory prohibition will be implied only if there is no express provision (whether or not in the tenancy) which prohibits or permits any form of assigning, sub-letting or parting with possession of the whole or any part of the dwelling.

The contrary conclusion, *i.e.* if it is said that the statutory term will be implied on all points not dealt with in the express terms, would give rise to curious results. It would mean that an express prohibition merely against sub-letting without the landlord's consent would be subject to the statutory proviso[25] that consent is not to be unreasonably withheld, whereas the statutory implied term prohibiting assignment without the landlord's consent would be free from that proviso. "All or nothing" at least avoids the inexplicable. But the effect is that, in the case of written tenancy agreements at least, the statutory term will only very rarely be implied, for it is uncommon for a written tenancy agreement to contain no provision at all about assignment or sub-letting of the demised premises.

(b) Premiums

The statutory prohibition will not be implied if "a premium is required to be paid on the grant or renewal of the tenancy".[26] The term "premium" here includes (a) "any fine or other like sum"; (b) "any other pecuniary consideration in addition to rent"; and (c) "any sum paid by way of deposit" unless it **11–08**

[24] *Cook v. Shoesmith* [1951] 1 K.B. 752, CA; and see *Esdaile v. Lewis* [1956] 1 W.L.R. 709, CA.
[25] Landlord and Tenant Act 1927, s.19(1).
[26] Act of 1988, s.15(3)(b).

"does not exceed one-sixth of the annual rent payable under the tenancy immediately after the grant or renewal in question".[27] With one qualification, this repeats the definition of premium in the Act of 1977.[28] The qualification is that under paragraph (c) there is here no requirement that the sum should be reasonable in relation to the potential liability in respect of which it is paid: the test under the Act of 1988 is purely arithmetical. Any benefit of financial advantage to the landlord is capable of being a fine.[29]

The purpose of this exception is to enable a tenant who has paid or will pay some premium over and above the rent under the tenancy to be able to alienate as freely as his bargain with his landlord permits. But if a contribution towards the cost of insuring the building or the provision of services is reserved as rent,[30] *semble* the exception does not apply and so, in the absence of an express provision as to alienation,[31] the landlord will be able lawfully to refuse consent to any proposed assignment, sub-letting or parting with possession of the whole or any part of the dwelling-house. A further contrast with the Act of 1977 is that for these purposes only a premium payable on the "grant or renewal" of the tenancy suffices; the word "continuance" that appears in the Act of 1977[32] is here omitted. Thus if a premium is paid in order to prevent the landlord from determining the tenancy, no new tenancy being granted,[33] that premium will not exclude the statutory implied term.

Sect. 3. Statutory Periodic Assured Tenancies

11–09 As stated above,[34] the statutory implied term that has just been considered applies to all periodic assured tenancies, whether original periodic tenancies or statutory periodic tenancies. The difference in effect between the two types of periodic tenancy is that the two exceptions for ordinary periodic tenancies just considered have no application to statutory periodic tenancies:[35] without exception, the statutory prohibition will be implied in every statutory periodic assured tenancy. Yet the terms of the former fixed term tenancy (including those which govern assignment, sub-letting or other dispositions) are by statute made terms of the statutory periodic tenancy;[36] and these may well differ from the statutory implied prohibition. The Act of 1988 makes no express provision for which of the two sets of terms is to prevail. Perhaps both would apply, with the more

[27] *ibid.*, s.15(4).
[28] Act of 1977, s.128(1), as amended by Housing Act 1980, s.79; Vol. 1, p. 682.
[29] *Barclays Bank plc v. Daejan Investments (Grove Hall) Ltd.* [1995] 1 E.G.L.R. 68, Ch.
[30] Which includes a provision that arrears may be recovered as if they were rent in arrear: *Escalus Properties Ltd. v. Robinson* [1996] Q.B. 321, CA.
[31] See *supra*.
[32] Act of 1977, s.119; Vol. 1, p. 688.
[33] See Vol. 1, p. 690.
[34] *Ante*, para. 11–03.
[35] Act of 1988, s.15(1), (3).
[36] *ibid*, ss.5(3)(e), 6(1)(b); *ante*, para. 7–12; and see *ante*, paras. 7–21 *et seq*. as to variation by rent assessment committees.

stringent in effect qualifying and prevailing over the more relaxed; but it is at least arguable that the more specific (in terms of making particular provision for the types of assignments or sub-lettings which are to be permitted, and the like) would prevail over the more general: *generalia specialibus non derogant*. On the other hand, the terms of the subsection which implies the term[37] are peculiarly emphatic, and perhaps the statutory term must prevail.

Sect. 4. Sub-tenancies

At common law, a sub-tenant's interest is normally extinguished automatically on the determination of the tenancy out of which it was carved.[38] But like the Rent Acts, the Act of 1988 has made provision for the protection of sub-tenants in these circumstances.[39] **11–10**

1. Conditions

Statutory protection under the Act of 1988 will apply if three conditions are satisfied. They are— **11–11**

(a) "A dwelling-house is for the time being lawfully let on an assured tenancy";
(b) "the landlord under the assured tenancy is himself a tenant under a superior tenancy"; and
(c) "the superior tenancy comes to an end".

The words "lawfully let" exclude any letting in breach of any term of the superior tenancy; but if the breach is subsequently waived, the letting thereupon becomes lawful,[40] a result emphasised by the words "for the time being". Though the sub-tenancy must itself be an assured tenancy, there is nothing to require the superior tenancy to be an assured tenancy. Nor does it matter how the superior tenancy has come to an end.

[37] Act of 1988, s.15(1).

[38] See Vol. 1, p. 322 and, more recently, *Pennell v. Payne* [1995] Q.B. 192, CA; but not in the case of a surrender of the superior interest, or of the service of a "consensual" notice to quit designed to destroy the sub-tenancy: *Barrett v. Morgan* [1998] 3 E.G.L.R. 3, CA.

[39] Following the decision of the Court of Appeal in *Wellcome Trust v. Hamad* [1998] Q.B. 638 that *Pittalis v. Grant* [1989] Q.B. 605, CA was decided *per incuriam*, the two statutory codes are placed on an even footing so far as the position of lawful sub-tenants is concerned.

[40] In the absence of any case decided on this point under the Act of 1988, the Rent Acts authorities must be relied upon: see Vol. 1, pp. 335–337. They emphasise that, in order to waive the unlawfulness of the sub-tenancy, the landlord must have full knowledge of the existence of a breach of covenant, and not just a suspicion: see, in particular, *Chrisdell Ltd. v. Johnson* (1987) 54 P. & C.R. 257, CA.

2. Operation

11–12 Where the above conditions are satisfied, the assured tenancy (*i.e.* the sub-tenancy) continues in existence "as a tenancy held of the person whose interest would, apart from the continuance of the assured tenancy, entitle him to actual possession of the dwelling-house at that time".[41] In short, the sub-tenant becomes the tenant of the next superior landlord. But this does not apply where the superior landlord is incapable[42] of being the landlord under an assured tenancy,[43] as where the landlord is a government department or local authority.[44] In such cases there is nothing in the Act of 1988 to preserve the sub-tenancy, though the sub-tenant may have other statutory or common law protection dependant on the method by which the superior tenancy was terminated.[45]

11–13 This provision for preservation of sub-tenancies applies even if a reversionary tenancy has been granted in circumstances in which, but for the effect of the Act of 1988 and this provision, the reversionary tenancy would or could have begun as a tenancy in possession. Instead, the reversionary tenancy takes effect as if it had been granted subject to the continuing periodic assured sub-tenancy, whether the reversionary tenancy was granted before or after the commencement of the Act of 1988.[46] This does not apply, however, if the assured sub-tenancy which continues beyond the beginning of the reversionary tenancy is a fixed term tenancy,[47] in which case, *semble*, the priorities must be determined according to the general law.

11–14 The position in this regard, which the Act does not permit to appear straightforward, may be summarised as follows. The landlord (L) grants a fixed term assured tenancy to a tenant (T). At a later date, L grants a tenancy of the same dwelling, or of that and other property (the reversionary tenancy), to another tenant (T2). If the reversionary tenancy is due to begin before the termination of T's fixed term tenancy, T2 will thereupon become T's landlord and will be subject to T's rights as an assured tenant, as L was before him. If, on the other hand, the reversionary tenancy is granted so as to begin on or after the date on which T's fixed term tenancy is due to expire, T2 would not, under the general law, become tenant subject to T's tenancy. But the Act of 1988 makes T2's interest subject to T's statutory periodic tenancy (assuming that one arises on the end of the fixed term[48]). If, alternatively, T's interest is a periodic tenancy (or will become such at a later time[49]) at the date of grant of the reversionary tenancy, and L could, but for the Act of 1988, have brought T's tenancy to an end before the commencement of the reversionary tenancy by the service of a notice to quit, T2's interest will be subject to the assured periodic tenancy.

[41] Act of 1988, s.18(1).
[42] By virtue of Act of 1988, Sched. 1.
[43] *ibid.*, s.18(2).
[44] See *ante*, pp. 50–54.
[45] See, *e.g.* Law of Property Act 1925, ss.139 (surrender or merger), 146(4) (forfeiture); n. 38, *supra* (4).
[46] Act of 1988, s.15(3), (4).
[47] *ibid.*
[48] As to which, see *ante*, paras. 7–01 *et seq.*
[49] For example, a term of one year certain and thereafter from year to year.

Even if a sub-tenant is not within the statutory provisions (for example because his sub-tenancy is not lawful, or is not assured), he will not necessarily be wholly unprotected. Thus he may be able to apply for relief against forfeiture, and even at common law (and now by statute) a surrender of a tenancy will not destroy a sub-tenancy.[50] **11–15**

Sect. 5. Transfer on Divorce

Under the Act of 1988, the position of transfers by court order in matrimonial cases is similar to that under the Rent Acts; and the Act similarly applies certain supplementary provisions for matrimonial cases. Since the Family Law Act 1996 replaced the Matrimonial Homes Act 1983 as the principal governing legislation in this area,[51] the court has had power to order transfers not just between spouses and former spouses but also between co-habitants and former co-habitants.[52] **11–16**

1. Transfer by order: Family Law Act 1996

The provisions of the Family Law Act 1996 relating to the transfer of "relevant tenancies" apply in cases of divorce, nullity or separation to assured tenancies and assured agricultural occupancies as they apply to *inter alia* protected and secure tenancies,[53] but only if the dwelling is or was a matrimonial home or, in the case of co-habitants, a home in which they lived together as man and wife.[54] The court may make an order (a "Part II order") directing that the estate or interest of one spouse or co-habitant in the dwelling-house under the lease or tenancy agreement and under any assignment shall be transferred to and vest in the other spouse or co-habitant, together with "all rights, privileges and appurtenances attaching to that estate or interest but subject to all covenants, obligations, liabilities and incumbrances to which it is subject".[55] The court may make such an order at any time when it has power to make a property adjustment **11–17**

[50] See, *e.g. Mellor v. Watkins* (1874) L.R. 9 QB 400, Ct. QB; Law of Property Act 1925, s.139.

[51] On October 1, 1997: S.I. 1997 No. 1892. Transitional provisions in the new Act preserve the effect of any application or order made, and applications pending, before that date: Family Law Act 1996, s.66(2), Sched. 9, paras. 7–10.

[52] The Family Law Act 1996 is the first Act of Parliament to use this concept. "Cohabitants" are defined by it as man and woman who, although not married to each other, are living together as husband and wife, and "former cohabitants" has a similar meaning, but excludes cohabitants who have subsequently married each other: *ibid.*, s.62(1).

[53] *ibid.*, s.53, Sched. 7, paras. 1–3. For the purposes of convenience, both interests are referred to in the text here as a "tenancy", except where a specific provision applicable only to assured agricultural occupancies is discussed.

[54] *ibid.*, para. 4.

[55] *ibid.*, para. 7. This wording is wide enough to include a personal covenant or obligation which, in the case of a tenancy entered into before January 1, 1996 (the date on which the Landlord and Tenant (Covenants) Act 1995 came into force), would not have passed to an assignee because it does not touch and concern the land, and in the case of a "new" tenancy granted on or after that date, would not have been transmitted to the assignee under that Act. The clear purpose is therefore to effect a substitution of the tenant, rather than an assignment of his interest.

order under sections 23A or 24 of the Matrimonial Causes Act 1973 with respect to the marriage, or when the co-habitants cease to live together as husband and wife.[56] In determining whether to make a Part II order or not, and if so in what manner, the court must have regard to *inter alia* the circumstances in which either spouse or co-habitant became tenant and the suitability of the parties as tenants.[57] Where the court makes such an order, the transfer and vesting takes effect by virtue of the order and without any further assurance, and from such date as may be specified in the order. And if the first spouse or co-habitant was an assignee of the tenancy, there is transferred to and vested in the other any liability of the first under an express or implied indemnity in the assignment.[58] If an order is made by the court, the first spouse's or co-habitant's liability under a covenant in the lease or tenancy agreement ''having reference to the dwelling-house'' which falls to be discharged or performed on or after the date specified in the order is not enforceable against him or her.[59]

11–18 Where a tenancy is transferred from the first spouse or co-habitant who is a successor in relation to the tenancy for the purposes of succession on death,[60] the other will also be deemed to be a successor for those purposes.[61] Further, when an assured agricultural occupancy is transferred, the agricultural worker condition[62] is fulfilled as long as the spouse or co-habitant to whom the occupancy is transferred continues to be the occupier under that occupancy, and it is deemed to be so fulfilled by virtue of the same statutory provision[63] as was applicable before the transfer.[64] The statutory ''matrimonial home rights'',[65] under which a spouse's occupation of a dwelling as a principal or only home is treated as being occupation by the other spouse as such for the purposes of the Act of 1988,[66] will normally cease to apply after a decree absolute of divorce.[67] An occupying spouse should accordingly apply for a transfer of an assured tenancy before decree absolute, and not after; for the right to apply for a transfer after that will be lost if the tenancy has by then ceased to be assured for want of occupation by the tenant.[68]

[56] Family Law Act 1996, Sched. 7, paras. 2(2), 3(2).

[57] *ibid.*, para. 5. The landlord is entitled to be heard before the court makes any Part II order: *ibid.*, para. 14(1); the Family Proceedings (Amendment No. 3) Rules 1997 (S.I. 1997 No. 1893), r. 2, substituting new rule 3.8 in the Family Proceedings Rules 1991 (S.I. 1991 No. 1247).

[58] *ibid.*, para. 7(1).

[59] *ibid.*, para. 7(2). The words in quotation marks are appropriate to a pre-January 1, 1996 tenancy rather than a ''new'' tenancy granted on or after that date (see n.55, *supra*), and the provision gives the first spouse or co-habitant a greater release than he or she would have obtained otherwise.

[60] Act of 1988, s.17; see *post*, para. 12–07.

[61] Family Law Act, s.53, Sched. 7, para. 7(4).

[62] See *ante*, para. 9–07.

[63] Of the paragraphs of Act of 1988, Sched. 3.

[64] Family Law Act 1996, s.53, Sched. 7, para. 7(5).

[65] Under *ibid.*, s.30(2).

[66] See *ante*, para. 3–24.

[67] Family Law Act 1996, s.30(8).

[68] A tenancy which is not an assured tenancy is not a ''relevant tenancy'' for the purposes of the transfer provisions of Family Law Act 1996, Sched. 7. See *Lewis v. Lewis* [1985] A.C. 828, a case under the Matrimonial Homes Act 1967 on the loss of a statutory tenancy.

2. Financial relief after overseas divorce: Matrimonial and Family Proceedings Act 1984

If outside the United Kingdom, the Channel Islands and the Isle of Man a marriage has been dissolved or annulled, or the parties have been legally separated, and the divorce, annulment or separation is entitled to be recognised as valid in England and Wales, either party may apply to the court for financial relief.[69] If one party is entitled to occupy a dwelling-house in England and Wales by virtue of (inter alia) an assured tenancy or assured agricultural occupancy, and at some time during the marriage that dwelling-house had been a matrimonial home of the parties, the court may make in respect of it any order transferring the tenancy which it could have made if a divorce or separation order, or a decree of nullity, had been made or granted in England and Wales.[70] **11–19**

3. Property adjustment order: Matrimonial Causes Act 1973

For the purposes of the court making a property adjustment order on or after granting a divorce or separation order or a decree of nullity,[71] a tenancy is "property",[72] and this plainly applies to assured tenancies. Thus, if there is no statutory or contractual prohibition against assignment,[73] the court may order one spouse to transfer the tenancy to the other, even if the landlord objects.[74] **11–20**

Sect. 6. Bankruptcy

Unlike statutory tenancies under the Rent Acts, assured tenancies under the Act of 1988 are necessarily contractual and not statutory; nevertheless they do not all vest in the bankrupt's trustee. Four classes of tenancy, which have little or no realisable commercial value, do not vest in the trustee unless he serves notice to the contrary on the bankrupt.[75] Other tenancies, other than tenancies held on trust,[76] vest in the trustee upon his appointment as such taking effect,[77] but **11–21**

[69] Matrimonial and Family Proceedings Act 1984, ss.12, 27; Interpretation Act 1978, Sched. 1.

[70] Matrimonial and Family Proceedings Act 1984, s.22 (as substituted by Family Law Act 1996, ss.66(1), 67(3), Sched. 8, para. 52; S.I. 1997 No. 1892); Family Law Act 1996, s.53, Sched. 7, paras. 4(a), 7.

[71] Under Matrimonial Causes Act 1973, ss.23A(1), 24(1), inserted and substituted respectively with effect from October 1, 1997 by Family Law Act 1996, ss.15, 67(3), Sched. 2, paras. 5, 6; S.I. 1997 No. 1892.

[72] *Hale v. Hale* [1975] 1 W.L.R. 931, CA (private landlord); *Thompson v. Thompson* [1976] Fam. 25, CA (council landlord).

[73] Which there may be in the case of periodic assured tenancies: Act of 1988, s.15; *ante*, paras. 11–03 *et seq.*

[74] See *Hale v. Hale, supra*, at pp. 936, 937; but see *Thompson v. Thompson, supra*, at p. 31 as to local authority tenants.

[75] Insolvency Act 1986, s.283(3A), added by Act of 1988, s.117(1).

[76] *ibid.*, s.283(3)(a).

[77] Insolvency Act 1986, s.306(1).

subject to his power of disclaimer. Assured tenancies and agricultural occupancies may fall into either category, depending on their terms.

1. Excluded from vesting

On the bankruptcy of a tenant, the following four classes of tenancy do not vest in his trustee of bankruptcy.

(a) Assured tenancy but assignment inhibited

11–22 First, there is an assured tenancy or an assured agricultural occupancy the terms of which ''inhibit an assignment''.[78] The terms of such a tenancy inhibit an assignment if they either—

(1) preclude an assignment; or
(2) permit it subject to a consent but exclude the statutory prohibition[79] against a payment in the nature of a fine; or
(3) permit it subject to a consent, but require in connection with a request for consent the making of an offer to surrender the tenancy.[80]

A periodic assured tenancy subject to the implied term limiting the right to assign, sub-let or part with possession[81] does not fall within any of these categories, and so would not on this basis be precluded from vesting in a trustee in bankruptcy. But a landlord does have the unqualified right to refuse consent to a proposed assignment of such a tenancy, and so it is unlikely to be of value to a trustee. A fixed term or original periodic assured tenancy, containing a standard term against alienation without the landlord's consent, will not fall within this class and accordingly will rest in the trustee automatically on bankruptcy.

(b) Protected occupancy but assignment inhibited

11–23 Secondly, there is a tenancy of a dwelling-house by virtue of which the tenant is a protected occupier of it within the meaning of the Act of 1976, if the terms of the tenancy ''inhibit an assignment'' of it.[82] This term has the same meaning as under the previous head.

(c) Protected tenancy but premium prohibited

11–24 Thirdly, there is a protected tenancy under the Act of 1977 in respect of which no premium can lawfully be required[83] as a condition of assignment.[84]

[78] Insolvency Act 1986, s.283(3A)(a), added by Act of 1988, s.117(1).
[79] In Law of Property Act 1925, s.144.
[80] Insolvency Act 1986, s.283(3A)(a), added by Act of 1988, s.117(1), applying Act of 1977, s.127(5), as amended by Housing Act 1980, s.78(1), (3).
[81] *Ante*, para. 11–03.
[82] Insolvency Act 1986, s.283(3A)(c), added by Act of 1988, s.117(1).
[83] By virtue of Act of 1977, ss.119–128.
[84] Insolvency Act 1986, s.283(3A)(b), added by Act of 1988, s.117(1). See Vol. 1, pp. 697–714.

(d) Unassignable secure tenancy

Fourthly, there is a secure tenancy,[85] which is not capable of being assigned except for very limited purposes (exchanges, property adjustment orders and qualifying successors).[86] This includes all secure tenancies except those granted for a term certain before November 5, 1982.[87] **11–25**

Like a statutory tenancy under the Rent Acts, these tenancies will accordingly remain vested in the bankrupt; but unlike in the case of a statutory tenancy, which is a purely personal right of occupation, a trustee in bankruptcy may cause these tenancies to vest in him. **11–26**

2. Vesting notices

If the trustee in bankruptcy serves on the bankrupt a notice in writing under these provisions, any tenancy excluded from vesting in the trustee under the previous paragraph to which the notice relates will vest in the trustee as part of the bankrupt's estate; and except against a purchaser in good faith, for value and without notice of the bankruptcy, the trustee's title to the tenancy will relate back to the commencement of the bankruptcy.[88] Except with the leave of the court, no such notice may be served more than 42 days after the tenancy first came to the knowledge of the trustee.[89] Once such a notice has been served, the trustee cannot disclaim the tenancy without the leave of the court.[90] **11–27**

3. Effect of vesting

If an assured tenancy vests in the trustee in bankruptcy, it will of necessity cease for the time being[91] to be an assured tenancy; for the dwelling-house will not then be occupied by the tenant as "his only or principal home".[92] But the tenancy may thereafter become an assured tenancy once more, upon satisfying the necessary requirements, and there may be a contest between a landlord determined to serve a notice to quit or forfeit and a trustee determined to secure a **11–28**

[85] Within Housing Act 1985, ss.79–117.

[86] Insolvency Act 1986, s.283(3A)(d), added by Act of 1988, s.117(1); Housing Act 1985, s.91(1), (3).

[87] Housing Act 1985, s.91(1).

[88] Insolvency Act 1986, s.308A, added by Act of 1988, s.117(2). The vesting in the bankrupt of any property which existed at the commencement of the bankruptcy relates back to that date; the difference here is that third party interests are not to be prejudiced by the trustee's later decision to cause the tenancy to vest in him.

[89] Insolvency Act 1986, s.309(1)(b), as amended by Act of 1988, s.117(3); and see Insolvency Act 1986, s.309(2) as to successive trustees and knowledge prior to appointment.

[90] Insolvency Act 1986, s.315(4), as amended by Act of 1988, s.117(4).

[91] From the date of actual vesting, not always the date of commencement of the bankruptcy.

[92] See *ante*, para. 3–24.

valuable assignment of the tenancy for the benefit of the creditors. If the assignment takes effect, and the assignee starts to reside in the dwelling before the expiry of a notice to quit, the notice will not have effect, and the tenancy will continue as a periodic assured tenancy.

Chapter 12

Transmission on Death

The Act of 1988 has both adopted and adapted the system under the Rent Acts for the transmission of tenancies on the death of the tenant. The changes are substantial. In general, while the rights of a surviving spouse have been maintained, those of surviving members of the family have been curtailed; and whereas "spouse" now bears an extended meaning, "members" of the "family", who remain undefined, are now required to have been resident for two years instead of six months. The changes require consideration under four main heads. **12–01**

First, there is the new system for assured tenancies under the Act of 1988. An assured tenancy can be transmitted on the tenant's death only if it is a periodic tenancy, only to the tenant's surviving spouse (and not to a member of his family), and only if there has been no previous transmission. If there is no such statutory transmission, the tenancy may devolve under the tenant's will or intestacy.

Secondly, there is the new system for assured agricultural occupancies under the Act of 1988. The system for assured agricultural occupancies differs from that for assured tenancies. Members of the family can still take, subject to two years' residence; the exclusion of second transmissions is not wholly clear; and the system operates not by transmitting the occupancy but by treating occupation by the surviving spouse or member of the family as satisfying the "agricultural worker condition".

Thirdly, there are revisions to the previous system for protected and statutory tenancies under the Act of 1977. For these, the existing system for transmission continues to apply, though with important modifications if the tenant dies on or after January 15, 1989. These modifications allow a statutory tenancy to be taken only by the tenant's surviving spouse, provided that there has been no previous transmission. Otherwise, only an assured tenancy will pass, whether to a surviving spouse or to a member of the family.

Fourthly, there are revisions to the previous system for protected occupiers and statutory tenants under the Rent (Agriculture) Act 1976. Their position is similar to that of protected and statutory tenancies. The existing system for transmission continues to apply, but with important modifications if the tenant or occupier dies on or after January 15, 1989. These modifications allow a statutory tenancy to be taken only by a surviving spouse, and only if there has been no previous transmission. Otherwise, only an assured agricultural occupancy will pass, whether to a surviving spouse or to a member of the family.

These four categories will now be considered in detail.

Sect. 1. Assured Tenancies

1. Requirements for transmission

12–02 If the tenant under an assured tenancy dies, there can be a transmission of his tenancy to his spouse, but only if four conditions are satisfied.

(a) Periodic assured tenancy

12–03 The tenancy must be a periodic assured tenancy at the time of the tenant's death;[1] no distinction is drawn here between original and statutory periodic tenancies, and both are within this condition. But fixed term assured tenancies are outside these provisions, and so are tenancies that had ceased to be assured tenancies before the tenant's death, for example by non-residence.

(b) Sole tenant

12–04 The provisions for transmission apply only to sole tenants.[2] If there are three or four joint tenants and one of them dies, the others take by survivorship at common law, and the Act of 1988 has no effect. Where there are only two joint tenants, the survivor similarly takes by survivorship outside the scope of these provisions; but in doing so, he is treated for their purposes as a "successor",[3] and accordingly when he dies the rule that there can now be only one transmission[4] will prevent there being any statutory transmission of his tenancy. Even if two joint tenants appear to die simultaneously, one (usually the younger[5]) will be taken to have survived the other, and this momentary survivorship, which makes him a "successor" for these purposes, will prevent his or her spouse from claiming a transmission.

(c) Occupation by spouse

12–05 "Immediately before" the tenant's death, the tenant's spouse must have been "occupying the dwelling-house as his or her only or principal home".[6] Unlike

[1] Act of 1988, s.17(1)(a).
[2] *ibid.*
[3] *ibid.*, s.17(2)(b).
[4] *Post*, para. 12–07.
[5] See Law of Property Act 1925, s.184.
[6] Act of 1988, s.17(1)(b).

under the Rent Acts,[7] there is no requirement here of any particular length of time during which the spouse so occupied the dwelling. Nor need the deceased tenant have been occupying the dwelling-house with the spouse, provided that the spouse's occupation sufficed to be treated as occupation by the tenant, so as to prevent the tenancy from ceasing to be assured by reason of non-occupation.[8]

For the purposes of transmission, "spouse" has been given an extended meaning, and "a person who was living with the tenant as his or her wife or husband shall be treated as the tenant's spouse".[9] This language necessarily excludes homosexual couples, however they regard each other or dress themselves, where neither would be commonly regarded as being the husband or wife of the other.[10] Those whose relationship is merely platonic, such as aunt and nephew, are also excluded.[11] But there is nothing to exclude a plurality of resident heterosexual cohabitants, and the Act of 1988 makes provision for them. If, "by virtue of" this extended definition of "spouse", there is on the death of the tenant "more than one person" who satisfies the requirement of being an occupying spouse, "such one of them as may be decided by agreement or, in default of agreement, by the county court shall be treated as the tenant's spouse" for these purposes.[12] **12–06**

This provision is similar to the provision made for multiple claimants as members of the tenant's family under the Rent Acts,[13] though here the problems for the county court may be more acute; for the relationship of the rival claimants to the deceased tenant which the court has to examine is not of blood but sexual. This jurisdiction of the county court also seems to apply if the claimants are a genuine spouse and a person who is to be "treated" as the tenant's spouse, for it is "by virtue of" the provision extending the meaning of "spouse" that there is more than one possible claimant. But competition between polygamous widows or polyandrous widowers continues to be left without resolution; for it is by marriage and not "by virtue of" the statutory provision extending the meaning of "spouse" that there are two or more rival claimants, and so their contest for succession does not literally fall within the jurisdiction of the county court specifically created by the Act of 1988.[14]

[7] See *post*, pp. 195–199 for a summary of the position under the Act of 1977, and Vol. 1, pp. 269–289 for a detailed treatment.

[8] See *ante*, para. 3–26.

[9] Act of 1988, s.17(4).

[10] See *Harrogate B.C. v. Simpson* (1984) 17 H.L.R. 205, CA (on "live together as husband and wife" within what is now Housing Act 1985, s.113(1)(a)), and *Fitzpatrick v. Sterling Housing Association Ltd.* [1998] Ch. 304, CA (on "living with the original tenant as his or her wife or husband" within Act of 1977, Sched. 1, para. 2(2)).

[11] Consider Vol. 1, p. 279.

[12] Act of 1988, s.17(5).

[13] *i.e.* Act of 1977, Sched. 1, para. 3.

[14] The dispute would have to be resolved according to the legality of the two (or more) marriages, but then one would be found to be the true "spouse" and the other(s), not being such, would presumably fall within the extended definition of "spouse" in the Act of 1988, and the county court would have a contest on which it could adjudicate. If there were also, for example, a competing mistress, she would benefit all by conferring jurisdiction on the county court in the first place. The temptation to find a decorous means of suppressing the "by virtue of" clause is considerable.

(d) Tenant not a "successor"

12–07 The broad rule is now that there can only be one succession under the Act of 1988. There can be no transmission of an assured tenancy if the deceased tenant was a "successor" as defined in the Act.[15] Because this restriction is statutory, a landlord cannot estop himself from relying on this rule.[16] For these purposes, there are five cases in which a tenant is, or is treated as, a "successor".

12–08 (i) TRANSMISSION UNDER THESE PROVISIONS: where the tenancy was transmitted to the deceased tenant under these provisions of the Act of 1988.[17]

(ii) TRANSMISSION UNDER THE RENT ACTS: where the deceased tenant had become entitled to the assured tenancy by transmission and conversion under the Act of 1977 or under the Rent (Agriculture) Act 1976.[18]

(iii) SUCCESSION UNDER WILL OR INTESTACY: where the tenancy became vested in the deceased tenant under the will or upon the intestacy of a previous tenant.[19]

(iv) SOLE SURVIVING JOINT TENANT: where, at some time before the tenant's death, the tenancy was a joint tenancy held by him and one or more persons, and prior to his death he had become the sole tenant by survivorship.[20]

(v) NEW TENANCY GRANTED TO SUCCESSOR: where a new tenancy was granted to a tenant who was already a successor. This head is more complex than the others. It applies where a tenant has been granted a tenancy of a dwelling-house (either alone or jointly with others) and two conditions are satisfied. First, before that tenancy ("the new tenancy") was granted, the tenant was a "successor" in relation to an earlier tenancy of the same (or substantially the same) dwelling-house; and, secondly, at all times since he became such a successor he has been a tenant (alone or jointly with others) of the dwelling-house let under the new tenancy, or of a dwelling-house which is substantially the same.[21] The status of being a "successor" is thus not affected by the grant to the tenant of a new tenancy of substantially the same dwelling-house, even, *semble*, if the new tenancy was granted to him jointly with persons other than those who were joint tenants under the earlier tenancy, and even if other tenancies were granted in between the tenancy to which the tenant succeeded and the tenancy vested in him at his death.

[15] Act of 1988, s.17(1)(c), (2), (3).
[16] *Daejan Properties Ltd. v. Mahoney* (1995) 28 H.L.R. 498, CA.
[17] Act of 1988, s.17(2)(a).
[18] *ibid.*, s.17(2)(c): *i.e.* by transmission and conversion under Act of 1977, Sched. 1, Pt. I, as amended by Act of 1988, s.39(2), (3), or under Act of 1976, s.4, as amended by Act of 1988, s.39(4). For these provisions, see *post*, paras. 12–18 *et seq.*, 12–30 *et seq.*
[19] Act of 1988, s.17(2)(a).
[20] *ibid.*, s.17(2)(b); for survivorship, see *ante*, para. 12–04.
[21] Act of 1988, s.17(3).

2. Effect of transmission

If the foregoing requirements are satisfied, the result is that on the death of the tenant the tenancy vests by virtue of the Act of 1988[22] in the spouse, and "does not devolve under the tenant's will or intestacy".[23] This explicit provision for statutory vesting removes many of the obscurities surrounding transmission under the Rent Acts, including those resulting from the transmission of contractual tenancies.[24] In place of a new statutory tenancy arising on the transmission, there is now the statutory vesting of the existing tenancy. There can now be no rivalry between the devolution of a contractual tenancy under the tenant's will or intestacy and any statutory transmission, for the statutory transmission will prevail. The result seems to be that, in contrast with the effect of transmission under the Rent Acts,[25] the spouse will take the existing assured tenancy with all its burdens and liabilities, including any liability for accrued disrepair,[26] and any pending proceedings for possession, or any order for possession. **12–09**

3. Devolution under will or intestacy

Where on the death of an assured tenant there is no transmission of the tenancy under these provisions, it will devolve under his will or intestacy in the normal way; assured tenancies are necessarily contractual tenancies.[27] On such a devolution, a statutory ground for possession will sometimes arise, and in other cases there may be consequences relating to other grounds for possession. **12–10**

(a) Periodic tenancy: one year rule (Ground 7)

Where a periodic assured tenancy (whether original or statutory) devolves under the will or intestacy of a deceased tenant, the landlord has a mandatory ground for seeking possession if he commences proceedings for possession not later than one year after the tenant's death;[28] and the court has power to extend this period so as to make time run from the date when the landlord (or any of the joint landlords) became aware of the tenant's death.[29] The ground does not arise if the assured tenancy is a fixed term tenancy. This ground for possession is fully considered later.[30] **12–11**

[22] *i.e.* Act of 1988, s.17.
[23] *ibid.*, s.17(1).
[24] Under the unhappy doctrine of *Moodie v. Hosegood* [1952] A.C. 61; See Vol. 1, pp. 284–289.
[25] See Vol. 1, pp. 281, 282; and see pp. 377, 378. The effect of a statutory transmission under the Matrimonial Homes Act 1983 however, was to transfer the statutory tenancy subject to the order for possession made before the transfer: *Church Commissioners for England v. Alemarah* (1996) 29 H.L.R. 351, CA.
[26] Consider *Granada Theatres Ltd. v. Freehold Investment (Leytonstone) Ltd.* [1959] Ch. 592, CA; and see the impersonal language of Ground 12: *post*, para. 15–21.
[27] See *ante*, para. 3–01.
[28] But a possession notice will have to be served at least two months before this date: see *post*, paras. 14–65 *et seq.*
[29] Act of 1988, Sched. 2, Pt. I, Ground 7.
[30] *Post*, Chap. 14, 258–260.

(b) Administration

12–12 Personal representatives are not subject to any special ground for possession; but in the administration of the estate of a deceased assured tenant whose tenancy has devolved upon them, they should bear Ground 12 in mind in disposing of the tenancy. All statutory periodic tenancies, and many ordinary periodic or fixed term tenancies, prohibit assignment of the tenancy, either absolutely or without the landlord's prior consent.[31] Although it was once said that a devise of a lease was no breach of such a prohibition,[32] today even an assent by the personal representatives to the beneficiary under a will or intestacy probably is;[33] and an assent or other disposition to some other person plainly will be.[34] Such breaches will invoke Ground 12,[35] a discretionary ground for possession, since there will be a breach of an obligation of the tenancy.[36]

Sect. 2. Assured Agricultural Occupancies

12–13 The provisions for the transmission of an assured agricultural occupancy on the death of the occupier operate in the same way as those governing assured tenancies. For the purposes of *inter alia* the statutory succession provisions for assured tenancies, every assured agricultural tenancy which is not an assured tenancy is treated as if it were one.[37] For an assured agricultural occupancy which is in its own right an assured tenancy,[38] no further supplementary provisions are required to give statutory protection to the successor, or to enable the occupancy to devolve under the will or intestacy of the occupier in cases where the statutory succession provision[39] does not apply. But for licences and for tenancies which are not assured tenancies in their own right, the continuation of these interests as deemed assured tenancies depends on the satisfaction of the agricultural worker condition for the time being; and upon the death of a sole tenant or licensee (called "the occupier"), that condition would no longer be satisfied. Where, on the other hand, the death is of one of two or more joint tenants each of whom satisfies the "agricultural worker condition", the tenancy will pass to the survivor or survivors, the condition will still be satisfied, and so the assured agricultural occupancy will continue.

[31] See *ante*, para. 11–04.
[32] See *Doe d. Goodbehere v. Bevan* (1815) 3 M. & S. 353 at 361, KB.
[33] See Administration of Estates Act 1925, s.36(2); and *Re Wright* [1949] Ch. 729, Ch.
[34] *Pazgate Ltd. v. McGrath* (1984) 17 H.L.R. 127, CA (though the decision was based mainly on Act on 1977, Case 6: Vol. 1, p. 412).
[35] Act of 1988, Sched. 2, Pt. II, Ground 12.
[36] For Ground 12, see *post*, para. 15–21.
[37] Act of 1988, s.24(3); *ante*, para. 9–17.
[38] An assured shorthold tenancy cannot be an assured agricultural occupancy: Act of 1988, s.24(2)(a).
[39] *i.e.* Act of 1988, s.17.

Accordingly, the Act of 1988 makes further provision for the continued satisfaction of the agricultural worker condition by a widow or widower or member of the occupier's family who was living in the dwelling-house at the time of the occupier's death. The ability of the occupancy to inure for successors depends on this provision. Put more fully, where there is an assured agricultural occupancy of a dwelling-house that is subject to a "relevant tenancy or licence", the Act of 1988 operates by providing that the occupation of the dwelling-house by "the qualifying widow or widower" of the "previous qualifying occupier", or by the "qualifying member" of the "previous qualifying occupier's family", will itself satisfy the "agricultural worker condition" where that condition was previously fulfilled, but had ceased to be fulfilled on the death of the occupier or one of the occupiers.[40] The effect of these provisions is to afford protection under the Act of 1988 in cases where the successors, whether statutory or otherwise, would not otherwise be deemed to be tenants under assured tenancies. So, a periodic assured agricultural occupancy vested solely in the occupier before his death will vest in the occupier's spouse, provided that the spouse lived in the dwelling-house as his or her only or principal home immediately before the death, and provided that the occupier was not himself a successor;[41] and thereafter the widow or widower's occupation will satisfy the agricultural worker condition. Otherwise, where the tenancy passes under the will or intestacy of the occupier, the occupation of the widow, widower or qualifying member of the family will satisfy the condition. 12–14

Most of these terms relating to assured agricultural occupancies have already been considered,[42] but some have not.

1. "Qualifying widow or widower"

A "qualifying widow or widower" is the widow or widower of the "previous qualifying occupier" of the dwelling-house if she or he was residing in it immediately before the death of the previous qualifying occupier.[43] The "previous qualifying occupier" is the occupier of the dwelling-house (or one of the joint occupiers) on whose death the agricultural worker condition ceased to be fulfilled.[44] A person who, immediately before the previous qualifying occupier's death, was living with him or her as his or her wife or husband is treated as being his or her widow or widower;[45] and if by virtue of this provision there is more than one person who would be the qualifying widow or widower of the previous qualifying occupier, it is to be decided by agreement or, in default, by 12–15

[40] Act of 1988, Sched. 3, para. 3(1).
[41] See *ante*, para. 12–07.
[42] *Ante*, Chap. 9, pp. 136, 137.
[43] Act of 1988, Sched. 3, para. 3(2).
[44] *ibid.*, para. 3(1).
[45] *ibid.*, para. 3(5).

the county court which of them is to be treated as the qualifying widow or widower for this purpose.[46]

2. "Qualifying member of the previous qualifying occupier's family"

12–16 A member of the family of the previous qualifying occupier of the dwelling-house is the qualifying member of the family only if the previous qualifying occupier left no qualifying widow or widower, and that member of the family had been residing with the qualifying occupier at the time of his death and for the previous two years.[47] If there is more than one member of the family who is a qualifying member of the family within this definition and who is the occupier of the dwelling-house, it must be decided by agreement (or, in default of agreement, by the county court) which is to be the qualifying member for the purposes of determining whether the agricultural worker condition is satisfied;[48] for there may be several qualifying members, each of whom could from time to time satisfy the agricultural worker condition.

3. Operation

12–17 Where these provisions apply they do not themselves effect any transmission of the occupancy, but instead merely operate so as to prevent it from ceasing to be assured. On the occupier's death the occupancy will no doubt often devolve upon the occupier's qualifying widow, widower or member of the family;[49] but if it devolves upon somebody else, the agricultural worker condition will not be satisfied and the occupancy will cease to be an assured tenancy. At first sight these provisions seem to be capable of repeated operation, without being limited to a single transmission, although there can be no more than one statutory transmission. The Act of 1976 provided for transmission only on the death of a protected occupier "in his own right",[50] and not one taking by succession; but the Act of 1988 omits any such restriction, and the contrast seems striking. But every devolution of a periodic tenancy under the will or intestacy of the tenant gives rise to a mandatory ground for possession;[51] and so the effect will be much the same subject to the landlord's taking the initive to terminate the tenancy upon a non-statutory transmission.

[46] *ibid.*, para. 3(6); see *ante*, para. 12–06.
[47] *ibid.*, para. 3(3). A widow or widower who is not "qualifying" thus does not exclude a member of the family.
[48] *ibid.*, para. 3(4).
[49] It is not clear how the provisions operate during the administration of the estate of the deceased occupier, while the "relevant tenancy or licence" is vested in his executors or administrators, or in the Public Trustee pending the grant of letters of administration, for "occupier" means the tenant or licensee under a relevant tenancy or licence: Act of 1988, Sched. 3, para. 1(1), (2).
[50] Act of 1976, ss.3(1), 4(2); see s.2(4).
[51] *Ante*, para. 12–11.

Sect. 3. Protected and Statutory Tenancies under the Act of 1977

Where a protected or statutory tenant within the Act of 1977 died before January 15, 1989, the rules for the transmission of his tenancy on his death remain unchanged.[52] But where the tenant dies on or after that date, those rules have been substantially modified by the Act of 1988.[53] The principal changes are the following. First, that although on a transmission to the original tenant's spouse (a term now used in an extended sense) that spouse will still become a statutory tenant, on a transmission to a member of the tenant's family that member will not become a statutory tenant but will take an assured tenancy. Secondly, on the death of a spouse who has become a statutory tenant by transmission, any second transmission will similarly confer not a statutory tenancy but an assured tenancy. Thirdly, the requisite period of residence with the tenant by a member of his or her family has been increased from six months to two years. **12–18**

The rules for transmission on the death of a tenant thus differ according to whether he is the "original tenant" (*i.e.* a person who at his death was either a protected tenant of the dwelling-house or else a statutory tenant of it by virtue of his previous protected tenancy[54]), or whether he was a "successor" (*i.e.* a person who had taken his interest by transmission). These rules will be considered in turn, together with the additional grounds for possession that apply to assured tenancies by succession.

1. DEATH OF ORIGINAL TENANT

Where a protected or statutory tenant dies on or after January 15, 1989, and he is an "original tenant" and not a "successor" within the Act of 1977, the provisions of the Act of 1977 for succession take effect as varied by the Act of 1988.[55] **12–19**

1. Person entitled

Surviving spouses and members of the tenant's family are now treated differently.

(a) Resident spouse

Here also, as with assured tenancies,[56] "spouse" has been given an extended meaning. For these purposes "a person who was living with the original tenant **12–20**

[52] See Vol. 1, pp. 269–289.
[53] See Act of 1988, ss.39, 141(3), Sched. 4.
[54] Act of 1977, Sched. 1, para. 1; Vol. 1, p. 270.
[55] See Act of 1988, Sched. 4, varying Act of 1977, Sched. 1.
[56] *Ante*, para. 12–06.

as his or her wife or husband shall be treated as the spouse of the original tenant''.[57] Similarly, where by virtue of this extension there is more than one person who satisfies the requirement of being a resident spouse, the one who is to be treated as the ''surviving spouse'' for these purposes is to be decided by agreement or, in default, by the county court.[58] The ''surviving spouse'', as thus ascertained, ''if residing in the dwelling-house immediately before the death of the original tenant'',[59] will take a statutory tenancy as the ''first successor''.

(b) Resident member of the family

12–21 If there is no ''surviving spouse'' who is entitled, there can be a transmission to a member of the tenant's family.[60]

(i) MEMBER OF THE FAMILY. The meaning of this expression[61] continues unchanged, except so far as the expanded meaning of ''spouse'' may have excluded more heterosexual cohabitants from being treated as members of the tenant's family. Where one of two homosexual partners died after 18 years of close and faithful cohabitation, the survivor was nevertheless not a member of the tenant's family.[62]

(ii) RESIDENCE IN DWELLING-HOUSE. The requirement that the member of the tenant's family should have been ''residing with him at the time of and for the period of 6 months immediately before his death''[63] has been amended by inserting the words ''in the dwelling-house'' after ''residing with him''.[64] This effects no change but makes explicit what had previously been achieved by judicial construction.[65] No longer is it arguable that residence with the tenant elsewhere will suffice.

(iii) THE TWO YEARS RULE. In the requirement of residence for a period of six months, the requirement of six months co-residence has now been replaced with a requirement of two years,[66] thereby excluding members of the family who do not begin to live with the tenant until his last days. This, however, is qualified by a transitional provision where the original tenant died on January 15, 1989, or within 18 months thereafter (*i.e.* by July 15, 1990). In such a case, a member

[57] Act of 1977, Sched. 1, para. 2(2), added by Act of 1988, Sched. 4, para. 2. See the discussion of this expression, *ante*, para. 12–06.

[58] Act of 1977, Sched. 1, para. 2(3), added by Act of 1988, Sched. 4, para. 2. See *ante*, para. 12–06, for some of the difficulties.

[59] Act of 1977, Sched. 1, para. 2, as substituted by Housing Act 1980, s.76(1); Vol. 1, pp. 274–276.

[60] Act of 1977, Sched. 1, para. 3.

[61] See Vol. 1, pp. 276–279.

[62] *Fitzpatrick v. Sterling Housing Association Ltd.* [1998] Ch. 304, CA. At the time of writing, there was an appeal to the House of Lords pending, and a reversal of this part of the decision would not be a surprise.

[63] Act of 1977, Sched. 1, para. 3.

[64] Act of 1988, Sched. 4, para. 3(a).

[65] See Vol. 1, p. 276.

[66] Act of 1988, Sched. 4, para. 3(b).

of the tenant's family who was residing with him in the dwelling-house on July 15, 1988, and who continued to reside with him there until he died, is taken as having satisfied the requirement of two years' residence.[67] The purpose of this amendment was to enable those who had completed the previously requisite six months' residence by January 15, 1989 to have only to continue that residence until the tenant died (however soon).

2. The tenancy transmitted

The tenancy thus transmitted on the death of the original tenant now differs according to whether it is taken by the surviving spouse or by a member of the tenant's family. As already seen,[68] the surviving spouse continues to take a statutory tenancy. But a member of the family takes instead "an assured tenancy of the dwelling-house by succession".[69] **12–22**

(a) Terms of assured periodic tenancy by succession

The assured tenancy is a periodic tenancy;[70] and its terms are substantially the same as those of a statutory periodic tenancy, with the adaptations needed to make it apply to the death of the original tenant instead of the ending of a fixed term tenancy. The tenancy is deemed to have been granted to the successor by the person who, immediately before the death of the "predecessor" (*i.e.* the protected or statutory tenant), was the predecessor's landlord under the tenancy;[71] the premises are the same dwelling-house as the predecessor occupied under the tenancy immediately before his death;[72] the tenancy takes effect in possession immediately after the predecessor's death;[73] the periods of the tenancy are the same as those for which rent was last payable by the predecessor under the tenancy;[74] and the other terms are the same as those on which the predecessor occupied the dwelling-house under the tenancy immediately before his death.[75] In addition, the tenancy is treated as being a statutory periodic tenancy for the purposes of the landlord's securing an increase in rent;[76] and if when he died the predecessor held under a fixed term tenancy, the provisions for varying the terms of a statutory periodic tenancy within a year of its being deemed to be granted[77] are made applicable (with appropriate modifications) to the assured periodic tenancy that the successor takes on the predecessor's death.[78] **12–23**

[67] Act of 1977, Sched. 1, paras. 3(2), 11A, inserted by Act of 1988, Sched. 4, paras. 3(d), 9.
[68] *Ante*. para. 12–18.
[69] Act of 1977, Sched. 1, para. 3, as amended by Act of 1988, Sched. 4, para. 3(c).
[70] Act of 1988, s.39(5)(a).
[71] *ibid.*, s.39(6)(b).
[72] *ibid.*, s.39(6)(c).
[73] *ibid.*, s.39(6)(a).
[74] *ibid.*, s.39(6)(d).
[75] *ibid.*, s.39(6)(e), applying subject to ss.13–15.
[76] *ibid.*, s.39(6)(f), applying s.13(2); see *post*, para. 17–04.
[77] *ibid.*, s.6; *ante*, paras. 7–14 *et seq.*
[78] *ibid.*, s.39(9).

(b) Assured shorthold tenancy

12–24 In one case, an assured periodic tenancy by succession takes a special form. Case 19 in the Act of 1977 provides a mandatory ground for possession in the case of protected shorthold tenancies or subsequent tenancies held by the former shorthold tenant.[79] If immediately before the death of the predecessor the landlord might have recovered possession under this case, the assured periodic tenancy to which the successor becomes entitled by transmission will be an assured shorthold tenancy, whether or not it fulfils the conditions[80] (where these apply) for such a tenancy.[81]

2. DEATH OF FIRST SUCCESSOR

12–25 Where a "first successor", that is to say the person who first succeeded to a protected or statutory tenancy under the Act of 1977, dies on or after January 15, 1989, the provisions of that Act governing further succession take effect as varied by the Act of 1988.[82] When he dies, the "first successor" may be holding a statutory tenancy or an assured tenancy. If he is holding an assured tenancy, there is no provision for any further transmission,[83] and the tenancy (which is necessarily contractual) will pass under the first successor's will or intestacy. If instead he is holding a statutory tenancy, there may be a further transmission[84] if the necessary requirements are satisfied.

1. Transmission

12–26 If at his death a first successor is a statutory tenant, there will be a further transmission if two requirements are satisfied.

(a) Membership of both families

The claimant must have been a member not only of the original tenant's family when he died, but also of the first successor's family when he died.[85] This will usually exclude the widow or widower of a first successor.

[79] See Vol. 1, p. 483.
[80] *i.e.* those in Act of 1988, s.20(1); *ante*, paras. 8–24 *et seq.*
[81] Act of 1988, s.39(7), as amended with effect from February 28, 1997 by Housing Act 1996, ss.104, 232(3), Sched. 8, para. 2(8); S.I. 1997 No. 225. From that date, the former requirements of Act of 1988, s.20(1) do not apply: see *ante*, para. 8–46.
[82] See Act of 1988, Sched. 4, varying Act of 1977, Sched. 1.
[83] See Act of 1977, Sched. 1, paras. 4, 5, as amended by Act of 1988, Sched. 4, paras. 4, 5.
[84] *ibid.*
[85] Act of 1977, Sched. 1, para. 6(1), as substituted by Act of 1988, Sched. 4, para. 6. For the most recent consideration of the meaning of "member of family" in the Act of 1977, see *Fitzpatrick v. Sterling Housing Association Ltd.* [1998] Ch. 304, CA (long-standing and devoted homosexual lover and partner not "family").

(b) Residence with first successor

The claimant must have been "residing in the dwelling-house with the first successor at the time of, and for the period of 2 years immediately before, the first successor's death".[86] But if the first successor died on January 15, 1989, or died within 18 months thereafter (*i.e.* by July 15, 1990), a member of his family who was residing with him in the dwelling-house on July 15, 1988, and continued to reside with him there until he died, is taken as having satisfied the requirement of two years' residence.[87]

2. The tenancy transmitted

A person who satisfies these requirements is "entitled to an assured tenancy of the dwelling-house by succession"; and if there are two or more such persons, it will be decided by agreement or, in default, by the county court which of them is to take.[88] The terms of such a tenancy are the same in principle as those where an assured tenancy is taken by a first successor, considered above.[89] **12–27**

3. No further transmission

The restrictions on entitlement to a succession tenancy being statutory and not contractual, a landlord cannot be bound by an agreement that a person is entitled to a succession tenancy under the Act, nor can he be estopped from relying on the terms of the statute.[90] But a landlord can agree, under the Act of 1977,[91] to a change in the identity of the statutory tenant; and so where the landlord had represented that he was treating the tenant (a second successor) and her daughter as the tenant, and the daughter had relied upon this to her detriment, the landlord was estopped from denying that mother and daughter were joint statutory tenants, and the daughter was entitled to remain in possession as tenant after the death of her mother.[92] **12–28**

3. ADDITIONAL GROUNDS FOR POSSESSION

Assured tenancies by succession are exposed not only to the grounds for possession under the Act of 1988[93] but also to six mandatory grounds for possession **12–29**

[86] Act of 1977, Sched. 1, para. 6(1), as substituted by Act of 1988, Sched. 4, para. 6.
[87] Act of 1977, Sched. 1, para. 6(2), substituted by Act of 1988, Sched. 4, para. 6. See also *ante*, para. 12–21.
[88] Act of 1977, Sched. 1, paras. 6(1), 11A, substituted by Act of 1988, Sched. 4, paras. 6, 9.
[89] *Ante*, para. 12–23.
[90] *Daejan Properties Ltd. v. Mahoney* (1995) 28 H.L.R. 498, CA. In principle, the same must apply to succession to assured tenancies under the Act of 1988.
[91] Sched. 1, para. 13.
[92] *Daejan Properties Ltd. v. Mahoney, supra.*
[93] For these, see *post*, pp. 240–302.

under the Act of 1977. "If and so long as a dwelling-house is subject to an assured tenancy to which the successor has become entitled by succession", the court "shall make an order for possession if satisfied that the circumstances are as specified in any of Cases 11, 12, 16, 17, 18 and 20"[94] in the Act of 1977.[95] These Cases may briefly be indicated as follows: lettings by owner-occupiers (Case 11); retirement homes (Case 12); dwelling required for agricultural worker (Case 16); redundant farmhouse on amalgamation (Case 17); farmhouse required for farmer (Case 18); and member of armed forces (Case 20).[96] There is also a further provision under which notices relating to certain mandatory grounds for possession under the Act of 1977 which were given to the predecessor are treated as having been given in relation to corresponding grounds for possession under the Act of 1988.[97] For assured tenancies by succession, there are three of these mandatory grounds: they may briefly be indicated as being holiday accommodation (Case 13 and Ground 3); student accommodation (Case 14 and Ground 4); and dwellings for ministers of religion (Case 15 and Ground 5).[98] The regulated tenancy of the predecessor is treated, for these purposes, as if it had been an earlier assured tenancy granted to the successor, such that the notice applies as if it had been given to the successor under the corresponding ground of the Act of 1988 immediately before the beginning of the succession tenancy.[99]

Sect. 4. Protected Occupancies and Statutory Tenancies under the Act of 1976

12–30 On the death of a protected occupier or statutory tenant under the Act of 1976, that Act made provisions for transmission that were closely similar to those for protected and statutory tenancies under the Act of 1977,[1] and these continue in force. But where the "original occupier" dies on or after January 15, 1989, these provisions are modified by the Act of 1988[2] in much the same way as the corresponding provisions of the Act of 1977 have been modified for protected and statutory tenancies under that Act.[3] The "original occupier" is a person who was, immediately before his death, a protected occupier or statutory tenant of the dwelling-house in his own right,[4] and not by succession. As the provisions for transmission under the Act of 1976 do not apply on the death of a protected occupier or statutory tenant by succession, only one transmission was (and is) possible.

94 In Act of 1977, Sched. 15.
95 Act of 1988, ss.7(3), 39(10), Sched. 4, para. 13(1).
96 See, generally, Vol. 1, pp. 465–480.
97 Act of 1988, Sched. 4, para. 15(1).
98 *ibid.*
99 Act of 1988, Sched. 4, para. 15(2), Sched. 2, Pt. IV, para. 8.
1 See Act of 1976, ss.3, 4.
2 Act of 1988, s.39(4), applying Sched. 4, Pt. II.
3 *Ante*, paras. 12–18 *et seq.*
4 Act of 1976, ss.2(4), 4(2), applied by Act of 1988, s.39(4).

1. Person entitled

The statutory provisions are similar to those made for protected and statutory tenants under the Act of 1977.[5]

(a) Resident spouse

Here too,[6] "spouse"[7] has been given an extended meaning. A person who was living with the original occupier as his or her wife or husband is for these purposes to be treated as the spouse of the original occupier;[8] and that person, if living in the dwelling-house immediately before the death of the original occupier, is to be the statutory tenant of it while occupying it as his or her residence.[9] If by virtue of this provision two or more persons are thus entitled, the one to take the statutory tenancy is to be decided by agreement or, in default, by the county court.[10] **12–31**

(b) Resident member of the family

If at his death the original occupier leaves no surviving spouse who is residing in the dwelling-house, but a member of his family was residing with him there and had been so residing for the two years immediately before his death, that member of the family becomes entitled to an assured tenancy of the dwelling-house by succession.[11] If there are two or more members of his family thus entitled, which of them is to take will be decided by agreement or, in default, by the county court.[12] The statutory changes here are the confirmation that residence must be in the dwelling-house, the substitution of "two years" for the previous "six months", and the substitution of an assured tenancy for a statutory tenancy. Here too there is a transitional provision whereby if the original occupier died during the period January 15, 1989 to July 15, 1990, a member of the family is taken to have satisfied the requirement of two years' residence if his residence had begun by July 15, 1988, and had continued until the death of the original occupier.[13] **12–32**

[5] *Ante*, paras. 12–19 *et seq.*
[6] See *ante*, paras. 12–06, 12–20.
[7] In fact, Act of 1976, ss.3(2) and 4(3) are drafted in terms of "widow", with a somewhat lame 35-word extension that includes widowers. The Act of 1988 prefers the mercifully comprehensive brevity of "spouse".
[8] Act of 1976, s.4(5A), added by Act of 1988, Sched. 4, para. 12.
[9] Act of 1976, s.4(3), as amended by Housing Act 1980, s.76(3). The meaning of occupation as his or her residence is the same as under the Rent Acts: *ibid.* s.4(5), as amended by Act of 1977, Sched. 23, para. 72.
[10] Act of 1976, s.4(5B), added by Act of 1988, Sched. 4, para. 12.
[11] Act of 1976, s.4(4), as amended by Housing Act 1980, s.76(3) and Act of 1988, Sched. 4, para. 11.
[12] *ibid.*
[13] Act of 1976, s.4(5C), added by Act of 1988, Sched. 4, para. 12; and see *ante*, para. 12–21.

2. The tenancy transmitted

(a) Nature

12–33 If the original occupier was a protected occupier or statutory tenant in his or her own right (and not by transmission),[14] the surviving spouse still becomes a protected occupier if he or she already has a ''relevant licence or tenancy'',[15] but otherwise becomes a statutory tenant.[16] A member of the family of the original occupier, on the other hand, will now take only an assured tenancy of the dwelling-house by succession. Where the original occupier was entitled by transmission, instead of being a protected occupier or statutory tenant ''in his own right'',[17] there continues to be no provision for transmission. As before, there is no second transmission.

(b) Terms

12–34 Where under these provisions for transmission[18] a person becomes entitled to an assured tenancy of a dwelling-house by succession, the tenancy is a periodic tenancy, and it is subject to the same terms as those which have already been considered[19] in relation to succession to an assured tenancy under the Act of 1977.[20]

(c) Assured agricultural occupancy

12–35 On the death of a protected occupier or statutory tenant, the assured periodic tenancy to which the successor becomes entitled will be an assured agricultural occupancy, whether or not it fulfils the conditions for such occupancies.[21]

3. Additional grounds for possession

12–36 Assured tenancies by succession are subject to certain additional mandatory grounds for possession.[22] Where, as will be the case,[23] the assured tenancy by succession under the Act of 1976 is an assured agricultural occupancy, the additional grounds for possession are different. They are only two grounds from the Act of 1976: Case XI (owner-occupiers) and Case XII (retirement homes).[24]

[14] Act of 1976, s.4(2), (3).
[15] For these, see *ante*, para. 9–06. No doubt this phrase has the same meaning as ''relevant tenancy or licence''.
[16] Act of 1976, s.3(2), 4(3), as amended by Housing Act 1980, s.76(3).
[17] Act of 1976, ss.3(1), 4(2).
[18] *i.e.*, Act of 1976, s.4, as amended: Act of 1988, s.39(5)(b).
[19] *Ante*, para. 12–23.
[20] Act of 1988, s.39(5)(b), (6), (9).
[21] *ibid.*, s.39(8). For these conditions, see *ante*, paras. 9–02 *et seq.*
[22] See *ante*, para. 12–29 in relation to assured tenancies by succession under Act of 1977.
[23] See *supra*.
[24] Act of 1988, s.39(10), Sched. 4, paras. 13(2), 14, referring to Act of 1976, Sched. IV, Pt. II, Cases XI and XII. See Vol. 1, p. 496.

Part Four

SECURITY OF OCCUPATION

The means by which the Act of 1988 provides security of occupation for the tenant of a dwelling-house held on an assured tenancy will be discussed in the next four chapters. Chapter 13 first considers the means by which an assured tenancy may be brought to an end, and the statutory fetters on the landlord's right to possession. The landlord cannot terminate an assured tenancy by means of a notice to quit, but must instead obtain an order for possession. Before he can do this, he must serve a notice on the tenant (a "possession notice"), warning him of his intention and stating the grounds on which he relies. As under the Rent Acts, the court is prohibited from making an order for possession against an assured tenant except on one of the statutory grounds.

Chapter 14 then examines the nine mandatory grounds for possession. These are grounds on which the landlord, on establishing that the requirements of the ground are satisfied, is entitled as of right to an order for possession. The ten discretionary grounds for possession are addressed in Chapter 15. Under these, the landlord must establish that the requirements of the ground are satisfied, and in addition the court must be persuaded that it is reasonable to make an order for possession.

Finally, Chapter 16 discusses the amplified provisions that protect residential tenants against harassment and eviction without an order of the court. The amendments and extensions made by the Act of 1988 include the creation of a new right of action for damages for unlawful eviction, and the protection of licensees; but certain types of tenancy and licence are excluded.

Chapter 13

Restrictions Upon the Landlord's Right to Possession

Sect. 1. Termination of Tenancies

1. Method of protection

13–01 Like the Rent Acts, the Act of 1988 sets out a number of grounds for possession upon which the court must, or may, make an order for possession, and also prohibits the court from making an order for possession except upon one or more of these grounds.[1] In other respects, however, the protection of the tenant's right to possession is provided by quite different means. The familiar system under the Rent Acts is not to interfere with the determination of the contractual tenancy, whether by the landlord or by effluxion of time, but to prohibit the court from making an order for possession except on one of the statutory grounds for possession. From this prohibition sprang the jurisprudential curiosity known as the statutory tenancy, a tenancy that is no true tenancy.[2] The Act of 1988 applies at the earlier stage of the determination of the tenancy, rather than on the making of the order for possession. Its method is to ensure that some type of contractual tenancy is always in place; the statutory tenancy of the Rent Acts has no part to play. The Act prevents the landlord from unilaterally determining an assured tenancy without an order of the court except in the one case of operation of a break clause; and in the latter case, and in other cases in which the assured tenancy expires or is terminated other than by the volition of the tenant, it gives the tenant a right to continue in possession under a new[3] periodic tenancy.[4]

[1] See Act of 1977, s.98(1); Act of 1988, s.7(1).

[2] See, *e.g.* Vol. 1, pp. 252–255 and Supplement, annotation thereto.

[3] Which the Act of 1988 calls a statutory periodic tenancy, not to be confused with a Rent Act statutory tenancy.

[4] See *ante*, p. 100.

2. The statutory prohibition

The main provision for security of tenure under the Act of 1988 may be set out[5] as follows. 13–02

> "An assured tenancy cannot be brought to an end by the landlord except"—
>
> (1) "by obtaining an order of the court in accordance with the following provisions of this Chapter or Chapter II below[6] or",
>
> (2) "in the case of a fixed term tenancy which contains power for the landlord to determine the tenancy in certain circumstances, by the exercise of that power
>
> and, accordingly, the service by the landlord of a notice to quit shall be of no effect in relation to a periodic assured tenancy".[7]

3. Scope of the prohibition

(a) "An assured tenancy"

The prohibition applies to all assured tenancies, but only to them. Thus if an assured tenancy ceases to be assured, whether by the dwelling-house ceasing to be occupied by the tenant as his only or principal home or otherwise,[8] the prohibition will cease to apply, and the normal rules for the determination of the tenancy will have effect. On the other hand, if while a notice to quit is running the requirements for an assured tenancy are once more satisfied (*e.g.*, by the tenant again occupying the dwelling-house as his only or principal home), it seems that the notice to quit would thereupon become ineffective to terminate the tenancy.[9] Yet once the notice to quit has expired, a resumption of occupation would be ineffective, since there would then no longer be any tenancy that could become assured. It is not clear what is the effect if an assured tenant is served with an appropriate statutory notice[10] seeking to terminate his tenancy and, before the notice expires, the tenancy ceases to be assured.[11] 13–03

(b) "Cannot be brought to an end"

What the prohibition applies to is the process of a landlord's bringing a tenancy 13–04

[5] The sub-division has been made for clarity, but the text is *verbatim*.

[6] *i.e.* Chap. I (ss.1–19) and Chap. II (ss.19A–23, dealing with assured shorthold tenancies) of Part I of the Act of 1988.

[7] Act of 1988, s.5(1), following the line taken for secure tenancies by Housing Act 1980, s.32(1) and Housing Act 1985, s.82(1).

[8] See *ante*, pp. 15, 30, 32–64; and consider *R. v. L.B. Croydon, ex p. Toth* (1986) 18 H.L.R. 493, QB; (1987) 20 H.L.R. 576, CA (on Housing Act 1985).

[9] Contrast Vol. 1, p. 63. Yet consider *Clarke v. Grant* [1950] 1 K.B. 104 at 105, CA.

[10] See Sect. 2, *post*.

[11] See *post*, para. 13–31.

to an end. Thus it will not apply to the ending of a fixed term tenancy by effluxion of time. But within these limits, it is perfectly general in its operation, except so far as limb (2) of the prohibition creates an exception for break clauses in fixed term tenancies.[12]

(c) "By the landlord"

13–05 The prohibition applies only to the landlord, and does not affect determination by the tenant.[13] Thus there is nothing to interfere with the operation of a notice to quit given by the tenant under a periodic tenancy, or the exercise of a "break clause" by the tenant, or a surrender by deed or by operation of law. Premeditated abuse by landlords in seeking to obtain possession by inducing the tenant to determine the tenancy is curtailed somewhat by the provision already considered,[14] although this is confined to actions on or before the grant of the tenancy. These various modes of terminating tenancies are now considered further.

4. Mode of termination of tenancy

13–06 The Act of 1988 is somewhat reticent about the method by which an assured tenancy will come to an end. It contains no explicit provision for the termination of any assured tenancies except statutory periodic tenancies. In all other respects, the methods of termination have to be deduced from—

(i) the ambit of the statutory prohibition above, and
(ii) the exception from that prohibition.

The result appears to be as follows.

(a) Termination by tenant

13–07 As mentioned above, the statutory prohibition does not apply to termination of the tenancy by the tenant, and so he is free to determine it in any way open to him under the general law. All assured tenancies will have been let as a dwelling,[15] and so for periodic tenancies a notice to quit served by a tenant[16] must be in writing and (in addition to satisfying the common law requirements) be given

[12] See *post*, paras. 13–10 *et seq.*
[13] See *Greenwich L.B.C. v. McGrady* (1982) 46 P. & C.R. 223, CA (Housing Act 1980, s.32(1), now Housing Act 1985, s.82(1) ("cannot be brought to an end by the landlord except . . ".)).
[14] Act of 1988, s.5(5); *ante*, para. 6–13.
[15] Act of 1988, s.1(1).
[16] See *Newlon Housing Trust v. Alsulaimen* [1998] 3 W.L.R. 451, HL: notice to quit served by one joint tenant not a "disposition" of property within Matrimonial Causes Act 1973, s.37(2)(b).

not less than four weeks before the date on which it is to take effect.[17] A valid notice to quit can be given by one (or more) of two or more joint tenants without the concurrence of the other(s).[18] At common law, a notice to quit served by a *mesne* landlord as tenant has the effect of automatically terminating any sub-tenancy in existence which was created out of it,[19] so that as against neither the head landlord nor the *mesne* landlord would the sub-tenant have a defence to a claim to possession. But, in view of the statutory prohibition,[20] such a notice to quit ought not to be effective to terminate the sub-tenancy vis-a-vis the *mesne* landlord;[21] and the sub-tenant can rely on the Act of 1988 for protection against the head landlord.[22] Both surrenders by deed and by operation of law are consensual acts,[23] and so the prohibition appears to be a prohibition on the landlord's unilaterally bringing an assured tenancy to an end. Termination by surrender certainly seems to be intended to be effective because the Act of 1988 provides that in such cases no new statutory periodic tenancy arises.[24] There is no obstacle to the tenant's terminating a fixed term tenancy by the exercise of a break clause.

(b) Periodic tenancies: determination by landlord

For periodic tenancies generally, the statutory prohibition is in terms that an assured tenancy "cannot be brought to an end by the landlord except by obtaining an order of the court";[25] and the orders of the court that are relevant here are orders for possession.[26] The inference from this language is that an order for possession is intended not only to do what it professedly does, ordering possession to be given to the landlord, but also to do something else, namely to terminate the tenancy. Unlike in the case of some statutory periodic tenancies,[27] **13–08**

[17] Protection from Eviction Act 1977, s.5(1). No information to be contained in a tenant's notice has ever been prescribed by the Secretary of State for the purposes of this subsection. Tenancies comprising dwellings will not be assured tenancies, however, if the dwelling-house is not "let as a dwelling", and to such tenancies Protection from Eviction Act, Pt. II will not apply: *National Trust for Places of Historic Interest or Natural Beauty v. Knipe* [1998] 1 W.L.R. 230, CA (agricultural holding including a dwelling-house).

[18] *Hammersmith & Fulham L.B.C. v. Monk* [1992] 1 A.C. 478, and *Newlon Housing Trust v. Alsulaimen, supra.* But a contractual break clause cannot be exercised by notice by one of two joint tenants where the purported exercise does not satisfy the common law and statutory requirements of a notice to quit: *Hounslow L.B.C. v. Pilling* (1993) 66 P. & C.R. 22, CA.

[19] *Pennell v. Payne* [1995] Q.B. 192, CA; unless, perhaps, the service is collusively for the purpose of destroying the rights of the sub-tenant: *Barrett v. Morgan* [1998] 3 E.G.L.R. 3, CA (appeal to House of Lords pending).

[20] Para. 13–02, *ante.*

[21] The contrary is arguable on the basis that the *mesne* landlord did not take any step in relation to the sub-tenancy which could be called the *mesne* landlord bringing it to an end within the terminology of the prohibition. See *Crawley B.C. v. Ure* (1995) 71 P. & C.R. 12, CA (service of notice to quit by one of two joint tenants not a "positive act" amounting to a breach of trust).

[22] Act of 1988, s.18.

[23] In the latter case, the court must be able to infer that both parties to the tenancy were accepting its termination and acted accordingly: see *Proudreed Ltd. v. Microgen Holdings plc* [1996] 1 E.G.L.R. 89, CA; *Filering Ltd. v. Taylor Commercial Ltd.* [1996] N.P.C. 79, CA; *Camden L.B.C. v. Alexandrou* (1997) 30 H.L.R. 534, CA.

[24] Act of 1988, s.5(2).

[25] Act of 1988, s.5(1); *ante*, paras. 6–09, 6–10.

[26] *ibid.* s.7(1), (2); *post*, para. 13–17.

[27] See *infra.*

there is no express provision for the termination of original assured tenancies, and the mode of termination, and the date of termination,[28] have to be inferred from the terms of the prohibition, and in particular the words "except by".

(c) Statutory periodic tenancies

13–09 Statutory periodic tenancies alone have explicit provision for determination in specified circumstances. The court is given power to "make an order for possession of a dwelling-house on grounds relating to a fixed term tenancy which has come to an end; and where an order is made in such circumstances, any statutory periodic tenancy which has arisen on the ending of the fixed term tenancy shall end (without any notice and regardless of the period) on the day on which the order takes effect".[29] There are thus two categories, depending upon the particulars of the ground or grounds on which the order for possession has been made:

(i) if those grounds relate to a fixed term tenancy which has come to an end, this provision applies, so that the resulting statutory periodic tenancy will come to an end on the day on which the order takes effect; and
(ii) if those grounds relate to a fixed term tenancy which is still running, or to the statutory periodic tenancy itself, the provision does not apply, and some other basis for the determination of the tenancy must be found.

The phrase "the day on which the order takes effect" seems to refer to the date for giving up possession that the order specifies, rather than the date on which the order is obeyed.[30] Because a statutory periodic tenancy is a contractual periodic tenancy, the tenant may determine it by service of a notice to quit, just as he may with an original assured periodic tenancy.[31]

(d) Fixed term tenancies: determination by landlord

13–10 In addition to the provisions affecting assured tenancies generally, assured fixed term tenancies are subject to a further provision relating to the determination of the tenancy.[32] It provides for the landlord to terminate a fixed term tenancy pursuant to a power in the tenancy to do so other than a provision for forfeiture or re-entry. It raises a number of difficulties. The wording of the exception to the general prohibition is: "except . . . in the case of a fixed term tenancy which

[28] *Post*, paras. 13–16 *et seq.*
[29] Act of 1988, s.7(7).
[30] "Is to take effect" would have been clearer. See the corresponding provision for secure tenancies in Housing Act 1985, s.82(2), where the words are "the date on which the tenant is to give up possession in pursuance of the order".
[31] *Ante*, para. 13–07.
[32] It is really in the nature of an exception to the general prohibition against the landlord's terminating assured tenancies except by court order.

contains power for the landlord to determine the tenancy in certain circumstances, by the exercise of that power . . ''.[33] This apparently general ability for the landlord to exercise a power of determination is, however, subject to an important qualification: ''For the avoidance of doubt, it is hereby declared that any reference in this Part of this Act[34] (however expressed) to a power for a landlord to determine a tenancy does not include a reference to a power of re-entry for forfeiture for breach of any term or condition of the tenancy''.[35] The effect of these provisions must now be considered, particularly in relation to break clauses and forfeiture clauses.

(i) ''IN CERTAIN CIRCUMSTANCES'': this expression has an aura of uncertainty. It plainly does not include an unrestricted power for the landlord to determine the tenancy at any time. ''Circumstances'' is very wide in its meaning, and is capable of including time, manner, cause, occasion, incident and occurrence, and much else besides, but not merely the desire of the landlord to determine the tenancy. Probably any objectively ascertainable limitation on the power would suffice, and the principal power for which Parliament must have intended to make provision is a break clause.[36] Nevertheless, the rationale of this is obscure. A right to break the tenancy at a particular date is obviously included, and it is difficult to see why an unrestricted power for the landlord to determine the tenancy at any time after the seventh year of the term had ended would not be included;[37] but what if the event specified as entitling the landlord to exercise the break is within the control or will of the landlord himself, or someone acting on his behalf? The answer here is unclear. If the landlord validly exercises the power, the Act of 1988 does not interfere with its operation as such; but upon termination, a statutory periodic tenancy will usually arise.[38] **13–11**

(ii) BREACH OF TERM OR CONDITION: as stated above, the landlord's power of determination under the Act does not include a ''power of re-entry or forfeiture for breach of any term or condition of the tenancy''.[39] A power for the landlord to determine the tenancy on the occurrence of a specified event will not fall within this exclusion if the occurrence of that event is no breach of any term or condition of the tenancy, and so the exercise of such a power will determine the tenancy. **13–12**

(iii) POWER OF RE-ENTRY OR FORFEITURE: the borderline between a break clause and a power of re-entry or forfeiture is not always clear; but the distinction is important in deciding whether or not an assured tenancy has been deter- **13–13**

33 Act of 1988, s.5(1).
34 *i.e.* Pt I (ss.1–45) of the Act of 1988.
35 *ibid.*, s.45(4).
36 Perhaps ''in certain circumstances'' was inserted to indicate this; it is difficult to see any other reason.
37 Even though it might be argued that after the seventh year, the power would thenceforth be unrestricted, and the circumstances of its exercise only uncertain. Nevertheless, the Act must be taken to be speaking in this respect from the date of grant of the tenancy, and not from time to time during it, and the certain circumstances are the expiry of the seventh year of the term.
38 *Ante*, p. 100.
39 Act of 1988, s.45(4).

mined. A tenancy may give the landlord power to determine the tenancy upon the tenant committing a breach of covenant, or upon events which include this, and the power may be drafted in terms that are very different from those of a clause of forfeiture or re-entry. In such cases the courts look to the substance rather than the wording. Whatever its terms, the courts will treat a power for the landlord to bring the tenancy to a premature end upon a breach by a tenant of the terms of the tenancy as being a forfeiture clause, even if the tenancy also contains a forfeiture clause in contrasting terms.[40] It is accordingly pointless for a landlord to dress up a forfeiture clause as being a break clause under which an assured fixed term tenancy can be ended under the Act of 1988. But a break clause will be effective if the specified events do not constitute breaches of the terms of the tenancy.[41]

13–14 (iv) RE-ENTRY OR FORFEITURE: the combined effect of these statutory provisions is that the landlord cannot bring any assured tenancy to an end by re-entry or forfeiture. Re-entry and forfeiture fall within the general prohibition that prevents the landlord from bringing any assured tenancy to an end except by obtaining an order of the court for possession under the Act of 1988; and the exception for a landlord's power to determine a fixed term tenancy does not include a power of re-entry or forfeiture for breach of a term or condition of the tenancy.[42] Instead, the landlord's remedy is to seek an order for possession on the ground of a breach of an obligation of the tenancy; but in relation to the mandatory ground based on prolonged rent arrears[43] and all the discretionary grounds other than suitable alternative accommodation and employment,[44] a proviso for re-entry in standard form will usually serve as the necessary provision for the tenancy to be brought to an end on such grounds, enabling the court to make an order for possession during the fixed term.[45] For this reason, it is common to find a proviso for re-entry in an assured tenancy.

13–15 (v) RELIEF AGAINST FORFEITURE: as an assured tenancy cannot be brought to an end by re-entry or forfeiture, the statutory provisions for relief against forfeiture[46] cannot apply. Instead, the tenant may be able to obtain a measure of relief in the proceedings for possession; for, with the exception of that relating to

[40] See *Richard Clarke & Co. Ltd. v. Widnall* [1976] 1 W.L.R. 8435, CA, as considered in *Clays Lane Housing Co-operative Ltd. v. Patrick* (1984) 49 P. & C.R. 72, CA. See also *Plymouth Corporation v. Harvey* [1971] 1 W.L.R. 549, Ch. (forfeiture disguised as surrender).

[41] *Supra.*

[42] Act of 1988, ss.5(1), 45(4); *ante*, para. 13–10.

[43] Act of 1988, Sched. 2, Pt. I, Ground 8.

[44] *i.e.* all the discretionary grounds except *ibid.*, Grounds 9 and 16: see *post*, Chap. 15.

[45] Act of 1988, s.7(6); *post*, para. 13–42.

[46] See Common Law Procedure Act 1852, ss.210–212; Law of Property Act 1925, s.146; County Courts Act 1984, ss.138–140; and see the concise statement of the law in Megarry and Wade's *The Law of Real Property* (5th ed.) pp. 676–683. It might be argued that relief could be granted on the footing that proceedings for possession are proceedings to ''enforce'' a forfeiture within Law of Property Act 1925, s.146(2) and County Courts Act 1984, s.138(1). But such an argument is difficult to sustain, and the language of Common Law Procedure Act 1852, ss.210–212, provides no foothold for any such contention. Any such argument was rejected in *Artesian Residential Investments Ltd. v. Beck* [1999] E.G.C.S. 46, CA (no relief against forfeiture where landlord proved Ground 8: no forfeiture).

prolonged non-payment of rent,[47] the relevant grounds for possession are discretionary and the court may refuse to make an order for possession if it is not reasonable to do so,[48] and may stay, suspend or postpone any order for possession that it makes.[49] Yet although this may often produce reasonable results as between landlord and tenant, it will bring little comfort to sub-tenants, including mortgagees of the tenancy. For upon a forfeiture, on whatever grounds, sub-tenants may apply to the court for relief, and the court may either grant relief to the tenant[50] or vest the premises in the sub-tenant for any term not exceeding that of the sub-tenancy;[51] and without a forfeiture there can be no relief. Where a sub-tenant is himself an assured tenant, the Act of 1988 protects him by making his sub-tenancy continue as a tenancy held from the superior landlord;[52] but this will be of no avail to a mortgagee, who would not be an assured tenant.

5. Date of termination

On the footing that, despite some lack of clarity, it is the order for possession that will terminate the tenancy, the question is when. Apart from orders for possession made on grounds relating to fixed term tenancies which have been succeeded by statutory periodic tenancies,[53] this is obscure. The two possible views are that this occurs— **13–16**

(i) when the order is made; or
(ii) when the order takes effect.

These views will be considered in turn.

(a) When the order is made

The statutory language is that the tenancy cannot be brought to an end by the landlord except "by obtaining" an order for possession.[54] On any ordinary use of language, a landlord "obtains" an order for possession when the court makes the order in his favour. If the intention had been to indicate the date when the order was to take effect, the words "by obtaining" could have been replaced by "under" or "in accordance with". Further, there is a pointed contrast between the phrase "by obtaining" and the express provision for certain statutory periodic tenancies to end on the day on which the order for possession "takes effect";[55] it seems improbable that such differing expressions would be used to express the same meaning. Again, if the general rule was intended to be **13–17**

[47] n. 43, *supra*.
[48] *Post*, pp. 279 *et seq*.
[49] *Post*, paras. 15–03 *et seq*.
[50] *Escalus Properties Ltd. v. Robinson* [1996] Q.B. 231, CA.
[51] See Megarry and Wade, *supra*, at p. 683.
[52] Act of 1988, s.18(1); *ante*, para. 11–11.
[53] *Ante*, para. 13–09.
[54] Act of 1988, s.5(1).
[55] *ibid*., s.7(7); *ante*, para. 13–09.

that assured tenancies end on the date on which orders for possession take effect, it is difficult to see why a specific provision to this effect should have been made for a limited category of assured periodic tenancies. For secure tenancies, the Housing Act 1985 makes a general provision, not confined to a narrow class of tenancy, that the tenancy is to end "on the date on which the tenant is to give up possession in pursuance of the order",[56] thereby avoiding (and contrasting with) the uncertainties of "by obtaining" and "takes effect". Yet again, there is the power of the court, before an order for possession is executed, to stay or suspend its execution, or to postpone the date of possession. In exercising this power, the court is usually required to impose conditions with regard to the payment of any arrears of rent, "and rent or payments in respect of occupation after the termination of the tenancy (*mesne* profits) . . ".[57] These latter words ill accord with any contention that the tenancy remains in existence after the order has been made.

(b) When the order takes effect

13–18 The natural expectation is that when a tenancy is to be ended by an order for possession, the tenancy should not be ended until the order takes effect. This is especially so in cases where orders for possession are almost invariably made for some future date, and the court has power, at any time before the execution of the order, to stay or suspend its execution, or to postpone the date of possession.[58] If the tenancy is to end when the order is made, the Act might well be expected to contain some provision regulating the position of the ex-tenant in the interim; but there is none. It seems unlikely, after 73 years' experience with statutory tenancies, that Parliament would wish to start again on a similar course. There is also the express provision for certain statutory periodic tenancies to end on the day when the order for possession "takes effect".[59] Apart from the verbal contrast already considered,[60] it is hard to see why this rule should be made for one particular category of assured tenancy if the same rule applies to all assured tenancies.

(c) Resolving the uncertainty

13–19 It is still impossible to say how this uncertainty will be resolved.[61] In many cases it may be of little practical significance; in others it may be important. For

[56] Housing Act 1985, s.82(2); see *e.g.*, *Thompson v. Elmbridge B.C.* [1987] 1 W.L.R. 1425, CA.

[57] Act of 1988, s.9(3); see *post*, paras. 13–49 *et seq*. This provision seems to be modelled on Act of 1977, s.100(3), which was appropriate enough for the different system under the Rent Acts.

[58] Act of 1988, s.9(2); *post*, para. 13–50. Under Housing Act 1985, Pt. IV (secure tenancies), where an order for possession is suspended on terms that the tenant comply with certain obligations, the tenancy ends when the obligations are broken: *Greenwich L.B.C. v. Regan* (1996) 72 P. & C.R. 470, CA (For what may happen thereafter by consent or by order of the court, see *Burrows v. Brent L.B.C.* [1996] 1 W.L.R. 1448, HL).

[59] Act of 1988, s.7(7); *ante*, para. 13–09.

[60] *Supra*.

[61] The first edition of this volume (1989) stated, at p. 134, that "At present, it is impossible to say how this uncertainty will be resolved". Ten years on, there has been no reported case under the

example, if the tenant dies after the order is made but before it takes effect, there can be no transmission of the tenancy unless it still exists.[62] On the language of the statute, the making of the order seems to be the most likely date. Yet the causes of simplicity and functional efficiency may persuade the court to adopt the date of the order taking effect, even though it is doubtful whether there is enough statutory material for even the most purposive process of statutory construction to produce this result.[63]

Sect. 2. Possession Notices

In general, no proceedings for possession of a dwelling-house which is let on an assured tenancy can be brought unless the landlord has served on the tenant a notice of his intention to bring the proceedings.[64] Such a notice, which for brevity may be called a "possession notice",[65] must comply with a number of requirements that will be examined in turn. Possession notices may be regarded as replacing landlords' notices to quit in the limited sense of warning the tenant of the impending termination of his tenancy; but they differ in many ways, for example in not themselves ending the tenancy, and in being required for all assured tenancies, whether periodic or fixed term. **13–20**

1. The notice

(a) Form

A possession notice must comply with the requirements of the Act of 1988[66] and in particular it must be in the prescribed form:[67] Form 3 or a form substantially to **13–21**

Act of 1988 which has decided the point although the statutory provisions discussed, *supra*, were considered in *Artesian Residential Investments Ltd. v. Beck* [1999] E.G.C.S. 46, CA. Remarkably, under the Housing Act 1985, the issue has been much litigated (in relation to the time at which a right to buy is lost, and to the effect of a revised agreement for payment of arrears of rent after default by the tenant in complying with the terms of a suspended order for possession: n58, *supra*); perhaps the time will come for the Act of 1988.

[62] See Vol. 1, pp. 272, 273. If it does still exist, however, the interest transmitted may be subject to the order for possession: see *Church Commissioners for England v. Alemarah* (1996) 29 H.L.R. 351, CA.

[63] Yet of one statute, Lord Reid said: "To achieve the obvious intention and produce a reasonable result we must do some violence to the words": *Luke v. Inland Revenue Commissioners* [1963] A.C. 557 at 577.

[64] Act of 1988, s.8. The assertion in the text is true also in relation to assured shorthold tenancies, but the notice considered here is of a different type, and is distinct from the requirements for claiming possession on the assured shorthold tenancy ground.

[65] The title in the statutory form (see n. 69, *infra*) is "Notice Seeking Possession of a Property Let on an Assured Tenancy", and correspondingly for assured agricultural occupancies. Under Housing Act 1985, s.83, the term "notice seeking possession" (or "N.S.P.") gained some currency, and the same phrase is commonly used in the county courts under the Act of 1988.

[66] *i.e.* s.8 of the Act.

[67] *ibid.*, s.8(3).

the same effect.[68] The form prescribed is now the same for assured tenancies and for assured agricultural occupancies,[69] and accordingly the form includes references to landlord/licensor and tenant/licensee and requires the landlord or his agent to cross out those parts of the text that do not apply. Under equivalent provisions of the Housing Act 1985, a form which differed from the prescribed form only by using the words, "The reasons for taking this action are . . ". instead of "Particulars of each ground are as follows . . ". and which included a full explanation of why each ground was being relied upon was a form substantially to the same effect as the prescribed form.[70] And where the notice contained the typescript "Director of Housing" but was not signed by the landlord, though a covering letter was signed by his servant, the notice was in a form substantially to the same effect as the prescribed form.[71]

(b) Contents

13–22 The notice must inform the tenant of four matters.[72] They are as follows—

(i) PROCEEDINGS: that "the landlord intends to begin proceedings for possession of the dwelling-house on one or more of the grounds specified in the notice".[73] In fact, the prescribed form, Form No. 3, does not so state in terms, but paragraphs 2 and 3 of it are to similar effect.[74]

13–23 (ii) GROUNDS: the notice must specify the ground or grounds on which possession is sought, with particulars of them.[75] The prescribed form requires the full text of each ground being relied upon to be set out, and a "full explanation" to be given of why each ground is being relied on. A purported possession notice which fails to set out the substance of all the provisions of the ground for possession relied upon is invalid.[76] The purpose of requiring this information to be stated in the notice is "to enable the relevant party to take steps to remedy

[68] The Assured Tenancies and Agricultural Occupancies (Forms) Regulations 1997 (S.I. 1997 No. 194), reg. 2. The statutory power to prescribe a form of notice includes power to require the notice to be in the prescribed form or in a form substantially to the same effect: *Dudley M.B.C. v. Bailey* (1990) 22 H.L.R. 424, CA.

[69] The Assured Tenancies and Agricultural Occupancies (Forms) Regulations 1997 (S.I. 1997 No. 194) ("the 1997 Forms Regulations"), reg.3(c), Sched., Form No. 3. Before February 28, 1997, when the 1997 Forms Regulations came into effect (*ibid.*, reg.1), there were separate forms for assured tenancies and assured agricultural occupancies: the Assured Tenancies and Agricultural Occupancies (Forms) Regulations 1988 (S.I. 1998 No. 2203), reg.3(3), (4), Sched., Form Nos. 3, 4. Nothing in the 1997 Forms Regulations affects the validity of notices, including possession notices, served before February 28, 1997 if, at the date of service, the notice was in the form then prescribed: 1997 Forms Regulations, reg.4(2).

[70] *Dudley M.B.C. v. Bailey, supra.*

[71] *City of London v. Devlin* (1995) 29 H.L.R. 58, CA (notice seeking possession under Housing Act 1985). See also, by analogy, *Panayi v. Roberts* (1993) 25 H.L.R. 421, CA.

[72] Act of 1988, s.8(2), (3).

[73] *ibid.*, s.8(3)(a).

[74] Form 3 is printed *post*, p. 660.

[75] *ibid.* s.8(2); paras. 3 and 4 in the prescribed form.

[76] *Mountain v. Hastings* (1993) 25 H.L.R. 427, CA (Ground 8 specified as "at least three months rent is unpaid").

the complaints so that he can be in as good a position as possible to avoid eviction''.[77] Under similar legislation, ''non-payment of rent'' has been held to be an insufficient statement of the particulars of the ground for possession;[78] but the notice need not specify the exact amount of arrears if sufficient information is provided that the tenant may readily calculate the correct figure for himself.[79] Where a breach of obligation is relied upon, ''the requirement of particulars is satisfied . . . if the landlord has stated in summary form the facts which he then intends to prove in support of the stated ground for possession'',[80] and accordingly an honest mistake as to the amount of rent arrears will not invalidate the notice.[81]

One of the ways in which a statutory possession notice differs from a notice to quit is the requirement to specify the ground on which possession is sought. In this respect, it is similar to a statutory notice to quit under the Agricultural Holdings Act 1986. Under that Act, a notice to quit was held to be a nullity where the landlord was reckless as to whether the breaches of covenant alleged in the notice had occurred.[82] In principle, such a challenge could be made to a possession notice under the Act of 1988, though in practice it is rarely likely to occur. Unlike the Agricultural Holdings Act 1986, the Act of 1988 does not restrict the tenant's right to challenge the notice, and it requires the ground or grounds for possession specified therein to be proved in court. **13–24**

(iii) NOT BEFORE: the notice must inform the tenant that proceedings for possession ''will not begin earlier than a date specified in the notice''.[83] This date is considered in detail below. If proceedings are begun too early and the point is taken at trial, the court may, in an appropriate case and in the exercise of its discretion, allow new proceedings to be started and abridge all time limits to allow the new proceedings to be tried on the same day.[84] **13–25**

(iv) NOT AFTER: the notice must inform the tenant that ''those proceedings will not begin later than twelve months from the date of service of the notice''.[85]

[77] *Kelsey Housing Association v. King* (1995) 28 H.L.R. 270, CA, *per* Aldous L.J. at 275. And see also *Mountain v. Hastings, supra*. But these observations must be considered in the context of the jurisdiction given to the court to dispense with such a notice, or to allow further grounds or particulars to be added to it: Act of 1988, s.8(1), (2).

[78] *Torridge D.C. v. Jones* (1985) 16 H.L.R. 107, CA (on the similar provisions of Housing Act 1980, s.33, now Housing Act 1985, s.83).

[79] *Marath v. MacGillivray* (1996) 28 H.L.R. 484, CA (''At a meeting between the landlord and the tenant on July 27, 1994 the arrears were agreed at £103.29 since the commencement of the tenancy. Since that date, no payments of rent have been made'': notice valid), explaining *dicta* of Oliver L.J. in *Torridge D.C. v. Jones, supra*.

[80] *Dudley M.B.C. v. Bailey* (1990) 22 H.L.R. 424, CA, *per* Ralph Gibson L.J. at 431 (notice seeking possession under Housing Act 1985, s.83).

[81] *ibid.*

[82] *Rous v. Mitchell* [1991] 1 W.L.R. 469, CA. See also *Luttenberger v. North Thoseby Farms Ltd.* [1993] 1 E.G.L.R. 3, CA, and *Omnivale Ltd. v. Boldan* [1994] E.G.C.S. 63, CA.

[83] Act of 1988, s.8(3)(b), as amended by Housing Act 1996, ss.151(1), (3); para. 5 in the prescribed form.

[84] *City of London v. Devlin* (1995) 29 H.L.R. 58, CA.

[85] *ibid.*, s.8(3)(c); under para. 5 in the prescribed form.

(c) Specified dates

13–26 The notice thus states that the proceedings will be begun "not before" one date and "not after" another. The "not after" date is simple enough: as stated above, it is 12 months from the date of service of the notice, and the printed details of the prescribed form so state. The "not before" date is more complex: there are four variants.

13–27 (i) GROUND 14: DATE OF SERVICE: if a possession notice specifies Ground 14, Nuisance or Illegal User,[86] the "not before" date specified in the notice cannot be earlier than the date of service of the notice. This is so even if other grounds are specified in the notice.[87] Accordingly, if the landlord personally serves a possession notice on his tenant, the date specified in the notice as the "not before" date may be that day, and the landlord may on the same day file a request for possession proceedings to be issued.[88]

13–28 (ii) TWO MONTHS FROM DATE OF SERVICE: if the notice specifies any of Grounds 1 (Landlord's Only or Principal Home), 2 (Required for Sale by Mortgagee), 5 (Required for Minister of Religion), 6 (Demolition, Reconstruction or Substantial Works), 7 (Periodic Tenancy on Death of Tenant), 9 (Suitable Alternative Accommodation) or 16 (Former Service Tenant),[89] the "not before" date specified in the notice cannot be earlier than two months from the date of service of the notice; and if the tenancy is a periodic tenancy, the date must also be not earlier than the earliest date on which (apart from the Act[90]) the tenancy could have been brought to an end by a notice to quit given by the landlord on the date on which the possession notice is served.[91] This is so even if another ground for possession (except Ground 14) not within this group is also specified in the possession notice.[92] If Ground 14 is specified too, the "not before" date is the date of service of the possession notice.[93]

[86] Considered *post*, paras. 15–24 *et seq*.

[87] Act of 1988, s.8(4), as substituted by Housing Act 1996, ss.151(1), (4), 232(3); S.I. 1997 No. 225. This provision is effective from February 28, 1997, but has no effect where either a possession notice was served before that date or (self-evidently) the court dispenses with the requirement of a possession notice and proceedings were started before that date. In the case of a possession notice served before February 28, 1997, the requirements of the "not before" date are as printed in the first edition (1989) of Volume 3 at pp. 138, 139; and the previous statutory provisions applicable are printed *post*, p. 390, in italics.

[88] Although this expedition is in accordance with Parliament's policy of curtailing anti-social conduct of tenants, there is a risk of abuse if a landlord specifies Ground 14 and another ground, and then at trial pursues only the other ground. The courts must be astute to detect such abuse, and the answer may be that if the landlord has no honest belief in the allegations of nuisance or illegal user particularised in the notice (as to which see *Rous v. Mitchell*, *supra*), it is ineffective so far as Ground 14 is relied upon and therefore defective also in relation to the other ground specified because the "not before" date is too early.

[89] For detailed treatment of these grounds, see *post*, Chaps 14, 15.

[90] *i.e.* Act of 1988, s.5(1); *ante*, p. 205.

[91] Act of 1988, s.8(4A), substituted with effect from February 28, 1997 by Housing Act 1996, ss.151(1), (4), 232(3); S.I. 1997 No. 225. See n. 87, *supra*, for the transitional provisions applicable to this amendment, which will only arise if Ground 14 is also specified in the possession notice.

[92] *ibid*.

[93] *Supra*.

(iii) TWO WEEKS FROM DATE OF SERVICE: in all other cases the ''not before'' date specified in the notice cannot be earlier than two weeks from the date of service of the notice.[94] Where a landlord wishes to claim possession on the basis of rent arrears or breach of obligation, therefore, he will be well advised not to specify also one of the grounds falling within group (ii) above. **13–29**

(iv) GROUND 14A: VIOLENCE OR THREATS OF VIOLENCE: this ground, which was added by the Housing Act 1996 with effect from February 28, 1997,[95] is unusual in its requirements relating to the service of a possession notice.[96] If the partner who has left the dwelling is a tenant under the tenancy, he or she will have to be served with the possession notice in the usual way, and the ''not before'' date applicable is two weeks from the date of service of the notice. If that partner is not a tenant under the tenancy, then in addition to the requirement of service of the possession notice on the tenant (with a ''not before'' date of at least two weeks, as above), the court will not entertain possession proceedings unless the landlord has served the possession notice on him or her, or taken all reasonable steps to do so, or unless the court considers it just and equitable to dispense with such service.[97] If the court allows Ground 14A to be added to a possession notice after proceedings for possession are begun,[98] there is a further requirement for the partner who left to be notified of the claim for possession.[99] But these requirements do not affect the requirements as to specified dates of the possession notice itself, and the ground properly falls within group (iii) above. **13–30**

(d) Validity as common law notice to quit

If the tenancy remains an assured tenancy, the possession notice is the appropriate first step for the landlord to take to terminate it, and a notice to quit is of no effect.[1] But if the tenancy ceases to be assured, for example because the tenant starts to occupy another property as his main residence, the tenancy, if periodic, is properly terminable by notice to quit. Sometimes a tenancy will lose its assured status without the actual knowledge of the landlord, and the question may later arise whether a possession notice under the Act of 1988 unwittingly and inappropriately served is effective as a common law notice to quit. Clearly, this will not be the case if the date specified as the ''not before'' date is less than four weeks after the date of service, for a notice to quit must be given at **13–31**

[94] Act of 1988, s.8(4B), substituted with effect from February 28, 1997 by Housing Act 1996, ss.151(1), (4), 232(3); S.I. 1997 No. 225. See n. 87, *supra*, for the transitional provisions applicable to this amendment, which will only arise if Ground 14 is also specified in the possession notice.

[95] Housing Act 1996, ss.149, 232(3); S.I. 1997 No. 225.

[96] For a discussion of the ground generally, see *post*, paras. 15–29 *et seq.*

[97] Act of 1988, s.8A(1), inserted by Housing Act 1996, ss.150, 232(3); S.I. 1997 No. 225. See *post*, para. 15–36.

[98] Under Act of 1988, s.8(2); *post*, para. 15–36.

[99] *ibid.*, s.8A(2), (3); see *post*, para. 15–36.

[1] Act of 1988, s.5(1).

least four weeks before the date on which it takes effect.[2] But a possession notice of at least two months' duration[3] will satisfy this requirement; and the question is whether the information contained in the prescribed form possession notice sufficiently encapsulates the information prescribed for notices to quit.[4] It could be that the failure of Form 3 to refer to assistance under the legal aid scheme, and to the possibility of advice from rent officers, will prevent it from having this desirable effect.

2. Service of notice

(a) Mode of service

13–32 The Act of 1988 unfortunately fails to make any provision for the mode of service of a possession notice, and the general statutory rules seem to be inapplicable.[5] The common law will thus apply. Under this, it would probably suffice to leave the notice, addressed to the tenant, at the dwelling-house,[6] or else to post it to him there and rely on a (rebuttable)[6a] presumption that it arrived in the ordinary course of post.[7] But such a presumption will not apply in the case of recorded delivery or registered post: such a letter is served only when it is delivered to a person at the address who signs the receipt, and not when the postman attends at the address but does not deliver the document because nobody is present who is available or willing to sign the receipt.[8] For a ''bed-sitter'' or flat, delivery through the letter box of the hall of the building containing it, being as far as the postman or the public could go, will normally suffice.[9]

[2] Protection from Eviction Act 1977, s.5(1). The prescribed form possession notice does not contain words such as ''or on the first date after four weeks from the service on you of this notice on which a complete period of your tenancy expires'' commonly found in notices to quit.

[3] *i.e.* one falling within group (ii), *supra.*

[4] Notices to Quit, etc. (Prescribed Information) Regulations 1988 (S.I. 1988 No. 2201), reg.2, Sched, made under Protection from Eviction Act 1977, s.5(1). The exact wording need not be included in a notice to quit as long as all the relevant information is provided: *Swansea C.C. v. Hearn* (1990) 23 H.L.R. 284, CA.

[5] Law of Property Act 1925, s.196 applies only to notices required or authorised to be served or given under that Act, or (by subs. (5)) to notices required to be served by any ''instrument'' (not ''Act'') affecting property executed or coming into operation after 1925. Interpretation Act 1978, s.7 applies only to Acts authorising or requiring documents to be served by post. The Act of 1988 has not made Landlord and Tenant Act 1927, s.23 applicable.

[6] See *Willowgreen Ltd. v. Smithers* [1994] 1 W.L.R. 832, CA (service of proceedings at demised premises good if defendant had continuing presence there).

[6a] Unlike the stronger statutory presumption under Interpretation Act 1978, s.7 (see *Lex Service plc v. Johns* (1989) 59 P. & C. R. 427, CA), this presumption can be rebutted by satisfactory evidence from the tenant that he did not receive the notice.

[7] Consider *Papillon v. Brunton* (1860) 5 H. & N. 518, Ct. Ex.; *Gresham House Estate Co. v. Rossa Grande Gold Mining Co.* [1870] W.N. 119, QB; and see *R. v. Inhabitants of Slawstone* (1852) 18 Q.B. 388, QB. *Quaere* what course of post is ordinary today, but see Practice Direction [1985] 1 W.L.R. 489, Q.B.

[8] *Stephenson & Son v. Orca Properties Ltd.* [1989] 2 E.G.L.R. 129, CA.

[9] *Trustees of Henry Smith's Charity v. Kyriakou* [1989] 2 E.G.L.R. 110, CA.

(b) Joint landlords and joint tenants

Where there are joint landlords, service of a possession notice by only one of them suffices.[10] But if there are joint tenants, the notice must be served on all of them.[11] **13–33**

3. Need for possession notice

In the first instance, the court has no jurisdiction to make an order for possession under the Act of 1988 unless a possession notice has been served, and even then the order can be made only on the grounds for possession stated in the notice. But the court has power to waive the requirement of a notice altogether, or to allow the grounds stated in a notice to be added to or altered. A notice relating to a fixed term tenancy may be effective for the subsequent statutory periodic tenancy. These points will be considered in turn. **13–34**

(a) Jurisdiction

Unless a possession notice has been duly served, "the court shall not entertain proceedings for possession of a dwelling-house let on an assured tenancy".[12] A provision that the court is not to "entertain" an application may be only procedural, and subject to waiver;[13] but in this context the provision appears to go to jurisdiction. It seems to mean that the court has sufficient jurisdiction to determine whether the statute has been complied with, but if it appears, either initially or thereafter, that there has been no compliance, the court's jurisdiction is at an end.[14] If a notice does not comply with the statute, the court is "prohibited from entertaining the proceedings at all".[15] If more than one possession notice has been served owing to a doubt about the validity of one of them, the landlord may proceed at trial without having to elect which of the two notices he is relying on.[16] **13–35**

(b) Grounds available

The court cannot make an order for possession except on one or more of the statutory grounds,[17] and then not unless "that ground and particulars of it" are **13–36**

[10] Act of 1988, s.8(1)(a).

[11] *ibid.*, ss.8(1)(a), 45(3).

[12] Act of 1988, s.8(1).

[13] *e.g.*, Landlord and Tenant Act 1954, s.29(3): *Kammins Ballrooms Co. Ltd. v. Zenith Investments (Torquay) Ltd.* [1971] A.C. 850.

[14] See *R. v. Kensington and Chelsea Rent Tribunal, ex p. MacFarlane* [1974] 1 W.L.R. 1486 at 1490, D.C.

[15] *Torridge D.C. v. Jones* (1985) 18 H.L.R. 107 at 115, CA, *per* Oliver L.J. (on similar provisions of Housing Act 1985). This bar is subject to the jurisdiction to dispense with or amend a possession notice, *infra*, and if the defendant is to seek to rely on the absence of a possession notice, any application to dismiss the proceedings must be made promptly, at about the same time that the defence is served, or even before: *Kelsey Housing Association v. King* (1995) 28 H.L.R. 270, CA.

[16] *City of London v. Devlin* (1995) 29 H.L.R. 58, CA.

[17] Act of 1988, s.7(1), referring to *ibid.*, Sched. 2.

specified in the possession notice; but "the grounds specified in such a notice may be altered or added to with the leave of the court".[18] The alteration of the grounds includes the alteration of the particulars of the grounds relied upon.[19] The nature and extent of any proposed alteration or addition to particulars or grounds will always be appraised by the court before deciding whether, in the circumstances of the case, it is just that leave should be granted.[20]

(c) Dispensing with notice

13–37 If the court considers it "just and equitable" to dispense with the requirement of serving a possession notice, it may do so.[21] When considering whether to dispense with the notice, the court must approach the question broadly, considering all the circumstances of the case, including those that happened after the proceedings had started; and the mere fact that some prejudice is caused to the tenant by failing to serve a notice does not preclude exercise of the power to dispense with the notice if in all the circumstances it is just and equitable to do so.[22] This power seems unlikely to be exercised if the tenant has in no way become aware of the intended proceedings for possession, unless, perhaps, his misconduct has been so grave as to invite proceedings for possession, in the sense of making such proceedings so likely that he may be taken to have expected them. But, importantly, this power of dispensation does not apply if the landlord is seeking to recover possession on Ground 8[23] (prolonged non-payment of rent).

(d) Statutory periodic tenancies

13–38 If a possession notice is served while the tenancy is let on a fixed term tenancy, or the notice is served after a fixed term tenancy has come to an end but the notice relates (either wholly or partially) to events occurring during that tenancy, the notice takes effect even though the tenant becomes or has become a tenant under a statutory periodic tenancy arising when the fixed term tenancy ended.[24]

Sect. 3. Jurisdiction to Make Orders for Possession

13–39 The Act of 1988 principally confers security of tenure on assured tenants by prohibiting the court from making an order against them except on one or more of the specified grounds for possession. Unlike the Rent Acts, the Act of 1988

[18] *ibid.*, s.8(2).
[19] *Camden L.B.C. v. Oppong* (1996) 28 H.L.R. 701, CA (leave to add particulars of nuisance), decided under identical words of Housing Act 1985, s.84(3).
[20] *ibid.* at 706, *per* Leggatt L.J.
[21] Act of 1988, s.8(1)(b).
[22] *Kelsey Housing Association v. King* (1995) 28 H.L.R. 270, CA.
[23] Act of 1988, s.8(5). For Ground 8, see *post*, paras. 14–70 *et seq.* In a case of serious rent arrears but no possession notice, therefore, the landlord would be well advised to abandon reliance on Ground 8 and seek instead an order for possession on the discretionary rent arrears ground (Ground 10).
[24] *ibid.*, s.8(6).

also imposes further prohibitions on the jurisdiction of the court to make orders for possession; but like those Acts it confers a discretion in some cases to adjourn possession proceedings or to stay, suspend or simply postpone any order for possession made. There are a number of subsidiary provisions to consider too.

1. The prohibitions

(a) The main prohibition

The main prohibition is that "the court shall not make an order for possession of a dwelling-house let on an assured tenancy except on one or more of the grounds set out in Schedule 2 to this Act".[25] These grounds are considered in the next two Chapters.[26] As under the Rent Acts, this prohibition prevents the court from making an order for possession merely because the tenant consents to it; but an order can be made if the tenant concedes the existence of specific facts which constitute a ground for possession, and also (where relevant) agrees that it is reasonable to make the order.[27] Such a concession will not automatically be read into an order made by consent; but where there was an issue to be tried as to whether the tenant enjoyed security of tenure at all,[28] and the judge heard some of the evidence relating to that issue, the Court of Appeal declined to set aside an order for possession made by consent without any concession or admission as to the tenant's status. It did so on the basis that it was open to the judge, when presented with the consent order, to infer that Counsel for the tenant thereby admitted that the tenant had no security of tenure.[29] **13–40**

(b) Subsidiary prohibitions

Two of the subsidiary prohibitions have already been considered;[30] the third and fourth have not. **13–41**

(i) NO NOTICE: as seen above, the court is prohibited from entertaining proceedings for possession unless a possession notice has been duly served on the tenant, or the court has waived this requirement.[31]

(ii) UNSPECIFIED GROUND: as seen above, the court is also prohibited from

[25] Act of 1988, s.7(1).

[26] *Post*, pp. 231, 279.

[27] See *R. v. Bloomsbury and Marylebone County Court, ex p. Blackburne* [1985] 2 E.G.L.R. 159, CA; *R. v. Newcastle Upon Tyne County Court, ex p. Thompson* (1988) 20 H.L.R. 430 at 437, QB.

[28] As opposed to whether one of the statutory grounds for possession is established.

[29] *R. v. Worthing B.C., ex p. Bruce* [1994] 1 E.G.L.R. 116, CA; *cp Hounslow L.B.C. v. McBride* (1998) 31 H.L.R. 143, CA (consent order in 5-minute hearing: no inference possible).

[30] There is also a limited prohibition for shared accommodation: *ante*, para. 3–20.

[31] *Ante*, paras. 13–34 *et seq.*

making an order for possession on any ground unless that ground, and particulars of it, are specified in the possession notice.[32]

13–42 (iii) FIXED TERM TENANCY: the court is further prohibited from making an order for possession of a dwelling-house to take effect at a time when it is let on an assured fixed term tenancy unless—

(1) the ground for possession is one of ten specified grounds, and
(2) the terms of the tenancy also make provision for it to be brought to an end on the ground in question, whether that provision takes the form of a provision for re-entry, for forfeiture, for determination by notice or otherwise.[33]

The specified grounds, with brief indications of their nature, are Grounds 2 (sale by mortgagee), 8 (prolonged non-payment of rent), 10 (arrears of rent), 11 (persistent delays in paying rent), 12 (breach of obligation, other than rent), 13 (deterioration of dwelling from neglect), 14 (nuisance or annoyance), 14A (violence or threats of violence), 15 (deterioration of furniture from ill-treatment), and 17 (false statement inducing grant).[34] Thus for assured fixed term tenancies, no mandatory ground is available apart from Nos. 2 and 8; but all the discretionary grounds are, except for Nos. 9 (alternative accommodation) and 16 (former service tenant). Clearly, for some of these grounds a standard form proviso for re-entry in the event of rent arrears or breach of obligation of the tenancy will suffice as the "provision" for the tenancy to be brought to an end on such grounds, and this is why, although an assured tenancy cannot be forfeited,[35] a proviso for re-entry is usually included in such a tenancy agreement. For others, such as Grounds 2 and 17, some more specific wording will be required in the tenancy agreement if the landlord is to be able to recover possession on those grounds during the fixed term of the tenancy. As has been seen,[36] an order for possession made on grounds relating to a fixed term tenancy that has come to an end is effective to terminate the succeeding statutory periodic tenancy.

13–43 (iv) LONG RESIDENTIAL TENANCIES: where a claim to possession is made under an assured periodic tenancy which was granted pursuant to Schedule 10 to the Local Government and Housing Act 1989 on the termination of a long residential tenancy,[37] the court is precluded from ordering possession on any of the following grounds—

(1) Grounds 1 (landlord's only or principal home), 2 (sale by mortgagee), 5 (required for minister of religion) and 16 (former service tenant); and

[32] *Ante*, para. 13–36. This prohibition will not apply if the court waives the requirement of a possession notice.
[33] Act of 1988, s.7(6).
[34] *ibid.* For details of these grounds, see *post*, pp. 242, 260, 288–299, 300.
[35] *Ante*, paras. 13–10 *et seq*.
[36] *Ante*, para. 13–38 (Act of 1988, s.7(7)).
[37] As to which, see *ante*, para. 10–33.

(2) if the assured periodic tenancy arose on the termination of a tenancy formerly governed by Part I of the Landlord and Tenant Act 1954, Ground 6 (demolition or reconstruction).[38]

(c) Mortgages

None of the prohibitions, and nothing else in Part I of the Act of 1988, applies to proceedings for possession of a dwelling-house let on an assured tenancy which are brought by a mortgagee[39] who has lent money[40] on the security of the assured tenancy.[41] This express provision meets a point which under the Rent Acts had given rise to some controversy.[42] **13–44**

2. Power to make orders for possession

Two statutory provisions confer express power on the court to make orders for possession.

(a) Mandatory grounds

Subject to the prohibitions considered above, "if the court is satisfied that any of the grounds in Part I of Schedule 2 to this Act[43] is established . . . the court shall make an order for possession".[44] The grounds in Part I are commonly called the "mandatory" grounds because the court is given no discretion but is bound to make the order. **13–45**

(b) Discretionary grounds

Subject to the prohibitions considered above, "if the court is satisfied that any of the grounds in Part II of Schedule 2 to this Act[45] is established . . . the court may make an order for possession if it considers it reasonable to do so".[46] The grounds in Part II are commonly called the "discretionary" grounds because the court is given a discretion to make an order if it is reasonable to do so, thus applying the concept of reasonableness that is so familiar under the Rent Acts. **13–46**

[38] Act of 1988, s.7(5A), inserted by Local Government and Housing Act 1989, ss.194(1), 195(2), Sched. 11, para. 101; S.I. 1990 No. 431.
[39] As defined by Law of Property Act 1925, s.205(1)(xvi).
[40] *e.g.*, to pay a premium for purchasing a long lease that is not precluded from being assured by being at a low rent: see *ante*, p. 56.
[41] Act of 1988, s.7(1). Contrast mortgagees of the reversion: Ground 2, *post*, p. 242.
[42] Vol. 1, pp. 735–737. See *Dudley and District Benefit Building Society v. Emerson* [1949] Ch. 707, CA and *Britannia Building Society v. Earl* [1990] 1 W.L.R. 422, CA.
[43] *i.e.* Grounds 1 to 8: *post*, pp. 240–264.
[44] Act of 1988, s.7(3).
[45] *i.e.* Grounds 9 to 17: *post*, pp. 282–302.
[46] Act of 1988, s.7(4).

Although the text of Volume 1 addresses the criterion and the authorities at some length,[47] it is also considered in summary in connection with the discretionary grounds for possession.[48]

(c) Establishing the grounds

13–47 Whether the ground is mandatory or discretionary, the order for possession can be made only if the court "is satisfied" that the ground "is established". Save where the ground otherwise specifies,[49] therefore, the facts and circumstances to be taken are thus those that exist at the time of the hearing, when the court is making the order for possession, and not when the proceedings were commenced, or at any anterior time.[50] The express requirement that the court should be "satisfied" does not appear to affect the normal rule that it is the usual civil standard of proof which applies.

(d) The order

13–48 (i) MANDATORY GROUNDS. Where an order for possession is made on one of the mandatory grounds, or in respect of an assured shorthold tenancy,[51] the court has been given no special powers of staying or suspending the order.[52] Instead, the court is prohibited from making an order or granting any suspension or stay of execution which postpones the giving up of possession for more than 14 days unless the tenant shows that exceptional hardship would be caused. Even if so satisfied, the court cannot postpone possession for more than six weeks after the order is made.[53] In a case concerning a claim for possession of a block of offices let at an annual rent of nearly £1 million, this provision was held not to apply to the High Court;[54] but the result could perhaps be better supported by holding that, although the provision binds the High Court as well as county courts, the context requires or enables it to be confined to dwellings.[55] This restriction on the court's discretion does not apply in five cases,[56] but only one of these can apply where possession is claimed from an assured tenant, and this is where "the court had power to make the order only if it considered it reasonable to make it".[57] This does not apply to any of the mandatory grounds for possession.

[47] pp. 387–393, and Supplement (Third Cumulative), pp. 76, 77.

[48] *Post*, paras. 15–03 *et seq.*

[49] As, *e.g.*, Ground 8 does ("at the date of service of the notice . . ").

[50] But if an issue arises as to whether a ground specified in a possession notice was honestly advanced (as to which, see *ante*, para. 13–24) the relevant time for deciding this is the date of serving the notice.

[51] See *post*, paras. 14–78 *et seq.*

[52] See Act of 1988, s.9(6), and contrast under discretionary grounds for possession, *infra*.

[53] Housing Act 1980, s.89(1).

[54] *Bain and Co. v. Church Commissioners for England* [1989] 1 W.L.R. 24, Ch.

[55] The point does not seem to have been argued. If the High Court is outside the restrictions of Housing Act 1980, s.89(1), it could hardly have had the extensive powers of suspension and postponement given by *ibid.*, ss. 87 (before its repeal) and 88.

[56] *ibid.*, s.89(2).

[57] *ibid.*, s.89(2)(c).

(ii) DISCRETIONARY GROUNDS. The jurisdiction to adjourn proceedings and to stay or suspend orders for possession or postpone them is considered below.

3. Adjournment, stay, suspension and postponement.

Where proceedings for possession are brought in reliance on a discretionary ground, the court has wide powers to adjourn the proceedings or to stay or suspend an order for possession or postpone the giving up of possession in pursuance of the order. These powers cannot be excluded by agreement between the parties,[58] but any such agreement might be a factor in the exercise of the court's discretion. The Court of Appeal has the same powers if, on allowing an appeal, it substitutes an order for possession for that made by the trial judge.[59] *Semble* the discretion does not arise if the court makes an order on a mandatory ground even though it had to waive service of a possession notice, or allow the terms of such notice to be amended, before doing so.[60] The Court of Appeal has inherent power at common law to stay a possession order pending appeal.[61] **13–49**

(a) The powers

First, the court "may adjourn for such period or periods as it thinks fit proceedings for possession of a dwelling-house let on an assured tenancy".[62] Secondly, "on the making of an order for possession . . . or at any time before the execution of such an order" the court may— **13–50**

(1) "stay or suspend execution of the order", or
(2) "postpone the date of possession"

"for such period or periods as the court thinks just".[63] Save for the references to assured tenancies and in one immaterial respect, these powers are identical to the powers under the Act of 1977.[64] Under those powers, the court has jurisdiction to make successive orders for suspension,[65] and the same must apply under the Act of 1988. Either party may apply to the court for a variation in the terms at any time before a warrant for possession is executed, or possession given.[66]

[58] See *Rossiter v. Langley* [1925] 1 K.B. 741, DC and *Mouat-Balthasar v. Murphy* [1967] 1 Q.B. 344, CA, decided under equivalent provisions of the Rent Acts.
[59] *R. F. Fuggle Ltd. v. Gadsden* [1948] 2 K.B. 236 at 245, CA, decided under the Rent Acts.
[60] For then the court, having assumed jurisdiction, must apply the terms of the grounds to see whether it is "satisfied" that the landlord is entitled to possession: see Act of 1988, s.9(6).
[61] *Bibby v. Partap* [1996] 1 W.L.R. 931, PC.
[62] Act of 1988, s.9(1).
[63] *ibid.*, s.9(2).
[64] Section 100.
[65] See Vol. 1, p. 374, n.8.
[66] Act of 1988, s.9(2).

(b) Conditions of exercise

13–51 If the court grants any such adjournment, stay, suspension or postponement then it must, unless it considers that to do so would cause exceptional hardship to the tenant or would otherwise be unreasonable, "impose conditions with regard to payment by the tenant of arrears of rent (if any) and rent or payments in respect of occupation after the termination of the tenancy (*mesne* profits)", and the court "may impose such other conditions as it thinks fit".[67] In practice, the court's powers are most frequently exercised where there are relatively modest rent arrears, or good prospects of the tenant's soon being able to discharge the arrears, and where the court is satisfied that justice will be done by suspending the order for possession which it is reasonable to make[68] on condition that the tenant discharges the arrears either within a specific time, or by payment of instalments in addition to the rent which thereafter falls due. There are no such powers if the mandatory ground for possession based on rent arrears[69] is proved, and now that this ground is satisfied by eight weeks' or two months' arrears, there is less scope for suspending orders for possession based on rent arrears. Further, "if any such conditions" (*i.e.* those within this paragraph) "are complied with, the court may, if it thinks fit, discharge or rescind any such order" for possession.[70] If the conditions of suspension are not complied with, the suspension automatically terminates,[71] and the tenancy, if it was not terminated by the making of the order,[72] then terminates.[73] In the county court, the landlord may thereupon obtain the issue of a warrant of possession merely by certifying the default, without seeking the leave of the court.[74] It is not an abuse of process or oppressive to proceed in this way without giving prior notice to the tenant.[75]

(c) Right of spouse, former spouse, cohabitant and former cohabitant to apply

13–52 Under the Matrimonial Homes Act 1983 previously, and now under the Family Law Act 1996,[76] the spouse and to some extent the former spouse of the tenant has statutory rights to occupy, and other rights in relation to, the matrimonial

[67] Act of 1988, s.9(3).

[68] In practice, the suspended order for possession is so much used and well known that the reasoning of the court often appears to be that it is not reasonable to make an "outright" order for possession and so a suspended order is made. This may be regarded as a satisfactory shorthand for the jurisdictional requirements of the Act of 1988, rather than a non-fulfilment of them.

[69] *ibid.*, Sched. 2, Pt. I, Ground 8; see *post*, paras. 14–70 *et seq.*

[70] *ibid.*, s.9(4).

[71] *Yates v. Morris* [1951] 1 K.B. 77, CA.

[72] See the rival arguments, *ante*, paras. 13–16 *et seq.*

[73] *Greenwich L.B.C. v. Regan* (1996) 72 P. & C.R. 470, CA; *Brent L.B.C. v. Knightley* [1997] E.G.C.S. 11, CA; and see *Burrows v. Brent L.B.C.* [1996] 1 W.L.R. 1448, HL, decided under equivalent provisions of Housing Act 1985, Pt. IV.

[74] *Scott-James v. Chehab* [1988] 2 E.G.L.R. 61, CA, distinguishing *Fleet Mortgage and Investment Co. Ltd. v. Lower Maisonette 46 Eaton Place Ltd.* [1972] 1 W.L.R. 765, Ch. (leave required in the High Court).

[75] *Leicester C.C. v. Aldwinckle* (1991) 24 H.L.R. 40, CA; at all events unless the landlord knows that the tenant is faultless in the circumstances in which the conditions have been broken: *Saint v. Barking & Dagenham L.B.C.* [1998] 11 C.L. 315, CA.

[76] Which repealed and replaced the former Act with effect from October 1, 1997.

home. For as long as the tenant is entitled to occupy the dwelling-house, the spouse has many of the rights and protections that the tenant has. But the termination of the tenancy has the effect of terminating those rights. Accordingly, the Act of 1988 makes provision[77] for further protection of a spouse or former spouse in occupation of the dwelling by giving him or her the same rights as the tenant has to apply under the Act of 1988 for an adjournment, stay, suspension or postponement, as the case might require. The rights arise in any case where the tenant's spouse or former spouse, who has matrimonial home rights under Part IV of the Family Law Act 1996,[78] is in occupation of the dwelling-house when proceedings for possession are brought and the assured tenancy is terminated as a result of the proceedings.[79] (But the spouse or former spouse is not given any better rights than the tenant, and the powers of stay and suspension, etc., do not apply if the order for possession is made on a mandatory ground under the Act of 1988).[80] In such case, the spouse or former spouse, so long as he or she remains in occupation, has the same rights in relation to adjournments, stays, suspensions or postponements under the Act of 1988 as he or she would have had but for the termination of the tenancy,[81] *i.e.* the making of the order for possession shall not deprive the spouse of the right, which existed before the making of that order, to apply for relief under the Act of 1988.[82]

Similar protection is given to a former spouse of a tenant, and to a cohabitant or former cohabitant of the tenant, where that person has no interest in a dwelling-house that either was or was intended to be the matrimonial home, or (as the case may be) was or was intended to be the home in which the cohabitants lived together at any time.[83] This protection only applies if the former spouse or the cohabitant or former cohabitant (as the case may be) has no entitlement, by virtue of any beneficial estate or interest or under a contract, or by virtue of any enactment, to remain in occupation[84]; and it applies where the court has made an order for possession of the dwelling-house of which that person is in occupation.[85] If, in any such case, the court had made an order under the Family Law Act 1996 conferring protection on that person and that order is in force, that person has the same rights to seek an adjournment, stay, **13–53**

[77] As the Rent Acts belatedly did upon amendment of Act of 1977, s.100 by Housing Act 1980, s.75(3), effective from November 28, 1980.

[78] Or, before October 1, 1997, rights of occupation under the Matrimonial Homes Act 1983.

[79] The Act clearly postulates actual occupation, and not merely rights, subject to court order, to go into occupation.

[80] Act of 1988, s.9(6).

[81] *ibid.* s.9(5), as amended by Family Law Act 1996, s.66(1), Sched. 8, para. 59(1), (2); S.I. 1997 No. 1892. The subsection reverses the position that the spouse's rights under the Family Law Act 1996, as under the Matrimonial Homes Act 1983, are terminated by an order for possession: see *Penn v. Dunn* [1970] 2 Q.B. 686, CA. *Quaere* the utility of being able to apply for an adjournment of the proceedings, as distinct from a stay, suspension or postponement, after an order for possession has been made (which *ex hypothesi* it must have been to terminate the assured tenancy).

[82] See *Penn v. Dunn, supra.*

[83] Family Law Act 1996, ss.35, 36.

[84] *ibid.*, ss.35(1)(a), (b), 36(1)(a), (b).

[85] Act of 1988, s.9(5A), inserted on October 1, 1997 by Family Law Act 1996, ss.66(1), 67(3), Sched. 8, para. 59(3); S.I. 1997 No. 1892.

suspension or postponement as he or she would have had if the possession order had not been made.[86]

Sect. 4. Other Provisions

Certain other provisions concerning orders for possession, some of which are considered in more detail elsewhere in the text, may for convenience be mentioned here.

1. Assured agricultural occupancies

13–54 As already seen, any assured agricultural occupancy that is not an assured tenancy is to be treated as if it were an assured tenancy.[87] This applies to proceedings for possession; and it also applies to the grounds for possession. Assured agricultural occupancies are subject to all these grounds except Ground 16 (former service tenant), though there is a minor variation in Ground 9 (suitable alternative accommodation). These matters are considered under the respective grounds.[88]

2. Assured shorthold tenancies

13–55 In addition to the eighteen grounds for possession set out in Schedule 2 to the Act of 1988, there are provisions which, though not included in that Schedule, constitute in effect a further mandatory ground for possession, namely the coming to an end or due termination of an assured shorthold tenancy. For convenience, this will be considered in conjunction with the mandatory grounds for possession.[89]

3. Shared accommodation

13–56 Where a tenant shares living accommodation with a person or persons other than his landlord under a deemed assured tenancy,[90] the court cannot make an order for possession of the shared accommodation unless a similar order is or has been made in respect of the separate accommodation.[91] But that restriction is without prejudice to the enforcement of any order made by the court on the

[86] Act of 1988, s.9(5A), *supra*. Once again, not in the case of mandatory grounds for possession: *ibid.*, s.9(6).
[87] Act of 1988, s.24(3); *ante*, para. 9–17.
[88] *Post*, paras. 15–09, 15–39.
[89] *Post*, paras. 14–78 *et seq.*
[90] Act of 1988, s.3(1).
[91] *ibid.*, s.10(1), (2). *Ante*, para. 3–20.

application of the landlord modifying the tenant's right to use the whole or any part of the shared accommodation, or terminating his right to use the whole or part of any non-living shared accommodation.[92]

4. Compensation for misrepresentation or concealment

Under the Rent Acts, provision is made for the landlord to pay compensation to the tenant if an order for possession is obtained by misrepresentation or concealment of material facts; but this applies only to two grounds for possession.[93] For assured tenancies, this applies[94] to all the grounds for possession.[95] "Where a landlord obtains an order for possession of a dwelling-house let on an assured tenancy on one or more of the grounds in Schedule 2 to this Act and it is subsequently made to appear to the court that the order was obtained by misrepresentation or concealment of material facts, the court may order the landlord to pay to the former tenant such sum as appears sufficient as compensation for damage or loss sustained by that tenant as a result of the order".[96] In its essentials this language is identical with that of the Act of 1977,[97] and accordingly the authorities cited in the text of Volume 1[98] appear to apply equally to the Act of 1988,[99] though the value of a lost assured tenancy at a full rack rent may well be much less than a statutory tenancy which enjoys the "fair rent" rent control of the Rent Acts. For joint tenants, any claim must now, it seems, be made by them all.[1] **13–57**

5. Orders and warrants

If a landlord dies after an order for possession has been made, the benefit of the order normally passes to his personal representatives;[2] and they are entitled to an order declaring them entitled to enforce the order for possession.[3] But the benefit of an order does not pass automatically on an assignment of the reversion, and it has been doubted whether it can be assigned.[4] **13–58**

92 *ibid.*, s.10(3).
93 Act of 1977, s.102, applying to Case 8 (required for landlord's employee) and Case 9 (required for landlord: greater hardship).
94 Act of 1988, s.12.
95 *i.e.* all those in Act of 1988, Sched. 2; not assured shortholds.
96 Act of 1988, s.12.
97 s.102.
98 pp. 440–442.
99 See also *Murray v. Lloyd* [1989] 1 W.L.R. 1060, CA (damages of £115,000 where solicitors negligently caused loss of right to become statutory tenant of freehold house worth £460,000 with vacant possession).
1 See Act of 1988, s.45(3); but if one of them fails or refuses to do so, it may be possible, despite the statute, to permit the others to do so: see *Lloyd v. Sadler* [1978] Q.B. 774, CA, considering the authorities.
2 *Goldthorpe v. Bain* [1952] 2 Q.B. 455, CA.
3 *ibid.*; County Court Rules 1981, Order 26, r.5.
4 *Chung Kwok Hotel Co. Ltd. v. Field* [1960] 1 W.L.R. 1112, CA, distinguishing *Goldthorpe v. Bain, supra.*

13–59 A warrant of possession issued by a county court in order to enforce a judgment or order for the possession of land or for the delivery of possession of land remains in force for one year; but by the leave of the court it can be renewed for a further year before it expires, and so on from time to time during the currency of the renewed warrant.[5] An irregularity in a request for a warrant of possession[6] will not render it and execution pursuant to it a nullity.[7] But a failure to obtain leave to issue a warrant more than six years after judgment was an abuse of process, and not an irregularity capable of being cured by exercise of the court's discretion.[8] Where a stay of execution is granted, difficulties with renewal of warrants of possession may be overcome by granting the stay on terms giving the plaintiff leave to renew the warrant as may be necessary.[9] If an order for possession is set aside, any execution of that order falls with it;[10] and execution may be set aside if the warrant had been obtained by fraud or if there was an abuse of process or oppression in its execution.[11] But a discretionary stay or suspension will not be granted where the warrant has already been executed.

[5] County Courts Act 1984, s.111(2); County Court Rules 1981, Order 26, rr.6, 17.

[6] County Court (Forms) Rules 1982, Sched., Form N325.

[7] *Tower Hamlets L.B.C. v. Azad* (1997) 30 H.L.R. 203, CA.

[8] *Hackney L.B.C. v. White* (1995) 28 H.L.R. 219, CA.

[9] *National Westminster Bank plc v. Powney* [1991] Ch. 339, CA. (a mortgage case).

[10] *Governors of the Peabody Donation Fund v. Hay* (1986) 19 H.L.R. 145, CA; *L.B. Tower Hamlets v. Abadie* (1990) 22 H.L.R. 264, CA.

[11] *Leicester C.C. v. Aldwinckle* (1991) 24 H.L.R. 40, CA; *Hammersmith and Fulham L.B.C. v. Hill* [1994] 2 E.G.L.R. 51, CA; *Hackney L.B.C. v. White*, *supra*; and see *National & Provincial Building Society v. Ahmed* [1995] 2 E.G.L.R. 127 at 129, CA and *Saint v. Barking & Dagenham L.B.C.* [1998] 11 C.L. 315, CA.

Chapter 14

Mandatory Grounds for Possession

There are eight grounds for possession from an assured tenant where, if any such ground is proved, the court *must* make an order for possession of the dwelling-house. Before turning to the requirements of each of the mandatory grounds for possession, certain general matters relating to the nature of the grounds, the procedure, and the need (for some grounds) for a warning notice to have been given at the outset of the tenancy, will be considered. **14–01**

In the Act of 1988 there are eight mandatory grounds for possession,[1] together with what are in effect further mandatory grounds for assured shorthold tenancies.[2] The grounds are varied in character, and some resemble Cases for possession under the Act of 1977. In five out of the eight[3] an essential requirement is that, not later than the beginning of the tenancy, the landlord gave the tenant notice that possession might be recovered on that ground. Only one of the mandatory grounds is based on any default by the tenant: that is Ground 8 (prolonged non-payment of rent). Of the others, four are based on possession being required for some particular person or purpose: the landlord (Ground 1), a minister of religion (Ground 5), sale by a mortgagee (Ground 2) and demolition or reconstruction (Ground 6); two assist in providing transitory accommodation: for holidays (Ground 3) and for students (Ground 4); and one (Ground 7) applies for a year after the death of a tenant. **14–02**

Sect. 1. Procedure and Notices

1. Procedure for recovering possession under mandatory grounds

Under the Rent Acts, an expedited procedure is available in the county court for cases where there is a mandatory ground for possession.[4] It was expected by **14–03**

[1] Act of 1988, Sched. 2, Pt. I.
[2] Under *ibid.*, s.21, which provisions are considered *post*, Sect. 10.
[3] Grounds 1–5.
[4] See Vol. 1, p. 461.

most[5] that a similar speedy procedure would be provided for the mandatory grounds under the Act of 1988 shortly after the Act of 1988 came into force; this expectation was met, in part, but not until 1993.[6] In one respect, however, the new procedure goes further than the expedited procedure under the Rent Acts: it enables a judge to make an order for possession without there being any hearing of the landlord's claim for possession. In order to distinguish it from the Rent Acts procedure, it will be referred to as the "accelerated" procedure.

(a) Availability of the accelerated procedure

14–04 The accelerated procedure is only available where the proceedings for possession are brought under Grounds 1, 3, 4 or 5.[7] Most notably, therefore, it is not available where possession is claimed on the ground[8] of prolonged non-payment of rent which, apart from the assured shorthold tenancy ground, is by far the most commonly invoked mandatory ground. Use of the accelerated procedure is not mandatory but at the election of the landlord, where available.[9] Its availability is further restricted by the following six requirements.

14–05 (i) ONLY POSSESSION CLAIMED: the accelerated procedure is only available where possession alone is being claimed in the proceedings.[10] So the landlord cannot use the accelerated procedure to claim arrears of rent, or *mesne* profits, in addition to possession. The rule does not make clear whether costs can also be claimed: on a literal construction of the rule they cannot, being "another claim" made in the proceedings. But the form of originating application and affidavit prescribed for use[11] does contain wording expressly claiming the court fee and solicitors' costs.[12]

14–06 (ii) TENANCY AGREEMENT MADE ON OR AFTER JANUARY 15, 1989: the tenancy, and any agreement for the tenancy, must have been entered into on or after January 15, 1989 if the accelerated procedure is to be used. This requirement, which appears otiose at first blush given that the procedure is only available for assured tenancies under the Act of 1988,[13] does exclude two limited categories of tenancies entered into before that date which can nevertheless be assured tenancies under that Act: "old" assured tenancies under the Housing Act 1980,[14]

[5] See the first edition of Vol. 3 (1989), p. 146.
[6] The procedure was brought into effect on November 1, 1993 by the County Court (Amendment No. 3) Rules 1993 (S.I. 1993 No. 2175), r. 18.
[7] County Court Rules 1981, Order 49, r. 6(3)(b). A similar procedure exists for assured shorthold tenancies: *post*, paras. 14–86 *et seq*.
[8] Ground 8.
[9] County Court Rules 1981, Order 49, r. 6(4) ("the landlord *may* bring possession proceedings under this rule").
[10] County Court Rules 1981, Order 49, r. 6(3)(c).
[11] Form N5A of the Schedule to the County Court (Forms) Rules 1982; see *post*, n. 32.
[12] And the prescribed form of reply gives the defendant limited opportunity to make representations as to how (if at all) the costs should be paid by him: see *post*, n. 40.
[13] Act of 1988, s.1(2), Sched. 1, para. 1 prevents any tenancy entered into before, or pursuant to a contract made before, the commencement of the Act being an assured tenancy: see *ante*, para. 4–48.
[14] See *ante*, para. 5–02.

and other tenancies that become assured tenancies under the Act of 1988 upon a change of landlord after the Act came into force.[15]

14–07 (iii) TENANCY AGREEMENT IN WRITING: if the assured tenancy is not itself the subject of a written agreement, it must be a statutory periodic tenancy arising under the Act of 1988[16] on the same terms (save as to rent) as an assured tenancy which was the subject of a written agreement, or alternatively it must relate to the same or substantially the same premises which were let to the same tenant and be on the same terms (save as to rent and duration) as a tenancy which was the subject of a written agreement.[17] These alternative requirements are not satisfied by a tenancy which is a statutory periodic tenancy arising upon the termination of an oral tenancy agreement.[18] But the requirement is satisfied by an oral tenancy expressly granted upon the termination of a written agreement; and even apparently by an oral tenancy which itself was granted upon the termination of an oral tenancy, provided that somewhere previously there was a written tenancy agreement of substantially the same premises made with the tenant from whom possession is claimed. In such cases, there is no requirement that the tenancy under the original written tenancy agreement be an assured tenancy.

14–08 (iv) ORIGINAL TENANT: accelerated proceedings can only be brought against the tenant to whom the warning notice[19] was given.[20] As we shall see, the mandatory ground may be available to a landlord even though the warning notice was given before the beginning of a previous tenancy, and not before the current tenancy began. In such a case, the accelerated procedure is still available to the landlord (subject to satisfaction of the other conditions) provided that the tenant from whom he is now claiming possession is the person to whom the warning notice was in fact given. Where the tenancy has been assigned by the person to whom the warning notice was given, the accelerated procedure is not available.

14–09 (v) WARNING NOTICE IN FACT GIVEN: closely allied to the previous condition is the requirement that a warning notice must in fact have been given no later than the commencement of the relevant tenancy.[21] So, where the landlord needs

[15] See *ante*, paras. 5–59, 5–65. These categories are more illusory that real when considered with the other requirements for the procedure to apply because, in relation to Grounds 1 and 5, the appropriate warning notice would not have been given prior to the grant of tenancies which were not originally assured tenancies under the Act of 1988, and, in relation to Grounds 3 and 4, the original tenancies not exceeding 8 and 12 months respectively would long since have expired by the time that the accelerated procedure came into effect. It is submitted, however, that an assured tenancy by succession coming into existence under the Rent Acts, on or after January 15, 1989, would not be excluded by this requirement because, under Act of 1988, s.39(6)(a), such a tenancy is deemed to have been granted, and therefore was "entered into" on or after that date. Apart from that, it is almost impossible to conceive of any of Grounds 1, 3, 4 or 5 being applicable to a Rent Acts succession tenancy.

[16] S. 5(2).

[17] County Court Rules 1981, Order 49, r. 6(3)(d).

[18] *ibid.*

[19] Called the "requisite notice" in the r. As to this notice, see *infra*.

[20] County Court Rules 1981, Order 49, r. 6(3)(e).

[21] *ibid.*, r. 6(3)(f).

to persuade the court that it is just and equitable to dispense with that requirement,[22] the accelerated procedure is not available.

14–10 (vi) POSSESSION NOTICE IN FACT GIVEN: a possession notice must in fact have been given to the tenant in accordance with the requirements of section 8 of the Act of 1988.[23] The court has jurisdiction (with one exception) to dispense with service of a possession notice where it is just and equitable to do so,[24] but in such a case the accelerated procedure is not available to the landlord. The accelerated procedure is not available where a possession notice was in fact served but the application was made before the time specified in the notice as being the earliest date for bringing proceedings.[25] It is noteworthy that for Grounds 1 and 5, two of the four grounds for which the accelerated procedure is available, the amount of notice required to be given by the landlord's possession notice is not less than two months, as opposed to two weeks for most of the discretionary grounds and other mandatory grounds.[26] Only for Grounds 3 and 4,[27] therefore, is there any prospect of the landlord taking swift action and recovering possession by court order within weeks rather than months.

(b) Form of the accelerated procedure

14–11 The process permitted by the accelerated procedure is an originating application instead of the usual summons process required by Order 6, rule 3 of the County Court Rules 1981.[28] The application must be made in the prescribed form in the local county court for the district in which the dwelling-house is situated.[29] The application is required to include various information and statements to substantiate the basis of the landlord's claim and have various documents attached to it, including the first written tenancy agreement and the current (or most recent) written tenancy agreement,[30] which statements and documents are required to be verified by the landlord on oath.[31] The prescribed form of applica-

[22] As seems to have happened quite often in practice where an attempt to create an assured shorthold tenancy prior to February 28, 1997 failed for want of the necessary shorthold notice: see *Boyle v. Verrall* (1996) 29 H.L.R. 436, CA and *Mustafa v. Ruddock* (1997) 30 H.L.R. 495, CA.

[23] County Court Rules 1981, Order 49, r. 6(3)(g).

[24] See *ante*, para. 13–37. The exception is where possession is claimed under Ground 8 (prolonged non-payment of rent).

[25] Although, in such a case, the tenant was given a possession notice, it was not given to him ''in accordance with section 8 of the 1988 Act'', and so the court would have to exercise its discretion to dispense with the notice before it could entertain proceedings for possession: see *Kelsey Housing Association v. King* (1995) 28 H.L.R. 270, CA. The wording of Order 49, r.6(14)(b) of the County Court Rules 1981 puts any argument beyond doubt.

[26] See *ante*, paras. 13–26 *et seq.*

[27] Dwelling-house used for holiday lettings or lettings to students.

[28] County Court Rules 1981, Order 49, r. 6(4).

[29] *ibid.*, r. 6(5).

[30] *ibid.*, r. 6(6), (7), as amended on September 28, 1998 by the County Court (Amendment) Rules 1998 (S.I. 1998 No. 1899), r.4(1).

[31] *ibid.*, r. 6(8).

tion, Form N5A,[32] contains both the form of an originating application[33] and the skeleton of an affidavit, which the landlord is required to complete. The form of affidavit provides for evidence to be given to prove the landlord's entitlement to possession and for the necessary documents to be exhibited to it marked "A", "A1", "B" and "C".[34] The prescribed form can be used "with such modifications as the circumstances may require".[35]

(c) The procedure

(i) SERVICE: a copy of the application (including the exhibits), together with a copy for each defendant, must be filed in the county court for the district in which the dwelling-house is situated.[36] The court then effects service by sending the application and exhibits by first class post to the defendant(s) at the address stated in the application.[37] Unless the contrary is shown, the date of service is deemed to be the seventh day after the date of posting.[38] The normal county court rule applying to return undelivered of the originating documents and alternative modes of service of the proceedings for recovery of land apply here too.[39] **14–12**

(ii) REPLY: the application and exhibits are sent by the court together with a form of reply to the application, which is itself a prescribed form.[40] A defendant who wishes to oppose the application must complete and deliver to the court office the form of reply. He must do so within 14 days after the service of the application on him.[41] The form of reply seeks to elicit from the defendant both the extent to which he agrees with the statements made by the plaintiff on oath and certain facts fundamental to the appropriateness of the accelerated procedure.[42] If the defendant does deliver a reply in time, the proper officer of the court **14–13**

[32] Prescribed by the County Court (Forms) Rules 1982 (S.I. 1982 No. 586), r.2, Sched, as amended on September 28, 1998 by the County Courts (Forms) (Amendment) Rules 1998 (S.I. 1998 No. 1900), r.2. Before that date, the form prescribed was that substituted by S.I. 1997 No. 1838 for the original Form 5A, inserted by S.I. 1993 No. 2174.

[33] Which is no more than a formal "cover" sheet identifying the parties and the dwelling-house.

[34] The prescribed form is reproduced *post*, pp. 565 *et seq*.

[35] County Court (Forms) Rules 1982, r.2(2). In some county courts, the practice has developed of requiring a deponent other than the landlord to set out his authority to act on behalf of the landlord.

[36] County Court Rules 1981, Order 49, r. 6(5).

[37] *ibid*., rule 6(9).

[38] *ibid*., Order 7, r.10(3), Order 49, r. 6(9).

[39] *ibid*., Order 7, rr.10(4), 15; Order 49, r.6(9).

[40] County Court (Forms) Rules 1982, r.2(1), Sched., Form 11A, originally inserted by S.I. 1993 No. 2174, substituted by S.I. 1997 No. 1838, and then amended by S.I. 1998 No. 1900, r.6(1). The form, as amended, is reproduced *post*, pp. 573, 574.

[41] County Court Rules 1981, Order 49, r. 6(10). So, unless the landlord can prove that the tenant in fact received the application through the post earlier than seven days after posting (which would be a very rare case), the tenant may safely deliver his reply within 21 days after the date of the postmark. The court must inevitably wait until that time has elapsed before taking any further step with the application.

[42] Such as whether the defendant had a tenancy of the dwelling-house prior to January 15, 1989.

sends a copy to the plaintiff and refers both application and reply to the judge.[43]

14–14 (iii) DEFAULT OF REPLY: where the defendant has not filed a form of reply within the time specified, the plaintiff may file a written request for an order for possession, and the proper officer must, without delay, refer the application to the judge.[44] Given that the plaintiff will not know (a) when the court posted the application to the defendant; (b) when the defendant in fact received the application; and (c) when the defendant in fact delivered the form of reply, he cannot know the precise time at which he is first entitled to make such a written request.[45] Probably most plaintiffs will apply too soon, thinking that the court posts the application immediately upon its being filed, that the defendant only has 14 days from posting or the day after posting to file the reply, and that he will hear immediately from the court if a reply is filed. In practice, most courts will probably allow plaintiffs a little latitude and keep the written request on file until the time for filing a reply has properly elapsed. But it is unsatisfactory that a step which is important given the purpose of the accelerated procedure, and one which is made procedurally significant,[46] is required to be taken by a plaintiff who cannot be sure when he is entitled to take it other than by delaying taking it for many days.[47]

14–15 (iv) LATE REPLY: where a reply is received more than 14 days after the service of the application but before the plaintiff has filed a request for an order for possession, the proper officer must ''without delay'' refer the application to the judge.[48] Thus the tenant is not disadvantaged by failing to reply in time unless the landlord has already requested an order for possession and had it determined by the judge. Unless and until the landlord makes such request, *semble* the application is not referred to the judge at all.

14–16 (v) DETERMINATION WITHOUT HEARING: in the first instance there is no hearing of the application, whether it be referred to the judge because the defendant filed a reply or because the plaintiff requested an order for possession. If the judge is satisfied of the plaintiff's entitlement to the order for possession, he makes such an order without requiring the attendance of the parties.[49] The date for delivering up possession,[50] and the incidence and time for payment of costs, are determined by the judge on paper on the basis of the defendant's reply, if any. In this respect, the accelerated procedure goes beyond the expedited proced-

[43] County Court Rules 1981, Order 49, r. 6(11). Here, as elsewhere in relation to the accelerated procedure, ''judge'' includes a district judge, who has power to hear and determine such an application: r.6(18).

[44] *ibid.*, r. 6(12).

[45] The prescribed form of application does not contain any helpful notes in this regard.

[46] If the defendant does not file a reply and the plaintiff does not request an order for possession, the application does not, *semble*, get referred to the judge for determination.

[47] It is difficult to understand why the application is not taken as a request for an order for possession in the event that the defendant does not file a reply in time.

[48] County Court Rules 1981, Order 49, r. 6(11).

[49] *ibid.*, r. 6(15).

[50] Which, by virtue of Housing Act 1980, s.89(1), cannot be delayed more than 14 days after the making of the order unless the court is satisfied that ''exceptional hardship'' will be caused to the tenant.

ure under the Rent Acts, which merely enabled a hearing to take place more quickly and the merits to be considered in open court but on affidavit evidence.[51]

If the judge is not satisfied as to: (a) the timely giving of the warning notice; (b) the service of a valid possession notice and the making of the application within the time specified in it; (c) due service of the application; or (d) the plaintiff's entitlement to possession under the Ground relied upon, or more than one of these, he must (through the proper officer) fix a date for hearing the application and give directions regarding the steps to be taken before and at the hearing.[52] It is clear, therefore, that the judge, when considering the application on paper, must either make an order for possession or direct a hearing. Indeed, the Rules go further and require the judge to make an order for possession where he is satisfied as to each of the matters (a) to (d) above.[53] There may, however, be reasons other than those listed why the accelerated procedure is not available to the landlord, for example if the mandatory Ground is being invoked against an assignee of the tenancy, the warning notice having been given to his predecessor in title.[54] In such cases, it could be argued, the accelerated procedure rule[55] does not apply at all because one of the conditions for its application has not been satisfied,[56] and the application should be dismissed as incompetent.[57]

(vi) DIRECTIONS FOR HEARING: where the judge has directed that a hearing take place, he may give directions regarding the steps to be taken at and before the hearing, as may appear to him to be necessary or desirable.[58] The proper officer of the court is required to give all parties not less than 14 days' notice of the day fixed. In so doing, the judge is, it is considered, not bound merely to add the application to the undefended hearing list or to direct a full trial, but can (and should in an appropriate case) direct that a particular issue, on which *ex hypothesi* he was not satisfied, be tried, or that the landlord adduce sufficient or better evidence of the date of service of one or more of the notices, or even that the tenant adduce evidence to support a contention raised in his reply. Depending on whether the issue in question, or the matter requiring further proof, is satisfactorily dealt with at the hearing, the judge may then give judgment, give further directions for a trial, or even dismiss the application if it has become clear that the landlord cannot prove one or more of the necessary facts. **14–17**

(vii) SETTING ASIDE ORDER FOR POSSESSION: in addition to the usual ground for setting aside a judgment where failure of postal service is established,[59] the Rules specifically provide that the court may, on application or of its own motion, set aside, vary or confirm any order for possession made pursuant to **14–18**

[51] See Vol. 1, p. 461.
[52] County Court Rules 1981, Order 49, r. 6(13), (14).
[53] *ibid.*, r. 6(15).
[54] See *ante*, para. 14–08.
[55] *i.e.* Order 49, r. 6.
[56] *ibid.*, r. 6(2).
[57] The same argument could, however, be said to apply to the giving of a warning notice or of a possession notice, yet these are, *semble*, matters which should lead the judge to direct a hearing under rule 6(14). There is an inconsistency here which cannot be smoothed out entirely.
[58] County Court Rules 1981, Order 49, r. 6(16)(b).
[59] See *ibid.*, Order 37, r. 3.

the accelerated procedure. Any application within this provision must be made on notice and within 14 days of service of the order.[60] The tenant therefore is given another chance, beyond the late submission of his form of reply, to have the merits of any defence considered. The fact that such application to set aside or vary is to be made on notice suggests that an oral hearing is contemplated this time, rather than a consideration on paper of the request. It is considered that this specific provision must override the principle that a warrant of possession, once executed, will only be set aside on grounds of fraud or oppression,[61] because it is the judgment itself which can be set aside.[61a]

2. Warning notice

(a) The requirement

14–19 For each of the grounds that require notice to be given not later than the beginning of the tenancy,[62] the provision (with one qualification[63]) is in the same terms. "Not later than the beginning of the tenancy the landlord gave notice in writing to the tenant that possession might be recovered on this ground".[64] A notice is given "not later than the beginning of the tenancy" if it is given "not later than the day on which the tenancy is entered into".[65] Thus if the the tenancy agreement is signed in the morning, a notice given that afternoon will suffice.[66] Where there are joint landlords, the notice may be given by any one or more of them;[67] but where there are joint tenants, it must be given to all of them.[68] There is no prescribed form for this warning notice; but it must be in writing and make it clear that possession might be recovered on the ground in question.[69]

(b) Waiver

14–20 Under two of the grounds, the court is given power to dispense with the requirement for a warning notice if the court is "of the opinion" (Ground 1), or "satis-

[60] County Court Rules 1981, Order 49, r.6(17).
[61] *Leicester City Council v. Aldwinckle* (1991) 24 H.L.R. 40, CA.
[61a] See *ante*, para. 13–59.
[62] Grounds 1–5.
[63] Ground 2 is variant: see *post*, para. 14–29.
[64] Act of 1988, Sched. 2, Grounds 1–5. The requirements for the notice in Sched. 2, Pt. IV, are given legislative effect by s.7(5).
[65] *ibid.*, Pt. IV, para. 11, excluding s.45(2) (references in Act to beginning of tenancy: when tenant is entitled to possession).
[66] Which is a curious provision: there may be considerable difference to the tenant in terms of value and desirability between an assured tenancy with full security of tenure and an assured tenancy subject to termination on a mandatory ground because, for example, the landlord previously occupied the dwelling-house as his home (Ground 1). See *Bradshaw v. Baldwin-Wiseman* (1985) 49 P. & C.R. 382 at 385, CA.
[67] Act of 1988, Sched. 2, Pt. IV, para. 7.
[68] *ibid.*, s.45(3).
[69] See *Fowler v. Minchin* (1987) 19 H.L.R. 224, CA and *Springfield Investments Ltd. v. Bell* (1990) 22 H.L.R. 440, CA; Vol. 1, p. 468, and Supplement, annotation to Vol. 1, p. 477.

fied'' (Ground 2)[70] that it is ''just and equitable to dispense with the requirement of notice'';[71] but there is no such power under Grounds 3, 4 and 5. A similar power of dispensation exists under the Rent Acts[72] where the court is of the opinion that ''it is just and equitable to make an order for possession''. A slight difference in wording is apparent. Rent Act authorities establish that the judge must consider all the circumstances of the case as they affect each party at the date of the hearing in deciding whether to dispense with the notice.[73]

The same approach has been adopted under the Act of 1988, notwithstanding the difference in wording.[74] The court is to consider all the circumstances of the case, not just the reasons why written notice was not given.[75] The giving of oral notice is a factor, not a prerequisite to exercise of the discretion; and there is no requirement of exceptional circumstances to justify dispensation if oral notice was not given.[76] The court is thus essentially engaged on an exercise of balancing the relative merits and hardships of the parties' positions at the date of the hearing.[77]

(c) Effect on a later tenancy

If a warning notice has been given for a tenancy, it may also take effect as if it had been given immediately before the beginning of a later tenancy of substantially the same dwelling-house. This will occur if the later tenancy takes effect immediately on the coming to an end of the earlier tenancy, and it was granted (or deemed to be granted)[78] to the person who was the tenant under the earlier tenancy immediately before it came to an end.[79] If there are joint tenants, they must be the same under each tenancy.[80] The landlord, however, may prevent the warning notice from having this double effect by giving notice in writing to the tenant ''not later than the beginning'' of the later tenancy that it is not one in respect of which possession can be recovered on the ground in question.[81] Where the warning notice has this double effect, certain adaptations are made to Ground 1,[82] and also to Grounds 3 and 4;[83] and these are considered under those grounds. **14–21**

The mandatory grounds will now be considered in turn.

[70] There seems to be no significance in this difference in language, for which no reason appears.
[71] Act of 1988, Sched. 2, Ground 1, Ground 2(c).
[72] Under Act of 1977, Sched. 15, Cases 11, 19, 20.
[73] See Vol. 1, p. 470 and Supplement, annotation to Vol. 1, p. 483.
[74] Which difference led the judge at first instance in *Mustafa v. Ruddock* (1997) 30 H.L.R. 495, CA, to conclude that it could not be just and equitable to dispense where the only argument advanced was the landlord's need for the dwelling-house, there being no reason why either written or oral notice was not given.
[75] *Boyle v. Verrall* (1996) 29 H.L.R. 436, CA; *Mustafa v. Ruddock* (1997) 30 H.L.R. 495, CA.
[76] *ibid.*
[77] See *post*, para. 14–23, for the two cases decided under Ground 1, and see also *White v. Jones* (1993) 26 H.L.R. 477, CA (decided under Act of 1977, Sched. 15, Case 11).
[78] See Act of 1988, s.5(3)(b); *ante*, para. 7–06. The circumstances under discussion will most commonly arise when a fixed term assured tenancy is succeeded by a statutory periodic assured tenancy.
[79] Act of 1988, Sched. 2, Pt. IV, para. 8(1), (2).
[80] Act of 1988, s.45(3).
[81] *ibid.*, Sched. 2, Pt. IV, para. 8(3).
[82] *ibid.*, para. 9.
[83] *ibid.*, para. 10.

Sect. 2. Landlord's Only or Principal Home: Ground 1

14–22 Ground 1 has four requirements,[84] but has two alternative bases of establishing the ground, and so requirements 1 and 2 alone, or alternatively 1, 3 and 4, will suffice. It combines some elements of Cases 9 and 11 under the Act of 1977,[85] but there are many differences. The ground cannot be the basis of an order for possession to take effect at a time when the dwelling-house is let on a fixed term tenancy.[86] The four requirements are now considered.

1. Warning notice given or waived

14–23 For each of the alternative bases of claim under this ground, the warning notice considered above[87] must have been duly given, or else the court must consider it just and equitable to dispense with it. A factor when considering waiver is if, to the knowledge of the tenant, the landlord intended to create an assured shorthold tenancy (but failed) and therefore did not give a formal warning notice under Ground 1.[88] In such circumstances, it was just and equitable to dispense with the requirement for the notice where the landlord had a genuine need to occupy and the tenant did not defend the claim;[89] and also (where the tenant did defend) where the landlord had given some oral intimation that the dwelling-house might be required in the future and the landlord's need for that particular house was greater than the tenant's.[90]

2. Prior occupation as only or principal home

14–24 "At some time before the beginning of the tenancy, the landlord who is seeking possession or, in the case of joint landlords seeking possession, at least one of them occupied the dwelling-house as his only or principal home". Here, "the beginning of the tenancy" means "the day on which the tenancy is entered into or, if it is later, the day on which, under the terms of any lease, agreement or other document, the tenant is entitled to possession under the tenancy";[91] this is different from the meaning for warning notices.[92] The ground merely requires occupation "at some time before" the beginning of the tenancy, not "immediately before", so that occupation many years earlier will be enough. Nor is there

[84] Act of 1988, Sched. 2, Pt. I, Ground 1.
[85] See Vol. 1, pp. 423–440, 465–471.
[86] Act of 1988, s.7(6); see *ante*, para. 13–42.
[87] *Ante*, para. 14–19.
[88] As was the case in *Boyle v. Verrall* (1996) 29 H.L.R. 436, CA and in *Mustafa v. Ruddock* (1997) 30 H.L.R. 495, CA.
[89] *Mustafa v. Ruddock, supra.*
[90] *Boyle v. Verrall, supra.*
[91] Act of 1988, s.45(2).
[92] *Ante*, para. 14–19. Act of 1988, Sched. 2, Pt. IV, para. 11 applies only to references to "a notice being given not later than the beginning of the tenancy", not to occupation as a home at some time before the beginning of the tenancy.

any restriction on the meaning of ''occupied'': occupation as a mere licensee will suffice,[93] provided it was as the occupant's only or principal home.[94] Merely temporary or intermittent occupation that would suffice for occupation ''as a residence''[95] may well be insufficient for occupation ''as his only or principal home''. It is not clear whether there must be complete identity between the dwelling-house occupied and the dwelling-house claimed; verbally there must,[96] but there seems to be little reason for excluding the ground where the dwelling-house claimed consists of most though not all of the dwelling-house occupied.[97]

3. Required as only or principal home for landlord or spouse

As an alternative to proving prior occupation as his only or principal home,[98] the landlord can seek to establish that ''the landlord who is seeking possession or, in the case of joint landlords seeking possession, at least one of them requires the dwelling-house as his or his spouse's only or principal home''. ''Requires'' is not qualified by the word ''reasonably'', and no more has to be established than that the landlord genuinely requires or seeks possession for the stated purpose, even if it is not reasonable to do so.[99] It is likely that the court will give an extended interpretation to the word ''landlord'' so that all normal emanations of the landlord, such as his wife and minor children, will qualify. The ground is wide enough to include a landlord who seeks possession in order to house his estranged wife or, perhaps, a housekeeper and his young children.[1] It has been held that a dwelling-house was ''required as a residence''[2] where a landlord living overseas intended to return and live in it only until he could sell it.[3] It is difficult to see how a different result could be reached under Ground 1 on these facts, but there would be a point of distinction if the landlord only intended to use the dwelling as a second home. **14–25**

4. Reversion not acquired for money or money's worth

Where this alternative basis for Ground 1[4] is relied upon, there is a further requirement, namely that certain persons must not have ''acquired the reversion on the tenancy for money or money's worth''. Those persons are— **14–26**

[93] The troublesome words ''owner–occupier'' in Case 11 of the Rent Acts (Vol. 1, p. 466) have rightly not been repeated.

[94] For the meaning of this requirement, see *ante*, para. 3–24.

[95] See *Naish v. Curzon* (1984) 51 P. & C.R. 229, CA; *Mistry v. Isidore* (1990) 22 H.L.R. 281, CA, and Supplement, annotation to Vol. 1, p. 467.

[96] And this construction is supported by the use elsewhere in the Act of 1988 of the distinct phrase ''substantially the same dwelling-house'', *e.g.* in Sched. 2, Pt. IV, para. 8(2)(c).

[97] See Vol. 1, p. 467 at n. 57.

[98] *i.e.* paragraph 2, *supra*.

[99] *Boyle v. Verrall* (1996) 29 H.L.R. 436, CA.

[1] See Vol. 1, p. 429, for decisions on similar wording under Act of 1977, Sched. 15, Case 9.

[2] Within the meaning of *ibid.*, Case 9.

[3] *Lipton v. Whitworth* (1993) 26 H.L.R. 293, CA, distinguishing *Rowe v. Truelove* (1976) 241 E.G. 533, CA.

[4] *i.e.* that under paragraph 3 *supra*.

(i) "the landlord",[5] or
(ii) "in the case of a joint landlord, any one of them", or
(iii) "any other person who, as landlord,[6] derived title under the landlord who gave" the warning notice.

14–27 Where a warning notice takes effect both for a tenancy and for a later tenancy of the same dwelling-house,[7] "reversion" here means the reversion both on the earlier tenancy and on any later tenancy for which the notice takes effect.[8] A person who acquired the freehold or any other interest in the dwelling for money or money's worth before the first tenancy was granted has plainly not acquired "the reversion on the tenancy" for money or money's worth, for there can be no "reversion" on a tenancy that has yet to be granted. But, by virtue of the extended definition of reversion which applies,[9] an acquisition of the reversion on the first tenancy is treated as an acquisition of the reversion on any qualifying later tenancy.[10] The corresponding provision under the Rent Act is "become landlord by purchasing",[11] and case law defined "purchasing" as acquiring for money or money's worth.[12] There should not, accordingly, be any difference between the meaning of this requirement in Ground 1 and the meaning of the corresponding words in the Rent Act. Accordingly, an acquisition by devise or gift, or under a marriage settlement, is not an acquisition for money or money's worth, nor is the grant of a lease of the reversion provided that no premium is paid for it.[13]

Sect. 3. Required for Sale by Mortgagee: Ground 2

14–28 This ground[14] applies where a mortgagee of the landlord's interest, or of any superior landlord's interest, is entitled to exercise a power of sale over the dwelling-house and requires vacant possession in order to do so. But the ground is available to a landlord claiming possession, not to a mortgagee. It does not apply where the assured tenancy itself has been mortgaged: a mortagee who has lent money on the security of the assured tenancy is not subject to any of the restrictions in the Act of 1988 on recovering possession.[15] An order for possession may be made to take effect on this ground during the subsistence of a fixed term assured tenancy, as well as in the case of a periodic tenancy, provided that the

[5] *Quaere* whether the context here excludes the definition of "landlord" in Act of 1988, s.45(1). It seems likely that it does because the landlord here referred to must be the same person as the "landlord who is seeking possession" earlier in the text of the ground.
[6] Here, *semble*, the context does not exclude the wider definition of "landlord".
[7] See *ante*, para. 14–21.
[8] Act of 1988, Sched. 2, Pt. IV, para. 9.
[9] *Supra*.
[10] For the conditions of qualifying later tenancies, see *ante*, para. 14–21.
[11] See Vol. 1, pp. 431, 432 (Case 9).
[12] *ibid.*, pp. 432, 433.
[13] See the case law summarised in Vol. 1 at pp. 433, 434.
[14] Act of 1988, Sched. 2, Pt. I, Ground 2.
[15] Act of 1988, s.7(1). See *ante*, para. 13–44.

terms of the tenancy so provide.[16] But the accelerated procedure for claiming possession under mandatory grounds in the county court is not available for this ground.[17]

This ground has no counterpart under the Rent Acts. It has four requirements.

1. Warning notice given or waived

A warning notice, as considered above,[18] must have been duly given, or else the court must consider it just and equitable to dispense with it. Under this ground, however, the warning notice differs from the notices under Grounds 1, 3, 4 and 5. For those grounds, the warning in each case must be that possession might be sought "on this ground", *i.e.* the particular ground in question. But here the provision is that "notice was given as mentioned in Ground 1 above",[19] and the Ground 1 notice must state that possession might be recovered on Ground 1, namely that the landlord previously occupied the dwelling-house as his only or principal home or that he requires it to use it as such. It therefore seems that to recover possession on Ground 2, the warning notice required is a notice in terms of Ground 1 rather than Ground 2. A notice in terms of Ground 1 may thus do double duty, enabling the landlord to recover possession for his own occupation under Ground 1, or, if he has been unable to sustain the mortgage, under Ground 2 in order to enable the mortgagee to sell with vacant possession. **14–29**

Where the tenancy is a fixed term tenancy, an order for possession to take effect during the fixed term cannot be made unless the terms of the tenancy make provision for it to be brought to an end on this ground.[20] In this respect, the tenancy must refer specifically to Ground 2, and not only to Ground 1. The warning notice procedure is rather odd in this respect, but provided that the tenant has been given due notice that what might be called "overriding landlord need" might lead to loss of his security of tenure, there does not seem to be a difference in principle between the two kinds of need. As under the Rent Acts, the courts will doubtless be astute to prevent a colourable claim of, or on behalf of, a mortgagee being used collusively to escape from the consequences of security of tenure.[21] Where the landlord has not previously occupied the dwelling-house as his only or principal home, however, a Ground 1 warning notice might be challenged, should it be invoked in a Ground 2 claim for possession, on the basis that at the time of giving it the landlord had no honest belief that he would ever require the dwelling-house as a home.[22]

[16] Act of 1988, s.7(6); see *ante*, para. 13–42.
[17] For this procedure, see *ante*, paras. 14–04 *et seq.*
[18] *Ante*, para. 14–19.
[19] Ground 2, *supra*, para. (c).
[20] Act of 1988, s.7(6).
[21] *Quennell v. Maltby* [1979] 1 W.L.R. 318, CA.
[22] A challenge of the type which succeeded in *Rous v. Mitchell* [1991] 1 W.L.R. 469, CA, a case on a notice to quit under the Agricultural Holdings Act 1986, where the landlord was found to have had no honest belief in the allegation of unlawful sub-letting made in the notice to quit. But probably that principle does not apply where, as here, the landlord would not be making an allegation of fact which was true of false, but would be exercising a right to provide for a state of affairs which might or might not arise in the future.

14–30 It is, however, a little difficult to see why the Act of 1988 did not require a specific Ground 2 notice to be given. One of the requirements of the ground is the existence of a prior mortgage of the dwelling-house, which is a question of fact; and for the ground to be of maximum effect, the terms of the tenancy must provide for its termination on Ground 2, otherwise an order can only be made on this Ground to take effect at a time when the tenancy will be periodic.[23] An alternative view of the meaning of the provision is that it merely refers to the manner of giving a warning notice, and not to its content. The notice, like the notice in Ground 1, is to be given "not later than the beginning of the tenancy"; for unlike the other grounds, Ground 2 says nothing about when the notice must be given, and it is not difficult to infer its content. Until this problem is solved,[24] probably the best course is to give a notice that warns of both grounds.

When considering whether it is just and equitable to dispense with the requirement of notice, the court will doubtless weigh all factors as they exist at the date of the hearing as with the same jurisdiction under Ground 1.[25]

2. Mortgage granted before beginning of tenancy

14–31 The dwelling-house must be "subject to a mortgage granted before the beginning of the tenancy". Here too "the beginning of the tenancy" means the day on which the tenancy was entered into or (if it is later) the day on which, under the terms of the lease, agreement or other document, the tenant is entitled to possession under the tenancy.[26] So if a tenancy agreement is made under which the term of the tenancy begins a week later, and in the meantime the landlord mortgages his interest in the dwelling-house, then if the landlord gives a Ground 1 warning notice[27] the tenant is vulnerable to a Ground 2 possession claim even though, at the time the tenancy agreement was entered into, there was no mortgage in existence.[28] A tenant should therefore make inquiry where the landlord serves a Ground 1 warning notice.[29] But if the tenant became entitled to possession under the tenancy agreement before or on the same day that the the mortgage was made, this ground has no application. "Mortgage" includes a charge, and "mortgagee" is construed accordingly. Nothing in this provision excludes an equitable chargee with an expressly granted power of sale. Such a chargee is

[23] See *supra*.

[24] Ground 2 appears to be rarely invoked in practice (see paragraph 2, *infra*). Certainly there has been no reported case on it during the first ten years of existence of assured tenancies under the Act of 1988.

[25] *Boyle v. Verrall* (1996) 29 H.L.R. 4436, CA; *Mustafa v. Ruddock* (1997) 30 H.L.R. 495, CA; see *ante*, para. 14–20. Given that the notice which is being waived is probably not a notice specific to Ground 2, it is arguable that the absence of notice, oral or written, is a less weighty factor than under Ground 1.

[26] Act of 1988, s.45(2).

[27] Assuming that the analysis at para. 14–29, *ante*, is correct, *i.e.* that a Ground 1 notice serves a dual function.

[28] For these purposes, a mortgage is probably "granted" when it is executed, even though a legal charge might only be registered at H.M. Land Registry with effect from a later date.

[29] The tenant should be making inquiry in any event as to whether the landlord's interest is mortgaged: if it is, then under a mortgage in standard modern terms the tenancy will not be binding on the mortgagee unless it has given written consent to the grant of the tenancy. See *infra*.

not entitled to possession, as opposed to an order for sale, and it is unclear whether all the requirements of the Ground can be satisfied in such a case.[30] There is no requirement for identity between the dwelling-house and the mortgaged property provided that the dwelling-house is subject to the mortgage.

If the mortgage excludes the mortgagor's power of leasing,[31] no subsequent tenancy will be binding on the mortgagee, and so he will need no help from this ground. But most commercial mortgages merely provide that the mortgagor is not to grant tenancies without the mortgagee's written consent, and so if such consent has been given, or the tenancy has in some other way become binding on the mortgagee,[32] this ground may be useful to him. Mortgagees should therefore, either in the mortgage or in giving consent, require the mortgagor to give a suitable warning notice before granting any tenancy, and to claim possession from the tenant under Ground 2 if and when the mortgagee requires to sell with vacant possession. There is much to be said in policy terms for this ground, in that it encourages mortgagees to give consent to lettings and mortgagors to seek it. It is unfortunate that the exact requirements of the warning notice for this ground are unclear. **14–32**

3. Mortgagee entitled to sell

The mortgagee must be ''entitled to exercise a power of sale conferred on him by the mortgage or by section 101 of the Law of Property Act 1925''. It is not enough that the power of sale has arisen under section 101, as it will upon default by the mortgagor; it must have become exercisable.[33] **14–33**

4. Required for sale with vacant possession

It must be shown that the mortgagee ''requires possession of the dwelling-house for the purpose of disposing of it with vacant possession in exercise of that power'', *i.e.* the power of sale. The word ''requires'' probably connotes no more than a genuine desire on the part of the mortgagee, reasonableness of that desire not being a relevant factor.[34] Where the mortgaged property comprised a number of dwelling-houses, it is considered that the ground would be satisfied regardless of whether vacant possession of the other dwelling-houses could be obtained, and even though the mortgagee intended to dispose of the whole property as one lot rather than of the dwelling-house alone. **14–34**

[30] In particular, paragraph (b) of the ground. If the charge was not appropriately registered or protected by caution or notice, the tenant would take his tenancy free from the prior equitable interest of the chargee. But, as stated *supra*, Ground 2 is a ground for possession for the landlord, not for the mortgagee.

[31] Under Law of Property Act 1925, s.99.

[32] Because the mortgagee has ''adopted'' the tenancy as binding on it: see *Taylor v. Ellis* [1960] Ch. 368, Ch.

[33] A power that has arisen under Law of Property Act 1925, s.101 becomes exercisable only in the circumstances stated in s. 103, unless otherwise provided in the mortgage.

[34] See *ante*, para. 14–25, in relation to the ''requirement'' of the landlord under Ground 1.

Sect. 4. Short Lettings of Holiday Accommodation: Ground 3

14–35 Ground 3[35] closely corresponds to Case 13 under the Rent Acts,[36] and like that Case it is complementary to the exclusion from statutory protection of holiday lettings.[37] It enables holiday accommodation to be let on short lettings "between seasons", with the assurance that even though the tenancy will be an ordinary assured tenancy, possession can be recovered in time for the next season. An order for possession pursuant to this ground cannot be made to take effect at a time at which the tenancy is a fixed term assured tenancy.[38] Ground 3 has only three requirements.

1. Warning notice given

14–36 A warning notice, stating that possession might be recovered on this ground, must have been duly given in accordance with the principles considered above.[39] Unlike Grounds 1 and 2, there is no power for the court to dispense with this requirement.

2. Recent holiday occupation

(a) Holiday occupation

14–37 "At some time within the period of twelve months ending with the beginning of the tenancy, the dwelling-house was occupied under a right to occupy it for a holiday". As under the Rent Acts, the "right to occupy" probably includes occupation under a licence or tenancy, but not occupation under a right of ownership.[40] Whether the right of occupation was "for" a holiday will probably, in the absence of any express (and genuine) term of a written agreement, be a matter of inference from all the circumstances. "Holiday" appears to have a fairly flexible meaning, including, it seems, a "working holiday".[41] Whether or not there must be exact correlation between the premises occupied under the assured tenancy and the premises occupied for a holiday is unclear. Literally there must; but there seems to be no policy reason why this ground should not avail the landlord if more extensive premises were the subject of the right to occupy for holiday purposes.

[35] Act of 1988, Sched. 2, Pt. I, Ground 3.
[36] See Vol. 1, p. 481.
[37] Act of 1988, Sched. 1, para. 9; *ante*, para. 4–65.
[38] *ibid.*, s.7(6).
[39] *Ante*, para. 14–19.
[40] See Vol. 1, p. 481.
[41] See the discussion in Vol. 1 at p. 188.

(b) Twelve months

The period of 12 months must be calculated so as to end on the day when the tenancy is entered into or, if it is later, on the day when the tenant is entitled to possession under the tenancy.[42] There is no minimum period during which the dwelling-house must have been so occupied, provided that the occupation was genuinely for a holiday purpose. If part only of the holiday falls within the period of 12 months, perhaps just the last day of it, *semble* the requirement is satisfied. Where a warning notice takes effect both for a tenancy and for a qualifying later tenancy of the same dwelling-house,[43] such later tenancy for the purpose of this ground is treated as beginning at the beginning of the earlier tenancy in respect of which the notice was actually given, and this has effect even if there are successive qualifying later tenancies.[44] The practical effect of this is that the grant of the later tenancy does not affect the identification of the period of 12 months, which will still be that ending with the beginning of the earlier tenancy. Thus, if once a "holiday letting" is granted, and within 12 months of its end an assured tenancy is granted with the warning notice having been duly given, any renewal or renewals of that tenancy with the same person as tenant, whether statutory or express, will preserve to the landlord this mandatory ground for possession. **14–38**

3. Letting for a short term

The assured tenancy must be "a fixed term tenancy for a term not exceeding eight months". The term of a tenancy starts on the date it is granted or, if later, the date on which the term is expressed to start[45] or on which the tenant is entitled to possession. There is nothing to require that the letting should be for any particular purpose, or that the landlord should require possession for any particular reason. Only the warning notice alerts the tenant to the fact that the landlord may be entitled to recover possession on a mandatory ground. **14–39**

Sect. 5. Short Lettings of Student Accommodation: Ground 4

Ground 4[46] closely resembles Case 13 under the Rent Acts,[47] and like that Case it is complementary to the exclusion from statutory protection of certain lettings to students.[48] It enables student accommodation to be let on short lettings when **14–40**

[42] Act of 1988, s.45(2).
[43] See *ante*, para. 14–21.
[44] Act of 1988, Sched. 2, Pt. IV, para. 10.
[45] *Bradshaw v. Pawley* [1980] 1 W.L.R. 10, Ch.
[46] Act of 1988, Sched. 2, Pt. I, Ground 4.
[47] See Vol. 1, p. 482.
[48] Act of 1988, Sched. 1, para. 8; *ante*, para. 4–18.

vacated by the students (during vacations, for example) or when not required for student accommodation in a particular academic year, but with the assurance that even though the tenancy will be an ordinary assured tenancy, possession can be recovered in time for further lettings to students. An order for possession pursuant to this ground cannot be made to take effect at a time at which the tenancy is a fixed term assured tenancy.[49] Ground 4 has only three requirements.

1. Warning notice given

14–41 A warning notice, stating that possession might be recovered on this ground, must have been duly given in accordance with the principles considered above.[50] Unlike Grounds 1 and 2, there is no power for the court to dispense with this requirement.

2. Recent student letting

(a) Student letting by specified institution

14–42 "At some time within the period of twelve months ending with the beginning of the tenancy, the dwelling-house was let on a tenancy falling within paragraph 8 of Schedule 1 to this Act", *i.e.* a tenancy within the provision excluding certain student lettings from being assured tenancies. This provision has already been considered.[51] Only a letting by the specified educational establishment providing the course of study being pursued by the student and a letting by another specified institution can create a tenancy falling within the provision, and accordingly this ground will not ordinarily be available to individual landlords.[52]

(b) Twelve months

14–43 The period of 12 months must be calculated so as to end on the day when the tenancy is entered into or, if it is later, on the day when the tenant is entitled to possession under the tenancy.[53] There is no minimum period during which the dwelling-house must have been so let, provided that the letting fell within the

[49] *ibid.*, s.7(6).
[50] *Ante*, para. 14–19.
[51] *Ante*, paras. 4–18 *et seq.*
[52] The ground does not, however, require that there be identity between the landlord who granted the student letting and the landlord who granted the assured tenancy. So if a specified institution sold the dwelling-house to an individual within 12 months of the last student letting, or (probably) if a specified institution granted a tenancy of a dwelling-house belonging to another such that there was a student letting by estoppel, the individual would in these cases be able to take advantage of this ground.
[53] Act of 1988, s.45(2).

terms of the student letting exclusion from being an assured tenancy. If part only of the student letting falls within the period of 12 months, perhaps just the last day of it, *semble* the requirement is satisfied. Where a warning notice takes effect both for a tenancy and for a qualifying later tenancy of the same dwelling-house,[54] such later tenancy for the purpose of this ground is treated as beginning at the beginning of the earlier tenancy in respect of which the notice was actually given. This is so even if there are successive qualifying later tenancies.[55] The position under this ground in this respect is the same as the position under Ground 3, namely that the grant of the later tenancy or tenancies does not affect the computation of the period of 12 months. Thus, if once a student letting is granted, and within 12 months of its end an assured tenancy is granted with the warning notice having been duly given, any renewal or renewals of that tenancy with the same person as tenant, whether statutory or express, will preserve to the landlord this mandatory ground for possession.

3. Letting for a short term

The tenancy granted must be "a fixed term tenancy for a term not exceeding twelve months". The difference between the university year and the customary holiday seasons might account for the maximum term being 12 months instead of the eight months under Ground 3.[56] The term of a tenancy starts on the date it is granted or, if later, the date on which the term is expressed to start[57] or on which the tenant is entitled to possession. Here too there is nothing to require that the letting should be for any particular purpose, or that the landlord should require possession for any particular reason. Only the warning notice alerts the tenant to the fact that the landlord may be entitled to recover possession on a mandatory ground. **14–44**

Sect. 6. Required for Minister of Religion: Ground 5

Like the two preceding grounds, Ground 5 has only three requirements.[58] Its language is for the most part identical with the wording of Case 15 under the Rent Acts.[59] As with Grounds 3 and 4, an order for possession pursuant to this ground cannot be made to take effect at a time at which the tenancy is a fixed term assured tenancy.[60] **14–45**

[54] See *ante*, para. 14–21.
[55] Act of 1988, Sched. 2, Pt. IV, para. 10.
[56] *Ante*, para. 14–39.
[57] *Bradshaw v. Pawley* [1980] 1 W.L.R. 10, Ch.
[58] Act of 1988, Sched. 2, Pt. I, Ground 5.
[59] See Vol. 1, p. 474.
[60] Act of 1988, s.7(6).

1. Warning notice given

14–46 A warning notice, stating that possession might be recovered on this ground, must have been duly given in accordance with the principles considered above.[61] There is no power for the court to dispense with this requirement.

2. Minister's residence

14–47 The dwelling-house must be "held for the purpose of being available for occupation by a minister of religion as a residence from which to perform the duties of his office". There is nothing to restrict the religion to any particular faith or denomination, though doubtless the religion must be one that is generally recognised as being a religion. Nor is there anything to exclude part-time ministers; but under a religion that regards every member as a minister, probably even full-time members are not ministers for this purpose, for they are not in any way set apart from other members.[62] The dwelling-house must in some way be allocated or set apart for the purpose of being occupied from time to time by a minister, not merely as a residence but as a residence "from which" to perform "the duties of his office". "From which" is clearly intended to be wider than "in which", and "the duties" seems to imply that the dwelling-house should have been intended to be the base for the minister's official activities.

3. Required for a minister

14–48 The court must be "satisfied that the dwelling-house is required for occupation by a minister of religion as such a residence", *i.e.* as a residence from which to perform the duties of his office. There is nothing to confine this requirement to ministers previously connected with the dwelling, or to the same religion or denomination as that for which it had previously been held. Grammatically, the requirement in question is that of the landlord and not the minister; and this, together with the requirement that the dwelling-house be held as such, suggests that it is ecclesiastical authorities that are likely to invoke this ground rather than individuals.

Sect. 7. Demolition, Reconstruction or Substantial Works: Ground 6

14–49 Ground 6 has no counterpart under the Rent Acts; its ancestry lies in a ground for opposing the renewal of business tenancies[63] and in a ground for possession

[61] *Ante*, para. 14–19.
[62] Consider *Walsh v. Lord Advocate* [1956] 1 W.L.R. 1002, HL (on the words "a regular minister of any religious denomination": Jehovah's Witnesses).
[63] Landlord and Tenant Act 1954, Pt. II, s.30(1)(f). Many of the cases cited in this section were decided under that subsection.

from secure tenants.[64] In essence, the landlord must prove that he needs possession in order to carry out substantial works to the dwelling-house or to the building, which could not reasonably be carried out if the tenancy continued. The detail of the ground is complex, however: it has five requirements.[65] An order for possession on this ground cannot be made to take effect at a time at which the tenancy is a fixed term assured tenancy.[66] This ground also has a special feature,[67] in that if an order for possession is made, the tenant is entitled to be paid a sum equal to his removal expenses.[68]

1. THE REQUIREMENTS

1. Demolition, reconstruction or substantial works

It must be shown that "the landlord . . . intends"— **14–50**

(1) "to demolish or reconstruct the whole or a substantial part of the dwelling-house", or
(2) "to carry out substantial works on the dwelling-house or any part thereof or any building of which it forms part".

For demolition or reconstruction under limb (1), the part of the dwelling to be demolished or reconstructed must be "substantial"; but for carrying out substantial works under limb (2), any part of the dwelling suffices, though the nature of the works (which must be "substantial") will usually prevent the part from being insignificant. Further, limb (2) can be satisfied without any works being carried out on the dwelling at all,[69] as where substantial works to a part of the block of flats other than the dwelling are to be carried out, for example the staircases and lifts which give access to it, or the main roofs above it. What is "substantial" is a question of fact and degree, having regard to the totality of what is involved,[70] but it seems clear that the word "substantial" must be used here in the sense of "considerable" and not as meaning only more than *de minimis*. "Reconstruct" requires a measure of demolition affecting the structure

[64] Housing Act 1985, Sched. 2, Pt. II, Ground 10. In *Wansbeck D.C. v. Marley* (1987) 20 H.L.R. 247, CA, it was accepted that authorities under Landlord and Tenant Act 1954, Pt. II were applicable to this ground.
[65] Act of 1988, Sched. 2, Pt. I, Ground 6.
[66] *ibid.*, s.7(6).
[67] In common with one discretionary ground for possession: Ground 9, Suitable Alternative Accommodation, as to which see *post*, para. 15–16.
[68] *Post*, p. 257.
[69] The key requirement will then be **3. Possession needed to do work**, *post*, para. 14–54.
[70] *Atkinson v. Bettison* [1955] 1 W.L.R. 1127, CA; *Bewlay (Tobacconists) Ltd. v. British Bata Shoe Co. Ltd.* [1959] 1 W.L.R. 45, CA and, more recently, *Barth v. Pritchard* [1990] 1 E.G.L.R. 109, CA (rewiring, new partitions, new central heating and new lavatories not "substantial work of construction" within Landlord and Tenant Act 1954, s.30(1)(f)).

followed by physical rebuilding, and not merely physical work that changes the character or identity of the dwelling.[71]

2. The landlord's intention

(a) The landlord

14–51 The requisite intention must be held by "the landlord who is seeking possession or, if that landlord is a registered housing association or charitable housing trust, a superior landlord". "Registered housing association" has the same meaning as in the Housing Associations Act 1985, and "charitable housing trust" means a housing trust (within the meaning of that Act) which is a charity within the meaning of the Charities Act 1993.[72] Where such a body is the landlord, the necessary intention may instead be held by a superior landlord, although the claim for possession is still made by the immediate landlord, *i.e.* the association or the trust. Whether or not the landlord can successfully "intend" to have the works carried out by a building lessee or by a contractual purchaser of the dwelling or of the building[73] is unclear.

(b) "Intends"

14–52 The expression "the landlord intends" has become familiar after its extensive exploration by the courts in relation to business tenancies.[74] What must be shown under that jurisdiction is that at the date of the hearing[75] there is not merely a hope or aspiration, or an exploration of the possibilities, but a genuine, settled intention on the part of the landlord to do something that, judged by the standard of the reasonable man, he has a reasonable prospect of being able to bring about.[76] The landlord does not need to prove on a balance of probabilities that he will be able to do that which he intends; merely that there is some reasonable chance that he will be able to do so; the sort of prospect that a reasonable landlord would take seriously.[77] It may be assumed that most of this learning

[71] *Percy E. Cadle & Co. Ltd. v. Jacmarch Properties Ltd.* [1957] 1 Q.B. 323, CA; *Barth v. Pritchard, supra*; and see *Houseleys Ltd. v. Bloomer-Holt Ltd.* [1966] 1 W.L.R. 1244, CA. For a fuller analysis of cases decided under Landlord and Tenant Act 1954, s.30(1)(f), see Woodfall's *Law of Landlord and Tenant* (28th (looseleaf) ed.), paras. 22.105 *et seq.*

[72] For these see *ante*, paras. 5–26, 5–27.

[73] As is the case under the equivalent provision of the Landlord and Tenant Act, Pt. II: *Gilmour Caterers Ltd. v. Governors of St. Bartholomew's Hospital* [1956] 1 Q.B. 387, CA; *Turner v. Wandsworth L.B.C.* (1994) 69 P. & C.R. 433, CA.

[74] Under Landlord and Tenant Act 1954, Pt. II, s.30(1)(f), (g). See generally Woodfall, *Landlord and Tenant, supra.*

[75] *Betty's Cafes Ltd. v. Phillips Furnishing Stores Ltd.* [1959] A.C. 20.

[76] *Reohorn v. Barry Corporation* [1956] 1 W.L.R. 845, CA; *Gregson v. Cyril Lord Ltd.* [1963] 1 W.L.R. 41, CA; *Westminster City Council v. British Waterways Board* [1985] A.C. 676. See, most recently, *Dolgellau Golf Club v. Hett* [1998] 2 E.G.L.R. 75, CA, referring to the earlier case of *Cadogan v. McCarthy & Stone Developments Ltd.* [1996] E.G.C.S. 94, CA.

[77] See *Cadogan v. McCarthy & Stone Developments, supra*, and *Dolgellau Golf Club v. Hett, supra.* These recent authorities have stressed the limited degree required to succeed in proving "intention".

will be applied in interpreting the requirements of Ground 6, but it is possible that the court will not go so far as to allow the landlord's intention to be proved at the hearing when there was no such settled intention until the date of the trial.[78] The wording of the requirement of Ground 6 is marginally different in this respect from the wording of the business tenancy provision.[79]

If the landlord is a limited company, a formal resolution of the board of directors as to the company's intention may not be essential[80] (provided that the intention can be proved *aliunde*), and it is not conclusive;[81] the true intention must be ascertained by considering all the relevant circumstances. But an undertaking to the court to take the requisite steps (*e.g.*, to carry out the demolition or reconstruction) will, if given by a responsible person or body, usually establish the requisite fixity of intention.[82] 14–53

3. Possession needed to do work

It must be established by evidence[83] that the intended work "cannot reasonably be carried out without the tenant giving up possession of the dwelling-house" because of one or more of four alternative reasons.[84] *Semble* that if the work cannot reasonably be carried out for another reason too, the requirement is not met. "Possession" here means legal possession, not merely physical occupation, so that the requirement will not be satisfied if the landlord is entitled under the terms of the tenancy or otherwise to sufficient physical possession for a sufficient time reasonably to enable the work to be carried out.[85] Whether works can or cannot reasonably be carried out will be a question of fact and degree in each case, but is clearly an objective test. 14–54

The four reasons one or more of which must make the carrying out of the work impracticable are considered below. The scheme of these reasons appears to be that (a) and (b) apply where only access or other facilities are needed by the landlord reasonably to be able to carry out the intended works, that (c) applies where a reduction in the dwelling-house (and possibly further access or

[78] As was the case in *Betty's Cafes Ltd. v. Phillips Furnishing Stores Ltd., supra.*

[79] Under Landlord and Tenant Act 1954, s.30(1)(f), the landlord must prove that "on the termination of the current tenancy [he] intends . . ", and similar wording exists in the ground for possession from a secure tenant in Housing Act 1985, Sched. 2, Pt. II, Ground 10 ("The landlord intends, within a reasonable time of obtaining possession of the dwelling-house to . ."), so that the application of the reasoning in the *Betty's Cafes* case, *supra*, to secure tenancies in *Wansbeck D.C. v. Marley* (1987) 20 H.L.R. 247, at 253, CA, is unsurprising. In the absence of any similar words in the Act of 1988, it might be thought that, to serve a valid possession notice under Act of 1988, s.8, a landlord must have the requisite intention at the date of service as well as at the hearing.

[80] *H. L. Bolton (Engineering) Co. Ltd. v. T. J. Graham & Sons Ltd.* [1957] 1 Q.B. 159, CA.

[81] *Fleet Electrics Ltd. v. Jacey Investments Ltd.* [1956] 1 W.L.R. 1027, CA.

[82] *Espresso Coffee Machine Co. Ltd. v. Guardian Assurance Co. Ltd.* [1959] 1 W.L.R. 250, CA; *London Hilton Jewellers Ltd. v. Hilton International Hotels Ltd.* [1990] 1 E.G.L.R. 112, CA.

[83] See *Wansbeck D.C. v. Marley* (1987) 20 H.L.R. 247, CA, a case on the similar ground for possession from secure tenants.

[84] These are to some extent derived from Landlord and Tenant Act 1954, s.31A, inserted by Law of Property Act 1969, s.7(1).

[85] See *Heath v. Drown* [1973] A.C. 498.

facilities over the reduced dwelling) is needed, and that (d) applies where even such a reduction and agreement as (c) postulates would not reasonably enable the landlord to carry out the works.[86] If this were not so, the landlord would be able to rely on reason (c) or (d) in a case where access, arrangements or other facilities in the dwelling might suffice.

(a) Tenant unwilling to agree variation

14–55 "The tenant is not willing to agree to such variation of the terms of the tenancy as would give such access and other facilities as would permit the intended work to be carried out". If the landlord has to rely on this reason, *semble* he must prove the tenant's unwillingness to agree, and not merely his (the landlord's) willingness to agree a variation. In practice, this will involve the landlord putting the terms of a suggested variation to the tenant, except perhaps in an extreme case where the tenant has already manifested his complete unwillingness to co-operate to any degree. Save where the tenancy was granted by a lease under seal, there is no formality required for the variation, and an oral agreement to allow the landlord all necessary access will suffice. Strictly, an agreement to extend the term granted effects a surrender and re-grant,[87] and is not just a variation in the existing tenancy; but it is difficult to see why an agreement by the tenant to vacate for (say) six months to enable the works to be done in return for an extension of his tenancy should not be a "variation" within the meaning of this provision.

(b) Variation not practicable

14–56 "The nature of the works is such that no such variation is practicable". This reason seems most likely to be invoked in cases where the landlord intends to demolish or reconstruct (or both) the dwelling-house. There is likely in practice to be some overlap between this reason and reason (d) below. But in a case where possession of part of the dwelling and access over the rest does not reasonably enable the work to be carried out,[88] this reason must necessarily be satisfied too. The difference between the two reasons is likely to arise if the works reasonably necessitate possession of part and access and other facilities over the rest but the tenant is only willing to agree to give access and other facilities, not possession.

(c) Refusal of tenancy of reduced part

14–57 "The tenant is not willing to accept an assured tenancy of such part only of the dwelling-house. . ". ("the reduced part") "as would leave in the possession of

[86] Although the word "reasonable" appears in reason (c) and not in reason (a), all four reasons are subject to the overriding requirement that the works cannot *reasonably* be carried out without possession, and so there seems to be no difference in substance here.
[87] *Friends Provident Life Office v. British Railways Board* [1996] 1 All E.R. 336, CA.
[88] *i.e.* the agreement postulated by reason (c).

his landlord so much of the dwelling-house as would be reasonable to enable the intended work to be carried out and, where appropriate, as would give such access and other facilities over the reduced part as would permit the intended work to be carried out''. This reason can only apply where recovery of possession of some part of the dwelling is reasonably necessary to permit the works to be carried out.[89] That too must be a matter for the landlord to prove if he seeks to rely on this reason. The reason will only be satisfied where the reduced part of the dwelling is itself ''a dwelling-house. . .let as a separate dwelling'',[90] otherwise the tenancy of the reduced part cannot be an assured tenancy.

(d) Tenancy of reduced part not practicable

''The nature of the intended work is such that such a tenancy is not practicable'', *i.e.* it is not reasonably practicable for the tenant to retain possession of part of the dwelling under an assured tenancy of the reduced part. *Semble* this reason would be satisfied where the part of the dwelling reasonably required by the landlord to carry out the works was so substantial that the reduced part would not be a dwelling-house let as a separate dwelling. **14–58**

4. Reversion not acquired for money or money's worth

This ground is not available where the interest of the landlord seeking possession has been acquired for money or money's worth after the grant of the tenancy. In substance, this is based on the familiar concept of becoming landlord by purchasing under the Rent Acts,[91] but there are material differences from the Rent Acts provision. Where it is the superior landlord who has the relevant intention to demolish or reconstruct, etc.,[92] it does not matter that that person ''became landlord by purchasing'' provided that the immediate landlord seeking possession did not. **14–59**

If the landlord seeking possession acquired his interest in the dwelling-house before the grant of the tenancy, this requirement is *ipso facto* satisfied.[93] It does not matter that, at the date of grant, the interest in question was not the immediate reversion on the newly granted tenancy,[94] but it is implicit that the interest in question is the one by virtue of which the landlord is claiming possession.[95]

[89] See *supra*.
[90] Within Act of 1988, s.1(1).
[91] See Vol. 1, pp. 430–434.
[92] *Ante*, para. 14–51.
[93] Whether or not he bought it for money or money's worth.
[94] See *ante*, para. 11–11, for the circumstances in which an assured tenancy will become binding on a superior landlord.
[95] So, for example, it would not suffice if the landlord had owned a superior reversionary interest since before the grant of the tenancy, but purchased the immediate reversion afterwards. If, however, the immediate reversion thereupon merged in the superior interest, it seems arguable that the requirement would be satisfied here—because the relevant interest of the landlord in the dwelling-house is that which he owned prior to the grant of the tenancy—even though such a landlord would have ''become landlord by purchasing'' under the differently-worded provisions of the Rent Acts.

For these purposes, "the grant of the tenancy" usually bears its ordinary meaning; but in two cases it refers to an earlier grant. First, if the tenant to whom the tenancy was granted (or any of them, if the grant was to joint tenants) was the tenant, or one of the joint tenants, of the dwelling-house concerned under an earlier assured tenancy, "the grant of the tenancy" means the grant of that earlier assured tenancy. Secondly, if the tenant to whom the tenancy was granted (or any of them, if the grant was to joint tenants) was the tenant, or one of the joint tenants, of the dwelling-house concerned under a tenancy to which Schedule 10 to the Local Government and Housing Act applied,[96] "the grant of the tenancy" means the grant of that earlier tenancy.

14–60 This requirement is also satisfied where the interest of the landlord was in existence at the time of grant of the tenancy[97] and neither he (or in the case of joint landlords any of them) nor any person who since that time acquired that interest, whether alone or jointly with others, acquired it for money or money's worth. Again, it is implicit that the interest in question which must not have been "purchased" either by him (or them) or by another in the period of time since the grant of the tenancy is that of the landlord claiming possession. A payment in kind by one of several joint landlords who are predecessors in title of the landlord claiming possession will disentitle that landlord to rely on this ground. The ground cannot apply at all where the interest of the landlord claiming possession was created after the date of grant.[98] The words "money or money's worth" mirror exactly judicial exegesis of the phrase "become landlord by purchasing" in the Rent Acts,[99] and include any consideration with a monetary value. Every acquisition by an approved body under Part IV of the Act of 1988 (change of landlord: secure tenants) is deemed to be an acquisition for money or money's worth, and special provisions apply where the landlord's interest under the tenant's previous tenancy was acquired under that Part.[1]

5. No assured tenancy by transmission

14–61 Ground 6 is not available if the tenancy is an assured tenancy by transmission under the Acts of 1976 or 1977, as amended by the Act of 1988.[2] This prevents an assured tenancy by transmission, which has its origin in the Acts of 1976 or

[96] A long tenancy at a low rent which has the potential, upon termination, to become an assured tenancy: see *ante*, Chap. 10.

[97] Which again has the extended meaning discussed, *supra*, in two particular cases.

[98] And so the "loophole" under the Rent Acts of granting a reversionary tenancy for no premium (*Powell v. Cleland* [1948] 1 K.B. 262, CA) does not exist for assured tenancies.

[99] See *Powell v. Cleland*, *supra*, and, generally, Vol. 1, pp. 432–434.

[1] Local Government and Housing Act 1989, ss.194(1), 194(2), Sched. 11, para. 109; S.I. 1989 No. 2445, adding a paragraph to Ground 6. Housing Act 1988, Pt. IV was repealed on October 1, 1996, but without affecting any extant applications to acquire housing not disposed of by that date: Housing Act 1996, ss.222, 232(3), (4), Sched. 18, para. 1; S.I. 1996 No. 2402. Accordingly, subject to that saving, there will be no more such acquisitions which are deemed to be for money or money's worth: *ibid.*, ss.227, 232(3), (4), Sched. 19, Pt. IX; S.I. 1996 No. 2402.

[2] *i.e.* it must not be an assured tenancy which had "come into being by virtue of any provision of Schedule 1 to the Rent Act 1977, as amended by Part I of Schedule 4 to [the Act of 1988] or, as the case may be, section 4 of the Rent (Agriculture) Act 1976, as amended by Part II of that Schedule". For these, see *ante*, paras. 12–22, 12–27, 12–33.

1977, from being exposed to a ground for possession which does not exist under those Acts.

2. REMOVAL EXPENSES

Where the court makes an order for possession of a dwelling-house let on an assured tenancy on Ground 6, the landlord is liable to pay the tenant a sum equal to his removal expenses.[3] This also applies to an order for possession made on Ground 9 (alternative accommodation),[4] but not on any other ground.[5] **14–62**

1. Amount

The landlord's liability is to pay the tenant "a sum equal to the reasonable expenses likely to be incurred by the tenant in removing from the dwelling-house".[6] A similar expression is used in quantifying disturbance payments on the compulsory acquisition of land,[7] with "likely to be incurred" here recognising prospective expenses as well as those actually incurred. The reference to expenses incurred "in removing" is wider and more generous than the expenses "of removing" or "of the removal".[8] The tenant is entitled to reasonable expenses, reasonably incurred as a direct and natural consequence of, and in, the removal, and he is not confined to the immediate expenses of the physical transfer of furniture, fixtures and fittings.[9] The question whether any particular expense is included is one of circumstance and degree;[10] and redecoration, rewiring, transferring the telephone, adapting carpets and furniture, and replacing a gas cooker by an electric cooker for an "all-electric" flat may all, in a proper case, be included.[11] **14–63**

2. Determination of amount

Any question as to the amount of the sum payable under this provision is to be determined by agreement between the landlord and the tenant or, in default of agreement, by the court.[12] Any sum payable to the tenant by virtue of this provision is recoverable as a civil debt due from the landlord.[13] **14–64**

[3] Act of 1988, s.11.
[4] See *post*, para 15–16.
[5] Act of 1988, s.11(1).
[6] *ibid.*
[7] Land Compensation Act 1973, s.38(1)(a); Land Compensation (Scotland) Act 1973, s.35(1)(a).
[8] *Glasgow Corporation v. Anderson* 1976 S.L.T. 225, IH, applied in detail in *Nolan v. Sheffield Metropolitan D.C.* (1979) 38 P. & C.R. 741, LT.
[9] *Glasgow Corporation v. Anderson, supra*, at pp. 229, 230.
[10] *ibid.*, at p. 229.
[11] *ibid.*, and *Nolan v. Sheffield Metropolitan D.C.*, *supra*.
[12] Act of 1988, s.11(2).
[13] *ibid.*, s.11(3).

Sect. 8. Periodic Tenancy on Death of Tenant: Ground 7

14–65 Ground 7 enables the landlord to prevent security of tenure being perpetuated by periodic tenancies devolving under the will or on the intestacy of a deceased periodic tenant. There are only limited statutory provisions for the transmission of periodic tenancies on death.[14] The ground has three requirements.[15]

1. Periodic tenancy

14–66 The tenancy must be a periodic tenancy (including a statutory periodic tenancy) and not a fixed term tenancy. The ground does not make explicit at what time the tenancy in question must have been a periodic tenancy, but *semble* on the death of the tenant, for otherwise a periodic tenancy would not have "devolved under the will or intestacy". The ground may accordingly be assumed to have no application where the tenancy was a fixed term tenancy at the date of death.[16]

2. Devolution under will or intestacy

14–67 The tenancy must have devolved under the will or intestacy of the former tenant on his death. If instead there has been a statutory transmission on the tenant's death,[17] which will exclude any devolution under the will or intestacy, Ground 7 has no application. Nor will this ground apply if the existing tenancy is different from the tenancy which devolved under the will or intestacy, as where a new tenancy has been granted. But for the purposes of this ground, the mere acceptance of rent by the landlord from a new tenant after the former tenant's death is not to be "regarded as creating a new periodic tenancy". It will not be so regarded "unless the landlord agrees in writing to a change (as compared with the tenancy before the death) in the amount of the rent, the period of the tenancy, the premises which are let or any other term of the tenancy".[17a] But a change in the period of the tenancy or an agreement to extend the premises let under the tenancy will, as a matter of law, amount to a surrender of the devolved tenancy and the re-grant of a new tenancy,[18] and in such a case the ground would in any event be inapplicable. This provision is in terms confined to the creation of a new periodic tenancy by the acceptance of rent, and so would not prevent a tenant from arguing that a new tenancy had been created under an agreement, even if it is merely oral. But the tenant cannot escape the con-

[14] See *ante*, paras. 12–02 *et seq.*
[15] Act of 1988, Sched. 2, Ground 7.
[16] The limitation here is quite different in kind from that which restricts orders for possession taking effect *at a time when* the tenancy is a fixed term tenancy: Act of 1988, s.7(6).
[17] Under Act of 1988, s.17; *ante*, para. 12–09.
[17a] *ibid.*, Sched. 2, Pt. I, Ground 7.
[18] *Friends Provident Life Office v. British Railways Board* [1996] 1 All E.R. 336, CA.

sequences of the mandatory ground by asserting that the landlord has impliedly granted him a new tenancy by accepting rent from him unless there is a written variation of the tenancy.

3. Proceedings begun within a year of death

''The proceedings for the recovery of possession'' must be ''begun not later than twelve months after the death of the former tenant''. It is not enough merely to serve a possession notice[19] within the 12 months, for that, although a prelude to proceedings for possession, commences no proceedings but merely gives warning of an intention to bring them on the specified grounds.[20] The use of the definite article (''the proceedings'') may suggest that the proceedings must be begun claiming possession on this ground, as opposed to amended subsequently;[21] but it is not clear whether the court can exercise its discretion to dispense with a possession notice or alter or add to the grounds specified in it[22] where possession is claimed on this ground.[23] **14–68**

The difficulty that landlords are often left in ignorance of the death of a tenant (sometimes deliberately) is met by a provision that if the court ''so directs'', the 12 months is to run from the date on which, in its opinion, the landlord (or in the case of joint landlords, any one of them) became aware of the former tenant's death. It does not appear how far, for this purpose, the awareness of an agent of the landlord is to be treated as the awareness of the landlord, but the usual principles of the law of agency will apply, and there may therefore be a difference between a mere rent collector and a managing agent.

Unless the court considers that it is just and equitable to dispense with the requirement of a possession notice,[24] the landlord must serve such a notice before commencing possession proceedings.[25] Such a notice must be served specifying a date for the commencement of proceedings not earlier than two months from the date of service, and not earlier than the earliest date on which the tenancy could[26] be terminated by a notice to quit given on the same date as the possession notice is served. The landlord must therefore act well in advance of the expiry of the 12 months if he is to take advantage of this ground. If the deceased tenant died testate, the notice is properly served on his executors; if the tenant died intestate, the notice must be served on the Public Trustee if **14–69**

[19] See *ante*, paras. 13–20 *et seq.*
[20] And see Ground 10 (*post*, p. 288), distinguishing between the date of service of the warning notice and the date on which proceedings for possession are begun.
[21] The tenant in such a case would have a strong argument for resisting any such amendment on the ground that it would defeat an accrued ''limitation'' type defence.
[22] Under Act of 1988, s.8(1)(b), (2); *ante*, paras. 13–36, 13–37.
[23] It is difficult to see why that jurisdiction, being one for the discretion of the court and exercisable according to the justice of the case, should be excluded by implication, at least where the landlord has started his proceedings relying on Ground 7.
[24] As to which, see *ante*, para. 13–37.
[25] Act of 1988, s.8(1).
[26] Apart from Act of 1988, s.5(1).

letters of administration have not yet been granted; and once they have, on the administrators.[27]

Sect. 9. Prolonged Non-Payment of Rent: Ground 8

14–70 Under the Rent Acts, non-payment of rent has always been a discretionary ground for possession; but assured tenancies under the Act of 1988 are unique in having a mandatory ground based on rent arrears. No amendment has been made to the Rent Acts to provide such a ground. Further, by amendment made by the Housing Act 1996,[28] the amount of arrears required to support a mandatory order for possession on this ground has been reduced. This ground, and the separate machinery for obtaining a mandatory possession order from an assured shorthold tenant,[29] are by far the most commonly invoked grounds in practice.[30] Ground 8 is available both for periodic tenancies and, like Ground 2, for tenancies which will be fixed term tenancies when the order takes effect, provided that the terms of the tenancy make provision for it to be brought to an end on this ground.[31] Where the landlord seeks to recover possession on this ground, the court has no power to dispense with the service of a possession notice.[32] But the inclusion in the particulars in the notice of sufficient facts from which the tenant can easily calculate the true amount of arrears is sufficient.[33]

The ground is simple in principle, and there are only two requirements,[34] but the first requirement is different where the possession notice was served before February 28, 1997.

1. Specified amount of rent unpaid

14–71 The Act sets out the amount of rent that must be in arrears or unpaid in specific terms for four categories according to the periods of the tenancy for which the rent is payable. As amended, it provides as follows—

(a) Rent payable weekly or fortnightly: ''at least eight weeks' rent is unpaid''.
(b) Rent payable monthly: ''at least two months' rent is unpaid''.

[27] Law of Property (Miscellaneous Provisions) Act 1994, s.14 (effective from July 1, 1995: S.I. 1995 No. 1317); Practice Direction (Probate: Notice to Quit) [1995] 1 W.L.R. 1120, Fam.
[28] ss.101, 232(3), (4); S.I. 1997 No. 225; see *intra*.
[29] *Post*, paras. 14–78 *et seq*.
[30] A claim based on Ground 8 is invariably coupled with a claim on one or more of the discretionary grounds for rent arrears (Grounds 10 and 11): for these, see *post*, pp. 288, 289.
[31] Act of 1988, s.7(6); a standard form proviso for re-entry will serve this purpose.
[32] Under Act of 1988, s.8: *ibid*., s.8(5); see *ante*, para. 13–37.
[33] *Marath v. MacGillivray* (1996) 28 H.L.R. 484, CA (agreed arrears at earlier date stated and assertion made that no rent paid since then).
[34] Act of 1988, Sched. 2, Ground 8.

(c) Rent payable quarterly: "at least one quarter's rent is more than three months in arrears".
(d) Rent payable yearly: "at least three months' rent is more than three months in arrears".

No provision is made for rent that is payable in respect of any other period, whether semi-annually, four-weekly or otherwise, leaving it undetermined whether in these comparatively rare cases the specific categories are to be applied *cy-pres* or whether the ground is inapplicable. In this ground, "rent" means "rent lawfully due from the tenant", but otherwise "rent" is not a term of art in the Act of 1988, nor defined for this particular purpose,[35] and accordingly any periodic sum payable by the tenant to the landlord under the terms of the tenancy for the use of the dwelling will be rent.

(a) "Lawfully due"

Rent is "lawfully due" as soon as the proper date for payment has arrived.[36] **14–72**
This is so even if, apart from an estoppel binding the landlord or a variation of the terms of the tenancy, late payment has long been accepted without protest and the tenant has not been warned to pay punctually in future.[37] Rent is not lawfully due if the landlord has failed by notice to furnish the tenant with an address in England and Wales at which notices (including notices in proceedings) may be served on him by the tenant.[38] No distinction is made between rent payable in advance and rent payable in arrear. Thus, where rent is payable quarterly in advance, the ground will be satisfied when one quarter's rent is three months overdue; but if the rent is payable quarterly in arrear,[39] at the time when the ground is satisfied six months will have passed without the tenant having paid any rent.

35 Elsewhere in Act of 1988, rent is defined for specific purposes as excluding any sum payable by the tenant as is expressed to be payable in respect of "rates, council tax, services, management, repairs, maintenance or insurance" (*ibid.*, Sched. 1, paras. 2(2), 3C). This suggests that such sums, even if expressed to be payable in respect of those matters, are otherwise "rent" for the purposes of the Act of 1988. (See also *ibid.*, s.14(4).)

36 See *Bird v. Hildage* [1948] 1 K.B. 91, CA; and see Vol. 1, p. 400.

37 *ibid.*

38 Landlord and Tenant Act 1987, s.48; *Marath v. MacGillivray* (1996) 28 H.L.R. 484, CA. The introduction of s.48 provoked a spate of litigation as to its true meaning and effect. It is now established by the Court of Appeal that: (1) the section, which came into force on February 1, 1988, applies to tenancies made and rent in arrears before that date: *Hussain v. Singh* [1993] 2 E.G.L.R. 70; (2) it applies to tenancies which consist of or include a dwelling, provided that Landlord and Tenant Act 1954, Pt. II does not apply: *Lindsey Trading Properties Inc. v. Dallhold Estates (UK) Pty Ltd.* (1993) 70 P. & C.R. 332; (3) once a valid notice is served, all previous arrears become due: *ibid.*; (4) the notice must be in writing: *Rogan v. Woodfield Building Services Ltd.* (1994) 27 H.L.R. 78; (5) a separate notice is not required, and accordingly a statement in a lease or tenancy agreement or a different notice of the landlord's address *simpliciter* suffices if a reasonable tenant would conclude that that address was one at which he could serve notices, including notices in proceedings: *ibid.*, and *Drew-Morgan v. Hamid-Zadeh* [1999] E.G.C.S. 72; (6) the giving of an agent's address suffices: *Marath v. MacGillivray*, *supra* (address for landlord's agents and address for his solicitors given in shorthold tenancy notice: valid s.48 notice).

39 Which would be a rarity for a tenancy granted on or after January 15, 1989.

(b) Recoupment and set off

14–73 If the tenant has a claim against the landlord for breach of covenant, it is not clear how far that claim, by being set against the rent, will prevent the rent from being "lawfully due". Where the tenant has paid for carrying out repairs which the landlord, in breach of covenant, has failed to do, the tenant has a common law right to recoup for himself the proper cost of the repairs out of future rent,[40] and also out of arrears of rent.[41] In such cases, the tenant is "entitled to treat the expenditure as a payment of rent",[42] and on this footing the exercise of the right of recoupment will prevent such rents from being lawfully due. In practice, the approach of the court will be akin to that under Order 14:[43] if the tenant satisfies the court that he has an arguable case of entitlement to recoup, directions will be given for trial of the recoupment claim and, if in dispute, the amount of the rent otherwise due to the landlord. Legally, the onus will be on the landlord to satisfy the judge on the hearing of the "undefended" listing that there is no arguable defence to his claim.[44]

14–74 Where instead the tenant merely has a claim for damages against the landlord which he could raise by way of set-off and defence in equity to an action by the landlord for rent,[45] he does not have any right of recoupment as such, and it is arguable that the rent remains "lawfully due" until the tenant's cross-claim has been quantified and established. It is suggested that such an argument is wrong in principle: where an equitable set off exists[46] at the date when the landlord's entitlement to rent accrues, it is a true defence to the landlord's claim,[47] and not just a cross-claim which calls for an account. Therefore, where a tenant has an arguable case of an entitlement to damages that reduces the amount owed to the landlord below the requisite amount of rent arrears, the court should adopt the same procedure as where a right of recoupment has arguably been exercised.[48] If, on the other hand, the tenant's claim for damages does not have that sufficiently close connection with the landlord's claim such that it can be said to "impugn" the landlord's right to bring his claim,[49] and so is merely a counterclaim and not a set off, the rent is still "lawfully due" and the court has no discretion but to make an order for possession, even where it is thought that judgment for the tenant on his cross-claim might result in a net balance of judgments in favour of the tenant. Thus, on the "undefended" hearing, the judge must decide not just whether the cross-claim is arguable as a claim and will reduce the amount owed to the landlord below the requisite amount of rent arrears, but also whether the tenant's claim is sufficiently closely

[40] *Lee-Parker v. Izzet* [1971] 1 W.L.R. 1688, Ch.
[41] *Asco Developments Ltd. v. Gordon* [1978] E.G.D. 376, Ch.
[42] *Melville v. Grapelodge Developments Ltd.* (1978) 39 P. & C.R. 179 at 186, QB, *per* Neill J.
[43] Of the Rules of the Supreme Court 1965.
[44] Consider *Asco Developments Ltd. v. Gordon, supra.*
[45] Within the well-known principle in *British Anzani (Felixstowe) Ltd. v. International Marine Management (U.K.) Ltd.* [1980] Q.B. 137, QB.
[46] Or indeed a set off of mutual debts at law: see, generally, *Hanak v. Green* [1958] 2 Q.B. 9, CA.
[47] See *British Anzani (Felixstowe) Ltd. v. International Marine Management (U.K.) Ltd., supra.*
[48] *Supra.* See *Televantos v. McCulloch* (1990) 23 H.L.R. 412, CA.
[49] See *British Anzani (Felixstowe) Ltd. v. International Marine Management (U.K.) Ltd., supra.*

linked to the claim for rent to amount to an equitable set off rather than just a counterclaim.

(c) Housing benefit

14–75 Delays in paying "housing benefit"[50] to a tenant are sometimes responsible for rent remaining unpaid. This is sometimes caused by delay in making or authenticating the claim; but sometimes it is the result of administrative delay by the local housing authority, despite the obligation to make the first payment within 14 days of the claim, or as soon as possible thereafter.[51] Yet even so, the liability to pay rent to the landlord remains the tenant's, even if payments of housing benefit are made directly to the landlord, whether under the duty or the power to do this;[52] and the landlord's claim appears to be in no way affected by any default of the local housing authority.[52a] Where the tenant lived with a partner, unknown to the landlord, and the local housing authority tendered money directly to the landlord in the name of the partner, the landlord was entitled to refuse to accept it, even though it would have brought the amount of arrears below the level required by Ground 8.[53]

(d) Possession notice served before February 28, 1997

14–76 As originally enacted, there was a requirement for at least three months' rent to be in arrears or unpaid, regardless of for what periods payments of rent were due under the tenancy.[54] That amount was reduced by amendment on February 28, 1997 in relation to tenancies under which rent is payable weekly or monthly.[55] In the case of possession notices served before that date, however, the requisite amounts of unpaid rent where the rent was payable weekly or monthly are 13 weeks' and three months' respectively,[56] even if the possession proceedings are started and heard after that date.[57] Thus, if a possession notice was served before February 28, 1997 not specifying Ground 8, but at trial the

[50] Under Housing Benefit (General) Regulations 1987 (S.I. 1987 No. 1971) as amended, made under Social Security Act 1986. That Act and other social security legislation was consolidated on July 1, 1992 in the Social Security Contributions and Benefits Act 1992 and the Social Security Administration Act 1992. The Regulations remain in force.

[51] See reg.88(3), as amended by S.I. 1996 No. 965, r. 6.; and for payment on account, see reg.91, as amended by S.I. 1995 No. 2868, reg. 6.

[52] See regs.93, 94.

[52a] But see *Saint v. Barking & Dagenham L.B.C.* [1998] 11 C.L. 315, CA.

[53] *Bessa Plus plc v. Lancaster* (1997) 30 H.L.R. 48, CA. It would not appear to make any difference to the outcome if the landlord had known of the partner's occupation: a landlord is entitled to be paid rent by his tenant and refuse to accept it from others unless they are lawfully tendering the rent on his behalf: see *ibid.*

[54] See the first edition of Vol. 3 (1989), pp. 160, 161.

[55] As shown *ante*, para. 14–71.

[56] The originally enacted amounts, as opposed to eight weeks' and two months' which now apply: see *ante*, para. 14–71.

[57] Housing Act 1996, ss.101, 232(3), (4); the Housing Act 1996 (Commencement No. 7 and Savings) Order 1997 (S.I. 1997 No. 225), art. 2, Sched., para. 1(a). Para. 1(b) does not apply here because the court cannot dispense with a possession notice where Ground 8 is relied upon: *ante*, para. 13–37.

landlord obtains leave to add Ground 8 to the notice,[58] and only two months' rent was unpaid at the date of the notice,[59] the landlord's claim under Ground 8 must fail because the only possession notice was served before the date of the amendment, and therefore three months' unpaid rent at *inter alia* that time would have to be proved. No presumptions of service apply to assist with the question when a possession notice is effectually served.[60]

2. Unpaid when notice served and at hearing

14–77 The requisite amount of rent must be unpaid or in arrears both "at the date of the service" of the possession notice[61] and "at the date of the hearing". So if a notice pursuant to section 48 of the Landlord and Tenant Act 1987 is not served prior to the date of service of the possession notice, the claim to possession cannot succeed,[62] even if one is later served before the hearing. If this requirement is satisfied at both those dates, it does not seem to matter if between them it was not, as where a weekly tenant with eight weeks' rent unpaid at the date of service of the notice promptly pays four weeks' rent, but then lapses, and more than eight weeks' rent is unpaid at the date of the hearing. No presumptions of service apply to assist with the question when a possession notice is effectually served, and so service satisfying the common law requirements[63] will have to be proved by the landlord. The tender of a cheque shortly before or even at the hearing probably means that, if the cheque is honoured on first presentation, payment was made on the date the cheque was tendered.[64] Because this ground is a mandatory ground, the court does not have the statutory discretion to adjourn the proceedings that it would have if possession were being claimed on a discretionary ground;[65] but if the rent will be proved to have been paid on that day, neither can it make an order for possession. The only sensible answer is for the court to exercise its general discretion of its own motion to adjourn the case,[66] for a week or so, to see whether the cheque is honoured.[67] If the ground for possession is proved, there is no jurisdiction to grant relief to the tenant; the relief against forfeiture jurisdiction does not apply because there is no forfeiture.[67a]

[58] Under Act of 1988, s.8(2).
[59] See *infra*.
[60] *Ante*, para. 13–32.
[61] *ibid.*
[62] *Marath v. MacGillivray* (1996) 28 H.L.R. 484, CA.
[63] *Ante*, para. 13–32.
[64] Consider *Hannaford v. Smallacombe* (1993) 69 P. & C.R. 399, CA (on the question whether rent due had been paid by a certain date for the purposes of Agricultural Holdings Act 1986, Sched. 3, Case D).
[65] Under Act of 1988, s.9(1).
[66] County Courts Act 1984, s.3(2); County Court Rules 1981, Order 13, r. 3(1).
[67] But in view of the wording of Act of 1988, ss.7(3), 9(6) and the general rule that tender of a cheque is not payment, there is an argument as to whether the court would be acting properly in so doing.
[67a] *Artesian Residential Investments Ltd. v. Beck* [1999] E.G.C.S. 46, CA.

Sect. 10. Assured Shorthold Tenancies

An assured shorthold tenancy, being an assured tenancy, is subject to all the grounds for possession that apply to other assured tenancies.[68] In addition, an assured shorthold tenancy is subject to what in effect are its own self-contained mandatory grounds for possession.[69] The requirements for these grounds depend on whether the assured shorthold is an old or a new assured shorthold tenancy,[70] and on whether it is a fixed term tenancy or a periodic tenancy.[71] Before February 28, 1997,[72] all original assured shorthold tenancies and some derivative assured shorthold tenancies were fixed term tenancies, and only derivative assured shorthold tenancies could be periodic;[73] but now periodic tenancies can be original assured shortholds. In all cases, the right to recover possession on these grounds depends on the landlord having given the tenant at least two months' notice that possession is required. Probably the landlord cannot start possession proceedings, whether by summons or by using the accelerated procedure,[74] until the notice has expired, at all events where the notice states that possession cannot be applied for until it has expired.[75] **14–78**

Essentially, the regime for recovering possession from an assured shorthold tenant is the same for old and new shorthold tenancies; and accordingly the regime applicable to old tenancies will be first considered, and the separate considerations applicable to new tenancies thereafter.

1. OLD ASSURED SHORTHOLD TENANCIES

1. Fixed term assured shorthold tenancy

On or after the coming to an end of an assured shorthold tenancy which was a fixed term tenancy, the court must make an order for possession of the dwelling-house if it is satisfied on four matters.[76] They are as follows. **14–79**

(a) Assured shorthold ended

The court must be satisfied that "the assured shorthold tenancy has come to an

[68] Act of 1988, s.21(1), (4).
[69] The general body of grounds for possession in Pt. I of Act of 1988 takes effect under s.7, in Chap. I of Pt. I, and Sched. 2, whereas for assured shorthold tenancies possession is dealt with under s.21, in Chap. II of Pt. I. But see n. 89, *post*.
[70] *Ante*, paras. 8–03 *et seq.*
[71] *Ante*, para. 8–45.
[72] When the amendments made by Housing Act 1996, ss.98, 99 came into force: the Housing Act 1996 (Commencement No. 7 and Savings) Order 1997 (S.I. 1997 No. 225), art. 2.
[73] See *ante*, para. 8–35 *et seq.*
[74] See *post*, paras. 14–86 *et seq.*
[75] *Lower Street Properties Ltd. v. Jones* (1996) 28 H.L.R. 877, CA.
[76] Act of 1988, s.21(1).

end''.[77] There is nothing to restrict this; determination by effluxion of time or by the landlord (so far as he is able)[78] or by the tenant will suffice.

(b) No further assured tenancy

14–80 The court must be satisfied that, with one exception, no further assured tenancy (whether shorthold or not) is for the time being in existence. Apart from the exception, this would prevent the court making an order for possession in any case except where there was a surrender or similar action on behalf of the tenant[79] or where the conditions for an assured tenancy were not satisfied, because a statutory periodic tenancy would arise on the coming to an end of the fixed term tenancy.[80] The exception therefore is that an assured shorthold periodic tenancy, whether statutory or not, will not prevent this condition being satisfied.[81] So, if the fixed term tenancy expires by effluxion of time or by exercise of a break clause (after the first six months), the coming into existence of a statutory assured periodic tenancy (which will be a shorthold[82]) will not prevent the landlord claiming possession, nor will an expressly granted periodic assured tenancy (which will also be a shorthold); but an expressly granted new fixed term assured tenancy will preclude an order for possession under this regime.

(c) Two months' notice requiring possession

14–81 The court must be satisfied that the landlord (or if there are joint landlords, at least one of them) has ''given to the tenant not less than two months' notice in writing stating that he requires possession of the dwelling-house'';[83] and if there are joint tenants, notice must be given to them all.[84] There is nothing to require the notice to be in any particular form,[85] nor need the notice specify any date for possession. But where a notice did specify a date more than two months thereafter on which it expired, it was also effective notice of desire to exercise a break clause, and no separate break notice was required.[86] Prior to February 28, 1997, there was no requirement for the notice to be in writing, and any

77 Act of 1988, s.21(1)(a).
78 See, *e.g.*, *Aylward v. Fawaz* (1996) 29 H.L.R. 408, CA (landlord's break clause exercised by shorthold possession notice).
79 Act of 1988, s.5(2).
80 *ibid.*
81 *ibid.*, s.21(1)(a), as amended by Local Government and Housing Act 1989, ss.194(1), 195(2), Sched. 11, para. 103; S.I. 1989 No. 2445 (effective January 16, 1990).
82 *Ante*, paras. 8–36 *et seq.*
83 Act of 1988, s.21(1)(b), as amended (''*in writing*'') by Housing Act 1996, ss.98, 232(3), (4); S.I. 1997 No. 225 (effective February 28, 1997).
84 Act of 1988, s.45(3).
85 Unlike the notice under s.21(4) (*post*, para. 14–84), this notice need not state that possession is required by virtue of s. 21.
86 *Aylward v. Fawaz, supra.*

notice given before that date is unaffected by the change.[87] This notice is quite distinct from the possession notice in the prescribed form that must be given before seeking possession on the usual grounds for possession,[88] which is not appropriate here.[89]

(d) Notice given before end of tenancy

The notice "may be given before or on the day on which the tenancy comes to an end".[90] Once the tenancy has ended, it is too late to give this notice, and the landlord must take whatever steps are apt for ending whatever tenancy (if any) then exists.[91] But a notice given before or on the day on which the tenancy ends is effective even though a statutory periodic tenancy arises at the end of the fixed term tenancy.[92] An order for possession made when the notice has expired and the assured shorthold tenancy has come to an end will determine such a statutory periodic tenancy "(without further notice and regardless of the period) on the day on which the order takes effect".[93] **14–82**

2. Periodic assured shorthold tenancy

Different provisions apply where the assured shorthold tenancy is already a periodic tenancy, whether statutory or not, when the landlord comes to give his notice requiring possession. In such a case, the court must make an order for possession of a dwelling-house let on an assured shorthold tenancy which is a periodic tenancy if the court is satisfied on two different matters.[94] This regime cannot apply to an original old assured shorthold tenancy, for such a tenancy is necessarily for a fixed term of not less than six months; but if, when it ends, a tenancy of the same premises between the same parties comes into existence, that tenancy will be a derivative assured shorthold tenancy. This is so even if the new tenancy is a periodic tenancy, in which case it will fall within this **14–83**

[87] The Housing Act 1996 (Commencement No. 7 and Savings) Order 1997 (S.I. 1997 No. 225), Sched., para. 2. The reference in that para. to notice under s. 8 of the Act is surely a mistake for notice under s. 21. But see n. 89, *infra*, for another (less credible) explanation.

[88] See *ante*, paras. 13–20 *et seq.*

[89] See *Panayi v. Roberts* (1993) 25 H.L.R. 421, CA (*obiter*). The positive terms of s.21(1), requiring the order to be made, plainly prevail over the negative terms of s.8(1), in Chap. I, prohibiting the court from entertaining proceedings for possession without service of a possession notice: *ante*, para. 13–35. The contrary argument (which has had some support, and which was advanced in *Panayi v. Roberts, supra*), namely that a possession notice under s.8(1) is required even where the ground for possession relied upon is s.21 in Chap. II, has derived some support from the terms of the saving provision in the statutory instrument cited in n.87, *supra*, but must be wrong.

[90] Act of 1988, s.21(2).

[91] In most cases this will be the notice to recover possession from a derivative assured shorthold tenant; see *infra*.

[92] Act of 1988, s.21(2).

[93] *ibid.*, s.21(3).

[94] *ibid.*, s.21(4).

head;[95] and similarly for a statutory periodic tenancy.[96] The two matters on which the court must be satisfied are as follows.

(a) Notice requiring possession

14–84 The court must be satisfied that the landlord (or, in the case of joint landlords, at least one of them) has given to the tenant a notice in writing stating that, after a date specified in the notice, possession of the dwelling-house is required by virtue of section 21;[97] and if there are joint tenants, notice must be given to them all.[98] There is nothing to require the notice to be in any particular form. Words stating that possession is required ''at the end of the period of your tenancy which will end after the expiry of two months from the service upon you of this notice'' are sufficient identification of a date for the purposes of the section.[99] The notice need not state the date on which is it given.[1] Before February 28, 1997, it was unclear whether or not the notice had to be in writing;[2] but this ambiguity was removed by amendment.[3] Any notice given before that date is unaffected by the change.[4] Again, this notice is distinct from the usual possession notice, and ousts the requirement for one.[5]

(b) Correct date in notice

14–85 The court must also be satisfied that the date specified in the notice is correct. The date must satisfy three requirements.

(1) It must be ''the last day of a period of the tenancy''.[6]
(2) It must not be ''earlier than two months after the date the notice was given''.[7]
(3) It must not be earlier than the earliest day on which, ignoring the landlord's inability to terminate an assured tenancy by a notice to quit,[8] the tenancy could be brought to an end by a notice to quit given by the landlord on the same date as the statutory notice is given.[9]

[95] *Ante*, para. 8–40.
[96] *Ante*, para. 8–37.
[97] Act of 1988, s.21(4)(a).
[98] *ibid.*, s.45(3).
[99] *Lower Street Properties Ltd. v. Jones* (1996) 28 H.L.R. 877, CA.
[1] *ibid.*
[2] Though thought likely that it had to be: see the first edition of Vol. 3 (1989) at p. 165, n. 43.
[3] Housing Act 1996, ss.98, 232(3), (4); S.I. 1997 No. 225.
[4] The Housing Act 1996 (Commencement No. 7 and Savings) Order 1997 (S.I. 1997 No. 225), Sched., para. 2. The reference in that para. to notice under s. 8 of the Act is surely a mistake for notice under s. 21.
[5] *Ante*, para. 14–81, n.89.
[6] Act of 1988, s.21(4)(a).
[7] *ibid.* The date when the notice was given may be proved by extrinsic evidence, if necessary: see *Lower Street Properties Ltd. v. Jones*, *supra.*
[8] Act of 1988, s.5(1).
[9] *ibid.*, s.21(4)(b).

3. Accelerated procedure for possession order

As under the Rent Acts,[10] a special speedy procedure by originating application rather than by summons for recovery of land is available in the county court for recovery of possession from assured shorthold tenants.[11] In one respect, however, the new procedure goes further than the expedited procedure under the Rent Acts: it enables a judge to make an order for possession without there being any hearing of the landlord's claim. In order to distinguish it from the Rent Acts procedure, it will be referred to as the "accelerated" procedure. **14–86**

(a) Availability of the accelerated procedure

Use of the accelerated procedure is not mandatory but at the election of the landlord, where available.[12] Its availability is further restricted by the following five requirements. **14–87**

(i) ONLY POSSESSION CLAIMED: the accelerated procedure is only available where possession alone is being claimed in the proceedings.[13] So the landlord cannot use the accelerated procedure to claim arrears of rent, or *mesne* profits, in addition to possession. The rule does not make clear whether costs can also be claimed: on a literal construction of the rule they cannot, being "another claim" made in the proceedings. But the form of originating application and affidavit prescribed for use[14] does contain wording expressly claiming the court fee and solicitors' costs.[15] **14–88**

(ii) TENANCY AGREEMENT MADE ON OR AFTER JANUARY 15, 1989: the tenancy, and any agreement for the tenancy, must have been entered into on or after January 15, 1989 if the accelerated procedure is to be used. This requirement is otiose given that the procedure is only available for assured shorthold tenancies under the Act of 1988.[16] Of the limited categories of tenancies entered into before that date which can nevertheless be assured tenancies under the Act,[17] none will be capable of being an assured shorthold tenancy.[18] **14–89**

[10] See Vol. 1, p. 461.

[11] County Court Rules 1981, Order 49, r. 6A, rather than *ibid.*, Order 6, r. 3. The procedure first came into effect only on November 1, 1993 by virtue of the County Court (Amendment No. 3) Rules 1993 (S.I. 1993 No. 2175), r. 18, and was amended with effect from September 28, 1998 by the County Court (Amendment) Rules 1998 (S.I. 1998 No. 1899), r.4(2).

[12] County Court Rules 1981, Order 49, r. 6A(4) ("the landlord *may* bring possession proceedings under this rule").

[13] *ibid.*, r. 6A(3)(b).

[14] Form N5B of the County Court Forms, prescribed by County Court (Forms) Rules 1982 (S.I. 1982 No. 586), r.2, Sched., as substituted on September 28, 1998 by County Court (Forms) (Amendment) Rules 1998 (S.I. 1998 No. 1900), r.2, Sched. 1.

[15] And the prescribed form of reply gives the defendant limited opportunity to make representations as to how (if at all) the costs should be paid by him: see *post*, para. 14–95, n.46.

[16] Act of 1988, s.1(2), Sched. 1, para. 1 prevents any tenancy entered into before, or pursuant to a contract made before, the commencement of the Act being an assured tenancy: see *ante*, para. 4–48.

[17] As to which, see *ante*, paras. 5–02, 5–59, 5–65.

[18] Because no shorthold notice will have been given under Act of 1988, s.20(1)(c), (2) in relation to old shorthold tenancies, and because new shorthold tenancies must have been granted on or after February 28, 1997.

14–90 (iii) SHORTHOLD TENANCY AGREEMENT IN WRITING: where possession is claimed on the expiry of a fixed term tenancy,[19] the tenancy in question must have been an assured shorthold tenancy complying with all the requirements for creating an assured shorthold tenancy, and the subject of a written agreement.[20] The accelerated procedure is therefore not available in the cases of an oral shorthold tenancy, or a shorthold tenancy which is such by virtue only of being a re-granted tenancy upon the expiry of a shorthold tenancy which did comply with all the requirements for creating an assured shorthold tenancy.[21] Where possession is claimed from a periodic assured shorthold tenant,[22] the requirement here is that the tenancy did not immediately follow an assured tenancy which was not an assured shorthold tenancy[23] and that the tenancy is either itself the subject of a written agreement, or is a statutory periodic tenancy arising under the Act of 1988[24] on the same terms (save as to rent) as an assured tenancy which was the subject of a written agreement, or in the further alternative is a tenancy which relates to the same or substantially the same premises which were let to the same tenant and is on the same terms (save as to rent and duration) as a tenancy which was the subject of a written agreement.[25] These alternative requirements are not satisfied by a tenancy which is a statutory periodic tenancy arising upon the termination of an oral tenancy agreement.[26] But the requirement is satisfied by an oral tenancy expressly granted by the same landlord to the same tenant upon the termination of a written agreement; and even apparently by an oral tenancy which itself was re-granted upon the termination of an oral tenancy, provided that somewhere previously there was a written shorthold tenancy agreement of substantially the same premises made with the tenant from whom possession is claimed.

14–91 (iv) DEFENDANT SERVED WITH SHORTHOLD NOTICE: closely allied to the previous condition is the requirement that a shorthold notice[27] must have been served on the tenant who is to be sued for possession. In the case of a fixed term assured shorthold tenancy, the tenancy itself will have been preceded by a shorthold notice by virtue of requirement (iii) above, and the effect of this requirement is that the accelerated procedure is not available against a successor in title of the original tenant.[28] In the case of a periodic shorthold tenancy, the requirement is that a shorthold notice must have been served on the tenant who is to

[19] *i.e.* under Act of 1988, s.21(1).

[20] County Court Rules, Order 49, r. 6A(3)(c).

[21] Pursuant to Act of 1988, s.20(4). C.C.R. Order 49, r.6A(3)(c) further states that the tenancy must not immediately have followed a tenancy which was not an assured shorthold tenancy. It does not specify whether or not the previous non-shorthold tenancy must have been of the same dwelling-house. But a tenancy cannot be a shorthold tenancy if the landlord of an assured tenant grants him a new tenancy, even if of a different dwelling-house: Act of 1988, s.20(3). The rule cannot mean that a previous assured tenancy of a different dwelling-house held from a different landlord disentitles the landlord under the shorthold tenancy to use the accelerated procedure. It is, in truth, difficult to see to what it is directed.

[22] *i.e.* Pursuant to Act of 1988, s.21(4).

[23] Which is impossible in the case of an old periodic assured shorthold tenancy: see *ante*, paras. 8–24, 8–40.

[24] S. 5(2).

[25] County Court Rules 1981, Order 49, r. 6A(3)(c).

[26] *ibid.*

[27] Pursuant to Act of 1988, s.20(1)(c), (2).

[28] County Court Rules, Order 49, r. 6A(3)(d).

be sued for possession in relation to the first assured shorthold tenancy of the premises,[29] but the effect is the same: if the tenancy is now vested in a different person, whether lawfully or unlawfully, the accelerated procedure cannot be used.

(v) WRITTEN SECTION 21 POSSESSION NOTICE GIVEN: a possession notice in writing in accordance with the Act of 1988[30] must have been given to the tenant.[31] This requirement only excludes from the accelerated procedure those cases in which oral notice was given prior to February 28, 1997.[32] **14–92**

(b) Form of the accelerated procedure

The process permitted by the accelerated procedure is an originating application instead of the usual summons process required by Order 6, rule 3 of the County Court Rules 1981.[33] The application must be made in the prescribed form in the local county court for the district in which the dwelling-house is situated.[34] The application is required to include various information and statements to substantiate the basis of the landlord's claim and to have various documents attached to it, including the first written tenancy agreement and the current (or most recent) written tenancy agreement.[35] The information and statements required differ slightly depending on whether possession is claimed from a tenant under an original fixed term tenancy or a tenant under a deriviative shorthold tenancy.[36] The statements and documents are required to be verified by the landlord on oath.[37] The prescribed form of application, Form N5B,[38] contains both the form of an originating application[39] and the skeleton of an affidavit, which the landlord is required to complete. The form of affidavit provides for evidence to be given to prove the landlord's entitlement to possession and for **14–93**

29 *ibid.*, r. 6A(9)(d).

30 Section 21(1)(b) in the case of fixed term tenancies; section 21(4)(a) in the case of periodic tenancies.

31 County Court Rules, Order 49, r. 6A(3)(e), (9)(e).

32 Housing Act 1996, ss.98, 232(3), (4); S.I. 1997 No. 225, art. 2, Sched., para. 2; and see para. 14–81, n.87, *ante*.

33 County Court Rules 1981, Order 49, r. 6A(4).

34 *ibid.*, r. 6A(5).

35 *ibid.*, r. 6A(6), (7), (10). Rule 6A(7) was amended on September 28, 1998 by the County Court (Amendment) Rules 1998 (S.I. 1998 No. 1899), r.4(2).

36 *ibid.*, r. 6A(9) seems to contemplate that such a derivative tenancy will be a periodic tenancy because it requires a notice in writing pursuant to Act of 1988, s.21(4) to have been given, which notice is not appropriate where the tenancy is a fixed term tenancy. So where a new, derivative fixed term shorthold tenancy is granted, which does not comply with the requirements of *ibid.*, s.20 for creating an original shorthold tenancy, but which nevertheless is a shorthold tenancy by virtue of *ibid.*, s.20(4), *semble* the landlord cannot use the accelerated procedure to claim possession except by waiting for the new tenancy to expire and then serving a s.21(4) notice; yet rule 6A(10)(b)(iii) shows that the accelerated procedure was intended to be available in the case of a derivative fixed term tenancy.

37 *ibid.*, r. 6A(8).

38 Prescribed by the County Court (Forms) Rules 1982 (S.I. 1982 No. 586), r.2, Sched., as substituted on September 28, 1998 by the County Courts (Forms) (Amendment) Rules 1998 (S.I. 1998 No. 1900), r.2, Sched. 1. Before that date, the prescribed form was that inserted into the 1982 Rules by S.I. 1997 No. 1838.

39 Which is no more than a formal "front" sheet identifying the parties and the dwelling-house.

the necessary documents to be exhibited to it marked "A", "A1", "B" and "C".[40] The prescribed form can be used "with such modifications as the circumstances may require".[41]

(c) The procedure

14–94 (i) SERVICE: a copy of the application (including the exhibits), together with a copy for each defendant, must be filed in the county court for the district in which the dwelling-house is situated.[42] The court then effects service by sending the application and exhibits by first class post to the defendant(s) at the address stated in the application.[43] Unless the contrary is shown, the date of service is deemed to be the seventh day after the date of posting.[44] The normal county court rules applying to return undelivered of the originating documents and to alternative modes of service of the proceedings for recovery of land apply here too.[45]

14–95 (ii) REPLY: the application and exhibits are sent by the court together with a form of reply to the application, which is itself a prescribed form.[46] A defendant who wishes to oppose the application must complete and deliver to the court office the form of reply. He must do so within 14 days after the service of the application on him.[47] The form of reply seeks to elicit from the defendant both the extent to which he agrees with the statements made by the plaintiff on oath and certain facts fundamental to the appropriateness of the accelerated procedure.[48] If the defendant does deliver a reply in time, the proper officer of the court sends a copy to the plaintiff and refers both application and reply to the judge.[49]

14–96 (iii) DEFAULT OF REPLY: where the defendant has not filed a form of reply within the time specified, the plaintiff may file a written request for an order for possession, and the proper officer must, without delay, refer the application to the judge.[50] Given that the plaintiff will not know (a) when the court posted the

[40] The prescribed form is reproduced *post*, p. 569 *et seq*.

[41] County Court (Forms) Rules 1982, r.2(2). In some county courts, the practice has developed of requiring a deponent other than the landlord to set out his authority to act on behalf of the landlord.

[42] County Court Rules 1981, Order 49, r. 6A(5).

[43] *ibid*., r. 6A(11).

[44] *ibid*., Order 7, r.10(3), Order 49, r. 6A(11).

[45] *ibid*., Order 7, rr.10(4), 15; Order 49, r.6A(11).

[46] County Court (Forms) Rules 1982, r.2(1), Sched., Form 11B, inserted by S.I. 1997 No. 1838 and amended by S.I. 1997 No. 2171 and by S.I. 1998 No. 1900, r.6(2). The form is reproduced, as amended, *post*, pp. 575, 576.

[47] County Court Rules 1981, Order 49, rule 6A(12). So, unless the landlord can prove that the tenant in fact received the application through the post earlier than seven days after posting (which would be a very rare case), the tenant may safely deliver his reply within 21 days after the date of the postmark. The court must inevitably wait until that time has elapsed before taking any further step with the application.

[48] Such as whether the defendant had a tenancy of the dwelling-house prior to January 15, 1989.

[49] *ibid*., r. 6A(13). Here, as elsewhere in relation to the accelerated procedure, "judge" includes a district judge, who has power to hear and determine such an application: r.6A(20).

[50] *ibid*., r. 6A(14).

application to the defendant; (b) when the defendant in fact received the application; and (c) when the defendant in fact delivered the form of reply, he cannot know the precise time at which he is first entitled to make such a written request.[51] Probably most plaintiffs will apply too soon, thinking that the court posts the application immediately upon its being filed, that the defendant only has 14 days from posting or the day after posting to file the reply, and that he will hear immediately from the court if a reply is filed. In practice, most courts will probably allow plaintiffs a little latitude and keep the written request on file until the time for filing a reply has properly elapsed. But it is unsatisfactory that a step which is important given the purpose of the accelerated procedure, and one which is made procedurally significant,[52] is required to be taken by a plaintiff who cannot be sure when he is entitled to take it other than by delaying for days in taking it.[53]

(iv) Late reply: where a reply is received more than 14 days after the service of the application but before the plaintiff has filed a request for an order for possession, the proper officer must ''without delay'' refer the reply to the judge.[54] Thus the tenant is not disadvantaged by failing to reply in time unless the landlord has already requested an order for possession and had it determined by the judge. Unless and until the landlord makes such request, *semble* the application is not referred to the judge at all. **14–97**

(v) Determination without hearing: in the first instance there is no hearing of the application, whether it be referred to the judge because the defendant filed a reply or because the plaintiff requested an order for possession. If the judge is satisfied of the plaintiff's entitlement to the order for possession, he makes such an order without requiring the attendance of the parties.[55] The date for delivering up possession,[56] and the incidence and time for payment of costs, are determined by the judge on paper on the basis of the defendant's reply, if any. In this respect, the accelerated procedure goes beyond the expedited procedure under the Rent Acts, which merely enabled a hearing to take place more quickly and the merits to be considered in open court but on affidavit evidence.[57] If the judge is not satisfied as to (a) the service of a shorthold notice in compliance with the Act,[58] (b) the giving of a written notice requiring possession in accordance with the Act,[59] (c) due service of the application, or (d) the plaintiff's entitlement to possession against the defendant under the Act, or as to more **14–98**

[51] The prescribed form of application does not contain any helpful notes in this regard.

[52] If the defendant does not file a reply and the plaintiff does not request an order for possession, *semble* the application does not get referred to the judge for determination.

[53] It is difficult to understand why the application is not taken as a request for an order for possession in the event that the defendant does not file a reply in time.

[54] County Court Rules 1981, Order 49, r. 6A(13). Presumably in such a case the landlord's application is referred together with the reply.

[55] *ibid.*, r. 6A(15)(a), (17).

[56] Which, by virtue of Housing Act 1980, s.89(1), cannot be delayed more than 14 days after the making of the order unless the court is satisfied that ''exceptional hardship'' will be caused to the tenant.

[57] See Vol. 1, p. 461.

[58] Act of 1988, s.20(1)(c), (2).

[59] *ibid.*, s.21(1)(b) or s.21(4)(a).

than one of these, he must (through the proper officer) fix a date for hearing the application and give directions regarding the steps to be taken before and at the hearing.[60] It is clear, therefore, that the judge, when considering the application on paper, must either make an order for possession or direct a hearing. Indeed, the Rules go further and require the judge to make an order for possession where he is satisfied as to each of the matters (a) to (d) above.[61] There may, however, be reasons other than those listed why the accelerated procedure is not available to the landlord, for example if the landlord is claiming possession from an assignee of the tenancy, the shorthold notice having been given to his predecessor in title.[62] In such cases, it could be argued, the accelerated procedure rule[63] does not apply at all because one of the conditions for its application has not been satisfied,[64] and the application should be dismissed as incompetent.[65]

14–99 (vi) DIRECTIONS FOR HEARING: where the judge has directed that a hearing take place, he may give such directions regarding the steps to be taken at and before the hearing as may appear to him to be necessary or desirable.[66] The proper officer of the court is required to give all parties not less than 14 days' notice of the day fixed.[67] In so doing, the judge is, it is considered, not bound merely to add the application to the undefended hearing list or to direct a full trial, but can (and should in an appropriate case) direct that a particular issue, on which *ex hypothesi* he was not satisfied, be tried, or that the landlord adduce sufficient or better evidence of the date of service of one or more of the notices, or even that the tenant adduce evidence to support a contention raised in his reply. Depending on whether the issue in question, or the matter requiring further proof, is satisfactorily dealt with at the hearing, the judge may then give judgment, give further directions for a trial, or even dismiss the application if it has become clear that the landlord cannot prove one or more of the necessary facts.

14–100 (vii) SETTING ASIDE ORDER FOR POSSESSION: in addition to the usual ground for setting aside a judgment where failure of postal service is established,[68] the Rules specifically provide that the court may, on application or of its own motion, set aside, vary or confirm any order for possession made pursuant to the accelerated procedure. Any application within this provision must be made on notice and within 14 days of service of the order.[69] The tenant therefore is given another chance, beyond the late submission of his form of reply, to have the merits of any defence considered. The fact that such application to set aside

[60] County Court Rules 1981, Order 49, r. 6A(15), (16).
[61] *ibid.*, r. 6A(17).
[62] See *ante*, para. 14–91.
[63] *i.e.* Order 49, r. 6A.
[64] *ibid.*, r. 6A(2).
[65] The same argument could, however, be said to apply to the giving of a shorthold notice or of a notice requiring possession, yet these are, *semble*, matters which should lead the judge to direct a hearing under r. 6A(14). There is an inconsistency here which cannot be smoothed out entirely.
[66] County Court Rules 1981, Order 49, r. 6A(18)(b).
[67] *ibid.*, r. 6A(18)(a).
[68] See CCR Order 37, r. 3.
[69] County Court Rules 1981, Order 49, r. 6A(19).

or vary is to be made on notice suggests that an oral hearing is contemplated this time, rather than a consideration on paper of the request. It is considered that this specific provision must override the principle that a warrant of possession, once executed, will only be set aside on grounds of fraud or oppression,[70] because it is the judgment itself which can be set aside, and not merely execution stayed or suspended.

2. NEW ASSURED SHORTHOLD TENANCIES

Most assured tenancies granted on or after February 28, 1997 are shorthold tenancies, whether they are periodic tenancies or fixed term tenancies, and regardless of the length of the term granted.[71] The requirement for a minimum fixed term of six months is no longer applicable, and therefore in principle a landlord under a periodic or very short term tenancy might be entitled to claim possession on the mandatory ground within about two months of the beginning of the tenancy. The Housing Act 1996 therefore modified the mandatory possession provisions of the Act of 1988 to ensure that possession could not be recovered on the shorthold ground before at least six months had elapsed after the beginning of the original shorthold tenancy. Essentially, the same machinery[72] and procedure[73] for recovering possession discussed above in relation to "old" tenancies applies to these "new" assured shorthold tenancies, and the text is equally applicable, subject only to the matters discussed below. The differences are addressed under the same headings. **14–101**

1. Fixed term assured shorthold tenancy

Where an order for possession of a dwelling-house let on a new assured shorthold fixed term tenancy is made,[74] the order may not be made so as to take effect earlier than a given time, which ensures that assured shorthold tenants are entitled (subject to compliance with the terms of the tenancy[75]) to enjoy at least six months in possession of the dwelling-house. Where the fixed term tenancy is not a "replacement tenancy", that time is six months after the beginning of the tenancy.[76] A "replacement tenancy" for these purposes is a tenancy which satisfies two criteria— **14–102**

(1) It comes into being on the coming to an end of an assured shorthold tenancy, and

[70] *Leicester City Council v. Aldwinckle* (1991) 24 H.L.R. 40, CA.
[71] See *ante*, para. 8–46 *et seq*.
[72] Under Act of 1988, s.21.
[73] *i.e.* the accelerated procedure.
[74] *i.e.* pursuant to Act of 1988, s.21(1).
[75] And to Act of 1988, Sched. 2, Ground 2 (mandatory mortgage ground for possession), if applicable.
[76] Act of 1988, s.21(5)(a), inserted by Housing Act 1996, ss.99, 232(3); S.I. 1997 No. 225 (with effect from February 28, 1997). For the meaning of "beginning of the tenancy" see *post*, para. 14–104.

(2) On its coming into being, the landlord and the tenant under it are the same as under the earlier tenancy when it came to an end, and the premises let under it are the same or substantially the same as those let under the earlier tenancy when it came to an end.[77]

If one of joint landlords or joint tenants under the earlier tenancy is not a landlord or tenant (as the case may be) under the later tenancy, or if a new person becomes a joint landlord or a joint tenant under the later tenancy, the later tenancy is not a replacement tenancy.[78] A statutory periodic tenancy will therefore be a replacement tenancy because the parties to the deemed grant and the demised premises are the same as under the previous tenancy when it expired.[79] A fixed term replacement tenancy will always have been expressly granted.

14–103 Where the fixed term tenancy is a replacement tenancy, the time before which an order for possession may not take effect is six months after the beginning of the "original tenancy".[80] Where the replacement tenancy came into being on the coming to an end of a tenancy which was not a replacement tenancy, the "original tenancy" is that earlier tenancy; where there have been successive replacement tenancies, the "original" tenancy is the tenancy which immediately preceded the first such replacement tenancy.[81] Thus, the period of six months will run from the beginning of the first fixed term shorthold tenancy, unless the second or any subsequent tenancy was either granted expressly by a different landlord or to a different tenant, or comprised premises which were not substantially the same as those let by the first tenancy. In such cases, the period of six months runs from the beginning of the second or subsequent tenancy, as the case might be.

14–104 The beginning of the tenancy for these purposes means the day on which the tenancy is entered into or, if later, the day on which the tenant is entitled to possession under the tenancy.[82]

14–105 Accordingly, if an assured tenancy which is not one falling within Schedule 2A of the Act of 1988[83] is granted for a fixed term of three months, the landlord may give his written notice requiring possession[84] at any time before the expiry of the term. If he gives it two months or more before the expiry of the term, he could start possession proceedings immediately after the term has expired,[85] using the accelerated procedure if he pleases; but if the judge were to make an order for possession on request made by the landlord, that order for possession could not be made so as to take effect before the expiry of six months from the

[77] Act of 1988, s.21(7), inserted by Housing Act 1996, ss.99, 232(3); S.I. 1997 No. 225 (with effect from February 28, 1997).

[78] *ibid.*, s.45(3).

[79] *ibid.*, s.5(3)(b), (c).

[80] *ibid.*, s.21(5)(b), inserted by Housing Act 1996, ss.99, 232(3); S.I. 1997 No. 225 (with effect from February 28, 1997).

[81] *ibid.*, s.21(6), inserted by Housing Act 1996, ss.99, 232(3); S.I. 1997 No. 225 (with effect from February 28, 1997).

[82] *ibid.*, s.45(2).

[83] The exceptions to "new" shorthold tenancies: see *ante*, paras. 8–06 *et seq.*

[84] Pursuant to *ibid.*, s.21(1).

[85] But probably not before then: see *Lower Street Properties Ltd. v. Jones* (1996) 28 H.L.R. 877, CA.

beginning of the tenancy, a time which could (in the example given) be two months or so later than the date when the application for possession was considered by the judge. In these circumstances it seems that the court probably must make an order for possession[86] but must postpone its operation until the period of six months has expired, notwithstanding the general provision, in the case of a mandatory ground for possession, that the giving up of possession "shall not in any event be postponed to a date later than six weeks after the making of the order".[87] If a landlord wishes to be able to recover possession before six months have elapsed, he must ensure that he has other mandatory grounds available to him, for the bar on possession orders taking effect is inapplicable to them.

2. Periodic assured shorthold tenancy

Where an order for possession of a dwelling-house let on a new assured shorthold periodic tenancy is made,[88] the order may similarly not be made so as to take effect earlier than six months after the beginning of the tenancy, or of the original tenancy, as the case may be. The bar here is precisely the same as that applicable to fixed term tenancies, considered above. Accordingly, the period of six months will run from the beginning of the first shorthold tenancy, whether fixed term or periodic, unless the second or any subsequent tenancy was either granted expressly by a different landlord or to a different tenant, or comprised premises which were not substantially the same as those let by the first tenancy. **14–106**

3. Accelerated procedure for possession order

(a) Availability of the accelerated procedure

The requirements for the availability of the accelerated procedure are modified in the case of a new assured shorthold tenancy. In the case of a new original shorthold tenancy, whether fixed term or periodic, the tenancy must still be the subject of a written agreement, but it must only satisfy the limited requirements for creating a new shorthold,[89] and not the requirements for an old shorthold.[90] In particular, there is no need to have served the prescribed form shorthold notice on the tenant before the tenancy was entered into. **14–107**

(b) Form of the accelerated procedure

The form of the procedure is the same as for old shorthold tenancies, but the statement that a shorthold notice was duly served does not have to be made, nor **14–108**

[86] Because the terms of Act of 1988, s.21(1) and (4) require it.
[87] Housing Act 1980, s.89(1).
[88] *i.e.* pursuant to Act of 1988, s.21(4).
[89] The conditions of Act of 1988, s.19A, inserted by Housing Act 1996, ss.96, 232(3); S.I. 1997 No. 225 (with effect from February 28, 1997); see *ante*, para. 8–46 *et seq.*
[90] *i.e.* those in Act of 1988, s.20(1).

any such notice exhibited.[91] In making the procedure available to new derivative assured shorthold tenancies,[92] the Rules Committee has made a minor error in stipulating, as a condition, that "[t]he tenancy in relation to which proceedings are brought. . .is an assured shorthold tenancy within the meaning of section 20 of the 1988 Act",[93] for that section expressly does not apply to new shorthold tenancies.[94]

(c) The procedure

14–109 The judge considering the application does not need to be satisfied that a prescribed form shorthold notice was served at any time.[95]

[91] County Court Rules, Order 49, r. 6A(6)(d), (7)(ii), (9)(d), (10)(e).
[92] As the Rules Committee clearly intended to do: see r. 6A(9)(d), (10)(e).
[93] *ibid.*, r. 6A(9)(c)(i).
[94] "... an assured tenancy which is not one to which section 19A above applies is a shorthold tenancy if . ." (Act of 1988, s.20(1), as substituted with effect from February 28, 1997 by Housing Act 1996, ss.104, 232(3), Sched. 8, para. 2(3); S.I. 1997 No. 225).
[95] County Court Rules, Order 49, r. 6A(16)(a).

Chapter 15

Discretionary Grounds for Possession

15–01 There are ten grounds on which, if the court is satisfied that the ground is established, it ''may''[1] make an order for possession. All the grounds are subject to the overriding requirement of reasonableness; even if the ground is established, the court can make an order for possession only ''if it considers it reasonable to do so''.[2] All except two of the grounds are based on some default by the tenant or someone else residing in or visiting the dwelling-house. The two exceptions are where suitable alternative accommodation is or will be available for the tenant (Ground 9), and where the dwelling-house was let to the tenant in consequence of his employment by the landlord and the tenant has ceased to be in that employment (Ground 16). The landlord must prove the ground for possession as well as reasonableness. None of the grounds require the type of warning notice that must be given for five of the mandatory grounds,[3] but for all of them a possession notice must have been served or the court must be persuaded that it is just and equitable to dispense with a possession notice.[4] It is doubtful if an order for possession can be made where there are two or more joint tenants and only one of them has been guilty of the default that satisfies the ground.[5] But in some cases, the wording of the ground in question may obviate the problem to some extent.[6] Where possession is claimed on one of these discretionary grounds, the court has power to adjourn the proceedings, to postpone the date for giving up possession, and to stay or suspend execution of any warrant of possession.[7]

15–02 Where a sub-tenant is in possession of the dwelling, the landlord must show the existence of one of the grounds, for ''tenant'' includes sub-tenants and others

[1] Act of 1988, s.7(4), Sched. 2, Pt. II.
[2] *ibid.*, s.7(4).
[3] *Ante*, para. 14–19.
[4] Under Act of 1988, s.8(1); *ante*, paras. 13–34 *et seq.*
[5] Act of 1988, s.45(3) compels the conclusion that a reference to ''the tenant'' in *ibid.*, Sched. 2 is, save where otherwise expressly stated, a reference to all such joint tenants. The point is thus even stronger than under the Rent Acts: see Vol. 1, p. 394 and Supplement, annotation to Vol. 1, p. 394.
[6] *e.g.*, under Ground 14, *post*, if ''the tenant'' is construed as meaning all the joint tenants, one of them may be ''a person residing . . . in the dwelling-house'' for the purposes of the ground.
[7] Act of 1988, s.9; see *ante*, paras. 13–49 *et seq.*

with derivative titles.[8] But the context of the grounds themselves probably implicitly requires that "tenant" means the tenant himself,[9] and so the default of the sub-tenant will not *ipso facto* satisfy one of the grounds.[10] But where there is a lawful assured sub-tenant, the landlord will also have to prove a ground against him.[11]

The requirement of reasonableness will be considered before turning to the individual grounds for possession, and then to the court's powers of adjournment and of staying or suspending orders for possession.

1. REASONABLENESS

1. The statute

15–03 The general statutory restrictions on terminating assured tenancies and the making of orders for possession have already been considered.[12] In the case of the discretionary grounds for possession,[13] if the court is satisfied that any of those grounds is established, then it "may make an order for possession if it considers it reasonable to do so".[14] But in the cases of Ground 9 (suitable alternative accommodation) and Ground 16 (employment letting), an order for possession cannot be made to take effect at a time when the tenancy is a fixed term tenancy, even if it is otherwise reasonable to do so; and in the cases of the other discretionary grounds, an order for possession cannot be made to take effect at a time when the tenancy is a fixed term tenancy unless the terms of the tenancy make provision for it to be brought to an end on such ground.[15]

2. "Reasonable"

15–04 In some 70 years[16] of litigation the courts have been working out the meaning and effect of the word "reasonable" in the context of orders for possession made under a system of rent control and allied security of tenure for tenants. The result has been summarised in six pages of the text of Volume 1.[17] The test is not whether the landlord's desire for possession is reasonable, but whether it

[8] Act of 1988, s.45(1).

[9] See *Enniskillen U.D.C. v. Bartley* [1947] N.I. 177, CA, *Lord Hylton v. Heal* [1921] 2 K.B. 438, DC and *Leith Properties Ltd. v. Byrne* [1983] Q.B. 443 at 442, CA, *per cur.* (Slade L.J.), all decided under the Rent Acts.

[10] Although it may do so: see the example given above in relation to Ground 14 (sub-tenant a "person residing in . . . the dwelling-house").

[11] Act of 1988, s.18(1); and see *Leith Properties Ltd. v. Byrne*, *supra*.

[12] Act of 1988, ss.5(1), 7(1); *ante*, Chap 13.

[13] *i.e.* those in *ibid.*, Sched. 2, Pt. II.

[14] *ibid.*, s.7(4).

[15] Act of 1988, s.7(6); *ante*, para. 13–42.

[16] The word first appeared in this context in the Increase of Rent, &c. (Amendment) Act 1919, s.1(1).

[17] pp. 387–393, and Supplement (Third Cumulative) pp. 76, 77.

is reasonable to make an order for possession.[18] Although the Act of 1988 does not, in conferring security of tenure, confer substantial benefits in terms of rent control,[19] the meaning of "reasonable" under it is being construed by the county courts,[20] unsurprisingly, in exactly the same way as in the numerous authorities under the Rent Acts.[21] The court must accordingly consider all relevant circumstances as they exist at the date of the hearing affecting the interest of the landlord and the tenant in the dwelling and their respective conduct, as well as the interests of the public. But the judge must not speculate on the likely outcome of an application by the tenant to be housed as homeless that may be expected to be made if the court orders possession.[22]

As with the Rent Acts, the county court cannot make an order for possession on a discretionary ground without considering the issue of reasonableness; if it fails to do so, the Court of Appeal may remit the case to the county court for the issue to be considered, or order a new trial, or, if satisfied that all relevant evidence on the issue is before it, decide the issue itself.[23] But in the case of an *ex tempore* judgment given in the county court on a possession list day, the Court of Appeal will be slow to infer that the issue was not considered from the absence of any express reference to it in the judgment.[24] If the judge did consider reasonableness, the Court of Appeal will not interfere with the exercise of his discretion, even if it might have exercised it differently, unless it considers that his decision is "plainly wrong". This may be because the judge failed to consider a relevant factor, or gave weight to an irrelevant one, or because his decision was one to which no reasonable judge could have come.[25] **15–05**

[18] *Shreeve v. Hallam* [1950] W.N. 140, CA, and see *Brown v. Davies* [1958] 1 Q.B. 117 at 129, CA, both decided under the Rent Acts.

[19] Originally, the Rent Acts conferred security of tenure as an ancilliary objective, in order to ensure that the rent controls were fully effective: see Vol. 1, p. 18. In latter years, rent control has become secondary, or at least less significant, and the Act of 1988 only entitles an original assured shorthold tenant, and a periodic assured tenant whose landlord has sought to increase the rent previously payable under his tenancy, to have the rent reviewed by a rent assessment committee: see *post*, Pt. V, Rent.

[20] No decision under Act of 1988 has gone to appeal and been reported on the question whether this approach is correct, probably for the reason that it manifestly is.

[21] And indeed under Housing Act 1985, Pt. IV, where the court, in determining the meaning of "reasonable" in *ibid*., s.84(2)(a), (c), has relied for guidance on the Rent Acts cases.

[22] *City of Bristol v. Mousah* (1997) 30 H.L.R. 32, CA; *Shrewsbury & Atcham B.C. v. Evans* (1997) 30 H.L.R. 123, CA, both decisions under the secure tenancies regime in Housing Act 1985, Pt. IV. *Aliter* if manifest that such application would succeed: *Lewisham L.B.C. v. Adeyemi* [1999] E.G.C.S. 74, CA (secure tenancy). For a more detailed consideration of other cases under the Rent Acts, see Vol. 1, pp 388–392.

[23] See, *e.g., Pickford v. Mace* [1943] K.B. 623 at 630, 632, CA, *Rhodes v. Cornford* [1947] 2 All E.R. 601 at 604 and *Redspring Ltd. v. Francis* [1973] 1 W.L.R. 134, CA, all cases decided under the Rent Acts.

[24] *White v. Wareing* [1992] 1 E.G.L.R. 271, CA.

[25] For recent examples of the policy of the Court of Appeal in this regard, see *Sheffield C.C. v. Green* [1993] E.G.C.S. 185 (rent arrears), *Woking B.C. v. Bistram* (1993) 27 H.L.R. 1 (nuisance: noise), *City of Bristol v. Mousah, supra* (breach of condition: drug dealing), *Green v. Sheffield C.C.* (1993) 26 H.L.R. 349 (breach of condition: dog), and *Sheffield C.C. v. Jepson* (1993) 25 H.L.R. 299 (breach of condition: dog), all decisions under Housing Act 1985, Pt. IV.

2. THE GROUNDS

Most of the ten discretionary grounds for possession under the Act of 1988 draw heavily on those under the Act of 1977,[26] though there are many differences. There has also been a measure of reorganisation, in that alternative accommodation is now integrated with the other discretionary grounds instead of being dealt with separately.[27] The grounds will be considered in turn.

Sect. 1. Suitable Alternative Accommodation: Ground 9

15–06 Ground 9 itself is expressed with brevity in almost unchanged language: "suitable alternative accommodation is available for the tenant or will be available for him when the order for possession takes effect".[28] As before, however, the ground itself is supplemented by a substantial body of further provisions which specifies what alternative accommodation is suitable and available within the meaning of the ground.[29] These provisions are expressed in language that is identical with that in the Act of 1977,[30] apart from matters such as the substitution of "assured tenancy" for "protected tenancy". As before,[31] the onus is plainly on the landlord, and he may discharge it either by producing a certificate of the local housing authority or by proving that suitable alternative accommodation is or will be available.

A. CERTIFICATE OF HOUSING AUTHORITY

15–07 A certificate of the local housing authority for the district in which the dwelling-house in question is situated,[32] certifying that the authority will provide suitable alternative accommodation for the tenant by a date specified in the certificate, is conclusive evidence that suitable alternative accommodation will be available for him by that date.[33] This language is identical with that of the Act of 1977. The certificate is conclusive both as to suitability and availability.[34] Any document purporting—

[26] Act of 1977, s.98(1)(a), (b), Sched. 15, Pt. I.
[27] It was not one of the numbered "Cases" under Act of 1977, though for convenience Vol. 1 previously called it "Case A.A": Vol. 1, p. 443.
[28] Act of 1988, Sched. 2, Pt. II, Ground 9; Act of 1977, s.98(1)(a).
[29] Act of 1988, s.7(5), Sched. 2, Pt. III.
[30] Act of 1977, Sched. 15, Pt. IV. See Vol. 1, pp. 443–458 and Supplement thereto.
[31] Vol. 1, p. 443.
[32] "Local housing authority" and "district" in relation to such an authority have the same meaning here as in the Housing Act 1985: Act of 1988, Sched. 2, Pt. III, para. 6.
[33] *ibid.*, para. 1.
[34] Compare the second type of certificate which may be given by a local authority under this ground (*post*, para. 15–12), which is conclusive as to size and rent of accommodation provided by the local authority to persons whose needs are similar to the tenant's, but not conclusive as to suitability: *Jones v. Cook* (1990) 22 H.L.R. 319, CA (decided under Act of 1977).

(a) to be a certificate of a local housing authority named therein and issued for the purposes of this provision, and
(b) to be signed by the proper officer of that authority

is receivable in evidence and deemed to be such a certificate without further proof unless the contrary is shown.[35] It is therefore unnecessary to call an officer of the local authority to give evidence. In practice, however, this head is rarely relied upon.

B. SUITABLE ALTERNATIVE ACCOMMODATION AVAILABLE

Where no certificate of the local housing authority is produced under the previous head, the landlord must prove *aliunde* that the alternative accommodation is suitable. Accommodation is "deemed to be suitable"[36] for these purposes if it satisfies three conditions. As under the Rent Acts, these conditions appear to be merely indicative and not exhaustive, so that they do not prevent accommodation from being suitable even if it does not satisfy them, for example an empty house owned by the tenant.[37] The three conditions (security of tenure, proximity to work and suitability to means and needs) will be considered first, before turning to availability and other matters. **15–08**

1. Security of tenure

Accommodation is deemed to be suitable so far as security of tenure is concerned if it consists of premises which are to be let as a separate dwelling either— **15–09**

(a) on an assured tenancy, other than (i) a tenancy in respect of which a warning notice[38] is given not later than the beginning of the tenancy that possession might be recovered on any of the mandatory Grounds 1 to 5[39] and (ii) an assured shorthold tenancy,[40] or
(b) on terms which will, in the opinion of the court, afford to the tenant security of tenure reasonably equivalent to the security afforded by an assured tenancy falling within (a) above.[41]

This too is substantially the same as the requirement under the Act of 1977.[42] Assured tenancies replace protected tenancies, and the exception of tenancies

[35] Act of 1988, Sched. 2, Pt. III, para. 5.
[36] *ibid.*, para. 2.
[37] See Vol. 1, p. 444.
[38] *Ante*, para. 14–19.
[39] See *ante*, Chap. 14.
[40] Act of 1988, Sched. 2, Pt. III, para. 2(a).
[41] *ibid.*, para. (2)(b).
[42] Act of 1977, Sched. 15, Pt. IV, para. 4.

subject to any of the first five mandatory grounds and assured shorthold tenancies takes the place of the exception of all the mandatory grounds under the Act of 1977, but otherwise the provisions are the same.[43] The additional mandatory grounds under the Act of 1988 do not depend on any step being taken which, prior to its beginning, makes the assured tenancy vulnerable to a claim to possession on a mandatory ground; they depend on circumstances which may or may not arise during the tenancy.

Reasonably equivalent security of tenure would certainly be afforded by a protected tenancy not subject to a mandatory ground for possession, but the creation of new such tenancies is now extremely rare. A secure tenancy[44] would doubtless afford wholly equivalent security of tenure, but an applicable statutory regime providing security has been held not to be essential in a few cases decided under the Rent Acts;[45] the security need only be reasonably equivalent, not identical.[46] In some circumstances, a lengthy term of years may suffice, if the identity of the landlord or some other factor means that the tenancy will not be an assured tenancy. Now that most new[47] assured tenancies are automatically assured shorthold tenancies, however, a landlord will either have to give an appropriate notice before the tenancy is entered into or include a suitable term in the tenancy agreement if an assured tenancy which is not a shorthold tenancy is to be granted.[48]

In the case of claims to possession under agricultural occupancies on this ground, references to an assured tenancy are to be read as including references to assured agricultural occupancies.[49]

2. Proximity to work

15–10 In addition to satisfying the condition considered above, the alternative accommodation must fulfil what are termed "the relevant conditions".[50] These are concerned with proximity to place of work and with the cost of the accommodation, its extent and its character. The language of the proximity to place of work condition is identical with the language of the Act of 1977: the accommodation must in the opinion of the court be "reasonably suitable to the needs of the tenant and his family as regards proximity to place of work".[51] The meaning may therefore be assumed to be unchanged,[52] and so "family" probably only extends to those members of the tenant's family who live with him in the dwelling. Others, such as lodgers and other relatives, may be relevant considerations when deciding whether it is reasonable to make an order for possession. "Place

[43] The provisions under the Rent Act are considered in Vol. 1, pp. 445–447.
[44] Under Housing Act 1985, Pt. IV.
[45] See *Fulford v. Turpin* [1955] J.P.L. 365, C.C. (term of 16 years sufficient); *Edwards v. Cohen* (1958) 108 L.J. News 556, C.C. (term of 10 years to couple in late 50s sufficient).
[46] Under the Rent Act, the grant of an assured tenancy instead of a protected tenancy has been held to be sufficient: *Laimond Properties Ltd. v. Al-Shakarchi* (1998) 30 H.L.R. 1099, CA.
[47] Granted on or after February 28, 1997, other than pusuant to a contract made before that date: see *ante*, Chap. 8.
[48] Act of 1988, s.19A, Sched. 2A, paras. 1, 3; *ante*, paras. 8–06, 8–08.
[49] *ibid.*, s.25(3).
[50] *ibid.*, Sched. 2, Pt. III, para. 2.
[51] *ibid.*, paras. 2, 3(1).
[52] See Vol. 1, pp. 447–449.

of work'' probably has a broad meaning, and can include more than one such place. Once again, the accommodation only has to be ''reasonably suitable'' in this respect, not as good as the premises of which possession is claimed.[53]

3. Reasonable suitability of accommodation

The remaining ''relevant conditions'', which are concerned with the cost of the accommodation and with its extent and character, may be satisfied in one of two ways.[54] These alternatives, which each comprise several constituent parts, cannot be mixed so as to satisfy one part of the requirement under one alternative and another part under the other.[55] Accordingly they are in substance one single requirement, capable of satisfaction in two alternative ways. But accommodation is not to be deemed suitable to the needs of the tenant and his family if the result of their occupation of it would be to make it an overcrowded[56] dwelling-house.[57] **15–11**

(a) Similar to local housing authority accommodation

The first way is by providing accommodation similar to what is provided by the local housing authority. For it to be satisfied, the court must consider that that accommodation is ''similar as regards rental and extent to the accommodation afforded by dwelling-houses provided in the neighbourhood by any local housing authority for persons whose needs as regards extent are, in the opinion of the court, similar to those of the tenant and of his family''.[58] In addition, if any furniture was provided for use under the assured tenancy, furniture must be provided for use in the alternative accommodation which, in the opinion of the court, ''is either similar to that so provided or is reasonably suitable to the needs of the tenant and his family''.[59] The reasonable suitability of the furniture is a different consideration from the overriding requirement of reasonableness. For these purposes, ''a certificate of a local housing authority stating— **15–12**

(a) the extent of the accommodation afforded by dwelling-houses provided by the authority to meet the needs of tenants with families of such number as may be specified in the certificate, and
(b) the amount of the rent charged by the authority for dwelling-houses affording accommodation of that extent''[60]

[53] Subject to reasonableness.
[54] As under Act of 1977, Sched. 15, Pt. IV, para. 5(1).
[55] *e.g.*, that the rent is reasonably suitable to the means of the tenant (under Act of 1988, Sched. 2, Pt. III, para. 3(1)(b)), and that the alternative accommodation is similar in extent to that provided by a local housing authority for persons whose needs as regards extent are similar to the tenant's, as certified (under *ibid.*, para. 3(1)(a)).
[56] *i.e.* for the purposes of Housing Act 1985, Pt. X.
[57] Act of 1988, Sched. 2, Pt. III, para. 4.
[58] *ibid.*, para. 3(1)(a).
[59] *ibid.*, para. 3(1).
[60] *ibid.*, para. 3(2).

is conclusive evidence of the facts so stated. The certificate is only conclusive evidence of the matters certified, however, not that the accommodation referred to in the certificate is similar as regards rental and extent to the alternative accommodation in question: that is for the court to decide.[61] Similarly, the court must decide whether the needs of the tenant are similar to those of the hypothetical tenant or family which is the subject of the certificate. The certificate may suffice for the statutory purpose even if no dimensions of rooms are given.[62] Any document purporting—

(a) to be a certificate of a local housing authority named therein and issued for the purposes of this provision, and
(b) to be signed by the proper officer of that authority

is receivable in evidence and deemed to be such a certificate without further proof unless the contrary is shown.[63] It is therefore unnecessary to call an officer of the local authority to give evidence. Where the requirement can be proved in this way, it is unnecessary to prove that the rent for the dwelling-house is suitable given the means of the tenant: if the rent is similar to that charged by a local housing authority for comparable accommodation, the dwelling is *ipso facto* considered suitable in that respect.

(b) Reasonably suitable to means and needs

15–13 The second way in which the requirement can be satisfied is by proving the reasonable suitability of the dwelling-house in respect of the tenant's means and needs. Here, the court must be of the opinion that the alternative accommodation is "reasonably suitable to the means of the tenant and to the needs of the tenant and his family as regards extent and character".[64] In addition, as with the first alternative, if any furniture was provided for use under the assured tenancy, furniture must be provided for use in the alternative accommodation which, in the opinion of the court, "is either similar to that so provided or is reasonably suitable to the needs of the tenant and his family".[65] Once again, what is reasonably suitable might be less in extent or quality than what is enjoyed under the assured tenancy.[66] The reasonable suitability of the alternative accommodation in each of the above respects is a different consideration from the overriding requirement of reasonableness.

Apart from "assured tenancy" replacing "protected or statutory tenancy", the language of these provisions in the two Acts concerned with the reasonable suitability of the accommodation is identical, and, in the absence of any reported

[61] *Jones v. Cook* (1990) 22 H.L.R. 319, CA, a case under the equivalent provisions of the Act of 1977.
[62] *ibid.*
[63] Act of 1988, Sched. 2, Pt. III, para. 5.
[64] *ibid.*, para. 3(1)(b).
[65] *ibid.*, para. 3(1).
[66] See, *e.g.*, *The Trustees of the Dame Margaret Hungerford Charity v. Beazeley* (1993) 26 H.L.R. 269, CA (3-bedroomed modern house suitable alternative to 17-roomed Grade I listed building), a decision under the equivalent provisions of the Act of 1977.

case decided under the Act of 1988, the meaning must be assumed to be have been intended to be unchanged.[67]

4. Reasonableness

As stated at the start of this Chapter,[68] all the discretionary grounds are subject to the overriding requirement that the court must consider separately whether it is reasonable to make an order for possession. This remains so under Ground 9 notwithstanding that the text of the provisions supplementing the ground[69] contains the adverb "reasonably" in four separate places. In practice, it is not uncommon for the court to conclude that it would not be reasonable to make an order for possession, for example because the tenant has lived in the dwelling-house for 20 or more years and the landlord is a commercial enterprise that has purchased subject to the tenancy, even though the alternative accommodation is suitable within the provisions of the Act. Environmental considerations may therefore be equally relevant in considering reasonableness where the alternative relied upon is (a) above[70] as where (b) is relied upon, even though alternative (a) does not refer to the character of the alternative accommodation.[71] **15–14**

5. Availability

As under the Act of 1977, the court must be satisfied that the accommodation "is available for the tenant or will be available for him when the order for possession takes effect".[72] Again the language is unaltered, and the meaning must be presumed to be unchanged.[73] Thus, the landlord can prove either that the accommodation is available at the time of the hearing or that it will be available when the order for possession takes effect. To protect the tenant in either case, the order is generally made conditionally on the accommodation being provided when the order takes effect.[74] The accommodation does not need to be provided by the landlord directly as long as it is proved that the owner of the accommodation will grant a suitable tenancy to the tenant. **15–15**

6. Removal expenses

When the landlord obtains an order for possession of a dwelling-house let on an assured tenancy on the ground of suitable alternative accommodation being **15–16**

[67] For a detailed consideration of the cases decided under the Act of 1977, see Vol. 1, pp. 450–456, and Supplement.
[68] *Ante*, para. 15–01.
[69] Act of 1988, Sched. 2, Pt. III.
[70] *Ante*, para. 15–12; Act of 1988, Sched. 2, Pt. III, para. 3(1)(a).
[71] *Dawncar Investments v. Plews* (1993) 25 H.L.R. 639, CA, decided under the equivalent provision of Act of 1977.
[72] Act of 1988, s.7(4), Sched. 2, Ground 9; Act of 1977, s.98(1)(a).
[73] For commentary on the provisions of the Act of 1977, see Vol. 1, pp. 456–458.
[74] Not so where head A is relied upon as the certificate of the local housing authority is conclusive on *inter alia* availability; see *ante*, para. 15–07.

available, he is liable to pay the tenant a sum equal to his removal expenses.[75] This provision has already been considered.[76]

Sect. 2. Unpaid Rent: Ground 10

15–17 Ground 10 is a version of Case 1 under the Act of 1977,[77] shorn of the provisions for breaches of obligations other than payment of rent[78] but expanded in its requirements. There are two of these.

1. Rent lawfully due

15–18 "Some rent lawfully due from the tenant"[79] must be unpaid. The meaning of "rent" and "rent lawfully due" have already been considered in relation to Ground 8,[80] and the meanings are the same here. Rent ostensibly payable at an increased rate under a sham agreement is not lawfully due.[80a]

2. Unpaid when notice served and when proceedings begun

15–19 Some rent must be—

(1) "unpaid on the date on which proceedings for possession are begun"; and
(2) "was in arrears at the date of the service of the notice under [section 8 of the Act] relating to those proceedings".[81]

Limb (2), however, does not apply[82] if the court considers it just and equitable to dispense with the requirement of a possession notice.[83] There is no requirement that the amount of arrears be the same on both dates, but the ground seems to imply[84] that some of the arrears at the date of the possession notice be still

75 Act of 1988. s.11.
76 Under Ground 6, *ante*, paras. 14–62 *et seq.*
77 Vol. 1, pp. 397–403.
78 Which now form a separate ground, Ground 12, *infra*.
79 Act of 1988, Sched. 2, Pt. II, Ground 10.
80 *Ante*, paras. 14–71 *et seq.*
80a *Bhopal v. Walia* [1999] E.G.C.S. 49, CA.
81 Act of 1988, Sched. 2, Pt. II, Ground 10.
82 *ibid.*, para. (b).
83 *Ante*, para. 13–37.
84 By the reverse chronological order of the relevant dates and the use of the words "some rent" as governing both paragraphs and dates.

outstanding at the date when proceedings are begun;[85] and so if the tenant clears the arrears specified in the possession notice before proceedings are begun, the fact that a further rent instalment has fallen due in the meantime would seem not to satisfy the ground.[85a] If the tenant has a counterclaim for damages which amounts to an equitable set off,[86] which has arisen by the time that the proceedings are begun, and which overtops the amount of the rent arrears, the ground will not be proved. For these purposes, possession proceedings in the county court are probably begun on the date on which the court enters the plaint in the records of the court and fixes the return date.[87] The date on which a possession notice is served has already been considered.[88]

In practice, Ground 10 is usually added to a possession notice and to the proceedings where Ground 8 is also relied upon, to prevent the claim being dismissed because the tenant has paid off just enough of the arrears to reduce them below the statutory minimum for that ground.

Sect. 3. Persistent Delays in Paying Rent: Ground 11

Even if no rent is in arrears, Ground 11 may be invoked if the tenant has persistently delayed in paying his rent; there is no corresponding ground under the Act of 1977.[89] The ground is that "whether or not any rent is in arrears on the date on which proceedings for possession are begun, the tenant has persistently delayed paying rent which has become lawfully due".[90] This ground thus cannot be defeated by the tenant paying all arrears of rent after receiving a possession notice but before proceedings are begun. Yet presumably the existence of a history of persistent delays is not intended to remain effective indefinitely, long after all arrears of rent have been paid, though, under the wording of the ground, this may be a factor that can only be assessed on the question of reasonableness. 15–20

[85] This construction would, it is submitted, best fulfil the statutory purpose of the possession notice: "The purpose of the requirement of statutory notice is to enable the [tenant] to take steps to remedy the complaints so that he can be in as good a position as possible to avoid eviction": *Kelsey Housing Association v. King* (1995) 28 H.L.R. 270 at 275, CA, *per* Aldous L.J. A contrary argument is that a landlord would then be in a better position if he had not served a possession notice, provided that he could satisfy the court that it was just and equitable to dispense with it. In any case, if the tenant did clear the arrears, unless the landlord long delayed in bringing proceedings the new arrears would be relatively small, and it is unlikely in such circumstances that the court would consider it reasonable to make an order for possession.

[85a] But Ground 11, *infra*, might assist.

[86] See *ante*, para. 14–74.

[87] County Court Rules 1981, Order 3, r. 3(2). The rival possibilities are the date when the plaintiff files the summons and particulars of claim with a request for service (*ibid.*, r. 3(1B)) and the date when the court posts the summons to the defendant (*ibid.*, Order 7, r. 10(1)(b)). Both seem unlikely: the former because the court will not have taken any step to start the action; the latter because a distinction has always been drawn between issue and service of court proceedings, and because the plaintiff can request return of the summons for personal service.

[88] *Ante*, para. 13–32.

[89] Under Case 1 there must be rent arrears when the proceedings are started: Vol. 1, p. 400.

[90] Act of 1988, Sched. 2, Pt. II, Ground 11. For "rent" and rent "lawfully due", see *ante*, paras. 14–71 *et seq.*; for the date on which proceedings are begun, see *supra*.

The ground is likely to be of particular use where the tenant has persistently paid arrears of rent only after service of a possession notice.[90a]

Sect. 4. Breach of Obligation: Ground 12

15–21 Ground 12 is that "any obligation of the tenancy (other than one relating to the payment of rent) has been broken or not performed".[91] This in substance corresponds to the part of Case 1 under the Act of 1977 that was excluded from Ground 10 under the Act of 1988. The commentary on this in the text of Volume 1[92] seems to be applicable to the Act of 1988. Where a lease contained a proviso for re-entry in the event of bankruptcy of the lessee, bankruptcy was a breach of an obligation of the tenancy.[92a] In secure tenancy cases decided on the equivalent ground for possession, there has been a noticeable hardening of the approach of the Court of Appeal in relation to breaches of obligations as a discretionary ground for ordering possession. In the case of a serious breach, or a breach that has been or will be persisted in, or both, there are likely to have to be exceptional circumstances for it to be unreasonable to make at least a suspended order for possession.[93]

Sect. 5. Deterioration of Premises by Waste or Neglect: Ground 13

15–22 Ground 13 is a modified version of Case 3 under the Act of 1977,[94] extended so as to include the common parts of any building that includes the dwelling-house. The ground has two limbs,[95] and in the case of the second limb there is a further requirement that has to be satisfied. The two limbs are—

(1) "The condition of the dwelling-house or any of the common parts has deteriorated owing to acts of waste by, or the neglect or default of, the tenant or any other person residing in the dwelling-house" other than a lodger or sub-tenant.
(2) Deterioration has occurred as in (1) above owing to acts of waste by, or the neglect or default of "a person lodging with the tenant or a sub-tenant of his" residing in the dwelling-house.

For this purpose, "common parts" means "any part of a building comprising

[90a] For a reported decision under Ground 11, see *Drew-Morgan v. Hamid-Zadeh* [1999] E.G.C.S. 72, CA.

[91] Act of 1988, Sched. 2, Ground 12.

[92] pp. 398–400.

[92a] *Cadogan Estates Ltd. v. McMahon* [1999] The Times, June 1, CA (decided under Act of 1977, Case 1).

[93] Consider *Sheffield C.C. v. Jepson* (1993) 25 H.L.R. 299, CA (keeping dog); *Green v. Sheffield C.C.* (1993) 26 H.L.R. 349, CA (keeping dog), *Woking B.C. v. Bistram* (1993) 27 H.L.R. 1, CA (creating noisy disturbances) and *City of Bristol v. Mousah* (1997) 30 H.L.R. 32, CA (dealing in Class A drugs). And see *West Kent Housing Association v. Davies* [1998] E.G.C.S. 103, CA, *post*, para. 15–24, n.11.

[94] Act of 1977, Sched. 15, Case 3.

[95] Act of 1988, Sched. 2, Ground 13.

the dwelling-house and any other premises which the tenant is entitled under the terms of the tenancy to use in common with the occupiers of other dwelling-houses in which the landlord has an estate or interest''.[96] ''Person residing in the dwelling-house'' has replaced ''person residing or lodging with him'' and is clearly wider than that phrase in being apt to include a sub-tenant or licensee to whom the tenant has sub-let or licensed the whole of the dwelling-house; but in general the authorities under the Act of 1977 appear to be applicable to this ground.[97] It is clear that a failure to act can suffice: ''neglect'' is used in the context of tenant-like conduct,[98] and does not betoken any breach of legal obligation.

The further requirement for the second limb is that the tenant has not taken ''such steps as he ought reasonably to have taken for the removal of the lodger or sub-tenant''.[99] Where a lodger[1] caused the deterioration, *semble* there is no reason why the lodger cannot be evicted forthwith, or at least after a period of notice, for he will be an excluded licensee[2] without the benefit of the provisions of the Protection from Eviction Act 1977 against eviction without due process of law and requiring the service of notice to quit of at least four weeks' duration.[3] Where the sub-tenant is an assured tenant, the reasonable steps will doubtless be the service of a possession notice and, so far as reasonable, the commencement and pursuit of possession proceedings. Subject to those cases, what steps are reasonable will be a question of mixed fact and law depending on the exact circumstances of the case. The reasonable steps must be directed to the removal of the lodger or sub-tenant, however, and not just to the remedying of the deterioration in condition.[4] **15–23**

Sect. 6. Nuisance or Illegal User: Ground 14

Ground 14, as originally enacted, read: ''The tenant or any other person residing in the dwelling-house has been guilty of conduct which is a nuisance or annoyance to adjoining occupiers, or has been convicted of using the dwelling-house or allowing the dwelling-house to be used for immoral or illegal purposes''. With one exception, that was identical to Case 2 under the Act of 1977.[5] The **15–24**

96 *ibid.*
97 Vol. 1, pp. 409, 410.
98 *Lowe v. Lendrum* (1950) 156 E.G. 423, CA, *per* Somervell L.J., a case under the Rent Acts.
99 Act of 1988, Sched. 2, Pt. II, Ground 13.
1 ''Lodger'' is not defined in the Act, but the meaning must be assumed to be that expounded in the speech of Lord Templeman in *Street v. Mountford* [1985] A.C. 809, in contradistinction to ''tenant''.
2 Within the meaning and by virtue of Protection from Eviction Act 1977, s.3A(2), (3).
3 *ibid.*, ss.3, 5. The tenant must not, however, use violence or threats of violence against any person in the premises who is opposed to the entry: Criminal Law Act 1977, s.6(1).
4 Though if the lodger or sub-tenant does effectually remedy the deterioration in response to a possession notice, it might not be reasonable to take the further step of issuing possession proceedings against him.
5 Act of 1977, Sched. 15, Case 2.

exception was that Case 2 applies to acts by the tenant "or any person residing or lodging with him or any sub-tenant of his" instead of the tenant "or any other person residing in the dwelling-house". Subject to that, the discussion in the text of Volume 1[6] appears to apply to the original Ground 14, and that ground, as enacted, continues to apply where a possession notice[7] was served before February 28, 1997, or where possession proceedings were started before that date and the court dispenses with the requirement of a possession notice.[8]

15–25 Subject to those savings, however, a new Ground 14 was substituted on and with effect from February 28, 1997,[9] which considerably extends the ambit of the ground, in particular to include the conduct of persons "visiting the dwelling-house". Apart from the proposition, implicit in the statutory wording, that a "visitor" is something less than a "resident", there is no limitation, express or obviously implicit, on the potentially wide meaning of "visitor":[10] overnight and longer temporary guests, guests for coffee mornings, lunch or dinner, nannies, dailies, workmen and salesmen would all, without contrivance, be said in ordinary English to be "visiting" the dwelling. In most of those instances, the degree of control that the tenant might be expected to exercise over such persons is much more limited that in the case of residents, and perhaps the intention of Parliament was to oust legalistic argument about the meaning of "resident" in favour of facilitating control of anti-social behaviour, subject to the safeguard of the reasonableness condition.[11] The new ground has two limbs.

1. Nuisance or annoyance

15–26 The ground is satisfied where the tenant or a person residing in or visiting the dwelling-house "has been guilty of conduct causing or likely to cause a nuisance or annoyance to a person residing, visiting or otherwise engaging in a lawful activity in the locality".[12] Here, the ground has been arguably extended in three respects. First, the conduct may be such as is *likely to cause* nuisance or annoyance, and need not actually have caused it. But under the old ground, as under the Rent Acts,[13] the focus is on the conduct rather than the reaction of adjoining occupiers, and the court could infer that conduct caused nuisance or annoyance

[6] pp. 403–408.

[7] Presumably specifying Ground 14.

[8] The Housing Act 1996 (Commencement No. 7 and Savings) Order 1997 (S.I. 1997 No. 225), arts. 1(2), 2, Sched., para. 1.

[9] Housing Act 1996, ss.148, 232(3), (4); S.I. 1997 No. 225, *supra*.

[10] The Occupiers' Liability Act 1957 is a possible, but rather far-fetched, aid to statutory construction, though the definition of "visitor" in *ibid.*, s.1(2) as meaning common law invitees and licensees does not narrow much the words of Ground 14 in any event.

[11] The tougher approach of the Court of Appeal where breaches of conditions are concerned has also been evident under this ground: see *West Kent Housing Association v. Davies* [1998] E.G.C.S. 103, CA (car repairs and racial abuse: judge wrong not to make possession order; *Kensington & Chelsea Royal L.B.C. v. Simmonds* (1996) 29 H.L.R. 507, CA (tenant answerable for nuisance caused by uncontrollable 13-year old son); *Camden L.B.C. v. Gilsenan* (1998) 31 H.L.R. 81, CA; cases under Housing Act 1985, Sched. 2, Ground 2).

[12] Act of 1988, Sched. 2, Pt. II, Ground 14(a), substituted by Housing Act 1996, ss.148, 232(3), (4); S.I. 1997 No. 225.

[13] Act of 1977, Sched. 15, Case 2.

without any positive evidence to that effect.[14] It is doubtful, therefore, whether any change in substance has been made here. Secondly, the persons likely to suffer the nuisance or annoyance have been more widely defined so as to include persons visiting or otherwise engaging in a lawful activity. Once again, "visitors" appears to have a wide meaning, and could include members of the public shopping in the building next door to the dwelling, and "persons engaging in a lawful activity" seems wider still. More remote premises, which might not be fairly described as having adjoining occupiers, will potentially be caught by these words. Thirdly, and connected with the second respect, the identification of those capable of suffering nuisance or annoyance appears to have been removed from a purely possessory context: where previously "adjoining occupiers" were the concern, now persons "in the locality" likely to be affected will suffice. "Locality" certainly seems to have been intended to have a broader meaning than "adjoining", even though that word was construed as being wider than "contiguous",[15] and the limiting word "occupiers" has been removed. What is "the locality" for these purposes is a question of fact for the judge. It may be "the part or the whole of a housing estate. It may straddle parts of two housing estates or include local shops serving the housing estate but within its boundaries".[15a] The applicable test may be what a resident of the area would say.[15b] The conduct in question does not have to be performed or done on the dwelling-house itself.[16]

2. Conviction

The ground is also satisfied if the tenant or a person residing in or visiting the dwelling-house has been convicted of an offence. A criminal conviction is required, and mere immorality which is not an offence, or an acquittal, does not satisfy the requirement.[17] There are two categories of offence for the purposes of the ground, and conviction of an offence falling within either suffices— **15–27**

(1) "using the dwelling-house or allowing it to be used for immoral or illegal purposes", or
(2) "an arrestable offence committed in, or in the locality of, the dwelling-house".[18]

The first of these categories is identical in substance to the old ground and with **15–28**

[14] *Frederick Platts Co. Ltd. v. Grigor* (1950) 66(1) T.L.R. 859, CA.

[15] *Cobstone Investments Ltd. v. Maxim* [1985] Q.B. 140, CA. Under Housing Act 1985, Sched. 2, Pt. I, Ground 2, prior to its amendment, the word used was "neighbours", which is wider than "adjoining occupiers", and persons living more than 100 yards from the dwelling-house were "neighbours": *Northampton B.C. v. Lovatt* [1998] 1 E.G.L.R. 15, CA.

[15a] *Manchester C.C. v. Lawler* (1998) 31 H.L.R. 119 at 124, CA, *per* Butler Sloss L.J. (decided under the equivalent, substituted wording of Housing Act 1985, Sched. 2, Ground 2).

[15b] *ibid.*

[16] *Northampton B.C. v. Lovatt*, *supra*, decided on the equivalent words in Housing Act 1985, Sched. 2, Ground 2.

[17] *Frederick Platts Co. Ltd. v. Grigor*, *supra*.

[18] Act of 1988, Sched. 2, Pt. II, Ground 14(b), substituted by Housing Act 1996, ss.148, 232(3), (4); S.I. 1997 No. 225.

part of Case 2 under the Rent Acts,[19] and also with the equivalent ground for possession from secure tenants under the Housing Act 1985 prior to its amendment.[20] The Rent Acts authorities, which it must be supposed will be equally applicable to this wording, establish that the ground will be satisfied when the offence has been committed on the premises, and if the premises have been used for the purpose of committing the offence;[21] it is not enough that the premises are incidentally the scene of an offence, such as an assault.[22] But it is not necessary that the use of premises be an ingredient in the offence itself.[23] A conviction for "allowing premises to be used . . ". is required;[24] it is not enough that someone who was not a visitor or resident was convicted of an offence related to the premises if the tenant (or a resident or visitor), although he permitted the unlawful conduct, has not been convicted of an offence.

The second category is new, and wider. Provided that the offence is an "arrestable offence",[25] and hence a reasonably serious one, its incidental commission on the premises will suffice; indeed, its incidental commission in the locality of the premises suffices. Again, the words "in the locality" are clearly designed to give a much wider effect to this ground than hitherto, and may perhaps be equated with "neighbourhood".[26]

Sect. 7. Domestic Violence: Ground 14A

15–29 Unlike all the other discretionary grounds for possession, Ground 14A[27] is only available to a limited, specified category of landlords: registered social landlords and charitable housing trusts. It was inserted in the Act of 1988 by amendment with effect from February 28, 1997.[28] The new ground enables that category of landlord to claim possession where one party to a domestic relationship has left the dwelling-house owing to actual or threatened violence from the other, and where one or other party is, or both are, the tenant. It does not apply in a case where a possession notice was served before February 28, 1997, or where the

[19] Act of 1977, Sched. 15, Case 2.

[20] Housing Act 1985, Sched. 2, Pt. I, Ground 2, substituted on February 12, 1997 by a new Ground 2 in terms identical with the new Ground 14 in Act of 1988: Housing Act 1996, ss.144, 232(3), (4); S.I. 1997 No. 66.

[21] See *S. Schneiders & Sons Ltd. v. Abrahams* [1925] 1 K.B. 301 at 310, CA, approved in *Abrahams v. Wilson* [1971] 2 Q.B. 88 at 92, 94, CA.

[22] *ibid.*

[23] *ibid.*

[24] Some such offences are noted in Vol. 1 at p. 407, n. 36.

[25] *i.e.* one punishable on conviction on indictment by a maximum sentence of not less than 5 years' imprisonment: Police and Criminal Evidence Act 1984, s.24(1).

[26] See *Northampton B.C. v. Lovatt*, *supra*, and para. 15–26, *supra*.

[27] Act of 1988, Sched. 2, Pt. II, Ground 14A, inserted by Housing Act 1996, ss.149, 232(3), (4); S.I. 1997 No. 225.

[28] A substantially identical ground under Housing Act 1985 was similarly inserted by Housing Act 1996, s.145 with effect from February 12, 1997: S.I. 1997 No. 66.

proceedings for possession were commenced before that date and the court dispenses with the requirement of a possession notice.[29]

The ground has six requirements in addition to the reasonableness criterion.

1. Registered social or charitable landlord

The landlord who is seeking possession must be a registered social landlord or a charitable housing trust.[30] For the purposes of this ground, "registered social landlord" means those bodies actually registered by the Housing Corporation or Housing for Wales (referred to here, as in the legislation, as "the Corporation") in their registers of social landlords under Part I of the Housing Act 1996.[31] The Corporation may register as a social landlord any body which is eligible for such registration and which meets the Corporation's criteria for registration.[32] Bodies eligible for registration as social landlords are— 15–30

(1) registered charities which are housing associations;[33]
(2) societies registered under the Industrial and Provident Societies Act 1965 which are non-profit making and housing-orientated, and
(3) companies registered under the Companies Act 1985 which are non-profit making and housing-orientated.[34]

"Charitable housing trust" for the purposes of this ground means a housing trust within the meaning of the Housing Associations Act 1985 which is a charity within the meaning of the Charities Act 1993.

2. Dwelling-house previously occupied by couple

The ground does not apply unless the dwelling-house "was occupied (whether alone or with others) by a married couple or a couple living together as husband and wife". For the tenancy to be an assured tenancy, it must be occupied by the tenant as his principal residence at least, and so the concept of "occupation" adds nothing except that the couple, whether or not both of them are the tenant, must have lived in the dwelling-house together. The phrase "as husband or wife" suggests that a gay or lesbian couple will not be at risk under this 15–31

[29] S.I. 1997 No. 225, *supra*, Sched., para. 1. Presumably this transitional provision implicitly provides that the new ground does not apply where a possession notice was served before February 28, 1997 and possession proceedings are being prosecuted *pursuant to it*; the new ground cannot have been intended to be disapplied to a tenancy forever merely because a possession notice was served before that date.

[30] Ground 14A, para. (b).

[31] Housing Act 1996, ss.1(1), 56(1), (2), (3).

[32] *ibid.*, ss.3(1), 5(1).

[33] Every housing association which immediately before October 1, 1996 was registered by the Corporation under Housing Associations Act 1985, Pt. I, became a registered social landlord under Housing Act 1996, Pt. I, on that date: Housing Act 1996, ss.1(2), 232(3), (4); S.I. 1996 No. 2402.

[34] *ibid.*, s.2(1), (2), (3).

ground,[35] unless the word "married" is to be construed as extending to same sex marriages permitted in other jurisdictions. And the word "couple" seems to exclude the type of relationship of heterosexual plurality accommodated elsewhere by the Act of 1988 in relation to succession by spouses to assured periodic tenancies,[36] though the fact that others were residing in the dwelling-house would not matter.

3. One or both partners tenant

15–32 The ground requires that "one or both of the partners is a tenant of the dwelling-house". Accordingly, it would not matter if one of the partners was a joint tenant with others, or if both were, but the ground does not apply if neither is a tenant.

4. Violence of threats of violence

15–33 "One partner has left the dwelling-house because of violence or threats of violence by the other towards—

(i) that partner, or
(ii) a member of the family of that partner who was residing with that partner immediately before the partner left".

For the purposes of this ground, "member of the family" has the same meaning as in Part I of the Housing Act 1996. There, a person is a member of another's family if either—

(a) "he is the spouse of that person or he and that person live together as husband and wife", or
(b) "he is that person's parent, grandparent, child, grandchild, brother, sister, uncle, aunt, nephew or niece";[37]

and for the purposes of (b) above a relationship by marriage is treated as a relationship by blood, a relationship of half-blood is treated as a relationship of the whole blood, and the stepchild of a person is treated as his child.[38] Given the context of this new ground, however, (a) above does not seem to apply: the "spouse" or common law husband or wife of the partner who has left must be the partner who remains, and it cannot have been intended that self-violence by

[35] See *Harrogate B.C. v. Simpson* (1984) 17 H.L.R. 205, CA ("live together as husband and wife" in Housing Act 1985, s.113(1)(a)); *Fitzpatrick v. Sterling Housing Association Ltd.* [1998] Ch. 304, CA (survivor of committed, long-term gay couple not "wife or husband" or member of same family within Act of 1977, Sched. 1, paras. 2(2), 3(1)). The case is due to be heard by the House of Lords on appeal during 1999.
[36] Act of 1988, s.17(4), (5); *ante*, para. 12–06.
[37] Housing Act 1996, s.62(1).
[38] *ibid.*, s.62(2).

one spouse would fall within the ground. But a child of both partners is certainly within the ground.

5. No return likely

The court must be satisfied that "the partner who has left is unlikely to return". It is not clear whether the unlikelihood of which the court must be satisfied is a balance of probabilities, or some lesser probability.[39] At all events, the landlord will have to prove something more than that the departed partner "might or might not" return, and this would seem to require it in practical terms either to call the departed partner to give evidence of his or her intentions, or to adduce some fairly convincing piece of hearsay evidence of the same.[40] **15–34**

6. Notice of proceedings given to partner who left

Where Ground 14A is specified in a possession notice, whether alone or in addition to other grounds, and the partner who has left the dwelling is not a tenant of it, then unless the court considers it just and equitable to dispense with service of that notice on him or her, the court shall not entertain proceedings for possession of the dwelling unless the landlord[41] either has served on him or her a copy of that notice or has taken all reasonable steps so to do.[42] What are reasonable steps for a landlord to take to serve a person who is not the tenant and who no longer lives at the dwelling is uncertain, but will be a matter of fact and degree for the individual case. The purpose of this notice may be to enable the court better to ascertain whether requirements 4. and 5. above are satisfied;[43] but more likely it is to give the partner who has left the opportunity to consider his or her position under Part IV of the Family Law Act 1996.[43a] That partner having left the dwelling, the purpose cannot be to give him or her the right to apply for an adjournment of the proceedings, or a stay, suspension or postponement of the order for possession.[43b] If the partner who left was a tenant, then there is no need for this extra requirement because the landlord must have served a possession notice on him or her prior to the start of the proceedings[44] unless the court can be persuaded to dispense with the requirement of a possession **15–35**

[39] The word "likely", and its synonyms, including "on the cards", have long been used by the courts as an approximation of the degree of foreseeability of loss required in the law of contract: see, *e.g.*, *The Heron II* [1969] 1 A.C. 350. There, it seems to connote something less than probability.

[40] Under the provisions of Civil Evidence Act 1995, ss.1(1), 2.

[41] Or, where there are joint landlords, at least one of them.

[42] Act of 1988, s.8A(1), inserted by Housing Act 1996, ss.150, 232(3), (4); S.I. 1997 No. 225.

[43] Although it is not usually the function of the court, but of the plaintiff, to assimilate the evidence necessary to prove a case.

[43a] See *ante*, paras. 11–16 *et seq*.

[43b] Under Act of 1988, s.9(5), (5A); see *ante*, paras. 13–52 *et seq*.

[44] Act of 1988, ss.8(1)(a), 45(3).

notice altogether, at which time it will have the opportunity, when exercising its discretion, to consider the position of the partner who left.[45]

15–36 If a possession notice was served before the proceedings were started but it did not specify Ground 14A, then, provided that that notice was not served before February 28, 1997,[46] the court has the usual discretion to allow other grounds, including Ground 14A, to be added to it.[47] If the court does give leave to add that ground after proceedings have been begun, and if the partner who left is not a party to the proceedings, then unless the court considers it just and equitable to dispense with service on him or her of an information notice, it must not continue to entertain the possession proceedings unless the landlord has either served on him or her an information notice or has taken all reasonable steps so to do.[48] In this case the requirement of notice or dispensation applies whether or not the partner who left was a tenant. The information notice[49] must state that proceedings for the possession of the dwelling-house have been begun, specify the ground or grounds on which possession is being sought, and give particulars of the ground or grounds.[50] There is no prescribed form for such an information notice; but the possession notice itself will not do, unless it is amended and re-dated, because *ex hypothesi* it will not specify Ground 14A and give particulars of it, nor will it state that proceedings have begun.

Sect. 8. Deterioration of Furniture from Ill-treatment: Ground 15

15–37 Ground 15 is substantially the same as Case 3 under the Act of 1977.[51] It has two limbs[52], and, as with Ground 13,[53] in the case of the second limb there is a further requirement that has to be satisfied. The two limbs are—

(1) "The condition of any furniture provided for use under the tenancy has, in the opinion of the court, deteriorated owing to ill-treatment by

[45] Act of 1988 s.8(1)(b). If the court does so dispense with the possession notice, Ground 14A cannot apply if the proceedings for possession were started before February 28, 1997: S.I. 1997 No. 225, Sched., para. 1(b).
[46] *ibid.*, para. 1(a).
[47] Act of 1988, s.8(2); *ante*, para. 13–36.
[48] Act of 1988, s.8A(2), inserted by Housing Act 1996, ss.150, 232(3), (4); S.I. 1997 No. 225. Even if the partner who left is a party to the proceedings, or is made such a party, the court might think it appropriate to exercise its power under Act of 1988, s.9 to adjourn the proceedings or stay or suspend any order for possession if the partner who left was not present or adequately represented when Ground 14A was added.
[49] So called in the text in order to identify the notice required, and to distinguish it from a possession notice under *ibid.*, s.8.
[50] *ibid.*, s.8A(3).
[51] Act of 1977, Sched. 15, Case 3. See Vol. 1, p. 410.
[52] Act of 1988, Sched. 2, Ground 15.
[53] *Ante*, para. 15–22.

the tenant or any other person residing in the dwelling-house'' other than a lodger or sub-tenant.

(2) Deterioration has occurred as in (1) above owing to ill-treatment by ''a person lodging with the tenant or a sub-tenant of his'' residing in the dwelling-house.

''Any other person residing in the dwelling-house'' has replaced ''person residing or lodging with him or any sub-tenant of his'' under the Rent Acts, and is perhaps slightly wider than those words as being apt to include a licensee to whom the tenant has licensed the whole of the dwelling-house and who does not share occupation with the tenant.[54]

The further requirement for the second limb is that the tenant has not taken such steps as he ought reasonably to have taken for the removal of the lodger or sub-tenant.[55] Where a lodger[56] caused the deterioration in the furniture, *semble* there is no reason why the lodger cannot be evicted forthwith, or at least after a period of notice, for he will be an excluded licensee[57] without the benefit of the provisions of the Protection from Eviction Act 1977 against eviction without due process of law and requiring the service of notice to quit of at least four weeks' duration.[58] Where the sub-tenant is an assured tenant, the reasonable steps will doubtless be the service of a possession notice and, so far as reasonable, the commencement and pursuit of possession proceedings. Subject to those cases, what steps are reasonable will be a question of mixed fact and law depending on the exact circumstances of the case. The reasonable steps must be directed to the removal of the lodger or sub-tenant, however, and not just to the remedying of the deterioration.[59] **15–38**

Sect. 9. Former Service Tenant: Ground 16

Ground 16 is that ''The dwelling-house was let to the tenant in consequence of his employment by the landlord seeking possession or a previous landlord under the tenancy and the tenant has ceased to be in that employment''.[60] This corre- **15–39**

[54] And ''the tenant has not taken'' now replaces ''where the court is satisfied that the tenant has not, before the making of the order in question, taken''; but plainly this has not affected the meaning.

[55] Act of 1988, Sched. 2, Pt. II, Ground 15.

[56] ''Lodger'' is not defined in the Act, but the meaning must be assumed to be that expounded in the speech of Lord Templeman in *Street v. Mountford* [1985] A.C. 809, in contradistinction to ''tenant''.

[57] Within the meaning and by virtue of Protection from Eviction Act 1977, s.3A(2), (3).

[58] *ibid.*, ss.3, 5. The tenant must not, however, use violence or threats of violence against any person in the premises who is opposed to the entry: Criminal Law Act 1977, s.6(1).

[59] Though if the lodger or sub-tenant does effectually remedy the deterioration in response to a possession notice, it might not be reasonable to take the further step of issuing possession proceedings against him.

[60] Act of 1988, Sched. 2, Pt. II, Ground 16.

sponds to one of the two main conditions of Case 8 under the Act of 1977.[61] The other condition, the landlord's reasonable requirement of possession for another employee, has not been included in the Act of 1988: it suffices that the employment has ended.[61a] To this extent, the authorities on Case 8 under the Act of 1977[62] appear to apply to Ground 16. So, provided the employment was *in fact* the motive which actuated the landlord to grant the tenancy, the tenant's knowledge of that, or that the tenancy might be brought to an end with the employment, and whether or not the tenancy was so determinable, appear to be irrelevant.[63] And it would not matter that the landlord claiming possession bought the property from the employer subject to the tenancy, provided that the tenant has ceased to be an employee of that employer. But Ground 16 does not apply to assured agricultural occupiers.[64]

For the purposes of this ground, at a time when the landlord is or was the Secretary of State for Health, employment by a health service body[65] is regarded as employment by the Secretary of State.[66]

Sect. 10. Grant of Tenancy Induced by False Statement: Ground 17

15–40 For secure tenancies it has always been a discretionary ground for possession that the tenant induced the grant of the tenancy by making a false statement.[67] With effect from February 28, 1997, there is now a similar discretionary ground for possession from assured tenants.[68] The ground is not available if a possession notice was served before that date, or, where the service of such a notice has been dispensed with by the court, if the possession proceedings were commenced before that date.[69] But subject to that it applies to assured tenancies, whenever granted. The ground has three requirements.

[61] Act of 1977, Sched. 15, Case 8.

[61a] Even, perhaps, if the tenant was unfairly dismissed: *Whitbread West Pennines Ltd. v. Reedy* (1988) 20 H.L.R. 642, CA.

[62] Vol. 1, pp. 419–422.

[63] Of course, if the "tenant" were a service occupier, because either his agreement with his employer expressly required him to live in the dwelling and so living materially assisted him in the performance of his duties or, although the agreement was silent on the point, it was necessary for him to live there in order to perform his duties (see Vol. 1, pp. 76–80 and annotation thereto in the Supplement), he would not be a tenant and therefore could not be an assured tenant.

[64] Act of 1988, s.25(2); *ante*, para. 9–21.

[65] As defined in National Health Service and Community Care Act 1990, s.60(7). A full list is set out in Supplement, annotation to Vol. 1, pp. 145, 146.

[66] Act of 1988, Sched. 2, Pt. II, Ground 16, as amended by National Health Service and Community Care Act 1990, s.60(2)(b), Sched. 8, para. 10. Note that in some circumstances a tenancy held of the Secretary of State for Health cannot be an assured tenancy: *ante*, paras. 4–38 *et seq*.

[67] Housing Act 1985, Sched. 2, Ground 5 (now extended on amendment by Housing Act 1996, ss.146, 232(3); S.I. 1997 No. 66).

[68] Act of 1988, Sched. 2, Pt. II, Ground 17, inserted by Housing Act 1996, ss.102, 232(3), (4); S.I. 1997 No. 225.

[69] S.I. 1997 No. 225, *supra*, Sched., para. 1. Presumably this transitional provision implicitly provides that the new ground does not apply in a case where a possession notice was served before February 28, 1997 and possession proceedings are being prosecuted *pursuant to it*; the new ground cannot have been intended to be disapplied to a tenancy forever merely because a possession notice was served before that date.

1. Original tenant

The ground is only available where "The tenant is the person, or one of the persons, to whom the tenancy was granted". So, if the tenancy has been assigned, the ground is not available against the assignee. Where the tenant is currently two or more persons, all of them must have been original grantees,[70] and so if the two original tenants assign the tenancy to themselves and another, the ground is not available. But it does not matter that another or others were joint grantees of the tenancy but are no longer tenants.[71] 15–41

2. False statement

A false statement must have been "made knowingly or recklessly by— 15–42

(a) the tenant, or
(b) a person acting at the tenant's instigation".

Once again, "the tenant" must include all joint tenants,[72] and so if the false statement was made by only one of the tenants, *semble* the ground cannot apply. *Aliter* if the court adjudges that the false statement was made by one of the joint tenants with the authority of the others, for then in law it will have been made by all of them. Where (b) applies, it is unclear if the tenant must have instigated the person to make the false statement, or whether it suffices if an agent instructed only to acquire a tenancy of a dwelling makes the false statement without any authority or approval from the tenant;[73] but the former seems to have been intended. If so, then once again all joint tenants must have "instigated" the making of the false statement. Knowledge or recklessness will include turning a blind eye to the truth, and making a statement without any honest belief in its truth or not caring whether it is true or not,[74] but probably not constructive notice. Any false statement will suffice,[75] subject to the next requirement and to consideration of reasonableness; but where the ground is established, the Court of Appeal will be slow to interfere with the trial judge's decision that it is reasonable to make an order for possession.[76]

[70] Act of 1988, s.45(3).
[71] As where three joint tenants assign the tenancy to two of their number. An assignment of a tenancy must be by deed, even if it is a short tenancy within Law of Property Act 1925, s.54(2) which was created by parol: *Crago v. Julian* [1992] 1 W.L.R. 372, CA.
[72] n. 70, *supra*.
[73] The words in question were only inserted in the equivalent ground under Housing Act 1985 with effect from February 12, 1997, and so there is no secure tenancy authority to assist here.
[74] See *Rous v. Mitchell* [1991] 1 W.L.R. 469, CA (reckless service of notice to quit under Agricultural Holdings Act 1986).
[75] No implied statement is made by an applicant for a tenancy that he is entitled lawfully to remain in the United Kingdom: *Akinbolu v. Hackney L.B.C.* [1996] *The Times*, May 13, CA.
[76] *Rushcliffe B.C. v. Watson* (1991) 24 H.L.R. 124, CA (a decision on the unamended Ground 5 in Housing Act 1985).

3. Induced grant of tenancy

15–43 The last requirement is that "the landlord was induced to grant the tenancy by [the] false statement". Where there are two or more joint landlords, they must all have been so induced.[77] As with the law of actionable misrepresentation, where it is not necessary to show more than that the misrepresentation was one of the matters that induced the representee to enter into the contract,[78] it is not necessary to show that the false statement was the only factor that induced the landlord to grant the tenancy provided that it was one of the factors.

3. ADJOURNMENT, STAY AND SUSPENSION

15–44 As under the Rent Acts, in claims for possession on any of the discretionary grounds, the court has been given wide powers of adjourning the proceedings, staying or suspending execution of an order for possession, and postponing the date for possession.[79] Apart from minor differences in grammar or arrangement, these provisions are in terms that are virtually identical with the corresponding provisions under the Act of 1977.[80] They are considered more fully in Chapter 12 above.[81]

[77] Act of 1988, s.45(3).
[78] See *Chitty on Contract* (27th ed.), para. 6–021.
[79] Act of 1988, s.9.
[80] Compare Act of 1977, s.100 (as amended) with Act of 1988, s.9. Subs. (1)–(4) in the two sections correspond almost exactly; Act of 1977, subs. (4A), (4B) have become subs. (5)(a), (b); subs. (5) is matched by the corresponding terms of subs. (6).
[81] paras. 13–49 *et seq.*

Chapter 16

Protection from Eviction

An assured tenancy, like a protected tenancy under the Rent Acts, is a contractual tenancy which, until its termination, carries with it the protection of contractual entitlement to possession of the dwelling. An assured tenant is therefore entitled to restrain any attempt by his landlord to evict him on the ground that so to do would be a breach of the covenant for quiet enjoyment and a trespass. He has the further protection that the landlord's attempt to evict him would be a criminal offence of unlawful eviction or harassment.[1] The protection from eviction afforded an assured tenant is not in principle different from that of the protected tenant, in that unless his tenancy is determined by an order of the court or by a surrender or some other act on the part of the tenant, there is a continuing entitlement to remain in possession.[2] Thus, the general principles of protection from eviction discussed in Volume 1[3] are equally applicable in the case of assured tenancies. **16–01**

However, the Act of 1988 has made a number of amendments to the Protection from Eviction Act 1977,[4] for the most part extending its provisions, but also limiting and otherwise changing it in a few respects. The most important of these amendments are of general application and are not limited to assured tenancies, but they are discussed here because they originate in the Act of 1988. They can be summarised under five main headings. **16–02**

(i) CRIMINAL HARASSMENT. The Act of 1988 created a further offence of harassment. It is closely related to the original offence of harassment under the Protection from Eviction Act 1977,[5] but is less stringent in some of its requirements.

[1] Under Protection from Eviction Act 1977, s.1(2), (3). See Vol. 1, pp. 381–383 and Supplement.

[2] Act of 1988, s.5(1), (2). In the case of an assured tenancy, the right is attributable to a new periodic contractual tenancy coming into existence by virtue of the Act; in the case of a statutory tenancy, it is attributable to the status of statutory tenant: see Vol. 1, Chap. 11, Sect. 2. In neither case does the tenant need the statutory protection afforded by Protection from Eviction Act 1977, s.3(1).

[3] pp. 380–387, as updated by the Supplement.

[4] For the origins, see Act of 1957, s.16; Protection from Eviction Act 1964; Act of 1965, Pt. III.

[5] Protection from Eviction Act 1977, s.1(3).

(ii) CRIMINAL EVICTION. The offences of criminal eviction and attempted criminal eviction[6] have been left unamended.

(iii) DAMAGES FOR UNLAWFUL EVICTION. A new statutory cause of action has been created, giving an unlawfully evicted residential occupier a right to damages calculated by reference to the increase in value of the landlord's interest in the property resulting from the removal of the residential occupier.

(iv) EVICTION WITHOUT AN ORDER OF THE COURT. The prohibition against evicting a residential tenant without an order of the court has been extended from tenancies to licences. But certain tenancies and licences, known as ''excluded'' tenancies and licences, are now outside the prohibition.

(v) NOTICES TO QUIT. The statutory requirement for four weeks' notice to quit in writing, containing the prescribed information, has been extended from dwellings let on tenancies to dwellings occupied under periodic licences. But ''excluded'' tenancies and licences are now outside the requirement.

A further criminal offence of harassment was created by the Protection from Harassment Act 1997.[7] This Act also created a further statutory tort of actual or threatened harassment.[8]

The five headings above and the new criminal offence and statutory tort of harassment will be considered in turn.

Sect. 1. Criminal Harassment

16–03 Under the Protection from Eviction Act 1977,[9] there is the criminal offence usually known as ''harassment''.[10] This is considered in Volume 1,[11] and it remains in force subject to a small but important amendment made by the Act of 1988.[12] The Act of 1988 created a further offence, also known as ''harassment'', which is substantially the same offence, though with a rather wider definition. For the sake of brevity and clarity, the two offences will be called the ''1977 offence'' and the ''1988 offence''.

[6] Protection from Eviction Act 1977, s.1(2).

[7] 1997 c.40. The relevant sections came into effect on June 16, 1997: *ibid.*, s.15(1); S.I. 1997 No. 1418; see *post*, p. 333.

[8] Protection from Harassment Act 1997, s.3(1), (2). These provisions also came into force on June 16, 1997: *ibid.*, s.15(2); S.I. 1997 No. 1498; *post*, p. 334.

[9] Section 1(3), replacing Act of 1965, s.30(2).

[10] See the marginal notes to Act of 1965, s.30 and Protection from Eviction Act 1977, s.1.

[11] pp. 382, 383, and Supplement. The offence is in Protection from Eviction Act 1977, s.1(3), printed *post*, Appendix 2, p. 474.

[12] See *infra*.

1. The 1977 offence

The 1977 offence remains unchanged[13] except for one word. For acts done after January 15, 1989, the phrase "calculated to interfere" now reads "likely to interfere".[14] "Calculated" is sometimes taken to mean "intended", although more usually it is held merely to mean "likely".[15] It is now clear that, at least as far as acts done on or after January 15, 1989 are concerned, the 1977 offence does not require the prosecution to prove that the person actually intended his acts to have the specified effect if, objectively, they were likely to have that effect. **16–04**

A person may be convicted of the 1977 offence of harassment even though his act or acts did not amount to a tort or breach of contract.[16]

2. The 1988 offence

The Act of 1988 created the 1988 offence by inserting new subsections into the Act creating the 1977 offence.[17] The penalties for each offence are the same.[18] Like the 1977 offence, the 1988 offence consists of doing certain acts with a particular state of mind; but unlike the 1977 offence, only the landlord of a residential occupier or the landlord's agent can be guilty of the offence. These aspects will be considered in turn. **16–05**

(a) Landlord or landlord's agent

"Landlord" here, in relation to a residential occupier of any premises, means the person who would be entitled to occupation of the premises in question but for either— **16–06**

"(a) the residential occupier's right to remain in occupation of the premises, or

(b) a restriction on the person's right to recover possession of the premises".

It also means any superior landlord under whom the landlord derives title.[19] This

[13] See Vol. 1, pp. 382, 383 and Supplement.

[14] Act of 1988, ss.29(1), 141(3), amending Protection from Eviction Act 1977, s.1(3).

[15] See, *e.g., Turner v. Shearer* [1972] 1 W.L.R. 1387, DC.

[16] *R. v. Burke* [1991] 1 A.C. 135 (landlord disconnected doorbell and padlocked lavatory, neither of which tenant had contractual right to use).

[17] Act of 1988, s.29(2), inserting subsections (3A), (3B) and (3C) in Protection from Eviction Act 1977, s.1.

[18] On summary conviction: a fine not exceeding the prescribed sum (at present £2,000) or not more than six months' imprisonment, or both; on conviction on indictment: a fine or not more than two years' imprisonment, or both: Protection from Eviction Act 1977, s.1(4), as amended by Magistrates' Courts Act 1980, ss.32(2), (9), 143; S.I. 1984 No. 477, art. 2(1). If a body corporate is guilty of an offence under the Protection from Eviction Act 1977, its officers may also be guilty: *ibid.*, s.1(6).

[19] Protection from Eviction Act 1977, s.1(3C), inserted by Act of 1988, s.29(2).

does not mean that any such superior landlord is automatically guilty of an offence if the immediate landlord is, but that the superior landlord may be guilty of the offence in his own right if he does the prescribed acts with the necessary state of mind.[20] "Residential occupier" means "a person occupying the premises as a residence, whether under a contract or by virtue of any enactment or rule of law giving him the right to remain in occupation or restricting the right of any other person to recover possession of the premises".[21] It is thus clear that "landlord" for the purposes of the 1988 offence can include a licensor and a person whose right to possession of the premises is delayed only by the requirement to recover possession by due process of law. An agent of the immediate "landlord" or of any superior landlord can be guilty of the offence in his own right if he does the acts in question.

(b) Acts

16–07 The *actus reus* of the 1988 offence has two limbs, namely if the "landlord" or his agent—

(a) "does acts likely to interfere with the peace or comfort of the residential occupier or members of his household", or
(b) "persistently withdraws or withholds services reasonably required for the occupation of the premises in question as a residence".[22]

With one exception, this provision is identical to the original corresponding provision for the 1977 offence.[23] The difference is that the phrase "likely to interfere" has replaced the original words "calculated to interfere" in the 1977 offence; and indeed the same change has been made in the wording of the 1977 offence itself, but only in respect of acts done on or after January 15, 1989.[24] Clearly, the word "acts" in the offence of 1988 is likely to be construed in the same way as the same word in the 1977 offence, and therefore the acts in question need not themselves be tortious or a breach of contract.[25]

(c) Knowledge

16–08 For the 1988 offence, the requisite *mens rea* is that in either limb (a) or limb (b) above the landlord or his agent "knows, or has reasonable cause to believe, that that conduct is likely to cause the residential occupier"—

[20] See, by analogy, *Jones v. Miah* [1992] 2 E.G.L.R. 50 at 52K, a decision on the true construction of similar wording of Act of 1988, s.27(9)(c).
[21] Protection from Eviction Act 1977, s.1(1); and see Vol. 1, p. 381 for "premises".
[22] *ibid.*, s.1(3A), inserted by Act of 1988, s.29(2).
[23] *ibid.*, s.1(3).
[24] Act of 1988, s.29(1); see *supra*.
[25] See *ante*, n.16.

(i) "to give up the occupation of the whole or part of the premises", or
(ii) "to refrain from exercising any right or pursuing any remedy in respect of the whole or part of the premises".[26]

The words "knows, or has reasonable cause to believe, that that conduct is likely to cause" have replaced the words "with intent to cause" that appeared, and still appear, in the 1977 offence;[27] and this specific intent[28] could be much more difficult to prove than the knowledge now required for the 1988 offence. On the other hand, unlike the 1988 offence, there is[29] no defence of "reasonable grounds" available where the specific intent is proved for the 1977 offence. In these respects the Act of 1988 has left the 1977 offence unchanged; but in all other respects the wording of this part of the 1977 and 1988 offences is identical.

(d) Defence

A person is not guilty of the 1988 offence if he proves that he had "reasonable grounds for doing the acts or withdrawing or withholding the services in question".[30] The statute appears to contain nothing to suggest that the standard of proof for this defence is higher than a balance of probabilities.[31] It seems perfectly possible in principle for a defence of reasonable grounds to succeed even where the landlord or his agent had the requisite knowledge for the offence, though such cases might prove to be rare in practice. **16–09**

Sect. 2. Criminal Eviction

The offence of criminal eviction, or attempted criminal eviction, of a residential occupier of premises, under the Protection from Eviction Act 1977,[32] remains in force, unchanged by the Act of 1988. The offence is committed if any person unlawfully deprives the residential occupier of any premises of his occupation of those premises or of any part of them, or attempts to do so, unless that person proves that he believed, and had reasonable cause to believe, that the residential occupier had ceased to reside in them.[33] **16–10**

[26] Protection from Eviction Act 1977, s.1(3A), added by Act of 1988, s.29(2).
[27] *ibid.*, s.1(3).
[28] See *McCall v. Abelesz* [1976] Q.B. 585 at 597, CA.
[29] Necessarily, in view of the specific intent which has to be proved.
[30] Protection from Eviction Act 1977, s.1(3B), added by Act of 1988, s.29(2).
[31] See *R. v. Dunbar* [1958] 1 Q.B. 1, CA.
[32] Protection from Eviction Act 1977, s.1(2).
[33] *ibid.* See Vol. 1, pp. 381, 382. For "residential occupier", see *ante*, para. 16–06. For the requisite standard of proof, see *supra*.

Sect. 3. Damages for Unlawful Eviction

16–11 Neither the original criminal offences of unlawful eviction and harassment, nor the new 1988 offence of harassment, give the residential occupier any civil right of action *per se*.[34] Neither do they prejudice any liability or remedy to which a person guilty of such an offence may be subject in civil proceedings.[35] Thus, where the residential occupier is a tenant, the landlord will *prima facie* be liable for breach of his covenant for quiet enjoyment and for trespass.[36] But where the tenancy has terminated and the occupier's only protection is the prohibition on eviction without due process of law,[37] the occupier may obtain an injunction restraining the eviction or harassment or requiring his reinstatement in the premises as the case might be,[38] but no claim in damages will lie.[39]

The Act of 1988 has remedied this lacuna by creating a new cause of action for damages based on the offences of unlawful eviction and harassment,[40] and has done so in such a way as to attempt to provide a serious deterrent to landlords minded to resort to self-help to obtain vacant possession of premises.[41] In effect, there is now a statutory tort of unlawful eviction.[42]

1. Application

16–12 The right of action arises ''if, at any time after June 9, 1988, a landlord (in this section referred to as ''the landlord in default'') or any person acting on behalf of the landlord in default'' does certain acts and certain consequences ensue.[43] June 9, 1988 was the first day of the Report Stage of the Housing Bill in the House of Commons, when many amendments were made to these provisions of the Bill.[44] Royal Assent for the Bill, as amended, was not given until November 15, 1988, and the Act of 1988 came into force on January 15, 1989. To that extent, therefore, the new statutory tort had limited retrospective effect. This was not, however, contrary to Article 7 of the European Convention for the Protection of Human Rights and Fundamental Freedoms of November 4, 1950 because, first, the remedy given is civil and not criminal, and secondly and in

[34] *McCall v. Abelesz* [1976] Q.B. 585, CA.
[35] Protection from Eviction Act 1977, s.1(5).
[36] See Vol. 1, pp. 383–386, and Supplement.
[37] Protection from Eviction Act 1977, s.3(1).
[38] *Luganda v. Service Hotels Ltd.* [1969] 2 Ch. 209, CA.
[39] *McCall v. Abelesz, supra.*
[40] Act of 1988, s.27.
[41] For reasons explained under ''The measure of damages'', *post*, para. 16–28, it is doubtful whether the new civil remedy provides an effective deterrent for those cases which previously fell through the net of liability in damages.
[42] A further statutort tort of harassment was created on June 16, 1997 by Protection from Harassment Act 1997: see *post*, para. 16–59.
[43] Act of 1988, s.27(1), (2). The necessary acts and consequences are addressed *infra*.
[44] (1988) 134 Hansard (H.C.) col. 993.

any event, the Convention has[45] no direct application to domestic law, its terms never having been embodied in any U.K. statute.[46]

In relation to a residential occupier, ''landlord'' means ''the person who, but for the occupier's right to occupy, would be entitled to occupation of the premises and any superior landlord under whom that person derives title''.[47] ''Residential occupier'', in relation to any premises, means ''a person occupying the premises as a residence, whether under a contract or by virtue of any enactment or rule of law giving him the right to remain in occupation or restricting the right of any other person to recover possession of the premises''.[48] ''The right to occupy'', in relation to a residential occupier, ''includes any restriction on the right of another person to recover possession of the premises in question''. The combined effect of these cumbersome definitions is to make clear that the necessary nexus between the occupier and the owner of premises exists, for the purposes of the right of action, provided at least that the occupier is in residence and is not yet entitled to be removed because due process of law has not yet been satisfied. We shall see[49] that this means that all licensees as well as tenants are residential occupiers for the purposes of the statutory tort unless they are ''excluded'' licensees or tenants. Similarly, a statutory tenant against whom an order for possession has been made but not yet lawfully executed is a ''residential occupier'' with a ''right to occupy''.[50] **16–13**

The definition of ''landlord'' does not without more make a superior landlord liable for the wrongs of the tortfeasor, but merely provides for statutory liability where such a person, although not himself entitled to occupation subject only to the residential occupier's right to occupy, commits the specified acts and the requisite consequences ensue.[51] But a person who is (subject to the residential occupier's rights) entitled to *occupation* as distinct from *possession* of the premises falls within the definition. Accordingly, a purchaser of the immediate landlord's reversionary interest, let into occupation by the vendor pending completion as a licensee pursuant to condition 8(1) of the National Conditions of Sale (20th edition), was held liable in damages.[52] But where there is no such contract of sale, and an intending purchaser has not been given a licence to occupy, that purchaser is not a ''landlord'' and cannot be liable for the statutory tort.[53] **16–14**

[45] At the date of writing, though it is imminently expected to become adopted as part of the domestic law of England and Wales.

[46] *Jones v. Miah* [1992] 2 E.G.L.R. 50, CA.

[47] Act of 1988, s.27(9)(c).

[48] *ibid.*, s.27(9)(a), applying Protection from Eviction Act 1977, s.1(1); see Vol. 1, p. 381.

[49] *Post*, Sect. 4, paras. 16–37 *et seq.*

[50] *Haniff v. Robinson* [1993] Q.B. 419, CA, holding that the words ''otherwise than by proceedings in the court'' in Protection from Eviction Act 1977, s.3(1) include the process of execution of a warrant of possession by a court bailiff.

[51] *Jones v. Miah* [1992] 2 E.G.L.R. 50, CA.

[52] *ibid.*

[53] *Francis v. Brown* (1997) 30 H.L.R. 143, CA.

16–15 Where damages for the statutory tort are claimed, the residential occupier is not also entitled to claim that his tenancy or licence continues, even though the eviction could not lawfully have terminated it.[54] The residential occupier has to elect at trial which remedy to pursue, and is not bound to do so before then.[55]

2. The acts and consequences

16–16 The cause of action arises if the landlord or person acting on his behalf does any of the following acts and, in the cases of paragraphs (2) and (3), the specified consequences ensue. The acts are—

(1) he unlawfully deprives the residential occupier of any premises of his occupation of the whole or any part of the premises;[56]
(2) he attempts unlawfully to deprive the residential occupier of any premises of his occupation of the whole or any part thereof;[57]
(3) knowing or having reasonable cause to believe that the conduct is likely to cause the residential occupier of any premises—

(i) to give up his occupation of the premises of any part thereof, or
(ii) to refrain from exercising any right or pursuing any remedy in respect of the premises of any part thereof,

he—

(a) does acts likely to interfere with the peace or comfort of the residential occupier or members of his household, or
(b) persistently withdraws or withholds services reasonably required for the occupation of the premises as a residence[58]

The specified consequences which must ensue in the cases of paragraphs (2) and (3) above are that, as a result of the conduct, the residential occupier gives up his occupation of the premises as a residence.[59]

16–17 The language of the statutory provisions is, in its essentials, identical with the language used in the Protection from Eviction Act 1977 in defining the offence of unlawful eviction and the 1988 offence of harassment.[60] In the case of paragraph (1), the right of action accrues[61] where the landlord or his agent evicts the occupier from the whole *or any part* of the premises occupied as a residence. In the cases of paragraphs (2) and (3), however, the attempted eviction and the conduct do not themselves evict the occupier, and for the statutory right of

[54] *Wandsworth L.B.C. v. Osei-Bonsu* [1999] 11 E.G. 167, CA.
[55] *ibid.*
[56] Act of 1988, s.27(1).
[57] *ibid.*, s.27(2)(a).
[58] *ibid.*, s.27(2)(b).
[59] *ibid.*, s.27(2).
[60] *Ante*, paras. 16–07, 16–08.
[61] Assuming, as must invariably be the case given the nature of the complaint, that some loss has been suffered: the cause of action is in tort: Act of 1988, s.27(4)(a).

action to accrue[62] it is necessary that the occupier give up his occupation of the premises as a residence as a result of the attempt or the conduct.[63] The language of the Act does indicate that occupation of the whole of the premises must have been given up in these cases before the right of action accrues.[64] At all events, if the occupier shows unusual fortitude and remains in the premises despite the conduct of the landlord or his agent, no cause of action arises unless the landlord or his agent does physically evict the occupier from at least part of the premises.

3. The right of action

Where the necessary acts on the part of the landlord or his agent are established and any necessary consequences have ensued,[65] the landlord in default is liable to pay damages to the former residential occupier in respect of the loss of his right to occupy the premises in question as his residence.[66] Even where the eviction was carried out by, or the conduct was that of, the agent of the landlord, only the landlord in default and not the agent is liable for the statutory measure of damages.[67] This is because the measure of damages, based on the increased value of the landlord's interest in the property attributable to vacant possession of the former residential occupier's residence,[68] is uniquely appropriate to the property-owning landlord himself. But *semble* if a landlord and a superior landlord conspire together to evict an occupier and the landlord does so as agent of the superior landlord, the landlord will be liable in his own capacity too. **16–18**

The liability in damages under the Act of 1988 is in addition to any liability arising apart from it, whether in tort, contract or otherwise.[69] So claims for damages for breach of a covenant for quiet enjoyment or for damages for trespass or for injunctive relief are unaffected by the new statutory remedy. Nothing in section 27 of the Act of 1988 affects the right of a residential occupier to enforce any right which arises apart from the section in respect of his loss of the right to occupy premises as his residence.[70] But damages cannot be awarded both in respect of a liability arising under the section and in respect of a liability

[62] See *supra*.
[63] Nice questions of causation may arise where the occupier gives up occupation a few weeks or so after acts or conduct on the part of the landlord: see, for example, *Murray v. Aslam* [1994] E.G.C.S. 160 (tenant evicted for two hours only and then resumed occupation, and left for home in Ireland a few weeks later: at least doubtful whether Act of 1988, s.27 applied). *Sed quaere* on the facts: if the occupier was in fact evicted then, subject to the defence of reinstatement (*post*, para. 16–23), the right of action accrued under paragraph (1) and the cause of the ultimate removal is irrelevant. The case is not adequately reported, and appears to be a decision on a procedural issue relating to a charging order.
[64] In Act of 1988, s.27(1), (2)(a) and (2)(b), express reference is made to the whole *or part* of the premises, but in the relevant part of section 27(2) the wording is ''gives up his occupation of the premises''. *Semble* an attempt to evict the occupier from the premises which results in the occupier giving up part only of the premises will not give him a right of action under the Act of 1988.
[65] See *supra*.
[66] Act of 1988, s.27(3).
[67] *Sampson v. Wilson* [1996] Ch. 39, CA, rejecting the earlier *obiter dicta* of Dillon and Leggatt L.JJ. in *Jones v. Miah* [1992] 2 E.G.L.R. 50, CA. See also *Francis v. Brown*, *supra*.
[68] See *post*, paras. 16–28 *et seq*.
[69] Act of 1988, s.27(4)(b).
[70] *ibid*., s.27(5).

arising elsewhere in respect of the same loss.[71] These provisions have given rise to some difficulty where a residential occupier has claimed damages, including aggravated and exemplary damages, for an eviction, with a claim to the new statutory damages in addition or in the alternative.

16–19 The starting point for analysis is that statutory damages are payable by the landlord in default in respect of the occupier's loss of the right to occupy the premises in question as his residence.[72] That provision naturally means the loss of the right to occupy during such future time as the occupier would otherwise have been entitled lawfully to occupy the premises, and that is appropriate because the measure of the damages is in effect the benefit to the landlord of his being able to occupy the premises during that period. One would not have expected, therefore, that the courts would see an overlap between general damages awarded for the injury, upset and anxiety caused by the eviction itself and any aggravated damages awarded to reflect the injury to dignity and pride caused by the nature of the eviction on the one hand,[73] and the statutory damages for loss of future occupation on the other.[74] Of course, general damages for breach of contract or trespass may be awarded to compensate for a period of time following the eviction during which the former occupier suffered loss through being homeless; in such a case there is potential for an overlap with the statutory damages for loss of the right to occupy the premises.

16–20 A series of decisions of the Court of Appeal made after the Act of 1988 came into force established a different and, it is submitted, less satisfactory distinction:[75] general damages for unlawful eviction[76] and aggravated damages had all to be "set off" against the statutory measure of damages,[77] but damages for breach of the covenant of quiet enjoyment did not.[78] Happily, a measure of certainty has been brought by the most recent decision of the Court of Appeal to consider the question.[79] A landlord, who intended to sell a house to her daughter, evicted the tenant of one of the flats in the house with the assistance of the daughter. The daughter, not being entitled to occupy the flat at the time of the eviction, could not herself be liable for the statutory measure of damages.[80] The landlord was liable for the statutory measure, and the question arose whether the daughter could be liable for exemplary damages at common law. The court

[71] Act of 1988, s.27(5).
[72] *ibid.*, s.27(3).
[73] As to which, see Vol. 1, pp. 383–385 and Supplement.
[74] The first edition of Vol. 3 (1989), at p. 179, expressed the view that "damages for any breach of contract, trespass, assault or other wrongs inflicted in the eviction" were distinct from the statutory measure of damages.
[75] Less satisfactory because (a) there is no clear logical basis for the distinction; (b) there are other cases where the court proceeded, apparently without hearing full argument on the point, on a different basis (*Jones v. Miah*, *supra*, at pp. 55J, 56B–C, E–F, H, as to which see *Mason v. Nwokorie*, *supra*, at p. 62H–J, and *King v. Jackson* [1998] 1 E.G.L.R. 30, CA); and (c) the use of the terminology "set off" seems wholly inapposite and liable to mislead: the point is that damages must not be awarded twice, not that anything needs to be deducted from the statutory measure of damages.
[76] As distinct from special damages.
[77] *Mason v. Nwokorie* [1994] 1 E.G.L.R. 59, CA.
[78] *Kaur v. Gill* [1995] *The Times*, June 15, CA.
[79] *Francis v. Brown* (1997) 30 H.L.R. 143, CA.
[80] See *ante*, para. 16–14.

held that the landlord herself could not be liable for exemplary damages in addition to the statutory measure of damages;[81] and therefore no exemplary damages could be awarded against the daughter, because the award of such damages against joint tortfeasors cannot exceed the lowest sum for which any of them can be held liable.[82] In addition, the court appears to have decided[83] that aggravated damages can be awarded in addition to the statutory measure of damages.[84] This decision seems clearly correct in principle. There is an obvious duplication of statutory and exemplary damages, but an award of aggravated damages is made to compensate the plaintiff for the particularly upsetting circumstances of his eviction,[85] and there is no overlap between that injury and the loss of the right after the eviction to occupy premises. Where there is an overlap between the statutory measure and common law damages, there is no need for the former residential occupier to "elect" which to pursue at any time prior to judgment,[86] although a claim to either or both of exemplary damages and statutory damages should be specifically pleaded.

4. Defences

The Act of 1988 creates three specific defences to an action for statutory damages, where the tort would otherwise be made out. **16–21**

(a) Reasonable belief

It is a defence to an action for statutory damages for the defendant "to prove that he believed, and had reasonable cause to believe" either of two matters.[87] These are— **16–22**

(1) "that the residential occupier had ceased to reside in the premises in question at the time when he was deprived of occupation" within paragraph (1) above,[88] "or, as the case may be, when the attempt was made or the acts were done as a result of which he gave up his occupation of those premises",[89] or
(2) "that where the liability would otherwise arise by virtue only of doing of acts or the withdrawal or withholding of services, he had reasonable grounds for doing the acts or withdrawing or withholding the services in question".[90]

[81] *Francis v. Brown, supra*, at p. 150.
[82] Applying the decision in *Broome v. Cassell & Co.* [1972] A.C. 1027.
[83] Only Sir Iain Glidewell addressed the point expressly in his judgment, but Peter Gibson and Simon Brown L.JJ. agreed on the amount of the judgment against the daughter, which included £1,000 for aggravated damages.
[84] Thereby distinguishing its earlier decision in *Mason v. Nwokerie, supra.*
[85] *e.g.*, if all his belongings are thrown out onto the street.
[86] *per* Hollis J. in *Mason v. Nwokorie, supra*, at 62M.
[87] Act of 1988, s.27(8).
[88] *Ante*, para. 16–16.
[89] Act of 1988, s.27(8)(a).
[90] *ibid.*, s.27(8)(b).

Thus, under paragraph (1) the critical time at which the reasonable belief must be proved to have been held is the time of the unlawful eviction, attempted unlawful eviction, or acts or omissions as a result of which the occupier removes from the premises,[91] as the case might be. Similarly, under paragraph (2), the critical time at which the reasonable belief in the existence of the reasonable grounds must be proved is the time of the doing of the acts or of the withholding or withdrawal of the services, as the case might be. In both cases, the belief must be objectively reasonable ("had reasonable cause to believe"), and not merely one which the landlord did in fact honestly have. Because the only defendant to an action for statutory damages is the landlord himself,[92] whether immediate or superior, the belief and knowledge in question has to be that of the landlord himself and not of his agent. A landlord who genuinely but mistakenly believed that, as a matter of civil law, he was entitled to take possession of a dwelling-house which was not being occupied at the time, was held not to have had reasonable cause so to believe because, first, the mistaken belief was not a reasonable mistake to have made and, secondly, the tenant was asserting his entitlement to reside there and the landlord did not start proceedings to resolve the dispute.[93] Nevertheless, in principle a mistake of the general law, as opposed to private right, can avail a defendant for the purposes of this statutory defence.[94]

(b) Reinstatement

16–23 It is a defence to show that the former residential occupier has been reinstated in the premises in time. For these purposes, "former residential occupier", in relation to any premises, means the person who was the residential occupier until he was deprived of his occupation[95] or gave up his occupation[96] of those premises in circumstances giving rise to *prima facie* liability in damages for the statutory tort.[97] This defence can arise in two different but related sets of circumstances.

16–24 First, no liability in damages for the statutory tort will arise if, before proceedings to enforce the liability are finally disposed of, the former residential occupier is reinstated in the premises in such circumstances that he becomes again the residential occupier of them.[98] For this purpose, proceedings to enforce the liability are "finally disposed of" on the earliest date by which the proceedings (including any proceedings on or in consequence of an appeal) have been determined and any time for appealing or further appealing has expired; except that if any appeal is abandoned, the proceedings are taken to be disposed of on the

[91] *i.e.* the three limbs of the cause of action, set out *ante*, p. 310.
[92] *Sampson v. Wilson* [1996] Ch. 39, CA; see *ante*, n.67.
[93] *Wandsworth L.B.C. v. Osei-Bonsu* [1999] 11 E.G. 167, CA.
[94] *ibid.*, doubting dicta to the contrary effect in *West Wiltshire D.C. v. Snelgrove* (1997) 30 H.L.R. 57 at 63, CA.
[95] Because the tort in Act of 1988, s.27(1) was committed.
[96] As a result of an attempt to evict him or of acts or conduct falling within Act of 1988, s.27(2).
[97] Act of 1988, s.27(9)(d).
[98] *ibid.*, s.27(6)(a).

date of the abandonment.[99] Thus, proceedings in the county court will not be finally disposed of for these purposes until 28 days after the court pronounces judgment[1] in the proceedings in any event, and for so long thereafter as any appeal to the Court of Appeal is pending. Difficult questions can arise where, for example, an appeal is made out of time against an order of the district judge striking out the proceedings, or an application is made to the Court of Appeal for an extension of time for service a notice of appeal.[2]

A landlord against whom an award of damages has been made may thus escape having to pay them if he offers to reinstate the former residential occupier and his offer is accepted and carried out in time. But if the occupier refuses reinstatement, however unreasonably,[3] this defence cannot succeed. For it to succeed, the circumstances of the reinstatement must be such that the occupier becomes again the residential occupier[4] of the premises in question. So the provision by the landlord of more limited rights of occupation than the occupier previously enjoyed, or equivalent rights but in different premises, would not appear sufficient for the purposes of this defence. Where the occupier has been reinstated, but then subsequently removes permanently from the premises, it will be a question primarily of fact whether the circumstances of the reinstatement were such as to amount to a resumption of residential occupation.[5] Where the premises had been wrecked during the course of the eviction, the mere proffering of the key to the premises did not constitute "reinstatement".[6]

Secondly, no liability in damages for the statutory tort will arise if, at the request of the former residential occupier, a court makes an order (whether in the nature of an injunction or otherwise) as a result of which he is reinstated in the premises in question in such circumstances that he becomes again the residential occupier of them.[7] This second set of circumstances is somewhat difficult precisely to construe. They must have been intended to add something to the first set, otherwise they are otiose. Regardless of whether an order of the court is made, if the occupier is fully reinstated before the proceedings are finally disposed of, the first set of circumstances is established and the defence is made out. The second set must therefore have been intended to cover the case where the proceedings for damages were finally disposed of, but thereafter the court made an order for reinstatement as a result of which reinstatement occurred. This might explain why the limiting words "at the request of the former residential occupier" are used: the landlord in default cannot take steps to escape his liability in this way. But it is hard to envisage circumstances in which the court, having awarded **16–25**

[99] Act of 1988, s.27(6)(a).

[1] And in proceedings in the High Court, 28 days after the order is sealed or otherwise perfected: RSC Order 59, r. 4(1), 19(3).

[2] For decisions on a similar provision in Landlord and Tenant Act 1954, s.64(2), see *Woodfall's Law of Landlord and Tenant* (28th (looseleaf) ed.), para. 22.095.

[3] Contrast the refusal of an offer of reinstatement made before proceedings are begun: *post*, para. 16–34.

[4] *i.e.* occupying them as his residence within the meaning of Protection from Eviction Act 1977, s.1: Act of 1988, s.27(6)(a), (9)(a).

[5] See the *obiter dicta* of the Court of Appeal in *Murray v. Aslam* [1994] E.G.C.S. 160 in this regard.

[6] *Tagro v. Cafane* [1991] 1 W.L.R. 378, CA, where an award of £31,000 damages was upheld.

[7] Act of 1988, s.27(6)(b).

damages to the former occupier, would accede thereafter to an application for reinstatement.[7a] As with the first set of circumstances, full reinstatement in the premises as a residential occupier is required for this defence to succeed.[8]

(c) The Crown

16–26 The Crown is not bound by the provisions for statutory damages,[9] and accordingly no action under this head can be brought against it.

5. The measure of damages

16–27 Damages for the statutory tort are payable for the loss of the right of the occupier to occupy the premises as his residence, and are based on the increase in the value of the landlord's interest in the premises resulting from the wrongful eviction. They are, therefore, closely related in type to an award of exemplary damages at common law for an assault or trespass carried out in the course of the unlawful eviction.[10] In effect, the Act of 1988 assumes that the eviction or acts or conduct were done for the purpose of generating a greater financial benefit for the landlord than any punishment arising from the wrongdoing[11]; and unless the landlord in default can bring himself within one of the statutory defences he will be at risk of being liable for a large measure of damages which would only normally result from an award of exemplary damages.[12]

(a) Difference in value

16–28 Damages for the statutory tort of wrongful eviction are based on a difference in values determined as at the time immediately before the residential occupier ceased to occupy the premises in question as his residence.[13] The difference to be taken is the difference at that time between "the value of the interest of the landlord in default" determined on the following assumptions, namely—

(a) "that the residential occupier continues to have the same right to occupy the premises as before that time", and
(b) "that the residential occupier has ceased to have that right".[14]

[7a] See *Wandsworth L.B.C. v. Osei-Bonsu, supra*; and *ante*, para. 16–15.
[8] See *supra*.
[9] Act of 1988, s.44(2)(a).
[10] As to which, see Vol. 1, pp. 384, 385 and Supplement.
[11] A matter which would have to be proved by the occupier in a claim for exemplary damages: see *Rookes v. Barnard* [1964] A.C. 1129.
[12] In *Tagro v. Cafane* [1991] 1 W.L.R. 378, the Court of Appeal upheld an award of £31,000 damages. Common law exemplary damages therefore cannot be recovered in addition to the statutory measure; nor, *semble*, can general damages for the loss of the right of future occupation: *ante*, paras. 16–19, 16–20.
[13] Act of 1988, s.28(1).
[14] *ibid.*

The crucial matters to identify, in addressing any claim for statutory damages, are (i) what is the nature of the right of the occupier, and (ii) what is the ''interest of the landlord in default'' for these purposes. The second of these matters is discussed in the next paragraph.[15] Where the parties and the judge had failed to identify first exactly what legal rights to remain in occupation the occupier had at the time of the eviction, the valuation evidence and the judge's assessment of damages were fundamentally flawed.[16] The valuation thus depends not simply on the difference in value with and without vacant possession, but on an examination of what rights the residential occupier had, and the increase in value of the landlord's interest resulting from the occupier's rights ceasing to exist. Where the displaced occupier is a statutory tenant under the Rent Acts, the difference in value is liable to be substantial; but if the occupier is a tenant under an assured shorthold tenancy, under which the landlord has already served a valid notice requiring possession[17] which expires shortly, the difference in value will *generally*[18] only be that which reflects the usual delay in recovering possession through court proceedings.[19] Where the interest of the landlord in default is subject to other residential occupiers, for example where a house contains several residential flats, there is no requirement in valuing the landlord's interest on the prescribed bases to disregard the effect on value of the other occupiers.[20]

(b) Interest of landlord in default

16–29 For these purposes, ''landlord in default'' has the same meaning as above,[21] *i.e.* the person who, but for the occupier's right to occupy, would be entitled to occupation of the premises, ''and any superior landlord under whom that person derives title''.[22] The effect of that definition is that a superior landlord, even though not the person immediately entitled to occupation, may be a landlord in default for these purposes. But that does not make him a landlord in default where the default has been that of the immediate landlord or his agent, and not the default of the superior landlord himself.[23] Nor does it extend the interest of

[15] See (b), *infra*.

[16] *King v. Jackson* [1998] 1 E.G.L.R. 30, CA: award of £11,000 damages where occupier only had legal right to remain for six further days was manifestly wrong; £1,500 damages in contract for breach of obligation for quiet enjoyment substituted; *Melville v. Bruton* (1996) 29 H.L.R. 319, CA: award of £15,000 where occupier assured shorthold tenant reduced to £500 on appeal. But where the parties had agreed the quantum of damages below, the Court of Appeal refused to interfere, even though there was strong evidence that the valuations had failed to take into account the precarious tenure of the occupier: *Wandsworth L.B.C. v. Osei-Bonsu, supra*.

[17] Under Act of 1988, s.21(1), or (4): see *ante*, paras. 14–81, 14–84.

[18] It is possible to envisage circumstances in which the difference could be greater: if, for example, a special purchaser has made an inflated offer to purchase the landlord's interest on condition that vacant possession is available within four weeks. *Mehta v. Royal Bank of Scotland plc* [1999] *The Times*, Jan. 25, Q.B., might have been such a case: statutory damages of £45,000 for a contractual licence terminable on four months' notice is difficult to explain otherwise.

[19] See, for example, *Melville v. Bruton* (1996) 29 H.L.R. 319 CA; *supra*, n. 16.

[20] *Melville v. Bruton* (1996) 29 H.L.R. 319, CA.

[21] *Ante*, para. 16–13.

[22] Act of 1988, s.28(4), applying s.27(9).

[23] *Jones v. Miah* [1992] 2 E.G.L.R. 50, CA.

the landlord in default, for valuation purposes, so as to include the interest of any superior landlords who have not been in default within the meaning of the Act.[24] Where the unlawful eviction, or the attempted eviction or conduct which led the occupier to vacate, was committed by a superior landlord or his agent, it is the superior landlord alone who is liable for the statutory damages, and the measure is based on the value of his interest alone.

16–30 The interest of the landlord in default in the premises in question is his interest in the building in which the premises in question are comprised (whether or not that building contains any other premises) together with its curtilage.[25] So, if a landlord in default had a whole building which was vacant except for one flat occupied by a residential occupier, the interest to be valued with and without that occupier's continued rights of occupation is the whole building including the flat, and not just the occupied flat. There may accordingly be a substantial difference between the damages for an evicted occupier who was the last tenant of a large house, so that the landlord thereupon obtained vacant possession of the whole, and an evicted occupier who is merely the first of many.[26]

(c) Valuation assumptions

16–31 In valuing the interest of the landlord in default in these cases, certain valuation assumptions have to be made.[27] They are the following.

(i) OPEN MARKET: the landlord in default ''is selling his interest[28] on the open market to a willing buyer''.[29]

(ii) OCCUPIER AND FAMILY NOT BUYING: ''neither the residential occupier nor any member of his family wishes to buy''. For these purposes ''member of his family'' has a very wide definition.[30]

(iii) NO SUBSTANTIAL DEVELOPMENT: ''it is unlawful to carry out any substantial development of any of the land in which the landlord's interest subsists or to demolish the whole or part of any building on that land''. For this purpose, all development is ''substantial development'' unless it is either—

(1) ''development for which planning permission is granted by a general development order[31] for the time being in force and which is carried

[24] *Jones v. Miah, supra*, at 52K.
[25] Act of 1988, s.28(2).
[26] Though note that the valuation assumptions preclude any ''substantial'' development: *infra*, (c)(iii).
[27] Act of 1988, s.28(3).
[28] For the extent of this interest, see (b), *supra*.
[29] The judgment of Simon Brown L.J. in *Wandsworth L.B.C. v. Osei-Bonsu, supra*, to the effect that the willing buyer concept ''helps to fix the respective valuations'' but that ''one postulates the landlord's continuing ownership in fact'' is not persuasive.
[30] Act of 1988, s.28(5), applying Housing Act 1985, s.113. For this, see *post*, para 16–47(i).
[31] Within the meaning of Town and Country Planning Act 1990, s.56(6). Other expressions also have the same meaning as in that Act: Act of 1988, s.28(6).

out so as to comply with any condition or limitation subject to which planning permission is so granted'',[32] or

(2) a change of use resulting in the building[33] in which the landlord's interest subsists or any part of it being used as, or as part of, one or more dwelling-houses.[34]

Thus, if the removal of the residential occupier results in an increase in value of the landlord's interest because a change of use falling within (2) above is now possible,[35] the landlord in default may be exposed to liability in damages reflecting this increase in value. Note, however, that the valuation assumption does not require any assumption that planning permission exists for the change of use defined in (2) above; the assumption is only that development except for that falling within (1) and (2) above is unlawful. In the case of (1), the development in question is by definition one for which planning permission is deemed to have been granted by the order; but in the case of (2), whether or not there is such additional value on the facts of a given case is a matter for the court to determine on the basis of factual evidence, or expert valuation evidence, or both.

(d) Mitigation of damages

In proceedings for the statutory measure of damages for unlawful eviction, **16–32**
there are two grounds on which the court ''may reduce the amount of damages which would otherwise be payable to such amount as it thinks appropriate''.[36] Any claim that damages should be so reduced should be pleaded and particularised.[37] The size of the reduction is a matter for judicial judgment, like the quantification of general damages, and a judge's assessment will not lightly be interfered with by the Court of Appeal.[38] The grounds are where it appears to the court that either of the following sets of circumstances is established.

(i) OCCUPIER'S CONDUCT. ''Prior to the event which gave rise to the liability, **16–33**
the conduct of the former residential occupier or any person living with him in the premises concerned was such that it is reasonable to mitigate the damages for which the landlord in default would otherwise be liable''.[39] ''Conduct'' in this provision means ''behaviour'' generally, and even a failure to pay rent is accordingly ''conduct''.[40] A mere subjective intention, such as an intention to

[32] Act of 1988, s.28(6)(a).

[33] *i.e.* the building in which the landlord's interest subsists within Act of 1988, s.28(2): *ibid.*, s.28(6).

[34] *ibid.*, s.28(6).

[35] For example, where the evicted occupier was the last tenant in a large house which can now be divided into several flats.

[36] Act of 1988, s.27(7).

[37] *Regalgrand Ltd. v. Dickerson* (1996) 74 P. & C.R. 312, CA.

[38] *ibid.*

[39] Act of 1988, s.27(7)(a). Subsequent conduct is thus not included.

[40] *Regalgrand Ltd. v. Dickerson, supra.*

move out of the premises, cannot be "conduct" unless it is clothed by some outward sign, but it might, provided "conduct" falling within the provision is otherwise proved, be relevant to the quantification of the reduction.[41] Thus, *semble*, once conduct of any kind sufficient to make it reasonable to reduce the amount of damages is proved, the appropriate amount for the award of damages is a matter for the wider discretion of the judge. In making such award, there is no need for the judge to identify an amount of reduction in respect of each piece of "conduct". So, where the tenant's rent had been about £700 in arrears before the eviction, and the damages that would otherwise have been awarded were reduced under this provision by £10,500 on the basis that the tenant was intending to leave very shortly in any event, the judge had not erred in principle in failing to make the amount of the reduction equate to the "cost"[42] to the landlord of the conduct in question.[43] Where the tenant's violent conduct led to his being ousted from the dwelling by injunction and precipitated the course of events leading to the unlawful dispossession, the court reduced the damages that would otherwise have been payable by two-thirds.[44]

16–34 (ii) UNREASONABLE REFUSAL OF REINSTATEMENT. "Before the proceedings were begun, the landlord in default offered to reinstate the former residential occupier in the premises in question", and either—

(1) "it was unreasonable of the former residential occupier to refuse that offer", or
(2) "if he had obtained alternative accommodation before the offer was made, it would have been unreasonable of him to refuse that offer if he had not obtained that accommodation".[45]

A landlord who, before proceedings are begun, discovers that an unlawfully evicted occupier has obtained satisfactory alternative accommodation may in this way be able to claim a reduction of the damages payable by offering reinstatement, without there being much risk of the offer being accepted; yet in such a case the reduction that the court "thinks appropriate" may be small. There is no requirement that the offer of reinstatement be in writing.

(e) Size of Award

16–35 Although the court has rejected an argument that it has any discretion as to the quantum of damages (at least where the jurisdiction to reduce the damages on the two specified grounds does not arise[46]), the statutory measure is intended to confiscate from the landlord the financial benefit accruing from his unlawful

[41] *Regalgrand Ltd. v. Dickerson, supra.*
[42] *i.e.* the amount of the arrears of rent and interest.
[43] *Regalgrand Ltd. v. Dickerson, supra.*
[44] *Wandsworth L.B.C. v. Osei-Bonsu* [1999] 11 E.G. 167, CA (£30,000 to £10,000).
[45] Act of 1988, s.27(7)(b). Contrast a refusal of an offer of reinstatement made before the proceedings are finally disposed of (ante, para. 16–24), where there is no requirement of reasonableness.
[46] See (d), *supra*.

conduct, and not to fine him. This is the explanation given[47] for apparently capricious results in terms of quantum of damages produced by the statutory remedy. For where the residential occupier's interest is about to terminate, or where he is only one of many such occupiers in a property, there may be no increase in value of the landlord's interest and accordingly no damages; yet in another case, where the nature of the eviction is no more distressing, the damages may be very substantial indeed. This apparent capriciousness of the statutory remedy serves only to underline that it is not intended to supplant the common law remedy in damages which most residential occupiers will have, and that such persons are well-advised not to ignore common law damages and to regard the statutory remedy as a gold mine or as a means of retribution which will avail them irrespective of the precise factual circumstances of the case.

6. Jurisdiction

Proceedings for damages for unlawful eviction may be brought in the county court[48] or in the High Court.[49] As seen above, such damages may well be for substantial sums, exceeding the relatively modest amounts that have been awarded in such cases under the general law of contract and tort, and in some cases High Court proceedings might be considered appropriate; in most cases, however, the local county court would be considered the most convenient forum. Where proceedings for damages for unlawful eviction are being brought in the county court, the court has jurisdiction to hear and determine any other proceedings joined with them, even though those other proceedings would otherwise be outside the court's jurisdiction.[50] 16–36

Sect. 4. Eviction without Order of Court

One of the main purposes of the Protection from Eviction Act 1977[51] is to prohibit the eviction of any residential tenant, after his tenancy has come to an end, by any method except by obtaining an order of the court and executing a warrant of possession. The Act does not apply to a "statutorily protected tenancy", such as a tenancy protected by the Rent Acts, for that already has its own protection under its own statute.[52] But for other tenancies, once the tenancy is at an end and the 16–37

[47] In *Melville v. Bruton* (1996) 29 H.L.R. 319, CA.

[48] Act of 1988, s.40(1).

[49] With effect from July 1, 1991, the jurisdictional limits of the county courts were removed and the county courts and the High Court are given co-extensive jurisdiction with power to transfer the proceedings to the most appropriate forum for trial: see *ante*, para. 2–01.

[50] As to which, see *ante*, para. 2–03; and see *Murray v. Lloyd* [1989] 1 W.L.R. 1060, Ch. (£115,000 for loss of right to statutory tenancy).

[51] Replacing provisions that originated in Protection from Eviction Act 1964.

[52] In *Haniff v. Robinson* [1993] Q.B. 419, CA, the Court of Appeal re-affirmed that a statutory tenancy does not terminate, even though an absolute order for possession is made, until the warrant of possession is executed (or the tenant gives up possession).

occupant has no right to remain, the Prevention from Eviction Act prevents his being lawfully evicted without an order of the court, save in some excepted cases.[53]

The Act of 1988 has amended these provisions in three main respects. First, licences have been brought within the ambit of the Protection from Eviction Act 1977,[54] subject to important exceptions. Previously, few licences had been included.[55] Second, as might be expected in view of the provisions governing their termination, assured tenancies and assured agricultural occupancies have been added to the category of "statutorily protected tenancy", and so are excluded from the prohibition in the Act of 1977 against eviction except by proceedings in court. Third, a number of tenancies and licences have been made "excluded tenancies and licences", and as such they too are excluded from the prohibition. But the Crown is bound by these provisions.[56]

1. LICENCES

16–38 The provisions against eviction except by proceedings in court apply in relation to any premises occupied as a dwelling under a licence as they apply in relation to premises let as a dwelling under a tenancy; and the words "let" and "tenancy" in those provisions are to be construed accordingly.[57] But wherethe premises are not occupied *as a dwelling* by the licensee, the protection against eviction provisions do not apply.[58] In any event, they do not apply to any "excluded licence".[59]

A corresponding addition has been made to the special provisions[60] relating to agricultural workers who are outside the protection of the Rent Acts.[61] For these, the references to a tenant under a former tenancy now include references to a licensee under a licence to occupy premises as a dwelling which has come to an end; and "tenancy" and "rent" and other expressions referable to a tenancy are to be construed accordingly.[62] Again, this does not apply to "excluded licences".[63]

2. STATUTORILY PROTECTED TENANCIES

16–39 Assured tenancies and assured agricultural occupancies have been added[64] to the list of statutorily protected tenancies,[65] as have a long residential tenancy to

[53] See Vol. 1, pp. 508–511.
[54] Called "the 1977 Act" in Act of 1988, Pt. I, Ch. IV: s.33(1).
[55] See Vol. 1, p. 509. The most important examples were restricted contracts that created a licence.
[56] Act of 1988, s.44(1).
[57] Protection from Eviction Act 1977, s.3(2B) (added by Act of 1988, s.30(2)), applying s.3(1), (2).
[58] *Brillouet v. Landless* (1995) 28 H.L.R. 836, CA (hotel rooms not occupied as dwelling by guest); but see *Mehta v. Royal Bank of Scotland plc [1999] The Times*, January 25, Q.B.
[59] *ibid.*; see *infra*.
[60] See Vol. 1, pp. 497–501.
[61] *i.e.* the Acts of 1976 and 1977.
[62] Protection from Eviction Act 1977, s.4(2A), added by Act of 1988, s.30(3).
[63] *ibid.*; see *infra*.
[64] By Act of 1988, s.33(2).
[65] In Protection from Eviction Act 1977, s.8(1).

which Schedule 10 to the Local Government and Housing Act 1989 applies[66] and an agricultural tenancy under the Agricultural Tenancies Act 1995.[67] Those holding over after the end of such tenancies or occupancies are accordingly outside the prohibition in the Protection from Eviction Act 1977 against eviction without an order of the court.

3. EXCLUDED TENANCIES AND LICENCES

Excluded tenancies and licences are also outside the prohibition under the Protection from Eviction Act 1977 against eviction without proceedings in court.[68] As long as the tenancy or licence continues, it provides its own protection against eviction; and the tenant or licensee, as a "residential occupier", has the protection of the Act against harassment and unlawful eviction. But once an excluded tenancy or licence has ended, there is nothing further to prevent the occupier from being lawfully evicted without an order of the court. **16–40**

For a tenancy or licence to take effect for these purposes[69] as an "excluded" tenancy or licence, two matters have to be considered. The first is whether the date on which the tenancy or licence was granted prevents its taking effect as an "excluded" tenancy or licence. The second is whether the nature of the tenancy or licence brings it within the statutory list of six categories of "excluded" tenancies and licences. Of these, five are either tenancies or licences, but the sixth is licences only.[70] These matters will be considered in turn.

1. Date of grant

Tenancies and licences require separate treatment.

(a) Tenancies

The prohibition against eviction except by proceedings in court applies to all premises let as a dwelling under a tenancy which is neither a statutorily protected tenancy "nor an excluded tenancy".[71] But this reference to an "excluded" tenancy does not apply to any such tenancy if it was entered into before January 15, 1989, or was entered into on or after that date but pursuant to a contract **16–41**

[66] By Local Government and Housing Act 1989, ss.194(1), 195(2), Sched. 11, para. 54; S.I. 1990 No. 431.

[67] By Agricultural Tenancies Act 1995, ss.40, 41(2), Sched., para. 29.

[68] Protection from Eviction Act 1977, s.3(1), as amended by Act of 1988, s.30(1).

[69] *i.e.* for the purposes of eviction without order of the court. The provisions for excluded tenancies and licences operate differently in relation to other provisions of the Protection from Eviction Act 1977; see *post*, paras. 16–55 *et seq.*

[70] Protection from Eviction Act 1977, ss.3A(1), 8(4), inserted by Act of 1988, ss.31, 33(3).

[71] *ibid.* s.3(1), as amended by Act of 1988, s.30(1).

made before that date.[72] The practical result is that any such tenancy entered into or contracted before January 15, 1989 which is not a "statutorily protected tenancy" enjoys the protection of the prohibition on eviction without due process. Any such tenancy entered into after that date (other than one contracted before it) will be excluded from that protection if it falls within the categories of "excluded" tenancies.[73] In the context of eviction without a court order, it does not matter whether premises comprised or included in an agricultural holding or a business tenancy were let as a dwelling within the meaning of the prohibition because such tenancies are "statutorily protected tenancies"[74] and thus excluded from this statutory protection in any event.[75]

16–42 This provision is supplemented by provisions relating to variations made in the terms of a tenancy. If, on or after January 15, 1989, the terms of an excluded tenancy entered into before that date are varied, and the variation affects the amount of rent which is payable under the tenancy, that tenancy must be treated as a new tenancy entered into at the time of the variation.[76] But for these purposes, there is no variation affecting the amount of the rent if there is merely a reduction or increase effected under the statutory provisions for regulating and registering rents, or a variation made by the parties which makes the rent expressed to be payable the same as the registered rent for the dwelling.[77] Where the variation does not affect the amount of the rent payable under the tenancy, the question whether the variation is such as to give rise to a new tenancy is left to the ordinary law, unaffected by the Act.[78] Thus, where additional premises are sought to be included in the tenancy, or where the length of the term granted is sought to be extended, the law infers the surrender of the existing tenancy and the grant of a new one; but otherwise it is a matter of construction of the contract of variation whether the parties intended to grant a new interest or merely to vary the terms of the existing tenancy and otherwise leave it in being.[79]

The practical effect of these provisions is that an excluded tenancy entered into before January 15, 1989, which therefore *prima facie* cannot be an excluded tenancy *for these purposes,*[80] may become one if after that date the rent is varied (other than in accordance with the registered rent provisions of the Rent Acts), the premises comprised in the tenancy are enlarged or the length of the term is

[72] Protection from Eviction Act 1977, s.3(2C), inserted by Act of 1988, s.30(2).
[73] See *infra*.
[74] Protection from Eviction Act 1977, s.8(1)(c), (d).
[75] But the difficulties posed by the decision in *National Trust for Places of Historic Interest or Natural Beauty v. Knipe* [1998] 1 W.L.R. 230, CA, are of direct application to notices to quit: see *post*, para. 16–53.
[76] Protection from Eviction Act 1977 s.8(6), inserted by Act of 1988, s.33(3). Note that the position in this regard is contrary to what would be the case at common law: see *Friends Provident Life Office v. British Railways Board* [1996] 1 All E.R. 336, CA.
[77] Protection from Eviction Act 1977, s.8(6).
[78] *ibid.*, s.8(5)(b). See *ante*, para. 5–22, where the similar provisions of Act of 1988, s.36(2), (3), are considered.
[79] *JW Childers Trustees v. Anker* [1996] 1 E.G.L.R. 1, CA; *Friends Provident Life Office v. British Railways Board* [1996] 1 All E.R. 336, CA.
[80] Note that a tenancy granted before January 15, 1989 and falling within one of the categories in Protection from Eviction Act 1977, s.3A (as to which, see *post*, paras. 16–45 *et seq.*) is an excluded tenancy for the purposes of that Act generally, although it is not treated as such, by virtue of *ibid.*, s.3(2C), for the purposes of the prohibition on eviction without due process.

extended, or if some other variation is effected which evinces an intention to create a new tenancy. Where a variation on or after January 15, 1989 does give rise to a new tenancy, then if it remains an excluded tenancy the prohibition against eviction except by proceedings in court will not apply to it. These provisions as to variations only apply where the tenancy varied was (a) entered into[81] before January 15, 1989 and (b) an excluded tenancy at the time of the variation. Thus, if the parties to a pre-January 15, 1989 tenancy not falling within the categories of ''excluded'' tenancies agree after that date to vary the rent (other than in accordance with the registered rent provisions of the Rent Acts) and other terms of the tenancy such that it becomes an ''excluded'' tenancy[82] within the meaning of section 3A of the Protection from Eviction Act 1977, the tenancy is not treated as a ''new'' tenancy for the purposes of the prohibition on eviction without a court order because, prior to the variation, the tenancy was not an ''excluded'' tenancy; and accordingly the prohibition on eviction without due process will continue to apply because the tenancy was entered into before January 15, 1989.

(b) Licences

The position of licences granted before January 15, 1989 is not wholly clear. On a straightforward reading of the statute, the provision discussed above which prevents ''old'' tenancies from having effect as ''excluded'' tenancies has no application to ''old'' licences, for the provision[83] is drafted in terms of ''tenancy'' alone, and not ''licence''. On this footing, every licence in the statutory list of ''excluded'' licences takes effect as an ''excluded'' licence, even if it was granted before January 15, 1989, and so will be outside the protection of the prohibition against eviction except by proceedings in court. Thus, for ''excluded'' tenancies and licences, ''old'' tenancies will be protected by the prohibition but ''old'' licences will not. A reason for this distinction appears to be that before January 15, 1989, the prohibition protected tenancies but not licences. In creating the categories of ''excluded'' tenancies and licences, the Act of 1988 accordingly refrained from taking away the protection from ''old'' tenancies. For licences, however, there was nothing to take away, but merely the question of which licences were to be left outside the newly-conferred protection, and so the new provisions applied to all licences, whatever the date. **16–43**

If this reasoning is correct, difficulties arise from the provisions, considered above in relation to tenancies, concerning the effect of a variation in the terms of an ''excluded'' tenancy or ''excluded'' licence entered into before January 15, 1989. These provisions are expressed in terms of both ''excluded'' tenancy and ''excluded'' licence;[84] and for ''excluded'' tenancies the date is plainly **16–44**

[81] The statutory provision does not here say ''. . . or entered into on or after January 15, 1989 pursuant to a contract made before that date . . .''.

[82] *e.g.*, by requiring part of the demised premises thenceforth to be shared with a member of the landlord's family.

[83] Protection from Eviction Act 1977, s.3(2C), added by Act of 1988, s.30(2).

[84] *ibid.*, s.8(5).

relevant. But if "excluded" licences are to take effect as such, whenever granted, it is difficult to see why they are included in these provisions. But if instead "old" licences are to be treated like "old" tenancies, this interpretative difficulty disappears. It is possible to construct an elaborate and tedious argument that this is the case;[85] but the better view seems to be that the literal meaning of the statute is to be preferred despite the curiosities of the provisions concerning variations in the terms of tenancies and licences. In short, "old" excluded tenancies are within the protection of the prohibition against eviction except by proceedings in court, but "old" licences are not.

2. Categories of excluded tenancies and licences

16–45 In addition to satisfying the provisions as to date considered above, a tenancy or licence will take effect as an excluded tenancy or licence only if it is included in the statutory list of "excluded" tenancies and licences. There are six categories in this list.[86] As stated above, five apply to tenancies and licences alike; the sixth applies only to licences. They vary considerably in purpose and complexity. In the first two categories, "occupier" not unexpectedly means, in relation to a tenancy, the tenant, and in relation to a licence, the licensee;[87] and if more than one person is the landlord or licensor, "landlord" or "licensor" means any one of them.[88] The following are the categories.

(a) Sharing with landlord or licensor

16–46 A tenancy or licence is an "excluded" tenancy or licence if two conditions are each satisfied.

(i) SHARED ACCOMMODATION: if under the terms of the tenancy or licence the occupier shares any accommodation with the landlord or licensor.[89] For this purpose, an occupier "shares" accommodation with another person if he has the use of it in common with that person, whether or not also in common with others.[90] There is no requirement that the accommodation shared should be

[85] The argument depends on provisions in Protection from Eviction Act 1977 which were inserted by Act of 1988, ss.30(1),(2), 31, 33(3). The basis of the argument is that in s.3(2C), which prevents "old" tenancies from taking effect as "excluded" tenancies, "tenancy" includes licence by virtue of s.3(2B). Yet the operative word in s.3(2C) is "tenancy" alone, and the reference in the same subsection to " "excluded tenancy" and "excluded licence" " provides a formidable contrast. The oddities of the drafting are compounded by the express reference in section 3(2C) to references in section 4(2A) to an excluded tenancy: section 4(2A) has only one reference to an excluded licence and none to an excluded tenancy.

[86] Protection from Eviction Act 1977, s.3A(2), (3), (6), (7), (8).

[87] *ibid.*, s.3A(5)(b).

[88] *ibid.*, s.3A(4).

[89] *ibid.*, s.3A(2)(a).

[90] *ibid.*, s.3A(4).

living accommodation;[91] any accommodation suffices except an area used for storage, or a staircase, passage, corridor or other means of access.[92]

(ii) PART OF ONLY OR PRINCIPAL HOME: if immediately before the tenancy or licence was granted, and also at the time it comes to an end, the landlord or licensee occupied as his only or principal home[93] premises of which the whole or part of the shared accommodation formed part.[94]

(b) Sharing with member of landlord's family

A tenancy or licence is also an ''excluded'' tenancy or licence if the following three conditions are satisfied. **16–47**

(i) SHARED ACCOMMODATION: if under the terms of the tenancy or licence the occupier shares any accommodation with a member of the family of the landlord or licensor.[95] ''Shares'' and ''accommodation'' have the same meaning as under paragraph (a) above.[96] ''Member of the family'' has a very wide meaning. It means spouse (including a person living with the landlord or licensor as husband or wife[97]), parent, grandparent, grandchild, brother, sister, uncle, aunt, nephew or niece; and for this purpose, a relationship by marriage is treated as a relationship by blood, the half-blood is treated as the whole blood, a stepchild is treated as a child, and an illegitimate child is treated as the legitimate child of his mother and reputed father.[98]

(ii) PART OF ONLY OR PRINCIPAL HOME: if immediately before the tenancy or licence was granted, and also at the time it comes to an end, the member of the family occupied as his only or principal home premises of which the whole or part of the shared accommodation formed part.[99]

(iii) LANDLORD'S HOME IN SAME BUILDING: if immediately before the tenancy or licence was granted, and also at the time it comes to an end, the landlord or licensor occupied as his only or principal home[1] premises in the same building as the shared accommodation, and that building is not a purpose-built block of flats.[2]

[91] Compare the requirement under Rent Act 1977, s.1, and under Act of 1988, s.1(1), that a dwelling house be let as a *separate* dwelling, which has been held to connote that living accommodation, such as a kitchen, has to be shared before the protection of these Acts is excluded: see Vol. 1, pp. 87–117.

[92] Protection from Eviction Act 1977, s.3A(5)(a).

[93] For ''only or principal home'', see *ante*, para. 3–24.

[94] Protection from Eviction Act 1977, s.3A(2)(b).

[95] *ibid.*, s.3A(3)(a).

[96] *ibid.*, s.3A(4), (5)(a).

[97] As to whether this phrase is apt to describe a committed, stable homosexual relationship, see *Fitzpatrick v. Sterling Housing Association Ltd.* [1988] Ch. 304, CA.

[98] Protection from Eviction Act 1977, s.3A(5), applying Housing Act 1985, s.113.

[99] *ibid.*, s.3A(3)(b).

[1] For ''only or principal home'', see *ante*, para. 3–24.

[2] *ibid.*, s.3A(3)(c). ''Purpose-built block of flats'' has the same meaning as in Act of 1988, Sched. 1, para. 22 (see *ante*, para. 4–22): Protection from Eviction Act 1977, s.3A(5)(c).

(c) Temporary expedient for trespasser

16–48 A tenancy or licence is an "excluded" tenancy or licence if it was granted as a temporary expedient to a person who entered the premises in question "or any other premises" as a trespasser.[3] This applies even if another tenancy or licence to occupy the premises, or any other premises, had previously been granted to that person,[4] and so there is no need for the tenant or licensee to be trespassing at the time of the grant of the tenancy or licence in question. The emphasis under this head is on the initial entry as a trespasser.

This provision appears to be directed to the concept that a "squat" is less burdensome to the owner of premises if it is subsequently controlled by a temporary licence than if it is left wholly unregulated. It may be that the literal width of the words "any other premises" would be tempered by reference to this underlying policy by confining it to premises which are in some way connected with the current, controlled squat. That is to say that the premises now comprised in the relevant tenancy or licence are either the same as or part of the premises initially squatted, or other premises owned by the owner of the premises initially squatted, or perhaps other premises in the close vicinity of those squatted, regardless of ownership. On the other hand, the emphasis in this category may be on the words "as a temporary expedient", so that provided a landlord or licensor can prove the expedience of the grant and its temporary nature, there need be no other connection at all with the premises initially squatted. Expedience may well be difficult to prove if the landlord or licensor has no connection at all with the squatted premises.

(d) Holiday tenancy or licence

16–49 A tenancy or licence is an "excluded" tenancy or licence if it confers on the tenant or licensee the right to occupy the premises for a holiday only.[5] This exclusion is complementary to the provision preventing such tenancies from being assured tenancies.[6]

(e) Free tenancy or licence

16–50 A tenancy or licence is an "excluded" tenancy or licence if it is granted otherwise than for money or money's worth.[7]

(f) Hostel licences

16–51 A licence is an "excluded" licence if it confers rights of occupation in certain hostels.[8] This category does not include tenancies. There are two requirements.

[3] Protection from Eviction Act 1977, s.3A(6).
[4] *ibid.*
[5] *ibid.*, s.3A(7)(a).
[6] *Ante*, para. 4–65.
[7] Protection from Eviction Act 1977, s.3A(7)(b).
[8] *ibid.*, s.3A(8).

(i) HOSTEL: the hostel must be a hostel within the meaning of the Housing Act 1985.[9] That Act defines ''hostel'' as meaning ''a building in which is provided, for persons generally or for a class or classes of persons—

(a) residential accommodation otherwise than in separate and self-contained sets of premises, and
(b) either board[10] or facilities for the preparation of food adequate to the needs of those persons, or both''.[11]

(ii) PROVIDED BY PUBLIC BODY: the hostel must be provided by certain specified public bodies.[12] They are as follows: the council of a county, county borough, district or London Borough; the Common Council of the City of London; the Council of the Isles of Scilly; the Inner London Education Authority; a ''joint authority'' or ''residuary authority'';[13] a development corporation;[14] the Commission for the New Towns; an urban development corporation;[15] a housing action trust;[16] the Development Board for Rural Wales (before October 1, 1998); the Housing Corporation or Housing for Wales (the latter before November 1, 1998); the Secretary of State[16a]; and a housing trust which is a charity or a registered social landlord.[17] In addition, this head applies if the hostel is provided by any other person who is (or who belongs to a class of persons which is) specified in an order made by the Secretary of State.[18] To date, the Secretary of State has only specified London Hostels Association Limited for these purposes.[19]

Sect. 5. Notices to Quit

For some 25 years, statute has invalidated any notice by a landlord or a tenant to quit any premises ''let . . . as a dwelling'' (whether or not protected by the Rent Acts) unless it is in writing and contains the prescribed information,[20] and **16–52**

[9] *ibid.*
[10] As to the general meaning of board, see Vol. 1, pp. 172, 173.
[11] Housing Act 1985, s.622.
[12] Protection from Eviction Act 1977, s.3A(8).
[13] Both within the meaning of Local Government Act 1985.
[14] Within the meaning of New Towns Act 1981.
[15] *i.e.* one established by an order under Local Government, Planning and Land Act 1980, s.135.
[16] *i.e.* one established under Act of 1988, Pt. III.
[16a] Under Housing Associations Act 1985, s.89.
[17] Within the meaning of Housing Act 1985: see *ante*, paras. 5–27, 5–36 *et seq.*
[18] Protection from Eviction Act 1977, s.3A(8). The power is exercisable by statutory instrument, and is subject to negative resolution: *ibid.* s.3A(9).
[19] With effect from October 31, 1991: Protection from Eviction (Excluded Licences) Order 1991 (S.I. 1991 No. 1943), printed *post*, p. 616.
[20] For the prescribed information to be given by landlords and licensors, see Notices to Quit etc. (Prescribed Information) Regulations 1988 (S.I. 1988 No. 2201, as amended by H.M.S.O. Correction Notice dated January, 1989), replacing Notices to Quit (Prescribed Information) Regulations 1980 (S.I. 1980 No. 1624: see Vol. 2, p. 1116) for notices given on or after January 15, 1989. Apart from advising tenants and licensees to get advice from a solicitor, etc., the prescribed information is mainly that the landlord or licensor must get an order from the court before the

it is given not less than four weeks before the date on which it is to take effect.[21] The Prescribed Information Regulations prescribe ''that [information] in the Schedule to these Regulations'',[22] and there is no express provision that information substantially to the same effect suffices.[23] Nevertheless, the exact wording of the prescribed information need not be used if all the relevant information is given.[24]

16–53 Where premises, which include a dwelling-house, are let as an agricultural holding, they are not ''let as a dwelling'' within the meaning of these notice to quit provisions of the Protection from Eviction Act 1977,[25] and accordingly a notice to quit served under the Agricultural Holdings Act 1986 does not need to contain the prescribed information under consideration. The same reasoning ought to apply to a business tenancy of premises which include a dwelling-house, otherwise every statutory notice[26] to terminate such a tenancy will have been invalid.[27]

Before the Act of 1988, the requirements for a valid notice to quit applied only to tenancies; but they have now been extended to some licences.

1. Extension to periodic licences

16–54 The same requirements for a valid notice to quit by a landlord or a tenant now apply also to any ''notice by a licensor or a licensee to determine a periodic licence to occupy premises as a dwelling'', whether the licence was granted before or after January 15, 1989.[28] This in terms applies only to periodic licences; other licences are unaffected. A service occupancy, which ends with

tenant or licensee can lawfully be evicted. No information has been prescribed for notices given by tenants or licensees.

[21] Protection from Eviction Act 1977, s.5(1), replacing Act of 1957, s.16, as amended by Housing Act 1974, s.123; see Vol. 1, pp. 232, 233.

[22] The Notices to Quit etc. (Prescribed Information) Regulations 1988, reg. 2.

[23] As is specifically provided in different contexts for notices relating to assured and protected tenancies: see, for example, the Assured Tenancies and Agricultural Occupancies (Forms) Regulations 1997 (S.I. 1997 No. 194), reg. 2.

[24] *Beckerman v. Durling* (1981) 6 H.L.R. 87, CA (on the 1980 Regulations); *Swansea City Council v. Hearn* (1990) 23 H.L.R. 284, CA (on the 1988 Regulations in relation to their application to a periodic licence).

[25] *National Trust for Places of Historic Interest or Natural Beauty v. Knipe* [1998] 1 W.L.R. 230, CA; leave to appeal refused: [1998] 1 W.L.R. 696, HL. The decision, whilst sensible, is not without its oddities. If premises including a dwelling-house intended as the tenant's residence let as an agricultural holding are not ''let as a dwelling'' under Protection from Eviction Act 1977, s.5(1), why does the definition of ''statutorily protected tenancy'' in *ibid.*, s.8(1), which relates to eviction from premises let as a dwelling without due process of law, need to include a tenancy of an agricultural holding?

[26] Served pursuant to Landlord and Tenant Act 1954, s.25(1).

[27] Support for this argument may be found in the reasoning in *Wagle v. Trustees of Henry Smith's Charity Kensington Estate* [1990] 1 Q.B. 42, CA, but this decision is difficult to reconcile with the later decision of the Court of Appeal in *Wellcome Trust v. Hamad* [1998] Q.B. 638. If a dwelling-house is let for residential purposes but on terms which do not preclude some business use, and after the date of grant the lessee starts to use the premises for a business to a substantial extent, the tenancy will become protected by Part II of the Landlord and Tenant Act 1954; but were the premises not let as a dwelling?

[28] Protection from Eviction Act 1977, s.5(1A), inserted by Act of 1988, s.32(2).

the employment, without notice, is not a periodic licence;[29] a guest's use of a hotel room probably is, but a hotel room is not licensed to the guest for occupation as a dwelling, and so the restrictions on termination of such a licence do not apply.[30] The length of notice required at common law to determine a licence has never become defined in the detailed way that it has for tenancies, where, of course, more than four weeks' notice is normally required for monthly, quarterly and yearly tenancies. In most cases the statutory minimum of four weeks' notice will probably satisfy the common law requirement of reasonable notice to determine a licence;[31] but if an express monthly or quarterly licence to occupy premises as a dwelling has been granted,[32] then a longer period of notice will be required.

2. Excluded tenancies and licences

The requirement of not less than four weeks' notice in writing containing the prescribed information does not apply to most of the "excluded" tenancies and licences contained in the six categories set out above.[33] **16–55**

(a) Tenancies

The requirement does not apply to premises let on an "excluded" tenancy within these categories if it was entered into on or after January 15, 1989 otherwise than pursuant to a contract made before that date.[34] "New" excluded tenancies are thus exempt from the requirement. But the requirement still applies to "old" tenancies (*i.e.* those entered into before that date), even though they are included in the list of "excluded" tenancies. **16–56**

As with the restrictions on eviction without due process of law,[35] this provision is supplemented by provisions relating to variations made in the terms of a tenancy. If, on or after January 15, 1989, the terms of an excluded tenancy entered into before that date are varied, and the variation affects the amount of rent which is payable under the tenancy, that tenancy must be treated as a new **16–57**

[29] *Norris v. Checksfield* [1991] 1 W.L.R. 1241, CA; see also *Burgoyne v. Griffiths* (1990) 23 H.L.R. 303, CA.

[30] *Brillouet v. Landless* (1995) 28 H.L.R. 836, CA.

[31] See, *e.g., Winter Garden Theatre (London) Ltd. v. Millennium Productions Ltd.* [1948] A.C. 173; and see Dawson and Pearce, *Licences Relating to the Occupation or Use of Land* (1979) pp. 85–89.

[32] In an ordinary case, it will be difficult to grant such an interest without, in law, creating a tenancy, but in some circumstances, for example where the grantee is a beneficiary under a trust or a contractual purchaser pending completion, it will be effective to create a periodic licence.

[33] Protection from Eviction Act 1977, s.3A(1) (*ante*, paras. 16–46 to 16–51); s.5(1) is now subject to s.5(1B): Act of 1988, s.32(1).

[34] Protection from Eviction Act 1977, s.5(1B)(a). Subs. 5(1A) and 5(1B) were inserted by Act of 1988, s.32(2).

[35] *Ante*, para. 16–42.

tenancy entered into at the time of the variation.[36] But for these purposes, there is no variation affecting the amount of the rent if there is merely a reduction or increase effected under the statutory provisions for regulating and registering rents, or a variation made by the parties which makes the rent expressed to be payable the same as the registered rent for the dwelling.[37] Where the variation does not affect the amount of the rent payable under the tenancy, the question whether the variation is such as to give rise to a new tenancy is left to the general law, unaffected by the Act.[38] Thus, where additional premises are sought to be included in the tenancy, or where the length of the term granted is sought to be extended, the law infers the surrender of the existing tenancy and the grant of a new one; but otherwise it is a matter of construction of the contract of variation whether the parties intended to grant a new interest or merely to vary the terms of the existing tenancy and otherwise leave it in being.[39]

The practical effect of these provisions is that an excluded tenancy entered into before January 15, 1989, which therefore *prima facie* cannot be an excluded tenancy *for these purposes,*[40] may become one if after that date the rent is varied (other than in accordance with the registered rent provisions of the Rent Acts), the premises comprised in the tenancy are enlarged or the length of the term is extended, or if some other variation is effected which evinces an intention to create a new tenancy. Where a variation on or after January 15, 1989 does give rise to a new tenancy, then if it remains an excluded tenancy the requirement of at least four weeks' written notice to quit containing the prescribed information will not apply to it. These provisions as to variations only apply where the tenancy varied was (a) entered into[41] before January 15, 1989 and (b) an excluded tenancy at the time of the variation.

(b) Licences

16–58 "Excluded" licences are different. The requirement does not apply to any "excluded" licence within the six categories.[42] This is so whether the licence was granted before, on or after January 15, 1989.[43] This does not deprive any existing licence of the benefit of the requirement, for until that date licences had not had that benefit. The exception of all "excluded" licences thus merely

[36] Protection from Eviction Act 1977, s.8(5), inserted by Act of 1988, s.33(3). Note that this is contrary to what would be the case at common law: see *Friends Provident Life Office v. British Railways Board* [1996] 1 All E.R. 336, CA.

[37] Protection from Eviction Act 1977, s.8(6).

[38] *ibid.*, s.8(5)(b). See *ante*, para. 5–22, where the similar provisions of Act of 1988, s.36(2), (3) are considered.

[39] *J.W. Childers Trustees v. Anker* [1996] 1 E.G.L.R. 1, CA; *Friends Provident Life Office v. British Railways Board supra.*

[40] Note that a tenancy granted before January 15, 1989 and falling within one of the categories in Protection from Eviction Act 1977, s.3A (as to which, see *ante*, paras. 16–46 to 16–51) is an excluded tenancy for the purposes of that Act generally, although it is not treated as such, by virtue of *ibid.*, s.5(1B)(a), for the purposes of the notices to quit provisions of the Act.

[41] The statutory provision does not here say "... or entered into on or after January 15, 1989 pursuant to a contract made before that date ...".

[42] Protection from Eviction Act 1977, s.5(1B)(b).

[43] The restriction as to date which appears in s.5(1B)(a) for excluded tenancies is omitted from s.5(1B)(b) for excluded licences.

reduced the number of licences which, "whether granted before or after" that date,[44] were to be given the benefit of the requirement; and for this purpose the date of the licence is irrelevant.[45]

Sect. 6. Protection from Harassment Act 1997

This Act ("the Act of 1997"), the relevant provisions of which came into force on June 16, 1997,[46] is not directed to harassment in a landlord and tenant context, but is quite general in its effect.[47] Although there are specific offences of criminal harassment and eviction and the new statutory tort of unlawful eviction,[48] the provisions of the Act of 1997 could well apply in the context of eviction or threatened eviction of a residential occupier. The Act creates a new offence of harassment, a statutory tort of harassment, and a supplementary offence of putting a person in fear of the use of violence against him. **16–59**

1. The offence of harassment

A person is guilty of an offence if he pursues a course of conduct which amounts to harassment of another and which he knows or ought to know amounts to harassment of the other.[49] There is no exhaustive definition of harassment, but harassing a person includes alarming the person or causing him distress.[50] Further, a course of conduct must involve conduct on at least two occasions,[51] and so an isolated incident causing a person alarm or distress will not amount to harassment for the purposes of this Act. Conduct includes speech.[52] For the purposes of the offence, a person whose conduct is in question ought to know that it amounts to harassment of another person if a reasonable person in the possession of the same information[53] would think that the course of conduct amounted to harassment of that person.[54] Neither a failure by a landlord to prevent his tenant from disturbing a neighbour, nor a refusal by a person to engage in normal neighbourly civilities, is an offence of harassment.[54a] **16–60**

44 Protection from Eviction Act 1977, s.5(1A).
45 Here, the express separate provision for excluded licences avoids the doubts regarding pre-January 15, 1989 licences in connection with the prohibition on eviction without an order of the court see *ante*, para. 16–43.
46 Protection from Harassment Act 1997, s.15(1), (2); S.I. 1997 No. 1418; S.I. 1997 No. 1498.
47 The origins of the Act were a number of unpleasant and widely-publicised occurrences of "stalking" of victims in public places.
48 See *ante*.
49 Protection from Harassment Act 1997, ss.1(1), 2(1).
50 *ibid.*, s.7(2).
51 *ibid.*, s.7(3).
52 *ibid.*, s.7(3).
53 Presumably the same information known to the harasser.
54 Protection from Harassment Act 1997, s.1(2).
54a *B. v. MHA Ltd.* [1999] 2 C.L. 372, CC; *Morris v. Knight* [1999] 2 C.L. 373, CC.

16–61 An offence of harassment is not made out if the person accused of it proves one of three defences. First, that the course of conduct was pursued for the purpose of preventing or detecting crime. Secondly, that the course of conduct was pursued under an enactment or rule of law, or that it was pursued to comply with any condition or requirement imposed by any person under any enactment. Thirdly, that the pursuit of the course of conduct was reasonable in the particular circumstances.[55]

16–62 A person guilty of the offence of harassment is liable on summary conviction to imprisonment for a term not exceeding six months, or a fine not exceeding level 5 on the standard scale, or both.[56] Harassment is an arrestable offence.[57]

2. Civil remedy

16–63 The Act of 1997 creates in effect a new statutory tort of actual or threatened harassment. It provides that an actual or apprehended commission of the offence of harassment may be the subject of a claim in civil proceedings by the person who is or may be the victim of the course of conduct in question.[58] So, where one of the statutory defences[59] is available to the person pursuing the course of conduct in question, no civil claim will lie either. Where such a claim does lie, the court may award damages for (amongst other things) any anxiety caused by the harassment and any financial loss resulting from the harassment.[60] So, *semble*, if a landlord twice telephones his tenant and threatens forcibly to evict him, the tenant may recover general damages for his anxiety and special damages for any expense incurred to protect himself, even if no actual or attempted eviction occurs. As with any threatened breach of statutory duty, the victim may obtain injunctive relief to prevent or alleviate the breach or threatened breach.

3. The offence of putting people in fear of violence

16–64 The Act of 1997 creates a further criminal offence, which is triable either way and punishable potentially more severely than the offence of harassment.[61] It is committed by a person whose course of conduct causes another to fear, on at least two occasions, that violence will be used against him and he knows or ought to know that his course of conduct will cause the other so to fear on each of those occasions.[62] The same definitions of ''course of conduct'', and the same objective test of what a person ought to know, apply as for the offence of

[55] Protection from Harassment Act 1997, s.1(3).
[56] *ibid.*, s.2(2).
[57] *ibid.*, s.2(3).
[58] *ibid.*, s.3(1). For the meaning of ''course of conduct'', see *ante*, para. 16–60.
[59] In Protection from Harrassment Act 1997, ss.1(3), 12(1): as to the latter, see *infra*.
[60] *ibid.*, s.3(2).
[61] On conviction on indictment by imprisonment for a term not exceeding five years, or a fine, or both; on summary conviction by imprisonment for a term not exceeding six months, or a fine not exceeding the statutory maximum, or both: Protection from Harassment Act 1997, s.4(4).
[62] *ibid.*, s.4(1).

harassment.[63] The offence of putting people in fear of violence is not made out if the person accused of it proves one of three defences. First, that his course of conduct was pursued for the purpose of preventing or detecting crime. Secondly, that his course of conduct was pursued under an enactment or rule of law, or that it was pursued to comply with any condition or requirement imposed by any person under any enactment. Thirdly, that the pursuit of his course of conduct was reasonable for the protection of himself or another, or for the protection of his or another's property.[64]

4. No offence or tort where Secretary of State certifies

There is a further exemption from the provisions of the Act, both criminal and civil, where the Secretary of State certifies that in his opinion anything done by a specified person on a specified occasion related to one or more of three matters was done on behalf of the Crown. The three matters are national security, the economic well-being of the United Kingdom, and the prevention or detection of serious crime.[65] The person and the occasion in question must be specified in the certificate;[66] and the certificate is conclusive evidence that the Act of 1997 does not apply to any conduct of that person on that occasion.[67] 16–65

[63] *ibid.*, ss.4(2), 7(3), (4).
[64] *ibid.*, s.4(3). Note than the third defence is narrower than the equivalent in the offence of harassment.
[65] Protection from Harassment Act 1997, s.12(1).
[66] *ibid.*, s.12(2).
[67] *ibid.*, s.12(1).

Part Five

RENT

1. INTRODUCTION

Under the Act of 1988, the restrictions on the amount of rent that a landlord may lawfully require his tenant to pay under an assured tenancy are much narrower and less stringent than those under the Rent Acts. There is no system of registered rents to limit the rent that can be charged on the grant of a tenancy, and the restrictions operate only by enabling certain assured tenants to refer their rents to the rent assessment committee.

There are two separate categories. First, there are assured periodic tenancies; and secondly, there are assured shorthold tenancies. Each has its own system, and each will be considered in a separate chapter. In this introduction, the two systems will each be briefly summarised, before setting out certain minor provisions that apply to rent generally. Chapters 17 and 18 will then examine the two systems.

2. THE TWO SYSTEMS: AN INTRODUCTION

1. Assured periodic tenancies

(a) Initial rent

There is no restriction on the amount of rent that may be charged on the grant of a periodic tenancy. If the rent exceeds £25,000 per annum the tenancy will not be assured; but then *a fortiori* there is no statutory restriction on quantum. Only if the landlord seeks to increase the rent under the statutory provisions for increase can the tenant refer the rent to the rent assessment committee.

(b) Increase by landlord

At any time after the first year of an assured periodic tenancy to which this provision applies, the landlord may increase the rent, by whatever amount he chooses, by duly serving a statutory notice of increase on the tenant. The increase, however, is subject to the tenant's right to refer the increased rent to the rent assessment committee. The provision applies to all statutory periodic tenancies. It also applies to all other assured periodic tenancies except those which are subject to some contractual provision for increasing the rent.

(c) Reference to committee

Where the landlord has served a valid statutory notice of increase, the tenant may refer the notice to the rent assessment committee before it is due to take effect. The committee will thereupon determine the open market rent for the dwelling-house; and this rent will normally become the rent under the tenancy from the date specified in the notice of increase.

(d) Open market rent

The committee will determine the open market rent on the basis of an assured tenancy of the dwelling-house, making certain assumptions and disregarding certain matters. But in contrast with the Rent Acts there is no provision for disregarding any "scarcity element".[1]

2. Assured shorthold tenancies

There are two classes of assured shorthold tenancy, depending (essentially) on whether they were granted before February 28, 1997 ("old shortholds"), or on or after that date ("new shortholds"). An original old assured shorthold tenancy[2] is necessarily a tenancy for a fixed term of not less than six months in respect of which a shorthold notice has been served. A new assured shorthold may be for a fixed term of any length, or periodic.

(a) Initial rent

There is no restriction as such on the amount of rent that may be charged on the grant of an assured shorthold tenancy.

[1] See Vol. 1, p. 558.
[2] See *ante*, paras. 8–23 *et seq.*

(b) Reference to committee

But the tenant under an original old assured shorthold tenancy has the right to refer the rent to the rent assessment committee as soon as the tenancy has been granted or at any time thereafter. Similarly, the tenant under a new shorthold tenancy has a period of six months from its beginning to refer the rent; and the rent determined by the committee will become the rent under the tenancy from the date specified by the committee, not being earlier than the date of the application. Tenants under derivative old assured shorthold tenancies[3] and new assured shorthold tenants after the expiry of six months lack this right, though if the tenancy is periodic and the landlord serves a notice of increase, the provisions of the first system[4] will apply.

(c) Rent reasonably to be expected

The rent determined by the committee is to be the rent that the landlord might reasonably be expected to obtain under the tenancy; but the committee must not make a determination unless the rent under the tenancy is ''significantly higher'' than this and there is also a sufficiency of comparables in the locality. There is no reference to an open market rent.

3. Other tenancies

There is no provision for referring the rents of any tenancies outside these categories to the committee. Except in the cases of original old assured shorthold tenancies and the first six months from grant of new assured shorthold tenancies, no rent under a fixed term tenancy can be referred to the committee, even if it is a derivative assured shorthold tenancy. Nor can the rent under a periodic tenancy which is subject to a rent increase clause be referred, however harsh the operation of the clause may be, unless it is a new assured shorthold tenancy and less than six months from the grant have expired.

3. GENERAL PROVISIONS

Two provisions that apply to rent generally will be considered here.

1. Distress

No distress for the rent of any dwelling-house let on an assured tenancy may be levied except with the leave of the county court.[5] On any application for leave,

[3] See *ibid.*
[4] *Ante*, p. 338.
[5] Act of 1988, s.19(1).

the court has the same powers with respect to adjournment, stay, suspension, postponement and otherwise as it has in proceedings for possession.[6] These provisions are in almost the same terms as those under the Rent Acts.[7] They do not apply, however, to the exercise of the landlord's right[8] to require a county court bailiff who is levying execution on the tenant to distrain for a limited amount of arrears of rent.[9]

2. Rent books

The provisions of the Landlord and Tenant Act 1985[10] which require landlords to give certain information to residential tenants and to provide rent books for weekly residential tenants are expressed in general terms that apply to assured tenancies. They are considered in Volume 1.[11] For assured tenancies and assured agricultural occupancies, a new form has been provided for insertion in rent books or other similar documents.[12]

[6] Act of 1988, s. 19(1); for these powers, see *ante*, paras. 13–49 *et seq*.
[7] Act of 1977, s.147(1); see Vol. 1, p. 524.
[8] Under County Courts Act 1984, s.102.
[9] Act of 1988, s.19(2).
[10] ss.1–7.
[11] pp. 525–530, and see annotation thereto in Supplement.
[12] Rent Book (Forms of Notice) (Amendment) Regulations 1988 (S.I. 1988 No. 2198), reg. 2, Sched., inserting Pt. IV into The Rent Book (Forms of Notice) Regulations 1982 (S.I. 1982 No. 1474), Sched. The form inserted in Pt. IV of the Schedule to the 1982 Regulations was further amended in consequence of the abolition of domestic rates and the introduction of council tax by amendment regulations: S.I. 1990 No. 1067, reg. 2; S.I. 1993 No. 656, reg. 2. For Pt. IV as so amended, see *post*, p. 582; for the 1982 Regulations, see Vol. 2, p. 1209.

Chapter 17

Rent Under Assured Periodic Tenancies

The rent under assured periodic tenancies will be considered in four sections:

1. Initial rent
2. Increase by landlord
3. Reference to rent assessment committee
4. Open market rent.

Sect. 1. Initial Rent

1. The agreed rent

Under the Act of 1988, the basic rule is that the rent under any assured tenancy will be whatever rent the parties have agreed. This rule is based on the absence of any provision to oust the common law; it is nowhere expressly enunciated. The rule applies even if a rent for the dwelling has been determined and registered under the Rent Acts, and even if under the Act of 1988 the rent assessment committee has previously determined the rent for the same dwelling under an earlier tenancy between the same or other parties. In contrast with the Rent Acts, the Act of 1988 contains no provision for a register of rents that will apply to subsequent tenancies of the dwelling, and there is nothing to give effect to any rents registered under the Rent Acts. The tenant must simply pay what he has agreed to pay. Not unless the landlord serves a notice of increase on the tenant can he refer the rent to the rent assessment committee; but then he may seek to mitigate the increase proposed by the landlord. 17–01

2. Continuance of initial rent

The initial rent will usually continue to be binding for a substantial period. Under a fixed term tenancy, there is no power for either party, in the absence of an express term providing for it, to seek to re-open or review the rent that 17–02 they agreed. Under a periodic tenancy, the landlord alone has a qualified right to seek to increase the rent. A tenant under an original old assured shorthold tenancy can refer his rent to the rent assessment committee forthwith;[1] but he has no such unilateral power under an assured periodic tenancy. Only if the landlord serves a notice of increase on the tenant can the tenant refer it to the committee. If the landlord is content with the amount of rent that he is receiving, or simply overlooks serving a notice of increase, the rent payable under the periodic tenancy will continue at the rate previously applying to it.

Sect. 2. Increase by Landlord

17–03 The system whereby landlords may increase the rent of assured periodic tenancies will now be examined under five heads. First, there are the types of tenancy that are within the system; second, there are the exceptions from the system; third, there is the method of making the increase, by serving a notice of increase; fourth, there is the effect of the notice; and fifth, there is the right of the tenant to refer the notice to the rent assessment committee. The fifth head is considered under Sect.3.[2]

1. Types of tenancy

17–04 Subject to the exceptions set out below, the statutory system for increasing rents applies to all assured periodic tenancies; it has no application to fixed term tenancies. For this purpose the Act of 1988 divides assured periodic tenancies into two categories, namely—

(1) ''a statutory periodic tenancy'', and
(2) ''any other periodic tenancy which is an assured tenancy''.[3]

No other type of tenancy is within the system. It does therefore apply in principle to periodic assured shorthold tenancies.[4] So even where the tenant has no, or no longer has the, right to challenge the rent payable under his assured shorthold tenancy, the landlord has the right to seek to have the rent payable under a periodic shorthold increased.

[1] As can a new assured shorthold tenant during the period of six months from the beginning of his original tenancy. For these, see *post*, paras. 18–26 *et seq*.
[2] *Post*, para. 17–16.
[3] Act of 1988, s.13(1).
[4] Act of 1988, ss.13(1), 14(9), the latter inserted on February 28, 1997 by Housing Act 1996, ss.104, 232(3), Sched. 8, para. 2(1), (2); S.I. 1997 No. 225. See *ante*, para. 8–40.

2. Exceptions

(a) The excepted tenancies

Certain assured periodic tenancies are excepted from the system. There are two heads. **17–05**

(i) EXEMPT LANDLORD. The system for increasing rents does not apply in the case of any statutory periodic tenancy which "cannot for the time being be an assured tenancy" because the interest of the landlord belongs to the Crown, or to a local authority, housing authority or housing action trust;[5] these stand outside the system altogether.[6]

(ii) RENT INCREASE CLAUSES. The statutory system does not apply in the case of "any other periodic tenancy" which is an assured tenancy "in relation to which there is a provision, for the time being binding on the tenant, under which the rent for a particular period of the tenancy will or may be greater than the rent for an earlier period".[7] The general effect is that if the tenancy is subject to its own contractual provision for increasing the rent, that provision will take effect to the exclusion of the statutory system for increasing rents. The terms of this exception make it clear that the right of a tenant during the period of six months from the beginning of a new assured shorthold tenancy to refer the amount of the rent to a rent assessment committee[8] is not a "provision" for these purposes. What is less clear is whether a statutory periodic assured shorthold tenancy, which arises on the termination of a fixed term assured shorthold tenancy which contained rent review provisions, itself contains those provisions,[9] and if so whether they oust the statutory system for increasing rents of periodic tenancies. A provision that will have this effect may for brevity be called a "rent increase clause"; and its meaning and effect are considered below.

(b) Effect of rent increase clause

As stated above, for any assured periodic tenancy except a statutory periodic tenancy, the presence of a rent increase clause will exclude the statutory system for increasing rents; only the rent increase clause will apply. This is clear; but for statutory periodic tenancies the position is less clear. In general, the terms of a statutory periodic tenancy "are the same as those of the fixed term tenancy" **17–06**

[5] *i.e.* tenancies that for the time being fall within Act of 1988, Sched. 1, paras. 11 or 12; *ante*, paras. 4–36, 4–43.

[6] Act of 1988, s.13(1)(a). Of course, for the time being such a tenancy is not an assured tenancy in any event, and so the implication seems to be that once a statutory periodic tenancy arises under the Act, the rent increase provisions of ss.13, 14 apply to it even if, for the time being, some other para. of Sched. 1 prevents the tenancy from being an assured tenancy. *Sed quaere*.

[7] Act of 1988, s.13(1)(b).

[8] *ibid*., s.22(1), (2), as amended by Housing Act 1996, ss.100, 104, 232(3), Sched. 8, para. 2(5); S.I. 1997 No. 225.

[9] *ibid*., s.5(3)(e); *ante*, para. 7–12.

which preceded it,[10] so that where there was a rent increase clause in the fixed term tenancy, that clause should become one of the terms of the statutory periodic tenancy. On that footing, questions would then arise about how the statutory system and the rent increase clause would work in harness.

The explicit provision which for other periodic tenancies makes the rent increase clause prevail is not matched by any corresponding provision for statutory periodic tenancies.[10a] By itself, this would not show that there is to be the opposite result for these tenancies; there is merely a silence. But this result could be produced in a different way, namely by preventing the rent increase clause from being included in the statutory periodic tenancy. This is at least a possible effect of the provision that it is only "subject to the following provisions of this Part of this Act" that the terms of the fixed term tenancy become terms of the ensuing statutory periodic tenancy,[11] so that it is only subject to the statutory system for increasing rents that the rent increase clause could become a term of the statutory periodic tenancy; for that system is laid down in the "following provisions of this Part of this Act".[12] Although the operation of the statutory system is not necessarily incompatible with the presence of a rent increase clause in the tenancy, there would be many difficulties, and so it seems probable that the somewhat delphic "subject to" is intended to exclude any rent increase clause from the statutory periodic tenancy. On that footing, the clear rule that for other periodic tenancies a rent increase clause will exclude the statutory system for increasing rent will have as its counterpart a less clear rule to the opposite effect for statutory periodic tenancies. In short, for other periodic tenancies the rent increase clause prevails, while for statutory periodic tenancies the statutory system prevails.

(c) Rent increase clauses

17–07 Over the last three decades, many variant contractual provisions for revising the rent under leases of commercial properties for fixed terms have become both commonplace and a fruitful source of litigation. Though not unknown,[13] they have been less prominent in periodic tenancies, and for obvious reasons they have been absent from tenancies within the Rent Acts. They are now becoming more common in longer assured tenancies of dwelling-houses, though somewhat rare in periodic assured tenancies. To be effective for the purposes of increases of rent under assured periodic tenancies, they must comply with the not very stringent requirements of the Act of 1988.[14]

[10] Act of 1988, s.5(3)(e), *supra*.

[10a] Probably it is implicit in the separation of statutory periodic tenancies and other periodic tenancies in the two sub-paras. of Act of 1988, s.13(1).

[11] *ibid.*, s.5(3)(e).

[12] By ss.13, 14.

[13] See, *e.g.*, *Greater London Council v. Connolly* [1970] 2 Q.B. 100, CA.

[14] Act of 1988, s.13(1)(b); see *ante*, p. 343, and *infra*.

(i) "IN RELATION TO WHICH THERE IS A PROVISION". The Act applies if "there is a provision" and that provision relates to the tenancy;[15] it does not require that the provision should be one of the terms of the tenancy agreement itself. Usually it will be; but an independent provision made after the tenancy was granted (but relating to it) will suffice if it satisfies the other requirements, *e.g.* as to being binding on the tenant.[16] **17–08**

(ii) "FOR THE TIME BEING". The provision must for the time being be binding on the tenant.[17] Thus, where the provision is to operate for only a limited period, the statutory system for increases will apply whenever that period is not running.

(iii) "BINDING ON THE TENANT". The provision must be binding on the tenant.[18] Under the general law, decisions on rent review clauses show that such clauses may be valid and binding on the tenant even though they condescend to very little particularity. Thus a provision that merely states that the rent "is liable to be increased or decreased on notice being given" is not void for uncertainty,[19] even though the amount of the rent depends, in a sense, on the whim of the landlord.[20] The courts are most reluctant to hold an agreement void for uncertainty, and will strive to give it meaning and effect.[21] Similarly, the requirement that a rent must be certain is satisfied if it has become certain by the time it is due for payment.[22] But an agreement to pay "such a rental as may be agreed upon between the parties", stating no basis on which the rent is to be determined, and providing no machinery for resolving a failure to agree, is void for uncertainty.[23] A successor in title of the original tenant who agreed the rent increase clause is likely to be bound by the term.[24]

(iv) FOR A PARTICULAR PERIOD OF THE TENANCY. This head would not include a provision whereby the rent could be increased for the whole period of the tenancy, as might be done under a provision making an increase of rent operate retrospectively.[25] Given that the tenancy is a periodic tenancy, so that any increase will operate indefinitely and for longer than a rent period of the ten-

[15] *ibid.*

[16] In relation to a tenancy made on or after January 1, 1996, such a provision would bind successors in title of the tenant as a "tenant covenant" of the tenancy, regardless of the fact that it was made outside the agreement itself: Landlord and Tenant (Covenants) Act 1995, ss.2(1), 3(2), 28(1). For tenancies granted or contracted before that date, the test is whether the review agreement touches and concerns the land, which any agreement to review the rent *prima facie* would do: see *P. & A. Swift Investments Ltd. v. Combined English Stores Group plc* [1989] A.C. 643.

[17] Act of 1988, s.13(1)(b).

[18] *ibid.*

[19] *Greater London Council v. Connolly, supra.*

[20] *ibid.*, at p. 109.

[21] *ibid.*, at p. 108; and see *Brown v. Gould* [1972] Ch. 53 at 56, 57, Ch.

[22] *Greater London Council v. Connolly, supra.*

[23] *King's Motors (Oxford) Ltd. v. Lax* [1970] 1 W.L.R. 426, Lanc. Ch., distinguished in *Corson v. Rhuddlan B.C.* (1990) 59 P. & C.R. 185, CA, where a maximum rent had been specified; and see *Brown v. Gould, supra.*

[24] See *supra*, n. 16.

[25] As in *C.H. Bailey Ltd. v. Memorial Enterprises Ltd.* [1974] 1 W.L.R. 728, CA, and *United Scientific Holdings Ltd. v. Burnley B.C.* [1978] A.C. 904.

ancy,[26] it is not easy to identify the "particular period"; nor is it obvious what is added by this provision.

(v) WILL OR MAY BE GREATER. This phrase is wide enough to include every type of provision for revising the rent, whether by pre-determined amounts (a "progressive rent"),[27] or by index-linking, valuation, arbitration, decision of the landlord or a third party, or anything else except a provision that can operate only to reduce the rent; for under any other provision the new rent at least "may" be greater than the old.

(d) Variable service charges

17–09 There is some uncertainty about the position of a tenancy under which the tenant is liable to pay a variable service charge, *i.e.* a charge for services which may vary according to the relevant costs.[28] Under the statutory system for increasing rents, the jurisdiction of the rent assessment committee is to determine the rent, including service charges, even if they are payable separately; but if these service charges are variable, the committee is required to determine the rent apart from them, for they are subject to their own system of control.[29] Yet a provision for a variable service charge plainly seems to be a provision under which the rent for a period of the tenancy may be greater than the rent for an earlier period; and as such it is arguably a rent increase clause that will exclude the statutory system for increasing rent,[30] and thus prevent the rent from ever reaching the committee. The statutory provisions in question[31] give no indication how this apparent conflict is to be resolved; but it seems more reasonable to treat a provision for a variable service charge as not being a rent increase clause than to exclude the rest of the rent from the jurisdiction that the statute appears intended to confer. Until the point is resolved in the courts, it therefore seems best to treat a provision for a variable service charge as not being a rent increase clause.

3. Notice of increase

17–10 The statutory system for increasing rent depends upon the landlord duly serving a notice of increase on the tenant.

(a) The notice

"For the purpose of securing an increase in the rent under a tenancy" within this system, "the landlord may serve on the tenant a notice in the prescribed

[26] As the expression is used in Act of 1988, s.5(3)(d). See *Greater London Council v. Connolly*, *supra*.
[27] See *ante*, para. 6–13.
[28] *Post*, para. 17–43.
[29] *Post*, paras. 17–43, 17–48.
[30] *Ante*, para. 17–05.
[31] Act of 1988, ss.13(1)(b), 14(4). There is nothing to suggest that either is to be subject to the other.

form[32] proposing a new rent to take effect at the beginning of a new period of the tenancy specified in the notice''.[33] For brevity, such a notice will be called a ''notice of increase''.

(b) Date for increase

The new period of the tenancy that is specified in the notice of increase must be a period beginning not earlier than the latest of three dates.[34] These dates are as follows.

(i) MINIMUM PERIOD. First, there is the end of the ''minimum period'' after the date of service of the notice.[35] The ''minimum period'' is six months for yearly tenancies, one month for tenancies where the period is less than a month, and a period equal to a period of the tenancy in any other case.[36] **17–11**

(ii) FIRST ANNIVERSARY OF TENANCY. Next, there is the first anniversary of the date on which the first period of the tenancy began.[37] But this does not apply to a statutory periodic tenancy;[38] thus, if such a tenancy arose at the end of a fixed term tenancy for a very short period, the date for the increase might be less than a year after the fixed term had begun. But statutory periodic tenancies must comply with the other conditions.

(iii) FIRST ANNIVERSARY OF PREVIOUS INCREASE. Finally, if the rent under the tenancy has previously been increased either by a notice under these provisions or by a rent assessment committee, there is the first anniversary of the date on which the increase took effect.[39] This head does not apply if the rent has been increased in any other way (such as by agreement), or if a reference to the rent assessment committee resulted in no increase being made.

(c) Introduction of council tax

On April 1, 1990, domestic rates were abolished[40] in favour of the community charge, which was not a property based tax. On April 1, 1993, the community **17–12**

[32] The Assured Tenancies and Agricultural Occupancies (Forms) Regulations 1997 (S.I. 1997 No. 194) (''the 1997 Forms Regulations''), reg.3(d), Sched., Form No. 4, or a form substantially to the same effect. The 1997 Forms Regulations revoked (by reg.4(1)) the Assured Tenancies and Agricultural Occupancies (Forms) Regulations 1988 (S.I. 1988 No. 2203) and successive amendment regulations, and the 1997 Forms Regulations came into effect on February 28, 1997. But the revocation of the 1988 Regulations, as amended, does not affect the validity of a notice in the then correct form served before that date. The original 1988 Regulations are printed in the first edition of Vol. 3 at pp. 324 *et seq.*, and the successive amendment regulations are noted in the Supplement. The final amended version of the 1988 Regulations, and the 1997 Forms Regulations, are printed *post*, pp. 588 *et seq*, 621 *et seq*.

[33] Act of 1988, s.13(2).

[34] *ibid.*

[35] *ibid.*, s.13(2)(a).

[36] *ibid.*, s.13(3).

[37] *ibid.*, s.13(2)(b).

[38] *ibid.*

[39] *ibid.*, s.13(2)(c).

[40] By Local Government Finance Act 1988, s.117(1), Sched. 13, Pt. I.

charge was in its turn abolished,[41] and was replaced by the council tax, which once again was essentially property based. The effect in many cases was that landlords of assured tenants, who had granted assured tenancies on the assumption that local taxes would be borne by the tenant as community charge, found themselves liable for the council tax for the dwelling-house. In other cases, however, the advance publicity for the commencement of council tax enabled landlords to include provisions in tenancy agreements for their tenants to make payments to them in respect of council tax for which they would be liable. For fixed term tenancies, the absence of any machinery in the Act of 1988 for variation of the rent prevails. But for periodic tenancies, the Secretary of State made two provisions under delegated legislation[42] to enable the rent payable to be revised to take into account the council tax liability.

First, the Act of 1988 was amended to provide that for notices of increase served on or after April 1, 1993, rent assessment committees to which any such notices were referred by assured tenants should, in determining the rent,[43] have regard to the amount of council tax for which the landlord or a superior landlord was liable in respect of the hereditament of which the dwelling-house formed part.[44] This provision is considered further below.[45] Secondly, in cases where a notice of increase had been served before April 1, 1993,[46] and either no increased rent had taken effect pursuant to it before that date or, if an increase had taken effect, the anniversary of that increase had not arrived,[47] the landlord was given the right to serve another notice of increase at any time before April 1, 1994.[48] This provision only applied where the terms of the tenancy, or an agreement collateral to the tenancy, made the tenant liable to make payments to the landlord in respect of council tax.[49] The procedure for this notice of increase was essentially the same as for a general notice of increase,[50] but a form for each of the notice of increase and the reference of the notice to the rent assessment committee was prescribed.[51]

Although the statutory provisions made were detailed, they are now of historic interest only owing to March 31, 1994 being the last day for serving this special notice of increase, and accordingly this summary of their effect must suffice.[52]

[41] By Local Government Finance Act 1992, Pt. III, s.100.

[42] Local Government Finance (Housing) (Consequential Amendments) Order 1993 (S.I. 1993 No. 651), coming into force on April 1, 1993, and made pursuant to Local Government Finance Act 1992, ss.113(1), 114.

[43] Under Act of 1988, s.14(1).

[44] Local Government Finance (Housing) (Consequential Amendments) Order 1993, *supra*, art. 1, Sched. 1, para. 17(1), (2), inserting subss. (3A), (3B) in Act of 1988, s.14 with effect from April 1, 1993.

[45] *Post*, para. 17–45.

[46] To which the amendment and statutory "regard" did not apply: *ibid*., art. 1(2)(c).

[47] Such that the landlord would have been able to serve another notice of increase.

[48] Local Government Finance (Housing) (Consequential Amendments) Order 1993, *supra*, art. 2(2), Sched. 2, para. 8, inserting ss.14A, 14B in Act of 1988 with effect from April 1, 1993.

[49] Act of 1988, s.14A(1)(b), as inserted.

[50] *Ante*, para. 17–10.

[51] Assured Tenancies and Agricultural Occupancies (Forms) (Amendment) Regulations 1993 (S.I. 1993 No. 654), reg.2(a), Sched., Forms Nos. 6A, 6B respectively.

[52] The Order (S.I. 1993 No. 651), so far as material, and the provisions inserted into the Act of 1988, are printed *post*, pp. 618–620.

4. Effect of notice

(a) Variation of rent

Where a notice of increase is served under these provisions, ''a new rent specified in the notice shall take effect as mentioned in the notice unless before the beginning of the new period specified in the notice'' either of two events occurs.[53] If neither event occurs in time, the existing rent is replaced by the rent stated in the notice as from the beginning of the new period of the tenancy specified in the notice.[54] If one of the events does occur in time, the notice does not have effect, though if the proposed increase is referred to the rent assessment committee,[55] the date specified in the notice for the increase of rent to take effect will be of potential significance.[56] **17–13**

(b) Variation excluded by reference or agreement

The two events mentioned above are— **17–14**

''(a) the tenant by an application in the prescribed form[57] refers the notice to a rent assessment committee;[58] or
(b) the landlord and the tenant agree on a variation of the rent which is different from that proposed in the notice or agree that the rent should not be varied''[59]

For either of these events to be effective, it must occur ''before the beginning of the new period specified in the notice''.[60] If it does not, the increase proposed in the notice of increase takes effect as mentioned in the notice. References to rent assessment committees will be considered under the next heading;[61] agreements are considered below.

(c) Agreements between landlord and tenant

If the landlord and the tenant are attempting to agree a variation of the rent, there is often a risk that time might expire while the variation is still in course of negotiation. It may thus be advisable for the tenant to make a precautionary reference to the rent assessment committee in due time, with a view to withdrawing it[62] if the negotiations ripen into an agreed variation. The Act of 1988 **17–15**

[53] Act of 1988, s.13(4), *infra*.
[54] *ibid.*
[55] *Infra.*
[56] *Post*, para. 17–21.
[57] The 1997 Forms Regulations (S.I. 1997 No. 194), *supra*, reg.3(e), Sched., Form No. 5.
[58] Act of 1988, s.13(4)(a).
[59] *ibid.*, s.13(4)(b).
[60] *ibid.*, s.13(4).
[61] *Post*, para. 17–16.
[62] See *post*, paras. 17–23 *et seq.*

specifically provides that nothing in this machinery for increasing rent[63] affects the right of the landlord or the tenant under an assured tenancy to vary by agreement any term of the tenancy, including a term relating to rent.[64] Any agreement should specify the date when the agreed new rent is to take effect, for the Act, though specific as to increases made by the notice of increase[65] or by the rent assessment committee,[66] makes no provision for variations made by agreement. But if the agreement is silent as to the date, it might be possible to infer that the agreed new rent is to run from the new period of the tenancy specified in the notice of increase.

Sect. 3. Reference to Rent Assessment Committee

1. The reference

17–16 A tenant may refer a notice of increase to the rent assessment committee by making an application to the committee in the prescribed form.[67] The application must be made "before the beginning of the new period specified" in the landlord's notice of increase;[68] and the committee has no power to extend the time. The tenant's application presumably "refers" the notice to the committee when his duly completed application in the prescribed form, with a copy of the landlord's notice,[69] is delivered to the committee.[70] For joint tenants, the prescribed form requires signature by all the tenants (or their agents), unless one signs on behalf of "the rest"[71] with their agreement.[72] In general, the procedure laid down for rent assessment committees under the Rent Acts has been made applicable to references under the Act of 1988;[73] but certain specific provisions have been made for the initial stages.

2. Representations

17–17 Where a reference to a rent assessment committee is made under the Act of

[63] *i.e.* in Act of 1988, ss.13, 14.
[64] *ibid.*, s.13(5).
[65] *Ante*, para. 17–13.
[66] *Post*, para. 17–21.
[67] The 1997 Forms Regulations (S.I. 1997 No. 194), *supra*, reg.3(e), Sched., Form No. 5.
[68] Act of 1988, s.13(4).
[69] See Form No. 5, *supra*, para. 12.
[70] Compare restricted contracts, where regulations (S.I. 1980 No. 1700, reg.3) state when a reference is deemed to have reached the tribunal: see Vol. 1, p. 765.
[71] And by implication himself.
[72] *Turley v. Panton* (1975) 29 P. & C.R. 397, DC; and see *R. v. Rent Officer for London Borough of Camden, ex p. Felix* (1988) 21 H.L.R. 34, QB.
[73] See *post*, para. 17–19.

1988, the first step must be taken by the committee.[74] This applies not only to a reference of a notice of increase under the present head, but also to a reference of the rent under an assured shorthold tenancy,[75] a reference of the rent under the special council tax provisions,[76] and to a reference to vary the terms of a statutory periodic tenancy.[77] The committee must serve on each party a notice specifying a period of not less than seven days from the service of the notice during which either representations in writing or "a request to make" oral representations may be made by that party to the committee;[78] and the notice served on the party who did not make the reference must be accompanied by a copy of the reference.[79] No time for serving this notice is specified. If within the seven days (or such further period as the committee may allow) a party makes a request to make oral representations, the committee must give him an opportunity of being heard in person or by a person authorised by him, whether or not of Counsel or a solicitor.[80] The committee must make such inquiry (if any) as they think fit, and consider any information supplied or representation made to them under these provisions.[81]

3. Information required by the committee

On a reference being made under any of these provisions,[82] the committee may by notice in the prescribed form[83] served on the landlord or the tenant require him to give the committee, within a specified period not less than 14 days from the service of the notice, "such information as they may reasonably require for the purposes of their functions".[84] Failure to comply with the notice is a summary offence.[85] In the case of an offence by a body corporate, any director, manager or secretary or other similar officer, or any person purporting to act as such, is also guilty of the offence and liable accordingly, if the offence is proved to have been committed with his consent or connivance, or to be attributable to any neglect by him.[86] **17–18**

[74] The Rent Assessment Committees (England and Wales) Regulations 1971 (S.I. 1971 No. 1065) ("the 1971 Regulations"), reg.2A(2). Reg. 2A was inserted by the Rent Assessment Committees (England and Wales) (Amendment) Regulations 1988 (S.I. 1988 No. 2200), reg.2(3) and amended successively by the Rent Assessment Committees (England and Wales) (Amendment) Regulations 1993 (S.I. 1993 No. 653), reg.2(b), and the Rent Assessment Committees (England and Wales) (Amendment) Regulations 1997 (S.I. 1997 No. 3007), reg.2. It is printed in its current form *post*, pp. 553, 554.
[75] *ibid.*, see *post*, para. 18–09.
[76] *Ante*, para. 17–12.
[77] *Ante*, paras. 7–14 *et seq.*
[78] The 1971 Regulations, *supra*, reg.2A(2).
[79] *ibid.*, reg.2A(3).
[80] *ibid.*, regs 2(3), 2A(4), the former as amended by The Rent Assessment Committees (England and Wales) (Amendment) Regulations 1988, *supra*, reg.2(2).
[81] The 1971 Regulations, reg.2A(5).
[82] *i.e.* those referred to in the previous paragraph.
[83] The 1997 Forms Regulations, *supra*, reg.3(g), Sched., Form No. 7.
[84] Act of 1988, s.41(2).
[85] *ibid.* s.41(3). Penalty: a fine not exceeding level 3 on the standard scale (£400: Criminal Justice Act 1982, s.37; S.I. 1984 No. 447, art. 2(4), Sched. 4).
[86] Act of 1988, s.41(4).

4. Procedure

17–19 As mentioned above,[87] references under the Act of 1988[88] have been brought[89] within the procedure for rent assessment committees under the Rent Acts.[90] This is considered in detail in Volume 1.[91]

5. Determination

17–20 Where a tenant has referred a notice of increase to the rent assessment committee, the committee must determine the rent at which they consider the dwelling-house might reasonably be expected to be let in the open market in accordance with a number of specified factors. This will be considered later in Sect. 4.[92] The committee must note in their determination the amount (if any which is more than negligible) of the rent which in their opinion is fairly attributable to the provision of services.[93]

6. Effect of determination

17–21 Where a notice of increase has been referred to a rent assessment committee, ''the rent determined by the committee . . . shall be the rent under the tenancy with effect from the beginning of the new period specified in the notice''.[94] This, however, is subject to two qualifications.

(a) Contrary agreement

This provision does not apply if ''the landlord and the tenant otherwise agree''.[95]

87 *Ante*, para. 17–16.
88 *i.e.* under Act of 1988, ss.3, 13, 14A and 22. And also references under Landlord and Tenant Act 1954, Pt. I, Sched. 5, para. 5, as applied by Local Government and Housing Act 1989, Sched. 10, para. 19, and under Local Government and Housing Act 1989, Sched. 10, paras. 6(2), 10(2): see *ante*, paras. 10–35, 10–42.
89 By S.I. 1988 No. 2200, *supra*, reg.2(1), as amended: see n. 74, *supra*.
90 Under the 1971 Regulations, *supra*, as amended. And see Act of 1977, s.74(1)(b)(ii), as amended by Leasehold Reform, Housing and Urban Development Act 1993, s.187, Sched. 21, para. 7. That Act, by ss.88, 91, extended further the jurisdiction of rent assessment committees to deal as leasehold valuation tribunals with enfranchisement issues under it and under the Leasehold Reform Act 1967.
91 pp. 616–625. The 1971 Regulations, as amended by S.I. 1988 No. 2200, reg.2(4), (5), make specific provision as to notice of the date of hearing and the supply of documents to the parties, in line with the provisions under the Rent Acts: see Vol. 1, pp. 617, 619.
92 *Post*, p. 356.
93 Act of 1988, s.41A, inserted by Social Security (Consequential Provisions) Act 1992, ss.4, 7(2), Sched. 2, para. 102.
94 Act of 1988, s.14(7).
95 *ibid*.

(b) Date: undue hardship

If it appears to the committee that it would cause "undue hardship" to the tenant for the new rent to be payable with effect from the beginning of the period specified in the notice, the committee may direct that the new rent should be payable from such a later date (not being later than the date of the determination) as the committee may direct.[96] The concept of "undue" hardship is difficult; little help is to be found in considering what degree of hardship is "due".[97] But there might well be "undue hardship" that would support a later date if a heavy increase of rent is made after the lapse of a substantial period between the application and the determination, and this produces greater arrears of rent than the tenant could fairly have been expected to provide for, perhaps even amounting to a mandatory ground for possession.[98]

7. Reduction of rent

When a notice of increase is referred to the committee, what has to be decided is not whether the increase is justified but what the open market rent would be. No doubt in most cases the main contentions will in substance turn on whether or not the increase is too great; but if the initial rent was excessive, or if the market has fallen substantially, the committee might conclude that the open market rent is less than the initial rent. In that case the landlord's attempt to increase the rent will result in its being reduced. 17–22

8. Withdrawal of reference

Despite the duty to determine the rent when a reference has been duly made, the committee is not required to continue with the determination if the tenancy has come to an end, or if the landlord and tenant give notice in writing that they no longer require such a determination.[99] Neither event terminates the reference or, *semble*, the jurisdiction of the committee; each of them merely releases the committee from the obligation to continue with the determination. More difficult questions as to the jurisdiction of the committee arise if, before they determine the rent, the tenancy ceases to be assured, or if the determination of the open market rent[1] would itself cause the tenancy to cease to be assured. These jurisdictional questions are addressed later.[2] 17–23

[96] *ibid.*, s.14(7).

[97] The same phrase was used, and the same difficulty of interpretation arose, in Arbitration Act 1950, s.27 (Power of court to extend time for commencing arbitration proceedings): see *Tote Bookmakers Ltd. v. Development and Property Holding Co. Ltd.* [1985] Ch. 261, Ch (hardship "undue" when not warranted by the circumstances). But under that Act, the applicant has been at fault, and so the implications may be different.

[98] See Ground 8; *ante*, paras. 14–70 *et seq.*

[99] Act of 1988, s.14(8).

[1] See *post*, paras. 17–30 *et seq.*

[2] *Post*, paras. 17–27, 17–28.

(a) Tenancy ended

17–24 Where the rent is less than the open market rent, and the tenancy comes to an end, a determination of the open market rent by the committee might show that a substantial sum for increased rent would be due for the period between the effective date in the notice of increase and the ending of the tenancy. In such a case the committee may consider that the process of determination ought to continue unless the landlord agrees that it should not.

(b) Joint notice

17–25 The committee presumably would not continue with the determination if the landlord and tenant had given written notice that they no longer required a determination. The determination would apply only to the particular tenancy, and would not become a registered rent that would apply to other tenancies and so operate *in rem*. There would thus be no public interest in proceeding to the determination such as under the Rent Acts may point against allowing the reference to be withdrawn.[3] But a landlord should be cautious in signing such a notice unless the tenant has agreed an increase of rent,[4] for the reference to the committee renders the notice of increase ineffective in the absence of a determination of the committee,[5] and so the landlord cannot obtain an increased rent unless he begins again. Although the language of the Act may indicate a single notice from both landlord and tenant, it is suggested that a separate letter from each would suffice; at all events, notice from one alone will not suffice.

(c) Unilateral withdrawal

17–26 There is no provision for the unilateral withdrawal of a reference. Although there seems to be no public interest that would require such a withdrawal to be rejected, the Act does not provide for it, and the withdrawal would arguably force the landlord to begin again,[6] and so delay the increase. The committee would doubtless refuse to permit it without the landlord's consent.

9. Jurisdiction of rent assessment committees

17–27 The committee's jurisdiction derives from the Rent Assessment Committees (England and Wales) Regulations 1971[7] and from the timeous service on it of a

[3] See *Hanson v. Church Commissioners for England* [1978] Q.B. 823, CA; Vol. 1, p. 622. *Quaere* if undue pressure for withdrawal was suspected: see *ante*, para. 7–21.
[4] Act of 1988, s.13(5).
[5] *Ante*, para. 17–14.
[6] Unless the effect of the withdrawal is that it is deemed never to have been referred, so that the increase in the notice takes effect: see Act of 1988, s.13(4). *Sed quaere*.
[7] S.I. 1971 No. 1065, as amended in particular by Amendment Regulations of 1988 (S.I. 1998 No. 2200), inserting reg.2A, and of 1997 (S.I. 1997 No. 3007), substituting new reg.2A(1).

valid application by the tenant referring a landlord's notice of increase.[8] Such a notice is arguably of no effect (unless the tenant agrees the proposed increase) if the tenancy is not an assured tenancy or an assured agricutural occupancy;[9] and if so the committee can have no jurisdiction if the landlord's notice of increase was not a notice within the Act, both for that reason and because the tenant's reference is not a reference "under subsection (4)(a) of section 13 above".[10] On the other hand, the landlord appears to be entitled to serve a notice of increase in the case of any statutory periodic tenancy other than one where Crown or exempted body ownership prevents the tenancy from being an assured tenancy for the time being.[11] The better conclusion therefore appears to be that a statutory periodic tenancy, *i.e.* one arising under the Act[12] upon the termination other than by an order of the court or by the tenant of an assured tenancy, is until it is terminated always susceptible to a notice of increase, even if it is for the time being not assured, except in the two cases of Crown and exempted body ownership just mentioned. Other periodic tenancies, however, must be assured tenancies for the right to serve and refer notices of increase to arise. It follows that in the former case, if a tenancy ceases to be an assured tenancy while the rent assessment committee is seised of the reference, its jurisdiction is not affected by the loss of assured status. But if the tenancy is not a statutory periodic tenancy, the loss of assured status would seem to deprive the committee of jurisdiction to continue with the determination.[13]

A similar problem arises where the rent assessment committee is seised of a reference and is minded to determine an open market rent which, either because it is very high or very low,[14] will result in the tenancy, after the determination comes into effect, not being able to be an assured tenancy from that time. It is now established that the committee must disregard the effect of the rental increase and determine the rent in accordance with the evidence of open market values.[15] **17–28**

10. Control of rent assessment committees

The Act of 1988 contains nothing to modify the existing provisions as to the **17–29**

[8] Act of 1988, ss.13(4), 14(1).
[9] *ibid.*, s.24(4).
[10] *ibid.*, s.14(1). Further, the prescribed forms assume that the tenancy is assured: Assured Tenancies and Agricultural Occupancies (Forms) Regulations 1997 (S.I. 1997 No. 194), reg.3(d), (e), Sched., Forms Nos. 4, 5.
[11] Act of 1988, s.13(1)(a), referring to Sched. 1, paras. 11, 12. The clear implication is that tenancies which, pursuant to other paras. of Sched. 1, are for the time being not assured tenancies are nevertheless statutory periodic tenancies for the purpose of service of a notice of increase; and some support for this conclusion is derived from s.5(2), (7) and the nature of such a tenancy as being contractual.
[12] s.5(2).
[13] The committee would otherwise have to determine the open market rent for a letting "by a willing landlord *under an assured tenancy*" (s.14(1), emphasis added), which would seem unfair on the tenant if in law he had no such secure status.
[14] See *ante*, paras. 4–07, 4–58.
[15] *R. v. London Rent Assessment Panel, ex p. Cadogan Estates Ltd.* [1998] Q.B. 398, QB (rent over £25,000 p.a.). See also *N. & D. (London) Ltd. v. Gadson* (1991) 24 H.L.R. 64, QB (rent £5 per month).

control of rent assessment committees and appeals from their decisions, and so the detailed commentary in Volume 1[16] will apply.

Sect. 4. Open Market Rent

17–30 Where a tenant refers the landlord's notice of increase to a rent assessment committee, the committee's duty is to determine the rent at which the committee considers that "the dwelling-house concerned might reasonably be expected to be let in the open market by a willing landlord under an assured tenancy"[17] which has certain characteristics, though disregarding certain matters. This requirement may be considered under the following heads.

1. Assumptions

17–31 In general, the assured tenancy to be considered by the committee is the same as the existing tenancy.[18] More specifically, the tenancy to be considered has the following characteristics.

(a) Identical dwelling-house

17–32 The committee must determine the rent at which "the dwelling-house concerned" might reasonably be expected to be let.[19] What is to be considered is thus the dwelling-house as it stands, even if it has been altered since the tenancy began. Subject to the "disregards", and especially to tenant's improvements and tenant's defaults,[20] the condition of the dwelling-house to be considered appears to be its condition at the beginning of the new period specified in the landlord's notice of increase.[21]

(b) Same periods

17–33 The tenancy to be considered is a periodic tenancy having the same periods as those of the tenancy to which the notice relates.[22] In the case of a statutory

[16] pp. 593–604, 807–820, as updated in the Supplement, including in particular references to the Tribunals and Inquiries Act 1992.
[17] Act of 1988, s.14(1); and see s.14(9) for assured shorthold tenancies which are periodic tenancies; *post*, paras. 18–05, 18–27.
[18] Though in some circumstances the existing tenancy might not be assured for the time being: see *ante*, para. 17–27.
[19] Act of 1988, s.14(1).
[20] See *post*, paras. 17–38 *et seq.*
[21] See Act of 1988, s.14(1)(b).
[22] *ibid.*, s.14(1)(a).

periodic tenancy, these derived from the periods for which rent was payable under the preceding fixed term tenancy.[23]

(c) Commencement

The tenancy to be considered is one that begins at the beginning of the new period specified in the notice of increase.[24] **17–34**

(d) Terms

The terms of the tenancy to be considered are the same terms as those of the tenancy to which the notice relates, apart from terms relating to the amount of rent.[25] But for statutory periodic tenancies there is a special rule if a reference of a notice of increase under this head and also a reference seeking a variation of the terms of the tenancy are both before the committee.[26] In that case, if the date for the variation of the terms of the tenancy[27] is not later than the first day of the period specified for the new rent to take effect, and the committee proposes to hear both references together, the committee must determine the reference for varying the terms first (and make any consequential adjustments of rent[28]), so that the rent will then be determined in relation to the terms as varied.[29] *Semble* the committee has a discretion as to whether to hear the two references together; and by implication, if the date for the variation of the terms is later that the start of the period for the new rent, the rent must be determined first, and then the new terms, with any appropriate adjustment to the rent in consequence of varied terms being made last. **17–35**

(e) Possession warning notices given

If any warning notices have been given under mandatory grounds for possession 1 to 5,[30] or have effect in relation to the periodic tenancy as if given,[31] the tenancy to be considered by the committee is to be one in respect of which the same notices have been given.[32] **17–36**

[23] *ibid.*, s.5(3)(d); *ante*, para. 7–11.
[24] *ibid.*, s.14(1)(b).
[25] *ibid.*, s.14(1)(c).
[26] Under Act of 1988, s.6; *ante*, para. 7–25.
[27] As specified in the notice under *ibid.*, s.6(2) proposing different terms.
[28] *ibid.*, s.6(5).
[29] Act of 1988, s.14(6); *ante*, para. 7–25. See *O'May v. City of London Real Property Co. Ltd.* [1983] 2 A.C. 726 on the interaction of rent and the terms of the tenancy (business tenancy).
[30] *Ante*, pp. 240–250 (landlord's only or principal home; mortgagee; holiday or student accommodation; minister of religion).
[31] Act of 1988, Sched. 2, Pt. IV, paras. 8–10; see *ante*, para. 14–21.
[32] Act of 1988, s.14(1)(d).

2. Disregards

In making a determination the committee must disregard the following matters.[33]

(a) Sitting tenant

17–37 The first disregard is "any effect on the rent attributable to the granting of a tenancy to a sitting tenant".[34] There is no express assumption of vacant possession,[35] and the effect of this disregard depends on whether the grant is with vacant possession. If it is, it disregards any additional value attributable to the bid of a special purchaser; if it is not, it excludes the substantial reduction in value that would normally result from the actual presence of a sitting tenant with statutory protection. Either way, it seems clear that what was intended was to determine the rent payable in the open market for a letting of the dwelling-house with vacant possession.

(b) Tenant's improvements

17–38 The second disregard is "any increase in the value of the dwelling-house attributable to a relevant improvement carried out by a person who at the time it was carried out was the tenant"[36] provided two requirements are satisfied.[37] This provision is needed because in determining the impersonal question of the market rent of any premises (*e.g.*, under a provision in a rent review clause for "a reasonable rent for the demised premises"), there is a presumption that the premises are valued as they stand, and this includes any improvements that have been made to them even if they were made or paid for by the tenant.[38]

There is no definition of the difficult term "improvement" in the Act of 1988, but the corpus of authorities on the term under the Rent Acts[39] and the general law[40] will provide at least some assistance. There is no provision for disregarding any alteration which, although an improvement from the tenant's point of view,[41] diminishes the value of the dwelling; nor, it seems, could any such diminution be set against an increase in value attributable to some other improvement.

This provision does not apply to improvements carried out by a person before he became "the tenant",[42] even if it was contemplated that a tenancy would be

[33] Act of 1988, s.14(2).
[34] *ibid.*, s.14(2)(a).
[35] *Quaere* whether this should be presumed: *Laura Investment Co. Ltd. v. Havering L.B.C. (No. 2)* [1993] 1 E.G.L.R. 124, Ch. In the statutory circumstances, it probably should, because otherwise the tenancy to be granted might not be an assured tenancy: Act of 1988, s.1(1)(b).
[36] Act of 1988, s.14(2)(b).
[37] For these requirements, see *infra*.
[38] See *Ponsford v. H.M.S. Aerosols Ltd.* [1979] A.C. 63. Contrast the "rent that it would be reasonable for the tenant to pay".
[39] See Vol. 1, pp. 521–524.
[40] See Woodfall's *Law of Landlord and Tenant* (28th (looseleaf) ed.), para. 11.261.
[41] See, *e.g.*, *Lambert v. F.W. Woolworth & Co. Ltd.* [1938] Ch. 883, CA.
[42] Act of 1988, s.14(2)(b).

granted to him,[43] and even, *semble*, if there was then a contract to grant him a tenancy at a future date. But once he becomes "the tenant" it is immaterial that he holds under a mere agreement for a lease and not a lease.[44]

The two requirements that must each be satisfied if an increase in value attributable to an improvement made by the tenant is to be disregarded are as follows.

(i) "RELEVANT IMPROVEMENT". An increase in value attributable to an improvement made by the tenant will be disregarded only if the improvement was a "relevant improvement".[45] There are two ways of establishing this. First, every improvement is a "relevant" improvement if "it was carried out during the tenancy to which the notice relates",[46] however long ago that was. Where the notice relates to a statutory periodic tenancy, improvements made during the preceding fixed term tenancy are not within this provision, for the two tenancies are distinct;[47] but such improvements may instead satisfy the next head. Secondly, an improvement will be a "relevant" improvement if three conditions are all satisfied. They are as follows. **17–39**

(1) The improvement was "carried out not more than twenty-one years before the date of service of the notice".[48] An improvement begun outside this period but completed within it would probably suffice.[49]
(2) "At all times during the period beginning when the improvement was carried out and ending on the date of service of the notice, the dwelling-house has been let under an assured tenancy".[50] Here, "was carried out" may mean "was being carried out" or it may mean "was completed", with the first meaning perhaps the more likely.
(3) On the coming to an end of an assured tenancy at any time during that period the tenant (or, if there are joint tenants, at least one of them) "did not quit".[51] Probably "quit" for this purpose includes departure under an order for possession, or a surrender to the landlord, quite apart from the continuity of tenancy required under the previous paragraph.

If, therefore, an improvement was carried out by the tenant at the time, but he later left the dwelling-house and it was re-let to another assured tenant without any break in continuity of tenancies, the improvement would not be a "relevant" improvement, and would not fall to be disregarded.

[43] Consider *Trustees of Henry Smith's Charity v. Hemmings* (1982) 45 P. & C.R. 377, CA.
[44] "Tenancy" includes "an agreement for a tenancy" (Act of 1988, s.45(1)), and so presumably a person holding under such an agreement is a "tenant", although the definition of "tenant" in the same subsection does not say so.
[45] Act of 1988, s.14(2)(b).
[46] *ibid.*, s.14(3).
[47] See *ante*, para. 7–06.
[48] Act of 1988, s.14(3)(a).
[49] Consider *R. v. Secretary of State for the Environment, ex p. Hackney L.B.C.* [1988] The Times, July 22, DC, contrasting "undertake" with "carry out".
[50] Act of 1988, s.14(3)(b).
[51] *ibid.*, s.14(3)(c).

17–40 (ii) IMPROVEMENT VOLUNTARY. For an increase in value to be disregarded, it is not enough for the improvement to be "relevant"; it must also in effect have been made voluntarily. An increase in value that is attributable to an improvement will not be disregarded if the tenant carried it out "in pursuance of an obligation to his immediate landlord".[52] There is nothing here to confine "obligation" to obligations under the tenancy. But this provision does not apply if the obligation "did not relate to the specific improvement concerned", but "arose by reference to consent given to the carrying out of that improvement".[53] Thus, if the tenant seeks the landlord's consent to carry out an improvement that he is not obliged to effect, and the landlord gives his consent in a formal document under which the tenant agrees to carry out the improvement in a particular manner, any increase in value attributable to the improvement will be disregarded.[54]

(c) Tenant's default

17–41 The third disregard is "any reduction in the value of the dwelling-house attributable to a failure by the tenant to comply with any terms of the tenancy".[55] This corresponds to a provision in the Act of 1977,[56] although that extends to "the tenant or any predecessor in title of his" instead of merely "the tenant".[57] The definition of "tenant" in the Act is wide enough to include the original tenant and the successor where the tenancy is transmitted to the spouse under the Act.[58] But where a new periodic assured tenancy by succession is deemed to have been granted to a successor to a Rent Act tenant,[59] the reference here to "the tenant" can only be to the successor himself, and so any default of the previous Rent Act tenant cannot be visited on the successor.[60]

3. Inclusions and exclusions

17–42 The rent determined by the rent assessment committee is required to be a rent properly so called; the committee does not have jurisdiction to determine a service charge in addition to the rent.[61] With one exception, which is no longer of actual relevance, the rent determined is to be inclusive of payment for additional matters for which the tenant might be paying his landlord, whether or not

[52] Act of 1988, s.14(2)(b)(i).
[53] *ibid.*, s.14(2)(b)(ii).
[54] A result that has been reached in the context of commercial rent review without the benefit of any statutory provision *Historic House Hotels Ltd. v. Cadogan Estates Ltd.* [1993] 2 E.G.L.R. 151, Ch., following *Godbold v. Martin the Newsagents Ltd.* [1983] 2 E.G.L.R. 128, Ch.
[55] Act of 1988, s.14(2)(c).
[56] Act of 1977, s.70(3)(a), where "any disrepair or other defect" appears in place of "any reduction in the value of the dwelling-house". See Vol. 1, pp. 562, 563.
[57] The relevant definitions of "tenant" in the two Acts are substantially the same: Act of 1977, s.152(1), Act of 1988, s.45(1).
[58] Act of 1988, s.17; *ante*, paras. 12–02 *et seq*.
[59] *Ante*, paras. 12–23, 12–27.
[60] *N. & D. (London) Ltd. v. Gadson* (1991) 24 H.L.R. 64, QB (rent assessment committee determined rent of £5 per month instead of market rent of £500 on account on disrepair of house).
[61] Act of 1988, s.14(4).

the sums so payable are separate from the rent payable for the occupation of the dwelling-house, and whether ot not they are payable under separate agreements.[62] The matters to be included in the determination of rent are considered first, before turning to the historic exclusions.

(a) Service charges

The rent to be determined by the rent assessment committee includes "any sums payable by the tenant to the landlord . . . for any of the matters referred to in subsection (1)(a)" of section 18 of the Landlord and Tenant Act 1985. Sums payable for these matters are usually called a "variable service charge", and are more commonly encountered with long leases of flats at low rents. Even if a variable service charge was payable under the fixed term assured tenancy (or indeed under a periodic assured tenancy which is not a statutory periodic tenancy), the Act requires the committee to determine a fixed rent which includes such sums. Service charge within subsection (1)(a) is sums payable, directly or indirectly, for services, repairs, maintenance, insurance, or the landlord's costs of management; and costs includes overheads.[63] Curiously, the prescribed form for a notice of increase[64] requires the landlord to indicate whether the new rent will include council tax and water rates only, and indicates that a rent determined by the committee will be inclusive of such matters. But the prescribed form for the tenant's application referring the landlord's notice to the committee[65] asks for details of all services provided, whether a separate charge is made for them, the amount of such charge, whether it is variable, and the incidence of repairing liability. **17–43**

(b) Furniture

The rent to be determined by the rent assessment committee is to include any sums payable by the tenant to the landlord "on account of the use of furniture", whether or not those sums are separate from the rent, or are payable under a separate agreement.[66] Accordingly, the prescribed form referring the notice of increase to the committee[67] asks for details of any furniture provided under the tenancy. **17–44**

(c) Council tax

Council tax replaced the community charge with effect from April 1, 1993.[68] Where the Act of 1988 made provision for rates to be excluded from the rent,[69] **17–45**

[62] *ibid.* And see s.14(7) (only amount in respect of rates to be added to amount determined by committee).
[63] Landlord and Tenant Act 1985, s.18(1), (3), as amended.
[64] 1997 Forms Regulations (S.I. 1997 No. 194), Sched., Form No. 4.
[65] *ibid.*, Form No. 5.
[66] Act of 1988, s.14(4).
[67] *Supra.*
[68] Local Government Finance Act 1992, Pt. I.
[69] See *infra.*

an amendment was required to provide for how the liability to pay council tax was to be taken into account. That tax is essentially property based, but does have personal elements.[70] In principle, the committee is required to determine a rent that includes any sums payable by the tenant to the landlord in respect of council tax[71]; but if the landlord's notice of increase was served before April 1, 1993, the determination on the reference of that notice was to disregard payments in respect of council tax.[72] Of course, if the tenant is liable to the billing authority to make payment in respect of council tax, the issue does not arise at all.

In so determining a rent inclusive of any sum payable to the landlord in respect of council tax, the committee is required to have regard to one matter, and to disregard a second.

(i) AMOUNT OF TAX FOR RELEVANT HEREDITAMENT. The committee shall have regard to the amount of the council tax which, at the date of the landlord's notice of increase, was set by the billing authority for the financial year in which that notice was served for the category of dwellings within which the relevant hereditament fell on that date.[73] "Hereditament", "billing authority" and "category of dwellings" have the same meanings here as in Part I of the Local Government Finance Act 1992.[74] In short, the committee must identify the council tax band within which the relevant hereditament falls and the amount of the tax set for that band in the year in question.

(ii) DISCOUNTS. The committee must disregard any discount or other reduction affecting the amount of council tax for the relevant hereditament actually payable for the year in question.[75] A billing authority must, if requested in writing by the committee, inform them whether or not the dwelling is, or was at any time specified in the request, an exempt dwelling for the purposes of the Local Government Finance Act 1992.[76]

(d) Rates

17–46 Where any rates in respect of the dwelling-house concerned were "borne by the landlord or a superior landlord", the rent assessment committee had to determine the rent as if the rates were not so borne.[77] The question is not whether the landlord or superior landlord was legally obliged to pay the rates but whether in fact he bore them. Rents determined by the committee were exclusive rents

[70] *e.g.*, discounts for single occupation and second homes.

[71] Act of 1988, s.14(4), as amended by the Local Government Finance (Housing) (Consequential Amendments) Order 1993 (S.I. 1993 No. 651), art. 2(1), Sched., para. 17(3).

[72] *ibid.*, art. 1(2)(c). Transitional provisions entitled a landlord to serve another notice of increase proposing a further increase to take account of the tenant's liability to make payments to the landlord in respect of council tax: see *ante*, para. 17–12.

[73] Act of 1988, s.14(3A), inserted by S.I. 1993 No. 651, *supra*, art. 2(1), Sched. 1, para. 17(1), (2).

[74] *ibid.*, s.14(3B), inserted by S.I. 1993 No. 651, art. 2(1), Sched. 1, para. 17(1), (2).

[75] *ibid.*, s.14(3A).

[76] *ibid.*, s.41B, inserted by S.I. 1993 No. 651, art. 2(1), Sched. 1, para. 18.

[77] *ibid.*, s.14(5).

in this regard, even if the tenant was paying an inclusive rent; but when a rent determined by the committee became the rent under a tenancy under which the landlord or superior landlord bore the rates, it did so with the addition of the appropriate amount in respect of rates.[78]

The exclusion of rates from the rent determined by the committee is now of historical importance only, for domestic rates were abolished with effect from April 1, 1990.[79]

4. Open market rent

Subject to these assumptions, disregards, inclusions and exclusions, the duty of the committee is, as stated above,[80] to "determine the rent at which . . . the committee consider that the dwelling-house concerned might reasonably be expected to be let in the open market by a willing landlord under an assured tenancy" of the nature considered above.[81] **17–47**

(a) The rent

The rent to be determined by the committee is the rent which, as seen,[82] includes any sums payable to the landlord on account of the use of furniture, in respect of council tax, or for services, repairs, maintenance or insurance, or the landlord's costs of management. The term "services" is not defined, but it probably has much the same meaning as under the Rent Acts.[83] In order to assist local authorities in their administration of the housing benefit scheme, where a rent is determined the committee must note in their determination the amount (if any more than negligible) of the rent which, in their opinion, is fairly attributable to the provision of services.[84] The amount so noted forms part of the specified information in the registers of rent.[85] **17–48**

(b) "Might reasonably be expected"

In the phrase "might reasonably be expected to be let", the word "reasonably" refers to the process of expectation; it in no way requires the rent to be subjectively reasonable. The concepts under the Rent Acts of a "fair rent"[86] or "such **17–49**

[78] *ibid.*, s.14(7). "Rates" includes water rates and charges, but not an owner's drainage rate: *ibid.*, s.45(1).
[79] See *ante*, para. 4–04.
[80] *Ante*, para. 17–30.
[81] Act of 1988, s.14(1). Compare business tenancies: Landlord and Tenant Act 1954, s.34(1) ("might reasonably be expected to be let in the open market by a willing lessor").
[82] *Supra*.
[83] See Vol. 1, pp. 567–570, 755–757.
[84] Act of 1988, s.41A, inserted on July 1, 1992 by Social Security (Consequential Provisions) Act 1992, ss.4, 7(2), Sched. 2, para. 103.
[85] Assured Tenancies and Agricultural Occupancies (Rent Information) Order 1988 (S.I. 1988 No. 2199), art. 3, Sched.; see para. 17–52.
[86] Act of 1977, s.70(1); Vol. 1, p. 554.

sum as they may . . . think reasonable''[87] have no application.[88] If by a process of reasonable expectation of the open market rent obtainable for the dwelling in question the committee reaches a rent which seems (subjectively) unfair or unreasonable, the committee has no discretion or other power to abate it. This appears to be so even though it has been recognised that ''in conditions of scarcity, the open market value may be forced up to a point which does exceed all reason'';[89] there may be circumstances in which it is reasonable to expect a letting to be at a rent which appears to be unreasonable.

(c) ''Willing landlord''

17–50 The postulate is that there is a hypothetical landlord who is able and ''willing'' to let the dwelling-house. The hypothetical landlord is not the actual landlord. He is neither reluctant, requiring to be tempted by a high rent, nor desperate, ready to accept any low rent in order to achieve a letting, but simply ''willing''; and he will let the dwelling-house for the best rent that he can obtain on the valuation date.[90] It is inherent in the concept of the hypothetical letting by a willing landlord that there is a market in which the hypothetical transaction takes place and parties who are willing to enter into it.[91]

(d) Assured tenancy

17–51 The tenancy to be assumed is an assured periodic tenancy, with the security of tenure that such tenancies have. This is a benefit that tends to increase the rent that a tenant would pay, and it must be taken into account accordingly.[92] If the tenancy referred to the committee is an assured shorthold tenancy, the tenancy to be assumed is an assured shorthold tenancy.[93] Presumably, if the reference is in relation to an original ''new'' periodic assured shorthold tenancy, it is such a tenancy that is valued; but if the tenancy is a derivative ''old'' assured shorthold tenancy, the valuation hypothesis probably requires the grant of a ''new''

[87] Act of 1977, s.78(2); Vol. 1, p. 771.

[88] See *Oriani v. Dorita Properties Ltd.* [1987] 1 E.G.L.R. 88, CA (to determine a ''fair and reasonable rent'' is wrong; to make a ''fair and reasonable assessment of the open market rental'' is right).

[89] *John Kay Ltd. v. Kay* [1952] 2 Q.B. 258 at 277, CA, *per* Jenkins L.J. (on Leasehold Property (Temporary Provisions) Act 1951).

[90] See *F.R. Evans (Leeds) Ltd. v. English Electric Co. Ltd.* (1977) 36 P. & C.R. 185 at 189, QB. It is implicit that the dwelling-house in not just exposed to the market for a single day, but that there has been an adequate ''lead in'' period of marketing to generate such interest as there is reasonably likely to be in the market: see *Dennis & Robinson v. Kiossos Establishment Ltd.* [1987] 1 E.G.L.R. 133, CA.

[91] *Dennis & Robinson v. Kiossos Establishment Ltd., supra.*

[92] See *Palmer v. Peabody Trust* [1975] Q.B. 604 at 609, DC. There is no question of disregarding it as ''personal circumstances'' (Act of 1977, s.70(1): see *Mason v. Skilling* [1974] 1 W.L.R. 1437 at 1441, HL), for unlike Act of 1977, Act of 1988 does not exclude them from consideration.

[93] Act of 1988, s.14(9), inserted by Housing Act 1996, ss.104, 232(3), Sched. 8, para. 2(1), (2); S.I. 1997 No. 225.

original assured shorthold tenancy to be assumed.[94] This may have some small impact on rent.[95] Where instead an assured agricultural occupancy is referred to the committee, it is an assured agricultural occupancy that is to be assumed.[96]

(e) Registers of rent

The president of every rent assessment panel[97] must keep and make publicly available specified information about rents under assured tenancies and assured agricultural occupancies that have been the subject of references or applications to rent assessment committees under the Act of 1988, or have been determined by them.[98] The method of keeping this information has not been prescribed, but for convenience the term "registers" may be used. This obligation applies to any determination of the open market rent on a notice of increase referred to the committee.[99] It also applies to the determination of the rent of an assured shorthold tenancy, and also to any case in which the committee has been precluded from making such a determination because of an insufficiency of comparables or because the rent is not "significantly higher" than the rent that the landlord might reasonably be expected to obtain.[1] The specified information thus does not include information about references or applications which are still pending. **17–52**

The specified information includes details of the rental period, liability for repairs and council tax[2] or rates, any services or furniture provided by the landlord or superior landlord, and the rent determined, the date of determination, and the amount fairly attributable to the provision of services.[3] The information must be kept available for public inspection during office hours at the office or principal office of the panel, free of charge.[4] A copy of any specified information, certified under the hand of an officer duly authorised by the president of the panel concerned, is receivable in evidence in any court in any proceedings.[5] These registers are a useful source of potential comparables for the rents of assured tenancies (including assured shorthold tenancies) and assured agricul-

[94] Act of 1988, s.14(1)(b).

[95] Given the provisions as to security of tenure and rent control for "new" shorthold tenancies: see *ante*, paras. 8–57, 14–101.

[96] Act of 1988, s.24(4).

[97] For the panels, see Vol. 1, pp. 589–591.

[98] Act of 1988, s.42(1).

[99] Assured Tenancies and Agricultural Occupancies (Rent Information) Order 1988 (S.I. 1988 No. 2199), art. 2, invoking Act of 1988, s.13(4).

[1] Assured Tenancies and Agricultural Occupancies (Rent Information) Order 1988 (S.I. 1988 No. 2199), art. 2, invoking Act of 1988, ss.22(1), (3); *post*, paras. 18–11, 18–12.

[2] By amendment with effect from April 1, 1993: Assured Tenancies and Agricultural Occupancies (Rent Information) (Amendment) Order 1993 (S.I. 1993 No. 657), art. 2.

[3] Specified by S.I. 1988 No. 2199 (*supra*), art. 3, Sched. The Order was made by the Secretary of State under Act of 1988, s.42(4). See now *ibid.*, s.41A, inserted by Social Security (Consequential Provisions) Act 1992, ss.4, 7(2), Sched. 2, para. 103. Such orders are subject to negative resolution by either House. They may make different provision for different cases or descriptions of case, including different provision for different areas: Act of 1988, s.42(3)(b).

[4] S.I. 1998 No. 2199 (*supra*), art. 4.

[5] Act of 1988, s.42(2), (3). Fee £1: S.I. 1988 No. 2199 (*supra*), art. 5, authorised by s.42(3)(a).

tural occupancies; but the primary duty of the tribunal is to have regard to open market evidence at the valuation date.[6]

(f) Methods of valuation

17–53 Several different methods of valuation became established in determining a "fair rent" under the Act of 1977.[7] The complication of eliminating the "scarcity element" that the Act of 1977 required[8] does not trouble the rent assessment committee under the Act of 1988. Because of the nature of the open market valuation exercise that the committee is required to undertake, the primary method of valuation must be by reference to comparables,[9] but there are others that might, unusually, be required.

17–54 (i) COMPARABLES. These will usually have to be established by the evidence of those concerned in letting residential property, and expert evidence generally. Committees are not bound by the strict rules of evidence,[10] but they should be slow to admit hearsay evidence (*e.g.*, as to particular transactions not within the witness's own knowledge), for the rents achieved can readily be affected by the terms of the tenancy, or of any collateral agreements made, or "side letters" exchanged, between landlord and tenant.[11] But expert opinion evidence as to the level of market rents and other matters may properly be based to a substantial degree on material of which the witness has only second-hand knowledge.[12] A secondary source of comparables may well be the records of the committees of other open market evidence produced to them previously in other references, and given that the strict rules of evidence do not apply, these can probably safely be used;[13] but the committees should not in the first instance rely on the specified information[14] from the registers kept by them,[15] for this is by its nature secondary and not best evidence of open market values.[16]

6 See *Spath Holme Ltd. v. Chairman of the Greater Manchester and Lancashire Rent Assessment Committee* (1995) 28 H.L.R. 107, CA; *Curtis v. London Rent Assessment Committee* [1999] Q.B. 92, CA.

7 See Vol. 1, pp. 571–580.

8 *ibid.*, pp. 558–562.

9 This is so even under the Rent Acts now: see *Curtis v. London Rent Assessment Committee, supra, Northumberland & Durham Property Trust Ltd. v. Chairman of the London Rent Assessment Committee* [1998] 3 E.G.L.R. 85 QB; *Northumberland & Durham Property Trust Ltd. v. London Rent Assessment Committee (No. 2)* [1998] 2 E.G.L.R. 99, QB.

10 After the Civil Evidence Act 1995 (first-hand hearsay admissible, subject to prior notice), the rules are not as strict in this respect as hitherto. Nevertheless, the Committee should always be aware of the dangers of admitting hearsay evidence: see the *English Exporters* case, *infra*.

11 In the commercial market, such leases have become referred to as having "headline" rents. As with newspapers, the real content is often masked by the headline.

12 See *English Exporters (London) Ltd. v. Eldonwall Ltd.* [1973] Ch. 415, Ch., Vol. 1, p. 618.

13 The committee's better course is always to disclose the information to the parties and ask for their comments before using such information.

14 Assured Tenancies and Agricultural Occupancies (Rent Information) Order 1988 (S.I. 1988 No. 2199), amended by S.I. 1993 No. 657, art. 2.

15 *Ante*, para. 17–52.

16 See the cases in n. 9, *supra*.

(ii) ABSENCE OF COMPARABLES. By 1999, there must, in respect of most types of dwelling-house and of most locations, be an adequate supply of comparables information available to the parties to the tenancy. But for unusual cases, or perhaps where the parties do not supply any comparables with their representations, the committee might have to have recourse to a secondary method of valuation. These might be use of previous determinations of the committee in approximately comparable cases of assured tenancies; rents registered for Rent Act tenancies, though here complex adjustments will have to be made to adjust for the ''scarcity element'' (if any) and the differences in security of tenure; or even licence fees for non-exclusive occupancies. It now seems unlikely that a rent assessment committee will ever have to have recourse to a return on capital valuation.[17] **17–55**

(iii) KNOWLEDGE AND EXPERIENCE. Under the Act of 1977, rent assessment committees, after giving the evidence such weight as they think fit, can properly rely upon their own knowledge and experience in determining the rent.[18] In principle, this plainly will apply to determining the rent for assured tenancies; but in most cases there will be little scope for such reliance, given the availability of market evidence, except of course in assessing the evidence put before the committee. **17–56**

[17] See the comments in the first edition of Vol. 3 (1989) at p. 216; and Vol. 1, pp. 577–579.
[18] See Vol. 1, pp. 571–573.

Chapter 18

Rent under Assured Shorthold Tenancies

18–01 In considering the rent under assured shorthold tenancies, it is necessary to distinguish between "old" assured shorthold tenancies, *i.e.* those granted before February 28, 1997 or after that date but pursuant to a contract made before that date, and "new" assured shorthold tenancies, granted on or after than date save pursuant to such a contract.[1] In the case of "old" shortholds, only tenants under "original" as opposed to "derivative" shortholds have the right to refer the rent to a rent assessment committee. In the case of new shortholds, the tenant has the right within six months of the beginning of the original tenancy so to refer the rent, and it does not matter whether at the time the original tenancy has ended and been succeeded by a replacement tenancy. Apart from this distinction, however, the jurisdiction of the rent assessment committee in relation to both types of shorthold tenancy is identical. Accordingly, this chapter will consider first rent under old shortholds, and then indicate in detail the differences of application in the case of new shortholds.

A. OLD ASSURED SHORTHOLD TENANCIES

18–02 An assured tenancy which is not a new assured shorthold tenancy is an old assured shorthold tenancy if the three pre-conditions for the creation of an assured shorthold tenancy[2] are satisfied, and if the tenancy is not a re-grant by the landlord to a non-shorthold assured tenant.[3] The rent under old assured shorthold tenancies will be considered in three sections. For the sake of avoiding tedious repetition, all references in this part "A" to assured shorthold tenancies are to old assured shorthold tenanies, save where expressly stated to the contrary.

[1] Act of 1988, ss.19A, 20(1). For a fuller analysis, see *ante*, Chap. 8, paras. 8–03 *et seq.*

[2] Length of fixed term; no power to determine before six months; shorthold notice: see *ante*, paras. 8–24 *et seq.*

[3] Act of 1988, s.20(1), as substituted on February 28, 1997 by Housing Act 1996, ss.104, 232(3), Sched. 8, para. 2(1), (3); S.I. 1997 No. 225.

Sect. 1. Initial Rent

Like all assured tenancies, whether periodic or fixed term, the initial rent under an original assured shorthold tenancy will be whatever rent the parties have agreed;[4] for there is nothing in the Act of 1988 to restrict it. But the parties to an original assured shorthold tenancy will doubtless bear in mind that the tenant has the right, as soon as the tenancy has been granted and at any time thereafter, to refer the rent to the rent assessment committee. **18–03**

Sect. 2. Application to Rent Assessment Committee

1. Tenants with the right to apply

(a) Original assured shorthold tenant

The right to apply to the rent assessment committee is a right given not to all tenants under assured shorthold tenancies, nor even to all tenants under fixed term assured shorthold tenancies, but only to tenants under "original assured shorthold tenancies". This is the name which for brevity may be given to an assured shorthold tenancy other than one arising by way of either deemed grant upon the expiry of a fixed term shorthold tenancy or express grant to an existing shorthold tenant.[5] It is only to tenants under these shorthold tenancies that the right is given to "make an application in the prescribed form to a rent assessment committee for a determination of the rent which, in the committee's opinion, the landlord might reasonably be expected to obtain under the assured shorthold tenancy".[6] Such a tenancy will of necessity be a fixed term tenancy for not less than six months under which the landlord has no power to determine the tenancy during the first six months.[7] **18–04**

(b) Derivative assured shorthold tenancy

A tenant under a derivative assured shorthold tenancy, which may possess none of the characteristics mentioned above,[8] has no right to apply to the committee under this head, even if he has a fixed term tenancy, and even if a shorthold notice was in fact given.[9] But if his tenancy is periodic, he will have the right, enjoyed by assured periodic tenants generally, to refer the rent to the rent assess- **18–05**

4 See *ante*, para. 17–01.
5 *i.e.* a shorthold tenancy falling within Act of 1988, s.20(4); see *ibid.*, s.22(2)(b).
6 Act of 1988, s.22(1).
7 *ibid.*, s.20(1), as substituted, *supra*; s.45(4).
8 *Ante*, paras. 8–35 *et seq.*.
9 Act of 1988, s.22(2)(b), applying *ibid.*, s.20(4).

ment committee if the landlord serves on him a prescribed form notice of increase.[10]

(c) Disapplication

18–06 The Secretary of State may by order made by a statutory instrument provide that this right to refer rents to the committee is not to apply "in such cases or to tenancies of dwelling-houses in such areas or in such other circumstances" as are specified in the order.[11] The order, which requires an affirmative resolution of each House of Parliament,[12] may contain such transitional, incidental and supplementary provisions as appear to the Secretary of State to be desirable.[13] No such order has yet been made.

2. Previous determination

18–07 Even the rent of an original assured shorthold tenancy cannot be referred to the committee if "the rent payable under the tenancy is a rent previously determined" under these provisions.[14] This does not mean that the tenant can make only one application; for on some applications the committee may make no determination of any rent,[15] and a fruitless application is no bar to a subsequent application. This provision does not prevent a tenant from referring his rent to the committee merely because it is of the same amount as the rent determined by the committee in respect of a previous tenancy: the rent determined by the committee is the rent for the particular tenancy,[16] and the terms of different tenancies may differ significantly.

3. Applications

18–08 The tenant under an original assured shorthold tenancy "may make an application in the prescribed form[17] to a rent assessment committee for a determination of the rent which, in the committee's opinion, the landlord might reasonably be

[10] Act of 1988, s.14(9); and see *ante*, paras. 17–04 *et seq.*
[11] *ibid.*, s.23(1).
[12] *ibid.*, s.23(3).
[13] *ibid.*, s.23(2).
[14] *ibid.*, s.22(2)(a), referring to rents determined under s.22.
[15] See *infra*.
[16] See Act of 1988, ss.22(1) ("obtain under the assured shorthold tenancy"), 22(4) ("rent for an assured shorthold tenancy") and 22(4)(b) ("rent so determined").
[17] Assured Tenancies and Agricultural Occupancies (Forms) Regulations 1997 (S.I. 1997 No. 194), reg. 3(f), Sched., Form No. 6 (a detailed three-page questionnaire), replacing and revoking Assured Tenancies and Agricultural Occupancies (Forms) Regulations 1988 (S.I. 1988 No. 2203), reg. 3(8), Sched., Form No. 8, as amended successively by Amendment Regulations of 1990 (S.I. 1990 No. 1532), reg. 2(a), (c), and by Amendment Regulations of 1993 (S.I. 1993 No. 654), reg. 2(g). The revocation of the 1988 Regulations, as amended, does not affect any notice served before February 28, 1997, when the 1997 Regulations came into force, if it was valid under the 1988 Regulations at the date of service: S.I. 1997 No. 194, reg. 4(2).

expected to obtain under the assured shorthold tenancy''.[18] There is nothing to restrict the time when the tenant can make his application, save that the tenancy must have been granted so that he has become ''the tenant''. For joint tenants, the prescribed form requires signature by all of them (or their agents) unless one signs on behalf of ''the rest''[19] with their agreement.[20] The basis on which the rent is to be assessed is considered later.[21]

4. Procedure

The procedure on a tenant's reference of a landlord's notice of increase to the rent assessment committee, considered above,[22] applies equally to an assured shorthold tenant's application under these provisions. This applies to representations, information required by the committee, and procedure generally.[23] **18–09**

5. Conditions precedent to determination

When a tenant has referred his rent to the committee, the committee is prohibited from determining the rent unless two conditions are each satisfied.[24] They are as follows. **18–10**

(a) Sufficiency of comparables

First, the committee must consider that ''there is a sufficient number of similar dwelling-houses in the locality let on assured tenancies (whether shorthold or not)''.[25] The inevitable question ''Sufficient for what?'' is presumably to be answered in some way such as ''sufficient to form a reasonable basis for a decision''. It will only be in the most unusual circumstances now that a committee is prohibited from determining the rent on this ground, given that assured tenancies have been being granted for upwards of ten years. The meaning of ''locality'' here is not clear. Under the Act of 1977 the word was used with two different meanings in the same section, a narrow meaning in relation to the physical condition of the dwelling, and a wider meaning in eliminating the scarcity element.[26] Here, unless there is some third meaning, the valuation context suggests that the wider meaning is the more apt, so that the ''locality'' will be a wide area. The matter is essentially one for the decision of the committee, with their local, and valuation, knowledge. **18–11**

[18] Act of 1988, s.22(1).
[19] And presumably of himself.
[20] See *Turley v. Panton* (1975) 29 P. & C.R. 397, D.C.; and see *R. v. Rent Officer for London Borough of Camden, ex p. Felix* (1988) 21 H.L.R. 34, QB.
[21] *Post*, para. 18–20.
[22] *Ante*, paras. 17–16 *et seq.*
[23] Considered at *ibid.*
[24] Act of 1988, s.22(3).
[25] *ibid.*, s.22(3)(a).
[26] Act of 1977, s.70(1), (2); Vol. 1, pp. 555, 560.

(b) "Significantly higher" rent

18–12 Secondly, the committee must also consider that the rent payable under the assured tenancy in question "is significantly higher than the rent which the landlord might reasonably be expected to be able to obtain under the tenancy, having regard to the level of rents payable under the tenancies referred to in paragraph (a) above",[27] *i.e.* the comparables. "Significant" appears to be a replacement for the long-serving "substantial" under the Rent Acts,[28] though it is certainly no more eloquent or precise. In the context, the meaning seems to be much the same; but as the matter appears to be essentially one for the committee and not the courts, probably "significantly" will continue to escape the close judicial scrutiny that "substantial" attracted.

6. Determination

18–13 When a tenant has duly made an application to the committee, and the conditions precedent are satisfied, the committee will normally proceed to determine the rent. The valuation basis on which this is to be done will be considered in the next section.[29] The president of every rent assessment panel[30] must keep and make publicly available specified information about rents under assured shorthold tenancies that have been the subject of references or applications to rent assessment committees under the Act of 1988, or have been determined by them.[31] In this respect, the commentary under references of notices of increase under periodic assured tenancies applies here.[32] And in particular, the requirement applies to any case in which the committee has been precluded from making such a determination because of an insufficiency of comparables or because the rent is not "significantly higher" than the rent that the landlord might reasonably be expected to obtain.[33] Where the committee is so precluded, the specified information in the register must indicate on which of those two grounds it was precluded.[34]

7. Effect of determination

(a) Effective date

18–14 When the committee has determined the rent for an original assured shorthold

[27] Act of 1988, s.22(3)(b).

[28] See Act of 1923, s.10(1); Vol. 1, pp. 176–182. The marginal note to Act of 1988, s.22 is "Reference of excessive rents to rent assessment committee". There is perhaps some echo here of Act of 1920, s.9(1) (rent yielding profit more than 25 per cent. in excess of normal profit).

[29] *Post*, paras. 18–20 *et seq.*

[30] For the panels, see Vol. 1, pp. 589–591.

[31] Act of 1988, s.42(1).

[32] *Ante*, para. 17–52.

[33] Assured Tenancies and Agricultural Occupancies (Rent Information) Order 1988 (S.I. 1988 No. 2199), art. 2, invoking Act of 1988, ss.22(1), (3); *supra*.

[34] Assured Tenancies and Agricultural Occupancies (Rent Information) Order 1990 (S.I. 1990 No. 1474), art. 2, amending Assured Tenancies and Agricultural Occupancies (Rent Information) Order 1988, *supra*, Sched, para. 11, with effect from August 20, 1990.

tenancy, "the determination shall have effect from such date as the committee may direct, not being earlier than the date of the application".[35] Unlike the provision for periodic tenancies, there is nothing stating that the rent determined by the committee "shall be the rent under the tenancy";[36] but the provision for excess rent considered below produces the same result when the rent has been reduced.[37] The committee's general discretion as to the date when the new rent will take effect is much wider here than under its limited powers for periodic tenancies.[38] With regard to what factors the committee is to exercise this wide discretion remains unclear.

(b) Excess rent

If when the determination takes effect the rent that would otherwise be payable under the tenancy thereafter exceeds the rent so determined, the excess is irrecoverable from the tenant.[39] No express provision has been made for the tenant to recover any overpayment of rent,[40] and so perhaps there is an analogy with an unenforceable fine for a licence to assign or for a change of use.[41] On the other hand, an overpayment might be recoverable if it was made under an operative mistake of law.[42] **18–15**

(c) Notice of increase

No notice of increase[43] may be served "with respect to a tenancy of the dwelling-house in question" until after the first anniversary of the date on which the determination on the assured shorthold tenant's application takes effect.[44] Such a notice could not be served in the case of a fixed term original assured shorthold tenancy of the premises, for notices of increase can be given only in respect of assured periodic tenancies.[45] But if the original assured shorthold tenancy ends and is succeeded by a derivative periodic tenancy, that periodic tenancy will enjoy what remains of the year's immunity from service of a notice of increase. **18–16**

8. Withdrawal of reference

The provisions concerning the withdrawal of a reference of a notice of increase, **18–17**

35 Act of 1988, s.22(4)(a).
36 *ibid.*, s.14(7).
37 And it avoids any unwitting increase of rent: compare *ante*, paras. 17–21, 17–22.
38 *Ante*, para. 17–21.
39 Act of 1988, s.22(4)(b).
40 Contrast the Rent Acts: Vol. 1, p. 538.
41 Law of Property Act 1925, s.144; Landlord and Tenant Act 1927, s.19(3); see *Andrew v. Bridgeman* [1908] 1 K.B. 596, CA (fine irrecoverable once paid).
42 See generally *Kleinwort Benson Ltd. v. Lincoln C.C.* [1998] 3 W.L.R. 1095, HL (mistake of law *in pari materia* with mistake of fact).
43 *i.e.* a notice served by the landlord under Act of 1988, s.13(2); *ante*, para. 17–10.
44 *ibid.*, s.22(4)(c).
45 *ibid.*, s.13(1); *ante*, para. 17–04.

considered above,[46] apply equally to the withdrawal of an application under this head.[47] But perhaps it is more odd here that a tenant who has applied for a reduction of rent cannot unilaterally withdraw his application.

9. Jurisdiction

18–18 Unlike references under periodic assured tenancies, there is no apparent ambiguity in this regard with applications by assured shorthold tenants. Only an assured shorthold tenant may make the application, and the committee has to be satisfied before determining a rent that "the rent payable under the assured shorthold tenancy in question is significantly higher ..." than can be reasonably expected.[48] Further, the effect of a determination of a rent by the committee only applies where what is determined is the "rent for an assured shorthold tenancy".[49] All these factors point to the conclusion that if the tenancy ceases to be an assured shorthold tenancy (*e.g.*, upon a change of landlord), the committee no longer has jurisdiction to determine a rent. This conclusion is reinforced by an express provision relating to new assured shorthold tenancies for continuation of the determination in such circumstances.[50]

10. Control of rent assessment committees

18–19 The Act of 1988 contains nothing to modify the existing provisions as to the control of rent assessment committees and appeals from their decisions, and so the detailed commentary in Volume 1[51] will apply.

Sect. 3. Rent Reasonably to be Expected

18–20 The rent to be determined by the committee under this head is "the rent which, in the committee's opinion, the landlord might reasonably be expected to obtain under the assured shorthold tenancy".[52] This raises five separate points.

[46] *Ante*, paras. 17–23 *et seq.*
[47] Act of 1988, s.22(5), applying *inter alia* s.14(8).
[48] *ibid.*, s.22(3)(b).
[49] *ibid.*, s.22(4).
[50] *ibid.*, s.22(5A), inserted by Housing Act 1996, ss.104, 232(3), Sched. 8, para. 2(1), (6); S.I. 1997 No. 225; *post*, para. 18–29.
[51] pp. 593–604, 807–820, as updated in the Supplement, including in particular references to the Tribunals and Inquiries Act 1992.
[52] Act of 1988, s.22(1).

1. The rent

As with references of landlords' notices of increase to the committee, "rent" for this purpose does not include rates,[53] but does include sums payable to the landlord on account of the use of furniture, in respect of council tax, or for services, repairs, maintenance, insurance, or the landlord's costs of management.[54] **18–21**

Whereas a rent referred to the rent assessment committee pursuant to a landlord's notice of increase must be a rent under a periodic tenancy, a rent application made by a tenant in respect of an assured shorthold tenancy will be under a fixed term tenancy, and possibly a term for a substantial period of years. The effect of a rent determination for such a tenancy may accordingly be to alter the basis of the tenant's payments under the tenancy from rent and separate service charge and insurance contributions to an inclusive rent. Where a rent is so determined, then from the date when the determination has effect, the landlord will not be able to recover from the tenant any sums in excess of the rent so determined, whether under the terms of the tenancy they were expressed as rent or otherwise; for under the Act, these included matters are all "rent".[55]

2. "The landlord"

The statutory language here may be contrasted with the language used for assessing the open market rent. The latter is in impersonal terms: what is to be assessed is the rent at which the dwelling might reasonably be expected to be let by "a willing landlord".[56] Here, the language is personal: it is the rent that "the landlord" might reasonably "be expected to obtain"; and the condition precedent relating to a "significantly higher" rent is in similar terms.[57] It thus seems that what must be considered is the actual landlord at the time, with all the advantages and disadvantages of ability and bargaining power that he has, and the rent that he might reasonably be expected to "obtain". Yet it is difficult to see any reason for requiring the committee to assess the landlord's capabilities as a negotiator, and the effect of the "significantly higher" condition[58] will probably prevent the point from having any real significance. The reason for using contrasting language remains obscure. Perhaps Parliament thought, consistently with the policy of the Act of 1988 as a whole, that rents freely entered into should not lightly be interfered with.[59] The experience of the first ten years of assured shorthold tenancies has shown that, in any event, this limited measure of rent control is toothless. **18–22**

[53] Which are in any event now defunct in the domestic context.

[54] Act of 1988, s.22(5), applying, *inter alia*, s.14(4), (5). The determination must note the amount (if any, more than negligible) which in the opinion of the committee is fairly attributable to the provision of services: Act of 1988, s.41A, inserted on July 1, 1992 by Social Services (Consequential Provisions) Act 1992, ss.4, 7(2), Sched. 2, para. 103.

[55] Act of 1988, s.22(4)(b), (5), referring to s.14(4).

[56] *ibid.*, s.14(1); *ante*, paras. 17–49, 17–50.

[57] *ibid.*, s.22(3)(b).

[58] *Ante*, para. 18–12.

[59] But then why provide a weak measure of rent control at all?

3. "Might reasonably be expected"

18–23 The comments already made on "might reasonably be expected" in relation to the open market rent[60] seem to be equally applicable here.

4. "Under the assured shorthold tenancy"

18–24 The tenancy to be considered is the actual shorthold tenancy under which the rent is payable, and not any hypothetical assured shorthold tenancy.

5. Methods of valuation

18–25 In general, what has been said about methods of valuation in relation to the open market rent appears to apply equally to the determination of the rent under this head. The words "reasonably be expected to obtain" provide an indefinite concept for the purposes of valuation, and the phrase "let in the open market" does not in terms appear. Nevertheless, it is difficult to see any other footing on which the reasonable expectation of the rent obtainable is to be assessed.

B. NEW ASSURED SHORTHOLD TENANCIES

18–26 A new assured shorthold tenancy is an assured tenancy that was either expressly entered into on or after February 28, 1997 other than pursuant to a contract made before that day, or a statutory periodic tenancy that was deemed to be granted on the coming to an end of such an expressly created tenancy. Thus, if a statutory periodic tenancy arises on the termination after February 28, 1997 of an old assured periodic tenancy, that periodic tenancy is an old assured shorthold tenancy. But if instead the parties expressly grant a new replacement tenancy, that tenancy is (if it otherwise satisfies the requirements for an assured shorthold tenancy) a new assured shorthold tenancy.[61] There are no other pre-conditions to the grant of a new assured shorthold tenancy, as there were with old original assured shorthold tenancies;[62] but there are some exceptional cases where the assured tenancy cannot be a new shorthold tenancy.[63]

The commentary in part "A" above applies equally to rent under new assured shorthold tenancies save in the particular respects addressed below, under the same headings as in part "A". For the sake of avoiding tedious repetition, all

[60] *Ante*, para. 17–49.

[61] Act of 1988, ss.19A, 20(1), (5A), as inserted and amended by Housing Act 1996, ss. 96, 104, Sched. 8, para. 2(1), (4). See *ante*, para. 8–16.

[62] *Ante*, para. 8–46.

[63] Act of 1988, Sched. 2A. Of these, the only particularly significant one for the purposes of this chapter is *ibid.*, para. 2 (after grant, landlord serves on tenant notice stating that tenancy is no longer an assured shorthold tenancy).

references in this part "B" to assured shorthold tenancies are to new assured shorthold tenanies, save where expressly stated to the contrary.

Sect. 4. Application to Rent Assessment Committee

1. Tenants with the right to apply

There is no distinction between original and derivative tenancies as such; nor is there a distinction between fixed term and periodic[64] assured shorthold tenancies. But there is a distinction of importance, for both rent control and security of tenure, between an "original tenancy" and a "replacement tenancy".[65] In relation to rent, this is because the tenant's right to apply to the rent assessment committee to determine a reasonable rent is limited to a period of six months starting with the beginning of the original tenancy.[66] Thus, it matters not if a short fixed term tenancy of (say) three months is followed by a replacement tenancy,[67] whether statutory or expressly granted: the right to apply to the committee remains exercisable during the first three months of the replacement tenancy. And if the original tenancy was a monthly periodic tenancy, the tenant has the right to apply within six months of the start of the tenancy. After the six months have expired, an assured periodic shorthold tenant will only have the right, enjoyed by assured periodic tenants generally, to refer the rent to the rent assessment committee if the landlord serves on him a prescribed form notice of increase.[68] **18–27**

3. Applications

As stated above, unlike with original old assured shorthold tenants, there is a time limit of six months in which to apply to the rent assessment committee. **18–28**

4. Jurisdiction

A landlord under an assured shorthold tenancy could effectually prevent the rent assessment committee from determining a reasonable rent under the tenancy by serving on the tenant a notice stating that the tenancy ceases to be an assured shorthold tenancy.[69] Of course, by serving such a notice before the tenancy was entered into,[70] the landlord could have avoided that risk, but at the expense of **18–29**

64 Now an original periodic tenancy can be an assured shorthold tenancy.
65 See *ante*, para. 8–48.
66 Act of 1988, s.22(2)(aa), inserted by Housing Act 1996, s.100(1), (2).
67 *ibid.*, s.21(7), inserted by Housing Act 1996, s.99.
68 Act of 1988, s.14(9); and see *ante*, para. 17–10.
69 Act of 1988, Sched. 2A, para. 2, inserted by Housing Act 1996, s.96: see *ante*, paras. 8–06, 8–07.
70 *ibid.*, para. 1.

greater security of tenure for the tenant. Parliament seems to have been determined not to allow the landlord to have the best of both worlds in the sense of waiting to see if the tenant applies to the committee and then converting the tenancy to a "full" assured tenancy. Where the landlord does serve such a notice after the tenancy has been entered into, and at the time of service there is pending before the rent assessment committee an application to determine a reasonable rent, the fact that by dint of the notice the tenancy ceases to be a shorthold tenancy "shall, in relation to that application, be disregarded for the purposes of" the provisions of the Act[71] relating to such rent determinations.[72] In short, the tenancy continues to be treated as an assured shorthold tenancy for all purposes relevant to the rent determination. *Semble* if on some other ground the tenancy ceases to be an assured shorthold tenancy, the jurisdiction of the committee to determine a rent is lost, even if an application is pending before it.

[71] s. 22.

[72] Act of 1988, s.22(5A), inserted by Housing Act 1996, s.104, Sched. 8, para. 2(1), (6).

APPENDICES

Explanatory Notes

1. Style

In printing the statutes, the Queen's Printer's copies of the Acts and statutory instruments have been departed from to the following extent only:

(a) The formal words of enactment of the Act have been omitted.
(b) Marginal notes have been set in bold type and moved into the text.
(c) Marginal and other references to the year and chapter number of Acts cited in the text of the Act have been omitted.

2. Repeals and amendments

Square brackets are used in the text of the statutes to indicate provisions that have been inserted or substituted; italics are used to indicate provisions that have been repealed.

3. S.I. Standard forms

Statutory instruments, which provide standard forms requiring to be completed, often use italics and square brackets as a guide to filling up the forms. These forms are here printed in accordance with that style, and so italics and square brackets here do not always have their usual significance.

Appendix 1

Housing Act 1988

A1–001

(1988 c.50)

ARRANGEMENT OF SECTIONS

PART I

RENTED ACCOMMODATION

CHAPTER I

ASSURED TENANCIES

Meaning of assured tenancy etc.

SECT. PAGE

Security of tenure

Rent and other terms

Miscellaneous

CHAPTER II

ASSURED SHORTHOLD TENANCIES

SECT. PAGE

CHAPTER III

ASSURED AGRICULTURAL OCCUPANCIES

CHAPTER IV

PROTECTION FROM EVICTION

CHAPTER V

PHASING OUT OF RENT ACTS AND OTHER TRANSITIONAL PROVISIONS

CHAPTER VI

GENERAL PROVISIONS

PART V

MISCELLANEOUS AND GENERAL

Leases

[.......]

Supplementary

[.......]

SCHEDULES

An Act to make further provision with respect to dwelling-houses let on tenancies or occupied under licences; to amend the Rent Act 1977 and the Rent

(Agriculture) Act 1976; to establish a body, Housing for Wales, having functions relating to housing associations; to amend the Housing Associations Act 1985 and to repeal and re-enact with amendments certain provisions of Part II of that Act; to make provision for the establishment of housing action trusts for areas designated by the Secretary of State; to confer on persons approved for the purpose the right to acquire from public sector landlords certain dwelling-houses occupied by secure tenants; to make further provision about rent officers, the administration of housing benefit and rent allowance subsidy, the right to buy, repair notices and certain disposals of land and the application of capital money arising thereon; to make provision consequential upon the Housing (Scotland) Act 1988; and for connected purposes.

[15th November 1988]

PART I

RENTED ACCOMMODATION

CHAPTER I

ASSURED TENANCIES

Meaning of assured tenancy etc.

Assured tenancies

A1–002 **1.**—(1) A tenancy under which a dwelling-house is let as a separate dwelling is for the purposes of this Act an assured tenancy if and so long as—

(a) the tenant or, as the case may be, each of the joint tenants is an individual; and
(b) the tenant or, as the case may be, at least one of the joint tenants occupies the dwelling-house as his only or principal home; and
(c) the tenancy is not one which, by virtue of subsection (2) or subsection (6) below, cannot be an assured tenancy.

(2) Subject to subsection (3) below, if and so long as a tenancy falls within any paragraph in Part I of Schedule 1 to this Act, it cannot be an assured tenancy; and in that Schedule—

(a) ''tenancy'' means a tenancy under which a dwelling-house is let as a separate dwelling;
(b) Part II has effect for determining the rateable value of a dwelling-house for the purposes of Part I; and
(c) Part III has effect for supplementing paragraph 10 in Part I.

[(2A) The Secretary of State may by order replace any amount referred to in paragraphs 2 and 3A of Schedule 1 to this Act by such amount as is specified in the order; and such an order shall be made by statutory instrument which shall be subject to annulment in pursuance of a resolution of either House of Parliament.]

ANNOTATION

Subsection (2A) was inserted as from April 1, 1990 by References to Rating (Housing) Regulations 1990 (S.I. 1990 No. 434), Sched., para. 27.

(3) Except as provided in Chapter V below, at the commencement of this Act, a tenancy—

(a) under which a dwelling-house was then let as a separate dwelling, and
(b) which immediately before that commencement was an assured tenancy for the purposes of sections 56 to 58 of the Housing Act 1980 (tenancies granted by approved bodies),

shall become an assured tenancy for the purposes of this Act.

(4) In relation to an assured tenancy falling within subsection (3) above—

(a) Part I of Schedule 1 to this Act shall have effect, subject to subsection (5) below, as if it consisted only of paragraphs 11 and 12; and
(b) sections 56 to 58 of the Housing Act 1980 (and Schedule 5 to that Act) shall not apply after the commencement of this Act.

(5) In any case where—

(a) immediately before the commencement of this Act the landlord under a tenancy is a fully mutual housing association, and
(b) at the commencement of this Act the tenancy becomes an assured tenancy by virtue of subsection (3) above, then, so long as that association remains the landlord under that tenancy (and under any statutory periodic tenancy which arises on the coming to an end of that tenancy), paragraph 12 of Schedule 1 to this Act shall have effect in relation to that tenancy with the omission of sub-paragraph (1)(h).

(6) If, in pursuance of its duty under—

(a) section 63 of the Housing Act 1985 (duty to house pending inquiries in case of apparent priority need),
(b) section 65(3) of that Act (duty to house temporarily person found to have priority need but to have become homeless intentionally), or
(c) section 68(1) of that Act (duty to house pending determination whether conditions for referral of application are satisfied),

a local housing authority have made arrangements with another person to provide accommodation, a tenancy granted by that other person in pursuance of the arrangements to a person specified by the authority cannot be an assured tenancy before the expiry of the period of twelve months beginning with the date specified in subsection (7) below unless, before the expiry of that period, the tenant is notified by the landlord (or, in the case of joint landlords, at least one of them) that the tenancy is to be regarded as an assured tenancy.

(7) The date referred to in subsection (6) above is the date on which the tenant received the notification required by section 64(1) of the Housing Act 1985 (notification of decision on question of homelessness or threatened homelessness) or, if he received a notification under section 68(3) of that Act (notification of which authority has duty to house), the date on which he received that notification.

ANNOTATION

Subsections (6) and (7) were repealed on January 20, 1997 by Housing Act 1996, ss.227, 232(3), (4), Sched. 19, Pt. VIII: S.I. 1996 No. 2959. The repeals do not apply in relation to an applicant whose application for accommodation or for assistance in obtaining accommodation was made before that date: *ibid.*, Sched., para. 1.

Letting of a dwelling-house together with other land

A1–003 **2.**—(1) If, under a tenancy, a dwelling-house is let together with other land, then, for the purposes of this Part of this Act,—

(a) if and so long as the main purpose of the letting is the provision of a home for the tenant or, where there are joint tenants, at least one of them, the other land shall be treated as part of the dwelling-house; and
(b) if and so long as the main purpose of the letting is not as mentioned in paragraph (a) above, the tenancy shall be treated as not being one under which a dwelling-house is let as a separate dwelling.

(2) Nothing in subsection (1) above affects any question whether a tenancy is precluded from being an assured tenancy by virtue of any provision of Schedule 1 to this Act.

Tenant sharing accommodation with persons other than landlord

A1–004 **3.**—(1) Where a tenant has the exclusive occupation of any accommodation (in this section referred to as ''the separate accommodation'') and—

(a) the terms as between the tenant and his landlord on which he holds the separate accommodation include the use of other accommodation (in this section referred to as ''the shared accommodation'') in common with another person or other persons, not being or including the landlord, and
(b) by reason only of the circumstances mentioned in paragraph (a) above, the separate accommodation would not, apart from this section, be a dwelling-house let on an assured tenancy,

the separate accommodation shall be deemed to be a dwelling-house let on an assured tenancy and the following provisions of this section shall have effect.

(2) For the avoidance of doubt it is hereby declared that where, for the purpose of determining the rateable value of the separate accommodation, it is necessary to make an apportionment under Part II of Schedule 1 to this Act, regard is to be had to the circumstances mentioned in subsection (1)(a) above.

(3) While the tenant is in possession of the separate accommodation, any term of the tenancy terminating or modifying, or providing for the termination or modification of, his right to the use of any of the shared accommodation which is living accommodation shall be of no effect.

(4) Where the terms of the tenancy are such that, at any time during the tenancy, the persons in common with whom the tenant is entitled to the use of the shared accommodation could be varied or their number could be increased; nothing in subsection (3) above shall prevent those terms from having effect so far as they relate to any such variation or increase.

(5) In this section "living accommodation" means accommodation of such a nature that the fact that it constitutes or is included in the shared accommodation is sufficient, apart from this section, to prevent the tenancy from constituting an assured tenancy of a dwelling-house.

Certain sublettings not to exclude any part of sub-lessor's premises from assured tenancy

4.—(1) Where the tenant of a dwelling-house has sub-let a part but not the whole of the dwelling-house, then, as against his landlord or any superior landlord, no part of the dwelling-house shall be treated as excluded from being a dwelling-house let on an assured tenancy by reason only that the terms on which any person claiming under the tenant holds any part of the dwelling-house include the use of accommodation in common with other persons. **A1–005**

(2) Nothing in this section affects the rights against, and liabilities to, each other of the tenant and any person claiming under him, or of any two such persons.

Security of tenure

Security of tenure

5.—(1) An assured tenancy cannot be brought to an end by the landlord except by obtaining an order of the court in accordance with the following provisions of this Chapter or Chapter II below or, in the case of a fixed term tenancy which contains power for the landlord to determine the tenancy in certain circumstances, by the exercise of that power and, accordingly, the service by the landlord of a notice to quit shall be of no effect in relation to a periodic assured tenancy. **A1–006**

(2) If an assured tenancy which is a fixed term tenancy comes to an end otherwise than by virtue of—

(a) an order of the court, or
(b) a surrender or other action on the part of the tenant,

then, subject to section 7 and Chapter 11 below, the tenant shall be entitled to remain in possession of the dwelling-house let under that tenancy and, subject to subsection (4) below, his right to possession shall depend upon a periodic tenancy arising by virtue of this section.

(3) The periodic tenancy referred to in subsection (2) above is one—

(a) taking effect in possession immediately on the coming to an end of the fixed term tenancy;
(b) deemed to have been granted by the person who was the landlord under the fixed term tenancy immediately before it came to an end to the person who was then the tenant under that tenancy;
(c) under which the premises which are let are the same dwelling-house as was let under the fixed term tenancy;
(d) under which the periods of the tenancy are the same as those for which rent was last payable under the fixed term tenancy; and
(e) under which, subject to the following provisions of this Part of this Act, the other terms are the same as those of the fixed term tenancy immediately before it came to an end, except that any term which makes provision for determination by the landlord or the tenant shall not have effect while the tenancy remains an assured tenancy.

(4) The periodic tenancy referred to in subsection (2) above shall not arise if, on the coming to an end of the fixed term tenancy, the tenant is entitled, by virtue of the grant of another tenancy, to possession of the same or substantially the same dwelling-house as was let to him under the fixed term tenancy.

(5) If, on or before the date on which a tenancy is entered into or is deemed to have been granted as mentioned in subsection (3)(b) above, the person who is to be the tenant under that tenancy—

(a) enters into an obligation to do any act which (apart from this subsection) will cause the tenancy to come to an end at a time when it is an assured tenancy, or
(b) executes, signs or gives any surrender, notice to quit or other document which (apart from this subsection) has the effect of bringing the tenancy to an end at a time when it is an assured tenancy,

the obligation referred to in paragraph (a) above shall not be enforceable or, as the case may be, the surrender, notice to quit or other document referred to in paragraph (b) above shall be of no effect.

(6) If, by virtue of any provision of this Part of this Act, Part I of Schedule 1 to this Act has effect in relation to a fixed term tenancy as if it consisted only of paragraphs 11 and 12, that Part shall have the like effect in relation to any

periodic tenancy which arises by virtue of this section on the coming to an end of the fixed term tenancy.

(7) Any reference in this Part of this Act to a statutory periodic tenancy is a reference to a periodic tenancy arising by virtue of this section.

Fixing of terms of statutory periodic tenancy

6.—(1) In this section, in relation to a statutory periodic tenancy,— **A1–007**

(a) "the former tenancy" means the fixed term tenancy on the coming to an end of which the statutory periodic tenancy arises; and
(b) "the implied terms" means the terms of the tenancy which have effect by virtue of section 5(3)(e) above, other than terms as to the amount of the rent;

but nothing in the following provisions of this section applies to a statutory periodic tenancy at a time when, by virtue of paragraph 11 or paragraph 12 in Part I of Schedule 1 to this Act, it cannot be an assured tenancy.

(2) Not later than the first anniversary of the day on which the former tenancy came to an end, the landlord may serve on the tenant, or the tenant may serve on the landlord, a notice in the prescribed form proposing terms of the statutory periodic tenancy different from the implied terms and, if the landlord or the tenant considers it appropriate, proposing an adjustment of the amount of the rent to take account of the proposed terms.

(3) Where a notice has been served under subsection (2) above,—

(a) within the period of three months beginning on the date on which the notice was served on him, the landlord or the tenant, as the case may be, may, by an application in the prescribed form, refer the notice to a rent assessment committee under subsection (4) below; and
(b) if the notice is not so referred, then, with effect from such date, not falling within the period referred to in paragraph (a) above, as may be specified in the notice, the terms proposed in the notice shall become terms of the tenancy in substitution for any of the implied terms dealing with the same subject matter and the amount of the rent shall be varied in accordance with any adjustment so proposed.

(4) Where a notice under subsection (2) above is referred to a rent assessment committee, the committee shall consider the terms proposed in the notice and shall determine whether those terms, or some other terms (dealing with the same subject matter as the proposed terms), are such as, in the committee's opinion, might reasonably be expected to be found in an assured periodic tenancy of the dwelling-house concerned, being a tenancy—

(a) which begins on the coming to an end of the former tenancy; and
(b) which is granted by a willing landlord on terms which, except in so far as they relate to the subject matter of the proposed terms, are those of

the statutory periodic tenancy at the time of the committee's consideration.

(5) Whether or not a notice under subsection (2) above proposes an adjustment of the amount of the rent under the statutory periodic tenancy, where a rent assessment committee determine any terms under subsection (4) above, they shall, if they consider it appropriate, specify such an adjustment to take account of the terms so determined.

(6) In making a determination under subsection (4) above, or specifying an adjustment of an amount of rent under subsection (5) above, there shall be disregarded any effect on the terms or the amount of the rent attributable to the granting of a tenancy to a sitting tenant.

(7) Where a notice under subsection (2) above is referred to a rent assessment committee, then, unless the landlord and the tenant otherwise agree, with effect from such date as the committee may direct—

(a) the terms determined by the committee shall become terms of the statutory periodic tenancy in substitution for any of the implied terms dealing with the same subject matter; and
(b) the amount of the rent under the statutory periodic tenancy shall be altered to accord with any adjustment specified by the committee;

but for the purposes of paragraph (b) above the committee shall not direct a date earlier than the date specified, in accordance with subsection (3)(b) above, in the notice referred to them.

(8) Nothing in this section requires a rent assessment committee to continue with a determination under subsection (4) above if the landlord and tenant give notice in writing that they no longer require such a determination or if the tenancy has come to an end.

Orders for possession

A1–008 **7.**—(1) The court shall not make an order for possession of a dwelling-house let on an assured tenancy except on one or more of the grounds set out in Schedule 2 to this Act; but nothing in this Part of this Act relates to proceedings for possession of such a dwelling-house which are brought by a mortgagee, within the meaning of the Law of Property Act 1925, who has lent money on the security of the assured tenancy.

(2) The following provisions of this section have effect, subject to section 8 below, in relation to proceedings for the recovery of possession of a dwelling-house let on an assured tenancy.

(3) If the court is satisfied that any of the grounds in Part I of Schedule 2 to this Act is established then, subject to [subsections (5A) and (6)] below, the court shall make an order for possession.

Annotation

The words in square brackets were substituted on April 1, 1990 by Local Government and Housing Act 1989, ss.194(1), 195(2), Sched. 11, para. 101: S.I. 1990 No. 431.

(4) If the court is satisfied that any of the grounds in Part II of Schedule 2 to this Act is established, then, subject to [subsections (5A) and (6)] below, the court may make an order for possession if it considers it reasonable to do so.

ANNOTATION

The words in square brackets were substituted on April 1, 1990 by Local Government and Housing Act 1989, ss.194(1), 195(2), Sched. 11, para. 101: S.I. 1990 No. 431.

(5) Part III of Schedule 2 to this Act shall have effect for supplementing Ground 9 in that Schedule and Part IV of that Schedule shall have effect in relation to notices given as mentioned in Grounds 1 to 5 of that Schedule.

[(5A) The court shall not make an order for possession of a dwelling-house let on an assured periodic tenancy arising under Schedule 10 to the Local Government and Housing Act 1989 on any of the following grounds, that is to say:

(a) Grounds 1, 2 and 5 in Part I of Schedule 2 to this Act;
(b) Ground 16 in Part II of that Schedule; and
(c) if the assured periodic tenancy arose on the termination of a former 1954 Act tenancy within the meaning of the said Schedule 10, Ground 6 in Part I of Schedule 2 to this Act.]

ANNOTATION

Subsection (5A) was inserted with effect from April 1, 1990 by Local Government and Housing Act 1989, ss.194(1), 195(2), Sched. 11, para. 101: S.I. 1990 No. 431.

(6) The court shall not make an order for possession of a dwelling-house to take effect at a time when it is let on an assured fixed term tenancy unless—

(a) the ground for possession is Ground 2 or Ground 8 in Part I of Schedule 2 to this Act or any of the grounds in Part II of that Schedule, other than Ground 9 or Ground 16; and
(b) the terms of the tenancy make provision for it to be brought to an end on the ground in question (whether that provision takes the form of a provision for re-entry, for forfeiture, for determination by notice or otherwise).

(7) Subject to the preceding provisions of this section, the court may make an order for possession of a dwelling-house on grounds relating to a fixed term tenancy which has come to an end; and where an order is made in such circumstances, any statutory periodic tenancy which has arisen on the ending of the fixed term tenancy shall end (without any notice and regardless of the period) on the day on which the order takes effect.

Notice of proceedings for possession

8.—(1) The court shall not entertain proceedings for possession of a dwelling-house let on an assured tenancy unless— **A1–009**

(a) the landlord or, in the case of joint landlords, at least one of them has served on the tenant a notice in accordance with this section and the proceedings are begun within the time limits stated in the notice in accordance with *subsections (3) and (4)* [subsections (3) to (4B)] below; or

(b) the court considers it just and equitable to dispense with the requirement of such a notice.

ANNOTATION

The words in square brackets were substituted by Housing Act 1996, ss.151(1), (2), 232(3), (4) on February 28, 1997, subject to savings where steps to claim possession had been taken before that date: S.I. 1997 No. 225.

(2) The court shall not make an order for possession on any of the grounds in Schedule 2 to this Act unless that ground and particulars of it are specified in the notice under this section; but the grounds specified in such a notice may be altered or added to with the leave of the court.

(3) A notice under this section is one in the prescribed form informing the tenant that—

(a) the landlord intends to begin proceedings for possession of the dwelling-house on one or more of the grounds specified in the notice; and

(b) those proceedings will not begin earlier than a date specified in the notice *which, without prejudice to any additional limitation under subsection (4) below, shall not be earlier than the expiry of the period of two weeks from the date of service of the notice* [in accordance with subsections (4) to (4B) below]; and

(c) those proceedings will not begin later than twelve months from the date of service of the notice.

ANNOTATION

The words in square brackets were substituted by Housing Act 1996, ss.151(1), (3), 232(3), (4), on February 28, 1997, subject to savings where steps to claim possession had been taken before that date: S.I. 1997 No. 225.

(4) If a notice under this section specifies, in accordance with subsection (3)(a) above, any of Grounds 1, 2, 5 to 7, 9 and 16 in Schedule 2 to this Act (whether with or without other grounds), the date specified in the notice as mentioned in subsection (3)(b) above shall not be earlier than—

(a) two months from the date of service of the notice; and

(b) if the tenancy is a periodic tenancy, the earliest date on which, apart from section 5(1) above, the tenancy could be brought to an end by a notice to quit given by the landlord on the same date as the date of service of the notice under this section.

[(4) If a notice under this section specifies in accordance with subsection (3)(a) above Ground 14 in Schedule 2 to this Act (whether with or without other grounds), the date specified in the notice as mentioned in subsection (3)(b) above shall not be earlier than the date of the service of the notice.

(4A) If a notice under this section specifies in accordance with subsection (3)(a) above, any of Grounds 1, 2, 5 to 7, 9 and 16 in Schedule 2 to this Act (whether without other grounds or with any ground other than Ground 14), the date specified in the notice as mentioned in subsection (3)(b) above shall not be earlier than—

(a) two months from the date of service of the notice; and
(b) if the tenancy is a periodic tenancy, the earliest date on which, apart from section 5(1) above, the tenancy could be brought to an end by a notice to quit given by the landlord on the same date as the date of service of the notice under this section.

(4B) In any other case, the date specified in the notice as mentioned in subsection (3)(b) above shall not be earlier than the expiry of the period of two weeks from the date of the service of the notice.]

ANNOTATION

Subsections (4), (4A) and (4B) were substituted by Housing Act 1996, ss.151(1), (4), 232(3), (4), on February 28, 1997, subject to savings where steps to claim possession had been taken before that date: S.I. 1997 No. 225.

(5) The court may not exercise the power conferred by subsection (1)(b) above if the landlord seeks to recover possession on Ground 8 in Schedule 2 to this Act.

(6) Where a notice under this section—

(a) is served at a time when the dwelling-house is let on a fixed term tenancy, or
(b) is served after a fixed term tenancy has come to an end but relates (in whole or in part) to events occurring during that tenancy,

the notice shall have effect notwithstanding that the tenant becomes or has become tenant under a statutory periodic tenancy arising on the coming to an end of the fixed term tenancy.

[Additional notice requirements: ground of domestic violence

8A.—(1) Where the ground specified in a notice under section 8 (whether with or without other grounds) is Ground 14A in Schedule 2 to this Act and the partner who has left the dwelling-house as mentioned in that ground is not a tenant of the dwelling-house, the court shall not entertain proceedings for possession of the dwelling-house unless— **A1–010**

(a) the landlord or, in the case of joint landlords, at least one of them has served on the partner who has left a copy of the notice or has taken all reasonable steps to serve a copy of the notice on that partner, or

(b) the court considers it just and equitable to dispense with such requirements as to service.

(2) Where Ground 14A in Schedule 2 to this Act is added to a notice under section 8 with the leave of the court after proceedings for possession are begun and the partner who has left the dwelling-house as mentioned in that ground is not a party to the proceedings, the court shall not continue to entertain the proceedings unless—

(a) the landlord or, in the case of joint landlords, at least one of them has served a notice under subsection (3) below on the partner who has left or has taken all reasonable steps to serve such a notice on that partner, or
(b) the court considers it just and equitable to dispense with the requirement of such a notice.

(3) A notice under this subsection shall—

(a) state that proceedings for the possession of the dwelling-house have begun,
(b) specify the ground or grounds on which possession is being sought, and
(c) give particulars of the ground or grounds.]

ANNOTATION

Section 8A was inserted (subject to savings) with effect from February 28, 1997: Housing Act 1996 ss. 150, 232(3), (4): Housing Act 1996 (Commencement No. 7 and Savings) Order 1997, (S.I. 1997 No. 225), arts. 1(2), 2, Sched., para. 1.

Extended discretion of court in possession claims

A1–011 **9.**—(1) Subject to subsection (6) below, the court may adjourn for such period or periods as it thinks fit proceedings for possession of a dwelling-house let on an assured tenancy.

(2) On the making of an order for possession of a dwelling-house let on an assured tenancy or at any time before the execution of such an order, the court, subject to subsection (6) below, may—

(a) stay or suspend execution of the order, or
(b) postpone the date of possession,

for such period or periods as the court thinks just.

(3) On any such adjournment as is referred to in subsection (1) above or on any such stay, suspension or postponement as is referred to in subsection (2) above, the court, unless it considers that to do so would cause exceptional hardship to the tenant or would otherwise be unreasonable, shall impose conditions with regard to payment by the tenant of arrears of rent (if any) and rent or

payments in respect of occupation after the termination of the tenancy (mesne profits) and may impose such other conditions as it thinks fit.

(4) If any such conditions as are referred to in subsection (3) above are complied with, the court may, if it thinks fit, discharge or rescind any such order as is referred to in subsection (2) above.

(5) In any case where—

(a) at a time when proceedings are brought for possession of a dwelling-house let on an assured tenancy, the tenant's spouse or former spouse, having *rights of occupation under the Matrimonial Homes Act 1983* [matrimonial home rights under Part IV of the Family Law Act 1996], is in occupation of the dwelling-house, and

(b) the assured tenancy is terminated as a result of those proceedings,

the spouse or former spouse, so long as he or she remains in occupation, shall have the same rights in relation to, or in connection with, any such adjournment as is referred to in subsection (1) above or any such stay, suspension or postponement as is referred to in subsection (2) above, as he or she would have if *those rights of occupation* [those matrimonial home rights] were not affected by the termination of the tenancy.

Annotation

The words in both sets of square brackets in subsection (5) were substituted with effect from October 1, 1997 by Family Law Act 1996, s.66(1), Sched. 8, para. 59(1), (2): S.I. 1997 No. 1892.

[(5A) In any case where—

(a) at a time when proceedings are brought for possession of a dwelling-house let on an assured tenancy—

(i) an order is in force under section 35 of the Family Law Act 1996 conferring rights on the former spouse of the tenant, or

(ii) an order is in force under section 36 of that Act conferring rights on a cohabitant or former cohabitant (within the meaning of that Act) of the tenant,

(b) that cohabitant, former cohabitant or former spouse is then in occupation of the dwelling-house, and

(c) the assured tenancy is terminated as a result of those proceedings,

the cohabitant, former cohabitant or former spouse shall have the same rights in relation to, or in connection with, any such adjournment as is referred to in subsection (1) above or any such stay, suspension or postponement as is referred to in subsection (2) above as he or she would have if the rights conferred by the order referred to in paragraph (a) above were not affected by the termination of the tenancy.]

Annotation

Subsection (5A) was inserted with effect from October 1, 1997 by Family Law Act 1996, s.66(1), Sched. 8, para. 59(1), (3): S.I. 1997 No. 1892.

(6) This section does not apply if the court is satisfied that the landlord is entitled to possession of the dwelling-house—

(a) on any of the grounds in Part I of Schedule 2 to this Act; or
(b) by virtue of subsection (1) or subsection (4) of section 21 below.

Special provisions applicable to shared accommodation

A1–012 **10.**—(1) This section applies in a case falling within subsection (1) of section 3 above and expressions used in this section have the same meaning as in that section.

(2) Without prejudice to the enforcement of any order made under subsection (3) below, while the tenant is in possession of the separate accommodation, no order shall be made for possession of any of the shared accommodation, whether on the application of the immediate landlord of the tenant or on the application of any person under whom that landlord derives title, unless a like order has been made, or is made at the same time, in respect of the separate accommodation; and the provisions of section 6 above shall have effect accordingly.

(3) On the application of the landlord, the court may make such order as it thinks just either—

(a) terminating the right of the tenant to use the whole or any part of the shared accommodation other than living accommodation; or
(b) modifying his right to use the whole or any part of the shared accommodation, whether by varying the persons or increasing the number of persons entitled to the use of that accommodation or otherwise.

(4) No order shall be made under subsection (3) above so as to effect any termination or modification of the rights of the tenant which, apart from section 3(3) above, could not be effected by or under the terms of the tenancy.

Payment of removal expenses in certain cases

A1–013 **11.**—(1) Where a court makes an order for possession of a dwelling-house let on an assured tenancy on Ground 6 or Ground 9 in Schedule 2 to this Act (but not on any other ground), the landlord shall pay to the tenant a sum equal to the reasonable expenses likely to be incurred by the tenant in removing from the dwelling-house.

(2) Any question as to the amount of the sum referred in subsection (1) above shall be determined by agreement between the landlord and the tenant or, in default of agreement, by the court.

(3) Any sum payable to a tenant by virtue of this section shall be recoverable as a civil debt due from the landlord.

Compensation for misrepresentation or concealment

12. Where a landlord obtains an order for possession of a dwelling-house let on an assured tenancy on one or more of the grounds in Schedule 2 to this Act and it is subsequently made to appear to the court that the order was obtained by misrepresentation or concealment of material facts, the court may order the landlord to pay to the former tenant such sum as appears sufficient as compensation for damage or loss sustained by that tenant as a result of the order. **A1–014**

Rent and other terms

Increase of rent under assured periodic tenancies

13.—(1) This section applies to— **A1–015**

(a) a statutory periodic tenancy other than one which, by virtue of paragraph 11 or paragraph 12 in Part I of Schedule 1 to this Act, cannot for the time being be an assured tenancy; and
(b) any other periodic tenancy which is an assured tenancy, other than one in relation to which there is a provision, for the time being binding on the tenant, under which the rent for a particular period of the tenancy will or may be greater than the rent for an earlier period.

(2) For the purpose of securing an increase in the rent under a tenancy to which this section applies, the landlord may serve on the tenant a notice in the prescribed form proposing a new rent to take effect at the beginning of a new period of the tenancy specified in the notice, being a period beginning not earlier than—

(a) the minimum period after the date of the service of the notice; and
(b) except in the case of a statutory periodic tenancy, the first anniversary of the date on which the first period of the tenancy began; and
(c) if the rent under the tenancy has previously been increased by virtue of a notice under this subsection or a determination under section 14 below, the first anniversary of the date on which the increased rent took effect.

(3) The minimum period referred to in subsection (2) above is—

(a) in the case of a yearly tenancy, six months;
(b) in the case of a tenancy wehre the period is less than a month, one month; and
(c) in any other case, a period equal to the period of the tenancy.

(4) Where a notice is served under subsection (2) above, a new rent specified in the notice shall take effect as mentioned in the notice unless, before the beginning of the new period specified in the notice,—

(a) the tenant by an application in the prescribed form refers the notice to a rent assessment committee; or
(b) the landlord and the tenant agree on a variation of the rent which is different from that proposed in the notice or agree that the rent should not be varied.

(5) Nothing in this section (or in section 14 below) affects the right of the landlord and the tenant under an assured tenancy to vary by agreement any term of the tenancy (including a term relating to rent).

Determination of rent by rent assessment committee

A1–016 **14.**—(1) Where, under subsection (4)(a) of section 13 above, a tenant refers to a rent assessment committee a notice under subsection (2) of that section, the committee shall determine the rent at which, subject to subsections (2) and (4) below, the committee consider that the dwelling-house concerned might reasonably be expected to be let in the open market by a willing landlord under an assured tenancy—

(a) which is a periodic tenancy having the same periods as those of the tenancy to which the notice relates;
(b) which begins at the beginning of the new period specified in the notice;
(c) the terms of which (other than relating to the amount of the rent) are the same as those of the tenancy to which the notice relates; and
(d) in respect of which the same notices, if any, have been given under any of Grounds 1 to 5 of Schedule 2 to this Act, as have been given (or have effect as if given) in relation to the tenancy to which the notice relates.

(2) In making a determination under this section, there shall be disregarded—

(a) any effect on the rent attributable to the granting of a tenancy to a sitting tenant;
(b) any increase in the value of the dwelling-house attributable to a relevant improvement carried out by a person who at the time it was carried out was the tenant, if the improvement—
    (i) was carried out otherwise than in pursuance of an obligation to his immediate landlord, or
    (ii) was carried out pursuant to an obligation to his immediate landlord being an obligation which did not relate to the specific improvement concerned but arose by reference to consent given to the carrying out of that improvement; and
(c) any reduction in the value of the dwelling-house attributable to a failure by the tenant to comply with any terms of the tenancy.

(3) For the purposes of subsection (2)(b) above, in relation to a notice which is referred by a tenant as mentioned in subsection (1) above, an improvement is

a relevant improvement if either it was carried out during the tenancy to which the notice relates or the following conditions are satisfied, namely—

(a) that it was carried out not more than twenty-one years before the date of service of the notice; and
(b) that, at all times during the period beginning when the improvement was carried out and ending on the date of service of the notice, the dwelling-house has been let under an assured tenancy; and
(c) that, on the coming to an end of an assured tenancy at any time during that period, the tenant (or, in the case of joint tenants, at least one of them) did not quit.

[(3A) In making a determination under this section in any case where under Part I of the Local Government Finance Act 1992 the landlord or superior landlord is liable to pay council tax in respect of a hereditament (''the relevant hereditament'') of which the dwelling-house forms part, the rent assessment committee shall have regard to the amount of council tax which, as at the date on which the notice under section 13(2) above was served, was set by the billing authority—

(a) for the financial year in which that notice was served, and
(b) for the category of dwellings within which the relevant hereditament fell on that date,

but any discount or other reduction affecting the amount of council tax payable shall be disregarded.

(3B) In subsection (3A) above—

(a) ''hereditament'' means a dwelling within the meaning of Part I of the Local Government Finance Act 1992.
(b) ''billing authority'' has the same meaning as in that Part of that Act, and
(c) ''category of dwellings'' has the same meaning as in section 30(1) and (2) of that Act.]

Annotation

Subsections (3A) and (3B) were inserted by Local Government Finance (Housing) (Consequential Amendments) Order 1993 (S.I. 1993 No. 651), art. 2(1), Sched. 1, para. 17(1), (2), with effect from April 1, 1993; but these amendments do not affect the determination of rent under Act of 1988, s.14 on a reference which relates to a notice served under *ibid.*, s.13(2) before that date: S.I. 1993 No. 651, *supra*, art. 1(2)(c).

(4) In this section ''rent'' does not include any service charge, within the meaning of section 18 of the Landlord and Tenant Act 1985, but, subject to that, includes any sums payable by the tenant to the landlord on account of the use of furniture [, in respect of council tax] or for any of the matters referred to in subsection (1)(a) of that section, whether or not those sums are separate from the sums payable for the occupation of the dwelling-house concerned or are payable under separate agreements.

ANNOTATION

The words in square brackets were inserted by Local Government Finance (Housing) (Consequential Amendments) Order 1993 (S.I. 1993 No. 651), art. 2(1), Sched. 1, para. 17(1), (3), with effect from April 1, 1993; but this amendment does not affect the determination of rent under Act of 1988, s.14 on a reference which relates to a notice served under *ibid.*, s.13(2) before that date: S.I. 1993 No. 651, *supra*, art.1(2)(c).

(5) Where any rates in respect of the dwelling-house concerned are borne by the landlord or a superior landlord, the rent assessment committee shall make their determination under this section as if the rates were not so borne.

(6) In any case where—

(a) a rent assessment committee have before them at the same time the reference of a notice under section 6(2) above relating to a tenancy (in this subsection referred to as ''the section 6 reference'') and the reference of a notice under section 13(2) above relating to the same tenancy (in this subsection referred to as ''the section 13 reference''), and

(b) the date specified in the notice under section 6(2) above is not later than the first day of the new period specified in the notice under section 13(2) above, and

(c) the committee propose to hear the two references together,

the committee shall make a determination in relation to the section 6 reference before making their determination in relation to the section 13 reference and, accordingly, in such a case the reference in subsection (1)(c) above to the terms of the tenancy to which the notice relates shall be construed as a reference to those terms as varied by virtue of the determination made in relation to the section 6 reference.

(7) Where a notice under section 13(2) above has been referred to a rent assessment committee, then, unless the landlord and the tenant otherwise agree, the rent determined by the committee (subject, in a case where subsection (5) above applies, to the addition of the appropriate amount in respect of rates) shall be the rent under the tenancy with effect from the beginning of the new period specified in the notice or, if it appears to the rent assessment committee that that would cause undue hardship to the tenant, with effect from such later date (not being later than the date the rent is determined) as the committee may direct.

(8) Nothing in this section requires a rent assessment committee to continue with their determination of a rent for a dwelling-house if the landlord and tenant give notice in writing that they no longer require such a determination or if the tenancy has come to an end.

[(9) This section shall apply in relation to an assured shorthold tenancy as if in subsection (1) the reference to an assured tenancy were a reference to an assured shorthold tenancy.]

ANNOTATION

Subsection (9) was inserted by Housing Act 1996, ss.104, 232(3), Sched. 8, para. 2(2), with effect from February 28, 1997: S.I. 1997 No. 225.

[Interim increase before 1st April 1994 of rent under assured periodic tenancies in certain cases where landlord is liable for council tax

14A.—(1) In any case where— **A1–017**

(a) under Part I of the Local Government Finance Act 1992 the landlord of a dwelling-house let under an assured tenancy to which section 13 above applies or a superior landlord is liable to pay council tax in respect of a dwelling (within the meaning of that Part of that Act) which includes that dwelling-house,

(b) under the terms of the tenancy (or an agreement collateral to the tenancy) the tenant is liable to make payments to the landlord in respect of council tax,

(c) the case falls within subsection (2) or subsection (3) below, and

(d) no previous notice under this subsection has been served in relation to the dwelling-house,

the landlord may serve on the tenant a notice in the prescribed form proposing an increased rent to take account of the tenant's liability to make payments to the landlord in respect of council tax, such increased rent to take effect at the beginning of a new period of the tenancy specified in the notice being a period beginning not earlier than one month after the date on which the notice was served.

(2) The case falls within this subsection if—

(a) the rent under the tenancy has previously been increased by virtue of a notice under section 13(2) above or a determination under section 14 or above, and

(b) the first anniversary of the date on which the increased rent took effect has not yet occurred.

(3) The case falls within this subsection if a notice has been served under section 13(2) above before 1st April 1993 but no increased rent has taken effect before that date.

(4) No notice may be served under subsection (1) above after 31st March 1994.

(5) Where a notice is served under subsection (1) above, the new rent specified in the notice shall take effect as mentioned in the notice unless, before the beginning of the new period specified in the notice—

(a) the tenant by an application in the prescribed form refers the notice to a rent assessment committee, or

(b) the landlord and the tenant agree on a variation of the rent which is different from that proposed in the notice or agree that the rent should not be varied.

(6) Nothing in this section (or in section 14B below) affects the rights of the landlord and the tenant under an assured tenancy to vary by agreement any term of the tenancy (including a term relating to rent).]

ANNOTATION

Section 14A was inserted by Local Government Finance (Housing) (Consequential Amendments) Order 1993 (S.I. 1993 No. 651), art. 2(2), Sched. 2, para. 8, with effect from April 1, 1993.

[Interim determination of rent by rent assessment committee

A1–018 **14B.**—(1) Where, under subsection (5)(a) of section 14A above, a tenant refers to a rent assessment committee a notice under subsection (1) of that section, the committee shall determine the amount by which, having regard to the provisions of section 14(3A) above, the existing rent might reasonably be increased to take account of the tenant's liability to make payments to the landlord in respect of council tax.

(2) Where a notice under section 14A(1) above has been referred to a rent assessment committee, then, unless the landlord and the tenant otherwise agree, the existing rent shall be increased by the amount determined by the committee with effect from the beginning of the new period specified in the notice or, if it appears to the committee that that would cause undue hardship to the tenant, with effect from such later date (not being later than the date the increase is determined) as the committee may direct.

(3) In any case where—

(a) a rent assessment committee have before them at the same time the reference of a notice under section 13(2) above relating to a tenancy (in this subsection referred to as "the section 13 reference") and the reference of a notice under section 14A(1) above relating to the same tenancy (in this subsection referred to as "the section 14A reference"); and

(b) the committee propose to hear the two references together,

the committee shall make a determination in relation to the section 13 reference before making their determination in relation to the section 14A reference, and if in such a case the date specified in the notice under section 13(2) above is later than the date specified in the notice under section 14A(1) above, the rent determined under the section 14A reference shall not take effect until the date specified in the notice under section 13(2).

(4) In this section "rent" has the same meaning as in section 14 above; and section 14(4) above applies to a determination under this section as it applies to a determination under that section.]

ANNOTATION

Section 14B was inserted by Local Government Finance (Housing) (Consequential Amendments) Order 1993 (S.I. 1993 No. 651), art. 2(2), Sched. 2, para. 8, with effect from April 1, 1993.

Limited prohibition on assignment etc. without consent

15.—(1) Subject to subsection (3) below, it shall be an implied term of every assured tenancy which is a periodic tenancy that, except with the consent of the landlord, the tenant shall not— **A1–019**

(a) assign the tenancy (in whole or in part); or
(b) sub-let or part with possession of the whole or any part of the dwelling-house let on the tenancy.

(2) Section 19 of the Landlord and Tenant Act 1927 (consents to assign not to be unreasonably withheld etc.) shall not apply to a term which is implied into an assured tenancy by subsection (1) above.

(3) In the case of a periodic tenancy which is not a statutory periodic tenancy [or an assured periodic tenancy arising under Schedule 10 to the Local Government and Housing Act 1989] subsection (1) above does not apply if—

(a) there is a provision (whether contained in the tenancy or not) under which the tenant is prohibited (whether absolutely or conditionally) from assigning or sub-letting or parting with possession or is permitted (whether absolutely or conditionally) to assign, sub-let or part with possession; or
(b) a premium is required to be paid on the grant or renewal of the tenancy.

ANNOTATION

The words in square brackets were inserted with effect from April 1, 1990 by Local Government and Housing Act 1989, ss.194(1), 195(2), Sched. 11, para. 102: S.I. 1990 No. 431.

(4) In subsection (3)(b) above "premium" includes—

(a) any fine or other like sum;
(b) any other pecuniary consideration in addition to rent; and
(c) any sum paid by way of deposit, other than one which does not exceed one-sixth of the annual rent payable under the tenancy immediately after the grant or renewal in question.

Access for repairs

16. It shall be an implied term of every assured tenancy that the tenant shall afford to the landlord access to the dwelling-house let on the tenancy and all reasonable facilities for executing therein any repairs which the landlord is entitled to execute. **A1–020**

Miscellaneous

Succession to assured periodic tenancy by spouse

A1–021 **17.**—(1) In any case where—

(a) the sole tenant under an assured periodic tenancy dies, and
(b) immediately before the death, the tenant's spouse was occupying the dwelling-house as his or her only or principal home, and
(c) the tenant was not himself a successor, as defined in subsection (2) or subsection (3) below,

then, on the death, the tenancy vests by virtue of this section in the spouse (and, accordingly, does not devolve under the tenant's will or intestacy).

(2) For the purposes of this section, a tenant is a successor in relation to a tenancy if—

(a) the tenancy became vested in him either by virtue of this section or under the will or intestacy of a previous tenant; or
(b) at some time before the tenant's death the tenancy was a joint tenancy held by himself and one or more other persons and, prior to his death, he became the sole tenant by survivorship; or
(c) he became entitled to the tenancy as mentioned in section 39(5) below.

(3) For the purposes of this section, a tenant is also a successor in relation to a tenancy (in this subsection referred to as "the new tenancy") which was granted to him (alone or jointly with others) if—

(a) at some time before the grant of the new tenancy, he was, by virtue of subsection (2) above, a successor in relation to an earlier tenancy of the same or substantially the same dwelling-house as is let under the new tenancy; and
(b) at all times since he became such a successor he has been a tenant (alone or jointly with others) of the dwelling-house which is let under the new tenancy or of a dwelling-house which is substantially the same as that dwelling-house.

(4) For the purposes of this section, a person who was living with the tenant as his or her wife or husband shall be treated as the tenant's spouse.

(5) If, on the death of the tenant, there is, by virtue of subsection (4) above, more than one person who fulfils the condition in subsection (1)(b) above, such one of them as may be decided by agreement or, in default of agreement, by the county court shall be treated as the tenant's spouse for the purposes of this section.

Provisions as to reversions on assured tenancies

18.—(1) If at any time— **A1–022**

(a) a dwelling-house is for the time being lawfully let on an assured tenancy, and
(b) the landlord under the assured tenancy is himself a tenant under a superior tenancy; and
(c) the superior tenancy comes to an end,

then, subject to subsection (2) below, the assured tenancy shall continue in existence as a tenancy held of the person whose interest would, apart from the continuance of the assured tenancy, entitle him to actual possession of the dwelling-house at that time.

(2) Subsection (1) above does not apply to an assured tenancy if the interest which, by virtue of that subsection, would become that of the landlord, is such that, by virtue of Schedule 1 to this Act, the tenancy could not be an assured tenancy.

(3) Where, by virtue of any provision of this Part of this Act, an periodic tenancy) continues beyond the beginning of a reversionary tenancy which was granted (whether before, on or after the commencement of this Act) so as to begin on or after—

(a) the date on which the previous contractual assured tenancy came to an end, or
(b) a date on which, apart from any provision of this Part, the periodic tenancy could have been brought to an end by the landlord by notice to quit,

the reversionary tenancy shall have effect as if it had been granted subject to the periodic tenancy.

(4) The reference in subsection (3) above to the previous contractual assured tenancy applies only where the periodic tenancy referred to in that subsection is a statutory periodic tenancy and is a reference to the fixed-term tenancy which immediately preceded the statutory periodic tenancy.

Restriction on levy of distress for rent

19.—(1) Subject to subsection (2) below, no distress for the rent of any dwelling-house let on an assured tenancy shall be levied except with the leave of the county court; and, with respect to any application for such leave, the court shall have the same powers with respect to adjournment, stay, suspension, postponement and otherwise as are conferred by section 9 above in relation to proceedings for possession of such a dwelling-house. **A1–023**

(2) Nothing in subsection (1) above applies to distress levied under section 102 of the County Courts Act 1984.

CHAPTER II

ASSURED SHORTHOLD TENANCIES

[Assured shorthold tenancies: post Housing Act 1996 tenancies

A1–024 **19A.** An assured tenancy which—

(a) is entered into on or after the day on which section 96 of the Housing Act 1996 comes into force (otherwise than pursuant to a contract made before that day), or
(b) comes into being by virtue of section 5 above on the coming to an end of an assured tenancy within paragraph (a) above,

is an assured shorthold tenancy unless it falls within any paragraph in Schedule 2A to this Act.]

ANNOTATION

Section 19A was inserted by Housing Act 1996, ss.96(1), 232(3) with effect from February 28, 1997: S.I. 1997 No. 225.

Assured shorthold tenancies

A1–025 ***20.**—(1) Subject to subsection (3) below, an assured shorthold tenancy is an assured tenancy—*

(a) which is a fixed term tenancy granted for a term certain of not less than six months; and
(b) in respect of which there is no power for the landlord to determine the tenancy at any time earlier than six months from the beginning of the tenancy; and
(c) in respect of which a notice is served as mentioned in subsection (2) below.

[Assured shorthold tenancies: pre-Housing Act 1996 tenancies

20.—(1) Subject to subsection (3) below, an assured tenancy which is not one to which section 19A above applies is an assured shorthold tenancy if—

(a) it is a fixed term tenancy granted for a term certain of not less than six months; and
(b) there is no power for the landlord to determine the tenancy at any time earlier than six months from the beginning of the tenancy; and
(c) a notice in respect of it is served as mentioned in subsection (2) below.]

ANNOTATION

The marginal note and subsection (1) were substituted by Housing Act 1996, ss.104, 232(3), Sched. 8, para. 2(3) with effect from February 28, 1997: S.I. 1997 No. 225.

(2) The notice referred to in subsection (1)(c) above is one which—

(a) is in such form as may be prescribed;
(b) is served before the assured tenancy is entered into;
(c) is served by the person who is to be the landlord under the assured tenancy on the person who is to be the tenant under that tenancy; and
(d) states that the assured tenancy to which it relates is to be a shorthold tenancy.

(3) Notwithstanding anything in subsection (1) above, where—

(a) immediately before a tenancy (in this subsection referred to as "the new tenancy") is granted, the person to whom it is granted or, as the case may be, at least one of the persons to whom it is granted was a tenant under an assured tenancy which was not a shorthold tenancy, and
(b) the new tenancy is granted by the person who, immediately before the beginning of the tenancy, was the landlord under the assured tenancy referred to in paragraph (a) above,

the new tenancy cannot be an assured shorthold tenancy.

(4) Subject to subsection (5) below, if, on the coming to an end of an assured shorthold tenancy (including a tenancy which was an assured shorthold but ceased to be assured before it came to an end), a new tenancy of the same or substantially the same premises comes into being under which the landlord and the tenant are the same as at the coming to an end of the earlier tenancy, then, if and so long as the new tenancy is an assured tenancy, it shall be an assured shorthold tenancy, whether or not it fulfils the conditions in paragraphs (a) to (c) of subsection (1) above.

(5) Subsection (4) above does not apply if, before the new tenancy is entered into (or, in the case of a statutory periodic tenancy, takes effect in possession), the landlord serves notice on the tenant that the new tenancy is not to be a shorthold tenancy.

[(5A) Subsections (3) and (4) above do not apply where the new tenancy is one to which section 19A above applies.]

ANNOTATION

Subsection (5A) was inserted by Housing Act 1996, ss.104, 232(3), Sched. 8, para. 2(4) with effect from February 28, 1997: S.I. 1997 No. 225.

(6) In the case of joint landlords—

(a) the reference in subsection (2)(c) above to the person who is to be the landlord is a reference to at least one of the persons who are to be joint landlords; and

(b) the reference in subsection (5) above to the landlord is a reference to at least one of the joint landlords.

(7) Section 14 above shall apply in relation to an assured shorthold tenancy as if in subsection (1) of that section the reference to an assured tenancy were a reference to an assured shorthold tenancy.

ANNOTATION

Subsection (7) was repealed pursuant to Housing Act 1996, ss.227, Sched. 19, Pt. IV with effect from February 28, 1997: S.I. 1997 No. 225.

[Post-Housing Act 1996 tenancies: duty of landlord to provide statement as to terms of tenancy

A1–026 **20A.—**(1) Subject to subsection (3) below, a tenant under an assured shorthold tenancy to which section 19A above applies may, by notice in writing, require the landlord under that tenancy to provide him with a written statement of any term of the tenancy which—

(a) falls within subsection (2) below, and
(b) is not evidenced in writing.

(2) The following terms of a tenancy fall within this subsection, namely—

(a) the date on which the tenancy began or, if it is a statutory periodic tenancy or a tenancy to which section 39(7) below applies, the date on which the tenancy came into being,
(b) the rent payable under the tenancy and the dates on which that rent is payable,
(c) any term providing for a review of the rent payable under the tenancy, and
(d) in the case of a fixed term tenancy, the length of the fixed term.

(3) No notice may be given under subsection (1) above in relation to a term of the tenancy if—

(a) the landlord under the tenancy has provided a statement of that term in response to an earlier notice under that subsection given by the tenant under the tenancy, and
(b) the term has not been varied since the provision of the statement referred to in paragraph (a) above.

(4) A landlord who fails, without reasonable excuse, to comply with a notice under subsection (1) above within the period of 28 days beginning with the date on which he received the notice is liable on summary conviction to a fine not exceeding level 4 on the standard scale.

(5) A statement provided for the purposes of subsection (1) above shall not

be regarded as conclusive evidence of what was agreed by the parties to the tenancy in question.

(6) Where—

(a) a term of a statutory periodic tenancy is one which has effect by virtue of section 5(3)(e) above, or

(b) a term of a tenancy to which subsection (7) of section 39 below applies is one which has effect by virtue of subsection (6)(e) of that section,

subsection (1) above shall have effect in relation to it as if paragraph (b) related to the term of the tenancy from which it derives.

(7) In subsections (1) and (3) above—

(a) references to the tenant under the tenancy shall, in the case of joint tenants, be taken to be references to any of the tenants, and

(b) references to the landlord under the tenancy shall, in the case of joint landlords, be taken to be references to any of the landlords.]

ANNOTATION

Section 20A was inserted by Housing Act 1996, ss.97, 232(3) with effect from February 28, 1997: S.I. 1997 No. 225.

Recovery of possession on expiry or termination of assured shorthold tenancy

21.—(1) Without prejudice to any right of the landlord under an assured shorthold tenancy to recover possession of the dwelling-house let on the tenancy in accordance with Chapter I above, on or after the coming to an end of an assured shorthold tenancy which was a fixed term tenancy, a court shall make an order for possession of the dwelling-house if it is satisfied— **A1–027**

(a) that the assured shorthold tenancy has come to an end and no further assured tenancy (whether shorthold or not) is for the time being in existence, other than [an assured shorthold periodic tenancy (whether statutory or not)]; and

(b) the landlord or, in the case of joint landlords, at least one of them has given to the tenant not less than two months' notice [in writing] stating that he requires possession of the dwelling-house.

ANNOTATION

The words in square brackets in subsection (1)(a) were substituted by Local Government and Housing Act 1989, ss.194(1), 195(2), Sched. 11, para. 103 with effect from January 16, 1990: S.I. 1989 No. 2445. The words in square brackets in subsection (1)(b) were inserted by Housing Act 1996, ss.98(1), (2), 232(3), (4) with effect from February 28, 1997, but the amendment has no effect where the notice was served before that date: S.I. 1997 No. 225.

(2) A notice under paragraph (b) of subsection (1) above may be given before or on the day on which the tenancy comes to an end; and that subsection shall

have effect notwithstanding that on the coming to an end of the fixed term tenancy a statutory periodic tenancy arises.

(3) Where a court makes an order for possession of a dwelling-house by virtue of subsection (1) above, any statutory periodic tenancy which has arisen on the coming to an end of the assured shorthold tenancy shall end (without further notice and regardless of the period) on the day on which the order takes effect.

(4) Without prejudice to any such right as is referred to in subsection (1) above, a court shall make an order for possession of a dwelling-house let on an assured shorthold tenancy which is a periodic tenancy if the court is satisfied—

(a) that the landlord or, in the case of joint landlords, at least one of them has given to the tenant a notice [in writing] stating that, after a date specified in the notice, being the last day of a period of the tenancy and not earlier than two months after the date the notice was given, possession of the dwelling-house is required by virtue of this section; and
(b) that the date specified in the notice under paragraph (a) above is not earlier than the earliest day on which, apart from section 5(1) above, the tenancy could be brought to an end by a notice to quit given by the landlord on the same date as the notice under paragraph (a) above.

ANNOTATION

The words in square brackets in subsection (4)(a) were inserted by Housing Act 1996, ss.98(1), (3), 232(3), (4) with effect from February 28, 1997, but the amendment has no effect where the notice was given before that date: S.I. 1997 No. 225.

[(5) Where an order for possession under subsection (1) or (4) above is made in relation to a dwelling-house let on a tenancy to which section 19A above applies, the order may not be made so as to take effect earlier than—

(a) in the case of a tenancy which is not a replacement tenancy, six months after the beginning of the tenancy, and
(b) in the case of a replacement tenancy, six months after the beginning of the original tenancy.

(6) In subsection (5)(b) above, the reference to the original tenancy is—

(a) where the replacement tenancy came into being on the coming to an end of a tenancy which was not a replacement tenancy, to the immediately preceding tenancy, and
(b) where there have been successive replacement tenancies, to the tenancy immediately preceding the first in the succession of replacement tenancies.

(7) For the purposes of this section, a replacement tenancy is a tenancy—

(a) which comes into being on the coming to an end of an assured shorthold tenancy, and

(b) under which, on its coming into being—
   (i) the landlord and tenant are the same as under the earlier tenancy as at its coming to an end, and
   (ii) the premises let are the same or substantially the same as those let under the earlier tenancy as at that time.]

ANNOTATION

Subsections (5), (6) and (7) were inserted by Housing Act 1996, ss.99, 232(3) on February 28, 1997: S.I. 1997 No. 225.

Reference of excessive rents to rent assessment committee

22.—(1) Subject to section 23 and subsection (2) below, the tenant under an assured shorthold tenancy *in respect of which a notice was served as mentioned in section 20(2) above* may make an application in the prescribed form to a rent assessment committee for a determination of the rent which, in the committee's opinion, the landlord might reasonably be expected to obtain under the assured shorthold tenancy. **A1–028**

ANNOTATION

The words in italics were repealed by Housing Act 1996, s.227, Sched. 19, Pt. IV with effect from February 28, 1997: S.I. 1997 No. 225.

(2) No application may be made under this section if—

(a) the rent payable under the tenancy is a rent previously determined under this section; *or*
[(aa) the tenancy is one to which section 19A above applies and more than six months have elapsed since the beginning of the tenancy or, in the case of a replacement tenancy, since the beginning of the original tenancy; or]
(b) the tenancy is an assured shorthold tenancy falling within subsection (4) of section 20 above (and, accordingly, is one in respect of which notice need not have been served as mentioned in subsection (2) of that section).

ANNOTATION

The word in italics was repealed by Housing Act 1996, s.227, Sched. 19, Pt. IV on February 28, 1997, and subsection (2)(aa) was inserted by Housing Act 1996, ss.100(1), (2), 232(3) on February 28, 1997: S.I. 1997 No. 225.

(3) Where an application is made to a rent assessment committee under subsection (1) above with respect to the rent under an assured shorthold tenancy, the committee shall not make such a determination as is referred to in that subsection unless they consider—

(a) that there is a sufficient number of similar dwelling-houses in the locality let on assured tenancies (whether shorthold or not); and

(b) that the rent payable under the assured shorthold tenancy in question is significantly higher than the rent which the landlord might reasonably be expected to be able to obtain under the tenancy, having regard to the level of rents payable under the tenancies referred to in paragraph (a) above.

(4) Where, on an application under this section, a rent assessment committee make a determination of a rent for an assured shorthold tenancy—

(a) the determination shall have effect from such date as the committee may direct, not being earlier than the date of the application;
(b) if, at any time on or after the determination takes effect, the rent which, apart from this paragraph, would be payable under the tenancy exceeds the rent so determined, the excess shall be irrecoverable from the tenant; and
(c) no notice may be served under section 13(2) above with respect to a tenancy of the dwelling-house in question until after the first anniversary of the date on which the determination takes effect.

(5) Subsections (4), (5) and (8) of section 14 above apply in relation to a determination of rent under this section as they apply in relation to a determination under that section and, accordingly, where subsection (5) of that section applies, any reference in subsection (4)(b) above to rent is a reference to rent exclusive of the amount attributable to rates.

[(5A) Where—

(a) an assured tenancy ceases to be an assured shorthold tenancy by virtue of falling within paragraph 2 of Schedule 2A to this Act, and
(b) at the time when it so ceases to be as assured shorthold tenancy there is pending before a rent assessment committee an application in relation to it under this section,

the fact that it so ceases to be an assured shorthold tenancy shall, in relation to that application, be disregarded for the purposes of this section.

(6) In subsection (2)(aa) above, the references to the original tenancy and to a replacement tenancy shall be construed in accordance with subsections (6) and (7) respectively of section 21 above.]

ANNOTATION

Subsections (5A) and (6) were inserted by Housing Act 1996, ss.100(1), (3), 104, 232(3), Sched. 8, para. 2(6) with effect from February 28, 1997: S.I. 1997 No. 225.

Termination of rent assessment committee's functions

A1–029 **23.**—(1) If the Secretary of State by order made by statutory instrument so provides, section 22 above shall not apply in such cases or to tenancies of dwelling-houses in such areas or in such other circumstances as may be specified in the order.

(2) An order under this section may contain such transitional, incidental and supplementary provisions as appear to the Secretary of State to be desirable.

(3) No order shall be made under this section unless a draft of the order has been laid before, and approved by a resolution of, each House of Parliament.

Chapter III

Assured Agricultural Occupancies

Assured agricultural occupancies

24.—(1) A tenancy or licence of a dwelling-house is for the purposes of this Part of this Act an "assured agricultural occupancy" if— **A1–030**

(a) it is of a description specified in subsection (2) below; and
(b) by virtue of any provision of Schedule 3 to this Act the agricultural worker condition is for the time being fulfilled with respect to the dwelling-house subject to the tenancy or licence.

(2) The following are the tenancies and licences referred to in subsection (1)(a) above—

(a) an assured tenancy which is not an assured shorthold tenancy;
(b) a tenancy which does not fall within paragraph (a) above by reason only of paragraph 3 [,3A,3B] or paragraph 7 of Schedule 1 to this Act ([or more than one of those paragraphs]) [and is not an excepted tenancy]; and
(c) a licence under which a person has the exclusive occupation of a dwelling-house as a separate dwelling and which, if it conferred a sufficient interest in land to be a tenancy, would be a tenancy falling within paragraph (a) or paragraph (b) above.

Annotation

The words in the first pair of square brackets in subsection (2)(b) were inserted and the words in the second pair of square brackets in that subsection were substituted by the References to Rating (Housing) Regulations 1990 (S.I. 1990 No. 434), reg. 2, Sched. para. 28. The words in subsection (2)(b) in the third pair of square brackets were inserted with effect from February 28, 1997 by Housing Act 1996, ss.103(2), 232(3); S.I. 1997 No. 225.

[(2A) For the purposes of subsection (2)(b) above, a tenancy is an excepted tenancy if it is—

(a) a tenancy of an agricultural holding within the meaning of the Agricultural Holdings Act 1986 in relation to which that Act applies, or
(b) a farm business tenancy within the meaning of the Agricultural Tenancies Act 1995.]

ANNOTATION

Subsection (2A) was inserted with effect from February 28, 1997 by Housing Act 1996, ss.103(3), 232(3): S.I. 1997 No. 225.

(3) For the purposes of Chapter I above and the following provisions of this Chapter, every assured agricultural occupancy which is not an assured tenancy shall be treated as if it were such a tenancy and any reference to a tenant, a landlord or any other expression appropriate to a tenancy shall be construed accordingly; but the provisions of Chapter I above shall have effect in relation to every assured agricultural occupancy subject to the provisions of this Chapter.

(4) Section 14 above shall apply in relation to an assured agricultural occupancy as if in subsection (1) of that section the reference to an assured tenancy were a reference to an assured agricultural occupancy.

Security of tenure

A1–031 **25.**—(1) If a statutory periodic tenancy arises on the coming to an end of an assured agricultural occupancy—

(a) it shall be an assured agricultural occupancy as long as, by virtue of any provision of Schedule 3 to this Act, the agricultural worker condition is for the time being fulfilled with respect to the dwelling-house in question; and
(b) if no rent was payable under the assured agricultural occupancy which constitutes the fixed term tenancy referred to in subsection (2) of section 5 above, subsection (3)(d) of that section shall apply as if for the words "the same as those for which rent was last payable under" there were substituted "monthly beginning on the day following the coming to an end of".

(2) In its application to an assured agricultural occupancy, Part II of Schedule 2 to this Act shall have effect with the omission of Ground 16.

(3) In its application to an assured agricultural occupancy, Part III of Schedule 2 to this Act shall have effect as if any reference in paragraph 2 to an assured tenancy included a reference to an assured agricultural occupancy.

(4) If the tenant under an assured agricultural occupancy gives notice to terminate his employment then, notwithstanding anything in any agreement or otherwise, that notice shall not constitute a notice to quit as respects the assured agricultural occupancy.

(5) Nothing in subsection (4) above affects the operation of an actual notice to quit given in respect of an assured agricultural occupancy.

Rehousing of agricultural workers etc.

A1–032 **26.**—In section 27 of the Rent (Agriculture) Act 1976 (rehousing: applications to housing authority)—

(a) in subsection (1)(a) after "statutory tenancy" there shall be inserted "or an assured agricultural occupancy"; and
(b) at the end of subsection (3) there shall be added "and assured agricultural occupancy has the same meaning as in Chapter III of Part I of the Housing Act 1988".

CHAPTER IV

PROTECTION FROM EVICTION

Damages for unlawful eviction

27.—(1) This section applies if, at any time after 9th June 1988, a landlord (in this section referred to as "the landlord in default") or any person acting on behalf of the landlord in default unlawfully deprives the residential occupier of any premises of his occupation of the whole or part of the premises. **A1–033**

(2) This section also applies if, at any time after 9th June 1988, a landlord (in this section referred to as "the landlord in default") or any person acting on behalf of the landlord in default—

(a) attempts unlawfully to deprive the residential occupier of any premises of his occupation of the whole or part of the premises, or
(b) knowing or having reasonable cause to believe that the conduct is likely to cause the residential occupier of any premises—
   (i) to give up his occupation of the premises or any part thereof, or
   (ii) to refrain from exercising any right or pursuing any remedy in respect of the premises or any part thereof,

   does acts likely to interfere with the peace or comfort of the residential occupier or members of his household, or persistently withdraws or withholds services reasonably required for the occupation of the premises as a residence,

and, as a result, the residential occupier gives up his occupation of the premises as a residence.

(3) Subject to the following provisions of this section, where this section applies, the landlord in default shall, by virtue of this section, be liable to pay to the former residential occupier, in respect of his loss of the right to occupy the premises in question as his residence, damages assessed on the basis set out in section 28 below.

(4) Any liability arising by virtue of subsection (3) above—

(a) shall be in the nature of a liability in tort; and
(b) subject to subsection (5) below, shall be in addition to any liability arising apart from this section (whether in tort, contract or otherwise).

(5) Nothing in this section affects the right of a residential occupier to enforce any liability which arises apart from this section in respect of his loss of the right to occupy premises as his residence; but damages shall not be awarded both in respect of such a liability and in respect of a liability arising by virtue of this section on account of the same loss.

(6) No liability shall arise by virtue of subsection (3) above if—

(a) before the date on which proceedings to enforce the liability are finally disposed of, the former residential occupier is reinstated in the premises in question in such circumstances that he becomes again the residential occupier of them; or
(b) at the request of the former residential occupier, a court makes an order (whether in the nature of an injunction or otherwise) as a result of which he is reinstated as mentioned in paragraph (a) above;

and, for the purposes of paragraph (a) above, proceedings to enforce a liability are finally disposed of on the earliest date by which the proceedings (including any proceedings on or in consequence of an appeal) have been determined and any time for appealing or further appealing has expired, except that if any appeal is abandoned, the proceedings shall be taken to be disposed of on the date of the abandonment.

(7) If, in proceedings to enforce a liability arising by virtue of subsection (3) above, it appears to the court—

(a) that, prior to the event which gave rise to the liability, the conduct of the former residential occupier or any person living with him in the premises concerned was such that it is reasonable to mitigate the damages for which the landlord in default would otherwise be liable, or
(b) that, before the proceedings were begun, the landlord in default offered to reinstate the former residential occupier in the premises in question and either it was unreasonable of the former residential occupier to refuse that offer or, if he had obtained alternative accommodation before the offer was made, it would have been unreasonable of him to refuse that offer if he had not obtained that accommodation,

the court may reduce the amount of damages which would otherwise be payable by such amount as it thinks appropriate.

(8) In proceedings to enforce a liability arising by virtue of subsection (3) above, it shall be a defence for the defendant to prove that he believed, and had reasonable cause to believe—

(a) that the residential occupier had ceased to reside in the premises in question at the time when he was deprived of occupation as mentioned in subsection (1) above or, as the case may be, when the attempt was made or the acts were done as a result of which he gave up his occupation of those premises; or
(b) that, where the liability would otherwise arise by virtue only of the doing of acts or the withdrawal or withholding of services, he had

reasonable grounds for doing the acts or withdrawing or withholding the services in question.

(9) In this section—

(a) ‘‘residential occupier’’, in relation to any premises, has the same meaning as in section 1 of the 1977 Act;
(b) ‘‘the right to occupy’’, in relation to a residential occupier, includes any restriction on the right of another person to recover possession of the premises in question;
(c) ‘‘landlord’’, in relation to a residential occupier, means the person who, but for the occupier's right to occupy, would be entitled to occupation of the premises and any superior landlord under whom that person derives title;
(d) ‘‘former residential occupier’’, in relation to any premises, means the person who was the residential occupier until he was deprived of or gave up his occupation as mentioned in subsection (1) or subsection (2) above (and, in relation to a former residential occupier, ‘‘the right to occupy’’ and ‘‘landlord’’ shall be construed accordingly).

The measure of damages

28.—(1) The basis for the assessment of damages referred to in section 27(3) above is the difference in value, determined as at the time immediately before the residential occupier ceased to occupy the premises in question as his residence, between— **A1–034**

(a) the value of the interest of the landlord in default determined on the assumption that the residential occupier continues to have the same right to occupy the premises as before that time; and
(b) the value of that interest determined on the assumption that the residential occupier has ceased to have that right.

(2) In relation to any premises, any reference in this section to the interest of the landlord in default is a reference to his interest in the building in which the premises in question are comprised (whether or not that building contains any other premises) together with its curtilage.

(3) For the purposes of the valuations referred to in subsection 15 above it shall be assumed—

(a) that the landlord in default is selling his interest on the open market to a willing buyer;
(b) that neither the residential occupier nor any member of his family wishes to buy; and
(c) that it is unlawful to carry out any substantial development of any of the land in which the landlord's interest subsists or to demolish the whole or part of any building on that land.

(4) In this section "the landlord in default" has the same meaning as in section 27 above and subsection (9) of that section applies in relation to this section as it applies in relation to that.

(5) Section 113 of the Housing Act 1985 (meaning of "members of a person's family") applies for the purposes of subsection (3)(b) above.

(6) The reference in subsection (3)(c) above to substantial development of any of the land in which the landlord's interest subsists is a reference to any development other than—

(a) development for which planning permission is granted by a general development order for the time being in force and which is carried out so as to comply with any condition or limitation subject to which planning permission is so granted; or

(b) a change of use resulting in the building referred to in subsection (2) above or any part of it being used as, or as part of, one or more dwelling-houses;

and in this subsection "general development order" [has the meaning given in section 56(6) of the Town and Country Planning Act 1990] and other expressions have the same meaning as in that Act.

ANNOTATION

The words in square brackets were substituted by Planning (Consequential Provisions) Act 1990, ss.4, 7(2), Sched. 2, para. 79(1), with effect from August 24, 1990.

Offences of harassment

A1–035 **29.**—(1) In section 1 of the 1977 Act (unlawful eviction and harassment of occupier), with respect to acts done after the commencement of this Act, subsection (3) shall have effect with the substitution, for the word "calculated", of the word "likely".

(2) After that subsection there shall be inserted the following subsections—

"(3A) Subject to subsection (3B) below, the landlord of a residential occupier or an agent of the landlord shall be guilty of an offence if—

(a) he does acts likely to interefere with the peace and comfort of the residential occupier or members of his household, or

(b) he persistently withdraws or withholds services reasonably required for the occupation of the premises in question as a residence,

and (in either case) he knows, or has reasonable cause to believe, that that conduct is likely to cause the residential occupier to give up the occupation of the whole or part of the premises or to refrain from exercising any right or pursuing any remedy in respect of the whole or part of the premises.

(3B) A person shall not be guilty of an offence under subsection (3A) above if he proves that he had reasonable grounds for doing the acts or withdrawing or withholding the services in question.

(3C) In subsection (3A) above ''landlord'', in relation to a residential occupier of any premises, means the person who, but for—

(a) the residential occupier's right to remain in occupation of the premises, or
(b) a restriction on the person's right to recover possession of the premises,

would be entitled to occupation of the premises and any superior landlord under whom that person derives title.''

Variation of scope of 1977 ss.3 and 4

30.—(1) In section 3 of the 1977 Act (prohibition of eviction without due process of law), in subsection (1) for the words ''not a statutorily protected tenancy'' there shall be substituted ''neither a statutorily protected tenancy nor an excluded tenancy.'' **A1–036**

(2) After subsection (2A) of that section there shall be inserted the following subsections—

''(2B) Subsections (1) and (2) above apply in relation to any premises occupied as a dwelling under a licence, other than an excluded licence, as they apply in relation to premises let as a dwelling under a tenancy, and in those subsections the expressions ''let'' and ''tenancy'' shall be construed accordingly.

(2C) References in the preceding provisions of this section and section 4(2A) below to an excluded tenancy do not apply to—

(a) a tenancy entered into before the date on which the Housing Act 1988 came into force, or
(b) a tenancy entered into on or after that date but pursuant to a contract made before that date,

but, subject to that, ''excluded tenancy'' and ''excluded licence'' shall be construed in accordance with section 3A below.''

(3) In section 4 of the 1977 Act (special provisions for agricultural employees) after subsection (2) there shall be inserted the following subsection—

''(2A) In accordance with section 3(2B) above, any reference in subsections (1) and (2) above to the tenant under the former tenancy includes a reference to the licensee under a licence (other than an excluded licence) which has come to an end (being a licence to occupy premises as a dwelling); and in the following provisions of this section the expressions ''tenancy'' and ''rent'' and any other expressions referable to a tenancy shall be construed accordingly.''

Excluded tenancies and licences

A1–037 **31.** After section 3 of the 1977 Act there shall be inserted the following section—

"Excluded tenancies and licences

3A.—(1) Any reference in this Act to an excluded tenancy or an excluded licence is a reference to a tenancy or licence which is excluded by virtue of any of the following provisions of this section.

(2) A tenancy or licence is excluded if—

(a) under its terms the occupier shares any accommodation with the landlord or licensor; and
(b) immediately before the tenancy or licence was granted and also at the time it comes to an end, the landlord or licensor occupied as his only or principal home premises of which the whole or part of the shared accommodation formed part.

(3) A tenancy or licence is also excluded if—

(a) under its terms the occupier shares any accommodation with a member of the family of the landlord or licensor;
(b) immediately before the tenancy or licence was granted and also at the time it comes to an end, the member of the family of the landlord or licensor occupied as his only or principal home premises of which the whole or part of the shared accommodation formed part; and
(c) immediately before the tenancy or licence was granted and also at the time it comes to an end, the landlord or licensor occupied as his only or principal home premises in the same building as the shared accommodation and that building is not a purpose-built block of flats.

(4) For the purposes of subsections (2) and (3) above, an occupier shares accommodation with another person if he has the use of it in common with that person (whether or not also in common with others) and any reference in those subsections to shared accommodation shall be construed accordingly, and if, in relation to any tenancy or licence, there is at any time more than one person who is the landlord or licensor, any reference in those subsections to the landlord or licensor shall be construed as a reference to any one of those persons.

(5) In subsections (2) to (4) above—

(a) ''accommodation'' includes neither an area used for storage nor a staircase, passage, corridor or other means of access;
(b) ''occupier'' means, in relation to a tenancy, the tenant and, in relation to a licence, the licensee; and
(c) ''purpose-built block of flats'' has the same meaning as in Part III of Schedule 1 to the Housing Act 1988;

and section 113 of the Housing Act 1985 shall apply to determine whether a person is for the purposes of subsection (3) above a member of another's family as it applies for the purposes of Part IV of that Act.

(6) A tenancy or licence is excluded if it was granted as a temporary expedient to a person who entered the premises in question or any other premises as a trespasser (whether or not, before the beginning of that tenancy or licence, another tenancy or licence to occupy the premises or any other premises had been granted to him).

(7) A tenancy or licence is excluded if—

(a) it confers on the tenant or licensee the right to occupy the premises for a holiday only; or
(b) it is granted otherwise than for money or money's worth.

(8) A licence is excluded if it confers rights of occupation in a hostel, within the meaning of the Housing Act 1985, which is provided by—

(a) the council of a county, district or London Borough, the Common Council of the City of London, the Council of the Isles of Scilly, the Inner London Education Authority, a joint authority within the meaning of the Local Government Act 1985 or a residuary body within the meaning of that Act;
(b) a development corporation within the meaning of the New Towns Act 1981;
(c) the Commission for the New Towns;
(d) an urban development corporation established by an order under section 135 of the Local Government, Planning and Land Act 1980;
(e) a housing action trust established under Part III of the Housing Act 1988;
(f) the Development Board for Rural Wales;
(g) the Housing Corporation or Housing for Wales;
(h) a housing trust which is a charity or a registered housing association, within the meaning of the Housing Associations Act 1985; or
(i) any other person who is, or who belongs to a class of person which is, specified in an order made by the Secretary of State.

(9) The power to make an order under subsection (8)(i) above shall be exercisable by statutory instrument which shall be subject to annulment in pursuance of a resolution of either House of Parliament.''

Notice to quit etc.

32.—(1) In section 5 of the 1977 Act (validity of notices to quit) at the beginning of subsection (1) there shall be inserted the words ''Subject to subsection (1B) below''. **A1–038**

(2) After subsection (1) of that section there shall be inserted the following subsections—

"(1A) Subject to subsection (1B) below, no notice by a licensor or a licensee to determine a periodic licence to occupy premises as a dwelling (whether the licence was granted before or after the passing of this Act) shall be valid unless—

(a) it is in writing and contains such information as may be prescribed, and

(b) it is given not less than 4 weeks before the date on which it is to take effect.

(1B) Nothing in subsection (1) or subsection (1A) above applies to—

(a) premises let on an excluded tenancy which is entered into on or after the date on which the Housing Act 1988 came into force unless it is entered into pursuant to a contract made before that date; or

(b) premises occupied under an excluded licence."

Interpretation of Chapter IV and the 1977 Act

A1–039 **33.**—(1) In this Chapter "the 1977 Act" means the Protection from Eviction Act 1977.

(2) In section 8 of the 1977 Act (interpretation) at the end of subsection (1) (statutory protected tenancy) there shall be inserted—

"(e) an assured tenancy or assured agricultural occupancy under Part I of the Housing Act 1988.".

(3) At the end of that section there shall be added the following subsections—

"(4) In this Act "excluded tenancy" and "excluded licence" have the meaning assigned by section 3A of this Act.

(5) If, on or after the date on which the Housing Act 1988 came into force, the terms of an excluded tenancy or excluded licence entered into before that date are varied, then—

(a) if the variation affects the amount of the rent which is payable under the tenancy or licence, the tenancy or licence shall be treated for the purposes of sections 3(2C) and 5(1B) above as a new tenancy or licence entered into at the time of the variation; and

(b) if the variation does not affect the amount of the rent which is so payable, nothing in this Act shall affect the determination of the question whether the variation is such as to give rise to a new tenancy or licence.

(6) Any reference in subsection (5) above to a variation affecting the amount of the rent which is payable under a tenancy or licence does not include a reference to—

(a) a reduction or increase effected under Part III or Part VI of the Rent Act 1977 (rents under regulated tenancies and housing association tenancies), section 78 of that Act (power of rent tribunal in relation to restricted contracts) or sections 11 to 14 of the Rent (Agriculture) Act 1976; or
(b) a variation which is made by the parties and has the effect of making the rent expressed to be payable under the tenancy or licence the same as a rent for the dwelling which is entered in the register under Part IV or section 79 of the Rent Act 1977.''.

CHAPTER V

PHASING OUT OF RENT ACTS AND OTHER TRANSITIONAL PROVISIONS

New protected tenancies and agricultural occupancies restricted to special cases

34.—(1) A tenancy which is entered into on or after the commencement of this Act cannot be a protected tenancy, unless— **A1–040**

(a) it is entered into in pursuance of a contract made before the commencement of this Act; or
(b) it is granted to a person (alone or jointly with others) who, immediately before the tenancy was granted, was a protected or statutory tenant and is so granted by the person who at that time was the landlord (or one of the joint landlords) under the protected or statutory tenancy; or
(c) it is granted to a person (alone or jointly with others) in the following circumstances—

(i) prior to the grant of the tenancy, an order for possession of a dwelling-house was made against him (alone or jointly with others) on the court being satisfied as mentioned in section 98(1)(a) of, or Case 1 in Schedule 16 to, the Rent Act 1977 or Case 1 in Schedule 4 to the Rent (Agriculture) Act 1976 (suitable alternative accommodation available); and
(ii) the tenancy is of the premises which constitute the suitable alternative accommodation as to which the court was so satisfied; and
(iii) in the proceedings for possession the court considered that, in the circumstances, the grant of an assured tenancy would not afford the required security and, accordingly, directed that the tenancy would be a protected tenancy; or

[(d) it is a tenancy under which the interest of the landlord was at the time the tenancy was granted held by a new town corporation, within the meaning of section 80 of the Housing Act 1985, and, before the date which has effect by virtue of paragraph (a) or paragraph (b) of subsection (4) of section 38 below, ceased to be so held by virtue of a disposal by the Commission for the New Towns made pursuant to a direction under section 37 of the New Towns Act 1981].

Annotation

Subsection (1)(d) was substituted by Local Government and Housing Act 1989, s.194(1), Sched. 11, para. 104, on November 16, 1989 (Royal Assent).

(2) In subsection (1)(b) above "protected tenant" and "statutory tenant" do not include—

(a) a tenant under a protected shorthold tenancy;
(b) a protected or statutory tenant of a dwelling-house which was let under a protected shorthold tenancy which ended before the commencement of this Act and in respect of which at that commencement either there has been no grant of a further tenancy or any grant of a further tenancy has been to the person who, immediately before the grant, was in possession of the dwelling-house as a protected or statutory tenant;

and in this subsection "protected shorthold tenancy" includes a tenancy which, in proceedings for possession under Case 19 in Schedule 15 to the Rent Act 1977, is treated as a protected shorthold tenancy.

(3) In any case where—

(a) by virtue of subsection (1) and (2) above, a tenancy entered into on or after the commencement of this Act is an assured tenancy, but
(b) apart from subsection (2) above, the effect of subsection (1)(b) above would be that the tenancy would be a protected tenancy, and
(c) the landlord and the tenant under the tenancy are the same as at the coming to an end of the protected or statutory tenancy which, apart from subsection (2) above, would fall within subsection (1)(b) above,

the tenancy shall be an assured shorthold tenancy (whether or not [, in the case of a tenancy to which the provision applies,] it fulfils the conditions in section 20(1) above) unless, before the tenancy is entered into, the landlord serves notice on the tenant that it is not to be a shorthold tenancy.

Annotation

The words in square brackets were inserted on February 28, 1997 by Housing Act 1996, ss. 104, 232(3), Sched. 8, para. 2(1), (7): S.I. 1997 No. 225.

(4) A licence or tenancy which is entered into on or after the commencement of this Act cannot be a relevant licence or relevant tenancy for the purposes of the Rent (Agriculture) Act 1976 (in this subsection referred to as "the 1976 Act") unless—

(a) it is entered into in pursuance of a contract made before the commencement of this Act; or
(b) it is granted to a person (alone or jointly with others) who, immediately before the licence or tenancy was granted, was a protected occupier or statutory tenant, within the meaning of the 1976 Act, and is so granted by the person who at that time was the landlord or licensor (or one of the joint landlords or licensors) under the protected occupancy or statutory tenancy in question.

(5) Except as provided in subsection (4) above, expressions used in this section have the same meaning as in the Rent Act 1977.

Removal of special regimes for tenancies of housing associations etc.

35.—(1) In this section "housing association tenancy" has the same meaning as in Part VI of the Rent Act 1977. **A1–041**

(2) A tenancy which is entered into on or after the commencement of this Act cannot be a housing association tenancy unless—

(a) it is entered into in pursuance of a contract made before the commencement of this Act; or
(b) it is granted to a person (alone or jointly with others) who, immediately before the tenancy was granted, was a tenant under a housing association tenancy and is so granted by the person who at that time was the landlord under that housing association tenancy; or
(c) it is granted to a person (alone or jointly with others) in the following circumstances—
    (i) prior to the grant of the tenancy, an order for possession of a dwelling-house was made against him (alone or jointly with others) on the court being satisfied as mentioned in paragraph (b) or paragraph (c) of subsection (2) of section 84 of the Housing Act 1985; and
    (ii) the tenancy is of the premises which constitute the suitable accommodation as to which the court was so satisfied; and
    (iii) in the proceedings for possession the court directed that the tenancy would be a housing association tenancy; or

[(d) it is a tenancy under which the interest of the landlord was at the time the tenancy was granted held by a new town corporation, within the meaning of section 80 of the Housing Act 1985, and, before the date which has effect by virtue of paragraph (a) or paragraph (b) of subsection (4) of section 38 below, ceased to be so held by virtue of a disposal by the Commission for the New Towns made pursuant to a direction under section 37 of the New Towns Act 1981].

ANNOTATION

Subsection (2)(d) was substituted on November 16, 1989 by the Local Government and Housing Act 1989, s.194(1), Sched. 11, para. 105 (Royal Assent).

(3) Where, on or after the commencement of this Act, a *registered housing association, within the meaning of the Housing Associations Act 1985* [registered social landlord, within the meaning of the Housing Act 1985 (see section 5(4) and (5) of that Act)] grants a secure tenancy pursuant to an obligation under section 554(2A) of the Housing Act 1985 (as set out in Schedule 17 to this Act) then, in determining whether that tenancy is a housing association tenancy, it shall be assumed for the purposes only of section 86(2)(b) of the Rent Act 1977 (tenancy would be a protected tenancy but for section 15 or 16 of that Act) that the tenancy was granted before the commencement of this Act.

ANNOTATION

The words in square brackets were substituted for the words in italics with effect from October 1, 1996 by Housing Act 1996 (Consequential Provisions) Order 1996 (S.I. 1996 No. 2325), art. 5(1), Sched. 2, para. 18(2).

(4) [Subject to section 38(4A) below] a tenancy or licence which is entered into on or after the commencement of this Act cannot be a secure tenancy unless—

(a) the interest of the landlord belongs to a local authority, a new town corporation or an urban development corporation, all within the meaning of section 80 of the Housing Act 1985, *a housing action trust established under Part III of this Act or the Development Board for Rural Wales* [or a housing action trust established under Part III of this Act]; or
(b) the interest of the landlord belongs to a housing co-operative within the meaning of section 27B of the Housing Act 1985 (agreements between local housing authorities and housing co-operatives) and the tenancy or licence is of a dwelling-house comprised in a housing co-operative agreement falling within that section; or
(c) it is entered into in pursuance of a contract made before the commencement of this Act; or
(d) it is granted to a person (alone or jointly with others) who, immediately before it was entered into, was a secure tenant and is so granted by the body which at that time was the landlord or licensor under the secure tenancy; or
(e) it is granted to a person (alone or jointly with others) in the following circumstances—

(i) prior to the grant of the tenancy or licence, an order for possession of a dwelling-house was made against him (alone or jointly with others) on the court being satisfied as mentioned in paragraph (b) or paragraph (c) of subsection (2) of section 84 of the Housing Act 1985; and
(ii) the tenancy or licence is of the premises which constitute the suitable accommodation as to which the court was so satisfied; and

(iii) in the proceedings for possession the court considered that, in the circumstances, the grant of an assured tenancy would not afford the required security and, accordingly, directed that the tenancy or licence would be a secure tenancy; or

(f) it is granted pursuant to an obligation under section 554(2A) of the Housing Act 1985 (as set out in Schedule 17 to this Act).

ANNOTATION

The words at the start of subsection (4) were added by Local Government and Housing Act 1989, s.194(1), Sched. 11, para. 105(2). The words in square brackets in subsection (4)(a) were substituted for the words in italics on October 1, 1998 by Government of Wales Act 1998, ss.129(2), 158(1), Sched. 15, para. 15: S.I. 1998 No. 2244.

(5) If, on or after the commencement of this Act, the interest of the landlord under a protected or statutory tenancy becomes held by a housing association, a housing trust, *the Housing Corporation or Housing for Wales* [or the Housing Corporation] [or, where that interest becomes held by him as the result of the exercise by him of functions under Part III of the Housing Association Act 1985, the Secretary of State,] nothing in the preceding provisions of this section shall prevent the tenancy from being a housing association tenancy or a secure tenancy and, accordingly, in such a case section 80 of the Housing Act 1985 (and any enactment which refers to that section) shall have effect without regard to the repeal of provisions of that section effected by this Act.

ANNOTATION

The words in the first pair of square brackets were substituted for the words in italics on November 1, 1998 by Government of Wales Act 1998, ss. 140(1), 158(1), Sched. 16, para. 60: S.I. 1998 No. 2244. The words in the second pair of square brackets were inserted on January 15, 1999 by Government of Wales Act 1998 (Housing) (Amendments) Order 1999 (S.I. 1999 No. 61), art. 2, Sched., para. 3(2).

(6) In subsection (5) above "housing association" and "housing trust" have the same meaning as in the Housing Act 1985.

New restricted contracts limited to transitional cases

36.—(1) A tenancy or other contract entered into after the commencement of this Act cannot be a restricted contract for the purposes of the Rent Act 1977 unless it is entered into in pursuance of a contract made before the commencement of this Act. **A1–042**

(2) If the terms of a restricted contract are varied after this Act comes into force then, subject to subsection (3) below,—

(a) if the variation affects the amount of the rent which, under the contract, is payable for the dwelling in question, the contract shall be treated as a new contract entered into at the time of the variation (and subsection (1) above shall have effect accordingly); and

(b) if the variation does not affect the amount of the rent which, under the contract, is so payable, nothing in this section shall affect the determination of the question whether the variation is such as to give rise to a new contract.

(3) Any reference in subsection (2) above to a variation affecting the amount of the rent which, under a contract, is payable for a dwelling does not include a reference to—

(a) a reduction or increase effected under section 78 of the Rent Act 1977 (power of rent tribunal); or
(b) a variation which is made by the parties and has the effect of making the rent expressed to be payable under the contract the same as the rent for the dwelling which is entered in the register under section 79 of the Rent Act 1977.

(4) In subsection (1) of section 81A of the Rent Act 1977 (cancellation of registration of rent relating to a restricted contract) paragraph (a) (no cancellation until two years have elapsed since the date of the entry) shall cease to have effect.

(5) In this section "rent" has the same meaning as in Part V of the Rent Act 1977.

No further assured tenancies under Housing Act 1980

A1–043 **37.**—(1) A tenancy which is entered into on or after the commencement of this Act cannot be an assured tenancy for the purposes of sections 56 to 58 of the Housing Act 1980 (in this section referred to as a "1980 Act tenancy").

(2) In any case where—

(a) before the commencement of this Act, a tenant under a 1980 Act tenancy made an application to the court under section 24 of the Landlord and Tenant Act 1954 (for the grant of a new tenancy), and
(b) at the commencement of this Act the 1980 Act tenancy is continuing by virtue of that section or of any provision of Part IV of the said Act of 1954,

section 1(3) of this Act shall not apply to the 1980 Act tenancy.

(3) If, in a case falling within subsection (2) above, the court makes an order for the grant of a new tenancy under section 29 of the Landlord and Tenant Act 1954, that tenancy shall be an assured tenancy for the purposes of this Act.

(4) In any case where—

(a) before the commencement of this Act a contract was entered into for the grant of a 1980 Act tenancy, but
(b) at the commencement of this Act the tenancy had not been granted,

the contract shall have effect as a contract for the grant of an assured tenancy (within the meaning of this Act).

(5) In relation to an assured tenancy falling within subsection (3) above or granted pursuant to a contract falling within subsection (4) above, Part I of Schedule 1 to this Act shall have effect as if it consisted only of paragraphs 11 and 12; and, if the landlord granting the tenancy is a fully mutual housing association, then, so long as that association remains the landlord under that tenancy (and under any statutory periodic tenancy which arises on the coming to an end of that tenancy), the said paragraph 12 shall have effect in relation to that tenancy with the omission of sub-paragraph (1)(h).

(6) Any reference in this section to a provision of the Landlord and Tenant Act 1954 is a reference only to that provision as applied by section 58 of the Housing Act 1980.

Transfer of existing tenancies from public to private sector

38.—(1) The provisions of subsection (3) below apply in relation to a tenancy which was entered into before, or pursuant to a contract made before, the commencement of this Act if,— **A1–044**

(a) at that commencement or, if it is later, at the time it is entered into, the interest of the landlord is held by a public body (within the meaning of subsection (5) below); and
(b) at some time after that commencement, the interest of the landlord ceases to be so held.

(2) The provisions of subsection (3) below also apply in relation to a tenancy which was entered into before, or pursuant to a contract made before, the commencement of this Act if,—

(a) at the commencement of this Act or, if it is later, at the time it is entered into, it is a housing association tenancy; and
(b) at some time after that commencement, it ceases to be such a tenancy.

(3) [Subject to subsections (4), (4A) and (4B) below] on and after the time referred to in subsection (1)(b) or, as the case may be, subsection (2)(b) above—

(a) the tenancy shall not be capable of being a protected tenancy, a protected occupancy or a housing association tenancy;
(b) the tenancy shall not be capable of being a secure tenancy unless (and only at a time when) the interest of the landlord under the tenancy is (or is again) held by a public body; and
(c) paragraph 1 of Schedule 1 to this Act shall not apply in relation to it, and the question whether at any time thereafter it becomes (or remains) an assured tenancy shall be determined accordingly.

ANNOTATION

The words in square brackets at the start of subsection (3) were originally inserted on November 16, 1989 by Local Government and Housing Act 1989, s.194(1), Sched. 11, para. 106(1) (Royal Assent). The words were further amended on January 15, 1999 by Government of Wales Act 1998 (Housing (Amendments) Order 1999 (S.I. 1999 No. 61), art. 2, Sched., para 3(3)(a).

(4) In relation to a tenancy under which, at the commencement of this Act or, if it is later, at the time the tenancy is entered into, the interest of the landlord is held by a new town corporation, within the meaning of section 80 of the Housing Act 1985 [and which subsequently ceases to be so held by virtue of a disposal by the Commission for the New Towns made pursuant to a direction under section 37 of the New Towns Act 1981], subsections (1) and (3) above shall have effect as if any reference in subsection (1) above to the commencement of this Act were a reference to—

(a) the date on which expires the period of two years beginning on the day this Act is passed; or
(b) if the Secretary of State by order made by statutory instrument within that period so provides, such other date (whether earlier or later) as may be specified by the order for the purposes of this subsection.

ANNOTATION

The words in square brackets were inserted on November 16, 1989 by Local Government and Housing Act 1989, s.194(1), Sched. 11, para. 106(2) (Royal Assent).

[(4A) Where, by virtue of a disposal falling within subsection (4) above and made before the date which has effect by virtue of paragraph (a) or paragraph (b) of that subsection, the interest of the landlord under a tenancy passes to a *registered housing association* [registered social landlord (within the meaning of the Housing Act 1985 (see section 5(4) and (5) of that Act))], then, notwithstanding anything in subsection (3) above, so long as the tenancy continues to be held by a body which would have been specified in subsection (1) of section 80 of the Housing Act 1985 if the repeal of provisions of that section effected by this Act had not been made, the tenancy shall continue to be a secure tenancy and to be capable of being a housing association tenancy.]

ANNOTATION

Subsection (4A) was inserted on November 16, 1989 by Local Government and Housing Act 1989, s.194(1), Sched. 11, para. 106(3), and subsequently amended on October 1, 1996 by Housing Act 1996 (Consequential Provisions) Order 1996 (S.I. 1996 No. 2325), art. 5(1), Sched. 2, para. 18(3) by substituting the words in further square brackets within the subsection for the words in italics.

[(4B) Where, by virtue of a disposal by the Secretary of State made in the exercise by him of functions under Part III of the Housing Associations Act 1985, the interest of the landlord under a secure tenancy passes to a registered social landlord (within the meaning of the Housing Act 1985) then, notwithstanding anything in subsection (3) above, so long as the tenancy continues to be held by a body which would have been specified in subsection (1) of section 80 of the Housing Act 1985 if the repeal of provisions of that section effected by this Act had not been made, the tenancy shall continue to be a secure tenancy and to be capable of being a housing association tenancy.]

ANNOTATION

Subsection (4B) was inserted on Janauary 15, 1999 by Government of Wales Act 1998 (Housing) (Amendments) Order 1999 (S.I. 1999 No. 61), art. 2, Sched., para. 3(3)(b).

(5) For the purposes of this section, the interest of a landlord under a tenancy is held by a public body at a time when—

(a) it belongs to a local authority, a new town corporation or an urban development corporation, all within the meaning of section 80 of the Housing Act 1985; or
(b) it belongs to a housing action trust established under Part III of this Act; or
(c) *it belongs to the Development Board for Rural Wales; or*
(d) it belongs to Her Majesty in right of the Crown or to a government department or is held in trust for Her Majesty for the purposes of a government department.

ANNOTATION

Paragraph (c) was repealed on October 1, 1998, by Government of Wales Act 1998, ss.152, 158(1), Sched. 18, Pt. IV: S.I. 1998 No. 2244.

(6) In this section—

(a) "housing association tenancy" means a tenancy to which Part VI of the Rent Act 1977 applies;
(b) "protected tenancy" has the same meaning as in that Act; and
(c) "protected occupancy" has the same meaning as in the Rent (Agriculture) Act 1976.

Statutory tenants: succession

39.—(1) In section 2(1)(b) of the Rent Act 1977 (which introduces the provisions of Part I of Schedule 1 to that Act relating to statutory tenants by succession) after the words "statutory tenant of a dwelling-house" there shall be inserted "or, as the case may be, is entitled to an assured tenancy of a dwelling-house by succession." **A1–045**

(2) Where the person who is the original tenant, within the meaning of Part I of Schedule 1 to the Rent Act 1977, dies after the commencement of this Act, that Part shall have effect subject to the amendments in Part I of Schedule 4 to this Act.

(3) Where subsection (2) above does not apply but the person who is the first successor, within the meaning of Part I of Schedule 1 to the Rent Act 1977, dies after the commencement of this Act, that Part shall have effect subject to the amendments in paragraphs 5 to 9 of Part I of Schedule 4 to this Act.

(4) In any case where the original occupier, within the meaning of section 4 of the Rent (Agriculture) Act 1976 (statutory tenants and tenancies) dies after the commencement of this Act, that section shall have effect subject to the amendments in Part II of Schedule 4 to this Act.

(5) In any case where, by virtue of any provision of—

(a) Part I of Schedule 1 to the Rent Act 1977, as amended in accordance with subsection (2) or subsection (3) above, or
(b) section 4 of the Rent (Agriculture) Act 1976, as amended in accordance with subsection (4) above,

a person (in the following provisions of this section referred to as "the successor") becomes entitled to an assured tenancy of a dwelling-house by succession, that tenancy shall be a periodic tenancy arising by virtue of this section.

(6) Where, by virtue of subsection (5) above, the successor becomes entitled to an assured periodic tenancy, that tenancy is one—

(a) taking effect in possession immediately after the death of the protected or statutory tenant or protected occupier (in the following provisions of this section referred to as "the predecessor") on whose death the successor became so entitled;
(b) deemed to have been granted to the successor by the person who, immediately before the death of the predecessor, was the landlord of the predecessor under his tenancy;
(c) under which the premises which are let are the same dwelling-house as, immediately before his death, the predecessor occupied under his tenancy;
(d) under which the periods of the tenancy are the same as those for which rent was last payable by the predecessor under his tenancy;
(e) under which, subject to sections 13 to 15 above, the other terms are the same as those on which, under his tenancy, the predecessor occupied the dwelling-house immediately before his death; and
(f) which, for the purposes of section 13(2) above, is treated as a statutory periodic tenancy;

and in paragraphs (b) to (e) above "under his tenancy", in relation to the predecessor, means under his protected tenancy or protected occupancy or in his capacity as a statutory tenant.

(7) If, immediately before the death of the predecessor, the landlord might have recovered possession of the dwelling-house under Case 19 in Schedule 15 to the Rent Act 1977, the assured periodic tenancy to which the successor becomes entitled shall be an assured shorthold tenancy (whether or not [, in the case of a tenancy to which the provision applies,] it fulfils the conditions in section 20(1) above).

ANNOTATION

The words in square brackets were added on February 28, 1997 by Housing Act 1996, ss.104, 232(3), Sched. 8, para. 2(8): S.I. 1997 No. 225.

(8) If, immediately before his death, the predecessor was a protected occupier or statutory tenant within the meaning of the Rent (Agriculture) Act 1976, the assured periodic tenancy to which the successor becomes entitled shall be an assured agricultural occupancy (whether or not it fulfils the conditions in section 24(1) above).

(9) Where, immediately before his death, the predecessor was a tenant under a fixed term tenancy, section 6 above shall apply in relation to the assured periodic tenancy to which the successor becomes entitled on the predecessor's death subject to the following modifications—

(a) for any reference to a statutory periodic tenancy there shall be substituted a reference to the assured periodic tenancy to which the successor becomes so entitled;
(b) in subsection (1) of that section, paragraph (a) shall be omitted and the reference in paragraph (b) to section 5(3)(e) above shall be construed as a reference to subsection (6)(e) above; and
(c) for any reference to the coming to an end of the former tenancy there shall be substituted a reference to the date of the predecessor's death.

(10) If and so long as a dwelling-house is subject to an assured tenancy to which the successor has become entitled by succession, section 7 above and Schedule 2 to this Act shall have effect subject to the modifications in Part III of Schedule 4 to this Act; and in that Part "the predecessor" and "the successor" have the same meaning as in this section.

CHAPTER VI

GENERAL PROVISIONS

Jurisdiction of county courts

40.—(1) A county court shall have jurisdiction to hear and determine any question arising under any provision of— **A1–046**

(a) Chapters I to III and V above, or
(b) sections 27 and 28 above,

other than a question falling within the jurisdiction of a rent assessment committee by virtue of any such provision.

(2) Subsection (1) above has effect notwithstanding that the damages claimed in any proceedings may exceed the amount which, for the time being, is the county court limit for the purposes of the County Courts Act 1984.

(3) Where any proceedings under any provision mentioned in subsection (1) above are being taken in a county court, the court shall have jurisdiction to hear and determine any other proceedings joined with those proceedings, notwith-

standing that, apart from this subsection, those other proceedings would be outside the court's jurisdiction.

(4) If any person takes any proceedings under any provision mentioned in subsection (1) above in the High Court, he shall not be entitled to recover any more costs of those proceedings than those to which he would have been entitled if the proceedings had been taken in a county court: and in such a case the taxing master shall have the same power of directing on what county court scale costs are to be allowed, and of allowing any item of costs, as the judge would have had if the proceedings had been taken in a county court.

(5) Subsection (4) above shall not apply where the purpose of taking the proceedings in the High Court was to enable them to be joined with any proceedings already pending before that court (not being proceedings taken under any provision mentioned in subsection (1) above).

ANNOTATION

Subsection (2) was repealed by High Court and County Courts Jurisdiction Order 1991 (S.I. 1991 No. 724), art. 2(8), Sched., Pt. I. Subsections (4) and (5) were repealed on July 1, 1991 by Courts and Legal Services Act 1990, s.125(7), Sched. 20: S.I. 1991 No. 1364.

Rent assessment committees: procedure and information powers

A1–047 **41.**—*(1) In section 74 of the Rent Act 1977 (regulations made by the Secretary of State) at the end of paragraph (b) of subsection (1) (procedure of rent officers and rent assessment committees) there shall be added the words "whether under this Act or Part I of the Housing Act 1988".*

ANNOTATION

Subsection (1) was repealed by Leasehold Reform, Housing and Urban Development Act 1993, ss. 187(2), 188(2), Sched. 22: S.I. 1993 No. 2134 (September 2, 1993).

(2) The rent assessment committee to whom a matter is referred under Chapter I or Chapter II above may by notice in the prescribed form served on the landlord or the tenant require him to give to the committee, within such period of not less than fourteen days from the service of the notice as may be specified in the notice, such information as they may reasonably require for the purposes of their functions.

(3) If any person fails without reasonable excuse to comply with a notice served on him under subsection (2) above, he shall be liable on summary conviction to a fine not exceeding level 3 on the standard scale.

(4) Where an offence under subsection (3) above committed by a body corporate is proved to have been committed with the consent or connivance of, or to be attributable to any neglect on the part of, any director, manager or secretary or other similar officer of the body corporate or any person who was purporting to act in any such capacity, he as well as the body corporate shall be guilty of that offence and shall be liable to be proceeded against and punished accordingly.

[Amounts attributable to services

41A. In order to assist authorities to give effect to the housing benefit scheme under Part VII of the Social Security Contributions and Benefits Act 1992, where a rent is determined under section 14 or 22 above, the rent assessment committee shall note in their determination the amount (if any) of the rent which, in the opinion of the committee, is fairly attributable to the provision of services, except where that amount is in their opinion negligible; and the amount so noted may be included in the information specified in an order under section 42 below.] **A1–048**

ANNOTATION

Section 41A was inserted on July 1, 1992 by Social Security (Consequential Provisions) Act 1992, ss. 4, 7(2), Sched. 2, para. 103.

[Provision of information as to exemption from council tax

41B. A billing authority within the meaning of Part I of the Local Government Finance Act 1992 shall, if so requested in writing by a rent officer or a rent assessment committee in connection with his or their functions under any enactment, inform the rent officer or rent assessment committee in writing whether or not a particular dwelling (within the meaning of Part I of the Local Government Finance Act 1992) is, or was at any time specified in the request, an exempt dwelling for the purposes of that Part of that Act.] **A1–049**

ANNOTATION

Section 41B was inserted on April 1, 1993 by Local Government Finance (Housing) (Consequential Amendments) Order 1993 (S.I. 1993 No. 651), art. 2(1), Sched. 1, para. 18, as amended by S.I. 1993 No. 1120.

Information as to determinations of rents

42.—(1) The President of every rent assessment panel shall keep and make publicly available, in such manner as is specified in an order made by the Secretary of State, such information as may be so specified with respect to rents under assured tenancies and assured agricultural occupancies which have been the subject of references or applications to, or determinations by, rent assessment committees. **A1–050**

(2) A copy of any information certified under the hand of an officer duly authorised by the President of the rent assessment panel concerned shall be receivable in evidence in any court and in any proceedings.

(3) An order under subsection (1) above—

(a) may prescribe the fees to be charged for the supply of a copy, including a certified copy, of any of the information kept by virtue of that subsection; and

(b) may make different provision with respect to different cases or descriptions of case, including different provision for different areas.

(4) The power to make an order under subsection (1) above shall be exercisable by statutory instrument which shall be subject to annulment in pursuance of a resolution of either House of Parliament.

Powers of local authorities for purposes of giving information

A1–051 **43.** In section 149 of the Rent Act 1977 (which, among other matters, authorises local authorities to publish information for the benefit of landlords and tenants with respect to their rights and duties under certain enactments), in subsection (1)(a) after sub-paragraph (iv) there shall be inserted—

''(v) Chapters I to III of Part I of the Housing Act 1988.''.

Application to Crown Property

A1–052 **44.**—(1) Subject to paragraph 11 of Schedule 1 to this Act and subsection (2) below, Chapters I to IV above apply in relation to premises in which there subsists, or at any material time subsisted, a Crown interest as they apply in relation to premises in relation to which no such interest subsists or ever subsisted.

(2) In Chapter IV above—

(a) sections 27 and 28 do not bind the Crown; and
(b) the remainder binds the Crown to the extent provided for in section 10 of the Protection from Eviction Act 1977.

(3) In this section ''Crown interest'' means an interest which belongs to Her Majesty in right of the Crown or of the Duchy of Lancaster or to the Duchy of Cornwall, or to a government department, or which is held in trust for Her Majesty for the purposes of a government department.

(4) Where an interest belongs to Her Majesty in right of the Duchy of Lancaster, then, for the purposes of Chapters I to IV above, the Chancellor of the Duchy of Lancaster shall be deemed to be the owner of the interest.

Interpretation of Part I

A1–053 **45.**—(1) In this Part of this Act, except where the context otherwise requires,—

''dwelling-house'' may be a house or part of a house;
''fixed term tenancy'' means any tenancy other than a periodic tenancy;
''fully mutual housing association'' has the same meaning as in Part I of the Housing Associations Act 1985;

"landlord" includes any person from time to time deriving title under the original landlord and also includes, in relation to a dwelling-house, any person other than a tenant who is, or but for the existence of an assured tenancy would be, entitled to possession of the dwelling-house;

"let" includes "sub-let";

"prescribed" means prescribed by regulations made by the Secretary of State by statutory instrument;

"rates" includes water rates and charges but does not include an owner's drainage rate, as defined in section 63(2)(a) of the Land Drainage Act 1976;

"secure tenancy" has the meaning assigned by section 79 of the Housing Act 1985;

"statutory periodic tenancy" has the meaning assigned by section 5(7) above;

"tenancy" includes a sub-tenancy and an agreement for a tenancy or sub-tenancy; and

"tenant" includes a sub-tenant and any person deriving title under the original tenant or sub-tenant.

(2) Subject to paragraph 11 of Schedule 2 to this Act, any reference in this Part of this Act to the beginning of a tenancy is a reference to the day on which the tenancy is entered into or, if it is later, the day on which, under the terms of any lease, agreement or other document, the tenant is entitled to possession under the tenancy.

(3) Where two or more persons jointly constitute either the landlord or the tenant in relation to a tenancy, then, except where this Part of this Act otherwise provides, any reference to the landlord or to the tenant is a reference to all the persons who jointly constitute the landlord or the tenant, as the case may require.

(4) For the avoidance of doubt, it is hereby declared that any reference in this Part of this Act (however expressed) to a power for a landlord to determine a tenancy does not include a reference to a power of re-entry or forfeiture for breach of any term or condition of the tenancy.

(5) Regulations under subsection (1) above may make different provision with respect to different cases or descriptions of case, including different provisions for different areas.

[. . . . .]

PART V

MISCELLANEOUS AND GENERAL

Leases

[. . . . .]

Certain tenancies excluded from bankrupt's estate

117.—(1) In section 283 of the Insolvency Act 1986 (definition of bankrupt's **A1–054**

estate) at the end of subsection (3) (property excluded from the estate) there shall be inserted the following subsection—

"(3A) Subject to section 308A in Chapter IV, subsection (1) does not apply to—

(a) a tenancy which is an assured tenancy or an assured agricultural occupancy, within the meaning of Part I of the Housing Act 1988, and the terms of which inhibit an assignment as mentioned in section 127(5) of the Rent Act 1977, or
(b) a protected tenancy, within the meaning of the Rent Act 1977, in respect of which, by virtue of any provision of Part IX of that Act, no premium can lawfully be required as a condition of assignment, or
(c) a tenancy of a dwelling-house by virtue of which the bankrupt is, within the meaning of the Rent (Agriculture) Act 1976, a protected occupier of the dwelling-house, and the terms of which inhibit an assignment as mentioned in section 127(5) of the Rent Act 1977, or
(d) a secure tenancy, within the meaning of Part IV of the Housing Act 1985, which is not capable of being assigned, except in the cases mentioned in section 91(3) of that Act.".

(2) After section 308 of that Act there shall be inserted the following section—

"**Vesting in trustee of certain tenancies**
308A. Upon the service on the bankrupt by the trustee of a notice in writing under this section, any tenancy—

(a) which is excluded by virtue of section 283(3A) from the bankrupt's estate, and
(b) to which the notice relates,

vests in the trustee as part of the bankrupt's estate; and, except against a purchaser in good faith, for value and without notice of the bankruptcy, the trustee's title to that tenancy has relation back to the commencement of the bankruptcy."

(3) in section 309 of that Act (time-limit for certain notices) in subsection (1)(b)—

(a) after the words "section 308" there shall be inserted "or section 308A"; and
(b) after the words "the property" there shall be inserted "or tenancy".

(4) In section 315 of that Act (disclaimer (general power)), in subsection (4)

after the words "reasonable replacement value)" there shall be inserted "or 308A".

[........]

Amendment of Landlord and Tenant Act 1987

119. The Landlord and Tenant Act 1987 shall have effect subject to the amendments in Schedule 13 to this Act. **A1–055**

[........]

Supplementary

Application to Isles of Scilly

139.—(1) This Act applies to the Isles of Scilly subject to such exceptions, adaptations and modifications as the Secretary of State may by order direct. **A1–056**

(2) The power to make an order under this section shall be exercisable by statutory instrument which shall be subject to annulment in pursuance of a resolution of either House of Parliament.

Amendments and repeals

140.—(1) Schedule 17 to this Act, which contains minor amendments and amendments consequential on the provisions of this Act and the Housing (Scotland) Act 1988, shall have effect *and in that Schedule Part I contains general amendments and Part II contains amendments consequential on the establishment of Housing for Wales*. **A1–057**

(2) The enactments specified in Schedule 18 to this Act, which include some that are spent, are hereby repealed to the extent specified in the third column of that Schedule, but subject to any provision at the end of that Schedule and to any saving in Chapter V of Part I of or Schedule 17 to this Act.

Annotation

The words in subsection (1) in italics were repealed on November 1, 1998 by Government of Wales Act 1998, ss.152, 158(1), Sched. 18, Pt. VI: S.I. 1998 No. 2244.

Short title, commencement and extent

141.—(1) This Act may be cited as the Housing Act 1988. **A1–058**

(2) The provisions of Parts II and IV of this Act and sections 119, 122, 124, 128, 129, 135 and 140 above shall come into force on such day as the Secretary

of State may by order made by statutory instrument appoint, and different days may be so appointed for different provisions or for different purposes.

(3) Part I and this Part of this Act, other than sections 119, 122, 124, 128, 129, 132, 133, 134, 135 and 138 onwards, shall come into force at the expiry of the period of two months beginning on the day it is passed; and any reference in those provisions to the commencement of this Act shall be construed accordingly.

(4) An order under subsection (2) above may make such transitional provisions as appear to the Secretary of State necessary or expedient in connection with the provisions brought into force by the order.

(5) Part I, III and IV of this Act and this Part, except sections 118, 128, 132, 134, 135 and 137 onwards, extend to England and Wales only.

(6) This Act does not extend to Northern Ireland.

SCHEDULES

A1–059

SCHEDULE I

TENANCIES WHICH CANNOT BE ASSURED TENANCIES

PART 1

THE TENANCIES

Tenancies entered into before commencement

1. A tenancy which is entered into before, or pursuant to a contract made before, the commencement of this Act.

Tenancies of dwelling-houses with high rateable values

2. A tenancy under which the dwelling-house has for the time being a rateable value which,—

(a) if it is in Greater London, exceeds £1,500; and
(b) if it is elsewhere, exceeds £750.

[**2.**—(1) A tenancy—

(a) which is entered into on or after 1st April 1990 (otherwise than, where the dwelling-house had a rateable value on 31st March 1990, in pursuance of a contract made before 1st April 1990), and
(b) under which the rent payable for the time being is payable at a rate exceeding £25,000 a year.

(2) In sub-paragraph (1) ''rent'' does not include any sum payable by the tenant as is expressed (in whatever terms) to be payable in respect of rates, [council tax,] services, management, repairs, maintenance or insurance, unless it could not have been regarded by the parties to the tenancy as a sum so payable.

2A. A tenancy—

(a) which was entered into before 1st April 1990 or on or after that date in pursuance of a contract made before that date, and

(b) under which the dwelling-house had a rateable value on the 31st March 1990 which, if it is in Greater London, exceeded £1,500 and, if it is elsewhere, exceeded £750.]

ANNOTATION

Paragraphs 2 and 2A were substituted for the words in italics by References to Rating (Housing) Regulations 1990 (S.I. 1990 No. 434), Sched., para. 29, with effect from April 1, 1990. Within paragraph 2(2), as so substituted, the words in further square brackets were inserted by The Local Government Finance (Housing) (Consequential Amendments) Order 1993 (S.I. 1993 No. 651), art. 2(1), Sched. 1, para. 19 with effect from April 1, 1993.

Tenancies at a low rent

3.—(1) A tenancy under which either no rent is payable or the rent payable is less than two-thirds of the rateable value of the dwelling-house for the time being.

(2) In determining whether the rent under a tenancy falls within sub-paragraph (1) above, there shall be disregarded such part (if any) of the sums payable by the tenant as is expressed (in whatever terms) to be payable in respect of rates, services, management, repairs, maintenance or insurance, unless it could not have been regarded by the parties to the tenancy as a part so payable.

[**3.** A tenancy under which for the time being no rent is payable.

3A. A tenancy—

(a) which is entered into on or after 1st April 1990 (otherwise than, where the dwelling-house had a rateable value on 31st March 1990, in pursuance of a contract made before 1st April 1990), and
(b) under which the rent payable for the time being is payable at a rate of, if the dwelling-house is in Greater London, £1,000 or less a year and, if it is elsewhere, £250 or less a year.

3B. A tenancy—

(a) which was entered into before 1st April 1990 or where the dwelling-house had a rateable value on 31st March 1990, on or after 1st April 1990 in pursuance of a contract made before that date, and
(b) under which the rent for the time being payable is less than two-thirds of the rateable value of the dwelling-house on 31st March 1990.

3C. Paragraph 2(2) above applies for the purposes of paragraphs 3, 3A and 3B as it applies for the purposes of paragraph 2(1).]

ANNOTATION

The paragraphs in square brackets were substituted for the paragraphs in italics on April 1, 1990 by References to Rating (Housing) Regulations 1990 (S.I. 1990 No. 434), Sched., para. 29.

Business tenancies

4. A tenancy to which Part II of the Landlord and Tenant Act 1954 applies (business tenancies).

Licensed premises

5. A tenancy under which the dwelling-house consists of or comprises premises licensed for the sale of intoxicating liquors for consumption on the premises.

Tenancies of agricultural land

6.—(1) A tenancy under which agricultural land, exceeding two acres, is let together with the dwelling-house.

(2) In this paragraph ''agricultural land'' has the meaning set out in section 26(3)(a) of the General Rate Act 1967 (exclusion of agricultural land and premises from liability for rating).

Tenancies of agricultural holdings

7. A tenancy under which the dwelling-house—

(a) is comprised in an agricultural holding (within the meaning of the Agricultural Holdings Act 1986); and

(b) is occupied by the person responsible for the control (whether as tenant or as servant or agent of the tenant) of the farming of the holding.

[Tenancies of agricultural holdings etc.

7.—(1) A tenancy under which the dwelling-house—

(a) is comprised in an agricultural holding, and

(b) is occupied by the person responsible for the control (whether as tenant or as servant or agent of the tenant) of the farming of the holding.

(2) A tenancy under which the dwelling-house—

(a) is comprised in the holding held under a farm business tenancy, and

(b) is occupied by the person responsible for the control (whether as tenant or as servant or agent of the tenant) of the management of the holding.

(3) In this paragraph—

''agricultural holding'' means any agricultural holding within the meaning of the Agricultural Holdings Act 1986 held under a tenancy in relation to which that Act applies, and

''farm business tenancy'' and ''holding'', in relation to such a tenancy, have the same meaning as in the Agricultural Tenancies Act 1995.]

Annotation

Paragraph 7 was substituted for the previous paragraph 7 (in italics) with effect from September 1, 1995 by Agricultural Tenancies Act 1995, ss.40, 41(2), Sched., para. 34.

Lettings to students

8.—(1) A tenancy which is granted to a person who is pursuing, or intends to pursue, a course of study provided by a specified educational institution and is so granted either by that institution or by another specified institution or body of persons.

(2) In sub-paragraph (1) above ''specified'' means specified, or of a class specified, for the purposes of this paragraph by regulations made by the Secretary of State by statutory instrument.

(3) A statutory instrument made in the exercise of the power conferred by subparagraph (2) above shall be subject to annulment in pursuance of a resolution of either House of Parliament.

Holiday lettings

9. A tenancy the purpose of which is to confer on the tenant the right to occupy the dwelling-house for a holiday.

Resident landlords

10.—(1) A tenancy in respect of which the following conditions are fulfilled—

(a) that the dwelling-house forms part only of a building and, except in a case where the dwelling-house also forms part of a flat, the building is not a purpose-built block of flats; and
(b) that, subject to Part III of this Schedule, the tenancy was granted by an individual who, at the time when the tenancy was granted, occupied as his only or principal home another dwelling-house which,—

 (i) in the case mentioned in paragraph (a) above, also forms part of the flat; or
 (ii) in any other case, also forms part of the building; and

(c) that, subject to Part III of this Schedule, at all times since the tenancy was granted the interest of the landlord under the tenancy has belonged to an individual who, at the time he owned that interest, occupied as his only or principal home another dwelling-house which,—

 (i) in the case mentioned in paragraph (a) above, also formed part of the flat; or
 (ii) in any other case, also formed part of the building; and

(d) that the tenancy is not one which is excluded from this sub-paragraph by sub-paragraph (3) below.

(2) If a tenancy was granted by two or more persons jointly, the reference in subparagraph (1)(b) above to an individual is a reference to any one of those persons and if the interest of the landlord is for the time being held by two or more persons jointly, the reference in sub-paragraph (1)(c) above to an individual is a reference to any one of those persons.
(3) A tenancy (in this sub-paragraph referred to as ''the new tenancy'') is excluded from sub-paragraph (1) above if—

(a) it is granted to a person (alone, or jointly with others) who, immediately before it was granted, was a tenant under an assured tenancy (in this subparagraph referred to as ''the former tenancy'') of the same dwelling-house or of another dwelling-house which forms part of the building in question; and
(b) the landlord under the new tenancy and under the former tenancy is the same person or, if either of those tenancies is or was granted by two or more persons jointly, the same person is the landlord or one of the landlords under each tenancy.

Crown tenancies

11.—(1) A tenancy under which the interest of the landlord belongs to Her Majesty in right of the Crown or to a government department or is held in trust for Her Majesty for the purposes of a government department.
(2) The reference in sub-paragraph (1) above to the case where the interest of the landlord belongs to Her Majesty in right of the Crown does not include the case where that interest is under the management of the Crown Estate Commissioners [or it is held by the Secretary of State as the result of the exercise by him of functions under Part III of the Housing Associations Act 1985].

ANNOTATION

The words in square brackets were added on January 15, 1999 by Government of Wales Act 1998 (Housing) (Amendments) Order 1999 (S.I. 1999 No. 61), art. 2, Sched., para. 3(4).

Local authority tenancies etc.

12.—(1) A tenancy under which the interest of the landlord belongs to—

(a) a local authority, as defined in sub-paragraph (2) below;

(b) the Commission for the New Towns;
(c) the Development Board for Rural Wales;
(d) an urban development corporation established by an order under section 135 of the Local Government, Planning and Land Act 1980;
(e) a development corporation, within the meaning of the New Towns Act 1981;
(f) an authority established under section 10 of the Local Government Act 1985 (waste disposal authorities);
(g) a residuary body, within the meaning of the Local Government Act 1985;
[(gg) the Residuary Body for Wales (Corff Gweddilliol Cymru);]
(h) a fully mutual housing association; or
(i) a housing action trust established under Part III of this Act.

ANNOTATION

The words in italics were repealed on October 1, 1998 by Government of Wales Act 1998, ss.152, 158(1), Sched. 18, Pt. IV: S.I. 1998 No. 2244. The words in square brackets were added on July 5, 1994 by Local Government (Wales) Act 1994, ss.39(2), 66(2)(b), Sched. 13, para. 31.

(2) The following are local authorities for the purposes of sub-paragraph (1)(a) above—

(a) the council of a county, [county borough,] district or London borough;
(b) the Common Council of the City of London;
(c) the Council of the Isles of Scilly;
(d) the Broads Authority;
[(da) a National Park authority;]
(e) the Inner London Education Authority; and
(f) a joint authority, within the meaning of the Local Government Act 1985; [and
(g) a police authority established under [section 3 of the Police Act 1996] [, the Service Authority for the National Criminal Intelligence Service and the Service Authority for the National Crime Squad].]

ANNOTATION

The words in square brackets in paragraph 12(2)(a) were inserted on April 1, 1996 by Local Government (Wales) Act 1994, ss.22(2), 66(3), Sched. 8, para. 9(2): S.I. 1996 No. 396. Paragraph 12(2)(da) was inserted on November 23, 1995 by Environment Act 1995, ss.78, 125(3), Sched. 10, para. 28: S.I. 1995 No. 2950. Paragraph 12(2)(g) and the word 'and' preceding it were inserted by Police and Magistrates' Courts Act 1994, ss.43, 94(1), Sched. 4, para. 62: S.I. 1994 No. 3262 (April 1, 1995). The words in the first square brackets in that sub-paragraph were substituted on August 22, 1996 by Police Act 1996, s.103(1), 104(1), Sched. 7, Pt. I, para. 1(1), (2), (2C); and the words in the second square brackets were added on October 31, 1997 by Police Act 1997, ss.134(1), 135(1), Sched. 9, para. 57: S.I. 1997 No. 2390.

Transitional cases

13.—(1) A protected tenancy, within the meaning of the Rent Act 1977.
(2) A housing association tenancy, within the meaning of Part VI of that Act.
(3) A secure tenancy.
(4) Where a person is a protected occupier of a dwelling-house, within the meaning of the Rent (Agriculture) Act 1976, the relevant tenancy, within the meaning of that Act, by virtue of which he occupies the dwelling-house.

PART II

A1–060 RATEABLE VALUES

14.—(1) The rateable value of a dwelling-house at any time shall be ascertained for the purposes of Part I of this Schedule as follows—

(a) if the dwelling-house is a hereditament for which a rateable value is then shown in the valuation list, it shall be that rateable value;

(b) if the dwelling-house forms part only of such a hereditament or consists of or forms part of more than one such hereditament, its rateable value shall be taken to be such value as is found by a proper apportionment or aggregation of the rateable values or values so shown.

(2) Any question arising under this Part of this Schedule as to the proper apportionment or aggregation of any value or values shall be determined by the county court and the decision of that court shall be final.

15. Where, after the time at which the rateable value of a dwelling-house is material for the purposes of any provision of Part I of this Schedule, the valuation list is altered so as to vary the rateable value of the hereditament of which the dwelling-house consists (in whole or in part) or forms part and the alteration has effect from that time or from an earlier time, the rateable value of the dwelling-house at the material time shall be ascertained as if the value shown in the valuation list at the material time had been the value shown in the list as altered.

16. Paragraphs 14 and 15 above apply in relation to any other land which, under section 2 of this Act, is treated as part of a dwelling-house as they apply in relation to the dwelling-house itself.

PART III

PROVISIONS FOR DETERMINING APPLICATION OF PARAGRAPH 10 (RESIDENT LANDLORDS) A1–061

17.—(1) In determining whether the condition in paragraph 10(1)(c) above is at any time fulfilled with respect to a tenancy, there shall be disregarded—

(a) any period of not more than twenty-eight days, beginning with the date on which the interest of the landlord under the tenancy becomes vested at law and in equity in an individual who, during that period, does not occupy as his only or principal home another dwelling-house which forms part of the building or, as the case may be, flat concerned;

(b) if, within a period falling within paragraph (a) above, the individual concerned notifies the tenant in writing of his intention to occupy as his only or principal home another dwelling-house in the building or, as the case may be, flat concerned, the period beginning with the date on which the interest of the landlord under the tenancy becomes vested in that individual as mentioned in that paragraph and ending—

(i) at the expiry of the period of six months beginning on that date, or

(ii) on the date on which that interest ceases to be so vested, or

(iii) on the date on which that interest becomes again vested in such an individual as is mentioned in paragraph 10(1)(c) or the condition in that paragraph becomes deemed to be fulfilled by virtue of paragraph 18(1) or paragraph 20 below,

whichever is the earlier; and

(c) any period of not more than two years beginning with the date on which the interest of the landlord under the tenancy becomes, and during which it remains, vested—

(i) in trustees as such; or

(ii) by virtue of section 9 of the Administration of Estates Act 1925, in [the Probate Judge or the Public Trustee.]

ANNOTATION

The words in square brackets were substituted on July 1, 1995 by Law of Property (Miscellaneous Provisions) Act 1994, ss.21(1), 23(1), Sched. 1, para. 11; S.I. 1995 No. 1317.

(2) Where the interest of the landlord under a tenancy becomes vested at law and in equity in two or more persons jointly, of whom at least one was an individual, sub-paragraph (1) above shall have effect subject to the following modifications—

(a) in paragraph (a) for the words from "an individual" to "occupy" there shall be substituted "the joint landlords if, during that period none of them occupies"; and

(b) in paragraph (b) for the words "the individual concerned" there shall be substituted "any of the joint landlords who is an individual" and for the words "that individual" there shall be substituted "the joint landlords".

18.—(1) During any period when—

(a) the interest of the landlord under the tenancy referred to in paragraph 10 above is vested in trustees as such, and
(b) that interest is *or, if it is held on trust for sale, the proceeds of its sale are* held on trust for any person who or for two or more persons of whom at least one occupies as his only or principal home a dwelling-house which forms part of the building or, as the case may be, flat referred to in paragraph 10(1)(a),

the condition in paragraph 10(1)(c) shall be deemed to be fulfilled and accordingly, no part of that period shall be disregarded by virtue of paragraph 17 above.

(2) If a period during which the condition in paragraph 10(1)(c) is deemed to be fulfilled by virtue of sub-paragraph (1) above comes to an end on the death of a person who was in occupation of a dwelling-house as mentioned in paragraph (b) of that sub-paragraph, then, in determining whether that condition is at any time thereafter fulfilled, there shall be disregarded any period—

(a) which begins on the date of the death;
(b) during which the interest of the landlord remains vested as mentioned in sub-paragraph (1)(a) above; and
(c) which ends at the expiry of the period of two years beginning on the date of the death or on any earlier date on which the condition in paragraph 10(1)(c) becomes again deemed to be fulfilled by virtue of sub-paragraph (1) above.

ANNOTATION

The words in italics in paragraph 18(1) were repealed on January 1, 1997 by Trusts of Land and Appointment of Trustees Act 1996, ss.25(2), 27(2), Sched. 4: S.I. 1996 No. 2974.

19. In any case where—

(a) immediately before a tenancy comes to an end the condition in paragraph 10(1)(c) is deemed to be fulfilled by virtue of paragraph 18(1) above, and
(b) on the coming to an end of that tenancy the trustees in whom the interest of the landlord is vested grant a new tenancy of the same or substantially the same dwelling-house to a person (alone or jointly with others) who was the tenant or one of the tenants under the previous tenancy,

the condition in paragraph 10(1)(b) above shall be deemed to be fulfilled with respect to the new tenancy.

20.—(1) The tenancy referred to in paragraph 10 above falls within this paragraph if the interest of the landlord under the tenancy becomes vested in the personal representatives of a deceased person acting in that capacity.

(2) If the tenancy falls within this paragraph, the condition in paragraph 10(1)(c) shall be deemed to be fulfilled for any period, beginning with the date on which the interest becomes vested in the personal representatives and not exceeding two years, during which the interest of the landlord remains so vested.

21. Throughout any period which, by virtue of paragraph 17 or paragraph 18(2) above, falls to be disregarded for the purpose of determining whether the condition in paragraph 10(1)(c) is fulfilled with respect to a tenancy, no order shall be made for possession of the dwelling-house subject to that tenancy, other than an order which might be made if that tenancy were or, as the case may be, had been an assured tenancy.

22. For the purposes of paragraph 10 above, a building is a purpose-built block of flats if as constructed it contained, and it contains, two or more flats; and for this purpose "flat" means a dwelling-house which—

(a) forms part only of a building; and
(b) is separated horizontally from another dwelling-house which forms part of the same building.

Section 7 SCHEDULE 2 **A1–062**

GROUNDS FOR POSSESSION OF DWELLING-HOUSES LET ON ASSURED TENANCIES

PART I

GROUNDS ON WHICH COURT MUST ORDER POSSESSION

Ground 1

Not later than the beginning of the tenancy the landlord gave notice in writing to the tenant that possession might be recovered on this ground or the court is of the opinion that it is just and equitable to dispense with the requirement of notice and (in either case)—

(a) at some time before the beginning of the tenancy, the landlord who is seeking possession or, in the case of joint landlords seeking possession, at least one of them occupied the dwelling-house as his only or principal home; or
(b) the landlord who is seeking possession or, in the case of joint landlords seeking possession, at least one of them requires the dwelling-house as his or his spouse's only or principal home and neither the landlord (or, in the case of joint landlords, any one of them) nor any other person who, as landlord, derived title under the landlord who gave the notice mentioned above acquired the reversion on the tenancy for money or money's worth.

Ground 2

The dwelling-house is subject to a mortgage granted before the beginning of the tenancy and—

(a) the mortgagee is entitled to exercise a power of sale conferred on him by the mortgage or by section 101 of the Law of Property Act 1925; and
(b) the mortgagee requires possession of the dwelling-house for the purpose of disposing of it with vacant possession in exercise of that power; and
(c) either notice was given as mentioned in Ground 1 above or the court is satisfied that it is just and equitable to dispense with the requirement of notice;

and for the purpose of this ground "mortgage" includes a charge and "mortgagee" shall be construed accordingly.

Ground 3

The tenancy is a fixed term tenancy for a term not exceeding eight months and—

(a) not later than the beginning of the tenancy the landlord gave notice in writing to the tenant that possession might be recovered on this ground; and
(b) at some time within the period of twelve months ending with the beginning of the tenancy, the dwelling-house was occupied under a right to occupy it for a holiday.

Ground 4

The tenancy is a fixed term tenancy for a term not exceeding twelve months and—

(a) not later than the beginning of the tenancy the landlord gave notice in writing to the tenant that possession might be recovered on this ground; and

(b) at some time within the period of twelve months ending with the beginning of the tenancy, the dwelling-house was let on a tenancy falling within paragraph 8 of Schedule 1 to this Act.

Ground 5

The dwelling-house is held for the purpose of being available for occupation by a minister of religion as a residence from which to perform the duties of his office and—

(a) not later than the beginning of the tenancy the landlord gave notice in writing to the tenant that possession might be recovered on this ground; and
(b) the court is satisfied that the dwelling-house is required for occupation by a minister of religion as such a residence.

Ground 6

The landlord who is seeking possession or, if that landlord is a *registered housing association* [registered social landlord] or charitable housing trust, a superior landlord intends to demolish or reconstruct the whole or a substantial part of the dwelling-house or to carry out substantial works on the dwelling-house or any part thereof or any building of which it forms part and the following conditions are fulfilled—

(a) the intended work cannot reasonably be carried out without the tenant giving up possession of the dwelling-house because—

(i) the tenant is not willing to agree to such a variation of the terms of the tenancy as would give such access and other facilities as would permit the intended work to be carried out, or
(ii) the nature of the intended work is such that no such variation is practicable, or
(iii) the tenant is not willing to accept an assured tenancy of such part only of the dwelling-house (in this sub-paragraph referred to as ''the reduced part'') as would leave in the possession of his landlord so much of the dwelling-house as would be reasonable to enable the intended work to be carried out and, where appropriate, as would give such access and other facilities over the reduced part as would permit the intended work to be carried out, or
(iv) the nature of the intended work is such that such a tenancy is not practicable; and

(b) either the landlord seeking possession acquired his interest in the dwelling-house before the grant of the tenancy or that interest was in existence at the time of that grant and neither that landlord (or, in the case of joint landlords, any of them) nor any other person who, alone or jointly with others, has acquired that interest since that time acquired it for money or money's worth; and
(c) the assured tenancy on which the dwelling-house is let did not come into being by virtue of any provision of Schedule 1 to the Rent Act 1977, as amended by Part I of Schedule 4 to this Act or, as the case may be, section 4 of the Rent (Agriculture) Act 1976, as amended by Part II of that Schedule.

For the purposes of this ground, if, immediately before the grant of the tenancy, the tenant to whom it was granted or, if it was granted to joint tenants, any of them was the tenant or one of the joint tenants [of the dwelling-house concerned] under an earlier assured tenancy *of the dwelling house concerned* [or, as the case may be, under a tenancy to which Schedule 10 to the Local Government and Housing Act 1989 applied], any reference in paragraph (b) above to the grant of the tenancy is a reference to the grant of that earlier assured tenancy [or, as the case may be, to the grant of the tenancy to which the said Schedule 10 applied.]

For the purposes of this ground *''registered housing association'' has the same meaning as in the Housing Associations Act 1985* [''registered social landlord'' has the same meaning as in the Housing Act 1985 (see section 5(4) and (5) of that Act)] and ''charitable housing trust'' means a housing trust, within the meaning of *the Charities Act 1960 that Act* [the Housing Associations Act 1985], which is a charity, within the meaning of the *Charities Act 1960* [the Charities Act 1993].

[For the purposes of this ground, every acquisition under Part IV of this Act shall be taken to be an acquisition for money or money's worth; and in any case where—

(i) *the tenancy (in this paragraph referred to as "the current tenancy") was granted to a person (alone or jointly with others) who, immediately before it was granted, was a tenant under a tenancy of a different dwelling-house (in this paragraph referred to as "the earlier tenancy"), and*

(ii) *the landlord under the current tenancy is the person who, immediately before that tenancy was granted, was the landlord under the earlier tenancy, and*

(iii) *the condition in paragraph (b) above could not have been fulfilled with respect to the earlier tenancy by virtue of an acquisition under Part IV of this Act (including one taken to be such an acquisition by virtue of the previous operation of this paragraph),*

the acquisition of the landlord's interest under the current tenancy shall be taken to have been under that Part and the landlord shall be taken to have acquired that interest after the grant of the current tenancy.]

ANNOTATION

(1) The words in the first, fifth, and sixth sets of square brackets were substituted for the words in italics on October 1, 1996 by Housing Act 1996 (Consequential Provisions) Order 1996 (S.I. 1996 No. 2325), art. 5(1), Sched. 2, para. 18(13).
(2) The words at end of this ground in italics were added on January 16, 1990 by Local Government and Housing Act 1989, ss.194(1), 195(2): S.I. 1989 No. 2445; and then repealed with effect from October 1, 1996 by Housing Act 1996, ss.227, 232(3), Sched. 19, Pt. IX: S.I. 1996 No. 2402.
(3) The words in the second and fourth sets of square brackets were added, and the words in the third set were substituted, on April 1, 1990 by Local Government and Housing Act 1989, ss.194(1), 195(2), Sched. 11, para. 108: S.I. 1990 No. 431.
(4) The substitution of the words in the penultimate set of square brackets for the words in italics was made on August 1, 1993 by Charities Act 1993, s.98(1), Sched. 6, para. 30.

Ground 7

The tenancy is a periodic tenancy (including a statutory periodic tenancy) which has devolved under the will or intestacy of the former tenant and the proceedings for the recovery of possession are begun not later than twelve months after the death of the former tenant or, if the court so directs, after the date on which, in the opinion of the court, the landlord or, in the case of joint landlords, any one of them became aware of the former tenant's death.

For the purposes of this ground, the acceptance by the landlord of rent from a new tenant after the death of the former tenant shall not be regarded as creating a new periodic tenancy, unless the landlord agrees in writing to a change (as compared with the tenancy before the death) in the amount of the rent, the period of the tenancy, the premises which are let or any other term of the tenancy.

Ground 8

Both at the date of the service of the notice under section 8 of this Act relating to the proceedings for possession and at the date of the hearing—

(a) if rent is payable weekly or fortnightly, at least [eight weeks] *thirteen weeks*' rent is unpaid;
(b) if rent is payable monthly, at least [two months] *three months*' rent is unpaid;
(c) if rent is payable quarterly, at least one quarter's rent is more than three months in arrears; and
(d) if rent is payable yearly, at least three months' rent is more than three months in arrears;

and for the purpose of this ground "rent" means rent lawfully due from the tenant.

ANNOTATION

The words in square brackets in paragraphs (a) and (b) were substituted for the words in italics on February 28, 1997 by Housing Act 1996, s.101, 232(3): S.I. 1997 No. 225. The amendment has no effect in a case where a notice under Act of 1988, s.8 was served before that date, nor where the court has dispensed with the requirement of such a notice and the proceedings for possession were started before that date: S.I. 1997 No. 225, art. 2, Sched., para. 1.

PART II

A1–063 GROUNDS ON WHICH COURT MAY ORDER POSSESSION

Ground 9

Suitable alternative accommodation is available for the tenant or will be available for him when the order for possession takes effect.

Ground 10

Some rent lawfully due from the tenant—

(a) is unpaid on the date on which the proceedings for possession are begun; and
(b) except where subsection (1)(b) of section 8 of this Act applies, was in arrears at the date of the service of the notice under that section relating to those proceedings.

Ground 11

Whether or not any rent is in arrears on the date on which proceedings for possession are begun, the tenant has persistently delayed paying rent which has become lawfully due.

Ground 12

Any obligation of the tenancy (other than one related to the payment of rent) has been broken or not performed.

Ground 13

The condition of the dwelling-house or any of the common parts has deteriorated owing to acts of waste by, or the neglect or default of, the tenant or any other person residing in the dwelling-house and, in the case of an act of waste by, or the neglect or default of, a person lodging with the tenant or a sub-tenant of his, the tenant has not taken such steps as he ought reasonably to have taken for the removal of the lodger or sub-tenant.

For the purposes of this ground, ''common parts'' means any part of a building comprising the dwelling-house and any other premises which the tenant is entitled under the terms of the tenancy to use in common with the occupiers of other dwelling-houses in which the landlord has an estate or interest.

Ground 14

The tenant or any other person residing in the dwelling-house has been guilty of conduct which is a nuisance or annoyance to adjoining occupiers, or has been convicted of using the dwelling-house or allowing the dwelling-house to be used for immoral or illegal purposes.

[Ground 14

The tenant or a person residing in or visiting the dwelling-house—

(a) has been guilty of conduct causing or likely to cause a nuisance or annoyance to a person residing, visiting or otherwise engaging in a lawful activity in the locality, or

(b) has been convicted of—

(i) using the dwelling-house or allowing it to be used for immoral or illegal purposes, or
(ii) an arrestable offence committed in, or in the locality of, the dwelling-house.]

ANNOTATION

Ground 14 was substituted by Housing Act 1996, ss.148, 232(3), (4) with effect from February 28, 1997, subject to savings where steps to claim possession had been taken before that date: S.I. 1997 No. 225; see *supra*, annotation to Ground 8.

[Ground 14A

The dwelling-house was occupied (whether alone or with others) by a married couple or a couple living together as husband and wife and—

(a) one or both of the partners is a tenant of the dwelling-house,
(b) the landlord who is seeking possession is a registered social landlord or a charitable housing trust,
(c) one partner has left the dwelling-house because of violence or threats of violence by the other towards—
    (i) that partner, or
    (ii) a member of the family of that partner who was residing with that partner immediately before the partner left, and
(d) the court is satisfied that the partner who has left is unlikely to return.

For the purposes of this ground "registered social landlord" and "member of the family" have the same meaning as in Part I of the Housing Act 1996 and "charitable housing trust" means a housing trust, within the meaning of the Housing Associations Act 1985, which is a charity within the meaning of the Charities Act 1993.]

ANNOTATION

Ground 14A was inserted by Housing Act 1996, ss.149, 232(3), (4) with effect from February 28, 1997, subject to savings where steps to claim possession had been taken before that date: S.I. 1997 No. 225; see *supra*, annotation to Ground 8.

Ground 15

The condition of any furniture provided for use under the tenancy has, in the opinion of the court, deteriorated owing to ill-treatment by the tenant or any other person residing in the dwelling-house and, in the case of ill-treatment by a person lodging with the tenant or by a sub-tenant of his, the tenant has not taken such steps as he ought reasonably to have taken for the removal of the lodger or sub-tenant.

Ground 16

The dwelling-house was let to the tenant in consequence of his employment by the landlord seeking possession or a previous landlord under the tenancy and the tenant has ceased to be in that employment.

[For the purposes of this ground, at a time when the landlord is or was the Secretary of State, employment by a health service body, as defined in section 60(7) of the National Health Service and Community Care Act 1990, shall be regarded as employment by the Secretary of State.]

ANNOTATION

The words in square brackets were inserted by National Health Service and Community Care Act 1990, s.60(2)(b), Sched. 8, para. 10; S.I. 1990 No. 1329.

[*Ground 17*

The tenant is the person, or one of the persons, to whom the tenancy was granted and the landlord was induced to grant the tenancy by a false statement made knowingly or recklessly by—

(a) the tenant, or
(b) a person acting at the tenant's instigation.]

ANNOTATION

Ground 17 was added by Housing Act 1996, ss.102, 232(3), (4) with effect from February 28, 1997, subject to savings where steps to claim possession had been taken before that date: S.I. 1997 No. 225; see *supra*, annotation to Ground 8.

PART III

A1–064

SUITABLE ALTERNATIVE ACCOMMODATION

1. For the purposes of Ground 9 above, a certificate of the local housing authority for the district in which the dwelling-house in question is situated, certifying that the authority will provide suitable alternative accommodation for the tenant by a date specified in the certificate, shall be conclusive evidence that suitable alternative accommodation will be available for him by that date.

2. Where no such certificate as is mentioned in paragraph 1 above is produced to the court, accommodation shall be deemed to be suitable for the purposes of Ground 9 above if it consists of either—

(a) premises which are to be let as a separate dwelling such that they will then be let on an assured tenancy, other than—

 (i) a tenancy in respect of which notice is given not later than the beginning of the tenancy that possession might be recovered on any of Grounds 1 to 5 above, or
 (ii) an assured shorthold tenancy, within the meaning of Chapter II of Part I of this Act, or

(b) premises to be let as a separate dwelling on terms which will, in the opinion of the court, afford to the tenant security of tenure reasonably equivalent to the security afforded by Chapter I of Part I of this Act in the case of an assured tenancy of a kind mentioned in sub-paragraph (a) above,

and, in the opinion of the court, the accommodation fulfils the relevant conditions as defined in paragraph 3 below.

3.—(1) For the purposes of paragraph 2 above, the relevant conditions are that the accommodation is reasonably suitable to the needs of the tenant and his family as regards proximity to place of work, and either—

(a) similar as regards rental and extent to the accommodation afforded by dwelling-houses provided in the neighbourhood by any local housing authority for persons whose needs as regards extent are, in the opinion of the court, similar to those of the tenant and of his family; or
(b) reasonably suitable to the means of the tenant and to the needs of the tenant and his family as regards extent and character; and

that if any furniture was provided for use under the assured tenancy in question, furniture is provided for use in the accommodation which is either similar to that so provided or is reasonably suitable to the needs of the tenant and his family.

(2) For the purposes of sub-paragraph (1)(a) above, a certificate of a local housing authority stating—

(a) the extent of the accommodation afforded by dwelling-houses provided by the authority to meet the needs of tenants with families of such number as may be specified in the certificate, and

(b) the amount of the rent charged by the authority for dwelling-houses affording accommodation of that extent,

shall be conclusive evidence of the facts so stated.

4. Accommodation shall not be deemed to be suitable to the needs of the tenant and his family if the result of their occupation of the accommodation would be that it would be an overcrowded dwelling-house for the purposes of Part X of the Housing Act 1985.

5. Any document purporting to be a certificate of a local housing authority named therein issued for the purposes of this Part of this Schedule and to be signed by the proper officer of that authority shall be received in evidence and, unless the contrary is shown, shall be deemed to be such a certificate without further proof.

6. In this Part of this Schedule ''local housing authority'' and ''district'', in relation to such an authority, have the same meaning as in the Housing Act 1985.

PART IV

NOTICES RELATING TO RECOVERY OF POSSESSION **A1–065**

7. Any reference in Grounds 1 to 5 in Part I of this Schedule or in the following provisions of this Part to the landlord giving a notice in writing to the tenant is, in the case of joint landlords, a reference to at least one of the joint landlords giving such a notice.

8.—(1) If, not later than the beginning of a tenancy (in this paragraph referred to as ''the earlier tenancy''), the landlord gives such a notice in writing to the tenant as is mentioned in any of Grounds 1 to 5 in Part I of this Schedule, then, for the purposes of the ground in question and any further application of this paragraph, that notice shall also have effect as if it had been given immediately before the beginning of any later tenancy falling within sub-paragraph (2) below.

(2) Subject to sub-paragraph (3) below, sub-paragraph (1) above applies to a later tenancy—

(a) which takes effect immediately on the coming to an end of the earlier tenancy; and
(b) which is granted (or deemed to be granted) to the person who was the tenant under the earlier tenancy immediately before it came to an end; and
(c) which is of substantially the same dwelling-house as the earlier tenancy.

(3) Sub-paragraph (1) above does not apply in relation to a later tenancy if, not later than the beginning of the tenancy, the landlord gave notice in writing to the tenant that the tenancy is not one in respect of which possession can be recovered on the ground in question.

9. Where paragraph 8(1) above has effect in relation to a notice given as mentioned in Ground 1 in Part I of this Schedule, the reference in paragraph (b) of that ground to the reversion on the tenancy is a reference to the reversion on the earlier tenancy and on any later tenancy falling within paragraph 8(2) above.

10. Where paragraph 8(1) above has effect in relation to a notice given as mentioned in Ground 3 or Ground 4 in Part I of this Schedule, any second or subsequent tenancy in relation to which the notice has effect shall be treated for the purpose of that ground as beginning at the beginning of the tenancy in respect of which the notice was actually given.

11. Any reference in Grounds 1 to 5 in Part I of this Schedule to a notice being given not later than the beginning of the tenancy is a reference to its being given not later than the day on which the tenancy is entered into and, accordingly, section 45(2) of this Act shall not apply to any such reference.

Section 19A

[SCHEDULE 2A

ASSURED TENANCIES: NON-SHORTHOLDS **A1–066**

Tenancies excluded by notice

1.—(1) An assured tenancy in respect of which a notice is served as mentioned in sub-paragraph (2) below.

(2) The notice referred to in sub-paragraph (1) above is one which—

(a) is served before the assured tenancy is entered into,
(b) is served by the person who is to be the landlord under the assured tenancy on the person who is to be the tenant under that tenancy, and
(c) states that the assured tenancy to which it relates is not to be an assured shorthand tenancy.

2.—(1) An assured tenancy in respect of which a notice is served as mentioned in sub-paragraph (2) below.

(2) The notice referred to in sub-paragraph (1) above is one which—

(a) is served after the assured tenancy has been entered into,
(b) is served by the landlord under the assured tenancy on the tenant under that tenancy, and
(c) states that the assured tenancy to which it relates is no longer an assured shorthand tenancy.

Tenancies containing exclusionary provision

3. An assured tenancy which contains a provision to the effect that the tenancy is not an assured shorthand tenancy.

Tenancies under section 39

4. An assured tenancy arising by virtue of section 39 above, other than one to which subsection (7) of that section applies.

Former secure tenancies

5. An assured tenancy which became an assured tenancy on ceasing to be a secure tenancy.

Tenancies under Schedule 10 to the Local Government and Housing Act 1989

6. An assured tenancy arising by virtue of Schedule 10 to the Local Government and Housing Act 1989 (security of tenure on ending of long residential tenancies).

Tenancies replacing non-shortholds

7.—(1) An assured tenancy which—

(a) is granted to a person (alone or jointly with others) who, immediately before the tenancy was granted, was the tenant (or, in the case of joint tenants, one of the tenants) under an assured tenancy other than a shorthold tenancy (''the old tenancy''),
(b) is granted (alone or jointly with others) by a person who was at that time the landlord (or one of the joint landlords) under the old tenancy, and
(c) is not one in respect of which a notice is served as mentioned in sub-paragraph (2) below.

(2) The notice referred to in sub-paragraph (1)(c) above is one which—

(a) is in such form as may be prescribed,
(b) is served before the assured tenancy is entered into,
(c) is served by the person who is to be the tenant under the assured tenancy on the person who is to be the landlord under that tenancy (or, in the case of joint landlords, on at least one of the persons who are to be joint landlords), and
(d) states that the assured tenancy to which it relates is to be a shorthold tenancy.

8. An assured tenancy which comes into being by virtue of section 5 above on the coming to an end of an assured tenancy which is not a shorthold tenancy.

Assured agricultural occupancies

9.—(1) An assured tenancy—

(a) in the case of which the agricultural worker condition is, by virtue of any provision of Schedule 3 to this Act, for the time being fulfilled with respect to the dwelling-house subject to the tenancy, and
(b) which does not fall within sub-paragraph (2) or (4) below.

(2) An assured tenancy falls within this sub-paragraph if—

(a) before it is entered into, a notice—

(i) in such form as may be prescribed, and
(ii) stating that the tenancy is to be a shorthold tenancy,

is served by the person who is to be the landlord under the tenancy on the person who is to be the tenant under it, and
(b) it is not an excepted tenancy.

(3) For the purposes of sub-paragraph (2)(b) above, an assured tenancy is an excepted tenancy if—

(a) the person to whom it is granted or, as the case may be, at least one of the persons to whom it is granted was, immediately before it is granted, a tenant or licensee under an assured agricultural occupancy, and
(b) the person by whom it is granted or, as the case may be, at least one of the persons by whom it is granted was, immediately before it is granted, a landlord or licensor under the assured agricultural occupancy referred to in paragraph (a) above.

(4) An assured tenancy falls within this sub-paragraph if it comes into being by virtue of section 5 above on the coming to an end of a tenancy falling within sub-paragraph (2) above.]

ANNOTATION

Schedule 2A was inserted by Housing Act 1996, ss.96(2), 232(3), Sched. 7 with effect from February 28, 1997: S.I. 1997 No. 225. Paragraphs 7(2)(a) and 9(2)(a) came into effect on August 23, 1996 for the purpose only of conferring on the Lord Chancellor or the Secretary of State powers to make orders, regulations or rules: S.I. 1996 No. 2212.

Section 24 SCHEDULE 3

AGRICULTURAL WORKER CONDITIONS **A1–067**

Interpretation

1.—(1) In this Schedule—

''the 1976 Act'' means the Rent (Agriculture) Act 1976;
''agriculture'' has the same meaning as in the 1976 Act; and
''relevant tenancy or licence'' means a tenancy or licence of a description specified in section 24(2) of this Act.

(2) In relation to a relevant tenancy or licence—

(a) ''the occupier'' means the tenant or licensee; and
(b) ''the dwelling-house'' means the dwelling-house which is let under the tenancy or, as the case may be, is occupied under the licence.

(3) Schedule 3 to the 1976 Act applies for the purposes of this Schedule as it applies for the purposes of that Act and, accordingly, shall have effect to determine—

(a) whether a person is a qualifying worker;
(b) whether a person is incapable of whole-time work in agriculture, or work in agriculture as a permit worker, in consequence of a qualifying injury or disease; and
(c) whether a dwelling-house is in qualifying ownership.

The conditions

2. The agricultural worker condition is fulfilled with respect to a dwelling-house subject to a relevant tenancy or licence if—

(a) the dwelling-house is or has been in qualifying ownership at any time during the subsistence of the tenancy or licence (whether or not it was at that time a relevant tenancy or licence); and
(b) the occupier or, where there are joint occupiers, at least one of them—
    (i) is a qualifying worker or has been a qualifying worker at any time during the subsistence of the tenancy or licence (whether or not it was at that time a relevant tenancy or licence); or
    (ii) is incapable of whole-time work in agriculture or work in agriculture as a permit worker in consequence of a qualifying injury or disease.

3.—(1) The agricultural worker condition is also fulfilled with respect to a dwelling-house subject to a relevant tenancy or licence if—

(a) that condition was previously fulfilled with respect to the dwelling-house but the person who was then the occupier or, as the case may be, a person who was one of the joint occupiers (whether or not under the same relevant tenancy or licence) has died; and
(b) that condition ceased to be fulfilled on the death of the occupier referred to in paragraph (a) above (hereinafter referred to as "the previous qualifying occupier"); and
(c) the occupier is either—
    (i) the qualifying widow or widower of the previous qualifying occupier; or
    (ii) the qualifying member of the previous qualifying occupier's family.

(2) For the purposes of sub-paragraph (1)(c)(i) above and sub-paragraph (3) below a widow or widower of the previous qualifying occupier of the dwelling-house is a qualifying widow or widower if she or he was residing in the dwelling-house immediately before the previous qualifying occupier's death.

(3) Subject to sub-paragraph (4) below, for the purposes of sub-paragraph (1)(c)(ii) above, a member of the family of the previous qualifying occupier of the dwelling-house is the qualifying member of the family if—

(a) on the death of the previous qualifying occupier there was no qualifying widow or widower; and
(b) the member of the family was residing in the dwelling-house with the previous qualifying occupier at the time of, and for the period of two years before, his death.

(4) Not more than one member of the previous qualifying occupier's family may be taken into account in determining whether the agricultural worker condition is fulfilled by virtue of this paragraph and, accordingly, if there is more than one member of the family—

(a) who is the occupier in relation to the relevant tenancy or licence, and
(b) who, apart from this sub-paragraph, would be the qualifying member of the family by virtue of sub-paragraph (3) above,

only that one of those members of the family who may be decided by agreement or, in default of agreement by the county court shall be the qualifying member.

(5) For the purposes of the preceding provisions of this paragraph a person who, immediately before the previous qualifying occupier's death, was living with the previous occupier as his or her wife or husband shall be treated as the widow or widower of the previous occupier.

(6) If, immediately before the death of the previous qualifying occupier, there is, by virtue of sub-paragraph (5) above, more than one person who falls within subparagraph (1)(c)(i) above, such one of them as may be decided by agreement or, in default of agreement, by the county court shall be treated as the qualifying widow or widower for the purposes of this paragraph.

4. The agricultural worker condition is also fulfilled with respect to a dwelling-house subject to a relevant tenancy or licence if—

(a) the tenancy or licence was granted to the occupier or, where there are joint occupiers, at least one of them in consideration of his giving up possession of another dwelling-house of which he was then occupier (or one of joint occupiers) under another relevant tenancy or licence; and

(b) immediately before he gave up possession of that dwelling-house, as a result of his occupation the agricultural worker condition was fulfilled with respect to it (whether by virtue of paragraph 2 or paragraph 3 above or this paragraph);

and the reference in paragraph (a) above to a tenancy or licence granted to the occupier or at least one of joint occupiers includes a reference to the case where the grant is to him together with one or more other persons.

5.—(1) This paragraph applies where—

(a) by virtue of any of paragraphs 2 to 4 above, the agricultural worker condition is fulfilled with respect to a dwelling-house subject to a relevant tenancy or licence (in this paragraph referred to as ‘‘the earlier tenancy or licence’’); and

(b) another relevant tenancy or licence of the same dwelling-house (in this paragraph referred to as ‘‘the later tenancy or licence’’) is granted to the person who, immediately before the grant, was the occupier or one of the joint occupiers under the earlier tenancy or licence and as a result of whose occupation the agricultural worker condition was fulfilled as mentioned in paragraph (a) above;

and the reference in paragraph (b) above to the grant of the later tenancy or licence to the person mentioned in that paragraph includes a reference to the case where the grant is to that person together with one or more other persons.

(2) So long as a person as a result of whose occupation of the dwelling-house the agricultural worker condition was fulfilled with respect to the earlier tenancy or licence continues to be the occupier, or one of the joint occupiers, under the later tenancy or licence, the agricultural worker condition shall be fulfilled with respect to the dwelling-house.

(3) For the purposes of paragraphs 3 and 4 above and any further application of this paragraph, where sub-paragraph (2) above has effect, the agricultural worker condition shall be treated as fulfilled so far as concerns the later tenancy or licence by virtue of the same paragraph of this Schedule as was applicable (or, as the case may be, last applicable) in the case of the earlier tenancy or licence.

Section 39 — SCHEDULE 4 — **A1–068**

STATUTORY TENANTS: SUCCESSION

PART I

AMENDMENTS OF SCHEDULE 1 TO RENT ACT 1977

1. In paragraph 1 the words ‘‘or, as the case may be, paragraph 3’’ shall be omitted.

2. At the end of paragraph 2 there shall be inserted the following sub-paragraphs—

‘‘(2) For the purposes of this paragraph, a person who was living with the original tenant as his or her wife or husband shall be treated as the spouse of the original tenant.

(3) If, immediately after the death of the original tenant, there is, by virtue of sub-paragraph (2) above, more than one person who fulfils the conditions in sub-paragraph (1) above, such one of them as may be decided by agreement or, in default of agreement, by the county court shall be treated as the surviving spouse for the purposes of this paragraph.’’

3. In paragraph 3—

(a) after the words "residing with him" there shall be inserted "in the dwelling-house"
(b) for the words "period of 6 months" there shall be substituted "period of 2 years";
(c) for the words from "the statutory tenant" onwards there shall be substituted "entitled to an assured tenancy of the dwelling-house by succession"; and
(d) at the end there shall be added the following sub-paragraph—

"(2) If the original tenant died within the period of 18 months beginning on the operative date, then, for the purposes of this paragraph, a person who was residing in the dwelling-house with the original tenant at the time of his death and for the period which began 6 months before the operative date and ended at the time of his death shall be taken to have been residing with the original tenant for the period of 2 years immediately before his death."

4. In paragraph 4 the words "or 3" shall be omitted.
5. In paragraph 5—

(a) for the words from "or, as the case may be" to "of this Act" there shall be substituted "below shall have effect"; and
(b) for the words "the statutory tenant" there shall be substituted "entitled to an assured tenancy of the dwelling-house by succession".

6. For paragraph 6 there shall be substituted the following paragraph—

"**6.**—(1) Where a person who—

(a) was a member of the original tenant's family immediately before that tenant's death, and
(b) was a member of the first successor's family immediately before the first successor's death,

was residing in the dwelling-house with the first successor at the time of, and for the period of 2 years immediately before, the first successor's death, that person or, if there is more than one such person, such one of them as may be decided by agreement or, in default of agreement, by the county court shall be entitled to an assured tenancy of the dwelling-house by succession.

(2) If the first successor died within the period of 18 months beginning on the operative date, then, for the purposes of this paragraph, a person who was residing in the dwelling-house with the first successor at the time of his death and for the period which began 6 months before the operative date and ended at the time of his death shall be taken to have been residing with the first successor for the period of 2 years immediately before his death."

7. Paragraph 7 shall be omitted.
8. In paragraph 10(1)(a) for the words "paragraphs 6 or 7" there shall be substituted "paragraph 6".
9. At the end of paragraph 11 there shall be inserted the following paragraph—

"**11A.** In this Part of this Schedule "the operative date" means the date on which Part I of the Housing Act 1988 came into force."

[For Act of 1977, Sched. 1, Pt. 1, as amended, see *post*, p. 471]

PART II

A1–069 AMENDMENTS OF SECTION 4 OF RENT (AGRICULTURE) ACT 1976

10. In subsection (2) the words "or, as the case may be, subsection (4)" shall be omitted.
11. In subsection (4)—

(a) in paragraph (b) after the words "residing with him" there shall be inserted "in the dwelling-house" and for the words "period of six months" there shall be substituted "period of 2 years"; and
(b) for the words from "the statutory tenant" onwards there shall be substituted "entitled to an assured tenancy of the dwelling-house by succession".

12. In subsection (5) for the words "subsections (1), (3) and (4)" there shall be substituted "subsections (1) and (3)" and after that subsection there shall be inserted the following subsections—

"(5A) For the purposes of subsection (3) above, a person who was living with the original occupier as his or her wife or husband shall be treated as the spouse of the original occupier and, subject to subsection (5B) below, the references in subsection (3) above to a widow and in subsection (4) above to a surviving spouse shall be construed accordingly.
(5B) If, immediately after the death of the original occupier, there is, by virtue of subsection (5A) above, more than one person who fulfils the conditions in subsection (3) above, such one of them as may be decided by agreement or, in default of agreement by the county court, shall be the statutory tenant by virtue of that subsection.
(5C) If the original occupier died within the period of 18 months beginning on the operative date, then, for the purposes of subsection (3) above, a person who was residing in the dwelling-house with the original occupier at the time of his death and for the period which began 6 months before the operative date and ended at the time of his death shall be taken to have been residing with the original occupier for the period of 2 years immediately before his death; and in this subsection 'the operative date' means the date on which Part I of the Housing Act 1988 came into force."

[For Act of 1976, s.4, as amended, see *post*, p. 468]

PART III

MODIFICATIONS OF SECTION 7 AND SCHEDULE 2 A1–070

13.—(1) Subject to sub-paragraph (2) below, in relation to the assured tenancy to which the successor becomes entitled by succession, section 7 of this Act shall have effect as if in subsection (3) after the word "established" there were inserted the words "or that the circumstances are as specified in any of Cases 11, 12, 16, 17, 18 and 20 in Schedule 15 to the Rent Act 1977".

(2) Sub-paragraph (1) above does not apply if, by virtue of section 39(8) of this Act, the assured tenancy to which the successor becomes entitled is an assured agricultural occupancy.

14. If by virtue of section 39(8) of this Act, the assured tenancy to which the successor becomes entitled is an assured agricultural occupancy, section 7 of this Act shall have effect in relation to that tenancy as if in subsection (3) after the word "established" there were inserted the words "or that the circumstances are as specified in Case XI or Case XII of the Rent (Agriculture) Act 1976".

15.—(1) In relation to the assured tenancy to which the successor becomes entitled by succession, any notice given to the predecessor for the purposes of Case 13, Case 14 or Case 15 in Schedule 15 to the Rent Act 1977 shall be treated as having been given for the purposes of whichever of Grounds 3 to 5 in Schedule 2 to this Act corresponds to the Case in question.

(2) Where sub-paragraph (1) above applies, the regulated tenancy of the predecessor shall be treated, in relation to the assured tenancy of the successor, as "the earlier tenancy" for the purposes of Part IV of Schedule 2 to this Act.

[........]

Section 119

SCHEDULE 13

AMENDMENTS OF LANDLORD AND TENANT ACT 1987 A1–071

[........]

2.—(1) In section 3 of that Act (qualifying tenants), in subsection (1) (paragraphs (a) to (c) of which exclude certain tenants) the word "or" immediately preceding paragraph (c) shall be omitted and at the end of that paragraph there shall be added "or

(d) an assured tenancy or assured agricultural occupancy within the meaning of Part I of the Housing Act 1988".

(2) In subsection (2) of that section (which excludes persons having interests going beyond a particular flat), for paragraphs (a) and (b) there shall be substituted the words "by virtue of one or

more tenancies none of which falls within paragraphs (a) to (d) of subsection (1), he is the tenant not only of the flat in question but also of at least two other flats contained in those premises''; and in subsection (3) of that section for ''(2)(b)'' there shall be substituted ''(2)''.

Section 140

SCHEDULE 17

A1–072

MINOR AND CONSEQUENTIAL AMENDMENTS

PART I

GENERAL AMENDMENTS

The Reserve and Auxiliary Forces (Protection of Civil Interests) Act 1951

1. In section 4 of the Reserve and Auxiliary Forces (Protection of Civil Interests) Act 1951 (recovery of possession of dwelling-houses in default of payment of rent precluded in certain cases) after subsection (2) there shall be inserted the following subsection—

''(2A) For the purposes of the foregoing provisions of this Act, a judgement or order for the recovery of possession of a dwelling-house let on an assured tenancy within the meaning of Part I of the Housing Act 1988 shall be regarded as a judgement or order for the recovery of possession in default of payment of rent if the judgement or order was made on any of Grounds 8, 10 and 11 in Schedule 2 to that Act and not on any other ground.''

2. For section 16 of that Act (protection of tenure of rented premises by extension of Rent Acts), as it applies otherwise than to Scotland, there shall be substituted the following section—

''**Protection of tenure of certain rented premises by extension of Housing Act 1988**

16.—(1) Subject to subsection (2) of section 14 of this Act and subsection (3) below, if at any time during a service man's period of residence protection—

(a) a tenancy qualifying for protection which is a fixed term tenancy ends without being continued or renewed by agreement (whether on the same or different terms and conditions), and
(b) by reason only of such circumstances as are mentioned in subsection (4) below, on the ending of that tenancy no statutory periodic tenancy of the rented family residence would arise, apart from the provisions of this section,

Chapter I of Part I of the Housing Act 1988 shall, during the remainder of the period of protection, apply in relation to the rented family residence as if those circumstances did not exist and had not existed immediately before the ending of that tenancy and, accordingly, as if on the ending of that tenancy there arose a statutory periodic tenancy which is an assured tenancy during the remainder of that period.

(2) Subject to subsection (2) of section 14 of this Act and subsection (3) below, if at any time during a service man's period of residence protection—

(a) a tenancy qualifying for protection which is a periodic tenancy would come to an end, apart from the provisions of this section, and
(b) by reason only of such circumstances as are mentioned in subsection (4) below that tenancy is not an assured tenancy, and
(c) if that tenancy had been an assured tenancy, it would not have come to an end at that time,

Chapter I of Part I of the Housing Act 1988 shall, during the remainder of the period of protection, apply in relation to the rented family residence as if those circumstances did not exist and, accordingly, as if the tenancy had become an assured tenancy immediately before it would otherwise have come to an end.

(3) Neither subsection (1) nor subsection (2) above applies if, on the ending of the tenancy qualifying for protection, a statutory tenancy arises.

(4) The circumstances referred to in subsections (1) and (2) above are any one or more of the following, that is to say—

(a) that the tenancy was entered into before, or pursuant to a contract made before, Part I of the Housing Act 1988 came into force;
(b) that the rateable value (as defined for the purposes of that Act) of the premises which are the rented family residence, or of a property of which those premises form part, exceeded the relevant limit specified in paragraph 2 of Schedule 1 to that Act;
(c) that the circumstances mentioned in paragraph 3 or paragraph 6 of that Schedule applied with respect to the tenancy qualifying for protection; and
(d) that the reversion immediately expectant on the tenancy qualifying for protection belongs to any of the bodies specified in paragraph 12 of that Schedule.''

[........]

4.—(1) Section 17 of that Act (provisions in case of rented premises which include accommodation shared otherwise than with landlord), as it applies otherwise than to Scotland, shall be amended in accordance with this paragraph.

(2) In subsection (1)—

(a) after the words ''qualifying for protection'' there shall be inserted ''which is a fixed term tenancy'';
(b) in paragraph (b) for the words from ''subsection (2)'' to ''1977'' there shall be substituted ''section 16(4) above, subsection (1) of section 3 of the Housing Act 1988'';
(c) for the words ''said section 22'' there shall be substituted ''said section 3''; and
(d) at the end there shall be added ''and, accordingly, as if on the ending of the tenancy there arose a statutory periodic tenancy which is an assured tenancy during the remainder of that period.''

(3) For subsection (2) there shall be substituted the following subsections—

''(2) Where, at any time during a service man's period of residence protection—

(a) a tenancy qualifying for protection which is a periodic tenancy would come to an end, apart from the provisions of this section and section 16 above, and
(b) paragraphs (a) and (b) of subsection (1) above apply,

section 3 of the Housing Act 1988 shall, during the remainder of the period of protection, apply in relation to the separate accommodation as if the circumstances referred to in subsection (1)(b) above did not exist and, accordingly, as if the tenancy had become an assured tenancy immediately before it would otherwise have come to an end.

(3) Neither subsection (1) nor subsection (2) above applies if, on the ending of the tenancy qualifying for protection, a statutory tenancy arises.''

[........]

6.—(1) In section 18 of that Act (protection of tenure, in connection with employment, under a licence or rent-free letting), in subsection (1), as it applies otherwise than to Scotland,—

(a) for the words ''Part VII of the Rent Act 1977'' there shall be substituted ''Chapter I of Part I of the Housing Act 1988''; and
(b) for the words ''subject to a statutory tenancy within the meaning of the Rent Act 1977'' there shall be substituted ''let on a statutory periodic tenancy which is an assured tenancy.''

[........]

(3) Subsection (2) of that section shall be omitted.

(4) In subsection (3) of that section, as it applies otherwise than to Scotland, at the end of paragraph (c) there shall be added ''or

(d) is a dwelling-house which is let on or subject to an assured agricultural occupancy within the meaning of Part I of the Housing Act 1988 which is not an assured tenancy.''

7. For section 19 of that Act (limitation on application of Rent Acts by virtue of sections 16 to 18), as it applies otherwise than to Scotland, there shall be substituted the following section—

"Limitation on application of Housing Act 1988 by virtue of sections 16 to 18

19. Where by virtue of sections 16 to 18 above, the operation of Chapter I of Part I of the Housing Act 1988 in relation to any premises is extended or modified, the extension or modification shall not affect—

(a) any tenancy of those premises other than the statutory periodic tenancy which is deemed to arise or, as the case may be, the tenancy which is for any period deemed to be an assured tenancy by virtue of any of those provisions; or
(b) any rent payable in respect of a period beginning before the time when that statutory periodic tenancy was deemed to arise or, as the case may be, before that tenancy became deemed to be an assured tenancy; or
(c) anything done or omitted to be done before the time referred to in paragraph (b) above."

[........]

9.—(1) Section 20 of that Act (modification of Rent Acts as respects occupation by employees), as it applies otherwise than to Scotland, shall be amended in accordance with this paragraph.
(2) In subsection (1) after the words "Case I in Schedule 15 to the Rent Act 1977" there shall be inserted "or Ground 12 in Schedule 2 to the Housing Act 1988."
(3) In subsection (2) after the words "Case 8 in the said Schedule 15" there shall be inserted "or, as the case may be, Ground 16 in the said Schedule 2" and for paragraph (b) there shall be substituted the following paragraph—

"(b) Chapter I of Part I of the Housing Act 1988 applies in relation to the premises as mentioned in section 18(1) of this Act and a dependant or dependants of the service man is or are living in the premises or in part thereof in right of the statutory periodic tenancy or assured tenancy referred to in section 19(a) of this Act."

(4) In subsection (3)—

(a) after the words "the Cases in Part I of the said Schedule 15" there shall be inserted "or, as the case may be, Grounds 10 to 16 in Part II of the said Schedule 2"; and
(b) after the words "section 98(1) of the Rent Act 1977" there shall be inserted "or, as the case may be, section 7(4) of the Housing Act 1988".

[........]

11. In section 22 of that Act (facilities for action on behalf of men serving abroad proceedings as to tenancies), as it applies otherwise than to Scotland, in subsection

(a) after the words "Rent Act 1977" there shall be inserted "or under Part I of the Housing Act 1988";
(b) for the words "Part V of that Act" there shall be substituted "Part V of the Rent Act 1977 or Part I of the Housing Act 1988"; and
(c) in paragraph (a) after the word "tenancy" there shall be inserted "or licence".

[........]

13.—(1) Section 23 of that Act (interpretation of Part II), as it applies otherwise than to Scotland, shall be amended in accordance with this paragraph.
(2) In subsection (1)—

(a) after the definition of "agricultural land" there shall be inserted—
" 'assured tenancy' has the same meaning as in Part I of the Housing Act 1988";
(b) after the definition of "dependant" there shall be inserted—
" 'fixed term tenancy' means any tenancy other than a periodic tenancy";
(c) for the definition of "landlord" and "tenant" there shall be substituted—
" 'in relation to a statutory tenancy or to a provision of the Rent Act 1977 'landlord' and 'tenant' have the same meaning as in that Act but, subject to that, those expressions have the same meaning as in Part I of the Housing Act 1988"; and
(d) after the definition of "relevant police authority" there shall be inserted—
" 'statutory periodic tenancy' has the same meaning as in Part I of the Housing Act 1988".

(3) At the end of subsection (1) there shall be inserted the following subsection—

"(1A) Any reference in this Part of this Act to Chapter I of Part I of the Housing Act 1988 includes a reference to the General Provisions of Chapter VI of that Part, so far as applicable to Chapter I."

(4) In subsection (3) after the words "Rent Act 1977" there shall be inserted "or Chapter I of Part I of the Housing Act 1988".

[........]

The Local Government, Planning and Land Act 1980

29. In Schedule 28 to the Local Government, Planning and Land Act 1980, in paragraph 10 after the words "Rent Act 1977" there shall be inserted "or the Housing Act 1988".

The Highways Act 1980

30. In Schedule 6 to the Highways Act 1980, in Part I, in paragraph 1(3)(b)(i) after the words "Rent Act 1977" there shall be inserted "and licensees under an assured agricultural occupancy within the meaning of Part I of the Housing Act 1988".

The New Towns Act 1981

31. In section 22 of the New Towns Act 1981 (possession of houses) after the words "Rent Act 1977" there shall be inserted "or Part I of the Housing Act 1988".

The Acquisition of Land Act 1981

32.—(1) In section 12(2) of the Acquisition of Land Act 1981 after the words "Rent (Agriculture) Act 1976" there shall be inserted "or a licensee under an assured agricultural occupancy within the meaning of Part I of the Housing Act 1988".

(2) In Schedule 1 to that Act, in paragraph 3(2) after the words "Rent (Agriculture) Act 1976" there shall be inserted "or a licensee under an assured agricultural occupancy within the meaning of Part I of the Housing Act 1988".

The Matrimonial Homes Act 1983

[........]

Annotation

Paragraphs 33 and 34 were repealed with effect from October 1, 1997 by Family Law Act 1996, s.66(3), Sched. 10: S.I. 1997 No. 1892.

The County Courts Act 1984

35.—(1) In section 66 of the County Courts Act 1984 (trial by jury: exceptions), in subsection (1) at the end of paragraph (b)(iii) there shall be inserted "or

(iv) under Part I of the Housing Act 1988".

(2) In section 77(6) of that Act (appeals: possession proceedings) after paragraph (e) there shall be inserted the following paragraph—

"(ee) section 7 of the Housing Act 1988, as it applies to the grounds in Part II of Schedule 2 to that Act; or".

The Matrimonial and Family Proceedings Act 1984

36. In section 22 of the Matrimonial and Family Proceedings Act 1984 (powers of the court in relation to certain tenancies of dwelling-houses), in paragraph (a) after the word "tenancy" there shall be inserted "or assured agricultural occupancy".

[........]

The Housing Act 1985

[........]

42. In section 171F of that Act (subsequent dealings after disposal of dwelling-house to private sector landlord: possession on grounds of suitable alternative accommodation) after "Rent Act 1977" there shall be inserted "or on Ground 9 in Schedule 2 to the Housing Act 1988".

43. In section 236 of that Act at the end of subsection (2) (meaning of "occupying tenant") there shall be added the words "or

(e) is a licensee under an assured agricultural occupancy."

44. In section 238 of that Act (index of defined expressions in Part VII) before the entry relating to "clearance area" there shall be inserted—

"assured agricultural occupancy ... section 622".

45. In section 247 of that Act (notification of certain disposals of land to the local housing authority), in subsection (5) (provision not to apply to certain disposals) after paragraph (c) there shall be inserted the following paragraph—

"(ca) the grant of an assured tenancy or assured agricultural occupancy, or of a tenancy which is not such a tenancy or occupancy by reason only of paragraph 10 of Schedule 1 to the Housing Act 1988 (resident landlords) or of that paragraph and the fact that the accommodation which is let is not let as a separate dwelling".

46. In section 263 of that Act (index of defined expressions in Part VIII) before the entry relating to "clearance area" there shall be inserted—

"assured agricultural occupancy .... section 622
assured tenancy .... section 622".

47. In Part IX of that Act (slum clearance) in the following provisions relating to the recovery of possession, namely, sections 264(5), 270(3), 276 and 286(3), after the words "Rent Acts" there shall be inserted "or Part I of the Housing Act 1988".

48. In section 309 of that Act (recovery of possession of premises for purposes of approved redevelopment), in paragraph (a) of subsection (1) after the words "the Rent Act 1977)" the following words shall be inserted "or let on or subject to an assured tenancy or assured agricultural occupancy"; and in the words following paragraph (b) of that subsection after the words "section 98(1)(a) of the Rent Act 1977" there shall be inserted "or section 7 of the Housing Act 1988."

49. In section 323 of that Act (index of defined expressions in Part IX) before the entry relating to "clearance area" there shall be inserted—

"assured agricultural occupancy .... section 622
assured tenancy .... section 622".

50. In section 368 of that Act (means of escape from fire: power to secure that part of house not used for human habitation), in subsection (6) after the words "Rent Acts" there shall be inserted "or Part I of the Housing Act 1988".

51. In section 381 of that Act (general effect of control order), in subsection (3) after the words "Rent Acts" there shall be inserted "and Part I of the Housing Act 1988".

52.—(1) In section 382 of that Act (effect of control order on persons occupying house) after subsection (3) there shall be inserted the following subsection—

"(3A) Section 1(2) of and paragraph 12 of Part I of Schedule 1 to the Housing Act 1988 (which exclude local authority lettings from Part I of that Act) do not apply to a lease or agreement under which a person to whom this section applies is occupying part of the house."

(2) In subsection (4) of that section after paragraph (b) there shall be inserted

"or (c) an assured tenancy or assured agricultural occupancy within the meaning of Part I of the Housing Act 1988";

and for the words "either of those Acts" there shall be substituted "any of those Acts".

53. In section 400 of that Act (index of defined expressions for Part XI) after the entry relating to "appropriate multiplier" there shall be inserted—

"assured tenancy .... section 622
assured agricultural occupancy .... section 622".

[........]

59. In section 533 of that Act (assistance for owners of defective housing; exceptions to eligibility) after the words "Rent (Agriculture) Act 1976" there shall be inserted "or who occupies the dwelling under an assured agricultural occupancy which is not an assured tenancy".

60.—(1) In section 553 of that Act (effect of repurchase of defective dwellings on certain existing tenancies) in subsection (2)—

(a) in paragraph (a) after the words "protected tenancy" there shall be inserted "or an assured tenancy";
(b) at the end of paragraph (b) there shall be added the words "or in accordance with any of Grounds 1, 3, 4 and 5 in Schedule 2 to the Housing Act 1988 (notice that possession might be recovered under that ground) or under section 20(1)(c) of that Act (notice served in respect of assured shorthold tenancies); and"; and

[........]

Annotation

Paragraph 60(c) was repealed on February 28, 1997 by Housing Act 1996, ss. 140(2), 141(2), Sched. 19, Pt. IV: S.I. 1997 No. 225.

61.—(1) In section 554 of that Act (grant of tenancy of defective dwelling to former owner-occupier) at the end of subsection (2) there shall be inserted the following subsection—

"(2A) If the authority is a registered housing association, other than a housing co-operative, within the meaning of section 27B, their obligation is to grant a secure tenancy if the individual to whom a tenancy is to be granted—

(a) is a person who, immediately before he acquired his interest in the dwelling-house, was a secure tenant of it; or
(b) is the spouse or former spouse or widow or widower of a person falling within paragraph (a); or
(c) is a member of the family, within the meaning of section 186, of a person falling within paragraph (a) who has died, and was residing with that person in the dwelling-house at the time of and for the period of twelve months before his death."

(2) In subsection (3) of that section, at the end of paragraph (b) there shall be inserted

"or (c) an assured tenancy which is neither an assured shorthold tenancy, within the meaning of Part I of the Housing Act 1988, nor a tenancy under which the landlord might recover possession on any of Grounds 1 to 5 in Schedule 2 to that Act.''

62. In section 577 of that Act (index of defined expressions for Part XVI) after the entry relating to ''associated arrangement'' there shall be inserted—

''assured agricultural occupancy .... section 622
assured tenancy .... section 622''.

63. In section 612 of that Act (exclusion of Rent Act protection) after the words ''the Rent Acts'' there shall be inserted ''or Part I of the Housing Act 1988''.

64. In section 622 of that Act (definitions: general) before the definition of ''bank'' there shall be inserted—

'' ''assured tenancy'' has the same meaning as in Part I of the Housing Act 1988;
''assured agricultural occupancy'' has the same meaning as in Part I of the Housing Act 1988''.

65. In Schedule 2 to that Act, in Part IV (grounds for possession: suitability of alternative accommodation) in paragraph 1, at the end of sub-paragraph (b) there shall be added

''or (c) which are to be let as a separate dwelling under an assured tenancy which is neither an assured shorthold tenancy, within the meaning of Part I of the Housing Act 1988, nor a tenancy under which the landlord might recover possession under any of Grounds 1 to 5 in Schedule 2 to that Act''.

[........]

The Landlord and Tenant Act 1985

67.—(1) In section 5 of the Landlord and Tenant Act 1985 (information to be contained in rent books), in subsection (1)(b) after the word ''tenancy'' there shall be inserted ''or let on an assured tenancy within the meaning of Part I of the Housing Act 1988''.

(2) In subsection (2) of that section after the word ''tenancy'' there shall be added ''or let on an assured tenancy within the meaning of Part I of the Housing Act 1988''.

[........]

The Agricultural Holdings Act 1986

69.—(1) In Schedule 3 to the Agricultural Holdings Act 1986 (cases where consent of Tribunal to operation of notice to quit is not required), in Part II (provisions applicable to Case A: suitable alternative accommodation), in paragraph 3 after paragraph (b) there shall be inserted

''or (c) premises which are to be let as a separate dwelling such that they will then be let on an assured tenancy which is not an assured shorthold tenancy (construing those terms in accordance with Part I of the Housing Act 1988), or

(d) premises to be let as a separate dwelling on terms which will afford to the tenant security of tenure reasonably equivalent to the security afforded by Chapter I of Part I of that Act in the case of an assured tenancy which is not an assured shorthold tenancy.''

(2) At the end of the said paragraph 3 there shall be added the following sub-paragraph—

''(2) Any reference in sub-paragraph (1) above to an assured tenancy does not include a reference to a tenancy in respect of which possession might be recovered on any of Grounds 1 to 5 in Schedule 2 to the Housing Act 1988.''

70. In Schedule 5 of that Act (notice to quit where tenant is a service man), in paragraph 2(2)(a) after the words ''Rent Act 1977'' there shall be inserted ''or paragraph 7 of Schedule 1 to the Housing Act 1988''.

[........]

Section 140 SCHEDULE 18

ENACTMENTS REPEALED **A1–073**

Chapter	Short Title	Extent of Repeal
14 & 15 Geo VI c. 65	The Reserve and Auxiliary Forces (Protection of Civil Interests) Act 1951	Section 18(2)
1976 c. 80	The Rent (Agriculture) Act 1976	In section 4(2) the words ''or, as the case may be, subsection (4)''. In section 13(3) the words ''68, 69'' and ''or Part II of Schedule 11 or Schedule 12 to that Act''. In Schedule 4, in Part I, paragraph 2(2).
1977 c. 42	The Rent Act 1977	Section 16A. Sections 19 to 21. In section 63, in subsection (1), paragraph (b) and the word ''and'' immediately preceding it; in subsection (2) in paragraph (a), the words ''and deputy rent officers'', in paragraph (b), the words ''or deputy rent officer'', in paragraph (d) the words ''and deputy rent officers'' and the word ''and'' at the end of the paragraph, and paragraph (e); in subsection (3), the words ''and deputy rent officers''; and in subsection (7)(b), the words ''and deputy rent officers''. In section 67, in subsection (5), the words ''and sections 68 and 69 of this Act'' and in subsection (7), the words ''Subject to section 69(4) of this Act.'' Sections 68 and 69. In section 74, in subsection (2), in paragraph (a) ''69'', in paragraph (b) the words ''or II'' and paragraph (c). In section 77(1) the words ''or the local authority''. In section 80(1) the words ''or the local authority''. Section 81A(1)(a). In section 87, in subsection (2), in paragraph (a) ''69'' and in paragraph (c) the words ''and 12''. In section 88(2) the words ''then, subject to section 89 of this Act''. Section 89. In section 103(1) the words ''or the local authority''. In section 137 the words ''this Part of ''

Chapter	Short Title	Extent of Repeal
1977 c. 42—*cont*	The Rent Act 1977—*cont*	In Schedule 1, in paragraph 1 the words ''or, as the case may be, paragraph 3'', in paragraph 4, the words ''or 3'', and paragraph 7. In Schedule 2, paragraph 6(3). Schedule 8. In Schedule 11, Part II. Schedule 12. In Schedule 14, paragraph 4. In Schedule 15, in Part IV, paragraph 4(2). In Schedule 20, paragraph 2(2). In Schedule 24, paragraph 8(3).
1977 c. 43	The Protection from Eviction Act 1977	In section 7(3)(c) the words from ''under'' to ''1977)''.
1980 c. 51	The Housing Act 1980	Section 52. Sections 56 to 68. Section 59(1). Section 60. Section 73(2). Section 76(2). In Schedule 9, paragraph 2. In Schedule 10, paragraph 2. In Schedule 25, paragraph 36, in paragraph 40 ''68(4)'' and paragraphs 46 and 63.
1985 c. 51	The Local Government Act 1985	In Schedule 13, in paragraph 21, the words from ''and section 19(5)(aa)'' onwards.
1985 c. 68	The Housing Act 1985	In section 80, in subsection (1) the words from ''the Housing Corporation'' to ''charity or'', the words ''housing association or'' and subsection (2). Sections 199 to 201. In Schedule 5, in paragraph 3 the word ''or'' immediately following the entry for section 55 of the Housing Associations Act 1985; paragraphs 6 and 8.
1985 c. 69	The Housing Associations Act 1985	In section 3(2) the words ''of housing associations maintained under this section''. In section 18(3) the words from ''and the Corporation'' onwards. In section 40, the entries relating to housing association grant and revenue deficit grant. Sections 41 to 57. Section 62. In section 73, the entries relating to approved development programme, hostel deficit grant, housing association grant, housing project, revenue deficit grant, shared ownership agreement and shared ownership lease. Section 75(1)(d).

Chapter	Short Title	Extent of Repeal
1985 c. 69—*cont*	The Housing Associations Act 1985—*cont*	In setion 87(1) the words "registered housing associations and other". In section 107, in subsection (3) the entries relating to sections 4, 44 and 45 and 52, and in subsection (4) the words "section 4(3)(h)". In Schedule 5, in paragraph 5(3) of Part I and in paragraph 5(3) of Part II, the words "at such times and in such places as the Treasury may direct, and" and the words "with the approval of the Treasury". In Schedule 6, paragraph 3(3)(b).
1986 c. 63	The Housing and Planning Act 1986	Section 7. Section 12. In section 13, subsections (1) to (3) and (5). Section 19. In Schedule 4, paragraphs 1(3) and 10. In Schedule 5, paragraph 8.
1987 c. 31	The Landlord and Tenant Act 1987	In section 3(1)(b) the word "or". Section 4(2)(a)(ii). Section 45. Section 60(2). In Schedule 4, paragraph 7.

1. The repeal of sections 19 to 21 of the Rent Act 1977 does not apply with respect to any tenancy or contract entered into before the coming into force of Part I of this Act nor to any other tenancy or contract which, having regard to section 36 of this Act, can be a restricted contract.

2. The repeal of section 52 of the Housing Act 1980 (protected shorthold tenancies) does not apply with respect to any tenancy entered into before the coming into force of Part I of this Act nor to any other tenancy which, having regard to section 34 of this Act, can be a protected shorthold tenancy.

3. The repeal of sections 56 to 58 of the Housing Act 1980 does not have effect in relation to any tenancy to which, by virtue of section 37(2) of this Act, section 1(3) of this Act does not apply.

4. The repeals in section 80 of the Housing Act 1985—

(a) have effect (subject to section 35(5) of this Act) in relation to any tenancy or licence entered into before the coming into force of Part I of this Act unless, immediately before that time, the landlord or, as the case may be, the licensor is a body which, in accordance with the repeals, would cease to be within the said section 80; and

(b) do not have effect in relation to a tenancy or licence entered into on or after the coming into force of Part I of this Act if the tenancy or licence falls within any of paragraphs (c) to (f) of subsection (4) of section 35 of this Act [; and

(c) do not have effect in relation to a tenancy while it is a housing association tenancy.]

ANNOTATION

Paragraph 4(c) was inserted by Local Government and Housing Act 1989, ss.194(1), 195(2), Sched. 11, para. 112: S.I. 1989 No. 2445, with effect from January 16, 1990.

Appendix 2

A2–001 **Rent (Agriculture) Act 1976, section 4**

(1976 c.80)

[Printed as amended by Act of 1988 as applying to the death on or after January 15, 1989 of the original occupier]

Statutory tenancies

Statutory tenants and tenancies

A2–002 **4.**—(1) Subject to section 5 below, where a person ceases to be a protected occupier of a dwelling-house on the termination, whether by notice to quit or by virtue of section 16(3) of this Act or otherwise, of his licence or tenancy, he shall, if and so long as he occupies the dwelling-house as his residence, be the statutory tenant of it.

(2) Subject to section 5 below, subsection (3), . . . below shall have effect for determining what person (if any) is the statutory tenant of a dwelling-house at any time after the death of a person (''the original occupier'') who was immediately before his death, a protected occupier or statutory tenant of the dwelling-house in his own right.

Annotation

The words omitted were omitted by virtue of Act of 1988, s. 39(4), Sched. 4, para. 10, and repealed by Act of 1988, s.140(2), Sched. 18.

(3) If the original occupier was a man who died leaving a widow who was residing [in the dwelling-house immediately before his death] then, after his death, unless the widow is a protected occupier of the dwelling-house by virtue of section 3(2) above, she shall be the statutory tenant if and so long as she occupies the dwelling-house as her residence.

This subsection is framed by reference to the case where the original occupier was a man, but is to be read as applying equally in the converse case where the original occupier was a woman.

ANNOTATION

The words in square brackets were substituted by Housing Act 1980, s.76(3) with effect in relation to deaths occurring after November 28, 1980: S.I. 1980 No. 1706.

(4) Where—

(a) the original occupier was not a person who died leaving a surviving spouse who was residing [in the dwelling-house immediately before his death], but

(b) one or more persons who were members of his family were residing with him [in the dwelling-house] at the time of and for the [period of 2 years] immediately before his death,

then, after his death, unless that person or, as the case may be, one of those persons is a protected occupier of the dwelling-house by virtue of section 3(3) above, that person or, as the case may be, such one of those persons as may be decided by agreement, or in default of agreement by the county court, shall be [entitled to an assured tenancy of the dwelling-house by succession.]

ANNOTATION

The words in the first set of square brackets were substituted by Housing Act 1980, s.76(3). The other insertions and substitutions were made by Act of 1988, s. 39(4), Sched. 4, para. 11.

(5) In [subsection (1) and (3)] above the phrase "if and so long as he occupies the dwelling-house as his residence" shall be construed in accordance with [section 2(3) of the Rent Act 1977] (construction of that phrase in the corresponding provisions of that Act).

ANNOTATION

The words in the first set of square brackets were substituted by Act of 1988, s.39(4), Sched. 4, para. 12. The words in the second set of square brackets were substituted by Rent Act 1977, s.155, Sched. 23, para. 72.

[(5A) For the purposes of subsection (3) above, a person who was living with the original occupier as his or her wife or husband shall be treated as the spouse of the original occupier and, subject to subsection (5B) below, the references in subsection (3) above to a widow and in subsection (4) above to a surviving spouse shall be construed accordingly.

(5B) If, immediately after the death of the original occupier, there is, by virtue of subsection (5A) above, more than one person who fulfils the conditions in subsection (3) above, such one of them as may be decided by agreement or, in default of agreement by the county court, shall be the statutory tenant by virtue of that subsection.

(5C) If the original occupier died within the period of 18 months beginning on the operative date, then, for the purposes of subsection (3) above, a person who was residing in the dwelling-house with the original occupier at the time of his death and for the period which began 6 months before the operative date and ended at the time of his death shall be taken to have been residing with the original occupier for the period of 2 years immediately before his death; and in this subsection "the operative date" means the date on which Part I of the Housing Act 1988 came into force.]

ANNOTATION

Subsections (5A), (5B) and (5C) were inserted by Act of 1988, Sched. 4, para. 12.

(6) A dwelling-house is, in this Act, referred to as subject to a statutory tenancy where there is a statutory tenant of it.

Rent Act, 1977, Schedule 1, Part I A2–003

(1977 c.42)

[Printed as amended by Act of 1988 as applying to the death on or after January 15, 1989 of the original tenant or the first successor.]

Sections 2 and 3

SCHEDULE 1

STATUTORY TENANCIES

PART I

STATUTORY TENANTS BY SUCCESSION

1. Paragraph 2 . . . below shall have effect, subject to section 2(3) of this Act, for the purpose of determining who is the statutory tenant of a dwelling-house by succession after the death of the person (in this Part of this Schedule referred to as "the original tenant") who, immediately before his death, was a protected tenant of the dwelling-house or the statutory tenant of it by virtue of his previous protected tenancy. **A2–004**

ANNOTATION

The words omitted were omitted by virtue of Act of 1988, s.39(2), Sched. 4, para. 1, and repealed by Act of 1988, s.140(2), Sched. 18.

2.—(1) The surviving spouse (if any) of the original tenant, if residing in the dwelling-house immediately before the death of the original tenant, shall after the death be the statutory tenant if and so long as he or she occupies the dwelling-house as his or her residence.

ANNOTATION

Paragraph 2(1) was substituted by Housing Act 1980, s.76(1) with effect in relation to deaths occurring after November 28, 1980: S.I. 1980 No. 1706.

[(2) For the purposes of this paragraph, a person who was living with the original tenant as his or her wife or husband shall be treated as the spouse of the original tenant.

(3) If, immediately after the death of the original tenant, there is, by virtue of sub-paragraph (2) above, more than one person who fulfils the conditions in sub-paragraph (1) above, such one of them as may be decided by agreement or, in default of agreement, by the county court shall be treated as the surviving spouse for the purposes of this paragraph.]

ANNOTATION

Sub-paragraphs (2) and (3) were inserted by Act of 1988, s.39(2), Sched. 4, para. 2.

3.—(1) Where paragraph 2 above does not apply, but a person who was a member of the original tenant's family was residing with him [in the dwelling-house] at the time of and for the [period of 2 years] immediately before his death then, after his death, that person or if there is more than one such person such one of them as may be decided by agreement, or in default of agreement by the county court, shall be [entitled to an assured tenancy of the dwelling-house by succession].

[(2) If the original tenant died within the period of 18 months beginning on the operative date, then, for the purposes of this paragraph, a person who was residing in the dwelling-house with the original tenant at the time of his death and for the period which began 6 months before the operative date and ended at the time of his death shall be taken to have been residing with the original tenant for the period of 2 years immediately before his death.]

ANNOTATION

Sub-paragraph (2) was inserted by Act of 1988, s.39(2), Sched. 4, para. 3. The additions and substitutions in paragraph 3(1) were also made by Act of 1988, s.39(2), Sched. 4, para. 3.

4. A person who becomes the statutory tenant of a dwelling-house by virtue of paragraph 2 . . . above is in this Part of this Schedule referred to as "the first successor".

ANNOTATION

The words omitted were omitted by virtue of Act of 1988, s.39(2), Sched. 4, para. 4, and repealed by Act of 1988, s.140(2), Sched. 18.

5. If, immediately before his death, the first successor was still a statutory tenant, paragraph 6 [below shall have effect] for the purpose of determining who is [entitled to an assured tenancy of the dwelling-house by succession] after the death of the first successor.

ANNOTATION

The substitutions in paragraph 5 were made by Act of 1988, s.39(3), Sched. 4, para. 5.

[6.—(1) Where a person who—

(a) was a member of the original tenant's family immediately before that tenant's death, and
(b) was a member of the first successor's family immediately before the first successor's death,

was residing in the dwelling-house with the first successor at the time of, and for the period of 2 years immediately before, the first successor's death, that person or, if there is more than one such person, such one of them as may be decided by agreement or, in default of agreement, by the county court shall be entitled to an assured tenancy of the dwelling-house by succession.

(2) If the first successor died within the period of 18 months beginning on the operative date, then, for the purposes of this paragraph, a person who was residing in the dwelling-house with the first successor at the time of his death and for the period which began 6 months before the operative date and ended at the time of his death shall be taken to have been residing with the first successor for the period of 2 years immediately before his death.]

ANNOTATION

Paragraph 6 was substituted for the previous paragraph 6 by Act of 1988, s.39(3), Sched. 4, para. 6.

Paragraph 7 was omitted by virtue of Act of 1988, s.39(3) Sched. 4, para. 7, and repealed by Act of 1988, Sched. 18., s.140(2), Paragraph 8 had previously been repealed by Housing Act 1980, s.152(3), Sched. 26.

9. Paragraphs 5 to 8 above do not apply where the statutory tenancy of the original tenant arose by virtue of section 4 of the Requisitioned Houses and Housing (Amendment) Act 1955 or section 20 of the Rent Act 1965.

10.—(1) Where after a succession the successor becomes the tenant of the dwelling-house by the grant to him of another tenancy, "the original tenant" and "the first successor" in this Part of this Schedule shall, in relation to that other tenancy, mean the persons who were respectively the original tenant and the first successor at the time of the succession, and accordingly—

(a) if the successor was the first successor, and, immediately before his death he was still the tenant (whether protected or statutory), paragraph 6 . . . above shall apply on his death,

(b) if the successor was not the first successor, no person shall become a statutory tenant on his death by virtue of this Part of this Schedule.

(2) Sub-paragraph (1) above applies—

(a) even if a successor enters into more than one other tenancy of the dwelling-house, and
(b) even if both the first successor and the successor on his death enter into other tenancies of the dwelling-house.

(3) In this paragraph ''succession'' means the occasion on which a person becomes the statutory tenant of a dwelling-house by virtue of this Part of this Schedule and ''successor'' shall be construed accordingly.

(4) This paragraph shall apply as respects a succession which took place before August 27, 1972 if, and only if, the tenancy granted after the succession, or the first of those tenancies, was granted on or after that date, and where it does not apply as respects a succession, no account should be taken of that succession in applying this paragraph as respects any later succession.

Annotation

The deletion in paragraph 10(1)(a) was made by Act of 1988, s.39(3), Sched. 4, para. 8.

11.—(1) Paragraphs 5 to 8 above do not apply where—

(a) the tenancy of the original tenant was granted on or after the operative date within the meaning of the Rent (Agriculture) Act 1976, and
(b) both that tenancy and the statutory tenancy of the first successor were tenancies to which section 99 of this Act applies.

(2) If the tenants under both of the tenancies falling within sub-paragraph (1)(b) above were persons to whom paragraph 7 of Schedule 9 to the Rent (Agriculture) Act 1976 applies, the reference in sub-paragraph (1)(a) above to the operative date shall be taken as a reference to the date of operation for forestry workers within the meaning of that Act.

[11A. In this Part of this Schedule ''the operative date'' means the date on which Part I of the Housing Act 1988 came into force.]

Annotation

Paragraph 11A was inserted by Act of 1988, s.39(3), Sched. 4, para. 9. Part I of the Housing Act 1988 came into force on January 15, 1989.

A2–005 # Protection from Eviction Act 1977

(1977 c.43)

[Printed as amended]

An Act to consolidate section 16 of the Rent Act 1957 and Part III of the Rent Act 1965, and related enactments.

[29th July 1977]

PART I

UNLAWFUL EVICTION AND HARASSMENT

Unlawful eviction and harassment of occupier

A2–006 **1.**—(1) In this section "residential occupier", in relation to any premises, means a person occupying the premises as a residence, whether under a contract or by virtue of any enactment or rule of law giving him the right to remain in occupation or restricting the right of any other person to recover possession of the premises.

(2) If any person unlawfully deprives the residential occupier of any premises of his occupation of the premises or any part thereof, or attempts to do so, he shall be guilty of an offence unless he proves that he believed, and had reasonable cause to believe, that the residential occupier had ceased to reside in the premises.

(3) If any person with intent to cause the residential occupier of any premises—

(a) to give up the occupation of the premises or any part thereof; of
(b) to refrain from exercising any right or pursuing any remedy in respect of the premises or part thereof;

does acts [likely] to interfere with the peace or comfort of the residential occupier or members of his household, or persistently withdraws or withholds services reasonably required for the occupation of the premises as a residence, he shall be guilty of an offence.

ANNOTATION

In subs. (3), Act of 1988, ss.29(1), 141(2) substituted "likely" for "calculated", with respect to acts done on or after January 15, 1989.

[(3A) Subject to subsection (3B) below, the landlord of a residential occupier or an agent of the landlord shall be guilty of an offence if—

(a) he does acts likely to interfere with the peace or comfort of the residential occupier or members of his household, or
(b) he persistently withdraws or withholds services reasonably required for the occupation of the premises in question as a residence,

and (in either case) he knows, or has reasonable cause to believe, that that conduct is likely to cause the residential occupier to give up the occupation of the whole or part of the premises or to refrain from exercising any right or pursuing any remedy in respect of the whole or part of the premises.

(3B) A person shall not be guilty of an offence under subsection (3A) above if he proves that he had reasonable grounds for doing the acts or withdrawing or withholding the services in question.

(3C) In subsection (3A) above "landlord", in relation to a residential occupier of any premises, means the person who, but for—

(a) the residential occupier's right to remain in occupation of the premises, or
(b) a restriction on the person's right to recover possession of the premises,

would be entitled to occupation of the premises and any superior landlord under whom that person derives title.]

ANNOTATION

Subs. (3A), (3B) and (3C) were inserted by Act of 1988, s.29(2).

(4) A person guilty of an offence under this section shall be liable—

(a) on summary conviction, to a fine not exceeding [the prescribed sum] or to imprisonment for a term not exceeding six months or to both;
(b) on conviction on indictment, to a fine or to imprisonment for a term not exceeding two years or to both.

ANNOTATION

In subs. (4)(a) the words in square brackets were substituted for "£400" by Magistrates' Courts Act 1980, ss.32(2)(a), 143. By S.I. 1984 No. 447, the current prescribed sum is £2,000.

(5) Nothing in this section shall be taken to prejudice any liability or remedy to which a person guilty of an offence thereunder may be subject in civil proceedings.

(6) Where an offence under this section committed by a body corporate is proved to have been committed with the consent or connivance of, or to be

attributable to any neglect on the part of, any director, manager or secretary or other similar officer of the body corporate or any person who was purporting to act in any such capacity, he as well as the body corporate shall be guilty of that offence and shall be liable to be proceeded against and punished accordingly.

Restriction on re-entry without due process of law

A2–007 **2.** Where any premises are let as a dwelling on a lease which is subject to a right of re-entry or forfeiture it shall not be lawful to enforce that right otherwise than by proceedings in the court while any person is lawfully residing in the premises or part of them.

Prohibition of eviction without due process of law

A2–008 **3.**—(1) Where any premises have been let as a dwelling under a tenancy which is [neither a statutorily protected tenancy nor an excluded tenancy] and—

(a) the tenancy (in this section referred to as the former tenancy) has come to an end, but
(b) the occupier continues to reside in the premises or part of them,

it shall not be lawful for the owner to enforce against the occupier, otherwise than by proceedings in the court, his right to recover possession of the premises.

ANNOTATION

In subs. (1), the words in square brackets were substituted for ''not a statutorily protected tenant'' by Act of 1988, s.30(1).

(2) In this section ''the occupier'', in relation to any premises, means any person lawfully residing in the premises or part of them at the termination of the former tenancy.

[(2A) Subsections (1) and (2) above apply in relation to any restricted contract (within the meaning of the Rent Act 1977) which—

(a) creates a licence; and
(b) is entered into after the commencement of section 69 of the Housing Act 1980;

as they apply in relation to a restricted contract which creates a tenancy.]

ANNOTATION

Subs. (2A) was inserted by Housing Act 1980, s.69(1) with effect from November 28, 1980; S.I. 1980 No. 1706.

[(2B) Subsections (1) and (2) above apply in relation to any premises occupied as a dwelling under a licence, other than an excluded licence, as they apply in relation to premises let as a dwelling under a tenancy, and in those subsections the expressions "let" and "tenancy" shall be construed accordingly.

(2C) References in the preceding provisions of this section and section 4(2A) below to an excluded tenancy do not apply to—

(a) a tenancy entered into before the date on which the Housing Act 1988 came into force, or
(b) a tenancy entered into on or after that date but pursuant to a contract made before that date,

but, subject to that, "excluded tenancy" and "excluded licence" shall be construed in accordance with section 3A below.]

ANNOTATION

Subss. (2B) and (2C) were inserted by Act of 1988, s.30(2).

(3) This section shall, with the necessary modifications, apply where the owner's right to recover possession arises on the death of the tenant under a statutory tenancy within the meaning of the Rent Act 1977 or the Rent (Agriculture) Act 1976.

[Excluded tenancies and licences

3A.—(1) Any reference in this Act to an excluded tenancy or an excluded licence is a reference to a tenancy or licence which is excluded by virtue of any of the following provisions of this section. **A2–009**

(2) A tenancy or licence is excluded if—

(a) under its terms the occupier shares any accommodation with the landlord or licensor; and
(b) immediately before the tenancy or licence was granted and also at the time it comes to an end, the landlord or licensor occupied as his only or principal home premises of which the whole or part of the shared accommodation formed part.

(3) A tenancy or licence is also excluded if—

(a) under its terms the occupier shares any accommodation with a member of the family of the landlord or licensor;
(b) immediately before the tenancy or licence was granted and also at the time it comes to an end, the member of the family of the landlord or licensor occupied as his only or principal home premises of which the whole or part of the shared accommodation formed part; and
(c) immediately before the tenancy or licence was granted and also at the time it comes to an end, the landlord or licensor occupied as his only or principal home premises in the same building as the shared accommodation and that building is not a purpose-built block of flats.

(4) For the purposes of subsections (2) and (3) above, an occupier shares accommodation with another person if he has the use of it in common with that person (whether or not also in common with others) and any reference in those subsections to shared accommodation shall be construed accordingly, and if, in relation to any tenancy or licence, there is at any time more than one person who is the landlord or licensor, any reference in those subsections to the landlord or licensor shall be construed as a reference to any one of those persons.

(5) In subsections (2) to (4) above—

(a) "accommodation" includes neither an area used for storage nor a staircase, passage, corridor or other means of access;
(b) "occupier" means, in relation to a tenancy, the tenant and, in relation to a licence, the licensee; and
(c) "purpose-built block of flats" has the same meaning as in Part III of Schedule 1 to the Housing Act 1988;

and section 113 of the Housing Act 1985 shall apply to determine whether a person is for the purposes of subsection (3) above a member of another's family as it applies for the purposes of Part IV of that Act.

(6) A tenancy or licence is excluded if it was granted as a temporary expedient to a person who entered the premises in question or any other premises as a trespasser (whether or not, before the beginning of that tenancy or licence, another tenancy or licence to occupy the premises or any other premises had been granted to him).

(7) A tenancy or licence is excluded if—

(a) it confers on the tenant or licensee the right to occupy the premises for a holiday only; or
(b) it is granted otherwise than for money or money's worth.

(8) A licence is excluded if it confers rights of occupation in a hostel, within the meaning of the Housing Act 1985, which is provided by—

(a) the council of a county, [county borough] district or London Borough, the Common Council of the City of London, the Council of the Isles of Scilly, the Inner London Education Authority, a joint authority within the meaning of the Local Government Act 1985 or a residuary body within the meaning of that Act;
(b) a development corporation within the meaning of the New Towns Act 1981;
(c) the Commission for the New Towns;
(d) an urban development corporation established by an order under section 135 of the Local Government, Planning and Land Act 1980;
(e) a housing action trust established under Part III of the Housing Act 1988;
(f) *the Development Board for Rural Wales*
(g) the Housing Corporation *or Housing for Wales*;

[(ga) the Secretary of State under Section 89 of the Housing Associations Act 1985;]

[(h) a housing trust (within the meaning of the Housing Associations Act 1985) which is a charity or a registered social landlord (within the meaning of the Housing Act 1985); or]

(i) any other person who is, or who belongs to a class of person which is, specified in an order made by the Secretary of State.

ANNOTATION

Section 3A was inserted by Act of 1988, s.31.

The words in square brackets in subsection (8)(a) were inserted on April 1, 1996 by Local Government (Wales) Act 1994, s.22(2), 66(3), Sched. 8, para. 4(1): S.I. 1996 No. 396.

Subsection (8)(h) was substituted for the words ''a housing trust which is a charity or a registered housing association, within the meaning of the Housing Associations Act 1985'' on October 1, 1996 by Housing Act 1996 (Consequential Provisions) Order 1996 (S.I. 1996 No. 2325), art. 5(1), Sched. 2, para. 7.

Subsection 8(f) was repealed on October 1, 1998 by Government of Wales Act 1998, ss.152, 158(1), Sched. 18, Pt. IV: S.I. 1998 No. 2244.

The words in subsection 8(g) were omitted and subsection 8(ga) was inserted by Government of Wales Act 1998, ss.140(1), 152, 158(1), Scheds. 16 (para. 2), 18, Pt. VI, with effect from November 1, 1998.

Special provisions for agricultural employees

4.—(1) This section shall apply where the tenant under the former tenancy (within the meaning of section 3 of this Act) occupied the premises under the terms of his employment as a person employed in agriculture, as defined in section 1 of the Rent (Agriculture) Act 1976, but is not a statutory tenant as defined in that Act. **A2–010**

(2) In this section ''the occupier'', in relation to any premises, means—

(a) the tenant under the former tenancy; or

(b) the widow or widower of the tenant under the former tenancy residing with him at his death or, if the former tenant leaves no such widow or widower, any member of his family residing with him at his death.

[(2A) In accordance with section 3(2B) above, any reference in subsections (1) and (2) above to the tenant under the former tenancy includes a reference to the licensee under a licence (other than an excluded licence) which has come to an end (being a licence to occupy premises as a dwelling); and in the following provisions of this section the expressions ''tenancy'' and ''rent'' and any other expressions referable to a tenancy shall be construed accordingly.]

ANNOTATION

Subs. (2A) was inserted by Act of 1988, s.30(3).

(3) Without prejudice to any power of the court apart from this section to postpone the operation or suspend the execution of an order for possession, if in proceedings by the owner against the occupier the court makes an order for

the possession of the premises the court may suspend the execution of the order on such terms and conditions, including conditions as to the payment by the occupier of arrears of rent, mesne profits and otherwise as the court thinks reasonable.

(4) Where the order for possession is made within the period of 6 months beginning with the date when the former tenancy came to an end, then, without prejudice to any powers of the court under the preceding provisions of this section or apart from this section to postpone the operation or suspend the execution of the order for a longer period, the court shall suspend the execution of the order for the remainder of the said period of 6 months unless the court—

(a) is satisfied either—

(i) that other suitable accommodation is, or will within that period be made, available to the occupier; or

(ii) that the efficient management of any agricultural land or the efficient carrying on of any agricultural operations would be seriously prejudiced unless the premises are available for occupation by a person employed or to be employed by the owner; or

(iii) that greater hardship (being hardship in respect of matters other than the carrying on of such a business as aforesaid) would be caused by the suspension of the order until the end of that period than by its execution within that period; or

(iv) that the occupier, or any person residing or lodging with the occupier, has been causing damage to the premises or has been guilty of conduct which is a nuisance or annoyance to persons occupying other premises; and

(b) considers that it would be reasonable not to suspend the execution of the order for the remainder of that period.

(5) Where the court suspends the execution of an order for possession under subsection (4) above it shall do so on such terms and conditions, including conditions as to the payment by the occupier of arrears of rent, mesne profits and otherwise as the court thinks reasonable.

(6) A decision of the court not to suspend the execution of the order under subsection (4) above shall not prejudice any other power of the court to postpone the operation or suspend the execution of the order for the whole or part of the period of 6 months mentioned in that subsection.

(7) Where the court has, under the preceding provisions of this section, suspended the execution of an order for possession, it may from time to time vary the period of suspension or terminate it and may vary any terms or conditions imposed by virtue of this section.

(8) In considering whether or how to exercise its powers under subsection (3) above, the court shall have regard to all the circumstances and, in particular, to—

(a) whether other suitable accommodation is or can be made available to the occupier;

(b) whether the efficient management of any agricultural land or the efficient carrying on of any agricultural operations would be seriously prejudiced unless the premises were available for occupation by a person employed or to be employed by the owner; and

(c) whether greater hardship would be caused by the suspension of the execution of the order than by its execution without suspension or further suspension.

(9) Where in proceedings for the recovery of possession of the premises the court makes an order for possession but suspends the execution of the order under this section, it shall make no order for costs, unless it appears to the court, having regard to the conduct of the owner or of the occupier, that there are special reasons for making such an order.

(10) Where, in the case of an order for possession of the premises to which subsection (4) above applies, the execution of the order is not suspended under that subsection or, the execution of the order having been so suspended, the suspension is terminated, then, if it is subsequently made to appear to the court that the failure to suspend the execution of the order or, as the case may be, the termination of the suspension was—

(a) attributable to the provisions of paragraph (a)(ii) of subsection (4), and

(b) due to misrepresentation or concealment of material facts by the owner of the premises,

the court may order the owner to pay to the occupier such sum as appears sufficient as compensation for damage or loss sustained by the occupier as a result of that failure or termination.

PART II

NOTICE TO QUIT

Validity of notices to quit

5.—(1) [Subject to subsection (1B) below] no notice by a landlord or a tenant to quit any premises let (whether before or after the commencement of this Act) as a dwelling shall be valid unless— **A2–011**

(a) it is in writing and contains such information as may be prescribed, and

(b) it is given not less than 4 weeks before the date on which it is to take effect.

ANNOTATION

The words in square brackets in subs. (1) were inserted by Act of 1988, s.32(1).

[(1A) Subject to subsection (1B) below, no notice by a licensor or a licensee to determine a periodic licence to occupy premises as a dwelling (whether the licence was granted before or after the passing of this Act) shall be valid unless—

(a) it is in writing and contains such information as may be prescribed, and
(b) it is given not less than 4 weeks before the date on which it is to take effect.

(1B) Nothing in subsection (1) or subsection (1A) above applies to—

(a) premises let on an excluded tenancy which is entered into on or after the date on which the Housing Act 1988 came into force unless it is entered into pursuant to a contract made before that date; or
(b) premises occupied under an excluded licence.]

ANNOTATION

Subss. (1A) and (1B) were inserted by Act of 1988, s.32(2).

(2) In this section ''prescribed'' means prescribed by regulations made by the Secretary of State by statutory instrument, and a statutory instrument containing any such regulations shall be subject to annulment in pursuance of a resolution of either House of Parliament.

(3) Regulations under this section may make different provision in relation to different descriptions of lettings and different circumstances.

PART III

SUPPLEMENTAL PROVISIONS

Prosecution of offences

A2–012 **6.**—Proceedings for an offence under this Act may be instituted by any of the following authorities:—

(a) councils of districts and London boroughs;
[(aa) councils of Welsh counties and county boroughs;]
(b) the Common Council of the City of London;
(c) the Council of the Isles of Scilly.

Annotation

Para. (aa) was inserted on April 1, 1996 by Local Government (Wales) Act 1994, ss.22(2), 66(3), Sched. 8, para. 4(2).

Service of notices

7.—(1) If for the purpose of any proceedings (whether civil or criminal) brought or intended to be brought under this Act, any person serves upon— **A2–013**

(a) any agent of the landlord named as such in the rent book or other similar document, or
(b) the person who receives the rent of the dwelling,

a notice in writing requiring the agent or other person to disclose to him the full name and place of abode or place of business of the landlord, that agent or other person shall forthwith comply with the notice.

(2) If any such agent or other person as is referred to in subsection (1) above fails or refuses forthwith to comply with a notice served on him under that subsection, he shall be liable on summary conviction to a fine not exceeding [level 4 on the standard scale], unless he shows to the satisfaction of the court that he did not know, and could not with reasonable diligence have ascertained, such of the facts required by the notice to be disclosed as were not disclosed by him.

Annotation

In subs. (2) the words in square brackets were substituted for ''£5'' by Criminal Justice Act 1982, s.39(2), Sched. 3. By Criminal Justice Act 1991, s.17(1), the current maximum fine for level 4 is £2,500.

(3) In this section ''landlord'' includes—

(a) any person from time to time deriving title under the original landlord,
(b) in relation to any dwelling-house, any person other than the tenant who is or, but for Part VII of the Rent Act 1977 would be, entitled to possession of the dwelling-house, and
(c) any person who [. . .] grants to another the right to occupy the dwelling in question as a residence and any person directly or indirectly derivin title from the grantor.

Annotation

In subs. (3)(c), the words ''under a restricted contract (within the meaning of the Rent Act 1977)'' were deleted by Act of 1988, Sched. 17, para. 26, Sched. 18.

Interpretation

8.—(1) In this Act ''statutorily protected tenancy'' means— **A2–014**

(a) a protected tenancy within the meaning of the Rent Act 1977 or a tenancy to which Part I of the Landlord and Tenant Act 1954 applies;

(b) a protected occupancy or statutory tenancy as defined in the Rent (Agriculture) Act 1976;

(c) a tenancy to which Part II of the Landlord and Tenant Act 1954 applies;

(d) a tenancy of an agricultural holding within the meaning of the [Agricultural Holdings Act 1986] [which is a tenancy in relation to which that Act applies].

[(e) an assured tenancy or assured agricultural occupancy under Part I of the Housing Act 1988.]

[(f) a tenancy to which Schedule 10 to the Local Government and Housing Act 1989 applies.]

[(g) a farm business tenancy within the meaning of the Agricultural Tenancies Act 1995].

ANNOTATION

In subs. (1)(d) the reference to the Agricultural Holdings Act 1986 in the first set of square brackets was substituted for a reference to the Agricultural Holdings Act 1948 by the 1986 Act, s.100, Sched. 14, para. 61, and the words in the second set of square brackets were inserted by Agricultural Tenancies Act 1995, s.40, Sched., para. 29. Subs. (1)(e) was inserted by Act of 1988, s.33(2). Subs. (1)(f) was added by Local Government and Housing Act 1989, ss.194(1), 195(2), Sched. 11, para. 54: S.I. 1990 No. 431. Subs. (1)(g) was added by Agricultural Tenancies Act 1995, s.40, Sched., para. 29.

(2) For the purposes of Part I of this Act a person who, under the terms of his employment, had exclusive possession of any premises other than as a tenant shall be deemed to have been a tenant and the expression ''let'' and ''tenancy'' shall be construed accordingly.

(3) In Part I of this Act ''the owner'', in relation to any premises, means the person who, as against the occupier, is entitled to possession thereof.

[(4) In this Act ''excluded tenancy'' and ''excluded licence'' have the meaning assigned by section 3A of this Act.

(5) If, on or after the date on which the Housing Act 1988 came into force, the terms of an excluded tenancy or excluded licence entered into before that date are varied, then—

(a) if the variation affects the amount of the rent which is payable under the tenancy or licence, the tenancy or licence shall be treated for the purposes of sections 3(2C) and 5(1B) above as a new tenancy or licence entered into at the time of the variation; and

(b) if the variation does not affect the amount of the rent which is so payable, nothing in this Act shall affect the determination of the question whether the variation is such as to give rise to a new tenancy or licence.

(6) Any reference in subsection (5) above to a variation affecting the amount of the rent which is payable under a tenancy or licence does not include a reference to—

(a) a reduction or increase effected under Part III or Part VI of the Rent Act 1977 (rents under regulated tenancies and housing association tenancies), section 78 of that Act (power of rent tribunal in relation to restricted contracts) or sections 11 to 14 of the Rent (Agriculture) Act 1976; or

(b) a variation which is made by the parties and has the effect of making the rent expressed to be payable under the tenancy or licence the same as a rent for the dwelling which is entered in the register under Part IV or section 79 of the Rent Act 1977.]

Annotation

Subss. (4), (5) and (6) were inserted by Act of 1988, s.33(3).

The court for purposes of Part I

9.—(1) The court for the purposes of Part I of this Act shall, subject to this section, be— **A2–015**

(a) the county court, in relation to premises with respect to which the county court has for the time being jurisdiction in actions for the recovery of land; and
(b) the High Court, in relation to other premises.

(2) Any powers of a county court in proceedings for the recovery of possession of any premises in the circumstances mentioned in section 3(1) of this Act may be exercised with the leave of the judge by any registrar of the court, except in so far as rules of court otherwise provide.

(3) Nothing in this Act shall affect the jurisdiction of the High Court in proceedings to enforce a lessor's right of re-entry or forfeiture or to enforce a mortgagee's right of possession in a case where the former tenancy was not binding on the mortgagee.

(4) Nothing in this Act shall affect the operation of—

(a) section 59 of the Pluralities Act 1838;
(b) section 19 of the Defence Act 1842;
(c) section 6 of the Lecturers and Parish Clerks Act 1844;
(d) paragraph 3 of Schedule 1 to the Sexual Offences Act 1956; or
(e) section 13 of the Compulsory Purchase Act 1965.

Application to Crown

10. In so far as this Act requires the taking of proceedings in the court for the recovery of possession or confers any powers on the court it shall (except in the case of section 4(10)) be binding on the Crown. **A2–016**

Application to Isles of Scilly

11.—(1) In its application to the Isles of Scilly, this Act (except in the case of section 5) shall have effect subject to such exceptions, adaptations and modifications as the Secretary of State may by order direct. **A2–017**

(2) The power to make an order under this section shall be exercisable by statutory instrument which shall be subject to annulment, in pursuance of a resolution of either House of Parliament.

(3) An order under this section may be varied or revoked by a subsequent order.

Consequential amendments, etc.

A2–018 **12.**—(1) Schedule 1 to this Act contains amendments consequential on the provisions of this Act.

(2) Schedule 2 to this Act contains transitional provisions and savings.

(3) The enactments mentioned in Schedule 3 to this Act are hereby repealed to the extent specified in the third column of that Schedule.

(4) The inclusion in this Act of any express saving, transitional provision or amendment shall not be taken to affect the operation in relation to this Act of section 38 of the Interpretation Act 1889 (which relates to the effect of repeals).

ANNOTATION

For Interpretation Act 1889, s.3, read Interpretation Act 1978, ss.16(1), 17(2), Sched. 2, para. 3: Interpretation Act 1978, s.25(2).

Short title, etc.

A2–019 **13.**—(1) This Act may be cited as the Protection from Eviction Act 1977.

(2) This Act shall come into force on the expiry of the period of one month beginning with the date on which it is passed.

(3) This Act does not extend to Scotland or Northern Ireland.

(4) References in this Act to any enactment are references to that enactment as amended, and include references thereto as applied by any other enactment including, except where the context otherwise requires, this Act.

SCHEDULES

Section 12 SCHEDULE 1

A2–020 CONSEQUENTIAL AMENDMENTS

Reserve and Auxiliary Forces (Protection of Civil Interests) Act 1951 (c.65)

1. In section 22(1) of the Reserve and Auxiliary Forces (Protection of Civil Interests) Act 1951, for "Part III of the Rent Act 1965" substitute "Part I of the Protection from Eviction Act 1977".

County Courts Act 1959 (c.22)

[. . . . .]

ANNOTATION

Para. 2 was repealed by County Courts Act 1984, s.148(3), Sched. 4 and replaced by s.66(1) of that Act.

Caravan Sites Act 1968 (c.52)

3. In section 5(5) of the Caravan Sites Act 1968 (provision of Part III of the Rent Act 1965 relating to protection against eviction etc. not to apply to caravans on protected sites) for the words "Part III of the Rent Act 1965" substitute "the Protection from Eviction Act 1977".

Rent (Agriculture) Act 1976 (c.80)

4. In Schedule 5 to the Rent (Agriculture) Act 1976, in paragraph 10(2) for "section 16 of the Rent Act 1957" substitute "section 5 of the Protection from Eviction Act 1977".

Section 12

SCHEDULE 2

Transitional Provisions and Savings A2–021

1.—(1) In so far as anything done under an enactment repealed by this Act could have been done under a corresponding provision of this Act, it shall not be invalidated by the repeal but shall have effect as if done under that provision.

(2) Sub-paragraph (1) above applies, in particular, to any regulation, rule, notice, or order.

2. The enactments mentioned in Schedule 6 to the Rent Act 1965 shall, notwithstanding the repeal of that Act by this Act, continue to have effect as they had effect immediately before the commencement of this Act.

SCHEDULE 3

Section 12

Repeals

Chapter	Short Title	Extent of Repeal
5 & 6 Eliz. 2. c.25	The Rent Act 1957	Section 16.
1965 c.75	The Rent Act 1965	The whole Act, so far as unrepealed.
1968 c.23	The Rent Act 1968	In section 108(2), the words "or under Part III of the Rent Act 1965." In section 109(3), the words "or Part III of the Rent Act 1965 (protection against harassment)". In Schedule 15, the entries relating to sections 32 and 34 of the Rent Act 1965.
1970 c.40	The Agriculture Act 1970	Section 99
1972 c.47	The Housing Finance Act 1972	In Schedule 9, paragraph 12(2) and in paragraph 12(3) the words "or to Part III of the Rent Act 1965".
1972 c.71	The Criminal Justice Act 1972	Section 30
1974 c.44	The Housing Act 1974	Section 123
1976 c.80	The Rent (Agriculture) Act 1976	In Schedule 8, paragraphs 13, 14 and 15.

A2–022

County Courts Act 1984

(1984 c.28)

An Act to consolidate certain enactments relating to county courts

[26 June 1984]

PART II

JURISDICTION AND TRANSFER OF PROCEEDINGS

Actions of contract and tort

A2–023 **General jurisdiction in actions of contract and tort**

15.—(1) Subject to subsection (2), a county court shall have jurisdiction to hear and determine any action founded on contract or tort [. . . .]

(2) A county court shall not, except as in this Act provided, have jurisdiction to hear and determine—

(a) [. . . .]
(b) any action in which the title to [. . .] any toll, fair, market or franchise is in question; or
(c) any action for libel or slander.

(3) [. . .]

ANNOTATION

The words omitted from subs. (1), (2) and the whole of subs. (3) were repealed by the High Court and County Courts Jurisdiction Order 1991 (S.I. 1991, No. 724), art. 2(8), Sched.

[. . . . .]

Recovery of land and cases where title in question

Actions for recovery of land and actions where title is in question

21.—(1) A county court shall have jurisdiction to hear and determine any action for the recovery of land . . . **A2–024**

(2) A county court shall have jurisdiction to hear and determine any action in which the title to any hereditament comes in question . . .

(3) Where a mortgage of land consists of or includes a dwelling-house and no part of the land is situated in Greater London then, subject to subsection (4), if a county court has jurisdiction by virtue of this section to hear and determine an action in which the mortgagee under that mortgage claims possession of the mortgaged property, no court other than a county court shall have jurisdiction to hear and determine that action.

(4) Subsection (3) shall not apply to an action for foreclosure or sale in which a claim for possession of the mortgaged property is also made.

(5), (6) . . .

(7) In this section—

"dwelling-house" includes any building or part of a building which is used as a dwelling;

"mortgage" includes a charge and "mortgagor" and "mortgagee" shall be construed accordingly;

"mortgagor" and "mortgagee" includes any person deriving title under the original mortgagor or mortgagee.

(8) The fact that part of the premises comprised in a dwelling-house is used as a shop or office or for business, trade or professional purposes shall not prevent the dwelling-house from being a dwelling-house for the purposes of this section.

(9) This section does not apply to a mortgage securing an agreement which is a regulated agreement within the meaning of the Consumer Credit Act 1974.

ANNOTATION

The words omitted from subsections (1) and (2) and the whole of subsections (5) and (6) were repealed by the High Court and County Courts Jurisdiction Order 1991 (S.I. 1991, No. 724), art. 2(8), Sched.

[. . . . .]

Exercise of jurisdiction and ancillary jurisdiction

[. . . . .]

Remedies available in county courts

[38.—(1) Subject to what follows, in any proceedings in a county court the court may make any order which could be made by the High Court if the proceedings were in the High Court. **A2–025**

(2) Any order made by a county court may be—

(a) absolute or conditional;
(b) final or interlocutory.

(3) A county court shall not have power—

(a) to order mandamus, certiorari or prohibition; or
(b) to make any order of a prescribed kind.

(4) Regulations under subsection (3)—

(a) may provide for any of their provisions not to apply in such circumstances or descriptions of case as may be specified in the regulations;
(b) may provide for the transfer of the proceedings to the High Court for the purpose of enabling an order of a kind prescribed under subsection (3) to be made;
(c) may make such provision with respect to matters of procedure as the Lord Chancellor considers expedient; and
(d) may make provision amending or repealing any provision made by or under any enactment, so far as may be necessary or expedient in consequence of the regulations.

(5) In this section ''prescribed'' means prescribed by regulations made by the Lord Chancellor under this section.

(6) The power to make regulations under this section shall be exercised by statutory instrument.

(7) No such statutory instrument shall be made unless a draft of the instrument has been approved by both Houses of Parliament.]

Annotation

Section substituted by Courts and Legal Services Act 1990, s.3, with effect from July 1, 1991: S.I. 1991 No. 1364.

Transfer of proceedings

[Transfer of proceedings to county court

A2–026 **40.**—(1) Where the High Court is satisfied that any proceedings before it are required by any provision of a kind mentioned in subsection (8) to be in a county court it shall—

(a) order the transfer of the proceedings to a county court; or
(b) if the court is satisfied that the person bringing the proceedings knew, or ought to have known, of that requirement, order that they be struck out.

(2) Subject to any such provision, the High Court may order the transfer of any proceedings before it to a county court.

(3) An order under this section may be made either on the motion of the High Court itself or on the application of any party to the proceedings.

(4) Proceedings transferred under this section shall be transferred to such county court as the High Court considers appropriate, having taken into account the convenience of the parties and that of any other persons likely to be affected and the state of business in the courts concerned.

(5) The transfer of any proceedings under this section shall not affect any right of appeal from the order directing the transfer.

(6) Where proceedings for the enforcement of any judgment or order of the High Court are transferred under this section—

(a) the judgment or order may be enforced as if it were a judgment or order of a county court; and
(b) subject to subsection (7), it shall be treated as a judgment or order of that court for all purposes.

(7) Where proceedings for the enforcement of any judgment or order of the High Court are transferred under this section—

(a) the powers of any court to set aside, correct, vary or quash a judgment or order of the High Court, and the enactments relating to appeals from such a judgment or order, shall continue to apply; and
(b) the powers of any court to set aside, correct, vary or quash a judgment or order of a county court, and the enactments relating to appeals from such a judgment or order, shall not apply.

(8) The provisions referred to in subsection (1) are any made—

(a) under section 1 of the Courts and Legal Services Act 1990; or
(b) by or under any other enactment.

(9) This section does not apply to family proceedings within the meaning of Part V of the Matrimonial and Family Proceedings Act 1984.]

ANNOTATION

Section substituted by Courts and Legal Services Act 1990, s.2(1), with effect from July 1, 1991: S.I. 1991 No. 1364.

Transfer to High Court by Order of High Court

41.—(1) If at any stage in proceedings commenced in a county court or transferred to a county court under section 40, the High Court thinks it desirable that the proceedings, or any part of them, should be heard and determined in the High Court, it may order the transfer to the High Court of the proceedings or, as the case may be, of that part of them. **A2–027**

(2) The power conferred by subsection (1) is without prejudice to section 29 of the Supreme Court Act 1981 (power of High Court to issue prerogative orders) [but shall be exercised in relation to family proceedings (within the meaning of Part V of the Matrimonial and Family Proceedings Act 1984) in accordance with any directions given under section 37 of that Act (directions as to distribution and transfer of family business and proceedings)].

[(3) The power conferred by subsection (1) shall be exercised subject to any provision made—

(a) under section 1 of the Courts and Legal Services Act 1990; or
(b) by or under any other enactment.]

ANNOTATION

The words in square brackets in subs. (2) were added by Matrimonial and Family Proceedings Act 1984, s.46(1), Sched. 1, para. 30. Subs. (3) was added by Courts and Legal Services Act 1990, s.2(2) with effect from July 1, 1991: S.I. 1991 No. 1364.

[Transfer to High Court by Order of a County Court

A2–028 **42.**—(1) Where a county court is satisfied that any proceedings before it are required by any provision of a kind mentioned in subsection (7) to be in the High court, it shall—

(a) order the transfer of the proceedings to the High Court; or
(b) if the court is satisfied that the person bringing the proceedings knew, or ought to have known, of that requirement, order that they be struck out.

(2) Subject to any such provision, a county court may order the transfer of any proceedings before it to the High Court.

(3) An order under this section may be made either on the motion of the court itself or on the application of any party to the proceedings.

(4) The transfer of any proceedings under this section shall not affect any right of appeal from the order directing the transfer.

(5) Where proceedings for the enforcement of any judgment or order of a county court are transferred under this section—

(a) the judgment or order may be enforced as if it were a judgment or order of the High Court; and
(b) subject to subsection (6), it shall be treated as a judgment or order of that court for all purposes.

(6) Where proceedings for the enforcement of any judgment or order of a county court are transferred under this section—

(a) the powers of any court to set aside, correct, vary or quash a judgment or order of a county court, and the enactments relating to appeals from such a judgment or order, shall continue to apply; and

(b) the powers of any court to set aside, correct, vary or quash a judgment or order of the High Court, and the enactments relating to appeals from such a judgment or order, shall apply.

(7) The provisions referred to in subsection (1) are any made—

(a) under section 1 of the Courts and Legal Services Act 1990; or
(b) by or under any other enactment.

(8) This section does not apply to family proceedings within the meaning of Part V of the Matrimonial and Family Proceedings Act 1984.]

ANNOTATION

Section substituted by Courts and Legal Services Act 1990, s.2(3), with effect from July 1, 1991; S.I. 1991 No. 1364..

[. . . . .]

PART IV

APPEALS ETC

Appeals

Appeals: general provisions

77.—(1) Subject to the provisions of this section and the following provisions of this Part of this Act, if any party to any proceedings in a county court is dissatisfied with the determination of the judge or jury, he may appeal from it to the Court of Appeal in such manner and subject to such conditions as may be provided by [Civil Procedure Rules]. **A2–029**

[(1A) Without prejudice to the generality of the power to make county court rules under section 75, such rules may make provision for any appeal from the exercise by a district judge, assistant district judge or deputy district judge of any power given to him by virtue of any enactment to be to a judge of a county court.]

(2) The Lord Chancellor may by order prescribe classes of proceedings in which there is to be no right of appeal under this section without the leave either of the judge of the county court or of the Court of Appeal.

(3) An order under subsection (2)—

(a) may classify proceedings according to the nature of those proceedings;
(b) may classify proceedings according to the amount or value or annual value of the money or other property which is the subject of those

proceedings or according to whether that amount or value or annual value exceeds a specified fraction of the relevant county court limit;
(c) may provide that the order shall not apply to determinations made before such date as may be specified in the order; and
(d) may make different provision for different classes of proceedings.

(4) The power to make an order under subsection (2) shall be exercisable by statutory instrument subject to annulment in pursuance of a resolution of either House of Parliament.

(5) Subject to the provisions of this section and the following provisions of this Part of this Act, where an appeal is brought under subsection (1) in any action, an appeal may be brought under that subsection in respect of any claim or counterclaim in the action notwithstanding that there could have been no such appeal if that claim had been the subject of a separate action.

(6) In proceedings in which either the plaintiff or the defendant is claiming possession of any premises this section shall not confer any right of appeal on any question of fact if by virtue of—

(a) section 13(4) of the Landlord and Tenant Act 1954; or
(b) Cases III to IX in Schedule 4 to the Rent (Agriculture) Act 1976; or
(c) section 98 of the Rent Act 1977, as it applies to Cases 1 to 6 and 8 and 9 in Schedule 15 to that Act, or that section is extended or applied by any other enactment; or
(d) section 99 of the Rent Act 1977, as it applies to Cases 1 to 6 and 9 in Schedule 15 to that Act; or
(e) [section 84(2)(a) of the Housing Act 1985]; or
[(ee) section 7 of the Housing Act 1988, as it applies to the grounds in Part II of Schedule 2 to that Act; or]
(f) any other enactment,

the court can only grant possession on being satisfied that it is reasonable to do so.

(7) This section shall not—

(a) confer any right of appeal from any judgment or oder where a right of appeal is conferred by some other enactment; or
(b) take away any right of appeal from any judgment or order where a right of appeal is so conferred,

and shall have effect subject to any enactment other than this Act.

(8) In this section—

"enactment" means an enactment whenever passed; and

"the relevant county court limit" means, in relation to proceedings of any description, the sum by reference to which the question whether a county court has jurisdiction to hear and determine the proceedings falls to be decided.

ANNOTATION

The words in subs. (1) were substituted by Civil Procedure Act 1997, Sched. 2, para. 2. Subs. (1A) was inserted by Courts and Legal Services Act 1990, s.125(2), Sched. 17, para. 15. The words in square brackets in subs. (6)(e) were substituted by Housing (Consequential Provisions) Act 1985, s.4, Sched. 2, para. 57(3). Subs. 6(ee) was inserted by Housing Act 1988, s.140(1), Sched. 17, para. 35(2).

Local Government and Housing Act 1989

(1989 c.42)

A2–030 An Act to make provision with respect to the members, officers and other staff and the procedure of local authorities; to amend Part III of the Local Government Act 1974 and Part II of the Local Government (Scotland) Act 1975 and to provide for a national code of local government conduct; to make further provision about the finances and expenditure of local authorities (including provision with respect to housing subsidies) and about companies in which local authorities have interests; to make provision for and in connection with renewal areas, grants towards the cost of improvement and repair of housing accommodation and the carrying out of works of maintenance, repair and improvement; to amend the Housing Act 1985 and Part III of the Local Government Finance Act 1982; to make amendments of and consequential upon Parts I, II and IV of the Housing Act 1988; to amend the Local Government Finance Act 1988 and the Abolition of Domestic Rates Etc. (Scotland) Act 1987 and certain enactments relating, as respects Scotland, to rating and valuation, and to provide for the making of grants; to make provision with respect to the imposition of charges by local authorities; to make further provision about certain existing grants and about financial assistance to and planning by local authorities in respect of emergencies; to amend sections 102 and 211 of the Local Government (Scotland) Act 1973; to amend the Local Land Charges Act 1975; to enable local authorities in Wales to be known solely by Welsh language names; to provide for the transfer of new town housing stock; to amend certain of the provisions of the Housing (Scotland) Act 1987 relating to a secure tenant's right to purchase his house; to amend section 47 of the Race Relations Act 1976; to confer certain powers on the Housing Corporation, Housing for Wales and Scottish Homes; to make provision about security of tenure for certain tenants under long tenancies; to provide for the making of grants and giving of guarantees in respect of certain activities carried on in relation to the construction industry; to provide for the repeal of certain enactments relating to improvement notices, town development and education support grants; to make, as respects Scotland, further provision in relation to the phasing of progression to registered rent for houses let by housing association or Scottish Homes and in relation to the circumstances in which rent increases under assured tenancies may be secured; and for connected purposes.

[16th November 1989]

PART IX

MISCELLANEOUS AND GENERAL

. . . .

Statutory references to rating

149.—(1) In the case of a provision which is made by or under any enactment and refers to a rate or a rateable value or any other factor connected with rating, the Secretary of State may make regulations— **A2–031**

(a) providing that the reference shall instead be to some other factor {whether or not connected with rating); or
(b) providing for the factor to be amended (whether by limiting its operation or in any other way);

and this section shall have effect in place of section 119 of the Local Government Finance Act 1988.

(2) Regulations under this section—

(a) may make provision in such manner as the Secretary of State thinks fit (whether by amending provisions or otherwise);
(b) may provide for a factor expressed by reference to valuation, rent, a premium, the length of a lease, anything connected with rating, or any other matter whatever;
(c) may provide for a factor expressed by reference to a combination of matters (whether expressed in terms of a formula or otherwise);
(d) may provide for a factor which includes a method of adjustment (whether by reference to indexation or otherwise);
(e) may make provision with respect to the resolution of disputes (whether by a court or otherwise); and
(f) may contain such supplementary, incidental, consequential or transitional provisions as appear to the Secretary of State to be necessary or expedient.

(3) A factor expressed by reference to rent may be by reference to ground rent, rent of premises at a market rate, rent as limited by law, or otherwise.

(4) Nothing in this section shall be construed as limiting the power conferred by section 14 of the Interpretation Act 1978 to revoke, amend or vary regulations previously made under this section.

(5) In this section "enactment" means an enactment contained in Schedule 10 to this Act, or in any other Act whether passed before or in the same Session as this Act; and for this purpose "Act" includes a private or local Act.

(6) Without prejudice to the generality of the powers conferred by this section, section 37 of the Landlord and Tenant Act 1954 (which provides for compensa-

tion by reference to rateable values) shall be amended in accordance with Schedule 7 to this Act.

ANNOTATION

S.149 came into force on November 16, 1989 (Royal Assent): s.195, *infra.*

[........]

Other provisions

[........]

Security of tenure on ending of long residential tenancies

A2–032 **186.**—(1) Schedule 10 to this Act shall have effect (in place of Part I of the Landlord and Tenant Act 1954) to confer security of tenure on certain tenants under long tenancies and, in particular, to establish assured periodic tenancies when such long tenancies come to an end.

(2) Schedule 10 to this Act applies, and section 1 of the Landlord and Tenant Act 1954 does not apply, to a tenancy of a dwelling-house—

(a) which is a long tenancy at a low rent, as defined in Schedule 10 to this Act; and
(b) which is entered into on or after the day appointed for the coming into force of this section, otherwise than in pursuance of a contract made before that day.

(3) If a tenancy—

(a) is in existence on 15th January 1999, and
(b) does not fall within subsection (2) above, and
(c) immediately before that date was, or was deemed to be, a long tenancy at a low rent for the purposes of Part I of the Landlord and Tenant Act 1954,

then, on and after that date (and so far as concerns any notice specifying a date of termination on or after that date and any steps taken in consequence thereof), section 1 of that Act shall cease to apply to it and Schedule 10 to this Act shall apply to it unless, before that date, the landlord has served a notice under section 4 of that Act specifying a date of termination which is earlier than that date.

(4) The provisions of Schedule 10 to this Act have effect notwithstanding any agreement to the contrary, but nothing in this subsection or that Schedule shall be construed as preventing the surrender of a tenancy.

(5) Section 18 of the Landlord and Tenant Act 1954 (duty of tenants of residential property to give information to landlords or superior landlords) shall apply in relation to property comprised in a long tenancy at a low rent, within

the meaning of Schedule 10 to this Act, as it applies to property comprised in a long tenancy at a low rent within the meaning of Part I of that Act, except that the reference in that section to subsection (1) of section 3 of that Act shall be construed as a reference to sub-paragraph (1) of paragraph 3 of Schedule 10 to this Act.

(6) Where, by virtue of subsection (3) above, Schedule 10 to this Act applies to a tenancy which is not a long tenancy at a low rent as defined in that Schedule, it shall be deemed to be such a tenancy for the purposes of that Schedule.

ANNOTATION

Section 186 came into force on April 1, 1990: s.195(2): S.I. 1990 No. 431, art. 4.

[. . . . . .]

Short title, commencement and extent

195.—(1) This Act may be cited as the Local Government and Housing Act 1989. **A2–033**

(2) The provisions of sections 1 and 2, 9, 10, 13 to 20 above, Parts II to V (with the exception in Part II of section 24), VII and VIII and (in this Part) sections 140 to 145, 156, 159, 160, 162, 164, 165, 167 to 173, 175 to 180, 182 and 183, 185, 186, and 194, except in so far as it relates to paragraphs 104 to 106 of Schedule 11, shall come into force on such day as the Secretary of State may by order made by statutory instrument appoint, and different days may be so appointed for different provisions or for different purposes.

(3) An order under subsection (2) above may contain such transitional provisions and savings (whether or not involving the modification of any statutory provision) as appear to the Secretary of State necessary or expedient in connection with the provisions brought into force by the order.

(4) Subject to subsection (5) below, this Act, except Parts I and II and sections 36(9), 140 to 145, 150 to 152, 153, 155, 157, 159, 161, 166, 168, 170, 171, 176 to 182, 185, 190, 192, 194(1), 194(4) and this section, extends to England and Wales only.

(5) Notwithstanding anything in subsection (4) above, any provision of Schedule 11 or Part II of Schedule 12 to this Act which amends or repeals any provision of the following enactments does not extend to Scotland—

(a) the Military Lands Act 1892;
(b) the Local Authorities (Expenditure Powers) Act 1983.

(6) This Act does not extend to Northern Ireland.

ANNOTATION

The Act was granted Royal Assent on November 16, 1989; all provisions, other than those identified in s.195(2) above and those separately identified in the Act, came into force on that date. Sched. 10 came into force on April 1, 1990: S.I. 1990 No. 431, art. 4.

Section 186 SCHEDULE 10

A2–034 SECURITY OF TENURE ON ENDING OF LONG RESIDENTIAL TENANCIES

Preliminary

1.—(1) This Schedule applies to a long tenancy of a dwelling-house at a low rent as respects which for the time being the following condition (in this Schedule referred to as "the qualifying condition") is fulfilled, that is to say, that the circumstances (as respects the property let under the tenancy, the use of that property and all other relevant matters) are such that, if the tenancy were not at a low rent, it would at that time be an assured tenancy within the meaning of Part I of the Housing Act 1988.

(2) For the purpose only of determining whether the qualifying condition is fulfilled with respects to a tenancy, Schedule 1 to the Housing Act 1988 (tenancies which cannot be assured tenancies) shall have effect with the omission of paragraph 1 (which excludes tenancies entered into before, or pursuant to contracts made before, the coming into force of Part I of that Act).

[(2A) For the purpose only of determining whether the qualifying condition is fulfilled with respect to a tenancy which is entered into on or after 1st April 1990 (otherwise than, where the dwelling-house has a rateable value on 31st March 1990, in pursuance of a contract made before 1st April 1990), for paragraph 2(1)(b) and (2) of Schedule 1 to the Housing Act 1988 there shall be substituted—

"(b) where (on the date the contract for the grant of the tenancy was made or, if there was no such contract, on the date the tenancy was entered into) R exceeded £25,000 under the formula—

$$R = \frac{P \times I}{1 - (1 + I)^{-T}}$$

where—

P is the premium payable as a condition of the grant of the tenancy (and includes a payment of money's worth) or, where no premium is so payable, zero,

I is 0.06,

T is the term, expressed in years, granted by the tenancy (disregarding any right to terminate the tenancy before the end of the term or to extend the tenancy).".]

ANNOTATION

Sub-para. (2A) was inserted, on the date when Schedule 10 came into force, by References to Rating (Housing) Regulations 1990 (S.I. 1990 No. 434), Sched., para. 31.

(3) At any time within the period of twelve months ending on the day preceding the term date, application may be made to the court as respects any long tenancy of a dwelling-house at a low rent, not being at the time of the application a tenancy as respects which the qualifying condition is fulfilled, for an order declaring that the tenancy is not to be treated as a tenancy to which this Schedule applies.

(4) Where an application is made under sub-paragraph (3) above—

(a) the court, if satisfied that the tenancy is not likely immediately before the term date to be a tenancy to which this Schedule applies but not otherwise, shall make the order; and
(b) if the court makes the order, then, notwithstanding anything in subparagraph (1) above the tenancy shall not thereafter be treated as a tenancy to which this Schedule applies.

(5) A tenancy to which this Schedule applies is hereinafter referred to as a long residential tenancy.

(6) Anything authorised or required to be done under the following provisions of this Schedule in relation to a long residential tenancy shall, if done before the term date in relation to a long tenancy of a dwelling-house at a low rent, not be treated as invalid by reason only that the time at which it was done the qualifying condition was not fulfilled as respects the tenancy.

(7) In determining for the purposes of any provision of this Schedule whether the property let under a tenancy was let as a separate dwelling, the nature of the property at the time of the creation of the tenancy shall be deemed to have been the same as its nature at the time in relation to which the question arises, and the purpose for which it was let under the tenancy shall be deemed to have been the same as the purpose for which it is or was used at the last-mentioned time.

[(8) The Secretary of State may by order replace the number in the definition of "I" in sub-paragraph (2A) above and any amount referred to in that sub-paragraph and paragraph 2(4)(b) below by such number or amount as is specified in the order; and such an order shall be made by statutory instrument which shall be subject to annulment in pursuance of a resolution of either House of Parliament.]

Annotation

Sub-para. (8) was inserted, on the date when Schedule 10 came into force, by References to Rating (Housing) Regulations 1990 (S.I. 1990 No. 434), Sched., para. 32.

2.—(1) This paragraph has effect for the interpretation of certain expressions used in this Schedule.

(2) Except where the context otherwise requires, expressions to which a meaning is assigned for the purposes of the 1988 Act or Part I of that Act have the same meaning in this Schedule.

(3) "Long tenancy" means a tenancy granted for a term of years certain exceeding 21 years, whether or not subsequently extended by act of the parties or by any enactment, but excluding any tenancy which is, or may become, terminable before the end of the term by notice given to the tenant.

[(4) A tenancy is "at a low rent" if under the tenancy—

(a) no rent is payable,
(b) where the tenancy is entered into on or after 1st April 1990 (otherwise than, where the dwelling-house had a rateable value on 31st March 1990, in pursuance of a contract made before 1st April 1990), the maximum rent payable at any time is payable at a rate of—
  (i) £1,000 or less a year if the dwelling-house is in Greater London and,
  (ii) £250 or less a year if the dwelling-house is elsewhere, or,
(c) where the tenancy was entered into before 1st April 1990 or (where the dwelling-house had a rateable value on 31st March 1990) is entered into on or after 1st April 1990 in pursuance of a contract made before that date, and the maximum rent payable at any time under the tenancy is less than two-thirds of the rateable value of the dwelling-house on 31st March 1990.]

Annotation

Sub-para. (4) was substituted for the former sub-para. (4) on the date when Schedule 10 came into force by References to Rating (Housing) Regulations 1990 (S.I. 1990 No. 434), Sched., para. 33. Sub-para. (4) previously read: "(4) a tenancy is 'at a low rent' if either no rent is payable under the tenancy or the maximum rent payable at any time is less than two-thirds of the rateable value for the time being of the dwelling-house under the tenancy."

(5) [Paragraph 2(2)] of Schedule 1 to the 1988 Act applies to determine whether the rent under a tenancy falls within sub-paragraph (4) above and Part II of that Schedule applies to determine the rateable value of a dwelling-house for the purposes of that sub-paragraph.

Annotation

The words in square brackets in subs. (5) were substituted for "Paragraph 3(2)" on the date when Schedule 10 came into force by References to Rating (Housing) Regulations 1990 (S.I. 1990 No. 434), Sched., para. 34.

(6) "Long residential tenancy" and "qualifying condition" have the meaning assigned by paragraph 1 above and the following expressions shall be construed as follows—

"the 1954 Act" means the Landlord and Tenant Act 1954;
"the 1988 Act" means the Housing Act 1988;

''assured periodic tenancy'' shall be construed in accordance with paragraph 9(4) below;
''the date of termination'' has the meaning assigned by paragraph 4(4) below;
''disputed terms'' shall be construed in accordance with paragraph 11(1)(a) below;
''election by the tenant to retain possession'' shall be construed in accordance with paragraph 4(7) below;
''former 1954 Act tenancy'' means a tenancy to which, by virtue of section 186(3) of this Act, this Schedule applies on and after 15th January 1999;
''the implied terms'' shall be construed in accordance with paragraph 4(5)(a) below;
''landlord'' shall be construed in accordance with paragraph 19(1) below;
''landlord's notice'' means a notice under sub-paragraph (1) of paragraph 4 below and such a notice is—

(a) ''a landlord's notice proposing an assured tenancy'' if it contains such proposals as are mentioned in sub-paragraph (5)(a) of that paragraph; and
(b) a ''landlord's notice to resume possession'' if it contains such proposals as are referred to in sub-paragraph (5)(b) of that paragraph;

''specified date of termination'', in relation to a tenancy in respect of which a landlord's notice is served, means the date specified in the notice as mentioned in paragraph 4(1)(a) below;
''tenant's notice'' shall be construed in accordance with paragraph 10(1)(a) below;
''term date'', in relation to a tenancy granted for a term of years certain, means the date of expiry of that term;
''the terms of the tenancy specified in the landlord's notice'' shall be construed in accordance with paragraph 4(6) below; and
''undisputed terms'' shall be construed in accordance with paragraph 11(2) below.

Continuation of long residential tenancies

3.—(1) A tenancy which, immediately before the term date, is a long residential tenancy shall not come to an end on that date except by being terminated under the provisions of this Schedule, and, if not then so terminated, shall subject to those provisions continue until so terminated and, while continuing by virtue of this paragraph, shall be deemed to be a long residential tenancy (notwithstanding any change in circumstances).

(2) Sub-paragraph (1) above does not apply in the case of a former 1954 Act tenancy the term date of which falls before 15th January 1999 but if, in the case of such a tenancy—

(a) the tenancy is continuing immediately before that date by virtue of section 3 of the 1954 Act, and
(b) on that date the qualifying condition (as defined in paragraph 1(1) above) is fulfilled,

then, subject to the provisions of this Schedule, the tenancy shall continue until terminated under those provisions and, while continuing by virtue of this paragraph, shall be deemed to be a long residential tenancy (notwithstanding any change in circumstances).

(3) Where by virtue of this paragraph a tenancy continues after the term date, the tenancy shall continue at the same rent and in other respects on the same terms as before the term date.

Termination of tenancy by the landlord

4.—(1) Subject to sub-paragraph (2) below and the provisions of this Schedule as to the annulment of notices in certain cases, the landlord may terminate a long residential tenancy by a notice in the prescribed form served on the tenant—

(a) specifying the date at which the tenancy is to come to an end, being either the term date or a later date; and
(b) so served not more than twelve nor less than six months before the date so specified.

(2) In any case where—

(a) a landlord's notice has been served, and
(b) an application has been made to the court or a rent assessment committee under the following provisions of this Schedule other than paragraph 6, and

(c) apart from this paragraph, the effect of the notice would be to terminate the tenancy before the expiry of the period of three months beginning with the date on which the application is finally disposed of,

the effect of the notice shall be to terminate the tenancy at the expiry of the said period of three months and not at any other time.

(3) The reference in sub-paragraph (2)(c) above to the date on which the application is finally disposed of shall be construed as a reference to the earliest date by which the proceedings on the application (including any proceedings on or in consequence of an appeal) have been determined and any time for appealing or further appealing has expired, except that if the application is withdrawn or any appeal is abandoned the reference shall be construed as a reference to the date of the withdrawal or abandonment.

(4) In this Schedule ''the date of termination'', in relation to a tenancy in respect of which a landlord's notice is served, means,—

(a) where the tenancy is continued as mentioned in sub-paragraph (2) above, the last day of the period of three months referred to in that sub-paragraph; and
(b) in any other case, the specified date of termination.

(5) A landlord's notice shall not have effect unless—

(a) it proposes an assured monthly periodic tenancy of the dwelling-house and a rent for that tenancy (such that it would not be a tenancy at a low rent) and, subject to sub-paragraph (6) below, states that the other terms of the tenancy shall be the same as those of the long residential tenancy immediately before it is terminated (in this Schedule referred to as ''the implied terms''); or
(b) it gives notice that, if the tenant is not willing to give up possession at the date of termination of the property let under the tenancy, the landlord proposes to apply to the court, on one or more of the grounds specified in paragraph 5(1) below, for the possession of the property let under the tenancy and states the ground or grounds on which he proposes to apply.

(6) In the landlord's notice proposing an assured tenancy the landlord may propose terms of the tenancy referred to in sub-paragraph (5)(a) above different from the implied terms; and any reference in the following provisions of this Schedule to the terms of the tenancy specified in the landlord's notice is a reference to the implied terms or, if the implied terms are varied by virtue of this sub-paragraph, to the implied terms as so varied.

(7) A landlord's notice shall invite the tenant, within the period of two months beginning on the date on which the notice was served, to notify the landlord in writing whether,—

(a) in the case of a landlord's notice proposing an assured tenancy, the tenant wishes to remain in possession; and
(b) in the case of a landlord's notice to resume possession, the tenant is willing to give up possession as mentioned in sub-paragraph (5)(b) above;

and references in this Schedule to an election by the tenant to retain possession are references to his notifying the landlord under this sub-paragraph that he wishes to remain in possession or, as the case may be, that he is not willing to give up possession.

5.—(1) Subject to the following provisions of this paragraph, the grounds mentioned in paragraph 4(5)(b) above are— **A2–035**

(a) Ground 6 in, and those in Part II of, Schedule 2 to the 1988 Act, other than Ground 16;
(b) the ground that, for the purposes of redevelopment after the termination of the tenancy, the landlord proposes to demolish or reconstruct the whole or a substantial part of the premises; and
(c) the ground that the premises or part of them are reasonably required by the landlord for occupation as a residence for himself or any son or daughter of his over eighteen years of age or his or his spouse's father or mother and, if the landlord is not the immediate landlord, that he will be at the specified date of termination.

(2) Ground 6 in Schedule 2 to the 1988 Act may not be specified in a landlord's notice to resume possession if the tenancy is a former 1954 Act tenancy; and in the application of that Ground in accordance with sub-paragraph (1) above in any other case, paragraph (c) shall be omitted.

(3) In its application in accordance with sub-paragraph (1) above, Ground 10 in Schedule 2 to the 1988 Act shall have effect as if, in paragraph (b)—

(a) the words "except where subsection (1)(b) of section 8 of this Act applies" were omitted; and
(b) for the words "notice under that section relating to those proceedings" there were substituted "landlord's notice to resume possession (within the meaning of Schedule 10 to the Local Government and Housing Act 1989)".

(4) The ground mentioned in sub-paragraph (1)(b) above may not be specified in a landlord's notice to resume possession unless the landlord is a body to which section 28 of the Leasehold Reform Act 1967 applies and the premises are required for relevant development within the meaning of that section; and on any application by such a body under paragraph 13 below for possession on that ground, a certificate given by a Minister of the Crown as provided by subsection (1) of that section shall be conclusive evidence that the premises are so required.

(5) The ground mentioned in sub-paragraph (1)(c) above may not be specified in a landlord's notice to resume possession if the interest of the landlord, or an interest which is merged in that interest and but for the merger would be the interest of the landlord, was purchased or created after 18th February 1966.

Interim rent

6.—(1) On the date of service of a landlord's notice proposing an assured tenancy, or at any time between that date and the date of termination, the landlord may serve a notice on the tenant in the prescribed form proposing an interim monthly rent to take effect from a date specified in the notice, being not earlier than the specified date of termination, and to continue while the tenancy is continued by virtue of the preceding provisions of this Schedule.

(2) Where a notice has been served under sub-paragraph (1) above—

(a) within the period of two months beginning on the date of service, the tenant may refer the interim monthly rent proposed in the notice to a rent assessment committee; and
(b) if the notice is not so referred, then, with effect from the date specified in the notice or, if it is later, the expiry of the period mentioned in paragraph (a) above, the interim monthly rent proposed in the notice shall be the rent under the tenancy.

(3) Where, under sub-paragraph (2) above, the rent specified in a landlord's notice is referred to a rent assessment committee, the committee shall determine the monthly rent at which, subject to sub-paragraph (4) below, the committee consider that the premises let under the tenancy might reasonably be expected to be let on the open market by a willing landlord under a monthly periodic tenancy—

(a) which begins on the day following the specified date of termination;
(b) under which the other terms are the same as those of the existing tenancy at the date on which was given the landlord's notice proposing an assured tenancy; and
(c) which affords the tenant security of tenure equivalent to that afforded by Chapter I of Part I of the 1988 Act in the case of an assured tenancy (other than an assured shorthold tenancy) in respect of which possession may not be recovered under any of Grounds 1 to 5 in Part I of Schedule 2 to that Act.

(4) Subsections (2) [,(3A)], (4) and (5) of section 14 of the 1988 Act shall apply in relation to a determination of rent under sub-paragraph (3) above as they apply in relation to a determination under that section to the modifications in sub-paragraph (5) below; and in this paragraph "rent" shall be construed in accordance with subsection (4) of that section.

(5) The modifications of section 14 of the 1988 Act referred to in sub-paragraph (4) above are that in subsection (2), the reference in paragraph (b) to a relevant improvement being carried out shall be construed as a reference to an improvement being carried out during the long residential tenancy and the reference in paragraph (c) to a failure to comply with any term of the tenancy shall be construed as a reference to a failure to comply with any term of the long residential tenancy.

(6) Where a reference has been made to a rent assessment committee under sub-paragraph (2) above, then, the rent determined by the committee (subject, in a case where section 14(5) of the 1988 Act applies, to the addition of the appropriate amount in respect of rates) shall be the rent under the tenancy with effect from the date specified in the notice served under sub-paragraph (1)

above or, if it is later, the expiry of the period mentioned in paragraph (a) of sub-paragraph (2) above.

ANNOTATION

The words in square brackets in sub-para. (4) were inserted by the Local Government Finance (Housing) (Consequential Amendments) Order 1993 (S.I. 1993 No. 651), art. 2(1), Sched. 1, para. 20.

7.—(1) Nothing in paragraph 6 above affects the right of the landlord and the tenant to agree the interim monthly rent which is to have effect while the tenancy is continued by virtue of the preceding provisions of this Schedule and the date from which that rent is to take effect; and, in such a case—

(a) notwithstanding the provisions of paragraph 6 above, that rent shall be the rent under the tenancy with effect from that date; and
(b) no steps or, as the case may be, no further steps may be taken by the landlord or the tenant under the provisions of that paragraph.

(2) Nothing in paragraph 6 above requires a rent assessment committee to continue with a determination under sub-paragraph (3) of that paragraph—

(a) if the tenant gives notice in writing that he no longer requires such a determination; or
(b) if the long residential tenancy has come to an end on or before the specified date of termination.

(3) Notwithstanding that a tenancy in respect of which an interim monthly rent has effect in accordance with paragraph 6 above or this paragraph is no longer at a low rent, it shall continue to be regarded as a tenancy at a low rent and, accordingly, shall continue to be a long residential tenancy.

Termination of tenancy by the tenant

8.—(1) A long residential tenancy may be brought to an end at the term date by not less than one month's notice in writing given by the tenant to his immediate landlord.
(2) A tenancy which is continuing after the term date by virtue of paragraph 3 above may be brought to an end at any time by not less than one month's notice in writing given by the tenant to his immediate landlord, whether the notice is given before or after the term date of the tenancy.
(3) The fact that the landlord has served a landlord's notice or that there has been an election by the tenant to retain possession shall not prevent the tenant from giving notice under this paragraph terminating the tenancy at a date earlier than the specified date of termination.

The assured periodic tenancy

9.—(1) Where a long residential tenancy (in this paragraph referred to as "the former tenancy") is terminated by a landlord's notice proposing an assured tenancy, then, subject to sub-paragraph (3) below, the tenant shall be entitled to remain in possession of the dwelling-house and his right to possession shall depend upon an assured periodic tenancy arising by virtue of this paragraph.
(2) The assured periodic tenancy referred to in sub-paragraph (1) above is one—

(a) taking effect in possession on the day following the date of termination;
(b) deemed to have been granted by the person who was the landlord under the former tenancy on the date of termination to the person who was then the tenant under that tenancy;
(c) under which the premises let are the dwelling-house;
(d) under which the periods of the tenancy, and the intervals at which rent is to be paid, are monthly beginning on the day following the date of termination;
(e) under which the rent is determined in accordance with paragraphs 10 to 12 below; and
(f) under which the other terms are determined in accordance with paragraphs 10 to 12 below.

(3) If, at the end of the period of two months beginning on the date of service of the landlord's notice, the qualifying condition was not fulfilled as respects the tenancy, the tenant shall not be

entitled to remain in possession as mentioned in sub-paragraph (1) above unless there has been an election by the tenant to retain possession; and if, at the specified date of termination, the qualifying condition is not fulfilled as respects the tenancy, then, notwithstanding that there has been such an election, the tenant shall not be entitled to remain in possession as mentioned in that sub-paragraph.

(4) Any reference in the following provisions of this Schedule to an assured periodic tenancy is a reference to an assured periodic tenancy arising by virtue of this paragraph.

Initial rent under and terms of assured periodic tenancy

A2–036 10.—(1) Where a landlord's notice proposing an assured tenancy has been served on the tenant—

(a) within the period of two months beginning on the date of service of the notice, the tenant may serve on the landlord a notice in the prescribed form proposing either or both of the following, that is to say,—

(i) a rent for the assured period tenancy different from that proposed in the landlord's notice; and
(ii) terms of the tenancy different from those specified in the landlord's notice,

and such a notice is in this Schedule referred to as a ''tenant's notice''; and
(b) if a tenant's notice is not so served, then, with effect from the date on which the assured periodic tenancy takes effect in possession—

(i) the rent proposed in the landlord's notice shall be the rent under the tenancy; and
(ii) the terms of the tenancy specified in the landlord's notice shall be terms of the tenancy.

(2) Where a tenant's notice has been served on the landlord under sub-paragraph (a) above—

(a) within the period of two months beginning on the date of service of the notice, the landlord may by an application in the prescribed form refer the notice to a rent assessment committee; and
(b) if the notice is not so referred, then, with effect from the date on which the assured periodic tenancy takes effect in possession,—

(i) the rent (if any) proposed in the tenant's notice, or, if no rent is so proposed, the rent proposed in the landlord's notice, shall be the rent under the tenancy; and
(ii) the other terms of the tenancy (if any) proposed in the tenant's notice and, in so far they do not conflict with the terms so proposed, the terms specified in the landlord's notice shall be terms of the tenancy.

11.—(1) Where, under sub-paragraph (2) of paragraph 10 above, a tenant's notice is referred to a rent assessment committee, the committee, having regard only to the contents of the landlord's notice and the tenant's notice, shall decide—

(a) whether there is any dispute as to the terms (other than those relating to the amount of the rent) of the assured periodic tenancy (in this Schedule referred to as ''disputed terms'') and, if so, what the disputed terms are; and
(b) whether there is any dispute as to rent under the tenancy;

and where the committee decide that there are disputed terms and that there is a dispute as to the rent under the tenancy, they shall make a determination under sub-paragraph (3) below before they make a determination under sub-paragraph (5) below.

(2) Where, under paragraph 10(2) above, a tenant's notice is referred to a rent assessment committee, any reference in this Schedule to the undisputed terms is a reference to those terms (if any) which—

(a) are proposed in the landlord's notice or the tenant's notice; and
(b) do not relate to the amount of the rent; and
(c) are not disputed terms.

(3) If the rent assessment committee decide that there are disputed terms, they shall determine whether the terms in the landlord's notice, the terms in the tenant's notice, or some other terms, dealing with the same subject matter as the disputed terms are such as, in the committee's opinion, might reasonably be expected to be found in an assured monthly periodic tenancy of the dwelling-house (not being an assured shorthold tenancy)—

(a) which begins on the day following the date of termination;
(b) which is granted by a willing landlord on terms which, except so far as they relate to the subject matter of the disputed terms, are the undisputed terms; and
(c) in respect of which possession may not be recovered under any of Grounds 1 to 5 in Part I of Schedule 2 to the 1988 Act;

and the committee shall, if they consider it appropriate, specify an adjustment of the undisputed terms to take account of the terms so determined and shall, if they consider it appropriate, specify an adjustment of the rent to take account of the terms so determined and, if applicable, so adjusted.

(4) In making a determination under sub-paragraph (3) above, or specifying an adjustment of the rent or undisputed terms under that sub-paragraph, there shall be disregarded any effect on the terms or the amount of rent attributable to the granting of a tenancy to a sitting tenant.

(5) If the rent assessment committee decide that there is a dispute as to the rent under the assured periodic tenancy, the committee shall determined the monthly rent at which, subject to sub-paragraph (6) below, the committee consider that the dwelling-house might reasonably be expected to be let in the open market by a willing landlord under an assured tenancy (not being an assured shorthold tenancy)—

(a) which is a monthly periodic tenancy;
(b) which begins on the day following the date of termination;
(c) in respect of which possession may not be recovered under any of Grounds 1 to 5 in Part I of Schedule 2 to the 1988 Act; and
(d) the terms of which (other than those relating to the amount of the rent) are the same as—
    (i) the undisputed terms; or
    (ii) if there has been a determination under sub-paragraph (3) above, the terms determined by the committee under that sub-paragraph and the undisputed terms (as adjusted, if at all, under that sub-paragraph).

(6) Subsections (2) [,(3A)], (4) and (5) of section 14 of the 1988 Act shall apply in relation to a determination of rent under sub-paragraph (5) above as they apply in relation to a determination under that section subject to the modifications in sub-paragraph (7) below; and in this paragraph "rent" shall be construed in accordance with subsection (4) of that section.

(7) The modifications of section 14 of the 1988 Act referred to in sub-paragraph (6) above are that in subsection (2), the reference in paragraph (b) to a relevant improvement being carried out shall be construed as a reference to an improvement being carried out during the long residential tenancy and the reference in paragraph (c) to a failure to comply with any term of the tenancy shall be construed as a reference to a failure to comply with any term of the long residential tenancy.

(8) Where a reference has been made to a rent assessment committee under sub-paragraph (2) of paragraph 10 above, then,—

(a) if the committee decide that there are no disputed terms and that there is no dispute as to the rent, paragraph 10(2)(b) above shall apply as if the notice had not been so referred,
(b) where paragraph (a) above does not apply the, so far as concerns the amount of the rent under the tenancy, if there is a dispute as to the rent, the rent determined by the committee (subject, in a case where section 14(5) of the 1988 Act applies, to the addition of the appropriate amount in respect of rates) and, if there is no dispute as to the rent, the rent specified in the landlord's notice or, as the case may be, the tenant's notice (subject to any adjustment under sub-paragraph (3) above) shall be the rent under the tenancy, and
(c) where paragraph (a) above does not apply and there are disputed terms, then, so far as concerns the subject matter of those terms, the terms determined by the committee under sub-paragraph (3) above shall be terms of the tenancy and, so far as concerns any undisputed terms, those terms (subject to any adjustment under sub-paragraph (3) above) shall also be terms of the tenancy,

with effect from the date on which the assured periodic tenancy takes effect in possession.

(9) Nothing in this Schedule affects the right of the landlord and the tenant under the assured periodic tenancy to vary by agreement any term of the tenancy (including a term relating to rent).

ANNOTATION

The words in sub-paragraph (6) were inserted by the Local Government Finance (Housing) (Consequential Amendments) Order 1993 (S.I. 1993 No. 651), art. 2(1), Sched. 1, para. 20.

12.—(1) Subsections (2) to (4) of section 41 of the 1988 Act (rent assessment committees:

information powers) shall apply where there is a reference to a rent assessment committee under the preceding provisions of this Schedule as they apply where a matter is referred to such a committee under Chapter I or Chapter II of Part I of the 1988 Act.

(2) Nothing in paragraph 10 or paragraph 11 above affects the right of the landlord and the tenant to agree any terms of the assured periodic tenancy (including a term relating to the rent) before the tenancy takes effect in possession (in this sub-paragraph referred to as "the expressly agreed terms"); and, in such case,—

(a) the expressly agreed terms shall be terms of the tenancy in substitution for any terms dealing with the same subject matter which would otherwise, by virtue of paragraph 10 or paragraph 11 above, be terms of the tenancy; and
(b) where a reference has already been made to a rent assessment committee under sub-paragraph (2) of paragraph 10 above but there has been no determination by the committee under paragraph 11 above,—
    (i) the committee shall have regard to the expressly agreed terms, as notified to them by the landlord and the tenant, in deciding, for the purposes of paragraph 11 above, what the disputed terms are and whether there is any dispute as to the rent; and
    (ii) in making any determination under paragraph 11 above the committee shall not make any adjustment of the expressly agreed terms, as so notified.

(3) Nothing in paragraph 11 above requires a rent assessment committee to continue with a determination under that paragraph—

(a) if the long residential tenancy has come to an end; or
(b) if the landlord serves notice in writing on the committee that he no longer requires such a determination;

and, where the landlord serves notice as mentioned in paragraph (b) above, then, for the purposes of sub-paragraph (2) of paragraph 10 above, the landlord shall be treated as not having made a reference under paragraph (a) of that sub-paragraph and, accordingly, paragraph (b) of that sub-paragraph shall, subject to sub-paragraph (2) above, have effect for determining rent and other terms of the assured periodic tenancy.

Landlord's application for possession

13.—(1) Where a landlord's notice to resume possession has been served on the tenant and either—

(a) there is an election by the tenant to retain possession, or
(b) at the end of the period of two months beginning on the date of service of the notice, the qualifying condition is fulfilled as respects the tenancy,

the landlord may apply to the court for an order under this paragraph on such of the grounds mentioned in paragraph 5(1) above as may be specified in the notice.

(2) The court shall not entertain an application under sub-paragraph (1) above unless the application is made—

(a) within the period of two months beginning on the date of the election by the tenant to retain possession; or
(b) if there is no election by the tenant to retain possession, within the period of four months beginning on the date of service of the landlord's notice.

(3) Where the ground or one of the grounds for claiming possession specified in the landlord's notice is Ground 6 in Part I of Schedule 2 to the 1988 Act, then, if on an application made under sub-paragraph (1) above the court is satisfied that the landlord has established that ground, the court shall order that the tenant shall, on the date of termination, give up possession of the property then let under the tenancy.

(4) Subject to sub-paragraph (6) below, where the ground or one of the grounds for claiming possession specified in the landlord's notice is any of Grounds 9 to 15 in Part II of Schedule 2 to the 1988 Act or the ground mentioned in paragraph 5(1)(c) above, then, if on an application made under sub-paragraph (1) above the court is satisfied that the landlord has established that ground

and that it is reasonable that the landlord should be granted possession, the court shall order that the tenant shall, on the date of termination, give up possession of the property then let under the tenancy.

(5) Part III of Schedule 2 to the 1988 Act shall have effect for supplementing Ground 9 in that Schedule (as that ground applies in relation to this Schedule) as it has effect for supplementing that ground for the purposes of that Act, subject to the modification that in paragraph 3(1), in the words following paragraph (b) the reference to the assured tenancy in question shall be construed as a reference to the long residential tenancy in question.

(6) Where the ground or one of the grounds for claiming possession specified in the landlord's notice is that mentioned in paragraph 5(1)(c) above, the court shall not make the order mentioned in sub-paragraph (4) above on that ground if it is satisfied that, having regard to all the circumstances of the case, including the question whether other accommodation is available for the landlord or the tenant, greater hardship would be caused by making the order than by refusing to make it.

(7) Where the ground or one of the grounds for claiming possession specified in the landlord's notice is that mentioned in paragraph 5(1)(b) above, then, if on an application made under sub-paragraph (1) above the court is satisfied that the landlord has established that ground and is further satisfied—

(a) that on that ground possession of those premises will be required by the landlord on the date of termination, and

(b) that the landlord has made such preparations (including the obtaining or, if that is not reasonably practicable in the circumstances, preparations relating to the obtaining of any requisite permission or consent, whether from any authority whose permission or consent is required under any enactment or from the owner of any interest in any property) for proceeding with the redevelopment as are reasonable in the circumstances,

the court shall order that the tenant shall, on the date of termination, give up possession of the property then let under the tenancy.

14.—(1) Where, in a case falling within sub-paragraph (7) of paragraph 13 above, the court is not satisfied as mentioned in that sub-paragraph but would be satisfied if the date of termination of the tenancy had been such date (in this paragraph referred to as "the postponed date") as the court may determine, being a date later, but not more than one year later, than the specified date of termination, the court shall, if the landlord so requires, make an order as mentioned in sub-paragraph (2) below.

(2) The order referred to in sub-paragraph (1) above is one by which the court specifies the postponed date and orders—

(a) that the tenancy shall not come to an end on the date of termination but shall continue thereafter, as respects the whole of the property let under the tenancy, at the same rent and in other respects on the same terms as before that date; and

(b) that, unless the tenancy comes to an end before the postponed date, the tenant shall on that date give up possession of the property then let under the tenancy.

(3) Notwithstanding the provisions of paragraph 13 above and the preceding provisions of this paragraph and notwithstanding that there has been an election by the tenant to retain possession, if the court is satisfied, at the date of the hearing, that the qualifying condition is not fulfilled as respects the tenancy, the court shall order that the tenant shall, on the date of termination, give up possession of the property then let under the tenancy.

(4) Nothing in paragraph 13 above or the preceding provisions of this paragraph shall prejudice any power of the tenant under paragraph 8 above to terminate the tenancy; and sub-paragraph (2) of that paragraph shall apply where the tenancy is continued by an order under sub-paragraph (2) above as it applies where the tenancy is continued by virtue of paragraph 3 above.

Provisions where tenant not ordered to give up possession

15.—(1) The provisions of this paragraph shall have effect where the landlord is entitled to make an application under sub-paragraph (1) of paragraph 13 above but does not obtain an order under that paragraph or paragraph 14 above. **A2–037**

(2) If at the expiration of the period within which an application under paragraph 13(1) above may be made the landlord has not made such an application, the landlord's notice to resume possession, and anything done in pursuance thereof, shall cease to have effect.

(3) If before the expiration of the period mentioned in sub-paragraph (2) above the landlord has made an application under paragraph 13(1) above but the result of the application, at the time when it is finally disposed of, is that no order is made, the landlord's notice to resume possession shall cease to have effect.

(4) In any case where sub-paragraph (3) above applies, then, if within the period of one month beginning on the date that the application to the court is finally disposed of the landlord serves on the tenant a landlord's notice proposing an assured tenancy, the earliest date which may be specified in the notice as the date of termination shall, notwithstanding anything in paragraph 4(1)(b) above, be the day following the last day of the period of four months beginning on the date of service of the subsequent notice.

(5) The reference in sub-paragraphs (3) and (4) above to the time at which an application is finally disposed of shall be construed as a reference to the earliest time at which the proceedings on the application (including any proceedings on or in consequence of an appeal) have been determined and any time for appealing or further appealing has expired, except that if the application is withdrawn or any appeal is abandoned the reference shall be construed as a reference to the time of withdrawal or abandonment.

(6) A landlord's notice to resume possession may be withdrawn at any time by notice in writing served on the tenant (without prejudice, however, to the power of the court to make an order as to costs if the notice is withdrawn after the landlord has made an application under paragraph 13(1) above).

(7) In any case where sub-paragraph (6) above applies, then, if within the period of one month beginning on the date of withdrawal of the landlord's notice to resume possession the landlord serves on the tenant a landlord's notice proposing an assured tenancy, the earliest date which may be specified in the notice as the date of termination shall, notwithstanding anything in paragraph 4(1)(b) above, be the day following the last day of the period of four months beginning on the date of service of the subsequent notice or the day following the last day of the period of six months beginning on the date of service of the withdrawn notice, whatever is the later.

Tenancies granted in continuation of long tenancies

16.—(1) Where on the coming to the end of a tenancy at a low rent the person who was the tenant immediately before the coming to an end thereof becomes (whether by grant or by implication of the law) the tenant under another tenancy at a low rent of a dwelling-house which consists of the whole or any part of the property let under the previous tenancy, then, if the previous tenancy was a long tenancy or is deemed by virtue of this paragraph to have been a long tenancy, the new tenancy shall be deemed for the purposes of this Schedule to be a long tenancy, irrespective of its terms.

(2) In relation to a tenancy from year to year or other tenancy not granted for a term of years certain, being a tenancy which by virtue of sub-paragraph (1) above is deemed for the purposes of this Schedule to be a long tenancy, the preceding provisions of this Schedule shall have effect subject to the modifications set out below.

(3) In sub-paragraph (6) of paragraph 2 above for the expression beginning "term date" there shall be substituted—

> " "term date", in relation to any such tenancy as is mentioned in paragraph 16(2) below, means the first date after the coming into force of this Schedule on which, apart from this Schedule, the tenancy could have been brought to an end by notice to quit given by the landlord".

(4) Notwithstanding anything in sub-paragraph (3) of paragraph 3 above, where by virtue of that paragraph the tenancy is continued after the term date, the provisions of this Schedule as to the termination of a tenancy by notice shall have effect, subject to sub-paragraph (5) below, in substitution for and not in addition to any such provisions included in the terms on which the tenancy had effect before the term date.

(5) The minimum period of notice referred to in paragraph 8(1) above shall be one month or such longer period as the tenant would have been required to give to bring the tenancy to an end at the term date.

(6) Where the tenancy is not terminated under paragraph 4 or paragraph 8 above at the term date, then, whether or not it would have continued after that date apart from the provisions of this Schedule, it shall be treated for the purposes of those provisions as being continued by virtue of paragraph 3 above.

Agreement as to the grant of new tenancies

17. In any case where, prior to the date of termination of a long residential tenancy, the landlord and the tenant agree for the grant to the tenant of a future tenancy of the whole or part of the property let under the tenancy at a rent other than a low rent and on terms and from a date specified in the agreement, the tenancy shall continue until that date but no longer: and, in such a case, the provisions of this Schedule shall cease to apply in relation to the tenancy with effect from the date of the agreement.

Assumptions on which to determine future questions

18. Where under this Schedule any question falls to be determined by the court or a rent assessment committee by reference to circumstances at a future date, the court or committee shall have regard to all rights, interests and obligations under or relating to the tenancy as they subsist at the time of the determination and to all relevant circumstances as those then subsist and shall assume, except in so far as the contrary is shown, that those rights, interests, obligations and circumstances will continue to subsist unchanged until that future date.

Landlords and mortgagees in possession

19.—(1) Section 21 of the 1954 Act (meaning of ''the landlord'' and provisions as to mesne landlords) shall apply in relation to this Schedule as it applies in relation to Part I of that Act but subject to the following modifications—

(a) any reference to Part I of that Act shall be construed as a reference to this Schedule; and
(b) subsection (4) (which relates to statutory tenancies arising under that Part) shall be omitted.

(2) Section 67 of the 1954 Act (mortgagees in possession) applies for the purposes of this Schedule except that for the reference to that Act there shall be substituted a reference to this Schedule.

(3) In accordance with sub-paragraph (1) above, Schedule 5 to the 1954 Act shall also apply for the purpose of this Schedule but subject to the following modifications—

(a) any reference to Part I of the 1954 Act shall be construed as a reference to the provisions of this Schedule (other than this sub-paragraph);
(b) any reference to section 21 of the 1954 Act shall be construed as a reference to that section as it applies in relation to this Schedule;
(c) any reference to subsection (1) of section 4 of that Act shall be construed as a reference to sub-paragraph (1) of paragraph 4 above;
(d) any reference to the court includes a reference to a rent assessment committee;
(e) paragraphs 6 to 8 and 11 shall be omitted;
(f) any reference to a particular subsection of section 16 of the 1954 Act shall be construed as a reference to that subsection as it applies in relation to this Schedule;
(g) any reference to a tenancy to which section 1 of the 1954 Act applies shall be construed as a reference to a long residential tenancy; and
(h) expressions to which a meaning is assigned by any provision of this Schedule (other than this sub-paragraph) shall be given that meaning.

Application of other provisions of the 1954 Act

20.—(1) Section 16 of the 1954 Act (relief for tenant where landlord proceeding to enforce covenants) shall apply in relation to this Schedule as it applies in relation to Part I of that Act but subject to the following modifications— **A2–038**

(a) in subsection (1) the reference to a tenancy to which section 1 of teh 1954 Act applies shall be construed as a reference to a long residential tenancy;
(b) in subsection (2) the reference to Part I of that Act shall be construed as a reference to this Schedule;

(c) subsection (3) shall have effect as if the words "(without prejudice to section ten of this Act)" were omitted; and
(d) in subsection (7) the reference to subsection (3) of section 2 of the 1954 Act shall be construed as a reference to paragraph 1(6) above.

(2) Section 55 of the 1954 Act (compensation for possession obtained by misrepresentation) shall apply in relation to this Schedule as it applies in relation to Part I of that Act.

(3) Section 63 of the 1954 Act (jurisdiction of court for purposes of Parts I and II of the 1954 Act and of Part I of the Landlord and Tenant Act 1927) shall apply in relation to this Schedule and section 186 of this Act as it applies in relation to Part I of that Act.

(4) Section 65 of the 1954 Act (provisions as to reversions) applies for the purposes of this Schedule except that for any reference to that Act there shall be substituted a reference to this Schedule.

(5) Subsection (4) of section 66 of the 1954 Act (service of notices) shall apply in relation to this Schedule as it applies in relation to that Act.

21.—(1) Where this Schedule has effect in relation to a former 1954 Act tenancy the term date of which falls before 15th January 1999, any reference (however expressed) in the preceding provisions of this Schedule to the dwelling-house (or the property) let under the tenancy shall have effect as a reference to the premises qualifying for protection, within the meaning of the 1954 Act.

(2) Notwithstanding that at any time section 1 of the 1954 Act does not, and this Schedule does, apply to a former 1954 Act tenancy, any question of what are the premises qualifying for protection or (in that context) what is the tenancy shall be determined for the purposes of this Schedule in accordance with Part I of that Act.

Crown application

22.—(1) This Schedule shall apply where—

(a) there is an interest belonging to Her Majesty in right of the Crown and that interest is under the management of the Crown Estate Commissioners, or
(b) there is an interest belonging to Her Majesty in right of the Duchy of Lancaster or belonging to the Duchy of Cornwall,

as if it were an interest not so belonging.

(2) Where an interest belongs to Her Majesty in right of the Duchy of Lancaster, then, for the purposes of this Schedule, the Chancellor of the Duchy of Lancaster shall be deemed to be the owner of the interest.

(3) Where an interest belongs to the Duchy of Cornwall, then, for the purposes of this Schedule, such person as the Duke of Cornwall, or other possessor for the time being of the Duchy of Cornwall, appoints shall be deemed to be the owner of the interest.

ANNOTATION

Schedule 10 came into force, as amended, on April 1, 1990: s.195(2); S.I. 1990 No. 431, art. 4.

Law of Property (Miscellaneous Provisions) Act 1994 A2–039

(1994 c.36)

An Act to provide for new covenants for title to be implied on dispositions of property; to amend the law with respect to certain matters arising in connection with the death of the owner of property; and for connected purposes

[3 November 1994]

. . . .

PART II

MATTERS ARISING IN CONNECTION WITH DEATH

ANNOTATION

Sections 14, 17, 18 and 19 were brought into force on July 1, 1995 by Law of Property (Miscellaneous Provisions) Act 1994 (Commencement No. 2) Order 1995 (S.I. 1995 No. 1317). A2–040

Vesting of estate in case of intestacy or lack of executors

14.—(1) For section 9 of the Administration of Estates Act 1925 (vesting of estate of intestate between death and grant of administration) substitute— A2–041

"**Vesting of estate in Public Trustee where intestacy or lack of executors**

9.—(1) Where a person dies intestate, his real and personal estate shall vest in the Public Trustee until the grant of administration.

(2) Where a testator dies and—

(a) at the time of his death there is no executor with power to obtain probate of the will, or

(b) at any time before probate of the will is granted there ceases to be any executor with power to obtain probate,

the real and personal estate of which he disposes by the will shall vest in the Public Trustee until the grant of representation.

(1994 c.36)

(3) The vesting of real or personal estate in the Public Trustee by virtue of this section does not confer on him any beneficial interest in, or impose on him any duty, obligation or liability in respect of, the property.''

(2) Any real or personal estate of a person dying before the commencement of this section shall, if it is property to which this subsection applies, vest in the Public Trustee on the commencement of this section.

(3) Subsection (2) above applies to any property—

(a) if it was vested in the Probate Judge under section 9 of the Administration of Estates Act 1925 immediately before the commencement of this section, or

(b) if it was not so vested but as at commencement there has been no grant of representation in respect of it and there is no executor with power to obtain such a grant.

(4) Any property vesting in the Public Trustee by virtue of subsection (2) above shall—

(a) if the deceased died intestate, be treated as vesting in the Public Trustee under section 9(1) of the Administration of Estates Act 1925 (as substituted by subsection (1) above); and

(b) otherwise be treated as vesting in the Public Trustee under section 9(2) of that Act (as so substituted).

(5) Anything done by or in relation to the Probate Judge with respect to property vested in him as mentioned in subsection (3)(a) above shall be treated as having been done by or in relation to the Public Trustee.

(6) So far as may be necessary in consequence of the transfer to the Public Trustee of the functions of the Probate Judge under section 9 of the Administration of Estates Act 1925, any reference in an enactment or instrument to the Probate Judge shall be construed as a reference to the Public Trustee.

[. . . . .]

Notices affecting land: absence of knowledge of intended recipient's death

A2–042 **17.**—(1) Service of a notice affecting land which would be effective but for the death of the intended recipient is effective despite his death if the person serving the notice had no reason to believe that he has died.

(2) Where the person serving a notice affecting land has no reason to believe that the intended recipient has died, the proper address for the purposes of section 7 of the Interpretation Act 1978 (service of documents by post) shall be what would be the proper address apart from his death.

(3) The above provisions do not apply to a notice authorised or required to be served for the purposes of proceedings before—

(a) any court,
(b) any tribunal specified in Schedule 1 to the Tribunals and Inquiries Act 1992 (tribunals within general supervision of Council on Tribunals), or
(c) the Chief Land Registrar or any district registrar or assistant district registrar;

but this is without prejudice to the power to make provision in relation to such proceedings by rules of court, procedural rules within the meaning of section 8 of the Tribunals and Inquiries Act 1992 or rules under section 144 of the Land Registration Act 1925.

Notices affecting land: service on personal representatives before filing of grant

18.—(1) A notice affecting land which would have been authorised or required to be served on a person but for his death shall be sufficiently served before a grant of representation has been filed if— **A2–043**

(a) it is addressed to "The Personal Representatives of" the deceased (naming him) and left at or sent by post to his last known place of residence or business in the United Kingdom, and
(b) a copy of it, similarly addressed, is served on the Public Trustee.

(2) The reference in subsection (1) to the filing of a grant of representation is to the filing at the Principal Registry of the Family Division of the High Court of a copy of a grant of representation in respect of the deceased's estate or, as the case may be, the part of his estate which includes the land in question.

(3) The method of service provided for by this section is not available where provision is made—

(a) by or under any enactment, or
(b) by an agreement in writing,

requiring a different method of service, or expressly prohibiting the method of service provided for by this section, in the circumstances.

Functions of Public Trustee in relation to notices, etc.

19.—(1) The Public Trustee may give directions as to the office or offices at which documents may be served on him— **A2–044**

(a) by virtue of section 9 of the Administration of Estates Act 1925 (as substituted by section 14(1) above), or
(b) in pursuance of section 18(1)(b) above (service on Public Trustee of copy of certain notices affecting land);

and he shall publish such directions in such manner as he considers appropriate.

(2) The Lord Chancellor may by regulations make provision with respect to the functions of the Public Trustee in relation to such documents; and the regulations may make different provision in relation to different descriptions of document or different circumstances.

(3) The regulations may, in particular, make provision requiring the Public Trustee—

(a) to keep such documents for a specified period and thereafter to keep a copy or record of their contents in such form as may be specified;
(b) to keep such documents, copies and records available for inspection at such reasonable hours as may be specified; and
(c) to supply copies to any person on request.

In this subsection ''specified'' means specified by or under the regulations.

(4) Regulations under this section shall be made by statutory instrument which shall be subject to annulment in pursuance of the resolution of either House of Parliament.

(5) The following provisions of the Public Trustee Act 1906, namely—

(a) section 8(5) (payment of expenses out of money provided by Parliament), and
(b) section 9(1), (3) and (4) (provisions as to fees),

apply in relation to the functions of the Public Trustee in realtion to documents as to which this section applies as in relation to his functions under that Act.

Family Law Act 1996

(1996 c.27)

An Act to make provision with respect to: divorce and separation; legal aid in connection with mediation in disputes relating to family matters; proceedings in cases where marriages have broken down; rights of occupation of certain domestic premises; prevention of molestation; the inclusion in certain orders under the Children Act 1989 of provisions about the occupation of a dwelling-house; the transfer of tenancies between spouses and persons who have lived together as husband and wife; and for connected purposes. **A2–045**

[4th July 1996]

[. . . . .]

Part IV

Family Homes and Domestic Violence

Rights to occupy matrimonial home

Rights concerning matrimonial home where one spouse has no estate, etc.

30.—(1) This section applies if— **A2–046**

(a) one spouse is entitled to occupy a dwelling-house by virtue of

(i) a beneficial estate or interest or contract; or
(ii) any enactment giving that spouse the right to remain in occupation; and

(b) the other spouse is not so entitled.

(2) Subject to the provisions of this Part, the spouse not so entitled has the following rights (''matrimonial home rights'')—

(a) if in occupation, a right not to be evicted or excluded from the dwelling-house or any part of it by the other spouse except with the leave of the court given by an order under section 33;
(b) if not in occupation, a right with the leave of the court so given to enter into and occupy the dwelling-house.

(3) If a spouse is entitled under this section to occupy a dwelling-house or any part of a dwelling-house, any payment or tender made or other thing done by that spouse in or towards satisfaction of any liability of the other spouse in respect of rent, mortgage payments or other outgoings affecting the dwelling-house is, whether or not it is made or done in pursuance of an order under section 40, as good as if made or done by the other spouse.

(4) A spouse's occupation by virtue of this section—

(a) is to be treated, for the purposes of the Rent (Agriculture) Act 1976 and the Rent Act 1977 (other than Part V and sections 103 to 106 of that Act), as occupation by the other spouse as the other spouse's residence, and
(b) if the spouse occupies the dwelling-house as that spouse's only or principal home, is to be treated, for the purposes of the Housing Act 1985 [, Part I of the Housing Act 1988 and Chapter I of Part V of the Housing Act 1996], as occupation by the other spouse as the other spouse's only or principal home.

(5) If a spouse ("the first spouse")—

(a) is entitled under this section to occupy a dwelling-house or any part of a dwelling-house, and
(b) makes any payment in or towards satisfaction of any liability of the other spouse ("the second spouse") in respect of mortgage payments affecting the dwelling-house,

the person to whom the payment is made may treat it as having been made by the second spouse, but the fact that that person has treated any such payment as having been so made does not affect any claim of the first spouse against the second spouse to an interest in the dwelling-house by virtue of the payment.

(6) If a spouse is entitled under this section to occupy a dwelling-house or part of a dwelling-house by reason of an interest of the other spouse under a trust, all the provisions of subsections (3) to (5) apply in relation to the trustees as they apply in relation to the other spouse.

(7) This section does not apply to a dwelling-house which has at no time been, and which was at no time intended by the spouses to be, a matrimonial home of theirs.

(8) A spouse's matrimonial home rights continue—

(a) only so long as the marriage subsists, except to the extent that an order under section 33(5) otherwise provides; and
(b) only so long as the other spouse is entitled as mentioned in subsection

(1) to occupy the dwelling-house, except where provision is made by section 31 for those rights to be a charge on an estate or interest in the dwelling-house.

(9) It is hereby declared that a spouse—

(a) who has an equitable interest in a dwelling-house or in its proceeds of sale, but
(b) is not a spouse in whom there is vested (whether solely or as joint tenant) a legal estate in fee simple or a legal term of years absolute in the dwelling-house,

is to be treated, only for the purpose of determining whether he has matrimonial home rights, as not being entitled to occupy the dwelling-house by virtue of that interest.

ANNOTATION

The words in square brackets in subs. (4)(b) were substituted on February 12, 1997 by Housing Act 1996 (Consequential Amendments) Order 1997 (S.I. 1997 No. 74), art. 2, Sched., para. 10(a).

Effect of matrimonial home rights as charge on dwelling-house

31.—(1) Subsections (2) and (3) apply if, at any time during a marriage, one spouse is entitled to occupy a dwelling-house by virtue of a beneficial estate or interest. **A2–047**

(2) The other spouse's matrimonial home rights are a charge on the estate or interest.

(3) The charge created by subsection (2) has the same priority as if it were an equitable interest created at whichever is the latest of the following dates—

(a) the date on which the spouse so entitled acquires the estate or interest;
(b) the date of the marriage; and
(c) 1st January 1968 (the commencement date of the Matrimonial Homes Act 1967).

(4) Subsections (5) and (6) apply if, at any time when a spouse's matrimonial home rights are a charge on an interest of the other spouse under a trust, there are, apart from either of the spouses, no persons, living or unborn, who are or could become beneficiaries under the trust.

(5) The rights are a charge also on the estate or interest of the trustees for the other spouse.

(6) The charge created by subsection (5) has the same priority as if it were an equitable interest created (under powers overriding the trusts) on the date when it arises.

(7) In determining for the purposes of subsection (4) whether there are any persons who are not, but could become, beneficiaries under the trust, there is to be disregarded any potential exercise of a general power of appointment exercis-

able by either or both of the spouses alone (whether or not the exercise of it requires the consent of another person).

(8) Even though a spouse's matrimonial home rights are a charge on an estate or interest in the dwelling-house, those rights are brought to an end by—

(a) the death of the other spouse, or
(b) the termination (otherwise than by death) of the marriage,

unless the court directs otherwise by an order made under section 33(5).

(9) If—

(a) a spouse's matrimonial home rights are a charge on an estate or interest in the dwelling-house, and
(b) that estate or interest is surrendered to merge in some other estate or interest expectant on it in such circumstances that, but for the merger, the person taking the estate or interest would be bound by the charge,

the surrender has effect subject to the charge and the persons thereafter entitled to the other estate or interest are, for so long as the estate or interest surrendered would have endured if not so surrendered, to be treated for all purposes of this Part as deriving title to the other estates or interest under the other spouse or, as the case may be, under the trustees for the other spouse, by virtue of the surrender.

(10) If the title to the legal estate by virtue of which a spouse is entitled to occupy a dwelling-house (including any legal estate held by trustees for that spouse) is registered under the Land Registration Act 1925 or any enactment replaced by that Act—

(a) registration of a land charge affecting the dwelling-house by virtue of this Part is to be effected by registering a notice under that Act; and
(b) a spouse's matrimonial home rights are not an overriding interest within the meaning of that Act affecting the dwelling-house even though the spouse is in actual occupation of the dwelling-house.

(11) A spouse's matrimonial home rights (whether or not constituting a charge) do not entitle that spouse to lodge a caution under section 54 of the Land Registration Act 1925.

(12) If—

(a) a spouse's matrimonial home rights are a charge on the estate of the other spouse or of trustees of the other spouse, and
(b) that estate is the subject of a mortgage,

then if, after the date of the creation of the mortgage (''the first mortgage''), the charge is registered under section 2 of the Land Charges Act 1972, the charge is, for the purposes of section 94 of the Law of Property Act 1925 (which regulates the rights of mortgagees to make further advances ranking in priority to subsequent mortgages), to be deemed to be a mortgage subsequent in date to the first mortgage.

(13) It is hereby declared that a charge under subsection (2) or (5) is not

registrable under subsection (10) or under section 2 of the Land Charges Act 1972 unless it is a charge on a legal estate.

Further provisions relating to matrimonial home rights

32. Schedule 4 re-enacts with consequential amendments and minor modifications provisions of the Matrimonial Homes Act 1983. **A2–048**

Occupation orders

Occupation orders where applicant has estate or interest etc. or has matrimonial home rights

33.—(1) If— **A2–049**

(a) a person ("the person entitled")—

(i) is entitled to occupy a dwelling-house by virtue of a beneficial estate or interest or contract or by virtue of any enactment giving him the right to remain in occupation, or

(ii) has matrimonial home rights in relation to a dwelling-house, and

(b) the dwelling-house—

(i) is or at any time has been the home of the person entitled and of another person with whom he is associated, or

(ii) was at any time intended by the person entitled and any such other person to be their home.

the person entitled may apply to the court for an order containing any of the provisions specified in subsections (3), (4) and (5).

(2) If an agreement to marry is terminated, no application under this section may be made by virtue of section 62(3)(e) by reference to that agreement after the end of the period of three years beginning with the day on which it is terminated.

(3) An order under this section may—

(a) enforce the applicant's entitlement to remain in occupation as against the other person ("the respondent");

(b) require the respondent to permit the applicant to enter and remain in the dwelling-house or part of the dwelling-house;

(c) regulate the occupation of the dwelling-house by either or both parties;

(d) if the respondent is entitled as mentioned in subsection (1)(a)(i), prohibit, suspend or restrict the exercise by him of his right to occupy the dwelling-house;

(e) if the respondent has matrimonial home rights in relation to the dwelling-house and the applicant is the other spouse, restrict or terminate those rights;

(f) require the respondent to leave the dwelling-house or part of the dwelling-house; or
(g) exclude the respondent from a defined area in which the dwelling-house is included.

(4) An order under this section may declare that the applicant is entitled as mentioned in subsection (1)(a)(i) or has matrimonial home rights.

(5) If the applicant has matrimonial home rights and the respondent is the other spouse, an order under this section made during the marriage may provide that those rights are not brought to an end by—

(a) the death of the other spouse; or
(b) the termination (otherwise than by death) of the marriage.

(6) In deciding whether to exercise its powers under subsection (3) and (if so) in what manner, the court shall have regard to all the circumstances including—

(a) the housing needs and housing resources of each of the parties and of any relevant child;
(b) the financial resources of each of the parties;
(c) the likely effect of any order, or of any decision by the court not to exercise its powers under subsection (3), on the health, safety or well-being of the parties and of any relevant child; and
(d) the conduct of the parties in relation to each other and otherwise.

(7) If it appears to the court that the applicant or any relevant child is likely to suffer significant harm attributable to conduct of the respondent if an order under this section containing one or more of the provisions mentioned in subsection (3) is not made, the court shall make the order unless it appears to it that—

(a) the respondent or any relevant child is likely to suffer significant harm if the order is made; and
(b) the harm likely to be suffered by the respondent or child in that event is as great as, or greater than, the harm attributable to conduct of the respondent which is likely to be suffered by the applicant or child if the order is not made.

(8) The court may exercise its powers under subsection (5) in any case where it considers that in all the circumstances it is just and reasonable to do so.

(9) An order under this section—

(a) may not be made after the death of either of the parties mentioned in subsection (1); and
(b) except in the case of an order made by virtue of subsection (5)(a), ceases to have effect on the death of either party.

(10) An order under this section may, in so far as it has continuing effect, be

made for a specified period, until the occurrence of a specified event or until further order.

Effect of order under s.33 where rights are charge on dwelling-house

34.—(1) If a spouse's matrimonial home rights are a charge on the estate or interest of the other spouse or of trustees for the other spouse— **A2–050**

(a) an order under section 33 against the other spouse has, except so far as a contrary intention appears, the same effect against persons deriving title under the other spouse or under the trustees and affected by the charge, and
(b) sections 33(1), (3), (4) and (10) and 30(3) to (6) apply in relation to any person deriving title under the other spouse or under the trustees and affected by the charge as they apply in relation to the other spouse.

(2) The court may make an order under section 33 by virtue of subsection (1)(b) if it considers that in all the circumstances it is just and reasonable to do so.

One former spouse with no existing right to occupy

35.—(1) This section applies if— **A2–051**

(a) one former spouse is entitled to occupy a dwelling-house by virtue of a beneficial estate or interest or contract, or by virtue of any enactment giving him the right to remain in occupation;
(b) the other former spouse is not so entitled; and
(c) the dwelling-house was at any time their matrimonial home or was at any time intended by them to be their matrimonial home.

(2) The former spouse not so entitled may apply to the court for an order under this section against the other former spouse (''the respondent'').

(3) If the applicant is in occupation, an order under this section must contain provision—

(a) giving the applicant the right not to be evicted or excluded from the dwelling-house or any aprt of it by the respondent for the period specified in the order; and
(b) prohibiting the respondent from evicting or excluding the applicant during that period.

(4) If the applicant is not in occupation, an order under this section must contain provision—

(a) giving the applicant the right to enter into and occupy the dwelling-house for the period specified in the order; and
(b) requiring the respondent to permit the exercise of that right.

(5) An order under this section may also—

(a) regulate the occupation of the dwelling-house by either or both of the parties;
(b) prohibit, suspend or restrict the exercise by the respondent of his right to occupy the dwelling-house;
(c) require the respondent to leave the dwelling-house or part of the dwelling-house; or
(d) exclude the respondent from a defined area in which the dwelling-house is included.

(6) In deciding whether to make an order under this section containing provision of the kind mentioned in subsection (3) or (4) and (if so) in what manner, the court shall have regard to all the circumstances including—

(a) the housing needs and housing resources of each of the parties and of any relevant child;
(b) the financial resources of each of the parties;
(c) the likely effect of any order, or of any decision by the court not to exercise its powers under subsection (3) or (4), on the health, safety or well-being of the parties and of any relevant child;
(d) the conduct of the parties in relation to each other and otherwise;
(e) the length of time that has elapsed since the parties ceased to live together;
(f) the length of time that has elapsed since the marriage was dissolved or annulled; and
(g) the existence of any pending proceedings between the parties—

(i) for an order under section 23A or 24 of the Matrimonial Causes Act 1973 (property adjustment orders in connection with divorce proceedings etc.);
(ii) for an order under paragraph 1(2)(d) or (e) of Schedule 1 to the Children Act 1989 (orders for financial relief against parents); or
(iii) relating to the legal or beneficial ownership of the dwelling-house.

(7) In deciding whether to exercise its power to include one or more of the provisions referred to in subsection (5) ("a subsection (5) provision") and (if so) in what manner, the court shall have regard to all the circumstances including the matters mentioned in subsection (6)(a) to (e).

(8) If the court decides to make an order under this section and it appears to it that, if the order does not include a subsection (5) provision, the applicant or any relevant child is likely to suffer significant harm attributable to conduct of the respondent, the court shall include the subsection (5) provision in the order unless it appears to the court that—

(a) the respondent or any relevant child is likely to suffer significant harm if the provision is included in the order; and
(b) the harm likely to be suffered by the respondent or child in that event is as great as or greater than the harm attributable to conduct of the respondent which is likely to be suffered by the applicant or child if the provision is not included.

(9) An order under this section—

(a) may not be made after the death of either of the former spouses; and
(b) ceases to have effect on the death of either of them.

(10) An order under this section must be limited so as to have effect for a specified period not exceeding six months, but may be extended on one or more occasions for a further specified period not exceeding six months.

(11) A former spouse who has an equitable interest in the dwelling-house or in the proceeds of sale of the dwelling-house but in whom there is not vested (whether solely or as joint tenant) a legal estate in fee simple or a legal term of years absolute in the dwelling-house is to be treated (but only for the purpose of determining whether he is eligible to apply under this section) as not being entitled to occupy the dwelling-house by virtue of that interest.

(12) Subsection (11) does not prejudice any right of such a former spouse to apply for an order under section 33.

(13) So long as an order under this section remains in force, subsections (3) to (6) of section 30 apply in relation to the applicant—

(a) as if he were the spouse entitled to occupy the dwelling-house by virtue of that section; and
(b) as if the respondent were the other spouse.

One cohabitant or former cohabitant with no existing right to occupy

36.—(1) This section applies if— **A2–052**

(a) one cohabitant or former cohabitant is entitled to occupy a dwelling-house by virtue of a beneficial estate or interest or contract or by virtue of any enactment giving him the right to remain in occupation;
(b) the other cohabitant or former cohabitant is not so entitled; and
(c) that dwelling-house is the home in which they live together as husband and wife or a home in which they at any time so lived together or intended so to live together.

(2) The cohabitant or former cohabitant not so entitled may apply to the court for an order under this section against the other cohabitant or former cohabitant (“the respondent”).

(3) If the applicant is in occupation, an order under this section must contain provision—

(a) giving the applicant the right not to be evicted or excluded from the dwelling-house or any part of it by the respondent for the period specified in the order; and
(b) prohibiting the respondent from evicting or excluding the applicant during that period.

(4) If the applicant is not in occupation, an order under this section must contain provision—

(a) giving the applicant the right to enter into and occupy the dwelling-house for the period specified in the order; and
(b) requiring the respondent to permit the exercise of that right.

(5) An order under this section may also—

(a) regulate the occupation of the dwelling-house by either or both of the parties;
(b) prohibit, suspend or restrict the exercise by the respondent of his right to occupy the dwelling-house;
(c) require the respondent to leave the dwelling-house or part of the dwelling-house; or
(d) exclude the respondent from a defined area in which the dwelling-house is included.

(6) In deciding whether to make an order under this section containing provision of the kind mentioned in subsection (3) or (4) and (if so) in what manner, the court shall have regard to all the circumstances including—

(a) the housing needs and housing resources of each of the parties and of any relevant child;
(b) the financial resources of each of the parties;
(c) the likely effect of any order, or of any decision by the court not to exercise its powers under subsection (3) or (4), on the health, safety or well-being of the parties and of any relevant child;
(d) the conduct of the parties in relation to each other and otherwise;
(e) the nature of the parties' relationship;
(f) the length of time during which they have lived together as husband and wife;
(g) whether there are or have been any children who are children of both parties or for whom both parties have or have had parental responsibility;
(h) the length of time that has elapsed since the parties ceased to live together; and
(i) the existence of any pending proceedings between the parties—

(i) for an order under paragraph 1(2)(d) or (e) of Schedule 1 to the

Children Act 1989 (orders for financial relief against parents); or

(ii) relating to the legal or beneficial ownership of the dwelling-house.

(7) In deciding whether to exercise its powers to include one or more of the provisions referred to in subsection (5) (''a subsection (5) provision'') and (if so) in what manner, the court shall have regard to all the circumstances including—

(a) the matters mentioned in subsection (6)(a) to (d); and
(b) the questions mentioned in subsection (8).

(8) The questions are—

(a) whether the applicant or any relevant child is likely to suffer significant harm attributable to conduct of the respondent if the subsection (5) provision is not included in the order, and
(b) whether the harm likely to be suffered by the respondent or child if the provision is included is as great as or greater than the harm attributable to conduct of the respondent which is likely to be suffered by the applicant or child if the provision is not included.

(9) An order under this section—

(a) may not be made after the death of either of the parties; and
(b) ceases to have effect on the death of either of them.

(10) An order under this section must be limited so as to have effect for a specified period not exceeding six months, but may be extended on one occasion for a further specified period not exceeding six months.

(11) A person who has an equitable interest in the dwelling-house or in the proceeds of sale of the dwelling-house but in whom there is not vested (whether solely or as joint tenant) a legal estate in fee simple or a legal term of years absolute in the dwelling-house is to be treated (but only for the purpose of determining whether he is eligible to apply under this section) as not being entitled to occupy the dwelling-house by virtue of that interest.

(12) Subsection (11) does not prejudice any right of such a person to apply for an order under section 33.

(13) So long as the order remains in force, subsections (3) to (6) of section 30 apply in relation to the applicant—

(a) as if he were a spouse entitled to occupy the dwelling-house by virtue of that section; and
(b) as if the respondent were the other spouse.

Neither spouse entitled to occupy

A2–053 **37.**—(1) This section applies if—

(a) one spouse or former spouse and the other spouse or former spouse occupy a dwelling-house which is or was the matrimonial home; but
(b) neither of them is entitled to remain in occupation—

(i) by virtue of a beneficial estate or interest or contract; or
(ii) by virtue of any enactment giving him the right to remain in occupation.

(2) Either of the parties may apply to the court for an order against the other under this section.

(3) An order under this section may—

(a) require the respondent to permit the applicant to enter and remain in the dwelling-house or part of the dwelling-house;
(b) regulate the occupation of the dwelling-house by either or both of the spouses;
(c) require the respondent to leave the dwelling-house or part of the dwelling-house; or
(d) exclude the respondent from a defined area in which the dwelling-house is included.

(4) Subsections (6) and (7) of section 33 apply to the exercise by the court of its powers under this section as they apply to the exercise by the court of its powers under subsection (3) of that section.

(5) An order under this section must be limited so as to have effect for a specified period not exceeding six months, but may be extended on one or more occasions for a further specified period not exceeding six months.

Neither cohabitant not former cohabitant entitled to occupy

A2–054 **38.**—(1) This section applies if—

(a) one cohabitant or former cohabitant and the other cohabitant or former cohabitant occupy a dwelling-house which is the home in which they live or lived together as husband and wife; but
(b) neither of them is entitled to remain in occupation—

(i) by virtue of a beneficial estate or interest or contract; or
(ii) by virtue of any enactment giving him the right to remain in occupation.

(2) Either of the parties may apply to the court for an order against the other under this section.

(3) An order under this section may—

(a) require the respondent to permit the applicant to enter and remain in the dwelling-house or part of the dwelling-house;
(b) regulate the occupation of the dwelling-house by either or both of the parties;
(c) require the respondent to leave the dwelling-house or part of the dwelling-house; or
(d) exclude the respondent from a defined area in which the dwelling-house is included.

(4) In deciding whether to exercise its powers to include one or more of the provisions referred to in subsection (3) (''a subsection (3) provision'') and (if so) in what manner, the court shall have regard to all the circumstances including—

(a) the housing needs and housing resources of each of the parties and of any relevant child;
(b) the financial resources of each of the parties;
(c) the likely effect of any order, or of any decision by the court not to exercise its powers under subsection (3), on the health, safety or well-being of the parties and of any relevant child;
(d) the conduct of the parties in relation to each other and otherwise; and
(e) the questions mentioned in subsection (5).

(5) The questions are—

(a) whether the applicant or any relevant child is likely to suffer significant harm attributable to conduct of the respondent if the subsection (3) provision is not included in the order; and
(b) whether the harm likely to be suffered by the respondent or child if the provision is included is as great as or greater than the harm attributable to conduct of the respondent which is likely to be suffered by the applicant or child if the provision is not included.

(6) An order under this section shall be limited so as to have effect for a specified period not exceeding six months, but may be extended on one occasion for a further specified period not exceeding six months.

. . . .

Transfer of tenancies

Transfer of certain tenancies

53. Schedule 7 makes provision in relation to the transfer of certain tenancies on divorce etc. or on separation of cohabitants. **A2–055**

. . . .

Section 53

SCHEDULE 7

A2–056 TRANSFER OF CERTAIN TENANCIES ON DIVORCE ETC. OR ON SEPARATION OF COHABITANTS

PART I
GENERAL

Interpretation

1. In this Schedule—

"cohabitant", except in paragraph 3, includes (where the context requires) former cohabitant;

"the court" does not include a magistrates' court,

"landlord" includes—

(a) any person from time to time deriving title under the original landlord; and
(b) in relation to any dwelling-house, any person other than the tenant who is, or (but for Part VII of the Rent Act 1977 or Part II of the Rent (Agriculture) Act 1976) would be, entitled to possession of the dwelling-house;

"Part II order" means an order under Part II of this Schedule;

"a relevant tenancy" means—

(a) a protected tenancy or statutory tenancy within the meaning of the Rent Act 1977;
(b) a statutory tenancy within the meaning of the Rent (Agriculture) Act 1976;
(c) a secure tenancy within the meaning of section 79 of the Housing Act 1985; [. . .]
(d) an assured tenancy or assured agricultural occupancy within the meaning of Part I of the Housing Act 1988; [or
(e) an introductory tenancy within the meaning of Chapter I of Part V of the Housing Act 1996;]

"spouse", except in paragraph 2, includes (where the context requires) former spouse; and

"tenancy" includes sub-tenancy.

ANNOTATION

The word omitted from sub-para. (c), and sub-para. (e), were inserted by Housing Act 1996 (Consequential Amendments) Order 1997 (S.I. 1997 No. 74) art. 2, Sched., para. 10(b).

Cases in which the court may make an order

2.—(1) This paragraph applies if one spouse is entitled, either in his own right or jointly with the other spouse, to occupy a dwelling-house by virtue of a relevant tenancy.

[(2) On granting a decree of divorce, a decree of nullity of marriage or a decree of judicial separation or at any time thereafter (whether, in the case of a decree of divorce or nullity of marriage, before or after the decree is made absolute), the court may make a Part II order.]

ANNOTATION

The words in square brackets were substituted by Family Law Act 1996 (Commencement No. 2) Order 1997 (S.I. 1997 No. 1892), art. 4(a).

3.—(1) This paragraph applies if one cohabitant is entitled, either in his own right or jointly with the other cohabitant, to occupy a dwelling-house by virtue of a relevant tenancy.

(2) If the cohabitants cease to live together as husband and wife, the court may make a Part II order.

4. The court shall not make a Part II order unless the dwelling-house is or was—

(a) in the case of spouses, a matrimonial home; or
(b) in the case of cohabitants, a home in which they lived together as husband and wife.

Matters to which the court must have regard

5. In determining whether to exercise its powers under Part II of this Schedule and, if so, in what manner, the court shall have regard to all the circumstances of the case including— **A2–057**

(a) the circumstances in which the tenancy was granted to either or both of the spouses or cohabitants or, as the case requires, the circumstances in which either or both of them became tenant under the tenancy;
(b) the matters mentioned in section 33(6)(a), (b) and (c) and, where the parties are cohabitants and only one of them is entitled to occupy the dwelling-house by virtue of the relevant tenancy, the further matters mentioned in section 36(6)(e), (f), (g) and (h); and
(c) the suitability of the parties as tenants.

Part II

Orders That May be Made

References to entitlement to occupy

6. References in this Part of this Schedule to a spouse or a cohabitant being entitled to occupy a dwelling-house by virtue of a relevant tenancy apply whether that entitlement is in his own right or jointly with the other spouse or cohabitant. **A2–058**

Protected, secure or assured tenancy or assured agricultural occupancy

7.—(1) If a spouse or cohabitant is entitled to occupy the dwelling-house by virtue of a protected tenancy within the meaning of the Rent Act 1977, a secure tenancy within the meaning of the Housing Act 1985 [, an assured tenancy] or assured agricultural occupancy within the meaning of Part I of the Housing Act 1988 [or an introductory tenancy within the meaning of Chapter I of Part V of the Housing Act 1996], the court may by order direct that, as from such date as may be specified in the order, there shall, by virtue of the order and without further assurance, be transferred to, and vested in, the other spouse or cohabitant—

(a) the estate or interest which the spouse or cohabitant so entitled had in the dwelling-house immediately before that date by virtue of the lease or agreement creating the tenancy and any assignment of that lease or agreement, with all rights, privileges and appurtenances attaching to that estate or interest but subject to all covenants, obligations, liabilities and incumbrances to which it is subject; and
(b) where the spouse or cohabitant so entitled is an assignee of such lease or agreement, the liability of that spouse or cohabitant under any covenant of indemnity by the assignee express or implied in the assignment of the lease or agreement to that spouse or cohabitant.

(2) If an order is made under this paragraph, any liability or obligation to which the spouse or cohabitant so entitled is subject under any covenant having reference to the dwelling-house in the lease or agreement, being a liability or obligation falling due to be discharged or performed on or after the date so specified, shall not be enforceable against that spouse or cohabitant.

(3) If the spouse so entitled is a successor within the meaning of Part IV of the Housing Act 1985, his former spouse or former cohabitant (or, [in the case of judicial separation], his spouse) shall be deemed also to be a successor within the meaning of that Part.

[(3A) If the Spouse or cohabitant so entitled is a successor within the meaning of section 132 of the Housing Act 1996, his former spouse or former cohabitant (or, if a separation order is in force, his spouse) shall be deemed also to be a successor within the meaning of that section.]

(4) If the spouse or cohabitant so entitled is for the purpose of section 17 of the Housing Act 1988 a successor in relation to the tenancy or occupancy, his former spouse or former cohabitant (or, [in the case of judicial separation], his spouse) is to be deemed to be a successor in relation to the tenancy or occupancy for the purposes of that section.

(5) If the transfer under sub-paragraph (1) is of an assured agricultural occupancy, then, for the purposes of Chapter III of Part I of the Housing Act 1988—

(a) the agricultural worker condition is fulfilled with respect to the dwelling-house while the spouse or cohabitant to whom the assured agricultural occupancy is transferred continues to be the occupier under that occupancy, and
(b) that condition is to be treated as so fulfilled by virtue of the same paragraph of Schedule 3 to the Housing Act 1988 as was applicable before the transfer.

[........]

ANNOTATION

The words in the first set of square brackets in sub-para. (1) were substituted, the words in the second set of brackets in sub-para. (1) were inserted and sub-para. (3A) was inserted with effect from February 12, 1997 by Housing Act 1996 (Consequential Amendments) Order 1997 (S.I. 1997 No. 74), art. 2, Sched., para. 10(b). The words in square brackets in sub-paras. (3) and (4) were substituted and sub-para. (6) was omitted on July 28, 1997 by Family Law Act 1996 (Commencement No. 2) Order 1997 (S.I. 1997 No. 1892), art. 4(b), (c).

Statutory tenancy within the meaning of the Rent Act 1977

8.—(1) This paragraph applies if the spouse or cohabitant is entitled to occupy the dwelling-house by virtue of a statutory tenancy within the meaning of the Rent Act 1977.

(2) The court may by order direct that, as from the date specified in the order—

(a) that spouse or cohabitant is to cease to be entitled to occupy the dwelling-house; and
(b) the other spouse or cohabitant is to be deemed to be the tenant or, as the case may be, the sole tenant under that statutory tenancy.

(3) The question whether the provisions of paragraphs 1 to 3, or (as the case may be) paragraphs 5 to 7 of Schedule 1 to the Rent Act 1977, as to the succession by the surviving spouse of a deceased tenant, or by a member of the deceased tenant's family, to the right to retain possession are capable of having effect in the event of the death of the person deemed by an order under this paragraph to be the tenant or sole tenant under the statutory tenancy is to be determined according as those provisions have or have not already had effect in relation to the statutory tenancy.

Statutory tenancy within the meaning of the Rent (Agriculture) Act 1976

9.—(1) This paragraph applies if the spouse or cohabitant is entitled to occupy the dwelling-house by virtue of a statutory tenancy within the meaning of the Rent (Agriculture) Act 1976.

(2) The court may by order direct that, as from such date as may be specified in the order—

(a) that spouse or cohabitant is to cease to be entitled to occupy the dwelling-house; and
(b) the other spouse or cohabitant is to be deemed to be the tenant or, as the case may be, the sole tenant under that statutory tenancy.

(3) A spouse or cohabitant who is deemed under this paragraph to be the tenant under a statutory tenancy is (within the meaning of that Act) a statutory tenant in his own right, or a statutory tenant by succession, according as the other spouse or cohabitant was a statutory tenant in his own right or a statutory tenant by succession.

PART III

SUPPLEMENTARY PROVISIONS

Compensation

A2–059 10.—(1) If the court makes a Part II order, it may by the order direct the making of a payment by the spouse or cohabitant to whom the tenancy is transferred ("the transferee") to the other spouse or cohabitant ("the transferor").

(2) Without prejudice to that, the court may, on making an order by virtue of sub-paragraph (1) for the payment of a sum—

(a) direct that payment of that sum or any part of it is to be deferred until a specified date or until the occurrence of a specified event, or
(b) direct that that sum or any part of it is to be paid by instalments.

(3) Where an order has been made by virtue of sub-paragraph (1), the court may, on the application of the transferee or the transferor—

(a) exercise its powers under sub-paragraph (2), or
(b) vary any direction previously given under that sub-paragraph,

at any time before the sum whose payment is required by the order is paid in full.

(4) In deciding whether to exercise its powers under this paragraph and, if so, in what manner, the court shall have regard to all the circumstances including—

(a) the financial loss that would otherwise be suffered by the transferor as a result of the order;
(b) the financial needs and financial resources of the parties; and
(c) the financial obligations which the parties have, or are likely to have in the foreseeable future, including financial obligations to each other and to any relevant child.

(5) The court shall not give any direction under sub-paragraph (2) unless it appears to it that immediate payment of the sum required by the order would cause the transferee financial hardship which is greater than any financial hardship that would be caused to the transferor if the direction were given.

Liabilities and obligations in respect of the dwelling-house

11.—(1) If the court makes a Part II order, it may by the order direct that both spouses or cohabitants are to be jointly and severally liable to discharge or perform any or all of the liabilities and obligations in respect of the dwelling-house (whether arising under the tenancy or otherwise) which—

(a) have at the date of the order fallen due to be discharged or performed by one only of them; or
(b) but for the direction, would before the date specified as the date on which the order is to take effect fall due to be discharged or performed by one only of them.

(2) If the court gives such a direction, it may further direct that either spouse or cohabitant is to be liable to indemnify the other in whole or in part against any payment made or expenses incurred by the other in discharging or performing any such liability or obligation.

Date when order made between spouses is to take effect

12.—(1) In the case of a decree of [divorce or] nullity of marriage, the date specified in a Part II order as the date on which the order is to take effect must not be earlier than the date on which the decree is made absolute.

[. . . . .]

Annotation

The words in square brackets were inserted and para. 12(2) was omitted on July 28, 1997 by Family Law Act 1996 (Commencement No. 2) Order 1997 (S.I. 1997 No. 1892), art. 4(d).

Remarriage of either spouse

13.—(1) If after *the making of a divorce order or* the grant of a decree [dissolving or] annulling a marriage either spouse remarries, that spouse is not entitled to apply, by reference to *the making of that order or* the grant of that decree, for a Part II order.

(2) For the avoidance of doubt it is hereby declared that the reference in sub-paragraph (1) to remarriage includes a reference to a marriage which is by law void or voidable.

ANNOTATION

The words in italics were omitted and the words in square brackets were inserted on July 28, 1997 by Family Law Act 1996 (Commencement No. 2) Order 1997 (S.I. 1997 No. 1892), art. 4(e).

Rules of court

14.—(1) Rules of court shall be made requiring the court, before it makes an order under this Schedule, to give the landlord of the dwelling-house to which the order will relate an opportunity of being heard.

(2) Rules of court may provide that an application for a Part II order by reference to an order or decree may not, without the leave of the court by which that order was made or decree was granted, be made after the expiration of such period from the order or grant as may be prescribed by the rules.

Saving for other provisions of Act

A2–060 15.—(1) If a spouse is entitled to occupy a dwelling-house by virtue of a tenancy, this Schedule does not affect the operation of sections 30 and 31 in relation to the other spouse's matrimonial home rights.

(2) If a spouse or cohabitant is entitled to occupy a dwelling-house by virtue of a tenancy, the court's powers to make orders under this Schedule are additional to those conferred by sections 33, 35 and 36.

Housing Act 1996 A2–061

(1996 c.52)

An Act to make provision about housing, including provision about the social rented sector, houses in multiple occupation, landlord and tenant matters, the administration of housing benefit, the conduct of tenants, the allocation of housing accommodation by local housing authorities and homelessness; and for connected purposes.

[24th July 1996]

PART I

SOCIAL RENTED SECTOR

CHAPTER I

REGISTERED SOCIAL LANDLORDS

Registration

The register of social landlords

1.—(1) The *Corporation* [Relevant Authority] shall maintain a register of **A2–062**
social landlords which shall be open to inspection at all reasonable times *at the head office of the Corporation.*

[(1A) In this Part "the Relevant Authority" means the Housing Corporation or the Secretary of State, as provided by section 56.

(1B) The register maintained by the Housing Corporation shall be maintained at its head office.]

(2) On the commencement of this section every housing association which immediately before commencement was registered in the register kept by the Corporation under Part I of the Housing Associations Act 1985 shall be registered as a social landlord.

ANNOTATION

The words in subs. (1) were substituted and repealed, subss. (1A) and (1B) were inserted and subs. (2) was repealed, with effect from November 1, 1998, by Government of Wales Act 1998, s.140(1), Sched. 16, paras. 82, 83: S.I. 1998 No. 2244.

Eligibility for registration

A2–063 **2.**—(1) A body is eligible for registration as a social landlord if it is—

(a) a registered charity which is a housing association,
(b) a society registered under the Industrial and Provident Societies Act 1965 which satisfies the conditions in subsection (2), or
(c) a company registered under the Companies Act 1985 which satisfies those conditions.

(2) The conditions are that the body is non-profit-making and is established for the purpose of, or has among its objects or powers, the provision, construction, improvement or management of—

(a) houses to be kept available for letting,
(b) houses for occupation by members of the body, where the rules of the body restrict membership to persons entitled or prospectively entitled (as tenants or otherwise) to occupy a house provided or managed by the body, or
(c) hostels,

and that any additional purposes or objects are among those specified in subsection (4).

(3) For the purposes of this section a body is non-profit-making if—

(a) it does not trade for profit, or
(b) its constitution or rules prohibit the issue of capital with interest or divident exceeding the rate prescribed by the Treasury for the purposes of section 1(1)(b) of the Housing Associations Act 1985.

(4) The permissible additional purposes or objects are—

(a) providing land, amenities or services, or providing, constructing, repairing or improving buildings, for its residents, either exclusively or together with other persons;
(b) acquiring, or repairing and improving, or creating by the conversion of houses or other property, houses to be disposed of on sale, on lease or on shared ownership terms;
(c) constructing houses to be disposed of on shared ownership terms;
(d) managing houses held on leases or other lettings (not being houses within subsection (2)(a) or (b)) or blocks of flats;
(e) providing services of any description for owners or occupiers of

houses in arranging or carrying out works of maintenance, repair or improvement, or encouraging or facilitating the carrying out of such works;

(f) encouraging and giving advice on the forming of housing associations or providing services for, and giving advice on the running of, such associations and other voluntary organisations concerned with housing, or matters connected with housing.

(5) A body is not ineligible for registration as a social landlord by reason only that its powers include power—

(a) to acquire commercial premises or businesses as an incidental part of a project or series of projects undertaken for purposes or objects falling within subsection (2) or (4);

(b) to repair, improve or convert commercial premises acquired as mentioned in paragraph (a) or to carry on for a limited period any business so acquired;

(c) to repair or improve houses, or buildings in which houses are situated, after a disposal of the houses by the body by way of sale or lease or on shared ownership terms.

(6) In this section—

''block of flats'' means a building containing two or more flats which are held on leases or other lettings and which are occupied or intended to be occupied wholly or mainly for residential purposes;

''disposed of on shared ownership terms'' means disposed of on a lease—

(a) granted on a payment of a premium calculated by reference to a percentage of the value of the house or of the cost of providing it, or

(b) under which the tenant (or his personal representatives) will or may be entitled to a sum calculated by reference directly or indirectly to the value of the house;

''letting'' includes the grant of a licence to occupy;

''residents'', in relation to a body, means persons occupying a house or hostel provided or managed by the body; and

''voluntary organisation'' means an organisation whose activities are not carried on for profit.

(7) The Secretary of State may by order specify permissible purposes, objects or powers additional to those specified in subsections (4) and (5).

The order may (without prejudice to the inclusion of other incidental or supplementary provisions) contain such provision as the Secretary of State thinks fit with respect to the priority of mortgages entered into in pursuance of any additional purposes, objects or powers.

(8) An order under subsection (7) shall be made by statutory instrument which shall be subject to annulment in pursuance of a resolution of either House of Parliament.

(1996 c.52)

Registration

A2–064 **3.**—(1) The [Relevant Authority] may register as a social landlord any body which is eligible for such registration.

(2) An application for registration shall be made in such manner, and shall be accompanied by such fee (if any), as the [Relevant Authority] may determine.

(3) As soon as may be after registering a body as a social landlord the Corporation shall give notice of the registration—

(a) in the case of a registered charity, to the Charity Commissioners,
(b) in the case of an industrial and provident society, to the appropriate registrar, and
(c) in the case of a company registered under the Companies Act 1985 (including such a company which is also a registered charity), to the registrar of companies,

who shall record the registration.

(4) A body which at any time is, or was, registered as a social landlord shall, for all purposes other than rectification of the register, be conclusively presumed to be, or to have been, at that time a body eligible for registration as a social landlord.

ANNOTATION

The words in subss. (1) and (2) were substituted, with effect from November 1, 1998, by Government of Wales Act 1998, s.140(1), Sched. 16, para. 82: S.I. 1998 No. 2244.

Removal from the register

A2–065 **4.**—(1) A body which has been registered as a social landlord shall not be removed from the register except in accordance with this section.

(2) If it appears to the [Relevant Authority] that a body which is on the register of social landlords—

(a) is no longer a body eligible for such registration, or
(b) has ceased to exist or does not operate,

the [Relevant Authority] shall, after giving the body at least 14 days' notice, remove it from the register.

(3) In the case of a body which appears to the [Relevant Authority] to have ceased to exist or not to operate, notice under subsection (2) shall be deemed to be given to the body if it is served at the address last known to the [Relevant Authority] to be the principal place of business of the body.

(4) A body which is registered as a social landlord may request the [Relevant Authority] to remove it from the register and the [Relevant Authority] may do so, subject to the following provisions.

(5) Before removing a body from the register of social landlords under subsection (4) the [Relevant Authority] shall consult the local authorities in whose area

the body operates; and the [Relevant Authority] shall also inform those authorities of its decision.

(6) As soon as may be after removing a body from the register of social landlords the [Relevant Authority] shall give notice of the removal—

(a) in the case of a registered charity, to the Charity Commissioners,
(b) in the case of an industrial and provident society, to the appropriate registrar, and
(c) in the case of a company registered under the Companies Act 1985 (including such a company which is also a registered charity), to the registrar of companies,

who shall record the removal.

ANNOTATION

The words in square brackets throughout this section were substituted, with effect from November 1, 1998, by Government of Wales Act 1998, s.140(1), Sched. 16, para. 82: S.I. 1998 No. 2244.

Criteria for registration or removal from register

5.—(1) The [Relevant Authority] shall establish (and may from time to time vary) criteria which should be satisfied by a body seeking registration as a social landlord; and in deciding whether to register a body the [Relevant Authority] shall have regard to whether those criteria are met. **A2–066**

(2) The [Relevant Authority] shall establish (and may from time to time vary) criteria which should be satisfied where such a body seeks to be removed from the register of social landlords; and in deciding whether to remove a body from the register the [Relevant Authority] shall have regard to whether those criteria are met.

(3) Before establishing or varying any such criteria the [Relevant Authority] shall consult such bodies representative of registered social landlords, and such bodies representative of local authorities, as it thinks fit.

(4) The [Relevant Authority] shall publish the criteria for registration and the criteria for removal from the register in such manner as the [Relevant Authority] considers appropriate for bringing the criteria to the notice of bodies representative of registered social landlords and bodies representative of local authorities.

ANNOTATION

The words in square brackets throughout this section were substituted, with effect from November 1, 1998, by Government of Wales Act 1998, s.140(1), Sched. 16, para. 82: S.I. 1998 No. 2244.

Appeal against decision on removal

6.—(1) A body which is aggrieved by a decision of the [Relevant Authority]— **A2–067**

(a) not to register it as a social landlord, or

(b) to remove or not to remove it from the register of social landlords, may appeal against the decision to the High Court.

(2) If an appeal is brought against a decision relating to the removal of a body from the register, the [Relevant Authority] shall not remove the body from the register until the appeal has been finally determined or is withdrawn.

(3) As soon as may be after an appeal is brought against a decision relating to the removal of a body from the register, the [Relevant Authority] shall give notice of the appeal—

(a) in the case of a registered charity, to the Charity Commissioners,
(b) in the case of an industrial and provident society, to the appropriate registrar, and
(c) in the case of a company registered under the Companies Act 1985 (including such a company which is also a registered charity), to the registrar of companies.

ANNOTATION

The words in square brackets throughout this section were substituted, with effect from November 1, 1998, by Government of Wales Act 1998, s.140, Sched. 16, para. 82: S.I. 1998 No. 2244.

[. . . . .]

CHAPTER II

DISPOSAL OF LAND AND RELATED MATTERS

[. . . . .]

Right of tenant to acquire dwelling

Right of tenant to acquire dwelling

A2–068 **16.**—(1) A tenant of a registered social landlord has the right to acquire the dwelling of which he is a tenant if—

(a) he is a tenant under an assured tenancy, other than an assured shorthold tenancy or a long tenancy, or under a secure tenancy,
(b) the dwelling was provided with public money and has remained in the social rented sector, and

(c) he satisfies any further qualifying conditions applicable under Part V of the Housing Act 1985 (the right to buy) as it applies in relation to the right conferred by this section.

(2) For this purpose a dwelling shall be regarded as provided with public money if—

(a) it was provided or acquired wholly or in part by means of a grant under section 18 (social housing grant),
(b) it was provided or acquired wholly or in part by applying or appropriating sums standing in the disposal proceeds fund of a registered social landlord (see section 25), or
(c) it was acquired by a registered social landlord after the commencement of this paragraph on a disposal by a public sector landlord at a time when it was capable of being let as a separate dwelling.

(3) A dwelling shall be regarded for the purposes of this section as having remained within the social rented sector if, since it was so provided or acquired—

(a) the person holding the freehold interest in the dwelling has been either a registered social landlord or a public sector landlord; and
(b) any person holding an interest as lessee (otherwise than as mortgagee) in the dwelling has been—
   (i) an individual holding otherwise than under a long tenancy; or
   (ii) a registered social landlord or a public sector landlord.

(4) A dwelling shall be regarded for the purposes of this section as provided by means of a grant under section 18 (social housing grant) if, and only if, the Corporation when making the grant notified the recipient that the dwelling was to be so regarded.

The Corporation shall before making the grant inform the applicant that it proposes to give such a notice and allow him an opportunity to withdraw his application within a specified time.

Right of tenant to acquire dwelling: supplementary provisions

17.—(1) The Secretary of State may by order— **A2–069**

(a) specify the amount of rate of discount to be given on the exercise of the right conferred by section 16; and
(b) designate rural areas in relation to dwellings in which the right conferred by that section does not arise.

(2) The provisions of Part V of the Housing Act 1985 apply in relation to the right to acquire under section 16—

(a) subject to any order under subsection (1) above, and
(b) subject to such other exceptions, adaptations and other modifications as may be specified by regulations made by the Secretary of State.

(3) The regulations may provide—

(a) that the powers of the Secretary of State under sections 164 to 170 of that Act (powers to intervene, give directions or assist) do not apply,
(b) that paragraphs 1 and 3 (exceptions for charities and certain housing associations), and paragraph 11 (right of appeal to Secretary of State), of Schedule 5 to that Act do not apply,
(c) that the provisions of Part V of that Act relating to the right to acquire on rent to mortgage terms do not apply,
(d) that the provisions of that Part relating to restrictions on disposals in National Parks, &c. do not apply, and
(e) that the provisions of that Part relating to the preserved right to buy do not apply.

Nothing in this subsection affects the generality of the power conferred by subsection (2).

(4) The specified exceptions, adaptations and other modifications shall take the form of textual amendments of the provisions of Part V of that Act as they apply in relation to the right to buy under that Part; and the first regulations, and any subsequent consolidating regulations, shall set out the provisions of Part V as they so apply.

(5) An order or regulations under this section—

(a) may make different provision for different cases or classes of case including different areas, and
(b) may contain such incidental, supplementary and transitional provisions as the Secretary of State considers appropriate.

(6) Before making an order which would have the effect that an area ceased to be designated under subsection (1)(b), the Secretary of State shall consult—

(a) the local housing authority or authorities in whose district the area or any part of it is situated or, if the order is general in its effect, local housing authorities in general, and
(b) such bodies appearing to him to be representative of registered social landlords as he considers appropriate.

(7) An order or regulations under this section shall be made by statutory instrument which shall be subject to annulment in pursuance of a resolution of either House of Parliament.

[. . . . .]

PART V

CONDUCT OF TENANTS

CHAPTER I

INTRODUCTORY TENANCIES

General provisions

Introductory tenancies

124.—(1) A local housing authority or a housing action trust may elect to operate an introductory tenancy regime. **A2–070**

(2) When such an election is in force, every periodic tenancy of a dwelling-house entered into or adopted by the authority or trust shall, if it would otherwise be a secure tenancy, be an introductory tenancy, unless immediately before the tenancy was entered into or adopted the tenant or, in the case of joint tenants, one or more of them was—

(a) a secure tenant of the same or another dwelling-house, or
(b) an assured tenant of a registered social landlord (otherwise than under an assured shorthold tenancy) in respect of the same or another dwelling-house.

(3) Subsection (2) does not apply to a tenancy entered into or adopted in pursuance of a contract made before the election was made.

(4) For the purposes of this Chapter a periodic tenancy is adopted by a person if that person becomes the landlord under the tenancy, whether on a disposal or surrender of the interest of the former landlord.

(5) An election under this section may be revoked at any time, without prejudice to the making of a further election.

Duration of introductory tenancy

125.—(1) A tenancy remains an introductory tenancy until the end of the trial period, unless one of the events mentioned in subsection (5) occurs before the end of that period. **A2–071**

(2) The "trial period" is the period of one year beginning with—

(a) in the case of a tenancy which was entered into by a local housing authority or housing action trust—

(i) the date on which the tenancy was entered into, or
(ii) if later, the date on which a tenant was first entitled to possession under the tenancy; or

(b) in the case of a tenancy which was adopted by a local housing authority or housing action trust, the date of adoption;

subject as follows.

(3) Where the tenant under an introductory tenancy was formerly a tenant under another introductory tenancy, or held an assured shorthold tenancy from a registered social landlord, any period or periods during which he was such a tenant shall count towards the trial period, provided—

(a) if there was one such period, it ended immediately before the date specified in subsection (2), and
(b) if there was more than one such period, the most recent period ended immediately before that date and each period succeeded the other without interruption.

(4) Where there are joint tenants under an introductory tenancy, the reference in subsection (3) to the tenant shall be construed as referring to the joint tenant in whose case the application of that subsection produces the earliest starting date for the trial period.

(5) A tenancy ceases to be an introductory tenancy if, before the end of the trial period—

(a) the circumstances are such that the tenancy would not otherwise be a secure tenancy,
(b) a person or body other than a local housing authority or housing action trust becomes the landlord under the tenancy,
(c) the election in force when the tenancy was entered into or adopted is revoked, or
(d) the tenancy ceases to be an introductory tenancy by virtue of section 133(3) (succession).

(6) A tenancy does not come to an end merely because it ceases to be an introductory tenancy, but a tenancy which has once ceased to be an introductory tenancy cannot subsequently become an introductory tenancy.

(7) This section has effect subject to section 130 (effect of beginning proceedings for possession).

Licences

A2–072 **126.**—(1) The provisions of this Chapter apply in relation to a licence to occupy a dwelling-house (whether or not granted for a consideration) as they apply in relation to a tenancy.

(2) Subsection (1) does not apply to a licence granted as a temporary expedi-

ent to a person who entered the dwelling-house or any other land as a trespasser (whether or not, before the grant of that licence, another licence to occupy that or another dwelling-house had been granted to him).

[........]

Part VII

Homelessness

[........]

Interim duty to accommodate

Interim duty to accommodate in case of apparent priority need

188.—(1) If the local housing authority have reason to believe that an applicant may be homeless, eligible for assistance and have a priority need, they shall secure that accommodation is available for his occupation pending a decision as to the duty (if any) owed to him under the following provisions of this Part. **A2–073**

(2) The duty under this section arises irrespective of any possibility of the referral of the applicant's case to another local housing authority (see sections 198 to 200).

(3) The duty ceases when the authority's decision is notified to the applicant, even if the applicant requests a review of the decision (see section 202).

The authority may continue to secure that accommodation is available for the applicant's occupation pending a decision on a review.

[........]

Duties to persons found to be homeless or threatened with homelessness

Duties to persons becoming homeless intentionally

190.—(1) This section applies where the local housing authority are satisfied that an applicant is homeless and is eligible for assistance but are also satisfied that he became homeless intentionally. **A2–074**

(2) If the authority are satisfied that the applicant has a priority need, they shall—

(a) secure that accommodation is available for his occupation for such period as they consider will give him a reasonable opportunity of securing accommodation for his occupation, and

(b) provide him with advice and such assistance as they consider appropriate in the circumstances in any attempts he may make to secure that accommodation becomes available for his occupation.

(3) If they are not satisfied that he has a priority need, they shall provide him with advice and such assistance as they consider appropriate in the circumstances in any attempts he may make to secure that accommodation becomes available for his occupation.

[........]

Referral to another local housing authority

[........]

Duties to applicant whose case is considered for referral or referred

A2–075 **200.**—(1) Where a local housing authority notify an applicant that they intend to notify or have notified another local housing authority of their opinion that the conditions are met for the referral of his case to that other authority—

(a) they cease to be subject to any duty under section 188 (interim duty to accommodate in case of apparent priority need), and
(b) they are not subject to any duty under section 193 (the main housing duty),

but they shall secure that accommodation is available for occupation by the applicant until he is notified of the decision whether the conditions for referral of his case are met.

(2) When it has been decided whether the conditions for referral are met, the notifying authority shall notify the applicant of the decision and inform him of the reasons for it.

The notice shall also inform the applicant of his right to request a review of the decision and of the time within which such a request must be made.

(3) If it is decided that the conditions for referral are not met, the notifying authority shall secure that accommodation is available for occupation by the applicant until they have considered whether other suitable accommodation is available for his occupation in their district.

If they are satisfied that other suitable accommodation is available for his occupation in their district, section 197(2) applies; and if they are not so satisfied, they are subject to the duty under section 193 (the main housing duty).

(4) If it is decided that the conditions for referral are met, the notified authority shall secure that accommodation is available for occupation by the applicant until they have considered whether other suitable accommodation is available for his occupation in their district.

If they are satisfied that other suitable accommodation is available for his occupation in their district, section 197(2) applies; and if they are not so satisfied, they are subject to the duty under section 193 (the main housing duty).

(5) The duty under subsection (1), (3) or (4) ceases as provided in that subsection even if the applicant requests a review of the authority's decision (see section 202).

The authority may continue to secure that accommodation is available for the applicant's occupation pending the decision on a review.

(6) Notice required to be given to an applicant under this section shall be given in writing and, if not received by him, shall be treated as having been given to him if it is made available at the authority's office for a reasonable period for collection by him or on his behalf.

[........]

Right of appeal to county court on point of law

204.—(1) If an applicant who has requested a review under section 202— **A2–076**

(a) is dissatisfied with the decision on the review, or
(b) is not notified of the decision on the review within the time prescribed under section 203,

he may appeal to the county court on any point of law arising from the decision or, as the case may be, the original decision.

(2) An appeal must be brought within 21 days of his being notified of the decision or, as the case may be, of the date on which he should have been notified of a decision on review.

(3) On appeal the court may make such order confirming, quashing or varying the decision as it thinks fit.

(4) Where the authority were under a duty under section 188, 190 or 200 to secure that accommodation is available for the applicant's occupation, they may continue to secure that accommodation is so available—

(a) during the period for appealing under this section against the authority's decision, and
(b) if an appeal is brought, until the appeal (and any further appeal) is finally determined.

[........]

Supplementary provisions

[........]

Discharge of functions: arrangements with private landlord

A2–077 **209.**—(1) This section applies where in pursuance of any of their housing functions under this Part a local housing authority make the arrangements with a private landlord to provide accommodation.

For this purpose a ''private landlord'' means a landlord who is not within section 80(1) of the Housing Act 1985 (the landlord condition for secure tenancies).

(2) If the housing function arises under section 188, 190, 200, or 204(4) (interim duties), a tenancy granted in pursuance of the arrangements to a person specified by the authority cannot be an assured tenancy before the end of the period of twelve months beginning with—

(a) the date on which the applicant was notified of the authority's decision under section 184(3) or 198(5), or
(b) if there is a review of that decision under section 202 or an appeal to the court under section 204, the date on which he is notified of the decision on review or the appeal is finally determined,

unless, before or during that period, the tenant is notified by the landlord (or, in the cases of joint landlords, at least one of them) that the tenancy is to be regarded as an assured shorthold tenancy or an assured tenancy other than an assured shorthold tenancy. A registered social landlord cannot serve such a notice making such a tenancy an assured tenancy other than an assured shorthold tenancy.

(3) Where in any other case a tenancy is granted in pursuance of the arrangements by a registered social landlord to a person specified by the authority—

(a) the tenancy cannot be an assured tenancy unless it is an assured shorthold tenancy, and
(b) the landlord cannot convert the tenancy to an assured tenancy unless the accommodation is allocated to the tenant under Part VI.

[. . . . .]

Part VIII

Miscellaneous and General Provisions

[. . . . .]

Final provision

[. . . . .]

Commencement

232.—(1) The following provisions of this Act come into force on Royal Assent— **A2–078**

section 110 (new leases: valuation principles),

section 120 (payment of housing benefit to third parties), and

sections 223 to 226 and 228 to 233 (general provisions).

(2) The following provisions of this Act come into force at the end of the period of two months beginning with the date on which this Act is passed—

sections 81 and 82 (restriction on termination of tenancy for failure to pay service charge),

section 85 (appointment of manager by the court),

section 94 (provision of general legal advice about residential tenancies),

section 95 (jurisdiction of county courts),

section 221 (exercise of compulsory purchase powers in relation to Crown land),

paragraph 24 (powers of local housing authorities to acqurie land for housing purposes), paragraph 26 (preserved right to buy) and paragraphs 27 to 29 of Schedule 18 (local authority assistance in connection with mortgages), and

sections 222 and 227, and Schedule 19 (consequential repeals), in so far as they relate to those paragraphs.

(3) The other provisions of this Act come into force on a day appointed by order of the Secretary of State, and different days may be appointed for different areas and different purposes.

(4) An order under subsection (3) shall be made by statutory instrument and may contain such transitional provisions and savings as appear to the Secretary of State to be appropriate.

Short title

233. This Act may be cited as the Housing Act 1996. **A2–079**

Appendix 3

Rules of the Supreme Court 1965 A3–001

S.I. 1965 No. 1776

[. . . . . .]

ORDER 59

APPEALS TO THE COURT OF APPEAL

Classes of case where leave to appeal is required

1B.—*(1) The classes of case prescribed for the purposes of section 18(1A) of the Act (appeals subject to leave) are the following—* **A3–002**

- *(a) a determination by a divisional court of any appeal to the High Court;*
- *(b) orders of the High Court or any other court or tribunal made with the consent of the parties or relating only to costs which are by law left to the discretion of the court or tribunal;*
- *(c) an order granting or refusing any relief made at the hearing of an application for judicial review;*
- *(d) orders which include the giving or refusing of possession of land;*
- *(e) orders including the grant or refusal of an application for the grant of a new tenancy under Part II of the Landlord and Tenant Act 1954;*
- *(f) interlocutory orders of the High Court or any other court or tribunal, except in the following cases, namely—*
  - *(i) where the liberty of the subject is concerned;*
  - *(ii) [. . .];*
  - *(iii) [. . .];*
  - *(iv) in the case of a decree nisi in a matrimonial cause.*

(g) an order made on an appeal to a judge from any order of a Master, the Admiralty Registrar or a District Judge of the Family Division or a District Registry;

(h) orders under section 42(1) of the Supreme Court Act 1981 (restriction of vexatious legal proceedings);

(i) orders relating to—

(i) the existence, position, form, extent or course of a boundary; or

(ii) the existence or terms of an easement.

(2) In this rule, "order" includes a judgment, decree, decision or direction.

(3) Leave to appeal to the Court of Appeal may be given by the court or tribunal from whose decision the appeal is sought or by the Court of Appeal.

[**1B.**—(1) Every appeal shall be subject to leave except an appeal against—

(a) the making of a committal order;

(b) a refusal to grant habeas corpus; or

(c) an order made under Section 25 of the Children Act 1989 (secure accommodation orders).

(2) Leave to appeal to the Court of Appeal may be given by the court below or by the Court of Appeal.]

ANNOTATION

The words in italics (added by S.I. 1993 No. 2133 and amended by S.I. 1995 No. 2206) were substituted by the words in square brackets with effect from January 1, 1999, subject to transitional provisions: Rules of the Supreme Court (Amendment No. 2) Rules 1998 (S.I. 1998 No. 3049), rr. 3, 4.

The Rent Assessment Committees (England and Wales) (Amendment) Regulations 1988 A3–003

S.I. 1988 No. 2200

Made 14th December 1988
Laid before Parliament 22nd December 1988
Coming into force 15th January 1989

The Secretary of State for the Environment, as respects England, and the Secretary of State for Wales, as respects Wales, in exercise of the powers conferred on them by section 74(1) of the Rent Act 1977, and of all other powers enabling them in that behalf, and after consultation with the Council on Tribunals, hereby make the following Regulations:

1. These Regulations may be cited as the Rent Assessment Committees (England and Wales) (Amendment) Regulations 1988 and shall come into force on 15th January 1989. **A3–004**

2. The Rent Assessment Committees (England and Wales) Regulations 1971 are amended as follows— **A3–005**

(1) insert at the end of the definition of "reference" in regulation 2(2) "or which is referred or made under section 6, 13[, 14A] or 22 of the Housing Act 1988 [or paragraph 6(2) or 10(2) of Schedule 10 to the Local Government and Housing Act 1989]";

(2) insert before "as the case may be" in regulation 2(3) "or regulation 2A(4) of these regulations";

(3) insert after regulation 2—

[1988 and 1989 Act references **A3–006**

2A.—(1) This regulation applies where a reference is made under:

—paragraph 5 of Schedule 5 to the Landlord and Tenant Act 1954 as applied by paragraph 19 of Schedule 10 to the Local Government and Housing Act 1989;

—section 6, 13, 14A or 22 of the Housing Act 1988; or

—paragraph 6(2) or 10(2) of Schedule 10 to the Local Government and Housing Act 1989.]

(2) The committee shall serve on each party a notice specifying a period of not less than 7 days from the service of the notice during which either representations in writing or a request to make oral representations may be made by that party to the committee.

(3) A notice served under paragraph (2) above on the party who did not make the reference shall be accompanied by a copy of the reference.

(4) Where a party makes a request to make oral representations within the period specified in paragraph (2) above (or such further period as a committee may allow), the committee shall give him an opportunity to be heard in person or by a person authorised by him, whether or not that person is of counsel or a solicitor.

(5) The committee shall make such inquiry, if any, as they think fit and consider any information supplied or representation made to them in pursuance of paragraph (2) above.";

(4) insert after "the Rent Act 1977" in regulation 3(4) "or regulation 2A(2) of these regulations";

(5) insert after "dwelling-houses" in regulation 5(1)(b) "or, as the case may be, to the terms (including rent) of assured tenancies or assured agricultural occupancies of other dwelling-houses where such tenancies or occupancies have been the subject of a reference to a committee and in either case", and omit the following "and".

EXPLANATORY NOTE

(This note is not part of the Regulations)

These Regulations amend the Rent Assessment Committees (England and Wales) Regulations 1971 (which regulate the procedure to be followed by rent assessment committees) to take account of the functions of rent assessment committees under Part I of the Housing Act 1988 in relation to assured tenancies and assured agricultural occupancies.

EDITORIAL NOTE

The Rent Assessment Committees (England and Wales) (Amendment) Regulations 1988 amended the Rent Assessment Committees (England and Wales) Regulations 1971. The 1971 Regulations are printed in Vol. 2 at p. 959. The 1971 Regulations, as amended by the 1988 Regulations, have been further amended by later amendment Regulations (S.I.s 1990 No. 427, 1993 No. 653, 1993 No. 2408, 1996 No. 2305, 1997 No. 1854 and 1997 No. 3007). The amendments made by these later amendment Regulations have been incorporated in the version of the 1988 Amendment Regulations reproduced here, for convenience, in so far as they affect the substantial amendment made by the 1988 Amendment Regulations. In reality, of course, the further amendment Regulations further amended the 1971 Regulations.

County Court Rules 1981 A3–007

S.I. 1981 No. 1687

[......]

ORDER 49

MISCELLANEOUS STATUTES

Housing Act 1988: assured tenancies

6.—(1) In this rule— A3–008

"the 1988 Act" means the Housing Act 1988;

"dwelling-house" has the same meaning as in Part I of the 1988 Act;

a Ground referred to by number means the Ground so numbered in Schedule 2 to the 1988 Act;

"the requisite notice" means such a notice as is mentioned in any of those Grounds and

"the relevant date" means the beginning of the tenancy.

(2) This rule applies to proceedings brought by a landlord to recover possession of a dwelling-house which has been let on an assumed tenancy in a case where all the conditions mentioned in paragraph (3) below are satisfied.

(3) The conditions referred to in paragraph (2) are these.

(a) The tenancy and any agreement for the tenancy were entered into on or after 15th January 1989.

(b) The proceedings are brought

(i) on Ground 1 (landlord occupation),
(ii) on Ground 3 (former holiday occupation),
(iii) on Ground 4 (former student letting) or
(iv) on Ground 5 (occupation by a minister of religion).

(c) The only purpose of the proceedings is to recover possession of the dwelling-house and no other claim is made in the proceedings (such as for arrears of rent).

(d) The tenancy is an assured tenancy within the meaning of the 1988 Act (and consequently is not a protected, statutory or housing association tenancy under the Rent Act 1977, and

(i) is the subject of a written agreement, or

(ii) is on the same terms (though not necessarily as to rent) as a tenancy which was the subject of a written agreement and arises by virtue of section 5 of the 1988 Act, or

(iii) relates to the same or substantially the same premises which were let to the same tenant and is on the same terms (though not necessarily as to rent or duration) as a tenancy which was the subject of a written agreement.

Where the tenancy in relation to which the proceedings are brought arises by virtue of section 5 of the 1988 Act but follows a tenancy which was the subject of an oral agreement, the condition mentioned in sub-paragraph (d)(ii) or (iii) above is not satisfied.

(e) The proceedings are brought against the tenant to whom the requisite notice was given.

(f) The tenant was given the requisite notice, not later than the relevant date.

(g) The tenant was given notice in accordance with section 8 of the 1988 Act that proceedings for possession would be brought.

(4) Where the conditions mentioned in paragraph (3) of this rule are satisfied, the landlord may bring possession proceedings under this rule instead of making a claim in accordance with Order 6, rule 3 (action for recovery of land by summons).

(5) The application must be made in the prescribed form and a copy of the application, with a copy for each defendant, must be filed in the court for the district in which the dwelling-house is situated.

(6) The application shall include the following information and statements.

(a) A statement identifying the dwelling-house which is the subject matter of the proceedings.

(b) A statement identifying the nature of the tenancy, namely—

(i) whether it is the subject of a written agreement; or

(ii) whether the tenancy arises by virtue of section 5 of the 1988 Act, or

(iii) where it is the subject of an oral agreement whether the tenancy is periodic or for a fixed term and, if for a fixed term, the length of the term and the date of termination.

(c) A statement that the dwelling-house (or another dwelling-house) was not let to the tenant by the landlord (or any of his predecessors) before 15th January 1989.

(d) The date on which and the method by which the requisite notice was given to the tenant.

(e) A statement identifying the Ground on which possession is claimed giving sufficient particulars to substantiate the plaintiff's claim to be entitled to possession on that Ground.

(f) A statement that a notice was served on the tenant in accordance with section 8 of the 1988 Act,

(i) specifying the date on which and the method by which the notice was served and

(ii) confirming that the period of notice required by section 8 of the 1988 Act has been given.

(g) The amount of rent which is currently payable.

(7) Copies of the following documents shall be attached to the application—

(i) [the first written tenancy agreement and] the current (or most recent) written tenancy agreement,

(ii) the requisite notice (referred to in paragraph (6)(d) above), and

(iii) the notice served in accordance with section 8 of the 1988 Act, together with any other documents necessary to prove the plaintiff's claim.

Annotation

The words in square brackets were inserted, with effect from September 28, 1998, by the County Court (Amendment) Rules 1998 (S.I. 1998 No. 1899), r. 4(1).

(8) The statements made in the application and any documents attached to the application shall be verified by the plaintiff on oath.

(9) Service of the application and of the attachments shall be effected by an officer of the court sending them by first-class post to the defendant at the address stated in the application and paragraphs (3) and (4) of Order 7, rule 10 (mode of service) and Order 7, rule 15 (service of summons for recovery of land) shall apply as they apply where service is effected under those rules.

(10) A defendant who wishes to oppose the plaintiff's application must, within 14 days after the service of the application on him, complete and deliver at the court office the form of reply which was attached to the application.

(11) On receipt of the defendant's reply the proper officer shall—

(a) send a copy of it to the plaintiff;

(b) refer the reply and the plaintiff's application to the judge,

and where a reply is received after the period mentioned in paragraph (10) but before a request is filed in accordance with paragraph (12) the reply shall be referred without delay to the judge.

(12) Where the period mentioned in paragraph (10) has expired without the defendant filing a reply, the plaintiff may file a written request for an order for possession and the proper officer shall without delay refer the plaintiff's application to the judge.

(13) After considering the application and the defendant's reply (if any), the judge shall either—

(a) make an order for possession under paragraph (15) or
(b) fix a day for a hearing under paragraph (14) and give directions regarding the steps to be taken before and at the hearing.

(14) The proper officer shall fix a day for the hearing of the application where the judge is not satisfied as to any of the following—

(a) that the requisite notice was given before the relevant date,
(b) that a notice was served in accordance with section 8 of the 1988 Act and that the time limits specified in the 1988 Act have been complied with,
(c) that service of the application was duly effected, or
(d) that the plaintiff has established that he is entitled to recover possession under the Ground relied on against the defendant.

(15) Except where paragraph (14) applies, the judge shall without delay make an order for possession without requiring the attendance of the parties.

(16) Where a hearing is fixed under paragraph (14)—

(a) the proper officer shall give to all parties not less than 14 days' notice of the day so fixed;
(b) the judge may give such directions regarding the steps to be taken before and at the hearing as may appear to him to be necessary or desirable.

(17) Without prejudice to Order 37, rule 3 (setting aside on failure of postal service), the court may, on application made on notice within 14 days of service of the order or of its own motion, set aside, vary or confirm any order made under paragraph (15).

(18) Without prejudice to Order 21, rule 5 and to Order 50, rule 3, a district judge shall have power to hear and determine an application to which this rule applies and references in this rule to the judge shall include references to the district judge.

Annotation

This rule was added with effect from November 1, 1993 by S.I. 1993 No. 2175.

Housing Act 1988: assured shorthold tenancies

A3–009 **6A.**—(1) In this rule, "the 1988 Act" means the Housing Act 1988 and "dwelling-house" has the same meaning as in Part I of the 1988 Act.

(2) This rule applies to the proceedings brought by a landlord under section 21 of the 1988 Act to recover possession of a dwelling-house let on an assured shorthold tenancy on the expiry or termination of that tenancy in a case where all the conditions mentioned in paragraph (3) below (or, as the case may be, paragraph (9)) are satisfied.

(3) The conditions referred to in paragraph (2) are these—

(a) The tenancy and any agreement for the tenancy were entered into on or after 15th January 1989.

(b) The only purpose of the proceedings is to recover possession of the dwelling-house and no other claim is made in the proceedings (such as for arrears of rent).

(c) The tenancy—

(i) was an assured shorthold tenancy and not a protected, statutory or housing association tenancy under the Rent Act 1977;

(ii) did not immediately follow an assured tenancy which was not an assured shorthold tenancy;

(iii) fulfilled the conditions provided by section 19A or section 20(1)(a) to (c) of the 1988 Act, and

(iv) was the subject of a written agreement.

(d) Where the tenancy and any agreement for the tenancy were entered into before 28th February 1997, a notice in writing was served on the tenant in accordance with section 20(2) of the 1988 Act and the proceedings are brought against the tenant on whom that notice was served.

(e) A notice in accordance with section 21(1)(b) of the 1988 Act was given to the tenant in writing.

(4) Where the conditions mentioned in paragraph (3) or paragraph (9) of this rule are satisfied, the landlord may bring possession proceedings under this rule instead of making a claim in accordance with Order 6, rule 3 (action for recovery of land by summons).

(5) The application must be made in the prescribed form and a copy of the application, with a copy for each defendant, shall be filed in the court for the district in which the dwelling-house is situated.

(6) The application shall include the following information and statements.

(a) A statement identifying the dwelling-house which is the subject matter of the proceedings.

(b) A statement that the dwelling-house (or another dwelling-house) was not let to the tenant by the landlord (or any of his predecessors) before 15th January 1989.

(c) A statement that possession is claimed on the expiry of an assured shorthold tenancy under section 21 of the 1988 Act giving sufficient particulars to substantiate the plaintiff's claim to be entitled to possession.

(d) Where the tenancy and any agreement for the tenancy were entered into before 28th February 1997, a statement that a written notice was served on the tenant in accordance with section 20(2) of the 1988 Act.

(e) A statement that a notice in writing was given to the tenant in accordance with section 21(1) of the 1988 Act specifying the date on which, and the method by which, the notice was given.

(f) In a case where the original fixed term tenancy has expired, a statement that no other assured tenancy is in existence other than an assured shorthold periodic tenancy (whether statutory or not).

(g) A statement confirming that there is no power under the tenancy agreement for the landlord to determine the tenancy (within the meaning given for the purposes of Part I of the 1988 Act by section 45(4) of the 1988 Act) at a time earlier than six months from the beginning of the tenancy.

(h) A statement that no notice under section 20(5) of the 1988 Act has been served.

(7) Copies of the following documents shall be attached to the application—

(i) the written tenancy agreement (or, in a case to which paragraph (9) applies, the current (or most recent) written tenancy agreement),

[(i) the first written tenancy agreement and the current (or most recent) written tenancy agreement,]

(ii) where the tenancy and any agreement for the tenancy were entered into before 28th February 1997 the written notice served in accordance with section 20(2) of the 1988 Act, and

(iii) the notice in writing given in accordance with section 21 of the 1988 Act,

together with any other documents necessary to prove the plaintiff's claim.

ANNOTATION

The words in italics were substituted by the words in square brackets, with effect from September 28, 1998, by the County Court (Amendment) Rules 1998 (S.I. 1998 No. 1899), r. 4(2).

(8) The statements made in the application and any documents attached to the application shall be verified by the plaintiff on oath.

(9) Where on the coming to an end of an assured shorthold tenancy (including a tenancy which was an assured shorthold but ceased to be assured before it came to an end) a new assured shorthold tenancy of the same or substantially the same premises (in this paragraph referred to as "the premises") comes into being under which the landlord and the tenant are the same as at the coming to an end of the earlier tenancy, then the provisions of this rule apply to that tenancy but with the following conditions instead of those in paragraph (3)—

(a) The tenancy and any agreement for the tenancy were entered into on or after 15th January 1989.

(b) The only purpose of the proceedings is to recover possession of the dwelling-house and no other claim is made in the proceedings (such as for arrears of rent).

(c) The tenancy in relation to which the proceedings are brought—

(i) is an assured shorthold tenancy within the meaning of section 20 of the 1988 Act and consequently is not a protected, statutory or housing association tenancy under the Rent Act 1977;

(ii) did not immediately follow an assured tenancy which was not an assured shorthold tenancy, and

(aa) is the subject of a written agreement, or

(ab) is on the same terms (though not necessarily as to rent) as a tenancy which was the subject of a written agreement and arises by virtue of section 5 of the 1988 Act, or

(ac) relates to the same or substantially the same premises which were let to the same tenant and is on the same terms (though not necessarily as to rent or duration) as a tenancy which was the subject of a written agreement.

Where the tenancy in relation to which the proceedings are brought arises by virtue of section 5 of the 1988 Act but follows a tenancy which was the subject of an oral agreement, the conditions mentioned in sub-paragraph (c)(ii)(ab) or (ac) above is not satisfied.

(d) Where the agreement and any agreement for the tenancy were entered into before 28th February 1997, a written notice was served in accordance with section 20(2) of the 1988 Act on the tenant in relation to the first assured shorthold tenancy of the premises and the proceedings are brought against the tenant on whom that notice was served.

(e) A notice in writing was given to the tenant in accordance with section 21(4) of the 1988 Act.

(10) In a case to which paragraph (9) applies, the application shall include the following information and statements.

(a) A statement identifying the dwelling-house which is the subject matter of the proceedings.

(b) A statement identifying the nature of the tenancy, namely—

(i) whether it is the subject of a written agreement;
(ii) whether the tenancy arises by virtue of section 5 of the 1988 Act, or
(iii) where it is the subject of an oral agreement, that the tenancy is periodic.

(c) A statement that the dwelling-house (or another dwelling-house) was not let to the tenant by the landlord (or any of his predecessors) before 15th January 1989.

(d) A statement that possession is claimed under section 21 of the 1988 Act giving sufficient particulars to substantiate the plaintiff's claim to be entitled to possession.

(e) Where the agreement and any agreement for the tenancy were entered into before 28th February 1997, a statement that a written notice was served in accordance with section 20(2) of the 1988 Act in relation to the first assured shorthold tenancy of the premises on the tenant against whom the proceedings are brought.

(f) A statement that a notice in writing was given to the tenant in accordance with section 21(4) of the 1988 Act specifying the date on which, and the method by which, the notice was given.

(g) In a case where the tenancy is a fixed term tenancy which has expired, a statement that no other assured tenancy is in existence other than an assured shorthold periodic tenancy (whether statory or not).

(h) A statement confirming that there was no power under the tenancy agreement for the landlord to determine (within the meaning given for the purposes of Part I of the 1988 Act by section 45(4) of the 1988 Act) the first assured shorthold tenancy of the premises to the tenant against whom the proceedings are brought at a time earlier than six months from the beginning of the tenancy.

(i) A statement that no notice under section 20(5) of the 1988 Act has been served.

(j) The amount of rent which is currently payable.

(11) Service of the application and of the attachments shall be effected by an officer of the court sending them by first-class post to the defendant at the address stated in the application and paragraphs (3) and (4) of Order 7, rule 10 (mode of service) and Order 7, rule 15 (service of summons for recovery of land) shall apply as they apply where service is effected under those rules.

(12) A defendant who wishes to oppose the plaintiff's application must, within 14 days after the service of the application on him, complete and deliver at the court office the form of reply which was attached to the application.

(13) On receipt of the defendant's reply the proper officer shall—

(a) send a copy of it to the plaintiff;
(b) refer the reply and the plaintiff's application to the judge

and where a reply is received after the period mentioned in paragraph (12) but before a request is filed in accordance with paragraph (14) the reply shall be referred without delay to the judge.

(14) Where the period mentioned in paragraph (12) has expired without the defendant filing a reply, the plaintiff may file a written request for an order for possession and the proper officer shall without delay refer any such request to the judge.

(15) After considering the application and the defendant's reply (if any), the judge shall either—

(a) make an order for possession under paragraph (17); or
(b) fix a day for a hearing under paragraph (16) and give directions regarding the steps to be taken before and at the hearing.

(16) The proper officer shall fix a day for the hearing of the application where the judge is not satisfied as to any of the following—

(a) where the tenancy and any agreement for the tenancy were entered into before 28th February 1997 that a written notice was served in accordance with section 20 of the 1988 Act,
(b) that a written notice was given in accordance with section 21 of the 1988 Act,
(c) that service of the application was duly effected, or
(d) that the plaintiff has established that he is entitled to recover possession under section 21 of the 1988 Act against the defendant.

(17) Except where paragraph (16) applies, the judge shall without delay make an order for possession without requiring the attendance of the parties.

(18) Where a hearing is fixed under paragraph (16)—

(a) the proper officer shall give to all parties not less than 14 days' notice of the day so fixed;
(b) the judge may give such directions regarding the steps to be taken before and at the hearing as may appear to him to be necessary or desirable.

(19) Without prejudice to Order 37, rule 3 (setting aside on failure of postal service), the court may, on application made on notice within 14 days of service of the order or of its own motion, set aside, vary or confirm any order made under paragraph (17).

(20) Without prejudice to Order 21, rule 5 and to Order 50, rule 3, a district judge shall have power to hear and determine an application to which this rule applies and references in this rule to the judge shall include references to the district judge.

ANNOTATION

This rule was added by S.I. 1993 No. 2175 with effect from November 1, 1993, and was amended on September 1, 1997 by S.I. 1997 No. 1837.

A3–010

County Court (Forms) Rules 1982

S.I. 1982 No. 586

A3–011. **1.** These Rules may be cited as the County Court (Forms) Rules 1982 and shall come into operation on 1 September 1982.

A3–012 **2.**—(1) The forms contained in the Schedule to these Rules shall be used in connection with proceedings in county courts to which the County Court Rules 1981 apply, subject to and in accordance with the provisions of this rule.

(2) The said forms shall be used in the several cases to which they apply with such variations as the circumstances may require.

(3) Where any of the County Court Rules 1981 re-enacts, with or without modification, a rule revoked by those rules, any form prescribed for use under the rule so revoked may, if substantially to the same effect as a form prescribed for use under provision so re-enacted, be used under that provision until the Lord Chancellor otherwise directs.

(4) Every form in the Schedule marked with the words "[Royal Arms]" shall have a replica of the Royal Arms printed, or embossed by an officer of the court, at the head of the first page.

(5) Every form in the Schedule marked with the word "Seal" shall bear the seal of the court.

SCHEDULE

[. . . . .]

A3–013 FORM N.5A

Application for Accelerated Possession Following Issue of a Notice under Section 8 of the Housing Act 1988

Case Number *Always quote this number*

In the

County Court

The court office is open from 10 am to 4 pm Monday to Friday

Telephone:

Plaintiff's full name and address.

Name and address for service and payment. *(if different from above)* Ref/Tel. no.

Defendant's name *(including title e.g. Mr. Mrs or Miss)* and address.

Seal

The Plaintiff (your Landlord) is **claiming possession** of

Court fee

Solicitor's costs

Total amount

Application issued on

What this means

- The court will be deciding whether or not you have to leave, and if you have to leave, when.

You must act immediately – there will not normally be a court hearing.

- **Read this application**, the information leaflet enclosed and the affidavit.
- **Get advice** from an advice agency (a list of agencies is attached) or a solicitor.
- **Fill in the form of reply** and return it to the court office.

More information about assured tenancies is available in Housing Booklet "Assured and Assured Shorthold Tenancies: A Guide for Tenants". The booklet is produced by the Department of the Environment. Your local Citizens Advice Bureau will have a copy.

N5A Application for Accelerated Possession Following Issue of a Notice under Section 8 of the Housing Act 1988 (Order 49, rule 6)

Affidavit to support my application for accelerated possession following issue of a notice under Section 8 of the Housing Act 1988

(The notes in the margin tell you when you have to delete part of the paragraph)

Paragraph 1.
Insert full name, address and occupation of person making this affidavit. Give the address of the property and delete words in brackets to show whether property is a house or part of one.

1 I,

make this affidavit to support my application for an order for possession of

which is a [dwelling-house] [part of a dwelling-house].

Paragraph 2.
Give the date of the first **written** tenancy agreement. Attach a copy of the agreement to this affidavit. It must contain all the terms of the agreement. Attach also a copy of the latest written agreement.

Delete the words in brackets if there was no previous landlord.

Delete as appropriate to show whether there is one or more Defendant. Give date when tenant(s) moved into the property.

2 On the day of [19] [20], I entered into a written tenancy agreement with the Defendant(s). A copy of the first agreement, marked 'A', is exhibited (attached) to this affidavit. A copy of the current written agreement, marked A1, is also attached.

I confirm that:

- both the tenancy and the agreement were made on or after 15 January 1989.
- I did not let the property mentioned above, or any other property, to the Defendant(s) before 15 January 1989, (and neither did any previous landlord).
- the Defendant(s) (is) (are) the original tenant(s) to whom the property was let under the assured shorthold tenancy agreement. The tenant(s) first occupied the property on

Paragraph 3.
Complete this section only if a new tenancy has been agreed **orally** (not in writing). Delete the words in brackets if the rent and duration of the tenancy are as set out in the written agreement. If either has changed, delete (i) or (ii) as appropriate.

3 The current agreement relates to the same, or substantially the same, property. The terms are the same as set out in the agreement at paragraph 2 (except for:

(i) the amount of rent to be paid. The current rent is £ per ;
(ii) the duration of the tenancy).

Paragraph 4.
Delete paragraphs (a) or (b) as appropriate to show how the latest tenancy agreement came about.

4 The tenancy is an assured tenancy.

(a) It is subject to the latest written agreement referred to in paragraph 2 above.

(b) The latest written agreement referred to in paragraph 2 has expired. There is now a further assured tenancy for an unspecified period. The terms of this tenancy are the same as in the latest written tenancy except as indicated at paragraph 3. Since the latest written agreement, there has not been a tenancy which was agreed orally and which was followed by a statutory periodic tenancy.

Paragraph 5.
Delete paragraphs (a)-(e) as appropriate to show the grounds on which you are claiming possession. If paragraph (b) applies, delete the options as applicable to show who bought the property and who intends to live there.

5 The tenancy is an assured tenancy and I am seeking an order for possession on the following grounds.

(a) at some time before the start of the tenancy (I) (a joint landlord) occupied the property as my main home. (The joint landlord's name is).

(b) I and/or a joint landlord bought the property before the tenancy started and I and/or my spouse, or a joint landlord and/or the joint landlord's spouse, intend(s) to live in it as the main home. (The joint landlord's name is).

(c) The tenancy was for a fixed term of eight months or less and, in the twelve months before the tenancy started, the property was let for a holiday.

(d) The tenancy was for a fixed term of twelve months or less and, in the twelve month period before the tenancy stated, the property was let to students by a specified educational establishment.

(e) The property is held for use by a minister of religion as a residence from which to carry out (his) (her) duties and is now needed for this purpose.

Paragraph 6.
Give the date on which the notice was served. A copy of the notice must be attached to this affidavit.

6 A notice was served on the Defendant[s] on the day of [19] [20] which said I might ask for possession on the ground(s) claimed in paragraph 5. A copy of this notice, marked 'B', is exhibited (attached) to this affidavit.

Paragraph 7.
Give details of how the notice (in paragraph 6) was served e.g. delivered personally, by post, etc. Attach any proof of service e.g. recorded delivery slip. Mark it 'B1'.

7

Paragraph 8.
Give the date on which the notice was served. A copy of the notice must be attached to this affidavit.

8 A further notice, under section 8 of the Housing Act 1988, was served on the Defendant[s] on the day of [19] [20] which said I intended to make an application for possession of the property on the grounds set out in paragraph 5. A copy of this notice, marked 'C', is exhibited (attached) to this affidavit. The notice of month(s) has expired.

Paragraph 9.
Give details of how the notice (in paragraph 8) was served e.g. delivered personally, by post, etc. Attach any proof of service e.g. recorded delivery slip. Mark it 'C1'.

9

Paragraph 10.
Give details of further evidence (if any) you wish to use to prove your claim for possession under one or more of the grounds set out in paragraph 5. Attach any written document(s) which support that evidence. Mark them 'D1', 'D2' and so on.

10

Paragraph 11.
Insert address of property and the time within which you want possession. You must not make any claim for rent arrears.

11 I ask the Court to grant me an order of possession of

within days and for payment of my costs of making this application.

Sworn at

in the

this day of [19] [20]

Before me

Officer of a court, appointed by the Circuit Judge to take affidavits.

Certificate of Service

I certify that the summons of which this is a true copy was served by me on:

by posting it to the Defendant on:

at the address stated on the summons

Officer of the Court

I certify that the summons has not been served for the following reasons:

Officer of the Court

ANNOTATION

The original Form N.5A was inserted by S.I. 1993 No. 2174. This was substituted by a different form by S.I. 1997 No. 1838, which in turn was substituted by the form printed above on September 28, 1998 by S.I. 1998 No. 1900.

A3–014 FORM N.5B

Application for Accelerated Possession Following Issue of a Notice under Section 21 of the Housing Act 1988

Case Number *Always quote this number*	
In the County Court	

The court office is open from 10 am to 4 pm Monday to Friday

Telephone:

Plaintiff's full name and address.

Name and address for service and payment. *(if different from above)* Ref/Tel. no.

Defendant's name *(including title e.g. Mr. Mrs or Miss)* and address.

Seal

The Plaintiff (your Landlord) is **claiming possession** of

Court fee	
Solicitor's costs	
Total amount	
Application issued on	

What this means

- The court will be deciding whether or not you have to leave, and if you have to leave, when.

You must act immediately - there will not normally be a court hearing.

- **Read this application**, the information leaflet enclosed and the affidavit.
- **Get advice** from an advice agency (a list of agencies is attached) or a solicitor.
- **Fill in the form of reply** and return it to the court office.

More information about assured tenancies is available in Housing Booklet "Assured and Assured Shorthold Tenancies: A Guide for Tenants". The booklet is produced by the Department of the Environment. Your local Citizens Advice Bureau will have a copy.

N5B Application for Accelerated Possession Following Issue of a Notice under Section 21 of the Housing Act 1988 (Order 49, rule 6A)

Affidavit to support my application for accelerated possession following issue of a notice under section 21 of the Housing Act 1988

(The notes in the margin tell you when you have to delete part of the paragraph)

Paragraph 1.
Insert full name, address and occupation of person making this affidavit. Give the address of the property and delete words in brackets to show whether property is a house or part of one.

1 I,

make this affidavit to support my application for an order for possession of

which is a [dwelling-house] [part of a dwelling-house].

Paragraph 2.
Give the date of the first **written** tenancy agreement. Attach a copy of the agreement to this affidavit. It must contain all the terms of the agreement.
Attach also a copy of the latest written agreement.

Delete the words in brackets if there was no previous landlord.

Delete as appropriate to show whether there is one or more Defendant. Give date when tenant(s) moved into the property.

2 On the day of [19] [20], I entered into a written tenancy agreement with the Defendant(s). A copy of the first agreement, marked 'A', is exhibited (attached) to this affidavit. A copy of the current written agreement, marked A1, is also attached.

I confirm that:

- both the tenancy and the agreement were made on or after 15 January 1989
- I did not let the property mentioned above, or any other property, to the Defendant(s) before 15 January 1989, (and neither did any previous landlord).
- the Defendant(s) (is) (are) the original tenant(s) to whom the property was let under the assured shorthold tenancy agreement. The tenant(s) first occupied the property on

Paragraph 3.
Complete this section only if a new tenancy has been agreed **orally** (not in writing).
Delete the words in brackets if the rent and duration of the tenancy are as set out in the written agreement. If either has changed, delete (i) or (ii) as appropriate.

3 The current agreement relates to the same, or substantially the same, property. The terms are the same as set out in the agreement at paragraph 2 (except for:

(i) the amount of rent to be paid. The current rent is
£ per

(ii) the duration of the tenancy).

Paragraph 4.
Delete paragraphs (a) or (b) as appropriate to show how the latest tenancy agreement came about.
If the tenancy is different from either of these two categories, you cannot use the Accelerated Possession Procedure.

4 The tenancy is an assured shorthold tenancy.

(a) The latest written agreement referred to in paragraph 2 has expired. There is now a further assured shorthold tenancy for an unspecified period. The terms of this tenancy are the same as in the latest written tenancy except as indicated at paragraph 3. Since the latest written agreement, there has not been a tenancy which was agreed orally and which was followed by a statutory periodic tenancy.

(b) It is subject to the latest written agreement referred to in paragraph 2 above, and it is not for a fixed term.

Paragraph 5.

5 The assured shorthold tenancy did not follow an assured non-shorthold tenancy.

Paragraph 6.

6 I did not serve a notice on the Defendant(s) before the previous assured shorthold tenancy expired, saying that any new tenancy would not be an assured shorthold tenancy, nor did the tenancy agreement contain a provision saying it was not an assured shorthold tenancy, nor is the tenancy an assured non-shorthold tenancy under any other provision of Schedule 2A to the Housing Act 1988.

Paragraph 7.
Delete this paragraph if the tenancy and/or any agreement for it was entered into on or after 28 February 1997.

7 A notice, under section 20 of the Housing Act 1988, was served on the Defendant[s] on the day of [19] [20] which said that the tenancy was to be an assured shorthold tenancy. A copy of this notice, marked 'B', is exhibited (attached) to this affidavit.

Paragraph 8.
Give details of how the notice (in paragraph 7) was served e.g. delivered personally, by post, etc. Attach any proof of service e.g. recorded delivery slip. Mark it 'B1'.

8

Paragraph 9.
Give the date on which the notice was served and the length of notice given. A copy of the notice must be attached to this affidavit.

9 A notice, under section 21 of the Housing Act 1988, was served on the Defendant[s] on the day of [19] [20] which said possession of the property was required. A copy of that notice, marked 'C', is exhibited (attached) to this affidavit. The notice of month(s) has expired.

Paragraph 10.
Give details of how the notice (in paragraph 9) was served e.g. delivered personally, by post, etc. Attach any proof of service e.g. recorded delivery slip. Mark it 'C1'.

10

Paragraph 11.
Give details of further evidence (if any) you wish to use to prove your claim for possession. Attach any written document(s) which support that evidence. Mark them 'D1', 'D2' and so on.

11

Paragraph 12.
Insert address of property and the time within which you want possession. You must not make any claim for rent arrears.

12 I ask the Court to grant me an order for possession of

within days and for payment of my costs of making this application.

Sworn at

in the

this day of [19] [20]

Before me

Officer of a court, appointed by the Circuit Judge to take affidavits.

Certificate of Service

I certify that the summons of which this is a true copy was served by me on:

by posting it to the Defendant on:

at the address stated on the summons

Officer of the Court

I certify that the summons has not been served for the following reasons:

Officer of the Court

ANNOTATION

Form N.5B was inserted by S.I. 1997 No. 1838, and was substituted by the form printed above on September 28, 1998 by S.I. 1998 No. 1900.

A3–015

FORM N.11A

Form of reply to application for accelerated possession [following issue of a notice] under section 8 of the Housing Act 1988 *(assured tenancies [including assured shorthold tenancies])*

- *Each of the questions in this form relates to a paragraph in the plaintiff's affidavit. You will find it easier to fill in if you have the affidavit open in front of you*
- *Use **black ink** when you fill in this form*
- *When you have filled it in sign it and send or take it to the court office shown on the application*

In the	Court
Case Number *Always quote this number*	
Plaintiff	
Defendant	

1 Are you the tenant named in the tenancy agreement attached to the plaintiff's affidavit? ☐ Yes ☐ No

2 Does the tenancy agreement referred to at paragraph 2 of the plaintiff's affidavit:

(a) set out the terms of your tenancy agreement with the plaintiff? ☐ Yes *If Yes, go to question 4* ☐ No *Give details below*

(b) set out the terms of your tenancy agreement except that the rent you pay, or the duration of the tenancy, have changed (as stated in paragraph 3 of the affidavit)? ☐ Yes *If Yes, go to question 4* ☐ No *Give details below*

3 If you have answered **No** to either part (a) or (b) of question 2, say which terms of the agreement are different, and how they differ

4 When did you move into the property? *Give date*

5 Did you have a tenancy agreement with the plaintiff (or the previous landlord) for the same, or substantially the same, property, (or another property) before 15 January 1989? ☐ Yes *If Yes, give details below* ☐ No

Say who the landlord was, and give the address of the property (and whether a house or a flat) and details of the previous tenancy (including the dates when you occupied the property). If you have a copy of the agreement, attach a copy to this reply.

6 Do you agree with the plaintiff's claim to be entitled to have possession of the property? ☐ Yes ☐ No *If No, give details below*

*You must have proper **legal** reasons for not agreeing with the claim for possession. Having nowhere else to live is not a legal reason*

N11A Form of reply to application for accelerated possession under section 8 of the Housing Act 1988 (assured tenancies [including assured shorthold tenancies]) (Order 49, rule 6)

7 Did you receive the notice referred to in paragraph 6 of the affidavit which stated that the plaintiff might ask for possession on the ground(s) given in paragraph 5?

☐ Yes *If Yes, give date below* ☐ No

Give date

8 Did you receive the notice referred to in paragraph 8 of the affidavit, which stated that the plaintiff intended to make an application for possession?

☐ Yes *If Yes, give date below* ☐ No

Give date

9 In the box below, say if you dispute any further evidence the plaintiff has given in paragraph 10 of the affidavit. If you do, say what you dispute and why.

10 If the court decides the plaintiff should have possession of the property, you will normally be told to leave in 14 days. However, if this would cause you exceptional hardship the court may allow up to 6 weeks (but no longer). If you think you would suffer exceptional hardship, say why in the box below.

11 If the court decides you should pay the plaintiff's costs of making this application would you prefer to pay the costs by instalments.

☐ Yes ☐ No

12

Give an address to which notices about this case should be sent to you	**Signed**
	(To be signed by you or your solicitor)
Postcode	**Dated**

ANNOTATION

The words in square brackets were inserted and the words in italics were omitted by The County Court (Forms) (Amendment) Rules 1998 (S.I. 1998 No. 1900), r.6.

A3–016 FORM N.11B

Form of reply to application for accelerated possession [following issue of a notice] under section 21 of the Housing Act 1988 *(assured shorthold tenancies only)*

- *Each of the questions in this form relates to a paragraph in the plaintiff's affidavit. You will find it easier to fill in if you have the affidavit open in front of you*
- *Use **black ink** when you fill in this form*
- *When you have filled it in sign it and send or take it to the court office shown on the application*

In the	Court
Case Number *Always quote this number*	
Plaintiff	
Defendant	

1 Are you the tenant named in the tenancy agreement attached to the plaintiff's affidavit? ☐ Yes ☐ No

2 Does the tenancy agreement referred to at paragraph 2 of the plaintiff's affidavit:

(a) set out the terms of your tenancy agreement with the plaintiff? ☐ Yes *If Yes, go to question 4* ☐ No *Give details below*

(b) set out the terms of your tenancy agreement except that the rent you pay, or the duration of the tenancy, have changed (as stated in paragraph 3 of the affidavit)? ☐ Yes *If Yes, go to question 4* ☐ No *Give details below*

3 If you have answered No to either part (a) or (b) of question 2, say which terms of the agreement are different, and how they differ

4 When did you move into the property? *Give date*

5 Did you have a tenancy agreement with the plaintiff (or the previous landlord) for the same, or substantially the same, property, (or another property) before 15 January 1989? ☐ Yes *If Yes, give details below* ☐ No

Say who the landlord was, and give the address of the property (and whether a house or a flat) and details of the previous tenancy (including the dates when you occupied the property). If you have a copy of the agreement, attach a copy to this reply.

6 Do you agree with the plaintiff's claim to be entitled to have possession of the property? ☐ Yes ☐ No *If No, give details below*

*You must have proper **legal** reasons for not agreeing with the claim for possession. Having nowhere else to live is not a legal reason*

N11B Form of reply to application for accelerated possession under section 21 of the Housing Act 1988 (assured shorthold tenancies only) (Order 49, rule 6A)

You only need to answer question 7 if the plaintiff says in paragraph 7 of the affidavit that he served a notice.

7 Did you receive the notice referred to in paragraph 7 of the affidavit which stated that the tenancy was to be an assured shorthold? *(This should only apply if your first tenancy, or any agreement for it, was entered into before 28 February 1997)*

☐ Yes *If Yes, give date below* ☐ No

Give date ______

8 Did you receive the notice referred to in paragraph 9 of the affidavit, [which stated that possession was required]

☐ Yes *If Yes, give date below* ☐ No

Give date ______

9 In the box below, say if you dispute any further evidence the plaintiff has given in paragraph 11 of the affidavit. If you do, say what you dispute and why.

10 If the court decides the plaintiff should have possession of the property, you will normally be told to leave in 14 days. However, if this would cause you exceptional hardship the court may allow up to 6 weeks (but no longer). If you think you would suffer exceptional hardship, say why in the box below.

11 If the court decides you should pay the plaintiff's costs of making this application would you prefer to pay the costs by instalments.

☐ Yes ☐ No

12

Give an address to which notices about this case should be sent to you	**Signed**
	(To be signed by you or your solicitor)
Postcode	**Dated**

ANNOTATION

The words in the title in square brackets were inserted and the words in italics were omitted by The County Courts (Forms) (Amendment) Rules 1998 (S.I. 1998 No. 1900), r.6. The words in square brackets in question 8 were substituted by The County Court (Forms) (Amendment No. 2) Rules 1997 (S.I. 1997 No. 2171), r.2.

A3–017 FORM N.119

Particulars of Claim for Possession
(Rented Property)

In the

County Court

Case Number

Notes to help you complete this form.

This form should only be used to recover possession of residential premises where one of the grounds is non-payment of rent. If you need more space, please continue on a separate sheet. Mark the sheet clearly with the names of the parties and the paragraph number(s) to which the information relates.

Plaintiff

Defendant[s]

Paragraph 1(a). Give the address of the property the Plaintiff wishes the Defendant to leave.

Paragraph 1(b). Delete the appropriate words in brackets to show whether the property is a dwelling-house or part of one.

1 **About the tenancy**

(a) The Plaintiff has a right to possession of the property at

(b) The property is a [dwelling-house] [part of a dwelling-house.]

Paragraph 2(a). Give the type of tenancy e.g. assured, protected, etc (or licence), the date of the agreement, amount of current rent and when it is payable e.g. weekly, fortnightly.

Paragraph 2(b). If the claim for possession is **not** based on forfeiture for non-payment of rent, delete this paragraph. If it is, give the daily rate at which unpaid rent should be calculated.

2 (a) The property is let to the Defendant[s] under a[n]

tenancy agreement [or licence]

which began on

The rent is £ per

(b) The daily rate at which any unpaid rent should be calculated is £ per day.

Paragraph 3(a). Say how much rent is outstanding up to the time the summons is issued, giving details of payments missed. If a schedule of payments missed or not made on time is attached, say so. Say whether payments generally have been made regularly and on time giving sufficient detail to support your claim for possession.

3 The reason the Plaintiff is asking for possession is:

(a) because the rent has not been paid as it should have under the terms of the tenancy agreement. Details are set out below.

N119 Particulars of Claim (Rented Property) (Order 6, rule 3(3))

Paragraph 3(b).
Delete this paragraph if the claim for possession is because of rent arrears only or you are claiming possession on statutory grounds. If not, give details of any other failure to comply with the tenancy agreement (or licence).

(b) because the Defendant[s] has failed to comply with the terms of the tenancy agreement in the following way:

Paragraph 3(c).
Delete this paragraph if you are **not** claiming possession on statutory grounds. If you are, say what the statutory grounds are.

(c) because:

Paragraph 4.
Give details of any steps taken to recover the arrears. If there have been previous court proceedings, give the date they were started and concluded, and the terms of any order(s) made.

4 The following steps have already been taken to recover the arrears:

Paragraph 5.
Give the date notice to quit (of breach of lease) (or seeking possession) was given to the Defendant[s]. Delete the words in brackets to show which type of notice was served.

5 The appropriate notice to quit [notice of breach of lease] [or notice seeking possession] was served on the Defendant[s] on

Paragraph 6.
Give what details you know of the Defendant's[s'] financial and other circumstances. Say in particular, whether Housing Benefit or arrears are paid direct to the Plaintiff by DSS and if so, how much.

6 **About the Defendant[s]**

The following information is known about the Defendant's[s'] circumstances:

Paragraph 7.
Delete this paragraph if you do not wish to give details of the Plaintiff's financial and other circumstances to support the claim for possession.

7 **About the Plaintiff**

The Plaintiff is asking the court to take the following information into account when making its decision whether or not to grant an order for possession:

Paragraph 8.
Delete this paragraph if the claim for possession is not based on forfeiture for non-payment of rent. If it is, delete (a) or (b) as appropriate. If (a) is deleted give the name and address of the person entitled to make a claim.

8 **(a) There is no underlessee [or mortgagee] entitled to claim relief against forfeiture.**

(b)

of

is entitled to claim relief against forfeiture as underlessee [or mortgagee].

What the court is being asked to do

Paragraph 9.
Delete paragraphs (a) – (c) as appropriate.

9 The Plaintiff is asking the court to make an order that the Defendant[s]:

(a) give the Plaintiff possession of the property [land] mentioned in paragraph 1:

(b) pay the unpaid rent due from

to the date of issue of this summons, and from the date of issue of the summons

to the date an order is made, at the rate of £ per

(c) pay the costs of making this application for possession.

Paragraph 10.
Delete if not applicable.

10 The Plaintiff is also asking that judgment is entered against the Defendant[s] for the total amount of the arrears outstanding up to the time an order is made [and costs].

Signed

(Solicitors for) Plaintiff

Date

Give an address where notices about this case can be sent to you

Postcode

N119 Particulars of Claim (Rented Property)

Rent Book (Forms of Notice) Regulations 1982 A3–018

S.I. 1982 No. 1474

Made 15th October 1982
In force 1st January 1983

The Secretary of State for the Environment, as respects England, and the Secretary of State for Wales, as respects Wales, in exercise of powers conferred by section 2(1) and 6(1)(b) of the Landlord and Tenant Act 1962 and now vested in them and of all other powers enabling them in that behalf, hereby make the following regulations:—

1. These regulations may be cited as the Rent Book (Forms of Notice) Regulations 1982 and shall come into operation on January 1, 1983. A3–019

2. In these regulations:— A3–020

"the 1962 Act" means the Landlord and Tenant Act 1962;
"the 1976 Act" means the Rent (Agriculture) Act 1976; and
"the 1977 Act" means the Rent Act 1977
[and
"the 1988 Act" means the Housing Act 1988]

Annotation

The words in square brackets were inserted on January 15, 1989 by The Rent Book (Forms of Notice) (Amendment) Regulations 1988 (S.I. 1988 No. 2198), reg. 2(1).

3.—(1) The prescribed form in which, under section 2(1) of the 1962 Act, notice or particulars are required to be contained in a rent book or other similar document provided in pursuance of section 1 of the 1962 Act shall be as follows:— A3–021

(a) if the premises are occupied by virtue of a restricted contract within the meaning of the 1977 Act, the form set out in Part I of the Schedule to these regulations;
(b) if the premises are a dwelling house let on or subject to a protected or statutory tenancy within the meaning of the 1977 Act,

the form set out in Part II of the Schedule to these regulations; and

(c) if the premises are a dwelling house subject to a statutory tenancy as defined in the 1976 Act, the form set out in Part III of the Schedule to these regulations

[(d) if the premises are a dwelling house let on an assured tenancy or an assured agricultural occupancy within the meaning of the 1988 Act, the form set out in Part IV of the Schedule to these regulations.]

or, in each case, a form substantially to the same effect.

(2) In the cases referred to in paragraphs [(a) to (d)] above, such rent book or similar document shall contain notice of the matters set out in the appropriate prescribed form, in addition to the name and address of the landlord and the particulars required by section 2(1) of the 1962 Act.

ANNOTATION

Reg. 3(1)(d) was inserted and the words in reg. 3(2) were substituted by The Rent Book (Forms of Notice) (Amendment) Regulations 1998 (S.I. 1988 No. 2198), reg. 2(2).

A3–022 **4.** The Rent Book (Forms of Notice) Regulations 1976 are hereby revoked.

SCHEDULE

[. . . . .]

PART IV

(FORM FOR RENT BOOK FOR ASSURED TENANCY OR ASSURED AGRICULTURAL OCCUPANCY)

IMPORTANT—PLEASE READ THIS
If the rent for the premises you occupy as your residence is payable weekly, the landlord must provide you with a rent book or similar document. If you have an assured tenancy, including an assured *shorthold* tenancy (*see* paragraph 7 below), or an assured agricultural occupancy, the rent book or similar document must contain this notice, properly filled in.

1. Address of premises . . . .
. . . .

*2. Name and address of landlord. . . . .
. . . .

*3. Name and address of agent (if any) . . . .
. . . .

*4. The rent payable [[**including council tax] [***and including rates]] is £ . . . per week.

5. Details of accomodation (if any) which the occupier has the right to share with other persons . . . .
. . . .

6. The other terms and conditions of the tenancy are . . . .
. . . .
. . . .

. . . .

. . . .

7. If you have an assured tenancy or an assured agricultural occupancy you have certain rights under the Housing Act 1988. These include the right not to be evicted from your home unless your landlord gets a possession order from the courts. Unless the property is let under an assured *shorthold* tenancy, the courts can only grant an order on a limited number of grounds. Further details regarding assured tenancies are set out in the Department of the Environment and Welsh Office booklet "Assured Tenancies" no. 19 in the series of housing booklets. These booklets are available from rent officers, council offices and housing aid centres, some of which also give advice.
8. You may be entitled to get help to pay your rent . . . through the housing benefit scheme. Apply to your local council for details.
9. It is a criminal offence for your landlord to evict you without an order from the court or to harass you or interfere with your possessions or use of facilities in order to force you to leave.
10. If you are in any doubt about your legal rights or obligations, particularly if your landlord has asked you to leave, you should go to a Citizens' Advice Bureau, housing aid centre, law centre or solicitor. Help with all or part of the cost of legal advice from a solicitor may be available under the Legal Aid Scheme.

*These entries must be kept up-to-date.
[**Cross out if council tax is not payable to the landlord.
***Cross out if rates are not payable to the landlord.]

ANNOTATION

Sched., Pt. IV inserted on January 15, 1989 by S.I. 1988 No. 2198, reg. 2(6). The words in square brackets in para. 4 were substituted on April 1, 1993 by S.I. 1993 No. 656, reg. (2)(a)(i). The words in para. 8 were omitted on April 1, 1990 by S.I. 1990 No. 1067, reg. 2(a). Notes substituted by S.I. 1993 No. 656, reg. 2(a)(ii) and (iii).

A3–023

The Assured Tenancies and Agricultural Occupancies (Rent Information) Order 1988

S.I. 1988 No. 2199

Made 14th December 1988
Laid before Parliament 22nd December 1988
Coming into force 15th January 1989

The Secretary of State for the Environment, as respects England, and the Secretary of State for Wales, as respects Wales, in exercise of the powers conferred upon them by section 42 of the Housing Act 1988, and of all other powers enabling them in that behalf, hereby make the following Order:

A3–024 **1.** This Order may be cited as the Assured Tenancies and Agricultural Occupancies (Rent Information) Order 1988 and shall come into force on 15th January 1989.

A3–025 **2.** This Order applies to cases where the rent assessment committee for an area have made a determination [on an application] under section 13(4) or 22(1) of the Housing Act 1988 or are precluded from making a determination on an application under section 22(1) by reason of section 22(3) of that Act.

ANNOTATION:

The words in square brackets were inserted by Assured Tenancies and Agricultural Occupancies (Rent Information) (Amendment) Order 1990 (S.I. 1990 No. 1474), art. 2(a).

A3–026 **3.** The President of the rent assessment panel for the area concerned shall, as respects those cases, make available for public inspection under section 42 of the Housing Act 1988 the information specified in the Schedule to this Order.

A3–027 **4.** The President of each rent assessment panel shall keep the specified information available for public inspection without charge during usual office hours at the office or principal office of that panel.

A3–028 **5.** A person requiring a copy of any specified information certified under the hand of an officer duly authorised by the President of the rent assessment panel concerned shall be entitled to obtain it on payment of a fee of £1 for the specified information relating to each determination or, where no determination is made, each application.

John Selwyn Gummer
Minister of State,
Department of the Environment

Signed by authority of the Secretary of State
13th December 1988

Peter Walker
Secretary of State for Wales

14th December 1988

SCHEDULE

Specified Information

1. Address of premises.
2. Description of premises.
3. Names and addresses of landlord and tenant.
4. If granted for a term, date of commencement of the tenancy and length of term.
5. The rental period.
6. Allocation between landlord and tenant of liabilities for repairs.
7. Whether any [Council Tax or rates] are borne by the landlord or a superior landlord.
8. Details of services provided by the landlord or a superior landlord.
9. Details of furniture provided by the landlord or a superior landlord.
10. Any other terms of the tenancy or notice relating to the tenancy taken into consideration in determining the rent.
11. The rent determined, the date it was determined and the amount (if any) of the rent which, in the opinion of the committee, is fairly attributable to the provision of services, except where that amount is in their opinion negligible, or, in the case where the committee are precluded from making a determination by section 22(3) of the Housing Act 1988, the rent currently payable under the assured shorthold tenancy [and whether the committee are so precluded by paragraph (a) or paragraph (b) of that subsection].

Annotation

The words in square brackets in para. 7 were substituted by The Assured Tenancies and Agricultural Occupancies (Rent Information) (Amendment) Order 1993 (S.I. 1993 No. 657), art. 2. The words in square brackets in para. 11 were inserted by The Assured Tenancies and Agricultural Occupancies (Rent Information) (Amendment) Order 1990 (S.I. 1993 No. 1474), art. 2(b).

EXPLANATORY NOTE

(This note is not part of the Order)

This Order specifies the information on rents of assured tenancies and assured agricultural occupancies which is to be made publicly available by the President of each rent assessment panel, the manner in which it is to be made available and the fee to be charged for the supply of a certified copy of such information.

A3–029 **The Notices to Quit etc. (Prescribed Information) Regulations 1988**

(S.I. 1988 No. 2201)

Made 14th December 1988
Laid before Parliament 22nd December 1988
Coming into force 15th January 1989

The Secretary of State for the Environment, as respects England, and the Secretary of State for Wales, as respects Wales, in exercise of the powers conferred upon them by section 5 of the Protection from Eviction Act 1977, and of all other powers enabling them in that behalf, hereby make the following Regulations:

A3–030 **1.** These Regulations may be cited as the Notices to Quit etc. (Prescribed Information) Regulations 1988 and shall come into force on 15th January 1989.

A3–031 **2.** Where, on or after the date these Regulations come into force, a landlord gives a notice to quit any premises let as a dwelling, or a licensor gives a notice to determine a periodic licence to occupy premises as a dwelling (and the premises are not let or occupied as specified in section 5(1B) of the Protection from Eviction Act 1977), the information prescribed for the purposes of section 5 of the Protection from Eviction Act 1977 shall be that in the Schedule to these Regulations.

A3–032 **3.** The Notices to Quit (Prescribed Information) Regulations 1980 are hereby revoked.

John Selwyn Gummer
Signed by authority of the Secretary of State — Minister of State,
13th December 1988 — Department of the Environment

Peter Walker
14th December 1988 — Secretary of State for Wales

SCHEDULE

PRESCRIBED INFORMATION

1. If the tenant or licensee does not leave the dwelling, the landlord or licensor must get an order for possession from the court before the tenant or licensee can lawfully be evicted. The landlord or licensor cannot apply for such an order before the notice to quit or notice to determine has run out.

2. A tenant or licensee who does not know if he has any right to remain in possession after a notice to quit or a notice to determine runs out can obtain advice from a solicitor. Help with all or part of the cost of legal advice and assistance may be available under the Legal Aid Scheme. He should also be able to obtain information from a Citizens' Advice Bureau, a Housing Aid Centre or a rent officer.

EXPLANATORY NOTE

(This note is not part of the Regulations)

These Regulations prescribe the information to be contained in a landlord's notice to quit given on or after the 15th January 1989 to determine a tenancy of premises let as a dwelling, or a licensor's notice given on or after that date to determine a periodic licence to occupy premises as a dwelling. They do not apply to the premises specified in section 5(1B) of the Protection from Eviction Act 1977 (premises subject to excluded licences or certain excluded tenancies). These Regulations replace the Notices to Quit (Prescribed Information) Regulations 1980, which applies only to tenancies.

A3–033 *The Assured Tenancies and Agricultural Occupancies (Forms) Regulations 1988*

S.I. 1988 No. 2203

EDITORIAL NOTE

These Regulations were revoked and superseded by The Assured Tenancies and Agricultural Occupancies (Forms) Regulations 1997, printed *post*, p. 621, on February 28, 1997. But nothing in the 1997 Regulations affects the validity of a notice served before that date, and accordingly the 1988 Regulations, printed here as amended from time to time, continue to apply to such notices.

The Secretary of State for the Environment, as respects England, and the Secretary of State for Wales, as respects Wales, in exercise of the powers conferred upon them by sections 6(2) and (3), 8(3), 13(2) and (4), 20(2), 22(1), 41(2) and 45(1) and (5) of the Housing Act 1988, and of all other powers enabling them in that behalf, hereby make the following regulations:

A3–034 *1. These Regulations may be cited as the Assured Tenancies and Agricultural Occupancies (Forms) Regulations 1988 and shall come into force on 15th January 1989.*

A3–035 *2. In these Regulations any reference to a section is to a section of the Housing Act 1988 and any reference to a numbered form is a reference to the form bearing that number in the Schedule to these regulations, or to a form substantially to the same effect.*

A3–036 *3. The forms prescribed for the purposes of Part I of the Housing Act 1988 shall be as follows:*

(1) for a notice under section 6(2) proposing terms of a statutory periodic tenancy different from the implied terms, form no. 1;
(2) for an application under section 6(3) referring a notice under section 6(2) to a rent assessment committee, form no. 2;
(3) for a notice under section 8 informing a tenant that the landlord intends to begin proceedings for possession of a dwelling-house let on an assured tenancy which is not an assured agricultural occupancy, form no. 3;

(4) *for a notice under section 8 informing a tenant that the landlord intends to begin proceedings for possession of a dwelling-house let on an assured agricultural occupancy, form no. 4;*

(5) *for a notice under section 13(2) proposing a new rent for an assured tenancy [or] an assured agricultural occupancy, form no. 5;*

(6) *for an application under section 13(4) referring to a rent assessment committee a notice under section 13(2) relating to an assured tenancy or an assured agricultural occupancy, form no. 6;*

[(6A) *for a notice under section 14A(1) proposing a new rent to take account of the tenant's liability to pay council tax for an assured tenancy or an assured agricultural occupancy, form no. 6A;*

(6B) *for an application under section 14A(5)(a) referring to a rent assessment committee a notice under section 14A(1), form no. 6B;]*

(7) *for a notice under section 20 of intention to grant an assured shorthold tenancy, form no. 7;*

(8) *for an application under section 22(1) to a rent assessment committee for a determination of rent under an assured shorthold tenancy, form no. 8; and*

(9) *for a notice under section 41(2) requiring a landlord or tenant to give information to a rent assessment committee, form no. 9.*

ANNOTATION

In reg. 3(5), the word in square brackets was substituted by The Assured Tenancies and Agricultural Occupancies (Forms) (Amendment) Regulations 1989 (S.I. 1989 No. 146), art. 2. Reg. 3(6A), (6B) was inserted on April 1, 1993 by The Assured Tenancies and Agricultural Occupancies (Forms) (Amendment) Regulations 1993 (S.I. 1993 No. 654), reg. 2(a).

Signed by authority of the Secretary of State
13th December 1988

John Selwyn Gummer
Minister of State,
Department of the Environment

14th December 1988

Peter Walker
Secretary of State for Wales

SCHEDULE

Housing Act 1988 section 6(2) FORM NO. 1 **A3–037**

Notice Proposing Different Terms for Statutory Periodic Tenancy

- Please write clearly in black ink.
- **This notice proposes changes to the terms of the statutory periodic tenancy. If you wish to refer it to a rent assessment committee, you must keep to the time limit set out in paragraph 2 below.**
- Please read this notice very carefully as it may alter the terms of the statutory periodic tenancy which arises when a fixed term assured tenancy runs out. It may also be used when a fixed term assured agricultural occupancy ends.
- It can be used by either a landlord or a tenant.
- This notice must be served no later than the first anniversary of the day the former fixed term tenancy or occupancy ended.

- Do not use this notice if you are a landlord only proposing an increase in rent.
- If you need help or advice about this notice, and what you should do about it, take it immediately to any of the following:
  - a Citizens' Advice Bureau
  - a housing aid centre
  - a law centre or a solicitor.

1. To: [ ] *Name(s) of landlord(s) or tenant(s)**

   of: [ ] *Address of premises*

2. This is to give notice that I/we* propose different terms of the statutory periodic tenancy from those in the fixed term assured tenancy which has now ended to take effect from

   [19]

   This date must be at least three months after this notice is served.

**Cross out whichever does not apply.*

- If you agree with the new terms and rent proposed, no nothing. They will become the terms of your tenancy agreement on the date specified in paragraph 2.
- If you don't agree with the proposed terms and any adjustment of the rent (see paragraph 4), and you are unable to reach agreement with your landlord/tenant, or if you do not wish to discuss it with him, you may refer the matter directly to your local rent assessment committee, **within three months of the date on which the notice is served**, using a special form.
- The committee will determine the proposed changes in the terms of the tenancy or some other different terms covering the same points, and the appropriate level of rent, if this applies.

3. Changes to the terms

   (a) The provisions of the tenancy to be changed are—
   Please attach relevant sections of the agreement if available.

   (b) The proposed changes are—
   (Continue on a separate sheet if necessary.)

4. *Changes to the rent, if applicable

   The existing rent is
   [This includes Council Tax*
   This includes rates*]

   £ per

   e.g. week, month, year

The new rent which takes into account the proposed changes in the terms of the tenancy will be—

£ per

e.g. week, month, year

[This includes Council Tax*
This includes rates*]

- Changes to the rent are optional. A proposal to adjust the rent to take account of the proposed new terms at paragraph 3 may be made if either the landlord or the tenant considers it appropriate.

To be signed by the landlord or his agent (someone acting for him) or the tenant or his agent. If there are joint landlords or joint tenants each landlord/tenant or the agent must sign unless one signs on behalf of the rest with their agreement.

Signed

Name(s) of landlord(s)/tenant(s)

Address of landlord(s)/tenant(s)

Tel:

If signed by agent, name and address of agent

Tel: *Date:* 19

**Cross out if this does not apply.*

ANNOTATION

The words in both sets of square brackets in para. 4 of Form No. 1 were substituted by The Assured Tenancies and Agricultural Occupancies (Forms) (Amendment) Regulations 1993 (S.I. 1993 No. 654), reg. 2(b).
See Editorial Note, *ante*, p. 588.

Housing Act 1988 section 6(3) FORM NO. 2 **A3–038**

Application Referring a Notice Under Section 6(2) to a Rent Assessment Committee

- Please write clearly in black ink.
- Please tick boxes where appropriate.
- When you have filled the form in please send it to the appropriate rent assessment panel.
- Make sure you also send a copy of the notice served on you proposing the new terms of the statutory periodic tenancy.
- This application may be used by a landlord or a tenant who has been served with a notice under section 6(2) of the Housing Act 1988, varying the terms of a statutory periodic tenancy. It may also be used where there was an earlier assured agricultural occupancy.

1. Address of premises

2. Name(s) of tenant(s)

3. Name(s) of landlord(s)

   Address of landlord(s)

4. Details of premises.

   (a) what type of property is it, e.g. house, flat or room(s)?

   (b) If it is a flat or room(s) say what floor(s) it is on.

   (c) Give the number and type of rooms, e.g. living room, bathroom.

   (d) Does the tenancy include any other facilities, e.g. garden, garage or other separate building or land? Yes ☐ No ☐

   (e) If Yes, please give details.

   (f) Is any of the accommodation shared?
   (i) with the landlord? Yes ☐ No ☐
   (ii) with another tenant or tenants? Yes ☐ No ☐

   (g) If Yes, please give details.

[5. (a) What is the current rent? £ per

e.g. week, month, year

   (b) Does this include any rates? Yes ☐ No ☐

   If Yes, please give details.]

   [(c) Does this include council tax? Yes ☐ No ☐

   If Yes, please give details.]

6. When did the statutory tenancy begin? | 19

7. Services

(a) Are any services provided under the tenancy (e.g. cleaning, lighting, heating, hot water or gardening)? Yes ☐ No ☐

(b) If Yes, please give details.

(c) Is a separate charge made for services, maintenance, repairs, landlord's costs of management or any other item? Yes ☐ No ☐

(d) What charge is payable? £

(e) Does the charge vary according to the relevant costs? Yes ☐ No ☐

(f) If Yes, please give details.

8. (a) Is any furniture provided under the tenancy? Yes ☐ No ☐

(b) If Yes, please give details. *(continue on a separate sheet if necessary).*

9. What repairs are the responsibility of

(a) the landlord?

(b) the tenant? *(continue on a separate sheet if necessary).*

10. (a) Give details of the other terms of the tenancy, e.g. whether the tenancy is assignable and whether a premium may be charged on an assignment *(continue on a separate sheet if necessary).*

(b) Please attach the tenancy agreement (or a copy), with a note of any variations, if you have one. It will be returned to you without delay.

11. I/We* attach a copy of the notice proposing changes to the statutory periodic tenancy and, if applicable, an adjustment of the amount of rent and apply to the rent assessment committee to consider it.

**Cross out whichever does not apply.*

To be signed by the landlord or his agent (someone acting for him) or by the tenant or his agent. If there are joint landlords or joint tenants each landlord/tenant or the agent must sign unless one signs on behalf of the rest with their agreement.

Signed

Name(s) of landlord(s)/tenant(s)

Address of landlord(s)/tenant(s)

Tel:

If signed by agent, name and address of agent

Tel: *Date:* 19

ANNOTATION

The words in the first set of square brackets in para. 5 of Form No. 2 were substituted by The Assured Tenancies and Agricultural Occupancies (Forms) (Amendment) Regulations 1990 (S.I. 1990 No. 1532), reg. 2(a).
The words in the second set of square brackets in para. 5 of Form No. 2 were inserted by The Assured Tenancies and Agricultural Occupancies (Forms) (Amendments) Regulations 1993 (S.I. 1993 No. 654), reg. 2(c).
See Editorial Note, *ante*, p. 588.

Housing Act 1988 section 8 FORM NO. 3

A3–039 *Notice Seeking Possession of a Property Let on an Assured Tenancy*

- Please write clearly in black ink.
- Do not use this form if possession is sought from an assured shorthold tenant under section 21 of the Housing Act 1988 of if the property is occupied under an assured agricultural occupancy.
- **This notice is the first step towards requiring you to give up possession of your home. You should read it very carefully.**
- If you need advice about this notice, and what you should do about it, take it as quickly as possible to any of the following—
  - a Citizens' Advice Bureau,
  - a housing aid centre,
  - a law centre,
  - or a solicitor.

You may be able to get Legal Aid but this will depend on your personal circumstances.

1. To: *Name(s) of tenant(s)*

2. Your landlord intends to apply to the court for an order requiring you to give up possession of—

Address of premises

- If you have an assured tenancy under the Housing Act 1988, which is not an assured shorthold tenancy, you can only be required to leave your home if your landlord gets an order for possession from the court on one of the grounds which are set out in Schedule 2 to the Act.
- If you are willing to give up possession of your home without a court order, you should tell the person who signed this notice as soon as possible and say when you can leave.

3. The landlord intends to seek possession on ground(s) [ ] in Schedule 2 to the Housing Act 1988, which reads

Give the full text of each ground which is being relied on. (Continue on a separate sheet if necessary.)

[ ]

- Whichever grounds are set out in paragraph 3 the court may allow any of the other grounds to be added at a later date. If this is done, you will be told about it so you can discuss the additional grounds at the court hearing as well as the grounds set out in paragraph 3.
- **4. Particulars of each ground are as follows—**
  Give a full explanation of why each ground is being relied on. (Continue on a separate sheet if necessary.)

[ ]

- If the court is satisfied that any of the grounds 1 to 8 is established it must make an order (but see below in respect of fixed term tenancies).
- Before the court will grant an order on any of the grounds 9 to 16, it must be satisfied that it is reasonable to require you to leave. This means that, if one of these grounds is set out in paragraph 3, you will be able to suggest to the court that it is not reasonable that you should have to leave, even if you accept that the ground applies.
- The court will not make an order under grounds 1, 3 to 7, 9 or 16, to take effect during the fixed term of the tenancy; and it will only make an order during the fixed term on grounds 2, 8 or 10 to 15 if the terms of the tenancy make provision for it to be brought to an end on any of these grounds.
- Where the court makes an order for possession solely on grounds 6 or 9, your landlord must pay your reasonable removal expenses.

5. The court proceedings will not begin until after

[19]

Give the date after which court proceedings can be brought.

- Where the landlord is seeking possession under grounds 1, 2, 5 to 7, 9 or 16 in Schedule 2, court proceedings cannot begin earlier than 2 months from this date this notice is served on you and not before the date on which the tenancy (had it not been assured) could have been brought to an end by a notice to quit served at the same time as this notice.
- Where the landlord is seeking possession on grounds 3, 4, 8 or 10 to 15, court proceedings cannot begin until 2 weeks after the date this notice is served.
- After the date shown in paragraph 5, court proceedings may be begun at once but not later than 12 months from the date this notice is served. After this time the notice will lapse and a new notice must be served before possession can be sought.

To be signed by the landlord or his agent (someone acting for him).

Signed

Name(s) of landlord(s)

Address of landlord(s)

Tel:

If signed by agent, name and address of agent

Tel: *Date:* 19

ANNOTATION

See Editorial Note, *ante*, p. 588.

Housing Act 1988 section 8 FORM NO. 4

A3–040 *Notice Seeking Possession of an Assured Agricultural Occupancy*

- Please write clearly in black ink.
- **This notice is the first step towards requiring you to give up possession of your home. You should read it very carefully.**
- If you need advice about this notice, and what you should do about it, take it as quickly as possible to any of the following—
- a Citizens' Advice Bureau,
- a housing aid centre,
- a law centre,
- or a solicitor.

You may be able to get Legal Aid but this will depend on your personal circumstances.

1. To: *Name(s) of tenant(s) or licensee(s)*

2. Your landlord or licensor intends to apply to the court for an order requiring you to give up possession of—

Address of premises

- If you have an assured agricultural occupancy under the Housing Act 1988, which is not an assured shorthold tenancy, you can only be required to leave your home if your landlord or licensor gets an order for possession from the court on one of the grounds which are set out in Schedule 2 to the Act, except ground 16.
- If you are willing to give up possession of your home without a court order, you should tell the person who signed this notice as soon as possible and say when you can leave.

3. The landlord or licensor intends to seek possession on ground(s) [ ] in Schedule 2 to the Housing Act 1988, which reads

Give the full text of each ground which is being relied on. (Continue on a separate sheet if necessary.)

[ ]

- Whichever grounds are set out in paragraph 3 the court may allow any of the other grounds to be added at a later date. If this is done, you will be told about it so you can discuss the additional grounds at the court hearing as well as the grounds set out in paragraph 3.

4. Particulars of each ground are as follows—

Give a full explanation of why each ground is being relied on. (Continue on a separate sheet if necessary.)

[ ]

- If the court is satisfied that any of grounds 1 to 8 is established it must make an order (but see below in respect of fixed term tenancies or licences).
- Before the court will grant an order on any of grounds 9 to 15, it must be satisfied that it is reasonable to require you to leave. This means that, if one of these grounds is set out in paragraph 3, you will be able to suggest to the court that it is not reasonable that you should have to leave, even if you accept that the ground applies.
- The court will not make an order under grounds 1, 3 to 7 or 9, to take effect during the fixed term of the tenancy or licence; and it will only make an order during the fixed term on grounds 2, 8 or 10 to 15 if the terms of the tenancy or licence make provision for it to be brought to an end on any of these grounds.
- Where the court makes an order for possession solely on ground 6 or 9, your landlord or licensor must pay your reasonable removal expenses.

5. The court proceedings will not begin until after

[19]

Give the date after which court proceedings can be brought.

- Where the landlord or licensor is seeking possession under grounds 1, 2, 5 to 7 or 9 in Schedule 2, court proceedings cannot begin earlier than 2 months from the date this notice is served on you and not before the date on which the tenancy or licence (had it not been an assured agricultural occupancy) could not have been brought to an end by a notice to quit or determine served at the same time as this notice.
- Where the landlord or licensor is seeking possession on grounds 3, 4, 8 or 10 to 15, court proceedings cannot begin until 2 weeks after the date this notice is served.
- After the date shown in paragraph 5, court proceedings may be begun at once but not later than 12 months from the date this notice is served. After this time the notice will lapse and a new notice must be served before possession can be sought.

To be signed by the landlord, the licensor or his agent (someone acting for him).

Signed [ ]

Name(s) of landlord(s) or licensor(s) [ ]

Address of landlord(s) or licensor(s) [ ]

Tel: [ ]

If signed by agent, name and address of agent

Tel: *Date:* 19

ANNOTATION

See Editorial Note, *ante*, p. 588.

Housing Act 1988 section 13(2) FORM NO. 5

A3–041 *Landlord's Notice Proposing a New Rent Under an Assured Periodic Tenancy or Agricultural Occupancy*

- Please write clearly in black ink.
- Do not use this form is there is a current rent fixing mechanism in the tenancy
- Do not use this form to propose a rent adjustment for a statutory periodic tenancy solely because of a proposed change of terms under section 6(2) of the Housing Act 1988.
- This notice may also be used to propose a new rent or licence for an assured agricultural occupancy. In such a case references to "landlord"/"tenant" can be read as references to "licensor"/"licensee' etc.

- **This notice proposes a new rent. If you want to oppose this proposal you must keep to the time limit set out in paragraph 2.**

Read this notice carefully. If you need help or advice take it immediately to:

- a Citizens' Advice Bureau,
- a housing aid centre,
- a law centre,
- or a solicitor.

[• Do not use this form to propose an interim increase of rent under an assured periodic tenancy or agricultural occupancy on account of council tax (use form no. 6A instead).]

1. To: *Name(s) of tenant(s)**

of: *Address of premises*

2. This is to give notice that as from 19

your landlord proposes to charge a new rent.
The new rent must take effect at the beginning of the new period of the tenancy and not earlier than any of the following—

(a) The minimum period after this notice was served,
(The minimum period is—
- in the case of a yearly tenancy, six months,
- in the case of a tenancy where the period is less than a month, one month, and,
- in any other case, a period equal to the period of the tenancy.)

(b) the first anniversary of the start of the first period of the tenancy except in the case of—
- a statutory periodic tenancy, which arises when a fixed term assured tenancy ends, or
- an assured tenancy which arose on the death of a tenant under a regulated tenancy,

(c) if the rent under the tenancy has previously been increased by a notice under section 13 or a determination under section 14 of the Housing Act 1988, the first anniversary of the date on which the increased rent took effect.

3. The existing rent is

£	per

[This includes council tax*
This includes rates*]

e.g. week, month, year

4. The proposed new rent will be

£	per

[This includes council tax*
This includes rates*]

e.g. week, month, year

[If you are required to include in your rent payments for council tax and you refer this notice to a rent assessment committee, the rent the committee determines will be inclusive of council tax.]

[* *Cross out if this does not apply.*]

[5. The landlord or superior landlord pays council tax in respect of the property*
Council tax is not payable in respect of the property*
A landlord may be liable for council tax if the property is in a house in multiple occupation, unless the property is an exempt dwelling. The main exemption is where the residents of such a dwelling are students or recent school or college leavers.]

[* *Cross out if this does not apply.*]

- If you agree with the new rent proposed do nothing. If you do not agree and you are unable to reach agreement with your landlord or do not want to discuss it directly with him, you may refer the notice to your local rent assessment committee before the beginning of the new period given in paragraph 2. The committee will consider your application and will decide whether the proposed new rent is appropriate.
- You will need a special form to refer the notice to a rent assessment committee.

To be signed by the landlord or his agent (someone acting for him). If there are joint landlords each landlord or his agent must sign unless one signs on behalf of the rest with their agreement.

Signed

Name(s) of landlord(s)

Address of landlord(s)

Tel:

If signed by agent, name and address of agent

Tel:

Date: 19

ANNOTATION

Words in square brackets substituted and inserted into Form No. 5 by The Assured Tenancies and Agricultural Occupancies (Forms) (Amendment) Regulations 1993 (S.I. 1993 No. 654), reg. 2(d). **See Editorial Note, *ante*, p. 588.**

Housing Act 1988 section 13(4) FORM NO. 6

A3–042 *Application Referring a Notice Proposing a New Rent Under an Assured Periodic Tenancy or Agricultural Occupancy to a Rent Assessment Committee*

- Please write clearly in black ink.
- Please tick boxes where appropriate.
- When you have filled in the form please send it to the appropriate rent assessment panel.
- You should use this form when your landlord has served notice on you proposing a new rent under an assured periodic tenancy.
- You will need to attach a copy of that notice to this form.
- This form may also be used to refer a notice proposing a new rent or licence fee for an assured agricultural occupancy. In such a case references to "landlord"/"tenant" can be read as references to "licensor"/ "licensee" etc.

1. Address of premises

2. Name(s) of landlord(s)

   Address of landlord(s)

3. Details of premises.

   (a) What type of property is it, e.g. house, flat or room(s)?

   (b) If it is a flat or room(s) say what floor(s) it is on.

   (c) Give the number and type of rooms, e.g. living room, bathroom.

   (d) Does the tenancy include any other facilities, e.g. garden, garage or other separate building or land? Yes ☐ No ☐

   (e) If Yes, please give details.

   (f) Do you share any accommodation?
   (i) with the landlord? Yes ☐ No ☐
   (ii) with another tenant or tenants? Yes ☐ No ☐

   (g) If Yes to either of the above, please give details.

[4. (a) What is the current rent? £ per

e.g. week, month, year

(b) Does this include any rates? Yes ☐ No ☐

If Yes, please give details.]

[(c) Does this include council tax? Yes ☐ No ☐

If Yes, please give details.]

5. (a) When did the present tenancy begin? 19

(b) When does the present tenancy end? 19

6. (a) Did you pay a premium? Yes ☐ No ☐

(b) If Yes, please give details.

7. Services

(a) Are any services provided under the tenancy (e.g. cleaning, lighting, heating, hot water or gardening)? Yes ☐ No ☐

(b) If Yes, please give details.

(c) Is a separate charge made for services, maintenance, repairs, landlord's costs of management or any other item? Yes ☐ No ☐

(d) What charge is payable? £

(e) Does the charge vary according to the relevant costs? Yes ☐ No ☐

(f) If Yes, please give details.

8. (a) Is any furniture provided under the tenancy? Yes ☐ No ☐

(b) If Yes, please give details.
(continue on a separate sheet if necessary).

9. Improvements

(a) Have you, or any former tenant(s) carried out improvements or replaced fixtures, fittings or furniture for which you or they were not responsible under the terms of the tenancy? Yes ☐ No ☐

(b) If Yes, please give details.
(continue on a separate sheet if necessary).

10. What repairs are the responsibility of

(a) the landlord?
(continue on a separate sheet if necessary).

(c) the tenant?
(continue on a separate sheet if necessary).

11. (a) Give details of the other terms of the tenancy, e.g. whether the tenancy is assignable and whether a premium may be charged on an assignment
(continue on a separate sheet if necessary).

(b) Please attach the tenancy agreement, or a copy (with a note of any variations), if you have one. It will be returned to you as quickly as possible.

12. Do you have an assured agricultural occupancy? Yes ☐ No ☐

13. I/We* attach a copy of the notice proposing a new rent under the assured periodic tenancy and I/we* apply for it to be considered by a rent assessment committee.

To be signed by the tenant or his agent (someone acting for him). If there are joint tenants, each tenant or his agent must sign, unless one signs on behalf of the rest with their agreement.

Signed

Name of tenant(s)

Address of tenant(s)

Tel:

If signed by agent, name and address of agent

Tel: *Date:* 19

**Cross out whichever does not apply.*

ANNOTATION

The words in the first set of square brackets in para. 4 of Form No. 6 were substituted by Assured Tenancies and Agricultural Occupancies (Forms) (Amendment) Regulations 1990 (S.I. 1990 No. 1532), reg. 2(a).

The words in the second set of square brackets in para. 4 of Form No. 6 were inserted by The Assured Tenancies and Agricultural Occupancies (Forms) (Amendment) Regulations 1993 (S.I. 1993 No. 654), reg. 2(c).

See Editorial Note, *ante*, p. 588.

Housing Act 1988 section 14A(1) FORM NO. 6A

Landlord's Notice Proposing an Interim Increase in Rent Under an Assured Periodic Tenancy or Agricultural Occupancy on account of Council Tax **A3–043**

- Please write clearly in black ink.
- This form should only be used to apply for an interim increase in rent to take into account the tenant's liability to make payments to the landlord in respect of council tax. It cannot be used after 31st March 1994 or if it has already been used or if council tax is not payable because the property is an exempt dwelling. It also cannot be used if an application for a determination of rent in other circumstances could be made.
- **This notice proposes a new rent to take account of council tax. If you want to oppose this proposal you must act before the date in paragraph 2.** Read this notice carefully. If you need help or advice take it immediately to:
  - a Citizens' Advice Bureau
  - a housing aid centre
  - a law centre
  - or a solicitor.
- This notice may also be used to propose a new rent or licence for an assured agricultural occupancy on account of council tax. In such a case references to "landlord"/"tenant" can be read as references to "licensor"/"licensee" etc.

1. To: *Name(s) of tenant(s)*

of: *Address of premises*

2. This is to give notice that as from 19

your landlord proposes to charge a new rent to include council tax.

The new rent must take effect at the beginning of a new period of the tenancy and not earlier than one month after this notice was served.

3. The existing rent is | £ per |

This includes rates* — *e.g. week, month, year*

4. The proposed new rent will be | £ per |

This includes council tax. — *e.g. week, month, year*
This includes rates*

- This form can only be used to increase the rent on account of the tenant's liability to pay council tax to the landlord.
- If you agree with the interim rent increase proposed do nothing. If you do not agree and you are unable to reach agreement with your landlord or do not want to discuss it directly with him, you may refer the notice to your local rent assessment committee before the beginning of the new period given in paragraph 2. The committee will consider your application and will decide whether the proposed interim rent increase is appropriate.
- You will need a special form to refer the notice to a rent assessment committee.

**Cross out if this does not apply.*

To be signed by the landlord or his agent (someone acting for him). If there are joint landlords each landlord or his agent must sign unless one signs on behalf of the rest with their agreement.

Signed

Name of landlord(s)

Address of landlord(s)

Tel:

If signed by agent, name and address of agent

Tel: *Date:* 19

Annotation

Form 6A was inserted on April 1, 1993 by Assured Tennancies and Agricultural Occupancies (Forms) (Amendment) Regulations 1993 (S.I. 1993 No. 654), reg. 2(e).
See Editorial Note, *ante*, p. 588.

Housing Act 1988
section 14A(5)(a)

FORM NO. 6B

Application Referring a Notice Proposing an Interim Increase in Rent on Account of Council Tax under an Assured Periodic Tendency or Agricultural Occupancy to a Rent Assessment Committee

- Please write clearly in black ink.
- Please tick boxes where appropriate.
- When you have filled in the form please send it to the appropriate rent assessment panel.
- You should use this form when your landlord has served notice in form 6A proposing a new rent on account of your liability to pay council tax.
- You will need to attach a copy of that notice to this form.
- This form may also be used to refer a similar notice for an assured agricultural occupancy. In such a case references to "landlord"/"tenant" can be read as references to "licensor"/"licensee" etc.

1. Address of premises

2. Name(s) of landlord(s)

   Address of landlord(s)

3. Details of premises.

   (a) What type of property is it, e.g. house, flat or room(s)?

   (b) If it is a flat or room(s) say what floor(s) it is on.

   (c) Give the number and type of rooms, e.g. living room, bathroom.

   (d) Does the tenancy include any other facilities, e.g. garden, garage or other separate building or land? Yes ☐ No ☐

   (e) If Yes, please give details.

   (f) Do you share accommodation?
   (i) with the landlord? Yes ☐ No ☐
   (ii) with another tenant or tenants? Yes ☐ No ☐

   (g) If Yes to either of the above, please give details.

4. (a) What is the existing rent? | £ per

e.g. week, month, year

(b) What is the proposed interim rent to take account of council tax? | £ per

e.g. week, month, year

5. Do you have an assured agricultural occupancy: Yes ☐ No ☐

6. I/We* attach a copy of the notice proposing an interim increase in rent on account of council tax under the assured periodic tenancy and I/we* apply for it to be considered by a rent assessment committee.

To be signed by the tenant or his agent (someone acting for him). If there are joint tenants, each tenant or his agent must sign, unless one signs on behalf of the rest with their agreement.

Signed

Name of tenant(s)

Address of tenant(s)

Tel:

If signed by agent, name and address of agent

Tel: *Date:* 19

**Cross out whichever does not apply.*

ANNOTATION

Form 6B was inserted on April 1, 1993 by The Assured Tenancies and Agricultural Occupancies (Forms) (Amendment) Regulations 1993 (S.I. 1993 No. 654), reg. 2(e).
See Editorial Note, *ante*, p. 588.

Housing Act 1988 section 20 FORM NO. 7

Notice of an Assured Shorthold Tenancy **A3–044**

- Please write clearly in black ink.
- If there is anything you do not understand you should get advice from a solicitor or a Citizens' Advice Bureau, before you agree to the tenancy.
- The landlord must give this notice to the tenant before an assured shorthold tenancy is granted. It does not commit the tenant to take the tenancy.
- **This document is important. Keep it in a safe place.**

To: [ ] *Name of proposed tenant. If a joint tenancy is being offered enter the names of the joint tenants.*

1. *You are proposing to take a tenancy of the dwelling known as:*

[ ]

from / /19 *to* / /19 *The tenancy must be for a term certain of at least six months.*

day month year day month year

2. This notice is to tell you that your tenancy is to be an assured shorthold tenancy. Provided you keep to the terms of the tenancy, you are entitled to remain in the dwelling for at least the first six months of the fixed period agreed at the start of the tenancy. At the end of this period, depending on the terms of the tenancy, the landlord may have the right to repossession if he wants.
3. The rent for this tenancy is the rent we have agreed. However, you have the right to apply to a rent assessment committee for a determination of the rent which the committee considers might reasonably be obtained under the tenancy. If the committee considers (i) that there is a sufficient number of similar properties in the locality let on assured tenancies and that (ii) the rent we have agreed is significantly higher than the rent which might reasonably be obtained having regard to the level of rents for other assured tenancies in the locality, it will determine a rent for the tenancy. That rent will be the legal maximum you can be required to pay from the date the committee directs.
   [If the rent includes a payment for council tax, the rent determined by the committee will be inclusive of council tax.]

4. *This notice was served on you on* 19

To be signed by the landlord or his agent (someone acting for him). If there are joint landlords each must sign, unless one signs on behalf of the rest with their agreement.

Signed [ ]

Name(s) of landlord(s) [ ]

Address of landlord(s)

Tel:

If signed by agent, name and address of agent

Tel: *Date:* 19

Special note for existing tenants

- Generally if you already have a protected or statutory tenancy and you give it up to take a new tenancy in the same or other accommodation owned by the same landlord, that tenancy cannot be an assured tenancy. It can still be a protected tenancy.
- But if you currently occupy a dwelling which was let to you as a protected shorthold tenant, special rules apply.
- If you have an assured tenancy which is not a shorthold under the Housing Act 1988, you cannot be offered an assured shorthold tenancy of the same or other accommodation by the same landlord.

ANNOTATION

Para. 4 of Form No. 7 was omitted by Assured Tenancies and Agricultural Occupancies (Forms) (Amendment) Regulations 1990 (S.I. 1990 No. 1532), reg. 2(b).
The words in square brackets in para. 3 of Form No. 7 were added by Assured Tenancies and Agricultural Occupancies (Forms) (Amendment) Regulations 1993 (S.I. 1993 No. 654), reg. 2(f).
See Editorial Note, *ante*, p. 588.

Housing Act 1988 section 22(1) FORM NO. 8

A3–045 *Application to a Rent Assessment Committee for a Determination of a Rent Under an Assured Shorthold Tenancy*

- Please write clearly in black ink.
- Please tick boxes where appropriate.
- A tenant with a fixed term assured shorthold tenancy may use this form to apply to the local rent assessment committee, during the fixed term, to have the rent reduced. This form cannot be used in the cases specified at the end of this form.
- [...]
- When you have filled the form in please send it to the appropriate rent assessment panel.

1. Address of premises

2. Name(s) of landlord(s)

Address of landlord(s)

3. Details of premises.

(a) What type of property is it, e.g. house, flat or room(s)?

(b) If it is a flat or room(s) say what floor(s) it is on.

(c) Give the number and type of rooms, e.g. living room, bathroom.

(d) Does the tenancy include any other facilities, e.g. garden, garage or other separate building or land? Yes ☐ No ☐

(e) If Yes, please give details.

(f) Do you share any accommodation?
(i) with the landlord? Yes ☐ No ☐
(ii) with another tenant or tenants? Yes ☐ No ☐

(g) If Yes to either of the above please give details.

[4. (a) What is the current rent? £ per

e.g. week, month, year

(b) Does this include any rates? Yes ☐ No ☐

If Yes, please give details.]

[(c) Does this include council tax? Yes ☐ No ☐

If Yes, please give details.]

5. (a) When did the present tenancy begin? 19

(b) When does the present tenancy end? 19

6. (a) Please confirm by ticking box that you received a notice saying that the tenancy was to be an assured shorthold tenancy before the agreement was entered into. ☐
   (b) Attach a copy of the notice if available. It will be returned without delay.

7. (a) Did you pay a premium? Yes ☐ No ☐

   (b) If Yes, please give details.

8. Services

   (a) Are any services provided under the tenancy (e.g. cleaning, lighting, heating, hot water or gardening)? Yes ☐ No ☐

   (b) If Yes, please give details.

   (c) Is a separate charge made for services, maintenance, repairs, landlord's costs of management or any other item? Yes ☐ No ☐

   (d) What charge is payable? £

   (e) Does the charge vary according to the relevant costs? Yes ☐ No ☐

   (f) If Yes, please give details.

9. (a) Is any furniture provided under the tenancy? Yes ☐ No ☐

   (b) If Yes, please give details. *(continue on a separate sheet if necessary).*

10. What repairs are the responsibility of

   (a) the landlord?

   (b) the tenant? *(continue on a separate sheet if necessary).*

11. (a) Give details of the other terms of the tenancy, e.g. whether the tenancy is assignable and whether a premium may be charged on an assignment *(continue on a separate sheet if necessary).*

(b) Please attach the tenancy agreement or a copy (with a note of any variations) if you have one. It will be returned to you without delay.

12. The existing rent is £ per

e.g. week, month, year

[This includes council tax*
This includes rates*] £ per

13. I/We* apply to the rent assessment committee to determine a rent for the above mentioned premises.

[*Cross out if this does not apply.*]

To be signed by the tenant or his agent (someone acting for him). If there are joint tenants each tenant or his agent must sign, unless one signs on behalf of the rest with their agreement.

Signed

Name(s) of tenant(s)

Address of tenant(s)

Tel:

If signed by agent, name and address of agent

Tel: *Date:* 19

- An application cannot be made if—
  - (a) the rent payable under the tenancy is a rent previously determined by a rent assessment committee; or
  - (b) the tenancy is an assured shorthold tenancy that came into being on the ending of a tenancy which had been an assured shorthold of the same, or substantially the same, property and the landlord and tenant under each tenancy were the same at that time.
- The rent assessment committee cannot make a determination unless it considers—
  - (a) that there is a sufficient number of similar dwelling-houses in the locality let on assured tenancies (whether shorthold or not); and
  - (b) that the rent payable under the shorthold tenancy in question is significantly higher than the rent which the landlord might reasonably be expected to get in comparison with other rents under the assured tenancies mentioned in (a) above.

ANNOTATION

Bullet point under heading was omitted by Assured Tenancies and Agricultural Occupancies (Forms) (Amendment) Regulations 1990 (S.I. 1990 No. 1532), reg. 2(c).
The words in the first set of square brackets in para. 4 of Form No. 8 were substituted by Assured Tenancies and Agricultural Occupancies (Forms) (Amendment) Regulations 1990 (S.I. 1990 No. 1532), reg. 2(a).
The words in the second set of square brackets in para. 4 of Form No. 8 were inserted by Assured Tenancies and Agricultural Occupancies (Forms) (Amendment) Regulations 1993 (S.I. 1993 No. 654), reg. 2(c).
The words in square brackets in para. 12 and the footnote in square brackets were substituted by Assured Tenancies and Agricultural Occupancies (Forms) (Amendment) Regulations 1993 (S.I. 1993 No. 654), reg. 2(g).
See Editorial Note, *ante*, p. 588.

Housing Act 1988 section 41(2) FORM NO. 9

A3–046 *Notice by Rent Assessment Committee Requiring Further Information*

To: __________ *Landlord(s)/tenant(s)**

of: __________ *Address of premises*

1. An application has been made to the rent assessment committee for consideration of—
   * the terms of a statutory periodic assured tenancy
   * an increase under an assured periodic tenancy
   * the rent under an assured shorthold tenancy
   * an increase in rent under an assured agricultural occupancy
   of the above property.
   The committee needs more information from you, to consider the application.

2. The information needed is __________

Please send it to __________

no later than __________ 19

3. If you fail to comply with this notice without reasonable cause you will be committing a criminal offence and may be liable to a fine.

Signed		Date	19

for the rent assessment committee

Cross our whichever does not apply.

ANNOTATION

See Editorial Note, *ante*, p. 588.

A3–047 **References to Rating (Housing) Regulations 1990**

S.I. 1990 No. 434

Made 5th March 1990
Laid before Parliament 9th March 1990
Coming into Force 1st April 1990

The Secretary of State for the Environment, as respects England, and the Secretary of State for Wales, as respects Wales, in exercise of the powers conferred upon them by section 117(8) of the Local Government Finance Act 1988, sections 149 and 190(1) of the Local Government and Housing Act 1989 and of all other powers enabling them in that behalf, hereby make the following Regulations—

A3–048 **1.** These Regulations may be cited as the References to Rating (Housing) Regulations 1990 and shall come into force on 1st April 1990.

A3–049 **2.** The enactments specified in the Schedule to these Regulations are amended as specified in that Schedule.

A3–050 **3.** Section 26(3)(a) (agricultural premises) of the General Rate Act 1967 shall continue to have effect after 31st March 1990 for the purposes of section 26 of the Rent Act 1977, sections 112 and 184 of the Housing Act 1985 and paragraph 6 of Schedule 1 to the Housing Act 1988 (land let with dwelling-house) as if section 117(1) (rates and precepts: abolition) of the Local Government Finance Act 1988 had not been enacted.

Chris Patten
5th March 1990 — Secretary of State for the Environment

Peter Walker
1st March 1990 — Secretary of State for Wales

SCHEDULE

[In consequence of the abolition of domestic rates, the Schedule makes detailed amendments to the Reserve and Auxiliary Forces (Protection of Civil Interests) Act 1951, the Landlord and Tenant Act 1954, the Leasehold Reform Act 1967, the Rent (Agriculture) Act 1976, the Rent Act 1977, the Housing Acts 1985 and 1988, and the Local Government and Housing Act 1989. The amendments that are relevant to this book have been set out in the annotations to the provisions in each of the Acts affected, and so they are not repeated here. The further amendment made by References to Rating (Housing) (Amendment) Regulations (S.I. 1990 No. 701) is not relevant to this book.]

EXPLANATORY NOTE

(This note is not part of the Regulations)

These Regulations amend certain housing legislation in consequence of the discontinuance of rating of domestic property. The enactments affected include those which relate to leasehold enfranchisement, assured tenancies, regulated tenancies, housing association tenancies, long tenancies at low rents, agricultural occupancies and statutory tenancies and control orders relating to houses in multiple occupation. Regulation 3 preserves a definition of agricultural land in the General Rate Act 1967 for the purposes of the Rent Act 1977, Parts IV and V of the Housing Act 1985 and paragraph 6 of the Schedule 1 to the Housing Act 1988.

A3–051 ## The Protection from Eviction (Excluded Licences) Order 1991

S.I. 1991 No. 1943

Made 28th August 1991
Laid before Parliament 5th September 1991
Coming into force 31st October 1991

The Secretary of State, in exercise of the powers conferred upon him by section 3A(8)(i) of the Protection from Eviction Act 1977, and of all other powers enabling him in that behalf, hereby makes the following Order:

Citation and commencement

A3–052 **1.** This Order may be cited as the Protection from Eviction (Excluded Licences) Order 1991 and shall come into force on 31st October 1991.

Specified person

A3–053 **2.** London Hostels Association, Limited is hereby specified for the purposes of section 3A(8) of the Protection from Eviction Act 1977 (licences which confer rights of occupation in hostels provided by certain persons).

Signed by the authority of the
Secretary of State for the Environment

G. S. K. Young
Minister of State,
Department of the Environment

28th August 1991

EXPLANATORY NOTE

(This note is not part of the Order)

The Protection from Eviction Act 1977 ("the 1977 Act") prohibits eviction without a court order (section 3), makes special provision for agricultural employees (section 4) and imposes requirements as to notices to quit (section 5). Excluded tenancies and licences are not subject to the requirements of these sections and section 3A of the 1977 Act provides which tenancies and licences are excluded. Subsection (8) of that section provides that a licence is excluded if it confers rights of occupation in a hostel provided by a body specified in the subsection or by a person or member of a class of person specified by order.

This Order specifies London Hostels Association, Limited for the purposes of section 3A(8).

A3–054 **The Local Government Finance (Housing) (Consequential Amendments) Order 1993**

S.I. 1993 No. 651

Made 11th March 1993
Laid before Parliament 11th March 1993
Coming into force 1st April 1993

The Secretary of State, in exercise of the powers conferred on him by sections 113(1) and 114 of the Local Government Finance Act 1992, and of all other powers enabling him in that behalf, hereby makes the following Order:

Citation, commencement and extent

A3–055 **1.**—(1) This Order may be cited as the Local Government Finance (Housing) (Consequential Amendments) Order 1993 and subject to paragraph (2) below, shall come into force on 1st April 1993.

(2) Paragraphs 5 to 10 and paragraph 17 of Schedule 1 to this Order shall not affect—

(a) the registration of rent under Part IV of the Rent Act 1977 on an application made under section 67 of that Act before 1st April 1993,
(b) the registration of rent under section 79 of that Act on a reference made under section 77 or 80 of that Act before that date, or
(c) the determination of rent under section 14 of the Housing Act 1988 on a reference which relates to a notice served under section 13(2) of that Act before that date.

(3) This Order extends to England and Wales only.

Amendment of enactments and interpretation

2.—(1) The enactments specified in Schedule 1 to this Order shall have effect subject to the amendments specified in that Schedule. **A3–056**

(2) The enactments specified in Schedule 2 to this Order shall have effect subject to the amendments specified in that Schedule (which make transitional provision in relation to the registration or determination of rent under or for the purposes of those enactments).

Michael Howard
One of Her Majesty's Principal Secretaries of State

Department of Environment
11th March 1993

Article 2(1)

SCHEDULE 1

AMENDMENTS

[...]

Housing Act 1988

17.—(1) Section 14 (determination of rent by rent assessment committee) is amended as follows. **A3–057**

(2) After subsection (3) insert—

"(3A) In making a determination under this section in any case where under Part I of the Local Government Finance Act 1992 the landlord or a superior landlord is liable to pay council tax in respect of a hereditament ("the relevant hereditament") of which the dwelling-house forms part, the rent assessment committee shall have regard to the amount of council tax which, as at the date on which the notice under section 13(2) above was served, was set by the billing authority—

(a) for the financial year in which that notice was served, and
(b) for the category of dwellings within which the relevant hereditament fell on that date,

but any discount or other reduction affecting the amount of council tax payable shall be disregarded.

(3B) In subsection (3A) above—

(a) "hereditament" means a dwelling within the meaning of Part I of the Local Government Finance Act 1992,
(b) "billing authority" has the same meaning as in that Part of that Act, and
(c) "category of dwellings" has the same meaning as in section 30(1) and (2) of that Act.".

(3) In subsection (4) after "furniture" insert ", in respect of council tax".

18. After section 41 insert—

"Provision of information as to exemption from council tax

41A. A billing authority within the meaning of Part I of the Local Government Finance Act 1992 shall, if so requested in writing by a rent officer or rent assessment committee in connection with his or their functions under any enactment, inform the rent officer or rent assessment committee in writing whether or not a particular dwelling (within the meaning of Part I of the Local Government Finance Act 1992) is, or was at any time specified in the request, an exempt dwelling for the purposes of that Part of that Act.".

19. In Schedule 1 (tenancies which cannot be assured tenancies), in paragraph 2(2) (tenancies of dwelling-houses with high rateable values), after "rates," insert "council tax,".

Local Government and Housing Act 1989

20. In Schedule 10 (security of tenure on ending of long residential leases) in paragraphs 6(4) and 11(6) after "Subsections (2)," insert "(3A),".

Article 2(2) SCHEDULE 2

A3–058 AMENDMENTS MAKING TRANSITIONAL PROVISION

[...]

EXPLANATORY NOTE

(This note is not part of the Order)

This Order amends certain housing legislation in consequence of the introduction of council tax under the Local Government Finance Act 1992. The Acts amended are the Landlord and Tenant Act 1954, the Rent (Agriculture) Act 1976, the Rent Act 1977, the Housing Act 1985, the Landlord and Tenant Act 1985, the Housing Act 1988 and the Local Government and Housing Act 1989.

The Assured Tenancies and Agricultural Occupancies (Forms) Regulations 1997 A3–059

S.I. 1997 No. 194

Made 29th January 1997
Coming into force 28th February 1997

The Secretary of State for the Environment, as respects England, and the Secretary of State for Wales, as respects Wales, in exercise of the powers conferred upon them by sections 6(2) and (3), 8(3), 13(2) and (4), 22(1), 41(2) and 45(1) and (5) of, and paragraphs 7(2)(a) and 9(2)(a)(i) of Schedule 2A to, the Housing Act 1988, and of all other powers enabling them in that behalf, hereby make the following Regulations:

Citation and commencement

1. These Regulations may be cited as the Assured Tenancies and Agricultural Occupancies (Forms) Regulations 1997 and shall come into force on 28th February 1997. A3–060

Interpretation

2. In these Regulations any reference to a section or Schedule is a reference to a section of, or Schedule to, the Housing Act 1988 and any reference to a numbered form is a reference to the form bearing that number in the Schedule to these Regulations, or to a form substantially to the same effect. A3–061

Prescribed forms

3. The forms prescribed for the purposes of Part I (rented accommodation) of the Housing Act 1988 are— A3–062

(a) for a notice under section 6(2) proposing terms of a statutory periodic tenancy different from the implied terms, Form No. 1;
(b) for an application under section 6(3) referring a notice under section 6(2) to a rent assessment committee, Form No. 2;
(c) for a notice under section 8 informing a tenant or licensee that the landlord intends to begin proceedings for possession of a dwelling-house let on an assured tenancy or an assured agricultural occupancy, Form No. 3;
(d) for a notice under section 13(2) proposing a new rent for an assured tenancy or an assured agricultural occupancy, Form No. 4;
(e) for an application under section 13(4) referring to a rent assessment committee a notice under section 13(2) relating to an assured tenancy or an assured agricultural occupancy, Form No. 5;
(f) for an application under section 22(1) to a rent assessment committee for a determination of rent under an assured shorthold tenancy, Form No. 6;
(g) for a notice under section 41(2) requiring a landlord or tenant to give information to a rent assessment committee, Form No. 7;
(h) for a notice under paragraph 7 of Schedule 2A, by the tenant to the landlord proposing that an assured tenancy be replaced by an assured shorthold tenancy, Form No. 8;
(i) for a notice under paragraph 9 of Schedule 2A, by the landlord to the prospective tenant, proposing an assured tenancy where the tenancy meets the conditions for an assured agricultural occupancy, Form No. 9.

Revocations and savings

A3–063 **4.**—(1) The Assured Tenancies and Agricultural Occupancies (Forms) Regulations 1988 ("the 1988 Regulations"), the Assured Tenancies and Agricultural Occupancies (Forms) (Amendment) Regulations 1989, the Assured Tenancies and Agricultural Occupancies (Forms) (Amendment) Regulations 1990 and the Assured Tenancies and Agricultural Occupancies (Forms) (Amendment) Regulations 1993 are hereby revoked.

(2) Nothing in paragraph (1) affects the validity of a notice served before the coming into force of these Regulations if, at the date of service of the notice, the notice was in the form then prescribed by the 1988 Regulations.

Signed by authority of the Secretary of State for the Environment

James Clappison

Parliamentary Under Secretary of State,
28th January 1997 — Department of Environment

William Hague

29th January 1997 — Secretary of State for Wales

Regulation 3 SCHEDULE

FORMS PRESCRIBED FOR THE PURPOSES OF PART I OF THE HOUSING ACT 1988 **A3–064**

FORM NO. 1

Housing Act 1988 section 6(2)

Notice proposing different terms for a Statutory Periodic Tenancy

- Please write clearly in black ink.
- Please tick boxes where appropriate and cross out text marked with an asterisk (*) that does not apply.
- This form can be used by either a landlord or a tenant to propose changes to the terms of a statutory periodic tenancy, which arises when a fixed term of an assured tenancy, an assured shorthold tenancy or an assured agricultural occupancy ends.
- This notice must be served on the landlord or tenant no later than the first anniversary of the day on which the former fixed term tenancy or occupancy ended.
- Do not use this notice if you are a landlord proposing only an increase in rent. Instead, you should use the form headed *Landlord's Notice proposing a new rent under an Assured Periodic Tenancy or Agricultural Occupancy*, which is available from a rent assessment panel or law stationers.

---

1. To: ....

*Name(s) of landlord(s)/tenant(s)**

Address of premises to which the tenancy relates:

....

....

....

---

2. This is to give notice that I/we* propose different terms for the statutory periodic tenancy from those of the fixed term assured tenancy which has now ended and that they should take effect from:

....

Insert date which must be at least three months after the date on which this notice is served.

---

3. Changes to the terms

(a) The existing provisions of the tenancy to be changed are:

....

....

....

Please attach relevant sections of the tenancy agreement if available

(b) The proposed changes are:

....

....

....

Continue on a separate sheet if necessary

---

4. Changes to the rent (if applicable). Go to section 5 if this does not apply.

- You should not propose a change to the rent on this form unless it is to take account of the proposed new terms at section 3. A change may be made if either the landlord or the tenant considers it appropriate.

(a) The existing rent is £....... per.......
(e.g. week, month, year)

(b) Does the rent include council tax? Yes ☐ No ☐

(c) If yes, the amount that is included for council tax is: £. . . . . . . per. . . . . . . *(e.g. week, month, year)*

(d) Does the rent include water charges? Yes ☐ No ☐

(e) If yes, the amount that is included for water charges is: £. . . . . . . per. . . . . . . *(e.g. week, month, year)*

(f) The new rent which takes into account the proposed changes in the terms of the tenancy will be: £. . . . . . . per. . . . . . . *(e.g. week, month, year)*

(g) Will the new rent include council tax? Yes ☐ No ☐

(h) If yes, the amount that will be included for council tax is: £. . . . . . . per. . . . . . . *(e.g. week, month, year)*

(i) Will the new rent include water charges? Yes ☐ No ☐

(j) If yes, the amount that will be included for water charges is: £. . . . . . . per. . . . . . . *(e.g. week, month, year)*

---

5. Name and address of landlord or tenant proposing the changes

To be signed and dated by the landlord or his agent (someone acting for him) or the tenant or his agent. If there are joint landlords or joint tenants each landlord/tenant or the agent must sign unless one signs on behalf of the rest with their agreement.

Signed . . . . *Date* . . . .
. . . .
. . . .

Please specify whether: landlord ☐ landlord's agent ☐ tenant ☐ tenant's agent ☐

Name(s) (Block Capitals) . . . .
. . . .
. . . .

Address
. . . .
. . . .
. . . .

Telephone: Daytime . . . . Evening . . . .

What to do if this notice is served on you

- If you agree with the new terms and rent proposed, do nothing. They will become the terms of the tenancy agreement on the date specified in section 2.
- If you don't agree with the proposed terms and any adjustment of the rent (see section 4), and you are unable to reach agreement with your landlord/tenant, or you do not wish to discuss it with him, you may refer the matter directly to your local rent assessment committee, before the date specified in section 2, using the form headed *Application referring a Notice proposing different terms for a Statutory Periodic Tenancy to a Rent Assessment Committee* which you can obtain from a rent assessment panel or a law stationer.
- The rent assessment committee will decide what, if any, changes should be made to the terms of the tenancy and, if applicable, the amount of the new rent.
- If you need help or advice about this notice and what you should do about it, take it immediately to a citizens' advice bureau, a housing advice centre, a law centre or a solicitor.

Form No. 2

Housing Act 1988 section 6(3)

Application referring a Notice proposing different terms for a Statutory Periodic Tenancy to a Rent Assessment Committee A3–065

- Please write clearly in black ink.
- Please tick boxes where appropriate and cross out text marked with an asterisk (*) that does not apply.
- This form should be used by a landlord or a tenant who has been served with a notice under section 6(2) of the Housing Act 1988, varying the terms of a statutory periodic tenancy which arises when a fixed term of an assured tenancy, an assured shorthold tenancy or an assured agricultural occupancy ends.
- When you have completed the form, please send it to your local rent assessment panel with a copy of the notice served on you proposing the new terms of the statutory periodic tenancy.

---

1. Name(s) of tenant(s):

....
....
....

---

2. Address of premises to which the tenancy relates:

....
....
....

---

3. Name(s) of landlord(s)/agent*:

....
....
....

Address of landlord(s)/agent*:

....
....
....

---

4. Details of premises.

(a) What type of accommodation is rented?

Room(s) ☐ Flat ☐ Terraced House ☐
Semi-Detached House ☐ Fully Detached House ☐ Other ☐ *(Please specify)*

(b) If it is a flat or room(s) what floor(s) is it on?

Ground ☐ First ☐ Second ☐ Other ☐ *(Please specify)*

(c) Give the number and type of rooms, e.g. living room, bathroom etc.

....
....

(d) Does the tenancy include any other facilities, e.g. garden, garage or other separate building or land?

Yes ☐ No ☐

(e) If yes, please give details:

....
....
....

(f) Is any of the accommodation shared with:

(i) the landlord? Yes ☐ No ☐
(ii) another tenant or tenants? Yes ☐ No ☐

(g) If yes, please give details:

....
....

5. When did the statutory periodic tenancy begin?

. . . .

6. Services.

(a) Are any services provided under the tenancy (e.g. cleaning, lighting, heating, hot water or gardening etc.)?

Yes ☐ No ☐

(b) If yes, please give details:

. . . .

. . . .

. . . .

(c) Is a separate charge made for services, maintenance, repairs, landlords' costs of management or any other item?

Yes ☐ No ☐

(d) If yes, what charge is payable? £ . . . . . . per. . . . . . .

(e.g. week, month, year)

(e) Does the charge vary according to the relevant costs?

Yes ☐ No ☐

(f) If yes, please give details:

. . . .

. . . .

. . . .

7. (a) Is any furniture provided under the tenancy?

Yes ☐ No ☐

(b) If yes, please give details. Continue on a separate sheet if necessary or provide a copy of the inventory.

. . . .

. . . .

. . . .

8. What repairs are the responsibility of:

(a) the landlord? Continue on a separate sheet if necessary.

. . . .

. . . .

. . . .

(b) the tenant? Continue on a separate sheet if necessary.

. . . .

. . . .

. . . .

9. Give details (if known) of the other terms of the tenancy, e.g. can you assign the tenancy (pass it on to someone else) and if so is a premium (a payment which is in addition to rent and equivalent to more than two months rent) payable on an assigment? Continue on a separate sheet if necessary.

. . . .

. . . .

. . . .

10. (a) Is there a written tenancy agreement? Yes ☐ No ☐

(b) If yes, please attach the tenancy agreement (with a note of any variations). It will be returned to you as soon as possible.

11. (a) I/We* attach a copy of the notice proposing changes to the statutory periodic tenancy and, if applicable, an adjustment of the amount of rent and apply for it to be considered by the rent assessment committee.

Signed .... *Date* ....
....
....

To be signed and dated by the landlord or his agent (someone acting for him) or the tenant or his agent. If there are joint landlords or joint tenants each landlord/tenant or the agent must sign unless one signs on behalf of the rest with their agreement.

Please specify whether: landlord ☐ landlord's agent ☐ tenant ☐ tenant's agent ☐

(b) Name and address of landlord or tenant referring to the rent assessment committee.

Name(s) (Block Capitals) ....
....
....

Address
....
....
....

Telephone: Daytime .... Evening ....

Form No. 3

Housing Act 1988 section 8 as amended by section 151 of the Housing Act 1996

Notice seeking possession of a property let on an Assured Tenancy or an Assured Agricultural Occupancy A3–066

- Please write clearly in black ink.
- Please tick boxes where appropriate and cross out text marked with an asterisk (*) that does not apply.
- This form should be used where possession of accommodation let under an assured tenancy, an assured agricultural occupancy or an assured shorthold tenancy is sought on one of the grounds in Schedule 2 to the Housing Act 1988.
- Do not use this form if possession is sought on the "shorthold" ground under section 21 of the Housing Act 1988 from an assured shorthold tenant where the fixed term has come to an end or, for assured shorthold tenancies with no fixed term which started on or after 28th February 1997, after six months has elapsed. There is no prescribed form for these cases, but you must give notice in writing.

---

1. To: ....
*Name(s) of tenant(s)/licensee(s)**

---

2. Your landlord/licensor* intends to apply to the court for an order requiring you to give up possession of:

....
....
....

Address of premises

---

3. Your landlord/licensor* intends to seek possession on ground(s) .... in Schedule 2 to the Housing Act 1988, as amended by the Housing Act 1996, which read(s):

....
....
....

Give the full text (as set out in the Housing Act 1988 as amended by the Housing Act 1996) of each ground which is being relied on. Continue on a separate sheet if necessary.

---

4. Give a full explanation of why each ground is relied on:

....

....

....

Continue on a separate sheet if necessary.

Notes on the grounds for possession

- If the court is satisfied that any of grounds 1 to 8 is established, it must make an order (but see below in respect of fixed term tenancies).
- Before the court will grant an order on any of grounds 9 to 17, it must be satisfied that it is reasonable to require you to leave. This means that, if one of these grounds is set out in section 3, you will be able to suggest to the court that it is not reasonable that you should have to leave, even if you accept that the ground applies.
- The court will not make an order under grounds 1, 3 to 7, 9 or 16, to take effect during the fixed term of the tenancy (if there is one) and it will only make an order during the fixed term on grounds 2, 8, 10 to 15 or 17 if the terms of the tenancy make provision for it to be brought to an end on any of these grounds.
- Where the court makes an order for possession solely on grounds 6 or 9, the landlord must pay your reasonable removal expenses.

---

5. The court proceedings will not begin until after:

....

Give the earliest date on which court proceedings can be brought

- Where the landlord is seeking possession on grounds 1, 2, 5 to 7, 9 or 16, court proceedings cannot begin earlier than 2 months from the date this notice is served on you (even where one of grounds 3, 4, 8, 10 to 13, 14A, 15 or 17 is specified) and not before the date on which the tenancy (had it not been assured) could have been brought to an end by a notice to quit served at the same time as this notice.
- Where the landlord is seeking possession on grounds 3, 4, 8, 10 to 13, 14A, 15 or 17, court proceedings cannot begin earlier than 2 weeks from the date this notice is served (unless one of 1, 2, 5 to 7, 9 or 16 grounds is also specified in which case they cannot begin earlier than two months from the date this notice is served).
- Where the landlord is seeking possession on ground 14 (with or without other grounds), court proceedings cannot begin before the date this notice is served.
- Where the landlord is seeking possession on ground 14A, court proceedings cannot begin unless the landlord has served, or has taken all reasonable steps to serve, a copy of this notice on the partner who has left the property.
- After the date shown in section 5, court proceedings may be begun at once but not later than 12 months from the date on which this notice is served. After this time the notice will lapse and a new notice must be served before possession can be sought.

---

6. Name and address of landlord/licensor*.

To be signed and dated by the landlord or licensor or his agent (someone acting for him). If there are joint landlords each landlord or the agent must sign unless one signs on behalf of the rest with their agreement.

Signed .... *Date* ....

....

Please specify whether: landlord ☐ licensor ☐ joint landlords ☐ landlord's agent ☐

Name(s) (Block Capitals) ....

....

....

Address

....

....

....

Telephone: Daytime .... Evening ....

What to do if this notice is served on you

- This notice is the first step requiring you to give up possession of your home. You should read it very carefully.
- Your landlord cannot make you leave your home without an order for possession issued by a court. By issuing this notice your landlord is informing you that he intends to seek such an order. If you are willing to give up possession without a court order, you should tell the person who signed this notice as soon as possible and say when you are prepared to leave.
- Whichever grounds are set out in section 3 of this form, the court may allow any of the other grounds to be added at a later date. If this is done, you will be told about it so you can discuss the additional grounds at the court hearing as well as the grounds set out in section 3.
- If you need advice about this notice, and what you should do about it, take it immediately to a citizens' advice bureau, a housing advice centre, a law centre or a solicitor.

FORM NO. 4

Housing Act 1988 section 13(2)

Landlord's Notice proposing a new rent under an Assured Periodic Tenancy or Agricultural Occupancy A3–067

- Please write clearly in black ink.
- Please tick boxes where appropriate.
- This form should be used to propose a new rent under an assured periodic tenancy, including an assured shorthold periodic tenancy.
- This form may also be used to propose a new rent or licence fee for an assured periodic agricultural occupancy. In such cases reference to "landlord"/"tenant" can be read as references to "licensor"/"licensee" etc.
- Do not use this form if there is a current rent fixing mechanism in the tenancy.
- Do not use this form to propose a rent adjustment for a statutory periodic tenancy solely because of a proposed change of terms under section 6(2) of the Housing Act 1988. You should instead use the form headed *Notice proposing different terms for a Statutory Periodic Tenancy* which you can obtain from a rent assessment panel or a law stationer.

---

1. To: ....

Name(s) of tenant(s)

---

2. Address of premises to which the tenancy relates:

....

....

....

3. This is to give notice that as from .... your landlord proposes to charge a new rent.

- The new rent must take effect at the beginning of a new period of the tenancy and not earlier than any of the following:
  - (a) the minimum period after this notice was served,
    (The minimum period is:
    —in the case of a yearly tenancy, six months;
    —in the case of a tenancy where the period is less than a month, one month;
    —in any other case, a period equal to the period of the tenancy;)
  - (b) the first anniversary of the start of the first period of the tenancy except in the case of:
    —a statutory periodic tenancy, which arises when a fixed term assured tenancy ends, or;
    —an assured tenancy which arose on the death of a tenant under a regulated tenancy;
  - (c) if the rent under the tenancy has previously been increased by a notice under section 13 or a determination under section 14 of the Housing Act 1988, the first anniversary of the date on which the increased rent took effect.

---

4. (a) The existing rent is: £. . . . . . per . . . . . . (*e.g. week, month, year*)

(b) Does the rent include council tax? Yes ☐ No ☐

(c) If yes, the amount that is included for council tax is: £. . . . . . per . . . . . . (*e.g. week, month, year*)

(d) Does the rent include water charges? Yes ☐ No ☐

(e) If yes, the amount that is included for water charges is: £. . . . . . per . . . . . . (*e.g. week, month, year*)

---

5. (a) The proposed new rent will be: £. . . . . . per . . . . . . (*e.g. week, month, year*)

(b) Will the new rent include council tax? Yes ☐ No ☐

(c) If yes, the amount that will be included for council tax will be: £. . . . . . per . . . . . . (*e.g. week, month, year*)

(d) Will the new rent include water charges? Yes ☐ No ☐

(e) If yes, the amount that will be included for water charges will be: £. . . . . . per . . . . . . (*e.g. week, month, year*)

---

6. Name and address of landlord.

To be signed and dated by the landlord or his agent (someone acting for him). If there are joint landlords each landlord or the agent must sign unless one signs on behalf of the rest with their agreement.

Signed . . . . *Date* . . . .

Please specify whether: landlord ☐ joint landlords ☐ landlord's agent ☐

Name(s) (Block Capitals) . . . .

Address
. . . .

Telephone: Daytime . . . . Evening . . . .

What to do if this notice is served on you

- You should treat this notice carefully. Your landlord is proposing a new rent.
- If you agree with the new rent proposed, do nothing. If you do not agree and you are unable to reach agreement with your landlord or do not want to discuss it directly with him, you may refer this notice to your local rent assessment committee prior to the date specified in section 3, using the form headed *Application referring a Notice proposing a new rent under an Assured Periodic Tenancy or Agricultural Occupancy to a Rent Assessment Committee*. You can obtain this form from a rent assessment panel or a law stationer.
- The rent assessment committee will consider your application and will decide what the rent for the premises will be. The committee may set a rent that is higher, lower or the same as the landlord has proposed in section 5.
- If you are required to include payments for council tax and water charges in your rent, the rent the committee determines will be inclusive of council tax and water charges.
- If you need help or advice please take this notice immediately to a citizens' advice bureau, a housing advice centre, a law centre or a solicitor.

FORM NO. 5

Housing Act 1988 section 13(4)

Application referring a Notice proposing a new rent under an Assured Periodic Tenancy or Agricultural Occupancy to a Rent Assessment Committee **A3–068**

- Please write clearly in black ink.
- Please tick boxes where appropriate and cross out text marked with an asterisk (*) that does not apply.
- This form should be used when your landlord has served notice on you proposing a new rent under an assured periodic tenancy, including an assured shorthold periodic tenancy.
- This form may also be used to refer a notice proposing a new rent or licence fee for an assured periodic agricultural occupancy. In such a case references to "landlord"/"tenant" can be read as references to "licensor"/"licensee" etc.
- This form must be completed and sent to your local rent assessment panel—with a copy of the notice served on you proposing the new rent—before the date it is proposed that the new rent will take effect.

---

1. Address of premises:

....

....

....

---

2. Name(s) of landlord(s)/agent*:

....

....

Address of landlord(s)/agent*:

....

....

....

....

---

3. Details of premises.

(a) What type of accommodation do you rent?

Room(s) ☐ Flat ☐ Terraced House ☐
Semi-Detached House ☐ Fully Detached House ☐ Other ☐ *(Please specify)*

(b) If it is a flat or room(s) what floor(s) is it on?

Ground ☐ First ☐ Second ☐ Other ☐ *(Please specify)*

(c) Give the number and type of rooms, e.g. living room, bathroom etc.

....

....

(d) Does the tenancy include any other facilities, e.g. garden, garage or other separate building or land?

Yes ☐ No ☐

(e) If yes, please give details:

....

....

....

(f) Do you share any accommodation with:

(i) the landlord? Yes ☐ No ☐
(ii) another tenant or tenants? Yes ☐ No ☐

(g) If yes to either of the above, please give details:

....

....

....

---

4. When did the present tenancy begin?

. . . .

---

5. (a) Did you pay a premium?

Yes ☐ No ☐

- a premium is a payment which is additional to rent and is equivalent to more than two months rent. It may give you the right to assign the tenancy (pass it on to someone else) unless the tenancy agreement states or implies otherwise.

(b) If yes, please give details:

. . . .
. . . .
. . . .

---

6. Services.

(a) Are any services provided under the tenancy (e.g. cleaning, lighting, heating, hot water or gardening)?

Yes ☐ No ☐

(b) If yes, please give details:

. . . .
. . . .
. . . .

(c) If yes, is a separate charge made for services, maintenance, repairs, landlords' costs of management or any other item?

Yes ☐ No ☐

(d) What charge is payable? £. . . . . per . . . .
(e.g. week, month, year)

(e) Does the charge vary according to the relevant costs?

Yes ☐ No ☐

(f) If yes, please give details:

. . . .
. . . .
. . . .

---

7. (a) Is any furniture provided under the tenancy?

Yes ☐ No ☐

(b) If yes, please give details. Continue on a separate sheet if necessary or attach a copy of the inventory:

. . . .
. . . .
. . . .

---

8. Improvements.

(a) Have you, or any former tenant(s) carried out improvements or replaced fixtures, fittings or furniture for which you or they were not responsible under the terms of the tenancy?

Yes ☐ No ☐

(b) If yes, please give details. Continue on a separate sheet if necessary:

. . . .
. . . .
. . . .

---

9. What repairs are the responsibility of:

(a) the landlord?

. . . .
. . . .
. . . .

(b) the tenant?

....

....

....

10. (a) Is there a written tenancy agreement? Yes ☐ No ☐

(b) If yes, please attach the tenancy agreement (with a note of any variations). It will be returned to you as soon as possible.

11. Do you have an assured agricultural occupancy?

Yes ☐ No ☐

12. (a) I/We* attach a copy of the notice proposing a new rent under the assured periodic tenancy and I/we* apply for it to be considered by the rent assessment committee.

Signed .... *Date* ....

....

To be signed and dated by the tenant or his agent. If there are joint tenants each tenant or the agent must sign unless one signs on behalf of the rest with their agreement.

Please specify whether: tenant ☐ joint tenants ☐ tenant's agent ☐

(b) Name and address of tenant(s) referring to the rent assessment committee.

Name(s) (Block Capitals) ....

....

....

Address

....

....

....

Telephone: Daytime .... Evening ....

Form No. 6

Housing Act 1988 section 22(1) as amended by section 100 of the Housing Act 1996

Application to a Rent Assessment Committee for a determination of a rent under an Assured Shorthold Tenancy A3–069

- Please write clearly in black ink.
- Please tick boxes where appropriate and cross out text marked with an asterisk (*) that does not apply.
- This form should be used by a tenant with an assured shorthold tenancy which began (or for which a contract had been made) before 28th February 1997, to apply to the local rent assessment committee, during the fixed term of the original tenancy, to have the rent reduced.
- This form should also be used by a tenant with an assured shorthold tenancy which began on or after 28th February 1997 (unless a contract had been made before that date), to apply to the rent assessment committee within six months of the beginning of the original tenancy, to have the rent reduced.
- This form cannot be used in the cases specified at the end of this form.
- When you have completed the form please send it to your local rent assessment panel.

1. Address of premises:

....

....

....

2. Name(s) of landlord(s)/agent*:

....

Address of landlord(s)/agent*:

....

....

....

---

3. Details of premises.

(a) What type of accommodation do you rent?

Room(s) ☐ Flat ☐ Terraced House ☐
Semi-Detached House ☐ Fully Detached House ☐ Other ☐ *(Please specify)*

(b) If it is a flat or room(s) what floor(s) is it on?

Ground ☐ First ☐ Second ☐ Other ☐ *(Please specify)*

(c) Give the number and type of rooms, e.g. living room, bathroom etc.

....

....

(d) Does the tenancy include any other facilities, e.g. garden, garage or other separate building or land?

Yes ☐ No ☐

(e) If yes, please give details:

....

....

....

(f) Do you share any accommodation with:

(i) the landlord? Yes ☐ No ☐
(ii) another tenant or tenants? Yes ☐ No ☐

(g) If yes to either of the above, please give details:

....

....

....

---

4. (a) What is the current rent? £...... per ......
(e.g. week, month, year)

(b) Does the rent include council tax? Yes ☐ No ☐

(c) If yes, the amount that is included for council tax is: £...... per ......
(e.g. week, month, year)

(d) Does the rent include water charges? Yes ☐ No ☐

(e) If yes, the amount that is included for water charges is: £...... per ......
(e.g. week, month, year)

---

5. (a) When did the present tenancy begin?

....

(b) When does the present tenancy end?

....

(c) Does the tenancy replace an original tenancy? Yes ☐ No ☐

If yes, when did the original tenancy begin ....

---

6. (a) If the tenancy began before 28th February 1997, please confirm by ticking the box that you received a notice saying that the tenancy was to be an assured shorthold tenancy before the agreement was entered into. ☐

(b) Attach a copy of the notice, if available. It will be returned to you as soon as possible.

---

7. (a) Did you pay a premium?

Yes ☐ No ☐

- a premium is a payment which is additional to rent and is equivalent to more than two months rent. It may give you the right to assign the tenancy (pass it on to someone else) unless the tenancy agreement states or implies otherwise.

(b) If yes, please give details:

. . . .
. . . .
. . . .

---

8. Services.

(a) Are any services provided under the tenancy (e.g. cleaning, lighting, heating, hot water or gardening)?

Yes ☐ No ☐

(b) If yes, please give details:

. . . .
. . . .
. . . .

(c) Is a separate charge made for services, maintenance, repairs, landlord's costs of management or any other item?

Yes ☐ No ☐

(d) If yes, what charge is payable? £ . . . . per. . . . .

(e.g. week, month, year)

(e) Does the charge vary according to the relevant costs?

Yes ☐ No ☐

(f) If yes, please give details:

. . . .
. . . .
. . . .

---

9. (a) Is any furniture provided under the tenancy?

Yes ☐ No ☐

(b) If yes, please give details. Continue on a separate sheet if necessary or provide a copy of the inventory.

. . . .
. . . .
. . . .

---

10. What repairs are the responsibility of:

(a) the landlord. Continue on a separate sheet if necessary:

. . . .
. . . .
. . . .

(b) the tenant. Continue on a separate sheet if necessary:

. . . .
. . . .
. . . .

---

11. (a) Give details (if known) of the other terms of the tenancy, e.g. whether the tenancy is assignable and whether a premium may be charged on an assignment. (Continue on a separate sheet if necessary).

. . . .
. . . .
. . . .

(b) Is there a written tenancy agreement? Yes ☐ No ☐

(c) If yes, please attach the tenancy agreement (with a note of any variations). It will be returned to you as soon as possible.

---

12. (a) I/we* apply to the rent assessment committee to determine a rent for the above mentioned premises.

Signed .... *Date* ....
....

To be signed and dated by the tenant or his agent. If there are joint tenants each tenant or the agent must sign unless one signs on behalf of the rest with their agreement.

Please specify whether: tenant ☐ joint tenants ☐ tenant's agent ☐

(b) Name and address of tenant(s) referring to the rent assessment committee.

Name(s) (Block Capitals) ....
....
....

Address
....
....
....

Telephone: Daytime .... Evening ....

Cases where this form should not be used

- An application cannot be made if—
  (a) the rent payable under the tenancy is a rent previously determined by a rent assessment committee; or
  (b) the tenancy is a replacement tenancy and more than six months have elapsed since the beginning of the original tenancy. A replacement tenancy is an assured shorthold tenancy that came into being on the ending of a tenancy which had been an assured shorthold of the same, or substantially the same, property and the landlord and tenant under each tenancy were the same at that time.
- The rent assessment committee cannot make a determination unless it considers—
  (a) that there is a sufficient number of similar properties in the locality let on assured tenancies (whether shorthold or not) for comparison; and
  (b) that the rent payable under the shorthold tenancy in question is significantly higher than the rent which the landlord might reasonably be expected to get in comparison with other rents for similar properties let on assured tenancies (whether shorthold or not) in the locality.

FORM NO. 7

Housing Act 1988 section 41(2)

A3-070 **Notice by Rent Assessment Committee requiring further information**

1. To: ....

☐ landlord(s) ☐ tenant(s)

of:

....
....
....

Addresses of premises

2. An application has been made to the rent assessment committee for consideration of:

☐ the terms of a statutory periodic assured tenancy
☐ an increase in rent under an assured periodic tenancy
☐ the rent under an assured shorthold tenancy
☐ an increase in rent under an assured agricultural occupancy

of the above property. The committee needs more information from you to consider the application.

3. The information needed is:

. . . .

. . . .

. . . .

. . . .

. . . .

. . . .

. . . .

4. Please send it to:

. . . .

. . . .

. . . .

. . . .

no later than . . . .

5. If you fail to comply with this notice without reasonable cause you will be committing a criminal offence and may be liable to a fine.

6. Signed on behalf of the rent assessment committee:

Signed. . . . . *Date* . . . .

Name (Block Capitals) . . . .

Address

. . . .

. . . .

. . . .

Telephone . . . .

Form No. 8

Housing Act 1988 Schedule 2A, paragraph 7(2) as inserted by Schedule 7 to the Housing Act 1996

Tenant's notice proposing that an Assured Tenancy be replaced by an Assured Shorthold Tenancy A3–071

- Please write clearly in black ink.
- Please cross out text marked with an asterisk (*) that does not apply.
- This notice should only be used by an assured tenant. You should only use this notice to notify your landlord that you wish your assured tenancy to be replaced by an assured shorthold tenancy.
- This notice must be served by a tenant on a landlord before an assured tenancy can be replaced by an assured shorthold tenancy.
- **You should be aware that by serving this notice, you will be giving up your right to stay in the property after the first six months of the assured shorthold tenancy or, if you agree a fixed term with your landlord, after the end of the fixed term.**
- **You do not have to complete the form even if your landlord has asked you to do so. Your existing security of tenure as an assured tenant will be unaffected if you do not complete it.**
- **If you are in any doubt about whether to complete this form, take it immediately to a citizens' advice bureau, housing advice centre, a law centre or a solicitor.**
- Once you are clear that you wish to issue this notice, complete the form and send it to your landlord.

1. To: . . . .
Name(s) of landlord(s)

2. I/We*, the tenant(s) of:
. . . .
. . . .
. . . .

Address of premises

give notice that I/we* propose that the assured tenancy to which this notice relates should be replaced by a shorthold tenancy.

---

3. I/We* propose that the new shorthold tenancy should commence on:

. . . . . . / . . . . . . / . . . . . .
day month year

- The new shorthold tenancy cannot commence until after the date this notice is served on the landlord.

---

4. (a) I/We* understand that under my/our* existing tenancy, I/we* can only be required to give up possession in accordance with the grounds set out in Schedule 2 to the Housing Act 1988, whereas under the new shorthold tenancy, the landlord(s) will be able to recover possession of the premises without being required to prove a ground for possession, after the first six months of the assured shorthold tenancy, or, if there is a fixed term for longer than 6 months, at the end of that fixed term, subject to two months' notice.

Signed . . . . *Date* . . . .
. . . .
. . . .

To be signed and dated by the tenant. If there are joint tenants each tenant must sign.

(b) Name and address of tenant.

Name(s) (Block Capitals) . . . .
. . . .
. . . .

Address
. . . .
. . . .
. . . .

Telephone: Daytime . . . . Evening . . . .

FORM NO. 9

Housing Act 1988 Schedule 2A, paragraph 9, as inserted by Schedule 7 to the Housing Act 1996

A3–072 **Landlord's notice proposing an Assured Shorthold Tenancy where the tenancy meets the conditions for an Assured Agricultural Occupancy**

- Please write clearly in black ink.
- Please tick boxes where appropriate.
- If the agricultural worker condition in Schedule 3 to the Housing Act 1988 is met with respect to the property to which the proposed assured tenancy relates, and the landlord wishes that tenancy to be an assured shorthold tenancy, he must serve this notice on the tenant before the tenancy is entered into.
- This notice cannot be used where the landlord has already granted to the prospective tenant (or, in the case of joint tenants, to at least one of them) a tenancy or licence under section 24 of the Housing Act 1988 (an assured agricultural occupancy).
- This notice does not commit the tenant to taking the tenancy.

---

1. To: . . . .
. . . .
. . . .

Name of the proposed tenant. If a joint tenancy is being offered, enter the names of the joint tenants.

2. You are proposing to take a tenancy at the following address:
....
....
....

commencing on ..../......./.......
day month year

---

3. This notice is to tell you that your tenancy is to be an assured shorthold tenancy.

- Provided you keep to the terms of the tenancy, you are entitled to remain in the property for at least six months after the start of the tenancy. Depending on the terms of the tenancy, once the first six months have elapsed, the landlord may have the right to seek possession at any time, subject to two months' notice.
- As an assured shorthold tenant, you have the right to apply to a rent assessment committee for the determination of a reasonable rent for the tenancy. An application to your local rent assessment committee must be made on the form headed *Application to a Rent Assessment Committee for a determination of a rent under an Assured Shorthold Tenancy* within six months of the beginning of the tenancy. You can obtain the form from a rent assessment panel or a law stationer.
- If you need help or advice about this notice, and what you should do about it, take it immediately to a citizens' advice bureau, a housing advice centre, a law centre or a solicitor.

---

4. Name and address of landlord.

To be signed and dated by the landlord or his agent (someone acting for him). If there are joint landlords each landlord or the agent must sign unless one signs on behalf of the rest with their agreement.

Signed .... *Date* ....
....
....

Please specify whether: landlord ☐ joint landlords ☐ agent ☐

Name(s) (Block Capitals) ....
....
....

Address:
....
....
....

Telephone: Daytime .... Evening ....

EXPLANATORY NOTE

(This note is not part of the Regulations)

These Regulations revoke and replace the Assured Tenancies and Agricultural Occupancies (Forms) Regulations 1988 ("the 1988 Regulations"). They prescribe forms for the purposes of various provisions of Part I of the Housing Act 1988 relating to assured tenancies and assured agricultural occupancies. The use for those purposes of forms substantially to the same effect as the prescribed forms is authorised by regulation 2.

Forms 3 and 4 prescribed by the 1988 Regulations have been amalgamated as new Form 3 with minor drafting amendments and with other amendments consequential on the Housing Act 1996. Forms 6A, 6B and 7 prescribed by the 1988 Regulations (Forms 6A and 6B were inserted by the Assured Tenancies and Agricultural Occupancies (Forms) (Amendment) Regulations 1993) have not been reproduced. Other forms prescribed by the 1988 Regulations have been reproduced with minor drafting amendments and with other amendments consequential on the Housing Act 1996. New Forms 8 and 9, which relate to the replacement of assured tenancies and assured agricultural occupancies by assured shorthold tenancies, are prescribed in consequence of amendments made to the Housing Act 1988 by the Housing Act 1996.

Regulation 4 revokes the 1988 Regulations, the Assured Tenancies and Agricultural Occupancies (Forms) (Amendment) Regulations 1989, the Assured Tenancies and Agricultural Occupancies (Forms) (Amendment) Regulations 1990 and the Assured Tenancies and Agricultural Occupancies (Forms) (Amendment) Regulations 1993.

The Housing Act 1996 (Commencement No. 7 and Savings) Order 1997 A3–073

S.I. 1997 No. 225

Made 28th January 1997

The Secretary of State, in exercise of the powers conferred on him by section 232(3) and (4) of the Housing Act 1996 and of all other powers enabling him in that behalf, hereby makes the following Order:

Citation and interpretation

1.—(1) This Order may be cited as the Housing Act 1996 (Commencement No. 7 and Savings) Order 1997. **A3–074**

(2) In this Order "the commencement date" means 28th February 1997.

Commencement and Savings

2. The following provisions of the Housing Act 1996 shall come into force on the commencement date, subject to the savings in the Schedule to this Order— **A3–075**

section 96 to the extent that it is not already in force,
sections 97 to 104,
sections 148 to 151, and
section 227 in so far as it relates to the repeals in Part IV of Schedule 19.

Article 2

SCHEDULE

SAVINGS

1. The insertion of section 8A in the Housing Act 1988 and the amendment to section 8 of and Schedule 2 to that Act (repossession: assured tenancies) shall have no effect in a case where— **A3–076**

(a) a notice under section 8 of that Act (notice of proceedings for possession) has been served before the commencement date; or

(b) the court has dispensed with the requirement of such a notice and the proceedings for possession were started before the commencement date.

2. The amendments to section 21(1) and (4) of the Housing Act 1988 (recovery of possession on expiry or termination of assured shorthold tenancy) shall have not effect in a case where a landlord has served a notice under section 8 of that Act (notice of proceedings for possession) before the commencement date.

Signed by the authority of the Secretary of State

James Clappison
Parliamentary Under-Secretary of State
Department of the Environment

28th January 1997

EXPLANATORY NOTE

(This note is not part of the Order)

Article 2 of this Order brings into force, on 28th February 1997, the following provisions of the Housing Act 1996 (subject to the savings in the Schedule to the Order)—

section 96, to the extent that it is not already in force;
sections 97 to 104 (assured tenancies);
sections 148 to 151 (repossession: assured tenancies); and
section 227, in so far as it relates to the repeals in Part IV of Schedule 19 (assured tenancies).

The amendments to sections 8 and 21(1) and (4) of and Schedule 2 to the Housing Act 1988 made by the provisions commenced in the Order are subject to the savings in the Schedule to the Order.

The Long Residential Tenancies (Supplemental Forms) Regulations 1997 A3–077

S.I. 1997 No. 3005

Made 16th December 1997
Laid before Parliament 22nd December 1997
Coming into force 15th January 1998

The Secretary of State for the Environment, as respects England, and the Secretary of State for Wales, as respects Wales, in exercise of the powers conferred on them by sections 18 and 66 of and paragraph 5 of Schedule 5 to the Landlord and Tenant Act 1954, as applied by section 186(5) of and paragraph 19 of Schedule 10 to the Local Government and Housing Act 1989, and now vested in them and of all other powers enabling them in that behalf, hereby make the following Regulations—

Citation and commencement

1. These Regulations may be cited as the Long Residential Tenancies (Supplemental Forms) Regulations and shall come into force on 15th January 1998. A3–078

Interpretation

2. In these Regulations— A3–079

"the 1954 Act" means the Landlord and Tenant Act 1954;

"the 1989 Act" means the Local Government and Housing Act 1989; and any reference to a numbered form is a reference to the form bearing that number in the Schedule, or to a form substantially to the same effect.

Forms

A3–080 **3.** The forms prescribed for the purposes specified below shall be as follows—

(a) for a notice under section 18 of the 1954 Act (as applied by section 186(5) of the 1989 Act) requiring information about sub-tenancies, form 7;
(b) for a notice under paragraph 5 of Schedule 5 to the 1954 Act (as applied by paragraph 19 of Schedule 10 to the 1989 Act) requiring a landlord to consent to the giving of a notice under paragraph 4(1) of Schedule 10 to the 1989 Act terminating a long residential tenancy, form 8; and
(c) for a notice under paragraph 5 of Schedule 5 to the 1954 Act (as applied by paragraph 19 of Schedule 10 to the 1989 Act) requiring a landlord to consent to the making of an agreement with the tenant under Schedule 10 to the 1989 Act, form 9.

Signed by authority of the Secretary of State

Hilary Armstrong
Minister of State,
Department of the Environment, Transport and the Regions

12th December 1997

Signed by authority of the Secretary of State for Wales

Win Griffiths
Parliamentary Under Secretary of State, Welsh Office

16th December 1997

Regulation 3

SCHEDULE

PRESCRIBED FORMS

FORM 7

A3–081 **Landlord's Notice Requiring Information about Sub-tenancies of Residential Property**

Section 18 of the Landlord and Tenant Act 1954 as applied by section 186(5) of the Local Government and Housing Act 1989

The landlord **must** *cross out any text in square brackets which does not apply.*

- This notice asks whether you have any sub-tenant of any part of the property described below.
- Please read this notice carefully. **There is a time limit which you must keep to.** If you need help or advice about this notice, you should take it immediately to any of the following:
  —a Citizens' Advice Bureau
  —a housing aid centre
  —a law centre
  —a solicitor.
- Please read the notes at the end of the form.

---

1. To: . . . .

Insert name[s] of tenant[s].

---

2. From: . . . .

of: . . . .

. . . .

. . . .

Insert name[s] and address of landlord[s].

(see note 1)

---

3. [I][We] require you to notify [me][us] whether you have a sub-tenant of the whole or any part of:

. . . .

. . . .

. . . .

Insert the address of the property to which the notice relates.

(see notes 2 to 4)

---

4. If you have a sub-tenant, [I][We] require you to state—

(a) what property is let under the sub-tenancy;

(b) if the sub-tenancy is for a fixed term, what is the term, or, if the sub-tenancy is terminable by notice, by what notice it can be terminated;

(c) the rent payable under the sub-tenancy;

(d) the full name of sub-tenant; and

(e) whether, to the best of your knowledge and belief, the sub-tenant occupies the property let under the sub-tenancy or any part of it, and, if not, what is the sub-tenant's address.

(see note 4)

---

5. I require you to give me the information requested in this notice **WITHIN ONE MONTH** of the giving of this notice.

(see note 5)

---

6. This Notice is given under the provisions of section 18 of the Landlord and Tenant Act 1954 as applied by section 186(5) of the Local Government and Housing Act 1989.

Signed . . . . Date . . . .

To be signed and dated by the landlord or the landlord's agent. If there are joint landlords, each landlord or the agent for that landlord must sign (but one can sign on behalf of another with his consent).

[The name and address of the agent is:

. . . .

. . . .

. . . .

Insert name and address of agent, if signed by an agent.]

Notes

Note 1: The landlord referred to in this notice is not necessarily the landlord to whom you pay the rent. It may be that landlord or a superior landlord.

Note 2: Section 18 of the Landlord and Tenant Act 1954, as applied by section 186(5) of the Local Government and Housing Act 1989, provides that a tenant or sub-tenant of any property let under a tenancy to which the section applies may be required to give information about sublettings by a notice from his immediate landlord or any superior landlord. Section 18 (as applied by the 1989 Act) will apply to you if you hold a long tenancy at a low rent or if you are a sub-tenant of a person holding such a tenancy. A long tenancy is normally a tenancy granted for more than 21 years. A tenancy is at a low rent:

(a) if no rent is payable; or

(b) where the tenancy was entered into before 1st April 1990, if the maximum rent payable at any time is less than two thirds of the rateable value of the property on 31st March 1990; or

(c) where the tenancy was entered into on or after 1st April 1990, if the maximum rent payable at any time is payable at a rate of:

(i) £1,000 or less a year if the property is in Greater London, or

(ii) £250 or less a year if the property is elsewhere.

The low rent test in (b) above applies (rather than the test in (c)) if the tenancy was entered into on or after 1st April 1990 in pursuance of a contract made before that date and the property had a rateable value on 31st March 1990.

Note 3: The information is required so that the landlord giving this notice can find out who will be in occupation when the current tenancy comes to an end. Where section 18 of the 1954 Act (as applied by the 1989 Act) applies, the landlord has a right to seek this information, but **NOT EARLIER THAN TWO YEARS** before the tenancy is due to end.

Note 4: If you have sublet to more than one sub-tenant, the information must be given in respect of each sub-tenancy (including any statutory tenancy under the Rent Act).

Note 5: If section 18 of the Landlord and Tenant Act 1954 applies to you (see note 2), you should **WITHIN ONE MONTH** of this notice having been given, supply the information asked for. Failing to give the information asked for or giving incorrect information could involve the landlord in loss for which you might in certain circumstances be held liable.

Form 8

A3–082 Landlord's Notice Requiring Consent of Other Landlord to Notice Terminating Long Residential Tenancy

Paragraph 5 of Schedule 5 to the Landlord and Tenant Act 1954 as applied by paragraph 19 of Schedule 10 to the Local Government and Housing Act 1989

*The landlord giving this notice **must** cross out any text in square brackets which does not apply.*

- This notice seeks your consent as another landlord with an interest in the property concerned, to a notice terminating the tenant's long residential tenancy and either proposing an assured monthly periodic tenancy or giving notice to resume possession.
- Please read this notice carefully. **There is a time limit which you must keep to.** If you need help or advice about this notice, you should take it immediately to any of the following—
  —a Citizens' Advice Bureau
  —a housing aid centre
  —a law centre
  —a solicitor.
- Please read the notes at the end of the form.

---

1. To: . . . .

Insert name[s] of other landlord[s].

---

2. From: . . . .

of: . . . .

. . . .

. . . .

Insert name[s] and address of the competent landlord[s] (who is giving this notice).

---

3. [I am] [We are] the landlord for the purposes of Schedule 10 to the Local Government and Housing Act 1989 of:

. . . .
. . . .
. . . .

Insert the address of the property let under the long residential tenancy.

and you are another landlord of that property.

(see notes 1 and 2)

---

4. [I][We] propose to give notice under paragraph 4(1) of Schedule 10 to the Local Government and Housing Act 1989 to:

. . . .
. . . .
. . . .

Insert name[s] of the tenant[s] under the long residential tenancy.

terminating the long residential tenancy of the property and

[proposing an assured monthly periodic tenancy.]
[stating that [I][we] propose to apply to court for possession.]

(see notes 3 and 4)

---

5. A copy of the proposed notice under paragraph 4(1) of Schedule 10 terminating the long residential tenancy is attached.

---

6. You are required **WITHIN ONE MONTH** after the service of this notice, to notify [me][us] in writing whether you consent to the notice referred to in paragraph 4 being given.

(see note 5)

---

7. This notice is given under paragraph 5 of Schedule 5 to the Landlord and Tenant Act 1954 as applied by paragraph 19 of Schedule 10 to the Local Government and Housing Act 1989.

Signed . . . .   Date . . . .

To be signed and dated by the landlord or the landlord's agent. If there are joint landlords, each landlord or the agent for that landlord must sign (but one can sign on behalf of another with his consent).

[The name and address of the agent is:

. . . .
. . . .
. . . .

Insert name and address of agent, if signed by an agent.]

Notes

Note 1: This notice requires you to consent to a landlord's notice being given under paragraph 4(1) of Schedule 10 to the Local Government and Housing Act 1989. That notice would terminate a long residential tenancy of property of which you are a superior landlord or an intermediate landlord.

Note 2: This notice is not appropriate if your interest in the property is due to end (or can be terminated by notice to quit) within the period of two months beginning on the relevant date (as defined in paragraph 3 of Schedule 5 to the Landlord and Tenant Act 1954).

Note 3: A notice under paragraph 4(1) of Schedule 10 to the 1989 Act, as well as terminating the long residential tenancy, will either propose an assured monthly periodic tenancy (form 1) or state that the landlord proposes to apply to court for possession (form 2).

Note 4: A notice under paragraph 4(1) of Schedule 10 to the 1989 Act can only be given to the tenant by the person who is the landlord for the purposes of that Schedule. Such a notice is binding on every superior and intermediate landlord. If you are a superior or intermediate landlord and you suffer loss as a result of such a notice having been given, you will be entitled to compensation unless your written consent to it has been obtained (but not if this notice should not have been served on you for the reason given in note 2).

Note 5: If you do not give your consent **WITHIN ONE MONTH** after this notice was served on you, or you consent subject to conditions which the rent assessment committee or county court considers unreasonable, the committee or court may (on the application of the landlord giving this notice) order that you shall be deemed to have consented. It may order that you shall be deemed to have consented either without qualification or subject to such conditions (including conditions as to the modification of the proposed notice or as to payment to you of compensation) as it may specify.

Form 9

A3–083 Landlord's Notice Requiring Consent of Other Landlord to Agreement with Tenant under Schedule 10 to Local Government and Housing Act 1989

Paragraph 5 of Schedule 5 to the Landlord and Tenant Act 1954 as applied by paragraph 19 of Schedule 10 to the Local Government and Housing Act 1989

*The landlord giving this notice **must** cross out any text in square brackets which does not apply.*

- This notice seeks your consent as another landlord with an interest in the property concerned, to an agreement to grant a new tenancy of the property to a tenant who has a long residential tenancy of the property.
- Please read this notice carefully. **There is a time limit which you must keep to.** If you need help or advice about this notice, you should take it immediately to any of the following:
  —a Citizens' Advice Bureau
  —a housing aid centre
  —a law centre
  —a solicitor.
- Please read the notes at the end of the form.

---

1. To: ....

Insert name[s] of other landlord[s].

---

2. From: ....

of: ....

....

....

Insert name[s] and address of the competent landlord[s] (who is giving this notice).

---

3. [I am] [We are] the landlord for the purposes of Schedule 10 to the Local Government and Housing Act 1989 of:

....

....

....

Insert the address of the property let under the long residential tenancy.

and you are another landlord of that property.

(see notes 1 and 2)

---

4. [I][We] propose to make an agreement under Schedule 10 to the Local Government and Housing Act 1989 for granting a tenancy of

[the whole of the property]

[the following part of the property, namely: ....

If the proposed agreement relates to only part of the property let under the long residential tenancy, describe that part.]

to:

. . . .

. . . .

. . . .

Insert name[s] of the tenant[s] under the long residential property.

---

5. A copy of the proposed agreement is attached.

(see note 3)

---

6. You are required **WITHIN ONE MONTH** after the service of this notice, to notify [me][us] in writing whether you consent to the making of the agreement.

(see note 4)

---

7. This notice is given under paragraph 5 of Schedule 5 to the Landlord and Tenant Act 1954 as applied by paragraph 19 of Schedule 10 to the Local Government and Housing Act 1989.

Signed . . . .   Date . . . .

To be signed and dated by the landlord or the landlord's agent. If there are joint landlords, each landlord or the agent for that landlord must sign (but one can sign on behalf of another with his consent).

[The name and address of the agent is:

. . . .

. . . .

. . . .

Insert name and address of agent, if signed by an agent.]

Notes

Note 1: This notice requires you to consent to an agreement under Schedule 10 to the Local Government and Housing Act 1989 in respect of property of which you are a superior or intermediate landlord.

Note 2: This notice is not appropriate if your interest in the property is due to end (or can be terminated by notice to quit) within the period of two months beginning on the relevant date (as defined in paragraph 3 of Schedule 5 to the Landlord and Tenant Act 1954).

Note 3: Under Schedule 10 to the Local Government and Housing Act 1989, the proposed agreement can only be made between the tenant and the person who is the landlord for the purposes of a Schedule. Such an agreement is binding on every superior and intermediate landlord. If you are a superior or intermediate landlord and suffer loss as a result of the making of the agreement, you will be entitled to compensation unless your written consent to it has been obtained (but not if this notice should not have been served on you for the reason given in note 2).

Note 4: If you do not give your consent **WITHIN ONE MONTH** after service of this notice, or you consent subject to conditions which the rent assessment committee or county court considers unreasonable, the committee or court may (on the application of the landlord giving this notice) order that you shall be deemed to have consented. It may order that you shall be deemed to have consented either without qualification or subject to such conditions (including conditions as to the modification of the proposed notice or as to payment to you of compensation) as it may specify.

EXPLANATORY NOTE

(This note is not part of the Regulations)

These Regulations prescribe forms of notice to be used for the purposes of section 186 of and Schedule 10 to the Local Government and Housing Act 1989 (security of tenure on ending of long residential tenancies). The forms prescribed are those specfied in regulation 3 and set out in the Schedule (or forms substantially to the same effect).

Forms 1 to 6 are prescribed for the purposes of Schedule 10 in the Long Residential Tenancies (Principal Forms) Regulations 1997.

The Long Residential Tenancies (Principal Forms) Regulations 1997 A3–084

S.I. 1997 No. 3008

Made 16th December 1997
Coming into force 15th January 1998

The Secretary of State for the Environment, as respects England, and the Secretary of State for Wales, as respects Wales, in exercise of the powers conferred on them by paragraphs 4(1), 6(1), 10 and 12(1) of Schedule 10 to the Local Government and Housing Act 1989 and of all other powers enabling them in that behalf, hereby make the following Regulations:

Citation and commencement

1. These Regulations may be cited as the Long Residential Tenancies (Principal Forms) Regulations and shall come into force on 15th January 1998. A3–085

Interpretation

2. In these Regulations, any reference to a numbered form is a reference to the form bearing that number in the Schedule, or to a form substantially to the same effect. A3–086

Forms

3. The forms prescribed for the purposes specified below shall be as follows— A3–087

(a) for a notice under paragraph 4(1) of Schedule 10 to the Local Government and Housing Act 1989 terminating a long residential tenancy and proposing an assured monthly periodic tenancy, form 1;

(b) for a notice under paragraph 4(1) of that Schedule terminating a long residential tenancy and proposing to apply to court for possession, form 2;
(c) for a notice under paragraph 6(1) of that Schedule proposing an interim monthly rent, form 3;
(d) for a notice under paragraph 10(1) of that Schedule proposing different rent or terms for an assured periodic tenancy, form 4;
(e) for a notice under paragraph 10(2) of that Schedule referring to a rent assessment committee a notice proposing different rent or terms for an assured periodic tenancy, form 5; and
(f) for a notice under section 41(2) of the Housing Act 1988, as applied by paragraph 12(1) of that Schedule, requiring a landlord or tenant to give information to a rent assessment committee, form 6.

Hilary Armstrong
Minister of State,
Department of the Environment, Transport and the Regions

12th December 1997

Win Griffiths
Parliamentary Under Secretary of State, Welsh Office

16th December 1997

Regulation 3

SCHEDULE

PRESCRIBED FORMS

FORM 1

A3–088 **Landlord's Notice Terminating Long Residential Tenancy and Proposing Assured Tenancy**

Paragraph 4(1) of Schedule 10 to the Local Government and Housing Act 1989

*The landlord **must** cross out any text in square brackets which does not apply.*

- This notice will end your existing long residential tenancy and contains a proposal to replace it with an assured periodic tenancy.
- Please read this notice carefully. **There are time limits which you must keep to.** If you need help or advice about this notice, you should take it immediately to any of the following:
  —a Citizens' Advice Bureau
  —a housing aid centre
  —a law centre
  —a solicitor.
- Please read the notes at the end of the form.

---

1. To: . . . .
Insert name[s] of tenant[s].

---

2. From: . . . .
of: . . . .
. . . .
. . . .
Insert name[s] and address of landlord[s].
(see note 1)

---

3. [I] [We] give you notice ending your long residential tenancy of:

. . . .

. . . .

. . . .

Insert address of property to which the notice relates.

on: . . . .

Insert the date at which the tenancy is to come to an end.

(see notes 2 and 4)

---

4. I believe that you are entitled to the protection of Schedule 10 to the Local Government and Housing Act 1989 in respect of

[the whole of the property]

[the following part of the property, namely: . . . .

If you consider only part of the property is protected, describe that part.]

(see note 5)

---

5. You are requested **WITHIN 2 MONTHS**, beginning on the date on which the notice was served, to notify [me] [us] in writing whether or not you wish to remain in possession.

(see notes 6 and 7)

Consequences of this notice if tenant claims the freehold or an extended lease or a new lease

6. If you are the tenant of a house, you may have the right to acquire the freehold or an extended lease of that house under Part I of the Leasehold Reform Act 1967. If you are the tenant of a flat, you may have the right to acquire a new lease of your flat under Part I of the Leasehold Reform, Housing and Urban Development Act 1993 and you may also have the right, collectively with the other tenants of flats in the same building, to acquire the freehold of that building under Part I of that Act.

(see note 8)

---

7. If you want to acquire the freehold under the 1967 Act or a lease under that Act or the 1993 Act, you must serve the appropriate notice for that **WITHIN 2 MONTHS** of the service of this notice. If you and other tenants of flats in the same building want to acquire the freehold of that building under the 1993 Act, you and other tenants must serve the notice for that **WITHIN 4 MONTHS** of the service of this notice. If you serve one of those notices, then this notice will not operate.

(see note 9)

---

8. If you serve one of those notices, then [I][we] [will][will not] be entitled to apply to the county court for possession of the property under:
[section 17 of the 1967 Act] [section 18 of the 1967 Act]
[section 23 of the 1993 Act] [section 47 of the 1993 Act]
[and [propose] [do not propose] to do so].

(see note 10)

---

9. The following are the names and addresses of other persons known or believed by [me] [us] to have an interest superior to your tenancy or to be the agent concerned with the property on behalf of a person having such an interest:

. . . .

. . . .

. . . .

Insert the name[s] and address[es] of any such person[s].

Consequences of this notice if tenant does not claim the freehold or an extended lease or a new lease

10. I propose that you should have an assured monthly periodic tenancy of the property specified in paragraph 4 at a rent of:

£ .... a month.

Insert the proposed monthly rent.

(see note 11)

and the other proposed terms of the tenancy are:

Insert the proposed terms or attach a copy of the proposed tenancy agreement. Continue on a separate sheet if necessary.

(see note 12)

---

11. If you want the terms of the new assured tenancy to be different from those proposed by the landlord in this notice, then you must serve a notice in **FORM 4** on [me] [us] **WITHIN 2 MONTHS** of the date this notice was served.

(see notes 13 and 14)

---

12. This notice is given under the provisions of paragraph 4(1) of Schedule 10 to the Local Government and Housing Act 1989.

(see note 15)

Signed .... Date ....

To be signed and dated by the landlord or the landlord's agent. If there are joint landlords, each landlord or the agent for that landlord must sign (but one can sign on behalf of another with his consent).

[The name and address of the agent is:

....

....

....

Insert name and address of agent, if signed by an agent.]

Notes

Note 1: The landlord referred to in this notice is not necessarily the landlord to whom you pay the rent. It is the person who is your landlord for the purposes of Schedule 10 to the Local Government and Housing Act 1989. That, broadly, will be your immediate landlord if he has a lease which is at least five years longer than your tenancy or, if not, the first superior landlord who has such a lease. If there is no landlord with such a lease, it will be the freeholder.

Note 2: Schedule 10 to the Local Government and Housing Act 1989 provides that a tenant of residential property under a long residential tenancy has a right, at the end of the original term of the tenancy, to continue as tenant on the same terms as before unless the tenant or the landlord ends the tenancy in accordance with the provisions of the Act. For this to apply, the tenancy must be a long tenancy at a low rent and the tenant must be occupying the property (as his only or principal home) on the relevant date. The relevant date is normally the day before the original term of the tenancy ends and a long residential tenancy is normally a tenancy granted for more than 21 years at a low rent. A tenancy is at a low rent:

(a) if no rent is payable; or
(b) where the tenancy was entered into before 1st April 1990, if the maximum rent payable at any time is less than two thirds of the rateable value of the property on 31st March 1990; or
(c) where the tenancy was entered into on or after 1st April 1990, if the maximum rent payable at any time is payable at a rate of:
    (i) £1,000 or less a year if the property is in Greater London, or
    (ii) £250 or less a year if the property is elsewhere.

The low rent test in (b) above applies (rather than the test in (c)) if the tenancy was entered into on or after 1st April 1990 in pursuance of a contract made before that date and the property had a rateable value on 31st March 1990.

Note 3: Schedule 10 does not apply if the property is excluded because of its high value; it does not apply:

(a) if the long residential tenancy was granted before 1st April 1990 and the rateable value of the property on 31st March 1990 was:
   (i) more than £1,500 if the property is in Greater London, or
   (ii) more than £750 if the property is elsewhere; or

(b) if the long residential tenancy was granted on or after 1st April 1990 and "R" under the formula in paragraph 1(2A) of Schedule 10 (which is based on the amount paid for the grant of the tenancy and the length of the tenancy) is more than £25,000.

The test in (a) above applies (rather than the test in (b)) if the tenancy was entered into on or after 1st April 1990 in pursuance of a contract made before that date and the property had a rateable value on 31st March 1990.

Note 4: The landlord can end the tenancy by notice which, as a general rule, must be served not more than 12 and not less than 6 months before the date of termination specified in the notice. This date must not normally be before the date on which the long residential tenancy expires. The landlord can serve a notice on you in form 3 proposing that you pay an interim monthly rent from a specified date which cannot be before the date specified in paragraph 3 of this notice. That notice may be served at the same time as this notice or later.

Note 5: Your right to remain in occupation is limited to parts of the property which you occupy at the end of the tenancy.

Note 6: If you wish to give up possession of the property, you should let the landlord know (in writing) **WITHIN 2 MONTHS** of the date this notice was served. Failing to notify the landlord may lead to an unnecessary application to the county court and consequent expense, which you may have to bear.

Note 7: If you do **not** wish to give up possession of the property, you should let the landlord know (in writing) **WITHIN 2 MONTHS** of the date this notice was served. If you fail to notify the landlord and are not in occupation of the property 2 months after this notice was served, you may lose the protection of the 1989 Act. However, if you fail to notify the landlord, but are in occupation (as your only or principal home) 2 months after this notice was served, you will not lose that protection.

Note 8: Your rights under the 1989 Act are in addition to any right you may have under the Leasehold Reform Act 1967 or the Leasehold Reform, Housing and Urban Development Act 1993.

Note 9: A landlord may, but does not have to, consent in writing to the deadline being extended.

Note 10: Sections 17 and 18 of the Leasehold Reform Act 1967 and sections 23 and 47 of the Leasehold Reform, Housing and Urban Development Act 1993 relate to cases where the landlord can apply to court for repossession if certain conditions are fulfilled (involving redeveloping the property or, under the 1967 Act, the landlord or a member of his family wanting to live in the property).

Note 11: The proposed rent must be at a level which is sufficient for the proposed tenancy to qualify as an assured tenancy and so must not be at a low rent. In this case, the tenancy would be at a low rent if no rent is payable or if the maximum rent payable at any time is payable at a rate of:

(a) £1,000 or less a year if the property is in Greater London, or
(b) £250 or less a year if the property is elsewhere.

Note 12: The landlord may specify terms which are the same as those of the long tenancy or different terms.

Note 13: If you do not agree with the rent or other terms proposed, you should serve a notice in **FORM 4** on the landlord proposing a different rent or terms. That notice must be served **WITHIN 2 MONTHS** of the service of this notice. The landlord may refer the matter to a rent assessment committee which will decide on any dispute about the rent or the other terms. If the dispute is referred to a rent assessment committee, this notice does not end your long residential tenancy until the last day of the period of three months starting with the date when the matter is finally disposed of. The assured tenancy will start on the day after.

Note 14: If you do not serve the notice referred to in note 13, the rent and terms proposed in this notice will be the rent and terms for the assured periodic tenancy (unless the landlord agrees a different rent or other terms with you). In that case, your long residential tenancy will end on the date specified in paragraph 3 of this notice and the assured tenancy will start on the day after.

Note 15: You may decide that you want your long residential tenancy to end at or after the date it would have ended under the terms of the tenancy. If so, you will need to give your immediate landlord not less than one month's notice in writing. Your immediate landlord will be the person to whom you pay your rent and may not be the landlord who has served this notice. It does not make any difference that this notice proposes an assured monthly periodic tenancy or that you have notified the landlord that you wished to remain in possession.

Form 2

A3-089 **Landlord's Notice Terminating Long Residential Tenancy and Seeking Possession**

Paragraph 4(1) of Schedule 10 to the Local Government and Housing Act 1989

*The landlord **must** cross out any text in square brackets which does not apply.*

- This notice will end your existing long residential tenancy and states that, if you are not willing to give up possession, the landlord proposes to apply to court for possession.
- Please read this notice carefully. **There are time limits which you must keep to.** If you need help or advice about this notice, you should take it immediately to any of the following:
  —a Citizens' Advice Bureau
  —a housing aid centre
  —a law centre
  —a solicitor.
- You may be able to get legal aid but this will depend on your personal circumstances.
- Please read the notes at the end of the form.

---

1. To: . . . .
Insert name[s] of tenant[s].

---

2. From: . . . .
of: . . . .
. . . .
. . . .
Insert name[s] and address of landlord[s].
(see note 1)

---

3. [I] [We] give you notice ending your long residential tenancy of:
. . . .
. . . .
. . . .
Insert address of property to which the notice relates.
on: . . . .
Insert the date at which the tenancy is to come to an end.
(see notes 2 and 4)

---

4. I believe that you are entitled to the protection of Schedule 10 to the Local Government and Housing Act 1989 in respect of

[the whole of the property]

[the following part of the property, namely: . . . .
If you consider only part of the property is protected, describe that part.]
(see note 5)

---

5. You are requested **WITHIN 2 MONTHS**, beginning on the date on which the notice was served, to notify [me] [us] in writing whether or not you wish to remain in possession.

(see notes 6 and 7)

Consequences of this notice if tenant claims the freehold or an extended lease or a new lease

6. If you are the tenant of a house, you may have the right to acquire the freehold or an extended lease of that house under Part I of the Leasehold Reform Act 1967. If you are the tenant of a flat, you may have the right to acquire a new lease of your flat under Part I of the Leasehold Reform, Housing and Urban Development Act 1993 and you may also have the right, collectively with the other tenants of flats in the same building, to acquire the freehold of that building under Part I of that Act.

(see note 8)

---

7. If you want to acquire the freehold under the 1967 Act or a lease under that Act or the 1993 Act, you must serve the appropriate notice for that **WITHIN 2 MONTHS** of the service of this notice. If you and other tenants of flats in the same building want to acquire the freehold of that building under the 1993 Act, you and other tenants must serve the notice for that **WITHIN 4 MONTHS** of the service of this notice. If you serve one of those notices, then this notice will not operate.

(see note 9)

---

8. If you serve one of those notices, then [I][we] [will][will not] be entitled to apply to the county court for possession of the property under:
[section 17 of the 1967 Act] [section 18 of the 1967 Act]
[section 23 of the 1993 Act] [section 47 of the 1993 Act]
[and [propose] [do not propose] to do so].

(see note 10)

---

9. The following are the names and addresses of other persons known or believed by [me] [us] to have an interest superior to your tenancy or to be the agent concerned with the property on behalf of a person having such an interest:

. . . .

. . . .

. . . .

Insert the name[s] and address[es] of any such person[s].

Consequences of this notice if tenant does not claim the freehold or an extended lease or a new lease

10. If you are not willing to give up possession of the property let under your long residential tenancy at the date of termination, I propose to apply to the county court for possession of the property on the following ground[s]—

. . . .

. . . .

. . . .

. . . .

Insert each ground on which you propose to apply to the court for possession and give the full text of each ground. Continue on a separate sheet if necessary.

(see notes 11 to 15)

---

11. This notice is given under the provisions of paragraph 4(1) of Schedule 10 to the Local Government and Housing Act 1989.

(see notes 16)

Signed . . . . Date . . . .

To be signed and dated by the landlord or the landlord's agent. If there are joint landlords, each landlord or the agent for that landlord must sign (but one can sign on behalf of another with his consent).

[The name and address of the agent is:

. . . .

. . . .

. . . .

Insert name and address of agent, if signed by an agent.]

Notes

Note 1: The landlord referred to in this notice is not necessarily the landlord to whom you pay the rent. It is the person who is your landlord for the purposes of Schedule 10 to the Local Government and Housing Act 1989. That, broadly, will be your immediate landlord if he has a lease which is at least five years longer than your tenancy or, if not, the first superior landlord who has such a lease. If there is no landlord with such a lease, it will be the freeholder.

Note 2: Schedule 10 to the Local Government and Housing Act 1989 provides that a tenant of residential property under a long residential tenancy has a right, at the end of the original term of the tenancy, to continue as tenant on the same terms as before unless the tenant or the landlord ends the tenancy in accordance with the provisions of the Act. For this to apply, the tenancy must be a long tenancy at a low rent and the tenant must be occupying the property (as his only or principal home) on the relevant date. The relevant date is normally the day before the original term of the tenancy ends and a long residential tenancy is normally a tenancy granted for more than 21 years at a low rent. A tenancy is at a low rent:

(a) if no rent is payable; or
(b) where the tenancy was entered into before 1st April 1990, if the maximum rent payable at any time is less than two thirds of the rateable value of the property on 31st March 1990; or
(c) where the tenancy was entered into on or after 1st April 1990, if the maximum rent payable at any time is payable at a rate of:
 (i) £1,000 or less a year if the property is in Greater London, or
 (ii) £250 or less a year if the property is elsewhere.

The low rent test in (b) above applies (rather than the test in (c)) if the tenancy was entered into on or after 1st April 1990 in pursuance of a contract made before that date and the property had a rateable value on 31st March 1990.

Note 3: Schedule 10 does not apply if the property is excluded because of its high value; it does not apply:

(a) if the long residential tenancy was granted before 1st April 1990 and the rateable value of the property on 31st March 1990 was:
 (i) more than £1,500 if the property is in Greater London, or
 (ii) more than £750 if the property is elsewhere; or
(b) if the long residential tenancy was granted on or after 1st April 1990 and "R" under the formula in paragraph 1(2A) of Schedule 10 (which is based on the amount paid for the grant of the tenancy and the length of the tenancy) is more than £25,000.

The test in (a) above applies (rather than the test in (b)) if the tenancy was entered into on or after 1st April 1990 in pursuance of a contract made before that date and the property had a rateable value on 31st March 1990.

Note 4: The landlord can end the tenancy by notice which, as a general rule, must be served not more than 12 and not less than 6 months before the date of termination specified in the notice. This date must not normally be before the date on which the long residential tenancy expires.

Note 5: Your right to remain in occupation is limited to parts of the property which you occupy at the end of the tenancy.

Note 6: If you wish to give up possession of the property, you should let the landlord know (in writing) **WITHIN 2 MONTHS** of the date this notice was served. Failing to notify the landlord may lead to an unnecessary application to the county court and consequent expense, which you may have to bear.

Note 7: If you do **not** wish to give up possession of the property, you should let the landlord know (in writing) **WITHIN 2 MONTHS** of the date this notice was served. If you fail to notify the landlord and are not in occupation of the property 2 months after this notice was served, you may lose the protection of the 1989 Act. However, if you fail to notify the landlord, but are in occupation (as your only or principal home) 2 months after this notice was served, you will not lose that protection.

Note 8: Your rights under the 1989 Act are in addition to any right you may have under the Leasehold Reform Act 1967 or the Leasehold Reform, Housing and Urban Development Act 1993.

Note 9: A landlord may, but does not have to, consent in writing to the deadline being extended.

Note 10: Sections 17 and 18 of the Leasehold Reform Act 1967 and sections 23 and 47 of the Leasehold Reform, Housing and Urban Development Act 1993 relate to cases where the landlord can apply to court for repossession if certain conditions are fulfilled (involving redeveloping the property or, under the 1967 Act, the landlord or a member of his family wanting to live in the property).

Note 11: The date of termination (referred to in paragraph 10 of this notice) is the date specified in paragraph 3 of this notice. Where the landlord applies to the county court for an order for possession of the property, the date of termination is the last day of the period of three months starting with the date when the application is finally disposed of.

Note 12: The landlord must state the ground or grounds on which he proposes to apply to court for possession. Only grounds specified in Schedule 10 to the Local Government and Housing Act 1989 may be included. Schedule 10 sets out some of the grounds in full and provides for some of the grounds set out in Schedule 2 to the Housing Act 1988 to apply (with some modifications). An outline of the grounds follows (but **not** the full text):

Schedule 2 to the Housing Act 1988

Ground 6: landlord intends to demolish or reconstruct a substantial part of the property or needs possession to carry out substantial works to the property; and the long residential tenancy was not formerly a tenancy under Part I of the Landlord and Tenant Act 1954.
Ground 9: suitable alternative accommodation available for tenant
Ground 10: some rent in arrears on date possession proceedings begun and on date this notice was served
Ground 11: tenant persistently delayed paying rent
Ground 12: obligation under tenancy, other than one related to the payment of rent, not complied with
Ground 13: condition of the property or common parts has deteriorated because of neglect or default by tenant or other person living at the property
Ground 14: nuisance or annoyance by tenant or other person living in or visiting the property or conviction for using the property for immoral or illegal purposes or an arrestable offence committed in, or in the locality of, the property
Ground 14A: landlord is a registered social landlord or housing action trust and there has been domestic violence or threat of violence
Ground 15: condition of furniture provided for use under the long residential tenancy deteriorated because of the ill-treatment by tenant or other person living at the property

Schedule 10 to the Local Government and Housing Act 1989

Paragraph 5(1)(b): landlord is a public body intending to demolish or reconstruct a substantial part of the property for purposes relevant to its functions
Paragraph 5(1)(c): landlord reasonably requires property to live in himself or for specified relations and landlord's interest in the property purchased or created before 19th February 1966.

Note 13: The landlord may apply to the county court for an order for possession on any of the grounds specified in paragraph 10 of this notice. In order for the application to succeed, the landlord must establish that ground. The landlord will also have to satisfy the court that it is reasonable to grant him possession (except for ground 6 in the 1988 Act and the ground in paragraph 5(1)(c) of Schedule 10 to the 1989 Act. However, if you are not occupying the property (as your only or principal home) at the date of the court hearing, the court will order possession. If the application succeeds, your long residential tenancy will end on the date of termination (see note 11).

Note 14: If you notify the landlord that you want to remain in possession of your property (see note 6), the landlord must apply to the court **WITHIN 2 MONTHS** of the date of service of that notification. If you do not notify the landlord that you want to remain in possession, then the application to the court must be **WITHIN FOUR MONTHS** of the date of service of this notice.

Note 15: If the landlord fails in his application for possession, this notice will lapse.

Note 16: You may decide that you want your long residential tenancy to end at or after the date it would have ended under the terms of the tenancy. If so, you will need to give your immediate landlord not less than one month's notice in writing. Your immediate landlord will be the person to whom you pay your rent and may not be the landlord who has served this notice. It does not make any difference that you have notified the landlord that you wished to remain in possession.

Form 3

A3–090 **Landlord's Notice Proposing an Interim Monthly Rent after Notice Terminating Long Residential Tenancy**

Paragraph 6(1) of Schedule 10 to the Local Government and Housing Act 1989

*The landlord **must** cross out any text in square brackets which does not apply.*

- This notice proposes that you pay an interim monthly rent after the date in paragraph 3.
- Please read this notice carefully. **There is a time limit which you must keep to.** If you need help or advice about this notice, you should take it immediately to any of the following:
  —a Citizens' Advice Bureau
  —a housing aid centre
  —a law centre
  —a solicitor.
- Please read the notes at the end of the form.

---

1. To: ....

Insert name[s] of tenant[s].

---

2. From: ....

of: ....

....

....

Insert name[s] and address of landlord[s].

(see note 1)

---

3. [I] [We] give you notice proposing that you pay an interim rent of:

£ .... a month

Insert the proposed monthly rent.

(see notes 2 to 5)

for:

....

....

....

Insert address of property let under the long residential tenancy.

to take effect on:

....

Insert the date on which the proposed interim rent is to take effect.

(see note 6)

---

4. This notice is given under the provisions of paragraph 6(1) of Schedule 10 to the Local Government and Housing Act 1989.

Signed .... Date ....

To be signed and dated by the landlord or the landlord's agent. If there are joint landlords, each landlord or the agent for that landlord must sign (but one can sign on behalf of another with his consent).

[The name and address of the agent is:

....

....

....

Insert name and address of agent, if signed by an agent.]

Notes

Note 1: The landlord referred to in this notice is not necessarily the landlord to whom you pay the rent. It is the person who is your landlord for the purposes of Schedule 10 to the Local Government and Housing Act 1989. That, broadly, will be your immediate landlord if he has a lease which is at least five years longer than your tenancy or, if not, the first superior landlord who has such a lease. If there is no landlord with such a lease, it will be the freeholder.

Note 2: In this notice, the landlord proposes that you pay an interim monthly rent for the property from the date specified (see note 6) until the termination date. The termination date is the date your long residential tenancy will end and is whichever is the later of:

(a) the date specified in the landlord's notice in form 1, and
(b) if any application is made to a rent assessment committee for the terms or rent of the assured tenancy to be set (apart from an application for an interim rent to be set), the last day of the period of three months starting with the date when the application is finally disposed of.

This notice may be served at the same time as the landlord's notice ending the long residential tenancy and proposing to replace it with an assured periodic tenancy (form 1) or at any time between then and the termination date.

Note 3: If you agree with the interim rent proposed, do nothing. The rent proposed in this notice will be the interim monthly rent which you will have to pay.

Note 4: If you do not agree with the interim rent proposed and are unable to reach agreement with the landlord (or do not want to discuss it directly with him), you may refer this notice to your local rent assessment committee. You cannot refer the notice to the committee if you have agreed an interim rent with the landlord (and the agreed interim rent will be the rent which you will have to pay). If you want to refer the notice to the committee, you must refer it **WITHIN TWO MONTHS** beginning on the date this notice is served on you.

Note 5: If you refer this notice to your local rent assessment committee, the committee may set a rent that is higher, lower or the same as the interim rent proposed in this notice. The rent set by the committee will be the rent at which the committee considers the property might reasonably be expected to be let on the open market by a willing landlord under a monthly periodic tenancy which:

(a) begins the day following the date for ending your tenancy specified in the landlord's notice in form 1;
(b) has the same terms as those in the long residential tenancy (as at the date on which the landlord's notice in form 1 was given); and
(c) gives the same security of tenure as a non-shorthold assured tenancy (the grounds 1 to 5 for possession of an assured tenancy in Part I of Schedule 2 to the Housing Act 1988 not applying).

In deciding the rent, the committee will disregard:

(a) the fact that the tenancy will be granted to a sitting tenant;
(b) any increase in the value of the property because of improvements carried out by the tenant during the long residential tenancy (subject to some exceptions); and

(c) any reduction in the value of the property caused by the tenant failing to comply with any term of the long residential tenancy.

The rent decided by the committee will not be inclusive of any variable service charge (as defined in section 18 of the Landlord and Tenant Act 1985). Subject to that, it will include any sums payable by the tenant to the landlord for council tax, the use of furniture, services, repairs, maintenance, insurance or management costs. If the landlord pays water rates for the property, the committee will determine the rent as if he did not, but an appropriate sum to reflect those payments may be added to the rent.

Note 6: The date to be specified:

(a) must be at least two months after the date of service of this notice; and
(b) must not be earlier than the date of termination specified in the landlord's notice in form 1.

Form 4

A3–091 **Tenant's Notice Proposing Different Terms or Rent for an Assured Tenancy**

Paragraph 10(1) of Schedule 10 to the Local Government and Housing Act 1989

The tenant giving this notice ***must*** *cross out any text in square brackets which does not apply.*

- This notice proposes changes to the terms of the assured monthly periodic tenancy proposed in your notice terminating a long residential tenancy.
- Please read this notice carefully. **There are time limits which must be kept.** If you need help or advice about this notice, you should take it immediately to any of the following:
  —a Citizens' Advice Bureau
  —a housing aid centre
  —a law centre
  —a solicitor.
- Please read the notes at the end of the form.

---

1. To: . . . .

of: . . . .

. . . .

Insert name[s] and address[es] of landlord[s]

---

2. From: . . . .

of: . . . .

. . . .

. . . .

Insert name[s] and address of tenant[s]

---

3. [I][We] give you notice that [I][we] propose:

[a different amount of rent]

[and]

[different terms (other than the amount of rent)]

for the assured monthly periodic tenancy proposed in your notice of . . . .

Insert the date of the landlord's notice.

(see notes 1 to 3)

---

4. [I][We] propose:

[an amount for rent of £. . . . . a month]

Insert the proposed monthly rent

[this [includes] [excludes] council tax [of £ . . . . a month]
[this [includes] [excludes] water rates [of £ . . . . a month]
If the rent includes council tax and/or water rates please insert the current monthly amounts.

[and]

[the following changes to the terms (apart from the amount of rent) set out in the landlord's notice:

Column 1 (Term proposed by landlord)	Column 2 (Term proposed by tenant)
. . . .	. . . .
. . . .	. . . .
. . . .	. . . .

Please set out in column 1 each term in the landlord's notice which you dispute and set out in column 2 the corresponding alternative term which you propose. Also include in column 2 any other terms which you propose. Continue on a separate sheet if necessary.]

(see notes 4 to 6)

---

5. This notice is given under the provisions of paragraph 10(1) of Schedule 10 to the Local Government and Housing Act 1989.

Signed . . . . Date . . . .

To be signed and dated by the tenant or the tenant's agent. If there are joint tenants each tenant or his agent must sign (but one can sign on behalf of another with his consent).

[The name and address of the agent is:

. . . .
. . . .
. . . .

Insert name and address of agent, if signed by an agent.]

Notes

Note 1: In this notice the tenant proposes a different amount of rent or other terms to those specified in your notice. This notice must be served by the tenant on you **WITHIN TWO MONTHS** starting on the date the landlord's notice proposing an assured tenancy was served on the tenant.

Note 2: If you agree with the new different amount of rent and/or other terms proposed by the tenant in this notice do nothing. From the date on which the assured periodic tenancy takes effect:

(a) the amount of rent will be:
  (i) the rent proposed in the tenant's notice, or
  (ii) if no amount of rent is proposed in the tenant's notice, the amount of rent is the amount proposed in the landlord's notice; and

(b) the other terms of the tenancy will be:
  (i) the terms proposed in the tenant's notice and, in so far as they do not conflict with the tenant's terms, any terms proposed in the landlord's notice, or
  (ii) if no other terms are proposed in the tenant's notice, the landlord's terms.

Note 3: If you do not agree with the different amount of rent and/or other different terms proposed by the tenant in this notice and you are unable to reach agreement with the tenant or you do not wish to discuss it with him, you may refer the matter directly to a local rent assessment committee by using **FORM 5 WITHIN TWO MONTHS** starting on the date on which this notice was served on you. The committee will determine whether there is any dispute over the rent and/or other terms and where there is a dispute made a determination. If the matter is referred to the committee, the long residential tenancy does not end until 3 months of the matter having been dealt with.

Note 4: Where the committee decide that there is a dispute about the amount of rent and the other terms of the tenancy, the committee will first decide whether the terms (apart from the amount of rent) in the landlord's notice, the tenant's notice, or some other terms dealing with the same subject matter might reasonably be expected to be found in an assured monthly periodic tenancy which:

(a) begins on the day following the date for ending the tenancy;
(b) gives the same security of tenure as a non-shorthold assured tenancy, (the grounds 1 to 5 for possession of an assured tenancy in Part I of Schedule 2 to the Housing Act 1988 not applying); and
(c) has the same terms as the undisputed terms or, if the committee has decided the terms, those terms and any undisputed terms.

In deciding the terms, the committee will disregard the fact that the tenancy will be granted to a sitting tenant.

Note 5: When the committee have decided the other terms of the tenancy, the committee will decide the amount of the rent. The rent set by the committee will be the rent which the committee considers the property might reasonably be expected to be let on the open market by a willing landlord under an assured monthly periodic tenancy on the same basis as set out in note 4.

In deciding the rent, the committee will disregard:

(a) the fact that the tenancy will be granted to a sitting tenant;
(b) any increase in the value of the property because of improvements carried out by the tenant during the long residential tenancy (subject to some exceptions); and
(c) any reduction in the value of the property caused by the tenant failing to comply with any term of the long residential tenancy.

The rent decided by the committee will not be inclusive of any variable service charge (as defined in section 18 of the Landlord and Tenant Act 1985). Subject to that, it will include any sums payable by the tenant to the landlord for council tax, the use of furniture, services, repairs, maintenance, insurance or management costs. If the landlord pays water rates for the property, the committee shall determine the rent as if he did not, but an appropriate sum to reflect those payments may be added to the rent.

Note 6: Referring this notice to a rent assessment committee does not affect the right to agree any terms of an assured periodic tenancy. If you and your tenant both notify the committee in writing (before it makes a determination) of any terms you have expressly agreed, the committee may not make any change to the agreed terms. The committee shall take account of those agreed terms in deciding what the disputed terms are and whether there is any dispute as to the amount of rent payable.

Form 5

A3–092 **Landlord's Application Referring Tenant's Notice Proposing Different Terms or Rent for a Proposed Assured Tenancy to a Rent Assessment Committee**

Paragraph 10(2) of Schedule 10 to the Local Government and Housing Act 1989

The landlord ***must*** *cross out any text in square brackets which does not apply and tick boxes where appropriate.*

- This application form should be used by a landlord who has been served with a notice under paragraph 10(1) of Schedule 10 to the Local Government and Housing Act 1989 in Form 4, proposing different rent and/or different terms to those proposed in his notice terminating the long residential tenancy.
- Please read this notice carefully. If you need help or advice about this form, you should take it immediately to any of the following:
  —a Citizens' Advice Bureau
  —a housing aid centre
  —a law centre
  —a solicitor.

- When you have filled in the form you must send it to the appropriate rent assessment committee **within two months** beginning on the date on which the tenant's notice (form 4) was served on you.
- The rent assessment committee will consider the landlord's notice (form 1) and the tenant's notice (form 4) and decide whether there is a dispute and, if so, what is in dispute. Both the landlord and the tenant will be notified of the date of the committee hearing to decide the matters which are in dispute.
- Please read the notes at the end of the form.

---

1. Name[s] of tenant[s]

. . . .

Address of tenant[s]

. . . .

. . . .

. . . .

Address of the property to which the application relates if different from the address of the tenant[s] given above.

. . . .

. . . .

. . . .

---

2. Name[s] of landlord[s]

. . . .

. . . .

. . . .

Address of landlord[s]

. . . .

. . . .

. . . .

---

3. Details of property

(a) What type of property is it?

Flat ☐ Terraced house ☐ Semi-detached house ☐

Fully detached house ☐

(b) If it is a flat, say what floor it is on.

Ground ☐ First ☐ Second ☐ Other ☐ *please specify*

. . . .

. . . .

. . . .

(c) Give the number and type of rooms, e.g. living room, bathroom etc.

. . . .

. . . .

. . . .

Please insert details

(d) Do the premises include any other facilities, e.g. garden, garage or other separate building or land? ☐ Yes ☐ No

(e) If 'Yes', please give details

. . . .

. . . .

. . . .

---

4. I attach:

(a) a copy of the lease under which the long residential tenancy was created;

(b) a copy of my notice under paragraph 4(1) of Schedule 10 dated . . . . *(insert date)* (form 1) terminating the tenant's long residential tenancy and proposing an assured periodic tenancy;

(c) a copy of the tenant's notice under paragraph 10(1) of Schedule 10 dated .... *(insert date)* (form 4) proposing different rent or other terms for the assured periodic tenancy.

IMPORTANT ***You must attach copies of documents (a), (b) and (c). If any proposed tenancy agreement was attached to the landlord's notice (form 1), you must attach a copy of that agreement.***

---

5. The amount of rent proposed in the landlord's notice is £ .... a month

Insert proposed monthly rent

This [includes][excludes] council tax [of £ .... a month]

This [includes][excludes] water rates [of £ .... a month]

If the rent includes council tax and/or water rates please insert the current monthly amounts.

Does the tenant dispute the amount of rent?

Yes ☐ No ☐

If 'Yes', please specify:

The amount of rent proposed in the tenant's notice £......... a month

Insert the proposed monthly rent

This [includes][excludes] council tax [of £ .... a month]

This [includes][excludes] water rates [of £ .... a month]

If the rent includes council tax and/or water rates please insert the current monthly amounts.

(see notes 1 and 3)

---

6. Does the tenant dispute any of the proposed terms (apart from the amount of rent)?

Yes ☐ No ☐

If 'Yes', please set out in Column 1 each term (apart from the amount of rent) proposed in the landlord's notice which is disputed by the tenant and set out in Column 2 the corresponding, alternative term (if any) proposed in the tenant's notice. Also include in Column 2 any other term proposed in that notice:

Column 1 (Landlord's term disputed by tenant)	Column 2 (Alternative term proposed by tenant)
....	....
....	....
....	....

Please continue on a separate sheet if necessary.

(see note 2)

IMPORTANT—*If, after this application to the rent assessment committee, the landlord and the tenant agree any terms for the assured periodic tenancy, the committee cannot change those terms provided that both the landlord and the tenant send the committee written notification of the agreed terms. The committee will take account of the agreed terms in deciding what the disputed terms are and whether there is any dispute as to the amount of the rent.*

---

7. [I][We] hereby refer the tenant's notice proposing rent or other terms for the assured periodic tenancy to the rent assessment committee to determine whether there is any dispute as to the proposed terms and/or rent and if there is any dispute to make a determination.

(see note 4)

---

8. This application is made under the provisions of paragraph 10(2) of Schedule 10 to the Local Government and Housing Act 1989.

Signed .... Date ....

To be signed and dated by the landlord or his agent. If there are joint landlords, each landlord or his agent must sign (but one can sign on behalf of another with his consent).

[The name, address and telephone number of the agent is:

. . . .

. . . .

. . . .

Insert name and address of agent, if signed by agent.]

Notes

Note 1: The rent decided by the committee will not be inclusive of any variable service charge (as defined in section 18 of the Landlord and Tenant Act 1985). Subject to that, it will include any sums payable by the tenant to the landlord for council tax, the use of furniture, services, repairs, maintenance, insurance or management costs. If the landlord pays water rates for the property, the committee shall determine the rent as if he did not, but an appropriate sum to reflect those payments may be added to the rent.

Note 2: Where the committee decide that there is a dispute about the amount of rent and the other terms of the tenancy, the committee will first decide whether the terms (apart from the amount of rent) in the landlord's notice, the tenant's notice, or some other terms dealing with the same subject matter might reasonably be expected to be found in an assured monthly periodic tenancy which:

(a) begins the day following the date for ending the tenancy;
(b) gives the same security of tenure as a non-shorthold assured tenancy, (the grounds 1 to 5 for possession of an assured tenancy in Part I of Schedule 2 to the Housing Act 1988 not applying); and
(c) has the same terms as the undisputed terms or, if the committee has decided the terms, those terms and any undisputed terms.

In deciding the terms, the committee will disregard the fact that the tenancy will be granted to a sitting tenant.

If the landlord and tenant agree any terms of an assured periodic tenancy before a determination by the committee and both of them notify the committee in writing of such expressly agreed terms, the committee may not make any change to the agreed terms. The committee shall take account of those agreed terms in deciding what the disputed terms are and whether there is any dispute as to the amount of rent payable.

Note 3: When the committee have decided the other terms of the tenancy the committee will decide the amount of the rent. The rent set by the committee will be the rent which the committee consider the property might reasonably be expected to be let on the open market by a willing landlord under an assured monthly periodic tenancy which:

(a) begins on the day following the date for ending the tenancy;
(b) gives the same security of tenure as a non-shorthold assured tenancy, (the grounds 1 to 5 for possession of an assured tenancy in Part I of Schedule 2 to the Housing Act 1988 not applying); and
(c) has the same terms as the undisputed terms or, if the committee has decided the terms, those terms and any undisputed terms.

In deciding the rent, the committee will disregard:

(a) the fact that the tenancy will be granted to a sitting tenant;
(b) any increase in the value of the property because of improvements carried out by the tenant during the long residential tenancy (subject to some exceptions); and
(c) any reduction in the value of the property caused by the tenant failing to comply with any term of the long residential tenancy.

Note 4: The rent assessment committee are not required to continue with a determination if the long residential tenancy has come to an end, or if the landlord serves notice in writing on the rent assessment committee that he no longer requires a determination. In such a case with effect from the date on which the assured periodic tenancy takes effect, the rent shall be the rent proposed in the tenant's notice unless no rent was proposed; in which case the rent will be the rent proposed in the landlord's notice. The other terms of the tenancy will be the terms proposed in the tenant's notice and, so far as they do not conflict with those terms, the terms specified in the landlord's notice. However, if the landlord and tenant agree other terms, those will be the terms of the tenancy.

FORM 6

A3–093 **Notice by Rent Assessment Committee Requiring Further Information**

Section 41(2) of the Housing Act 1988 as applied by paragraph 12(1) of Schedule 10 to the Local Government and Housing Act 1989

The rent assessment committee ***must*** *cross out any text in square brackets which does not apply.*

- This notice is from a rent assessment committee and is asking you for information.
- Please read this notice carefully. **There is a time limit which must be kept to.** If you need help or advice about this notice, you should take it immediately to any of the following:
  —a Citizens' Advice Bureau
  —a housing aid centre
  —a law centre
  —a solicitor.

---

1. To: . . . .
of: . . . .
. . . .
. . . .

Insert the name[s] and address of the [tenant[s]] [landlord[s]].

---

2. An application has been made to the rent assessment committee about:
. . . .
. . . .
. . . .

Insert the address of the property.
for consideration of:

[the amount of rent under an assured periodic tenancy replacing a long residential tenancy.]

[the terms (other than the amount of rent) of an assured periodic tenancy replacing a long residential tenancy.]

[the amount of rent and other terms of an assured periodic tenancy replacing a long residential tenancy.]

[an interim rent while a long residential tenancy is continuing under Schedule 10 to the Local Government and Housing Act 1989.]

---

3. The information needed is:
. . . .
. . . .
. . . .

Insert information which is needed.

---

4. Please send it to:
. . . .
. . . .
. . . .

Insert address to which the information is to be sent.

no later than:
. . . .

Insert the date by which the information must be sent. Thus must be at least 14 days from the service of this notice.

---

5. If you fail to comply with this notice without reasonable cause you will be committing a criminal offence and may be liable to a fine.

---

6. This notice is given under the provisions of section 41(2) of the Housing Act 1988 as applied by paragraph 12(1) of Schedule 10 to the Local Government and Housing Act 1989.

---

7. Signed on behalf of the rent assessment committee.

Signed: . . . . Date: . . . .

Name of committee: . . . .

Name of person signing: . . . .

Address: . . . .

To be signed and dated on behalf of the rent assessment committee. Insert the name of the committee, the name of the person signing and the address of the committee.

EXPLANATORY NOTE

(This note is not part of the Regulations)

These Regulations prescribe forms of notice to be used for the purposes of Schedule 10 to the Local Government and Housing Act 1989 (security of tenure on ending of long residential tenancies). The forms prescribed are those specified in regulation 3 and set out in the Schedule (or forms substantially to the same effect).

Additional forms are prescribed for the purposes of section 186 of and Schedule 10 to the 1989 Act in the Long Residential Tenancies (Supplemental Forms) Regulations 1997.

A3–094 **The Assured and Protected Tenancies (Lettings to Students) Regulations 1998**

S.I. 1998 No. 1967

Made 11th August 1998
Laid before Parliament 11th August 1998
Coming into force 1st September 1998

In exercise of the powers conferred on the Secretary of State by section 8 of the Rent Act 1977 and paragraph 8 of Schedule 1 to the Housing Act 1988, the Secretary of State for Education and Employment, as respects England, and the Secretary of State for Wales, as respects Wales, hereby make the following Regulations:

A3–095 **1.** These Regulations may be cited as the Assured and Protected Tenancies (Lettings to Students) Regulations 1998 and shall come into force on 1st September 1998.

A3–096 **2.** In these Regulations—

"assisted" has the same meaning as in section 579(5) and (6) of the Education Act 1996;
"further education" has the meaning assigned to it by section 2(3) and (5) of the Education Act 1996;
"higher education" means education provided by means of a course of any description mentioned in Schedule 6 to the Education Reform Act 1988;
"publicly funded" refers to an institution which is—

(a) provided or assisted by a local education authority;
(b) in receipt of grant under regulations made under section 485 of the Education Act 1996;
(c) within the higher education sector (within the meaning of section 91(5) of the Further and Higher Education Act 1992), other than a university; or
(d) within the further education sector (within the meaning of section 91(3) of the Further and Higher Education Act 1992), and

"the relevant enactments" means section 8 of the Rent Act 1977 and paragraph 8 of Schedule 1 to the Housing Act 1988 (lettings to students).

3. The following institutions are hereby specified as educational institutions for the purposes of the relevant enactments, that is to say— **A3–097**

(a) any university or university college and any constituent college, school or hall or other institution of a university;
(b) any other institution which provides further education or higher education or both and which is publicly funded;
(c) the David Game Tutorial College, London.

4. The following bodies of persons (whether unincorporated or bodies corporate) are hereby specified as bodies for the purposes of the relevant enactments, that is to say— **A3–098**

(a) the governing body of any educational institution specified in regulation 3 above;
(b) the body, other than a local education authority, providing any such educational institution; and
(c) a body listed in Schedule 1 to these Regulations.

5. The following bodies of persons (whether unincorporated or bodies corporate) are hereby specified as bodies for the purposes of paragraph 8 of Schedule 1 to the Housing Act 1988, that is to say— **A3–099**

(a) any housing association (as defined in section 1 of the Housing Associations Act 1985) which is registered by the Housing Corporation or Housing for Wales in accordance with Part I of the Housing Associations Act 1985 and which is not listed in Schedule 1 to these Regulations; and
(b) a body listed in Schedule 2 to these Regulations.

6. The Regulations specified in Schedule 3 to these Regulations are hereby revoked to the extent detailed in that Schedule. **A3–100**

Tessa Blackstone
7th August 1998 — Minister of State, Department for Education and Employment

Peter Hain
11th August 1998 — Parliamentary Under Secretary of State, Welsh Office

Regulation 4(c) SCHEDULE 1

SPECIFIED BODIES UNDER REGULATION 4(C) **A3–101**

International Students House
The London Goodenough Trust for Overseas Graduates

Regulation 5(b) SCHEDULE 2

A3–102 SPECIFIED BODIES UNDER REGULATION 5(B)

AFSIL Limited
Derbyshire Student Residences Limited
Friendship Housing
Hull Student Welfare Association
International Lutheran Student Centre
International Students Club (Church of England) Limited
International Students' Club (Lee Abbey) Limited
International Students Housing Society
Oxford Brookes Housing Association Limited
Oxford Overseas Student Housing Association Limited
St. Brigid's House Limited
St. Thomas More Housing Society Limited
The House of St. Gregory and St. Macrina Oxford Limited
The London Mission (West London) Circuit Meeting of the Methodist Church
The London School of Economics Housing Association
The Royal London Hospital Special Trustees
The Universities of Brighton and Sussex Catholic Chaplaincy Association
The Victoria League for Commonwealth Friendship
University of Leicester Students' Union
Wandsworth Students Housing Association Limited
York Housing Association Limited

Regulation 6 SCHEDULE 3

A3–103 REVOCATIONS

(1) *Regulations revoked*	*(2)* *References*	*(3)* *Extent of revocation*
The Assured and Protected Tenancies (Lettings to Students) Regulations 1988	S.I. 1988/2236	The whole Regulations
The Assured and Protected Tenancies (Lettings to Students) (Amendment) Regulations 1989	S.I. 1989/1628	The whole Regulations
The Assured and Protected Tenancies (Lettings to Students) (Amendment) Regulations 1990	S.I. 1990/1825	The whole Regulations
The Assured and Protected Tenancies (Lettings to Students) (Amendment) Regulations 1991	S.I. 1991/233	The whole Regulations
The Assured and Protected Tenancies (Lettings to Students) (Amendment) Regulations 1992	S.I. 1992/515	The whole Regulations
The Further and Higher Education Act 1992 (Consequential Amendments) Regulations 1993	S.I. 1993/559	Regulation 6
The Assured and Protected Tenancies (Lettings to Students) (Amendment) Regulations 1993	S.I. 1993/2390	The whole Regulations
The Assured and Protected Tenancies (Lettings to Students) (Amendment) Regulations 1996	S.I. 1996/458	The whole Regulations
The Assured and Protected Tenancies (Lettings to Students) (Amendment) (No. 2) Regulations 1996	S.I. 1996/2198	The whole Regulations

EXPLANATORY NOTE

(This note is not part of the Regulations)

Section 8 of the Rent Act 1977 and paragraph 8 of Schedule 1 to the Housing Act 1988 except from the definition of "protected tenancy" and "assured tenancy" in section 1 of the respective Acts a tenancy granted to a person who is pursuing, or intends to pursue, a course of study provided by a specified educational institution. The tenancy must be granted either by that institution or by another specified institution or body of persons. These Regulations specify the educational institutions and other bodies for the purposes of those provisions.

These Regulations consolidate the earlier Regulations specifying institutions and bodies for the purposes of the said section 8 and paragraph 8 with minor and drafting amendments to take account of the change in name of certain bodies listed therein and delete references to certain other bodies.

Index